Introduction to
SACRAMENTAL
THEOLOGY

Introduction to

SACRAMENTAL THEOLOGY

Signs of Christ in the Flesh

JOSÉ GRANADOS

Translated by Michael J. Miller | Foreword by David W. Fagerberg

THE CATHOLIC UNIVERSITY OF AMERICA PRESS
Washington, D.C.

Originally published in 2016 in Spanish as José Granados García,
Tratado General de los Sacramentos
(Madrid: Biblioteca de Autores Cristianos)

The paper used in this publication meets the minimum requirements of
American National Standards for Information Science—Permanence of Paper for
Printed Library Materials, ANSI Z39.48-1984.

∞

Design and composition by Kachergis Book Design

Names: Granados, José, 1970– author. | Miller, Michael J., translator. |
Fagerberg, David W., 1952– other.
Title: Introduction to sacramental theology : signs of Christ in the flesh / José Granados ;
translated by Michael J. Miller ; foreword by David W. Fagerberg.
Other titles: Tratado general de los sacramentos. English
Description: Washington, D.C. : The Catholic University of America Press, 2021. |
"Originally published in 2016 in Spanish as José Granados García,
Tratado General de los Sacramentos (Madrid: Biblioteca de Autores
Cristianos)" | Includes bibliographical references and index.
Identifiers: LCCN 2021025975 | ISBN 9780813233925 (paperback) |
ISBN 9780813233932 (ebook)
Classification: LCC BX2200 .G6613 2021 | DDC 234/.16—dc23
LC record available at https://lccn.loc.gov/2021025975

TO FR. LUIS F. LADARIA, SJ

Contents

CONTENTS

PART 3 ❧ TOWARD A
SACRAMENTAL WAY OF LIVING

Foreword

David W. Fagerberg

The sacraments are so familiar to us that their awesomeness has been diluted. We know that they are essential to the Church and important for our lives, but how? This comprehensive book goes a long way toward shaking us out of our lethargy about sacraments by refreshing traditional modes of thought and making them newly applicable. And what is most amazing is that Prof. Granados restores freshness not by personal novelty and idiosyncrasy, but by bringing the full heritage of sacramental theology to bear upon our modern needs.

From out of the numerous remarkable elements in this book, I will choose three to emphasize.

First, Prof. Granados *thinks with* sacramental theologians from all across the tradition. I mean that both in the sense of thinking "alongside of" and in the sense of "by means of" our theological predecessors. It is very rare, indeed, to find an author who can avoid prejudicing one era over another, and it is as refreshing as it is rare. He is a time traveler! He moves at ease through different periods of the Church: patristic East, patristic West, medieval scholastics, Protestant reformers and the Council of Trent, theologians of the 19th century, the second Vatican Council, and our most recent sacramental theologians. He accumulates wisdom from his sojourn with them to report to us. He is a host who is able to set up a table in the presence of his readers where invited guests from the long tradition can sit and hold discussion. There are theologians and philosophers and biblical scholars at the table; there are patristic players who maintain fundamental concerns; there are scholastic participants who add their organizational talents; and there are modern contributors who keep current challenges before our eyes. In his hands, the development of doctrine does not mean the replacement of an old doctrine by a newfangled one. In his hands, doctrines develop toward producing a full picture, as if on a canvas the size of a wall of the castle's great hall. Here some artists specialize in faces while others specialize in landscapes; here some eras have worked the lower left corner while other eras have worked the upper center (and there is still empty space on the canvas for future generations). Prof. Granados is truly appreciative for patristic ecclesiality, and at the same time finds value in the taxonomic skills of the Middle Ages.

This brings me to a second remarkable feature of this book. He states that treatises on the sacraments in general (*de sacramentis in genere*) did not appear until the 12th century, and they have fallen out of favor recently. Indeed, I was taught in my education four decades ago that such an approach is now fruitless, and one should ignore the genus in favor of the species—specific liturgies, specific rituals, specific sacraments. Prof. Granados disagrees and has reasons why. Discovering what those reasons are is a pleasure that awaits the reader, but I will summarily say that he presents a general sacramentology for four reasons: to be a formal order, a logic that guides revelation, an enrichment to all theology when examined in a sacramental key, and a way to situate sacraments in our human life. General sacramentology is not an exercise in abstraction, it is finding how sacraments rooted in our created condition will purify and strengthen our spiritual growth.

Third, this is not simply a history text. Prof. Granados *supersedes* the history of sacramental theology that he tells: the word means "to sit on top of." Only because he sits atop historical sacramental theology does his constructive sacramental theology become insightful. The book progresses from scriptural roots (both Old and New Testaments, since typology is not taboo for him), to the appearance of sacraments in the flesh of Christ, which signs and symbols have been elaborated through a hundred investigations. He thus arrives at our own set of modern problems (secularism, materialism, individualism, etc.) and, upon analysis, proposes the emphasis that our own generation needs: an emphasis upon our incarnate condition. Sacrament will release us from our postmodern condition because sacrament must always be thought of on the basis of our incarnate state, something forgotten by modern, regurgitated Gnosticism. Upon assuming flesh, Jesus brought us into the network of relations he had as Son of God and Son of Man, and made the sacraments an expansion of his presence throughout history. If I may express it by means of emphasis, when Jesus left us this new space of relations mediated by him in the Eucharist, he was not only saying "take my *body*," he was saying "take *my* body." Therefore, Prof. Granados concludes, the Eucharist is the fundamental sacrament, and the other six are always interpreted as expansions of the Eucharistic space into the life of the Christian.

Sacramental theology thereby becomes an outlook, a grammar, a ground from which theology can be done. We should learn to speak from the viewpoint of sacraments before we speak about sacraments. Doing so is Prof. Granados' significant and substantial offering.

Preface

Dante, in his *Divine Comedy* (*Paradiso* XXXI.103–8), tells of the astonishment of the pilgrim who arrives at St. Peter's Basilica in Rome and contemplates Veronica's veil and, on it, the features of Jesus' face. And he does not tire of looking at the face again and again, seeking to leave imprinted on his memory the Savior's likeness: "Jesus Christ, was Your face like that, then?" These lines by the poet intrigued Jorge Luis Borges. Although he does not share the pilgrim's vision, he too desires, nevertheless, to look into Jesus' eyes, and comments:

Men have lost a face, an irretrievable face, and they all wish to be that pilgrim who in Rome ... sees the face cloth of Veronica and murmurs in faith: "Jesus Christ, my God, true God, was Your face like that, then?" If we really knew what He was like, then the key to the parables would be ours and we would know whether the son of the carpenter was also the Son of God.[1]

"If we really knew what He was like." Borges, in his blindness, intuits a great truth. The meaning of Jesus' parables, the intention that inspired his travels and miracles, the very enterprise that he attempted in dying on the cross, his ultimate mystery as Son of God; all this we can know through the Gospels and faith assures us of it, but at the same time it becomes blurred and ambiguous without the concrete encounter with the Teacher, without the space opened up by his presence. If we could only converse with him face to face for a few hours, Borges seems to say, his eyes and the tone of his voice would show us once and for all whether his clear truths and his high moral standards can rule the concrete steps of a life.

This is, in fact, one of the great challenges facing Christianity today. We have his parables, we lack the sight of him; we have his commandments, we lack his voice; we have the strength of his commission, we lack the touch of his arms. Without the second, the first loses its foundations: doctrine that

---

1. Jorge L. Borges, "Paradiso, XXXI, 108," in his *El hacedor* (*1960*), in *Obras completas*, vol. 2: *1923–1972* (Buenos Aires: Emecé, 1974), 800.

is clear but abstract; morality that is superior but utopian; mission that is great but irrelevant.

Theology's answer to these questions passes through the treatise on the sacraments. For in them, from generation to generation, opens up the space of the encounter with Christ in the communion of the church. The sacraments tell us that the message of Jesus is always rooted in the concrete relations that we form in our flesh; that this is where the profession of faith resounds and his commandments are articulated, which therefore always stay at the level of our earthly journey. And so the clear doctrine and the high moral standards of Jesus appear, not as the final limit to which we tend asymptotically, but rather as the concrete foundations on which to build life, apart from which our building will not stand.

An axiom of the Church Fathers, implicit in their statements, says that the Son of God never abandoned the flesh once he had assumed it (*quod semel adsumpsit nunquam dimisit*).[2] Certainly the sentence applies to Jesus, who never left his flesh behind, for it ascended with him into heaven and remains forever at the right hand of God. But to the Fathers' way of thinking this flesh is ours too: the flesh of the whole human family, the flesh in which we are born, love one another, mature, suffer, generate life. And we must say, therefore, that Jesus did not abandon *our* flesh either, which he configured to himself in the sacraments. The encounter with him keeps happening in the space of the body, where we encounter the world and other human beings.

Someone who settles on this sacramental framework of the faith inhabits the space where the truth of Jesus proves to be not an abstract imposition, but rather light for the journey; nor are his commandments utopian morality, but rather a gift that embraces us and sustains us in our work; nor is his missionary command a quixotic gesture, but rather the building of a Christian culture that serves the common good of mankind. From this perspective, as I will show, the treatise on the sacraments acquires a strategic position, for it offers us the viewpoint from which to contemplate all together the different facets of the mystery.

Therefore the loss of that face that Borges lamented is not irreparable, a loss that turns the Christian message and morality into an abstraction. For as Pope Leo had said: "Whatever of our Redeemer was manifested has

---

2. See Antonio Orbe, "Al margen del misterio: los axiomas cristológicos," in his *En torno a la encarnación* (Santiago de Compostela: Instituto Teológico Compostelano, 1985), 205–21. A formulation of the axiom can be seen in Bonaventure, *In III Sententiarum*, d. 21, a. 1, q. 1, in *Opera Omnia* (Quaracchi: Collegii a S. Bonaventura, 1882, 1885, 1887, 1889) [hereafter Quaracchi], 3:437, who attributes it to St. Augustine and to St. John Damascene.

passed into the sacraments."[3] This is confirmed by the insight of another poet, Charles Péguy, who says that if a Christian envies those parishes in the Holy Land through which Jesus walked and preached, it is because he does not know the greatness of his own vocation: "You eat God directly, you are nourished by God directly. And there is nothing closer than the sense of touch. There is nothing closer than food: than the incorporation, than the incarnation of food."[4]

Theology, then, always needs sacramental spaces of communion where the mystery is manifested and communicated. And the pages of this treatise could not be an exception. They have found this space, on the one hand, in the Pontifical John Paul II Institute for Studies on Marriage and Family, both in the headquarters in Rome and in the different sections scattered throughout the world. If this book contains any light, it was kindled either in the common work with my colleagues and fellow professors, or in teaching our students, for theological truth is assimilated correctly only in the measure in which it is given.

Within that same Institute, the International Area for Research in Sacramental Theology, the direction of which was entrusted to me at its founding by the then-president of the John Paul II Institute, Msgr. Livio Melina, has been in a special way a luminous space. I am grateful to him for his generosity, and also to the vice-director, Professor Alexandra Diriart, with whom I have shared toils and initial fruits, in the hope that this Area for Research, inspired by the teaching of St. John Paul II, might continue its work of formation and of academic and cultural dialogue, contributing its luminous thread to the tapestry of sacramental theology.

In addition to the university environment of the John Paul II Institute, I have been accompanied in the fraternal environment of my community, the Disciples of the Hearts of Jesus and Mary. The insights in these pages matured in the harmony of our common friendship with the Lord. My thanks to all of my confreres, and especially to our Superior General, Fr. José Noriega Bastos, for their encouragement, support, and inspiration while I was working on this treatise.

The poet Dante, shortly after recalling Veronica, turns to the Virgin Mary, who will bestow on him the grace to gaze without distractions at that same face that is imprinted indistinctly on the cloth. The poet invokes Mary as the fixed goal of God's eternal designs (in other words, of his mystery or

---

3. Leo the Great, *Sermo* LXXIV.2 (Corpus Christianorum: Series Latina [hereafter CCL] 138A:42): "Quod itaque redemptoris nostri conspicuum fuit, in sacramenta transiuit."
4. Charles Péguy, *Le Mystère de la Charité de Jeanne d'Arc* (Paris: Gallimard, 1944), 35–36.

sacrament), which had to pass through her when her Son was born in the flesh. The mother of Jesus thus prepared the original environment in which the Word was received, the first sacramental space. Therefore Pope Leo the Great could consider her virginal womb in parallel with the waters of baptism, as they receive a similar gift: "He gave to the water what He gave to the Mother."[5] To her, the Star of the Sea, who sets a course for the economy of the flesh, which is the economy of the sacraments, I entrust the fruitfulness of this work.

Rome, December 8, 2016
Feast of the Immaculate Conception of Mary

5. Leo the Great, *Sermo* XXV: "dedit aquae quod dedit matri" (CCL 138:130).

Abbreviations

AAS	*Acta Apostolicae Sedis*
ACW	Ancient Christian Writers
ANF	Ante-Nicene Fathers (ed. Roberts et al.)
BFSMA	Bibliotheca Franciscana Scholastica Medii Aevi
BLE	*Bulletin de littérature ecclésiastique*
CCCM	Corpus Christianorum: Continuatio Mediaevalis
CCL	Corpus Christianorum: Series Latina
CIC	*Codex Iuris Canonici*
CSEL	Corpus Scriptorum Ecclesiasticorum Latinorum
CT	*Concilium Tridentinuum: Diariorum, actorum, epistularum tractatum*
CV	*Hugonis de Sancto Victore de sacramentis Christianae fidei* (ed. Berndt)
DH	*Enchiridion Symbolorum* (ed. Denzinger)
DTC	*Dictionnaire de Théologie Catholique* (ed. Vacant et al.)
FOTC	Fathers of the Church (The Catholic University of America Press)
GCS	Die griechischen christlichen Schriftsteller der ersten drei Jahrhunderte
GS	*Gaudium et Spes* (Vatican Council II)
LG	*Lumen Gentium* (Vatican Council II)
NPNF	Nicene and Post-Nicene Fathers (ed. Schaff)
Parma	*Commentum in quatuor libros sententiarum* (Aquinas)
PG	Patrologia Graeca (ed. Migne)
PL	Patrologia Latina (ed. Migne)

PTS	Patristische Texte und Studien
Quaracchi	*Opera Omnia* (Bonaventure)
SC	Sources Chrétiennes
SCG	*Summa Contra Gentiles* (Aquinas)
Sent.	*Libri Sententiarum* (Lombard)
SpBon	Spicilegium Bonaventurianum
SSC	*Sacrosanctum Concilium* (Vatican Council II)
ST	*Summa Theologiae* (Aquinas)

Introduction to
SACRAMENTAL
THEOLOGY

1 ❧ THE SACRAMENTS, A PLACE IN WHICH TO CONTEMPLATE THE MYSTERY

The treatise on the sacraments is usually one of the last that theology undertakes. This is justified if we look at the course of sacred history in the light of its fulfillment in Jesus. First we must talk about man, who was created in Christ and established in God's favor, about his Fall, about how he slowly became accustomed to the coming of the Messiah, about the redemptive incarnation of the Son, which makes his church present to himself as his body and bride. Only then do we arrive at the salvific signs that communicate grace; they prolong the life of Christ in man, incorporate him into his church, and permit him to participate in his work, disposing him for eternal salvation.

This sequence is correct because the task of theology, as St. Irenaeus of Lyons teaches, is to investigate the cadence of history, explaining its eras one by one.[1] In this system the sacraments propagate the work of Jesus: they engraft us into his vital movement, into his great journey from the Father to the Father. Therefore, according to the classical medieval order, after studying them, all that remained was to treat the final truths or the last things. This is the structure of the *Sentences* of Peter Lombard (d. 1160), which his myriad medieval commentators would imitate.

Still, there is another way of looking at the sacraments. Rather than as bits of theological knowledge, they can be considered as meeting places with the living Jesus, spaces where the spark of his presence flies up. As a result, then, the order is inverted and they come to have the role of initiating us into all of theology. Only then, surrounded by the glory of the risen Lord,

1. Irenaeus of Lyons, *Adversus haereses* I, 28 (SC 264:163–65).

I

are our minds opened to decipher God's plan (Lk 24:45). The doors of the mystery, it has been said rightly, open only from inside,[2] and that is precisely where the sacraments situate us—inside the mystery—so as to allow us to taste it.

The sacraments, therefore, are not just another subject that theology seeks to illuminate. They are, before anything else, windows through which to look at the gospel; promontories from which the whole plan of God can be surveyed. This means that the sacraments belong to the theological method, to the way in which faith contemplates the mystery. And only by considering this, their primordial role, can we correctly define them.

This insight will be the point of departure for my treatise. It will be necessary, first, to (1) prove that the sacrament, from Easter on, displays the original space of the meeting with Christ, the space from which it is possible to understand his person and work. In the next step, I will show (2) some features of what I want to call the sacramental outlook or perspective, which are useful in order to know not only the revealed mystery, but also (3) the way in which to propose it to the modern world. In light of this I will be able to raise the question that will demarcate my task: (4) what is the field of study and what is the method of general sacramental theology?

The Sacraments, the Original Space of the Encounter with Christ

Already in the New Testament the church's worship is revealed as the primary place of access to the life and work of Jesus. Indeed, before scripture speaks *about* the sacraments, it talks *in terms of* the sacraments, as especially in terms of the Eucharist. The link between the Eucharistic rite and the encounter with the glorified Christ already appears in the accounts of the resurrection. Think, for example, of the scene in Emmaus: the risen Lord is recognized in the breaking of the bread, which makes other modes of his presence redundant.[3] The apparition to Mary Magdalene too (Jn 20:11–18) is written in a sacramental key: in it, a new way of "touching" Jesus is revealed that will follow when he has ascended to the Father; Thomas, in placing his hand into Jesus' side and professing the most profound faith, will

---

2. The Lutheran theologian Eberhard Jüngel, "Sakrament und Repräsentation: Wesen und Funktion der sakramentalen Handlung," in his *Ganz Werden: Theologische Erörterungen* (Tübingen: Mohr Siebeck, 2003), 5:274–88.

3. J.-N. Aletti, "Signes, accomplissement et temps," *Recherches de science religieuse* 75, no. 2 (1987): 305–20.

complete this movement: blessed are they who believe without having seen, because they see and touch sacramentally (Jn 20:24–29).[4]

Later on, the apostles would base their authority as witnesses of Jesus on an experience with Eucharistic overtones: they "ate and drank with Him after He rose from the dead" (Acts 10:41). St. Paul, for his part, after being dazzled by the light and hearing the voice of Christ along the road to Damascus, received baptism and, with it, the ability to hear the gospel and to proclaim it (Acts 9:17–18; 22:17). And when St. Peter declares, "without having seen Him [Jesus Christ] you love Him" (1 Pt 1:8), this is situated also in a baptismal context: this experience is possible because Christians, reborn through the word, possess a new way of knowing (1 Pt 1:3–9, 23).

Moreover it is likely that the oldest professions of faith that are recorded in the New Testament matured in a liturgical soil (Phil 2:6–11; 1 Cor 8:6, 15:3–5; 1 Tm 3:16, etc.). The sacraments, especially the Eucharist, are the ambiance in which the community experiences Christ's presence and proclaims him as *Kyrios*, as the risen, all-powerful Lord. The word of faith will not be transmitted if it resounds outside of this sphere, just as a voice does not carry without the vibrating air. This outlook continues along a line that came from the Old Testament, as is shown, for example, by the "little historical creed" (Dt 26:1–5), where the profession of faith accompanies the offering of the first-fruits in the temple.[5]

In fact, contemporary scholarship is finding more and more evidence for the thesis that all the New Testament scriptures were written with worship as the point of departure, which suggests a corollary: its pages must be read in terms of worship. Thus, the Letter to the Corinthians opens with a liturgical greeting, and its final verses recall the beginning of the Eucharistic rite.[6] In Ephesians, to cite another example, the church is presented to us as a cultic community: someone who enters into this ecclesial space discovers the mystery of God revealed in Christ.[7] The Acts of the Apostles preserved for us the memory of a Eucharist that was prolonged well into the night,

---

4. André Feuillet, "La recherche du Christ dans la Nouvelle Alliance d'après la Christophanie de Jo. 20,11–18," in his *L'Homme devant Dieu: mélanges offerts au Père Henri de Lubac* (Paris: Aubier, 1963), 1:93–112, at 110.

5. Antonio Bonora, "Dalla storia e dalla natura alla professione di fede e alla celebrazione (Dt 26, 1–5)," *Parola di Spirito e Vita* 25 (1992): 27–39; Scott Hahn, "Canon, Cult and Covenant: The Promise of Liturgical Hermeneutics," in *Canon and Biblical Interpretation*, ed. C. G. Bartholomew (Grand Rapids, Mich.: Zondervan, 2006), 207–35.

6. Günther Bornkamm, "Zum Verständnis des Gottesdienstes bei Paulus," in his *Das Ende des Gesetzes: Paulusstudien* (Munich: Kaiser Verlag, 1958), 113–32.

7. Franz Mussner, "Die Kirche als Kultgemeinde nach dem Neuen Testament," in his *Praesentia Salutis: Gesammelte Studien zu Fragen und Themen des Neuen Testaments* (Düsseldorf: Patmos-Verlag, 1967), 253–67.

with the prolix homily of St. Paul, and concluded with the breaking of the bread (Acts 20:7–12).[8] We can suppose that on other occasions, when the Apostle was absent, his discourse would be replaced by the reading of his letters, which made him present among the faithful.

We get a glimpse of this in other New Testament writings too. The Letter to the Hebrews is designed to be read in a liturgical celebration;[9] and John narrates his revelation one Sunday, thus linking his experience of Christ to worship, in which Jesus appears as "the Living One" (Rv 1:18).[10] Some maintain that the Synoptic Gospels were written in order to be proclaimed in the liturgy, and that this context explains important elements of their structure.[11] John's Gospel, for its part, which catches a glimpse of the signs and the glory of Jesus, takes the sacramental viewpoint as the one best suited to approach the life of Christ.[12]

The patristic period sowed in those same furrows. Justin Martyr mentions the Gospels (which he calls "memoirs of the apostles") right when he is describing the Eucharistic memorial of Jesus.[13] Many other Church Fathers explain theology in a baptismal context, as "mystagogues," who enlighten the believer about the mysteries in which he is starting to participate.[14] St. Irenaeus of Lyons, to cite another example, argues that sound theological doctrine has to be based on a solid Eucharistic foundation. Therefore he rebukes the Gnostics, who were hostile toward God's creation, for continuing to celebrate the Eucharist, because it contains bread and wine, gifts of the creator. The church's doctrine, on the contrary, "is in harmony with the Eucharist and the Eucharist, for its part, confirms our doctrine."[15]

St. Augustine continues this line of argument in a new key by defining the sacraments as "visible words" with which God communicates to us. In them, therefore, we have the language of the faith or the grammar of all transmission of the mystery. The Sentences of Peter Lombard (written in the

---

8. John Paul Heil, *The Letters of Paul as Rituals of Worship* (Eugene, Ore.: Cascade, 2011); Martin Vahrenhorst, *Kultische Sprache in den Paulusbriefen* (Tübingen: Mohr Siebeck, 2008).

9. John Paul Heil, *Worship in the Letter to the Hebrews* (Eugene, Ore.: Wipf and Stock, 2011).

10. Fergus King, "*Lex orandi, lex credendi*: worship and doctrine in Revelation 4–5," *Scottish Journal of Theology* 67, no. 1 (2014): 33–49.

11. Denis Farkasfalvy, "The Eucharistic Provenance of the Christian Bible," in his *Inspiration and Interpretation: A Theological Introduction to Sacred Scripture* (Washington, D.C.: The Catholic University of America Press, 2010), 63–87.

12. See the discussion in chapter 3, below.

13. Justin Martyr, *1 Apologiae* 67, 3 (Patristische Texte und Studien [hereafter PTS] 38:129).

14. Vittorino Grossi, "*Regula veritatis* e *narratio* battesimale in sant'Ireneo," *Augustinianum* 12, no. 3 (1972): 437–63.

15. Irenaeus of Lyons, *Adversus haereses* IV, 18, 5 (Sources Chrétiennes [hereafter SC] 100:610). St. Basil the Great uses a similar way of reasoning when he proves faith in the Holy Spirit by the practice of baptism: Basil, *On the Holy Spirit*, XII (SC 17:156–57).

twelfth century), which were omnipresent during the Middle Ages, would reflect this insight by the very way in which they were arranged. The master follows the Augustinian division of theological teaching. This refers, in the first place, to revealed "realities" (*res*) as the object of its study. In the second place it is about the "signs" (*signa*) with which these realities are communicated, signs that make up the language in which God has shown himself to us.[16] Peter Lombard dedicates three of his four books to exploring the "realities": God, creation, Christ. The fourth volume is reserved for the signs that enable us to understand these salvific realities, and it deals precisely with the sacraments.[17] The sacraments, therefore, do not correspond strictly speaking to subject matter that is discussed, but rather to the language or grammar that enable us to understand and to communicate any theological matter.

Contemporary theology, starting with the liturgical movement, continued the patristic and medieval line of inquiry that was just sketched.[18] The sacraments, centered on the Eucharist, are the space or place where we experience the living, tangible presence of Jesus among men, thus accepting his mysteries; and, given that every theological outlook starts from this encounter with the risen Lord, the sacraments establish the vantage point from which to study theology. Their primary function, therefore, is not to be seen, but rather to teach us to see; and also to hear, touch, and taste, inasmuch as the sacramental space welcomes the whole person, with all his senses. As long as theology is united with the sacraments, it will never be an abstract theory, but rather a kind of knowledge rooted in the body, in the communal space in which salvation history is lived out.

It makes sense, then, that the sacraments are not confined to the field occupied by the seven salvific rites and that they extend their influence to the other treatises. In order to speak about man and God, in order to speak about the church and the cosmos, in order to preserve the memory of creation and to glimpse the glorious future, it will be necessary to situate ourselves in the area that they display. Some have proposed, therefore, that theology should always be sacramental theology, born and bred in the area

16. Augustine, *De doctrina christiana*, I, 2, 2 (CCL 32:7): "Omnis doctrina uel rerum est uel signorum, sed res per signa discuntur" (Every doctrine is either about realities or about signs, but the realities are learned through the signs).

17. Peter Lombard, *Libri IV Sententiarum* [hereafter *Sent.*] IV, prol., Spicilegium Bonaventurianum 4 (Rome: Collegii S. Bonaventurae Ad Claras Aquas, 1971) [hereafter SpBon], 5:231: "His tractatis quae ad doctrinam rerum pertinent, quibus fruendum est, et quibus utendum est, et quae fruuntur et utuntur, ad doctrinam signorum accedamus" (Having discussed these things that pertain to the doctrine about the realities, which ones are to be enjoyed and which ones are to be used and which ones enjoy and use, we turn now to the doctrine of signs).

18. Joris Geldhof, "Liturgy as Theological Norm: Getting Acquainted with 'Liturgical Theology,'" *Neue Zeitschrift für Systematische Theologie und Religionsphilosophie* 52, no. 2 (2010): 155–76.

of worship.[19] This is the point of the maxim *lex orandi, lex credendi*: the *lex credendi*, Christian doctrine, is a light that emanates from the fire of a sacramental experience, governed by the *lex orandi*.[20]

A Sacramental Viewpoint for the Study of Theology

The sacraments, therefore, open the space from which to have a sort of outlook, which we can call the sacramental outlook, which is capable of receiving the divine light and reflecting it to others. They contain the "Christian perspective" that makes it possible to define the essence of our faith.[21] What are the features of such a perspective? The task of this manual will be to get to know them in detail; let us list now the most prominent ones.

The Sacramental Outlook, from the Space of the Body of Jesus

Looking at things in terms of the sacraments means looking at them in terms of a space, the space opened up by the encounter with Christ. Its structure is given to us in the rites established by Jesus, particularly the Eucharist. And we notice right away that the sacramental space is a space founded in the flesh, into which we enter with all our senses. The sacraments, in fact, are rooted in tangible elements, beginning with the bread and wine that are changed into body and blood. The matter of the sacrament refers, therefore, to the presence of a body, Christ's, in which Christians participate. The rest of the sacramental economy will continue this logic: water poured out, oil that anoints, hands that cover the head, and so on—these are different ways of being assimilated into the body of Jesus. The word (*logos*) of theo-*logy* will have to be pronounced (as the word or form of each sacrament) over the concrete matter of our life in the flesh, thus tying it to the flesh of the Savior.

This inclusion of matter in the rite coincides with a fundamental datum of the encounter with the Paschal Christ. His apparitions revolve around corporeal experiences: eating, drinking, touching Jesus so as to verify that he is substantial. He is not a phantom: he really is present among things and possesses a concrete story, with living memories and a plan for the future. One can give it fish to eat, one can put a hand into its wound; it comes and

---

19. Here we have one of the major contributions of the work of Odo Casel: Arno Schilson, *Theologie als Sakramententheologie: die Mysterientheologie Odo Casels* (Mainz: Matthias Grünewald, 1987).

20. Paul de Clerck, "*Lex orandi, lex credendi*: sens originel et avatars historiques d'un adage équivoque," *Questions liturgiques et paroissiales* 59, no. 4 (1978): 193–212.

21. Julián Marías, *La perspectiva cristiana* (Madrid: Alianza Editorial, 1999).

goes from one location to another, becoming involved with the events of the world. Thus it becomes clear that the ultimate destination of Jesus' path is not a life beyond the body, but rather the glorious transformation of its corporeal presence.

This datum of faith illuminates our original experience of the body, which Jesus took on and expanded. The body is, in fact, the first space that is given to us to situate us between things and persons and to form bonds with them. In the body we recognize that we are debtors, recipients of an original gift, understanding that someone generated us; in the body we know that we are sharers in a communion that welcomes us, first in the maternal womb, then in the familial home. The body invites us to keep building this communion, now in the spousal surrender, now in the generation and education of children, now in the service of the common good, and so on.

The corporeal setting of the risen Lord, in which we participate in the sacraments, proves to be, in this light, a setting of communion. To speak about the flesh of Jesus is to speak about the environment of personal relationships that he started, in giving light to the church. In order to see sacramentally, one must place oneself in this relational setting of Jesus, a setting dominated—like the magnetic field surrounding a lodestone—by his presence and by the bonds that he establishes. Because it is rooted in the body, the sacramental outlook therefore proves to be an outlook in common, the specific outlook of "us." It does not just contemplate the love that God has shown for us, but rather contemplates "in terms of" this love, allowing oneself to be surrounded by it, receiving it and responding to it.

The sacramental perspective is opposed, therefore, to the outlook of the solitary individual, who observes objects while being entrenched in his subjectivity. One cannot know sacramentally if one knows only from outside, situating oneself at a safe distance, with the attitude of a spectator. The stained windows of the church, seen from the street, seem gray and formless; the sacramental outlook, on the contrary, is a participatory outlook in which one allows oneself to be surrounded by the light and discovers its beauty. Thus St. Irenaeus taught: "those who see the light are in the light and perceive its brightness."[22] We can conclude that someone who contemplates revelation in terms of the sacraments does not attain his knowledge by abstracting from the flesh, but rather by delving more deeply into the relations that open up to us in it.[23]

22. Irenaeus of Lyons, *Adversus haereses* IV, 20, 5 (SC 100:640).
23. José Granados, "Taste and See: the Body and the Experience of God," *Communio* 37, no. 2 (Summer 2010): 292–308.

The Sacramental Outlook, in Terms of the
Time Spent on Earth by Jesus

The sacramental outlook is not just situated in a setting, but is also passing through a story. In order to prove this, it is enough, once again, to look at the Eucharist, the place of memory and of hope. There the life of Jesus is recalled, with its origin in God; and yearning for his parousia is communicated, as the risen life that he received from the Father is anticipated for us. Every disciple who partakes of the sacrament is Thomas (Jn 20:28), who touches the open wounds (past) and professes that Christ (present) is his God and definitive Savior (future). After the sacraments, the word (*logos*) of theo-*logy* will always be a word that tells a story.

As for the *past*, the sacrament participates in the memory of Jesus, who instituted it ("in memory of Me"). In turn, Jesus himself recalled in his rite the story of the people after their liberation from Egypt. And this memory takes us back in time to gratitude for all creation, which is included in the bread and wine. Thus he confessed to his Father, as the most original, immemorial, and unforgettable memory, that he is in the beginning of all human knowledge.

Furthermore, the light that is perceived in the sacrament comes to us from a *future* time: the time of the risen Jesus, which anticipates in itself the end of history. The Eucharist, in effect, situates us in the presence of the definitive expectation of the Kingdom: "Maranatha!" (1 Cor 16:22).[24] The sacramental outlook helps to discover that life, in the light of its fruit perfected in Jesus, is full of productive seeds. Thus it allows us to grasp the promising aspect of every thing and of every event, noticing the increase of reality with which everything is sown.

This corresponds to the experience of the disciples who, upon encountering the glorified Christ, professed him as the fullness of time. The one who anticipated the end of the ages, leading history to an unsuspected goal at God's right hand, could not but possess also the secret of its beginning. In the warmth of the Paschal experience was born the profession of faith in Jesus as the preexisting Son of the Father, and as Lord who will come to judge us in glory.

In conclusion, the sacrament infuses in us a knowledge that takes the shape of a story, according to the temporal rhythm of the celebration (from Sunday to Sunday, from Easter to Easter, from Jubilee to Jubilee). The sac-

---

24. 1 Cor 16:22; *Didache* X, 6 (SC 248:182): the expression appears in a clearly Eucharistic context.

ramental outlook is capable of seeing only when it enters into the course of the ages: it sees in the measure in which it travels on.[25] In fact, it is by recounting the beneficent deeds of Yahweh that we can spell out his name and discover for ourselves the covenant to which he calls us.

It is not surprising, in light of what has been said, that the perspective of the sacraments, starting from their concentration on Christ, can be extended to all of salvation history, thus forming an axis by which to orient oneself in the course of the ages.[26] According to Hugh of St. Victor, the author of the first systematic treatise on the sacraments, God has left no step of sinful man's path unaccompanied by them.[27]

Let us summarize the points that have just been sketched. In the first place, the sacraments open up to us *a space* established by the presence of Christ, which is a communal space rooted in the flesh. Moreover, secondly, the sacraments introduce us *into a history*: the recollection of the life of Jesus and the anticipation of its fullness.[28] The Eucharist combines these two features: it is about (1) entering into the space opened up by the body of Jesus in his embrace of love ("take, My body; drink, My blood"); and (2) remembering with him the work of the Father ("do this in memory of Me") in the hope of a fulfillment ("until He comes [again]" in order to "drink of the fruit of the vine in the Kingdom" [1 Cor 11:26; Lk 22:18]). By joining these two aspects we can conclude: the space opened up by the sacraments is a dynamic space. Does not the whole Bible narrate "the history of a place," in other words, the building in time of a space—the flesh of a family, the Garden of Eden, the temple, the holy city and the Holy Land— in which God dwells with men? The sacramental outlook teaches us: only someone who dwells in this space and adopts the rhythm of its construction can understand scripture and the mystery to which it testifies for us.

---

25. Francis, *Lumen Fidei*, Encyclical Letter, June 29, 2013, par. 9; in *Acta Apostolicae Sedis* [hereafter *AAS*] 105 (2013): 559.

26. Joseph Ratzinger, "Zum Begriff des Sakramentes," in his *Gesammelte Schriften*, vol. 11: *Theologie der Liturgie* (Freiburg im Breisgau: Herder, 2008), 215–32; translated as "On the Concept of Sacrament" in his *Collected Works: Theology of the Liturgy* (San Francisco, Calif.: Ignatius Press, 2014), 11:169–84.

27. Hugh of St. Victor, *De sacramentis* I, 8, 12, in Patrologia Latina, ed. J.-P. Migne (Paris, 1841–55) [hereafter PL], 176:313. Also in *Hugonis de Sancto Victore de sacramentis Christianae fidei*, ed. R. Berndt (Frankfurt: Aschendorff, 2008) [hereafter *CV*], 1:204: "Si quis igitur quaerat tempus institutionis sacramentorum sciat quia quamdiu morbus est, tempus est medicinae" (Therefore if someone asks the time of the institution of the sacraments, let him know that as long as there is sickness, it is time for medicine).

28. This approach avoids reducing the sacraments to their merely anthropological side—a danger into which some of contemporary reflection has fallen. See Giuseppe Colombo, "Dove va la teologia sacramentaria?," *La Scuola Cattolica* 102 (1974): 673–717.

Sacramental Outlook and Man's Original Experience

If the sacramental outlook is acquired by entering into the space and passing through the time inaugurated by Jesus, it is important to add that this space and this story of the Savior will be glimpsed with the space and the story that we share with all human beings. Once again, this is confirmed for us by the Eucharist, which contains bread and wine, witnesses of a tradition of work and art; and it accommodates the pilgrimage of Israel, pursued for generations after its Passover.

This reflects a distinctive feature of the encounter with Christ in the sacraments. Given that he assumed our flesh and entered into the concrete setting of our familial and social relations, the sacramental space of his body and blood is situated within the cosmos and in the midst of the common life of human beings. The new place or house that Jesus inaugurated by dwelling among us (Jn 1:14) was the same house that God promised to David in days of yore (2 Sm 7:11), which in turn rose upon that first house of clay that God arranged for man by shaping him out of the earth (Gn 2:7). If this is so, then the sacrament, in opening the space of corporeal communion with Jesus, situates us in a new way in creation and among men; the sacramental vantage point allows us to look more deeply at all things with eyes that are more open.

What was said about *space* applies also to sacramental *time*. For the story of Christ, condensed in the Eucharist, is intertwined with the course of the generations from the beginning of the world: he is the son of Mary, a daughter of Abraham, son of Adam (Lk 3:38). Therefore, when the sacrament introduces us into the life of Jesus, it enables us to recover the memory of creation and to gain a full insight into its destiny. The celebration thereof, in terms of the memory of the master and hope in him, sharpens our vision so as to understand the movement of all things and the development of all events.

This implies that the Christian sacramental outlook is not situated on the margin of the other areas of life. For entering into the space of the sacraments changes our way of living in the world by providing a new perspective on reality. Thus we acquire an outlook that produces a culture, as culture is born when there is among human beings a common setting of life and a shared form of passing through history, celebrating the origin together and imagining the future. It is no accident that the words "culture" and "cultivate" have the same root. Just as the farmer is concerned above all with the soil that receives the seed and the microclimate of sunlight and water that will cause it to germinate, so too human culture starts, not from the human being in his isolated awareness, but rather from the relations that surround and sustain him and from the narratives that accompany him through the generations—relations and narratives engendered precisely by the sacraments.

Hence, inasmuch as the sacramental outlook is born in the encounter with Christ and in terms of the company of his recapitulating narrative, it calls for a cultural dialogue with the personal perspective of each human being in every time and place. This demand is becoming particularly dramatic in our postmodern condition, which is characterized, as we shall see, by the loss of welcoming spaces and of narratable times that humanize life. The analysis that follows will show us, on the one hand, the urgency of the sacramental method in the hour that is tolling; it will make us see, on the other hand, that a renewal of the Christian outlook is precisely what will attract postmodern man.

The Sacramental Viewpoint in Postmodern Culture

The sacramental outlook, as I have said, is always situated in a space, a space from which it is possible to recall the origin and to have a presentiment of the future, a space comparable to a garden in which traces of the sowing remain and one looks forward to the sure fruit. I will prove, as I have just pointed out, that this outlook is much needed in our culture, where there is a lack of habitable spaces and passable times for human beings. Rooted here, in this growing narrowness of space and time, is the deeper cause of contemporary secularization; therefore the sacramental viewpoint is ideal for the new evangelization, which proposes the Christian message in a postmodern context.

Reduction of Spaces and Impoverishment of Symbols

The major transformations of the modern world have resulted in a new way of considering space. Biblical culture, and with it all of antiquity, always kept man associated with his setting. What a man was and what his life consisted of could be known only by knowing the place where he lived, the persons who surrounded him, the relations that sheltered him. Hence God prepared for the children of Adam, when he fashioned them and gave them names, a cultivated garden; and he promised them a land in which to build houses and to dwell in them, to plant vineyards and to eat of their fruit. The first space in which man dwelt was his body, which already included within it the elements of the cosmos; next came the space of the family, the foundations of which were established by God; and then the city, the people, the whole world.

In the modern world man's destiny has ceased to be linked to his setting, and the latter has been reduced to the abstract space of physical science. Space, in the Cartesian view, is a specific feature of matter or *res extensa*, detached from what is specifically human, in other words, from the thinking mind.[29] Its coordinates are abstract; it is devoid of form; it has no center. All spaces end up being equal and in none of them can we feel welcomed. In this new perspective the person is discovered only against the vast infinity of the stars, and he will be seized with the terror that frightened Pascal.[30] This leads to an individualistic view of man who, deprived of a habitable setting, is reduced to the isolated point of his own reflection.

Each view of space (the ancient one of welcoming space or the modern one of extraneous space) is connected with a specific way of considering the relations of objects among themselves and with man. We can call this reference between some things and others, and of all of them to the human subject, *symbol*. As we will see, this is an important term for the way in which theology has thought about the sacraments. The concept is slippery, as its scope changes depending on how man understands his way of being settled in the world and of relating with things.[31] I will describe three stages in which the openness of beings among themselves and toward man is perceived in different ways depending on how belonging to space is experienced; in this openness their symbolism resides.

First, the cosmos of ancient man constituted *an abode* full of objects that were related with one another and with human destiny. For things spoke about a memory and about an inheritance, like old paintings or furniture in a family mansion. And they contained paths on which to walk through life, just as the name received from one's ancestors points to a vocation and a destiny. In deciphering this language, each person deciphered himself, the way in which belonging to a home determines who we are and how we approach life. The relation between things (their symbolism) was known by connaturality, in other words, by entering into relation with them, accepting them cordially as we accept our native language. Insofar as this home, just like all homes, was open to the mystery of the creator, it could be considered

29. About the lack of surroundings or setting in which Descartes reasoned, Maurizio Vitta, "La stufa di Cartesio," in his *Dell'abitare: Corpi spazi oggetti immagini* (Turin: Einaudi, 2008), 34–40.

30. Blaise Pascal, *Pensées* (Paris: Edition Sellier, Le Livre de Poche, 1992), nos. 102 (874) and 233 (951).

31. Charles Taylor, *The Ethics of Authenticity* (Cambridge, Mass.: Harvard University Press, 1991).

as a great temple: from this perspective the Jews saw in the sanctuary in Jerusalem a miniature of the cosmos and at the same time the columns that sustained it.[32]

Second, the modern subject also conceived of the world as an immense net in which all things were linked, but he decided to situate himself in an observatory that distanced him from them so as to keep them under control. In effect, after the scientific and technological revolution we have looked at the universe as a homogenous region, with precise movements governed by equations that can be determined with great precision. In them no conscious, free force intervened, as the laws of mechanics were already fixed in advance: man could only examine the universe from outside, suspecting that when he had answered all the questions of science he would nevertheless not have begun to unveil the mystery of human life.[33] Nature, far from reminding us of a home, resembled instead a hieroglyphic, or perhaps *a labyrinth*. For the labyrinth is a place full of symbols, understood as enigmas that it is important to unravel, which impede our knowledge of our origin and destiny. Moreover, although the symbols of the home are revealed to the one who dwells in it, those of the labyrinth are mastered only from outside, from a bird's-eye view, by escaping from its enclosures. These are the symbols belonging to modern man, symbols from which he always keeps his distance and in which one personally has no stake.

Third, the vanishing point that this process tends toward is clear: abandoning the labyrinth of symbols, getting rid of it, being able to look at it from outside. Our postmodern society is reaching that point, to the extent to which it dissociates the subject from the language of his own body, the ultimate interference of the cosmos in personal identity. All symbols today tend to be reduced to the symbols of the digital culture, to those malleable avatars that modify our face to suit our fancy. Outside the labyrinth, man now feels capable of redesigning the form of his walls, making it a looking-glass for himself. Symbols are created and recreated at his pleasure; absolute liberation is achieved in this way.

Are we talking about a true liberation? A short story by Borges denounces the illusory character of this final step.[34] A king of Babylon built a labyrinth full of twists and turns and invited one of his guests, the monarch of Arabia, to enter into it, thinking that he would make fun of his gullibility.

---

32. Stefan Heid, *Kreuz. Jerusalem. Kosmos. Aspekte frühchristlicher Staurologie* (Münster: Aschendorff, 2001).

33. Ludwig Wittgenstein, *Tractatus Logico-Philosophicus* (New York: Routledge, 2005), VI, 52 (186).

34. Jorge Luis Borges, "Los dos reyes y los dos laberintos," in his *El Aleph*, 1:607.

The latter could not manage to get out, feared for his life, and finally, sweating profusely, escaped miraculously by calling upon God, and he silently swore to take vengeance. If you have the opportunity, he said to the illustrious king, travel to my land, where there is a labyrinth much more ingenious than this one. Fortune smiled on the monarch of Arabia who, as he went back to his country, conquered the nearby lands until he took the Chaldean prisoner and led him in handcuffs to his estates. Then he assembled a group of camels and rode for three days into the desert. There he abandoned the foreigner, ordering him: Try to get out of this labyrinth of mine, in which there are no walls, nor hiding-places, nor doors!

Let us review these images. The manner in which we conceive of space will be our way of understanding the symbol. The symbols of home, those of the labyrinth, and those of the desert are very different. In the first case the symbols are linked with the life of man, who knows them through connaturality by dwelling among them. It is expected, on the contrary, that the symbol-labyrinth will be seen from outside, as a purely mathematical relation that is extrinsic to man's identity. Escaping from the labyrinth leads to the desert, where every symbol is a mirage, a projection of capricious subjectivity. And this desert, as Borges teaches us, is not liberation from the labyrinth, but rather the definitive victory of inextricability.

There seems to be no exit and no return from this situation. Of course, no one can restore the premodern vision of a world that appeared as a harmonious village in which everything had its place. The scientific revolution made impossible the naive outlook that discerns the "kingdoms" of nature. Only on the basis of the subject's experience is it possible now to colonize the universe, repopulating it with symbols that make it habitable. But why does this experience not inevitably lead to the desert of mirages in which the individual projects himself onto the world?

We have to answer: another way out is possible, which changes the labyrinth back into a dwelling and not into a desert. If modernity has failed in this task it is because it supposed that the human way of knowing was the way of the isolated mind, uncontaminated by matter. But if we again take man's experience in all its breadth, clearly it includes corporeality and, with it, the familiar relation between man and the universe. Our embodied condition offers us a viewpoint that is bound up with the cosmos, from which it is possible, once again, to discover the intrinsic symbolism of things—the dwelling in symbols—while recovering our place among them.[35]

35. Gabriel Marcel, "L'être incarné, repère central de la réflexion métaphysique," in his *Du refus à l'invocation* (Paris: Gallimard, 1940), 19–54.

This is precisely the space that the sacraments display. In fact, starting from the corporeal encounter with the risen Lord, the sacramental outlook takes the perspective of the body as the primary space of presence among things and of relation among human beings; as the first place in which one settles and participates in the world. This is the space where all beings can start speaking again and can reveal an order in which the person successfully situates himself and understands his vocation. From the Christian sacramental outlook one discovers then a way to remedy the deficit of habitable space in which to live.

The Sacramental Outlook, a Response to Secularization

What has been said about the reduction of habitable spaces for man (the passage from the dwelling to the labyrinth and to the desert) is at the root of contemporary secularization. Given that the dwelling opens onto the temple, to tear down one is to demolish the other. What has been terminated is not only the sacramental space of relation between man and things, but also that of the relation of everything with its God.

In fact, a connection has been verified between the secularization of society and the decline of the sacraments. It is certain, on the one hand, that the sacraments are in crisis because people have lost the lively experience of God and take no pleasure in rites or ceremonies.[36] On the other hand, the converse is true too, and more interesting: the loss of the sacramental practice (in the family, in the workplace, in leisure, in politics, etc.), the one thing capable of opening up habitable spaces where God manifests himself, has caused our lack of faith. God has gone away, as he abandoned the sanctuary in the prophet's vision (Ezek 10:15–19), not because man has thrown him out of the depths of man's mind—which is, in fact, the only place that modern men have been kept at his disposal—but rather because man has stopped cultivating settings that are hospitable for him: dwellings, streets, squares, lands.

This is confirmed for us by a reading of the book *A Secular Age*, in which the Canadian philosopher Charles Taylor describes the principal features of secularization, while distinguishing three senses of the term.[37] In the most obvious sense, "secularization" implies that God is absent because *the people practice their religion less*, attend worship less, while their interest in rituals declines. It is true that in some parts of the world we observe a revival of

---

36. Michel de Certeau, "La faiblesse de croire," in his *La faiblesse de croire* (Paris: Seuil, 1987), 299–305, at 302.

37. Charles Taylor, *A Secular Age* (Cambridge, Mass.: Harvard University Press, 2007).

religious sentiment that appears to belie this fact. Taylor opines, nevertheless, that this revival does not change the secularized situation of the world,
because there are other meanings of the word that show the persistence of
the phenomenon.

Indeed, in a more precise sense, modern "secularization" means that
God is *absent from the public square*: from government, from the sciences,
from technology, etc., and this exclusion comes to be required as a necessary
hypothesis for coexistence. One can believe in God, they say, and practice
one's faith, but without harboring any claims that this faith can modify
common life. In all public settings, even if one is a believer, it is necessary
to act as though God did not exist.[38] We should understand that, even if
religious practice increases, secularization in this second sense will continue
to be present: the exclusion of God from the public square and from the
concrete unfolding of events. If the supposed religious revival stops short
without transforming this second idea of secularity, it will have little weight.
Although God will be present, he will not matter for the common life, nor
will he shape the spaces of relations in which our identity is forged.

What makes matters worse is that there is, according to Taylor, *a third
sense of secularization*, which will continue unchanged even if the other two
are overcome. Today faith is thought of, in a pluralistic society, as one option
among many: one can choose to believe or not, to believe in this God or in
some other one. This means that faith is no longer one of the foundational
realities, but rather one of the realities founded on something else. Now, for
the Christian, faith is not just another option that one can embrace or not,
but rather the radical substratum which constitutes the person, which cannot be denied without denying oneself. Biblical faith, in fact, means to rely
totally on God, to establish him as the foundation of one's whole existence.
Faith, therefore, does not open up secondary spaces in which to broaden
life, but rather constitutes the original, fundamental space without which
every other space ends up turning into a labyrinth or a desert. Is it possible
to recover this vision of faith as the foundation of every other cultural edifice that is fit for human habitation?

From Taylor's analysis we can conclude that secularization concerns not
so much the question of whether or not one believes in God, but rather
more exactly: (1) the question about the influence of faith in the social and
cosmic world (this is the question about *the exteriority of faith*); (2) the question about faith's ability to be the foundation of man's space and the coor-

38. Livio Melina, "The Eclipse of the Sense of God and of Man," *Communio* 34, no. 1 (2007):
100–116.

dinates of his time (this is the question about *the radical character of faith*). According to this analysis, any return to religion that is a flight into interiority is only an accessory form of secularization; for in reality this is the type of religion that a secularized society promotes. Some contemporary phenomena of religious "revival" could be understood, from this perspective and paradoxically, as a prolongation of the loss of the sacred that is typical of the modern era.[39]

Well, then, the sacraments are essential to illuminate *point (1) about the exteriority of faith*: they tell us that faith is not played out in the subjective certainty of a private conviction, whether it be an opinion or a sentiment, but rather in common actions that concern man's body and his time, thus inaugurating a space of new relations with God and among ourselves. Recall that the Christian liturgy from its beginnings took on elements of the cult of the emperor, proclaiming Jesus as universal king. This revealed the claims of the new religion: to transform the concrete space of the public square, giving it the form of filial and familiar communion, not of despotic dominion.[40]

In this way the sacraments also elucidate *point (2) about the radical character of faith*: if faith is sacramental then it concerns and shapes the original corporeal space of our belonging to the world, to the place where the relations that constitute us as persons are brought forth, beginning with sonship and brotherhood. It is characteristic of faith to establish this space in a foundational relation with the Father. The life setting that is open for faith cannot be, therefore, just another accessory plan for a high-rise construction, but rather the foundational way of dwelling in the world and of passing through time, starting from the covenant with Yahweh. Therefore faith is situated at a deeper level than the judgments and choices that we make because these judgments and choices are always accomplished in terms of a concrete placement among things, the foundation of which is laid by faith. Sacramental faith, before being the fruit of human desiring and knowing, precedes this very desiring and knowing, generating and sustaining it. One does not lose faith as a wristwatch is lost; one abandons the faith as one abandons one's homeland for a gloomy exile.

In light of what has been said, the sacraments prove to be the key for proposing the faith again to a secularized culture, thus revitalizing that

---

39. Thus I disagree with the analysis by Peter L. Berger, "The Desecularization of the World: A Global Overview," in Berger (ed.), *The Desecularization of the World: Resurgent Religion and World Politics* (Grand Rapids, Mich.: Eerdmans, 1999).

40. Erik Peterson, *Das Buch von den Engeln: Stellung und Bedeutung der heiligen Engel im Kultus* (Leipzig: Jakob Hegner, 1935).

same culture. A well-known theologian from the past century warned: the Christian of the future will be mystical or he will not be a Christian.[41] This insight has to be made concrete, avoiding the misunderstanding of mystical experience as the spiritualization of the isolated conscience. For the mystery was made flesh in the concrete world, within a framework of relations and stories. And therefore it is more appropriate to say: the Christianity of the future will be sacramental or it will not be Christian.

The Treatise of General Sacramental Theology

We began by considering the sacraments not only as a concrete field that theology illuminates, but as spaces of relations from which it is possible to contemplate the mystery and to delve into it.[42] This sacramental point of view turns out to illuminate also the most original human experience and the cultural situation in which we live, especially in matters concerning the way to revive the presence of God. Let us examine from this perspective the guiding principles of this treatise, which has features in common with fundamental theology.[43]

Objective of a General Sacramental Theology

The treatise on the sacraments in general (*de sacramentis in genere*) appeared rather late: it entered the curriculum only in the twelfth century, when it was clearly defined what a sacrament is and the seven that fit the definition were enumerated. The Church Fathers in fact had no overarching concept that included within it the sacraments as species of one and the same genus.[44] Following scripture, they speak instead about specific sacraments, especially about baptism and the Eucharist, yet they were aware that these salvific rites share many features. For this reason we can understand this delay in elaborating a system: the sacraments are, as we have shown, a point of view about the revealed mystery and therefore the last thing that theological reflection considers; similarly, the final reality that the eye looks at is the light that surrounds it. This explains also why the Fathers use the word "sacrament" to refer not only to the Christian rites but to the whole mystery of salvation, which the sacraments display for us to see.

41. Karl Rahner, "Frömmigkeit heute und morgen," *Geist und Leben* 39, no. 5 (1966): 326–42, at 335.
42. José Granados, "Los sentidos de la fe," in *El que cree ve: Reflexiones en torno a la enciclica Lumen fidei*, ed. José Granados and Juan de Dios Larrú (Burgos: Monte Carmelo, 2014), 29–49.
43. The importance of the worship experience for fundamental theology is explored by Pierangelo Sequeri, *Il Dio affidabile: Saggio di teologia fondamentale* (Brescia: Queriniana, 1996), 733–70.
44. Granados, "Los sentidos de la fe."

The Middle Ages carried out a synthesizing effort which led, as I said, to a definition of sacrament. Concise formulas arose ("an efficacious sign of grace"), its composition of matter and form was determined, the way in which it causes grace was explained. Each sacrament was studied as a particular case of this overall view. At first the term included the rites of the Old Testament, and little by little it concentrated on those of the New Law. Thus we have a notion of sacrament that can be applied to each one of the seven, and only to the seven, the complete list of which would be provided by the Council of Trent.[45] Throughout this process it was not forgotten that the sacraments are very different from each other and that they are organically connected, with the Eucharist in the center.

Several critiques of this approach, which starts from the generic sacrament, have been presented. In the first place, it is not an easy task to include all seven under a single concept, given the differences between them. Formulating a general definition involves the risk of putting the sacraments into a straitjacket in which the unique features of each salvific sign are lost. The matter and form, for example, are easy to discover in baptism and the Eucharist; but it takes some mental acrobatics to identify them in the sacraments of matrimony or penance. In view of this, some contemporary authors propose abolishing the treatise on general sacramental theology. There are some, for example, who want to integrate it into the treatise on baptism, which would then be the privileged reference point for understanding the sacraments.[46]

In the second place, general sacramental theology has been criticized for starting from an abstract definition of sacrament and then concentrating on the elements essential for the validity of the rite, and for thus forgetting the liturgical context of the celebrations, which is reduced to an ornament. Contemporary theology is sensitive to this critique, as it favors liturgical celebration as the point of departure for any presentation of the sacraments.[47] General sacramental theology would not seem to be very pertinent to this approach, because there is no such thing as the celebration of a "sacrament in general" or a "general celebration" of the sacraments.

What can we say about the difficulties that have been mentioned? While conceding that there is a grain of truth in them, a general study of the sacraments continues to be necessary. In fact, there is a paradox: the twentieth

---

45. Council of Trent, Session VII, *Decree on the Sacraments*, canon 1 (DH 1601).

46. Jean-Paul Revel, *Traité des sacrements*, vol. 1: *Baptême et sacramentalité: Origine et significa-tion du Baptême* (Paris: Cerf, 2004), 20; our view will be centered instead on the Eucharist.

47. Cesare Giraudo, *In unum corpus: Trattato mistagogico sull'eucaristia* (Rome: San Paolo, 2000).

century, in which there were plenty of objections to any global sacramental theology, developed, along other lines, an extension of the term "sacrament" to all creation and to the whole context of salvation, which makes the overall outlook more urgent. Far from losing its relevance, this treatise is of even greater interest; let us examine the tasks that justify its existence.

First, *the task of general sacramental theology is to order the sacraments among themselves, starting with the Eucharist.* If the sacraments are spaces from which to contemplate the mystery, these spaces have to have among themselves an organic unity, like the rooms of a house or the squares and streets of a city. This order starts, concretely, from the Eucharist, the key to worship in the New Testament and the central rite instituted by Jesus.[48] From the beginning, this is where the disciples experienced the encounter with the risen Lord and participated in the relations inaugurated by his body. The sacramental space therefore unfolds around the Eucharistic body and grows from it as its point of departure. Therefore systematic reflection on this order and harmony among the sacraments is necessary; without this reflection it would be impossible to understand each one of them separately. In light of this, it is up to general sacramental theology to explore the connection of each sacrament with the Eucharist, as the original place where the church is born and where the landmarks of her pilgrimage are displayed, starting from the life of Jesus. This is not so much about elaborating an abstract concept of sacrament as it is about identifying the connection that associates each sacrament with the Eucharist and all the sacraments with each other. In other words: the general concept of sacrament is not a generic concept but rather an *organic* one, which investigates the specific participation of each one of them in the Eucharistic fullness.

Second, *general sacramental theology is concerned with discovering the sacramental logic that guides all revelation; the global concept of sacrament attempts to reflect this logic.* We have seen that the Eucharist, along with the sacraments associated with it, is not simply another sector of the Christian faith but rather the setting for the encounter with Christ, in terms of which his entire plan of salvation is understood. Then the question arises about the features of the *sacramental outlook or logic* to which the concept of sacrament is linked. It is up to general sacramental theology to study, therefore, not only what the seven sacraments have in common, but also the sacramental features of Christian life. Therefore this discipline is called today to turn

---

48. Jerzy Klinger, "La *koinonia* comme sacramentelle: Perspectives actuelles," *Istina* 20 (1975): 100–111; Sergio Ubbiali, "Eucaristia e sacramentalità: Per una teologia del sacramento," *La Scuola Cattolica* 110 (1982): 540–76.

into a "fundamental sacramental theology" that is at the same time the substratum of fundamental theology.[49] This is not so much a matter of speaking about generalities shared by the seven but rather of laying the foundations (both theological and cultural) of a complete sacramental discourse that embraces all aspects of the faith.

Third, *the task of general sacramental theology is to enrich each theological treatise by examining it in a sacramental key.* If a sacrament is a place of access to the mystery, if it constitutes the space and time from which revelation is known, then sacramental theology will make itself present in all areas of dogma. Its concern is then to mark out the lines of a sacramental (and especially Eucharistic) reading of the other treatises.[50] This is obvious with regard to Christology. The Eucharist constitutes, in a singular manner, the space from which one can remember Jesus ("do this in memory of me") and penetrate into his mystery; he has body and blood, given for mankind; he pleases the Father as his only-begotten Son alone can, and furthermore it asks of the Father the supreme gift: to divinize the flesh by filling it with the Holy Spirit.[51] We see as well the importance of the sacramental factor in knowing who the church is, the community that springs up in the space generated by the sacraments, which has been called the "universal sacrament of salvation."[52] Protology (creation theology) and eschatology can be accessed also from the time of memory and hope in which we participate through the sacraments: they speak to us about the original creational space and about the definitive space that is already anticipated in the Eucharistic body and in the other sacraments. And of course the matter concerns the question about God: what are the features of his face, given that he desired to reveal himself sacramentally, in other words, by pitching his tent among us and telling us about his name through a concrete human narrative? The sacraments paste together the ideal cloth on which to imprint the image of the triune God who, because he is a communion of Persons, lives in a relational space.

---

49. This is a fact widely acknowledged in contemporary theology: Giuseppe Colombo, "Teologia sacramentaria e teologia fondamentale," *Teologia* 19, no. 3 (1994): 238–62; Schilson, *Theologie als Sakramententheologie*; Andrea Grillo, "L'esperienza rituale come 'dato' della teologia fondamentale: Ermeneutica di una rimozione," in *Liturgia e incarnazione*, ed. Aldo N. Terrin (Padua: EMP, 1997), 167–224; Edward Schillebeeckx, "La liturgia, lugar teológico," in his *Revelación y teologia* (Salamanca: Sigueme, 1968), 211–14; Achille M. Triacca, "'Liturgia' 'locus theologicus' o 'Theologia' 'locus liturgicus'? Da un dilemma verso una sintesi," in *Paschale mysterium: Studi in memoria dell'Abate Prof. Salvatore Marsili (1910–1983)*, ed. Giustino Farnedi (Rome: Studia Anselmiana, 1986), 193–233.

50. Antonio Miralles, *Los sacramentos cristianos: curso de sacramentaria fundamental* (Madrid: Palabra, 2006).

51. I will develop these aspects in chapters 2 and 5, below.

52. I will study this point in chapter 15, below.

Fourth, *the task of general sacramental theology is to situate the sacraments in relation to the original creational experience of being human and to explain the fruitfulness that they possess to generate society and culture.* Given that the sacraments are rooted in our created condition, a condition that they take on, purify, and strengthen, it will be the task of general sacramental theology to explore the connection between the logic of the sacraments and the original experiences of the children of Adam. In order to understand both, it is necessary to adopt a sacramental outlook, in other words, one that is situated within the space opened by God to man so as to reveal himself. Our first parents were already placed in a beneficent setting, the garden designed by the creator. In paradise, where their experience of living in the body was prolonged, they enjoyed the presence of God, who walked through their lawns. The Lord promised from the beginning a land in which to live, and a temple that would be built in the middle of that land so as to make it holy. The story of salvation history can be told as the patient building of this common dwelling. It is up to general sacramental theology to associate this original setting with the new sacramental setting instituted by Jesus and inaugurated in his body. In this way it is evident that the sacraments build up the habitat in which full human life flourishes, in other words, construct culture and the common good. The sacrament of matrimony acquires special relevance here, because through it the creational experience is taken up into the salvific order of Jesus and his church. The original space of the family, where each person is welcomed upon coming into the world, is a structuring dimension of the space of the sacraments.

At this point, finally, I can pose a methodological question. Should general sacramental theology precede the study of each sacrament, as Scholasticism preferred, going from the general to the particular? Or is it better for the study of it to follow discussion of the other sacraments? Both routes are possible and we should speak perhaps about a luminous circle. On the one hand, by starting with the concrete sacraments we avoid forgetting the distinctive features of each one, and this allows us to stay closer to the biblical and patristic data. On the other hand, starting with the combined view will then help to consider each one of the seven, to situate them in their correct relation within the whole, as each sacrament needs the others in order to be manifested in its truth. In this volume, prompted by the weight of this last-mentioned reason, I posit that the study of general sacramental theology precedes that of the seven sacraments. However, at the same time, I anticipate some basic concepts about each concrete sacrament, insofar as they are necessary in order to contemplate the whole and to outline the very definition of sacrament—thus, for example, the priestly order will clarify the role of ministry, and matrimony will shed light on the creational root of the salvific signs.[53] The point of departure, moreover, will always be the sacrament of the Eucharist, the radical or fundamental sacrament from which we have access to the rest.

General Sacramental Theology and Liturgical Theology

I have situated the task of general sacramental theology in relation to the treatises on each specific sacrament. Now another question arises: what is its connection with liturgical theology?[54] The question is relevant if we consider the influence that the liturgical movement had, throughout the twentieth century, in renewing understanding of the salvific rites.

The study of the liturgy is established by a theological commonplace: *lex orandi, lex credendi.* I have already pointed out the profound meaning of this assertion: the liturgical space is the ideal one in which to contemplate the mystery; the form of the celebration is the form of the revelation. It is not enough to speak, therefore, about a "theology of the liturgy"; it is important to refer to "liturgical theology" as a foundational dimension of all theology.[55]

It is certain that theology since the Council of Trent has tended to understand the axiom *lex orandi, lex credendi* as though the liturgy were a mere quarry from which to extract dogmatic facts. This was combined with an almost exclusive interest in the acts that are indispensable for the validity of the sacrament (for example, in the case of the Mass, the words and gestures of the consecration), while regarding the rest of the liturgy only as a contribution to its solemnity. In this way everything was focused on the precise action of the rite, and there was a tendency to forget that the liturgy opens a communal space in which Christ makes himself present. Compensating for this defect was the existence of a sacramental Christian culture, which ruled all the spaces of human coexistence. Even though theology did not adequately reflect on the space that the sacraments open up, this space was

---

53. Such expressions were found already in Gulielmo [Wilhelm] Van Roo, *De sacramentis in genere* (Rome: Typis Pontificiae Universitatis Gregorianae, 1957), v–vi.

54. Pedro Fernández, "Liturgia y teología: La historia de un problema metodológico," *Ciencia Tomista* 99 (1972): 135–79; Albert Houssiau, "La liturgie, lieu privilegié de la théologie sacramentaire," *Questions liturgiques et paroissiales* 54 (1973): 7–12; Andrea Bozzolo, *Il rito di Gesù: Temi di teologia sacramentaria* (Rome: Libreria Ateneo Salesiano, 2013), 7.

55. Aidan Kavanagh, *On Liturgical Theology* (Collegeville, Minn.: Liturgical Press, 1992); Alexander Schmemann, *Introduction to Liturgical Theology* (Crestwood, N.Y.: St. Vladimir's Seminary Press, 2003) and *Liturgy and Tradition: Theological Reflections of Alexander Schmemann* (Crestwood, N.Y.: St. Vladimir's Seminary Press, 1990); David W. Fagerberg, *Theologia Prima: What is Liturgical Theology?* (Chicago: Hillenbrand Books, 2004); Geldhof, "Liturgy as Theological Norm."

in fact present and was encountered in the life of the faithful; even so, it lost solidity with the advance of modern times.

The great theological contribution of the liturgical movement—above all from the proposal of Odo Casel—consisted in recovering the liturgy as a place from which to gain access to the mystery. This means that liturgy is properly speaking the *locus theologicus*, as it not only furnishes data by which to know dogma, but also opens up the setting in which to receive the divine revelation. Liturgical science, insofar as it studies the "form" of the celebration, thus proves to be indispensable for the theology of the sacraments, as it describes the coordinates of the sacramental space, where the revelation takes place and where it can be understood and transmitted.[56]

It is certain that we must avoid, on the other hand, the tendency to consider the liturgical aspect as an absolute, while forgetting the dogmatic content.[57] Pius XII, in his encyclical letter *Mediator Dei* on the sacred liturgy, emphasized that, although the liturgy teaches us what we must believe, dogma too determines our manner of praying: *lex credendi* and *lex orandi* influence each other.[58] It is not right, therefore, to pit an intellectualist outlook (the sacrament as sign) against a practical outlook, which would be the province of liturgical science: as though the "theoretical sign" were opposed to the "practical rite."[59]

Certainly liturgical science, as a theological science, cannot be sought only in the description of the phenomenon (the experience of the rite) without moving on to its foundation. To do that it is called to take into account the historical development of worship, distinguishing the new elements in each era; it is called to verify the correspondence between the celebration and the Gospel and Catholic doctrine; it is called to investigate the liturgy's connection with man's primordial experiences (study of primitive rites); it is called to delve into the cultural roots of the celebration; and so on.[60]

56. For a proposal that presents liturgy and sacramental theology combined, see Dionisio Borobio (ed.), *La celebración en la Iglesia*, 3 vols. (Salamanca: Sigueme, 1987–90); Borobio explains the overall project in the introduction (25–32).

57. Joseph Ratzinger, "Gestalt und Gehalt der eucharistischen Feier," in his *Gesammelte Schriften*, 11:359–82 (Freiburg: Herder, 2008); translated as "Form and Content of the Eucharistic Celebration," in *Collected Works: Theology of the Liturgy* (San Francisco, Calif.: Ignatius Press, 2014), 11:299–318.

58. Pius XII, *Mediator Dei*, Encyclical Letter, November 20, 1947; available in *AAS* 39 (1947): 528–50, at 540–41.

59. A certain Protestant perspective, on the other hand, tends to insist on the precedence of doctrine over rite, in keeping with the reduction of the concept of sacrament to the preaching of the word, which is the distinctive feature of the Reformation: "praecipuus cultus Dei est docere Evangelium" (the chief worship of God is to teach the Gospel): Eberhard Jüngel, "Der evangelisch verstandene Gottesdienst," in his *Wertlose Wahrheit: Zur Identität und Relevanz des christlichen Glaubens: Theologische Erörterungen* (Munich: Kaiser, 1999), 3:16–77.

60. David N. Power, "Unripe Grapes: The Critical Function of Liturgical Theology," *Worship* 52, no. 5 (1978): 386.

Do general sacramental theology and liturgical theology tackle different subjects?[61] Sometimes it would seem that the two sciences can be identified and that one of them is superfluous. In that case it would lead us to get rid of general sacramental theology, which is more abstract and has greater risks of forgetting the priority of the revealed data over speculation. Moreover the liturgy, always anchored in the celebration, is less prone to reduce the sacraments to the cultural categories of the secular world. Some have gone so far as to suggest, therefore, that dogmatic theologians abandon the field of the sacraments and leave it to the liturgists.[62]

I think, nevertheless, that there is a key difference between the two sciences, a difference based on the objects that they study. The distinguishing feature of liturgical theology is its interest in the rite or the celebrative aspect.[63] The sacrament, for its part, does contain the rite as its essential element, but goes beyond it so as to extend to all the spaces of human and Christian life; to all the spheres of creation and redemption.

We could say that the rite, which is the central element of liturgical study, is only one aspect of the object of sacramental theology. From this perspective, contemporary proposals to define the sacrament as a type of ritual prove to be inadequate.[64] In reality we have to say that the sacrament refers not only to the liturgical space, but to man's entire living space: to the space of relations inaugurated by Christ inasmuch as it receives in itself all the settings (familial, workplace, cultural) of a believer's life. The rite, as I will show below in chapter 11, unfolds the sacramental space, a space that is prolonged beyond the celebration.

To illustrate this point, recall that the Church Fathers used the term baptism to refer not primarily to the immersion in water, but rather to the permanent transformation accomplished in the baptized person. Therefore they insistently recommend: "preserve your baptism," or "preserve your seal," which was much more than an admonition to keep alive the memory

61. Julián López Martín, *La liturgia de la Iglesia*: *Teología, historia, espiritualidad pastoral* (Madrid: Biblioteca de autores cristianos, 1996).

62. Giuseppe Colombo, "Introduzione," in Andrea Bozzolo, *La teologia sacramentaria dopo Rahner*: *il dibattito e i problemi* (Rome: Libreria Ateneo Salesiano, 1999), 7.

63. Martín, *La liturgia de la Iglesia*, 9: "Liturgy, as an aspect of the economy of salvation and an action of Christ and of the Church in the mediation of the signs, is the object of fundamental sacramental theology also, so that it is possible to treat liturgy and sacraments together in one discipline. Nonetheless, liturgical science focuses especially on the way in which the mystery of salvation is expressed and realized in sacramentality and in the other significant and esthetic elements of the celebration." Further on the author explains that liturgical science refers "to the dynamic elements of the celebration of the sacraments" and to "the basic lines of the respective rituals" (188).

64. Andrea Grillo, "La nozione di sacramento: da Trento al Vaticano II fino al Terzo Millennio: Dal 'sacramentum in genere signi' al 'sacramentum in genere ritus'?," *Annali di studi religiosi* 1 (2000): 239–63.

of having participated in the rite.[65] Another example: the sacrament of matrimony, in and of itself, needs no ceremony; it can exist without one, being anchored in a more original liturgy: the liturgy of the human body which, in the love of man and woman or in the generation and raising of children, opens up spaces for the presence and grace of God.

To summarize: general sacramental theology extends beyond the frontiers of liturgical studies, with which it is closely related. One of its tasks, for example, is to explain the connection between the celebration and the permanent transformation of the believer (through the sacramental character; chapter 12); between the ritual action and moral action (chapter 8); between the liturgical space and the communal and cosmic space (chapter 6).

Plan of the Treatise

What I have said above helps to organize this treatise in a suitable way. *Part 1* will identify the terrain on which the sacraments are founded, which is the space generated by Jesus' life in the flesh. The point of departure will be the institution of his Eucharistic and baptismal rite, in which the master concentrated the meaning of his life and word (chapter 2). By participating in this rite the apostles communicated immediately not only the description of this or that sacrament, but the central features of the sacramental outlook or logic. We will encounter those features, both in the Johannine writings (which relate for us the *signs and works* of Jesus: chapter 3), and in the Pauline letters (starting with the theology of the *mysterion*: chapter 4). I will then be able to undertake (chapter 5) a reflection on the roots of the sacraments in Christ, who instituted them. The sacraments will appear to be connected, not only to this or that act of his life, but to the totality of his history in the flesh, a history that inaugurated a new space of relations with God, men, and the world.

Part 2 will investigate the definition of sacrament, thereby exploring the distinct spheres of relations between men which, after having been present since the origins of the world, were taken up by Jesus in his rite. We will see first the vital connection of the sacraments with creation, where matrimony plays the leading role (chapter 6). I will then recall the history of the Old Testament: there the liturgical space, founded on the sacrifices offered to Yahweh, matures to the fullness of the body of Christ that was offered up for us (chapter 7). Finally, the rites instituted by Jesus, integrating the preceding history into themselves, will allow me to outline the definition of the Christian sacrament, thereby following the theological development from

---

65. See chapter 12, below.

St. Augustine and the medieval period, via the Protestant Reformation and the Council of Trent, down to our day (chapters 8 to 10). It will then be possible to show by way of synthesis (chapter 11) that a sacrament is the opening up, in the life of the faithful, of the generative spaces of relations (relations with the Father, one's brothers, and creation) that Jesus inaugurated.

Part 3 will be centered on the way in which these sacraments transform Christian existence, communicating their form to all spaces of life. The sacramental character (chapter 12) will appear as a permanent placement of the believer in Jesus' own sphere of relations. From this context [*trasfondo*] the whole moral activity of the Christian, who is the subject of the sacraments, will acquire sacramental traits (chapter 13). I will consider next the figure of the minister, whose presence configures the sacramental space, so that it is oriented toward Jesus, its source and its head (chapter 14). Finally the entire church will appear as a sacrament, in other words, as a space of relations built upon the columns of the seven sacraments and called to expand the sacramental logic to all society and to the whole cosmos (chapter 15).

PART 1

THE SACRAMENTS, DEEPLY ROOTED IN THE FLESH OF JESUS

The point of departure for studying the sacraments can only be the central rite instituted by Jesus in the context of his preaching and works. This invites us to focus our outlook on the Eucharist and, in relation to it, on baptism; from there I will identify several distinctive features so as to define what a sacrament is (chapter 2). Next I will examine the first two attempts to offer a unified view of the sacraments in terms of the life of Christ: St. John, who speaks to us about the signs and works of Jesus (chapter 3); and St. Paul, who deals with the revelation of the *mysterion-sacramentum* (chapter 4). These premises will enable us to establish the root of the sacraments in Christ; he instituted them when, throughout his life in the flesh, he opened a new space of relations animated fully by the love of God (chapter 5).

2 ❧ THE ORIGIN OF THE SACRAMENTS IN THE RITE OF JESUS

A conviction emerged from chapter 1: in the New Testament the sacraments open up the setting in which we can encounter the risen Lord—see his face, hear his voice, touch his wounds. Therefore, if every object of study has its suitable method, the sacraments are the ideal method for the object of theology: God, revealed in Christ for the salvation of mankind. Or also: if an organ corresponds to each sensation (and it would be absurd to attempt to taste chocolate with the tip of a finger), the organs appropriate for tasting the Christian mystery are the sacraments.

How can we inquire into the central features of the sacramental outlook? To answer that question, recall that the New Testament usually deals with the seven sacraments, not in general, but one by one: the Eucharist, baptism, penance, the anointing of the sick ... yet, given the central position of the Eucharist in the early church, and its constitutive place in the story of Jesus, we cannot avoid starting with it. We will see that the Eucharist gives us the key with which to unlock the secret of the other sacraments. They will be sacraments to the extent that they draw near to it and participate in it, as the fundamental sacrament that it is; in turn, each sacrament will illuminate and reinforce a key aspect of the Eucharist.

After the Eucharist, the next in order of importance is baptism, the second major rite attested in the life of Jesus and of the early church. I will conclude, on the one hand, that baptism and the Eucharist, even with the clear differences between them, share many common elements: in this resemblance the first features of a sacramental outlook are revealed. Moreover, baptism will prove to be oriented to the Eucharist, as the concrete way in which the latter breaks into the life of Christians. In fact, baptism, the portal sacrament, will give us the key through which to associate the rest of the sacraments with the body offered by Jesus and his outpoured blood.

From the Eucharistic Rite to the Sacramental Organism

If the Eucharist opens up to us the space in which to encounter Christ, to participate in his work, to hear and proclaim his word, we now ask ourselves: what is the structure of this space inaugurated by Jesus, as it can be inferred from the celebration of the rite?[1] Before answering, it is important to note that the Eucharistic rite not only is our way of gaining access to the mystery of Christ, but also constitutes for Jesus himself the framework that marked out his mission, in the sight of the Father and of mankind, "before He suffered" (Lk 22:15). In fact, Jesus did not invent the rite from scratch; there was a received component of it, too. It was received in the traditions of his people, although he would then transform them profoundly in keeping with the fullness that is his own; received, ultimately, from his Father, the origin of Israel's liturgy and of the sacred sense of all creation.[2] The space into which the rite introduces us will be, therefore, the very same space in which Jesus lived and which he fashioned during his life, death, and resurrection.

The Context: The Jewish Passover and the *todah* Sacrifice

The context in which Jesus celebrates his rite is constituted, on the one hand, by the supper of the Jewish Passover (*pesach*), the eating of the lamb that recalls the liberation from Egypt. Exegetes, of course, debate whether the Last Supper was a Paschal meal. For while the Synoptics present it in this way, St. John follows another chronology: the *pesach* fell that year, according to him, on Good Friday, so that the death of Jesus coincided with the sacrifice of the lambs in the Temple.[3] In any case, we can say with certainty that Jesus' supper shares many features with the *pesach*. The same Gospel situates the bread of life discourse (where the words of institution, more or less, appear) around the celebration of the Jewish Passover (Jn 6:4).

What are the Paschal features of Jesus' celebration? In the first place we have the festive and ritual character of this meal: hence the use of wine,

---

1. Ratzinger, "Gestalt und Gehalt der eucharistischen Feier."

2. In this section I draw from Heinz Schürmann, "Die Gestalt der urchristlichen Eucharistiefeier," *Münchener Theologische Zeitschrift* 6, no. 2 (1955): 107–31; Peter Stuhlmacher, "Das neutestamentliche Zeugnis zum Herrenmahl," *Zeitschrift für Theologie und Kirche* 84, no. 1 (1987): 1–35; Ferdinand Hahn, "Zum Stand der Erforschung des urchristlichen Herrenmahls," *Evangelische Theologie* 35 (1975): 553–63; and Michael Theobald, "Das Herrenmahl im Neuen Testament," *Theologische Quartalschrift* 183, no. 4 (2003): 257–80.

3. For a summary of the debate, see Joseph Ratzinger, *Jesus of Nazareth*, vol. 2: *Holy Week: From the Entrance into Jerusalem to the Resurrection* (San Francisco, Calif.: Ignatius Press, 2011), 106–15.

which was reserved for such occasions. The *pesach* was, specifically, a memorial: those eating it gratefully recalled Yahweh's mighty deed when he gave birth to Israel by bringing his people out of Egypt. Jesus too remembered the gifts from his Father, within the memory of his people, asking the disciples to preserve the memory of him (Lk 22:19). And this was not to be just a nostalgic remembrance: ritual commemoration, as the Bible understands it, makes present what happened, again making God's saving arm felt.[4]

Moreover, in the Passover they sacrificed the lamb, the substitute for the firstborn sons of Israel, who were rescued from a deadly plague by the blood that marked the doorposts. By liberating the firstborn son, God confirmed the blessing of fertility that he pronounced over our first parents (Gn 1:28), a blessing that was the prefiguration of all his further promises and made possible the grateful memory and the full future of the people. The rite was offered, therefore, with the filial attitude of someone who knows that he is generated by Yahweh and, by acknowledging in him the origin of life, can conquer the power of death and be transformed into a father. In light of this, Jewish tradition would identify the lamb with a specific person who entrusts himself radically to God and professes him as the origin of paternity—for example, Isaac or the Servant of Yahweh. The firstborn sons were rescued, thus, not by the blood of irrational animals but rather on the basis of a filial life which, by offering itself for the chosen people, revived their hope. Jesus situates himself in this context of gratitude toward the Father, handing over his body as food and pouring out his blood for the sins of the multitude (Mt 26:28). He, as the firstborn Son, takes up the logic of the Passover rite so as to fulfill it.

Once we have accepted the context of the *pesach*, we must nevertheless ask ourselves: is Jesus' rite directly derived from it? There are many elements that lead us to distinguish between what was celebrated by Jesus and the Jewish Passover. For what the master leaves to his disciples, and what he orders them to repeat ("do this in memory of me") is not the entire supper, but rather two particular moments: the offering of the bread and wine with the words that accompany them.[5] It turns out that these moments, which Jesus innovated, do not belong to the *pesach*. Moreover, in the Upper Room definitive features of the Hebrew Passover disappear; and thus, for example,

---

4. Max Thurian, *L'eucharistie: Mémorial du Seigneur: Sacrifice d'action de grâce et d'intercession* (Neuchatel: Delachaux et Niestlé, 1963); Enrico Galbiati, "I segni sacri dell'Antico Testamento," *Sacra Doctrina* 45 (1967): 13–36.

5. Although for a time the Eucharist was celebrated within the context of an ordinary meal, soon it was understood that the latter was incidental, as Paul already points out to the Corinthians (1 Cor 11:17–22).

a lamb is not mentioned. The differences increase in the church's practice of celebrating the Eucharist, not once a year, but rather every Sunday; this is an important change, given that the *pesach* was connected with the rhythm of the people's life.[6]

A question is justified, then: because of this concentration on the offering of bread and wine, is Jesus taking into account some other rite of the Old Testament? There are plenty of indications that the master reinterpreted the Last Supper on the basis of what was called a sacrifice of *todah*, or of praise [and thanksgiving] (Lv 7:12–18).[7] Situated at the center of this sacrifice is not the life of a sacrificed animal, but rather the very existence of the one who offers it, who is in mortal danger: this is precisely the existential context of the Last Supper, celebrated "on the night when [Jesus] was betrayed" (1 Cor 11:23). In the *todah*, moreover, a man, after escaping from death, fulfills in the presence of God his vow with an offering that includes bread, symbol of the everyday life that the votary shares with his friends; the shared bread is, therefore, the sign of victory: a life has been recovered and is given to the brethren.[8] Finally, such a sacrifice of praise [and thanksgiving] or *todah* is part of the core of the spirituality of the Psalter: of interest in this light is Psalm 22(21), precisely the one that Jesus recited during his passion.[9] In this psalm, after the first part in which the afflictions of death are described (vv. 1–22), the Psalmist gives thanks to God for the salvation that he has received, offering his praise in the midst of the brethren (vv. 23–32).

The connection with the *todah* neatly explains why Christians later called the Christian rite the Eucharist (thanksgiving). Now, the new thing in Jesus' *todah* is the fact that his gratitude refers to a future act: he praises God, not after having received life, but rather with a death sentence imminent. This is explained only in terms of the unique relation of Jesus with his Father to which the Gospels testify. Christ's trust in God, whom he dares to call "Abba," is so deeply rooted that his gratitude anticipates everything in the future, including moreover the "non-future" of death. He overflows with such thankfulness that it precedes the benefit that he hopes to receive.

6. Ratzinger, "Form and Content of the Eucharistic Celebration," 307–8.

7. Hartmut Gese, "Die Herkunft des Herrenmahls," in his *Zur biblischen Theologie: Alttestamentliche Vorträge* (Munich: Kaiser Verlag, 1983), 107–27; Cesare Giraudo, *La structura letteraria della Preghiera eucaristica: Saggio sulla genesi letteraria di una forma: Toda veterotestamentaria, Beraka giudaica, Anafora cristiana*, Analecta Biblica 92 (Rome: Biblical Institute Press, 1981); Xavier Léon-Dufour, *Le partage du pain eucharistique selon le Nouveau Testament* (Paris: Seuil, 1982), 54.

8. Aletti, "Signes," 314: "the breaking of the bread confirms that there has been a victory, since the living person invites others to share in his life."

9. Hartmut Gese, "Psalm 22 und das Neue Testament: der älteste Bericht vom Tode Jesu und die Entstehung des Herrenmahles," *Zeitschrift für Theologie und Kirche* 65, no. 1 (1968): 1–22; see also Pss 50:14, 66:13, 69:30.

He behaved similarly in multiplying the loaves and in raising Lazarus: he thanked God in poverty before receiving his favors.[10]

Jesus offers the *todah* of the Last Supper, we must conclude, not only for what God had given him, but also for what God was about to generate in him: the eternal life of his risen body, a life that would be poured out upon those who were his own.[11] This means that the Christian Eucharist, in the strict sense, is celebrated only after the resurrection and can be defined as "the *todah* of the Risen Lord."[12] The second part of Psalm 22(21), which was recited on the cross, adopts this eschatological perspective, which hints at the resurrection: "Yes, to Him shall all the proud of the earth bow down; before Him shall bow all who go down to the dust" (Ps 22:30). It is not surprising that Sunday proved to be the ideal day for the Eucharistic celebration.

It is important to emphasize that there is no contradiction between Jesus' *todah* and the context of the Jewish *pesach* (Passover supper). In both cases there is a memorial of thanksgiving for the son's rescue; and of a life handed over which, in obedience to the Father and in love for the brethren, is recovered so as to establish a new family. We could say that, in Jesus, the *pesach* is manifested as *todah*; in Christ it is revealed that the heart of the Jewish Passover was a sacrifice of praise [and thanksgiving]. Whereas with the *pesach* God began the journey of the chosen people, generating it to a new life, now the journey concludes with a definitive birth that also liberates from death.

The fact that the Eucharist is the *todah* of the risen Lord has a wealth of theological consequences. In the first place, the words spoken over the body and the blood will have to be understood in light of the glorified body, filled with the Spirit (Jn 6:63; Rom 8:11). In the second place, Jesus' rite, in pointing to his glorious Pasch, indicates the future when life has been recovered and the *todah* or praise [and thanksgiving] is offered; this means that through memory (*pesach*) the prospect of the definitive future is displayed (*todah* of the risen Lord). This then sets up two axes along which the central elements of the Eucharistic rite are situated and which demarcate the definition of the sacrament: the axis *flesh-Spirit* and the axis *memory-fulfillment*.

---

10. Albert Vanhoye, *Tanto amó Dios al mundo: Lectio sobre el sacrificio di Cristo* (Madrid: San Pablo, 2005).

11. According to *Pesikta de-Rav Kahana* 79a of the Mandelbaum edition (New York: Jewish Theological Seminary of America, 1962), 1:159, all sacrifices will cease at the end of time, as well as all songs; but the *todah* sacrifice and the *todah* song will never cease.

12. Gese, "Die Herkunft des Herrenmahls."

The First Axis of the Rite: Bread and Wine—
The Flesh and the Spirit

Keeping in mind the ritual form of the *todah*, let us begin to consider the center of Jesus' liturgy: the words spoken over the bread and the wine, with the gestures that accompany them. When Jesus distributes the bread he refers it to his body, which is "My body ... given for you" (Lk 22:19). It is easy to discover the Old Testament subtext of this phrase. The flesh, in the biblical view of man, is a continual reminder that the human person is not an isolated being. Let us recall several biblical expressions, individually applied to the familial connections of sonship, brotherhood, espousal: flesh of my flesh (Gn 2:23), one flesh (Gn 2:24), my/our own flesh (Gn 29:14; 37:27), and so on. Because they are flesh, Adam and his sons are defined in terms of the setting in which they are rooted; therefore, in order to encounter their genuine identity, they need to relate to their neighbors, with the people as a whole. It is understandable then that Jesus would later speak about his *body* "for you" (and not simply about his *life* for you). This is because the body is the place where one belongs to others, where one lives with others and for others, where life, finally, breaks through its isolation by mutual giving and receiving.[13] Inasmuch as Jesus took on our life so as to give it back to us renewed, this offering had to pass through the flesh.

Jesus channels this relational opening of the body primarily toward God the Father, as emphasized by the context of thanksgiving (*todah*) of the Last Supper. As the first bond that is forged in the flesh is a bond with the origin, whoever has a body cannot forget that someone engendered him, and he cannot deny the connection with his ancestors and, through them, with the creator, who formed us in our mother's womb (Jer 1:5). This explains why Jesus, in the Letter to the Hebrews, understanding that God "prepared a body" for him, feels moved to make an offering (Heb 10:6).

In terms of the original relation with God, the experience of the body speaks a language of unity with other human beings. For in the body the husband lives for his wife and the wife for her husband; the lives of parents are directed toward their children, and the lives of children come from their parents. Thus it is possible, for someone who accepts his embodied condition, to share the lot of the other, as attested by the concept of the "corporate person" that we encounter in scripture. Recall, in this regard,

---

13. Unless explicitly noted otherwise, I will use "body" and "flesh" as synonyms, fully aware that authors use them differently; in this regard see José Granados, *Teología de la carne: el cuerpo en la historia de su salvación* (Burgos: Monte Carmelo, 2012), 24.

the Servant of Yahweh (Is 53:12), who receives in himself the destiny of the people, so as to give them life. And also Isaac who, according to the Jewish tradition of the *akedah* (binding), participates actively in the sacrifice by letting himself be bound (Jn 18:12) and offers himself for the sin of all Israel. Jesus brings this journey to fulfillment: his words over the bread—"for you"—give expression to the language of donation that is inscribed in the flesh, which will attain fulfillment in the glorified body that will be fully communicative.

This perspective is rounded out with the words that Jesus pronounced in handing over the one chalice. According to the biblical view, life is contained in the blood (Dt 12:23); life which, in turn, is communicated to man by the divine breath (Gn 2:7), which is a participation in the spirit or breathing of Yahweh (*ruah*: Gn 6:3). This connection between blood and respiration is confirmed precisely in sacrifices, when steam from the outpoured blood is seen.[14] Hence a common mentality spread during antiquity: by means of blood, the vital or spiritual principle that proceeds from God comes into contact with human flesh.[15] In light of this, the gift of Jesus' blood would be associated with the outpouring of the Holy Spirit, as the Letter to the Hebrews attests (Heb 9:14; 13:20).[16]

This relation blood-Spirit is confirmed if we pay attention to the key term in the words pronounced over the cup: *covenant*. Mark and Matthew speak about the "blood of the covenant," referring to the sacrifice of Moses, who sprinkled blood on the people (Ex 24:8), after which the leaders of Israel ate and drank with God (Ex 24:11). Luke and Paul for their part mention "the new covenant," following the prophetic tradition (Jer 31:31) and adding "in My blood." If the covenant is associated with blood (including when the new panorama of the prophets is assumed, as in Paul and Luke), it is because blood, as communication of life and Spirit to man, signifies communion between the creature and God. So it is understood in the insight of St. Ignatius of Antioch: "I desire the drink of God, namely His blood, which is incorruptible love and eternal life."[17]

The binomial "flesh-blood," symbolized by the bread and the wine, re-

---

14. Vanhoye, *Tanto amó Dios al mundo* and *Accogliamo Cristo nostro sommo sacerdote: esercizi spirituali con Benedetto XVI* (Vatican City: LEV, 2008).

15. One witness to this mentality is Irenaeus of Lyons, *Adversus haereses* V, 3, 2 (SC 153:48): "aliud arteriae et venae, sanguinis et spiritus transitoria" (another [part of the flesh became] arteries and veins, passages for the blood and the air). The English translation is taken from the Ante-Nicene Fathers series (hereafter ANF), ed. Alexander Roberts et al. (London: T and T Clark, 1867–85), 1:529b.

16. Albert Vanhoye, "Par la tente plus grande et plus parfaite," *Biblica* 46 (1965): 1–28.

17. Ignatius of Antioch, *Ad Romans* VII, 3 (SC 10:136; ANF 1:77); also Melito, *Peri Pascha* 32 (SC 123:76): "Tell me, angel, what frightened you? ... The *blood* of the lamb or the *Spirit* of the Lord?"

fers us, therefore, to the pair "flesh-Spirit." The first axis of the Eucharist endorses the biblical view of man, who is formed of the earth (flesh) and open to the gift and to the action of the divine breath (Spirit) (Gn 2:7).[18] We can understand now that the Eucharist, by its emphasis on the flesh and blood, unfolds before mankind, so to speak, a space of relations; I mean the space of Jesus' body (his concrete way of being situated in the world and open to the Father and to his brethren) which was forged during his earthly life and is permeated with the Spirit of communion. It is a space that the resurrection consummated and sealed, through which Jesus was able to introduce those who are his own into it, feeding them with his body and blood. The Spirit's province is to impel history toward its end; given that he acts in this space, this must be a dynamic space that is growing toward its maturity, when the flesh will become fully spiritual. Thus we come to the other axis along which the rite moves: an axis that runs through the ages.

The Second Axis of the Rite: From Memory
to Eschatological Anticipation

The space inaugurated in the body and blood of Jesus is not a static space but rather ripens productively. Indeed, from it one gains access to the past and to the future, to the memory of the first gift and to the hope for the consummated gift.

In the first place, the Eucharistic space opens up to the past through memory. Jesus, in his rite, participates in the memorial of the people and entrusts his action to the memory of the disciples: "do this is memory of Me."[19] Memory, in the Bible, keeps alive the presence of Yahweh as the one who gave his people their origin by rescuing them. The privileged place of memory is worship, where these salvific deeds are made present. Hence Israel was constituted as such in the liturgy: only by remembering God's redeeming action, his mighty deeds [*hazañas*] for the benefit of its forefathers, can it recognize itself as chosen and loved by Yahweh. Therefore memory is the obligatory passage through which to know the God of the Bible, who reveals himself by acting in history and binds his name to the name and destiny of his own. To forget these past deeds is to forget who he is.

This memory reaches its zenith in the Eucharist of Jesus, his *todah*. Any *todah* sacrifice, being praise [and thanksgiving] for God's benefits, is an ex-

---

18. Carlos Granados, "El Espíritu de Yahvé y el dinamismo de la creación en el Antiguo Testamento," *Anthropotes* 26 (2010): 45–65.

19. Thurian, *L'eucharistie*.

ercise of memory, the organ of filial gratitude. All the more so the *todah* of the risen Son: in light of the definitive and insuperable gift of the Father, who placed all things into his hands (Jn 13:3), Jesus professes that all being and all becoming has its origin in God. Therefore the Eucharist, together with the entire life of Jesus, recapitulates the broad history of Israel, which goes back to the molding of man; and it also contains the memory of the creation of the cosmos, represented by the bread and wine, fruits of the earth and of human work.

In the second place, this space of relations inaugurated by Christ in the Eucharist also points toward the future. This already occurred in the liturgy of Israel: the memorial, being the memorial of a promise, was the memorial of a future action of God that surpassed the previous ones. Therefore, just as the liturgy made the past present, so too it anticipated the future. Tomorrow proved to be just as real as the oath made by Yahweh to save his people; the future could be touched as one touches the fruit sown in the earth and the child stirring in the womb.

Jesus' rite, too, at the Last Supper, anticipates the future of the resurrection. Therefore Jesus mentions the fruit of the vine, which he will drink again only in his Father's Kingdom (Mt 26:29). St. John, in his discourse on the bread of life, corroborates this view, while concentrating on the eternal life received by those who are fed by the body and blood of Christ.[20] And the Eucharist celebrated by the church preserves this eschatological tension ("Maranatha! Come, Lord Jesus!"), which not only hopes for but also anticipates the definitive Passover of history. Someone who enters into the space inaugurated by Jesus in the Eucharist is capable of tasting and assimilating the final fruit of time: a future beyond which God has nothing greater left to promise.

St. Paul sums up this temporal Eucharistic axis when he states (1 Cor 11:26): "As often as you eat this bread and drink the chalice [present], you proclaim the Lord's death [past] until He comes [future]." By eating the bread and drinking the wine, we unite our time with Christ's time, making the past present and anticipating the future.[21] We should understand it in this sense when St. Irenaeus of Lyons calls the Eucharistic chalice *compendii poculum*, the cup in which the ages are summarized.[22]

---

20. Jn 6:35, 39, 40, 44, 48; the Eucharist is different from the manna, which does not give eternal life (Jn 6:49); anyone who eats of the former will live forever (6:51), and already has eternal life (6:53, 57).

21. The last phrase, "until He comes," can be explained in the active sense: "so that He may come again"; Otfried Hofius, "'Bis dass er kommt' I.Kor XI.26," *New Testament Studies* 14 (1967–68): 439–41.

22. Irenaeus of Lyons, *Adversus haereses* III, 16, 7 (SC 211:314; ANF 1:443a).

All this implies that the Eucharist is, along with the real presence of the body and blood of Christ, also the real presence of his action in time. This means that in it we not only come into contact with Jesus, but also with his whole history, from his birth until his death and resurrection. Credit goes to the Benedictine monk Odo Casel (1886–1948) for reviving this view of the liturgy as participation in the mysteries of the life of Jesus.[23] For in the sacrament not only do the effects of Christ's bygone work reach us, but we also enter into the very action of Christ, inheriting his way of living in time.

Summary: Central Features of the Eucharistic Rite

We have now managed to sift out the central features of the Eucharistic rite inaugurated by Jesus, which are the features of the sacramental outlook. The whole rite is concentrated in the body of Jesus and in its ability to forge bonds, with the Father (to whom his thanks are directed) and with his brethren ("for you," "for the life of the world"). The words of institution refer the bread that is shared to the flesh of Jesus, to his relational way of living together with human beings and of directing everything to the Father; and they refer the wine poured out to his blood, where we encounter the Spirit, who enlivens the relations of communion between God and his own. In light of this, the material elements that are used in the rite acquire meaning also: the bread and the wine are placed at the service of the relational body of Christ, make it visible and tangible, and mediate man's assimilation of it as food. To celebrate the Eucharist, therefore, is to enter into the space of relations inaugurated by Jesus in his body, so as to receive in this space the bond of love that is his Spirit.

The rite is framed in a vital narrative: it contains within itself the memory of an origin and opens up a perspective of the ultimate future, as Jesus, the Alpha and Omega, experienced them. Moreover, given that Christ brings with him the fullness of time, the rite is capable of condensing all of history into his journey from the Father to the Father. The space of relations that opens up in the Eucharist is a space that unfolds, therefore, according to the rhythm with which Christ completed his passage through his earthly life. From the Eucharist we derive the coordinates by which to understand the other sacraments, which incorporate human beings into the new relations inaugurated by Jesus in his flesh, and into the dynamism with which they make their way to maturity.

23. Odo Casel, *Das christliche Kultmysterium* (Regensburg: Pustet, 1935).

Baptism, Being Born into the Body of Jesus

Together with the Eucharist, we encounter in the New Testament an abundance of testimonies referring to another rite: baptism. What is the relation between the two? One difference with the Eucharist hits the reader in the eye: Christian baptism appears to be spoken about, above all, in texts later than Easter. According to Matthew, Jesus ordered his disciples to baptize when he was already risen, as he was saying goodbye to them (Mt 28:19): "Go therefore and make disciples of all nations, baptizing them in the name of the Father and of the Son and of the Holy Spirit." Baptism appears also as part of their mission in the canonical conclusion of Mark (Mk 16:16).[24]

Some, relying on historical criticism, have said that these texts by themselves offer little basis for assurance that Jesus instituted the sacrament.[25] Would it not have been logical that, in discussing such an important mandate, all the sources would have attested it more clearly? So it is, in fact, with the Eucharist, as we have seen. And why does Jesus not speak about baptism during his public ministry? How is it that he does not baptize, just like John baptized?

On the other hand, without clear support in the teaching of Jesus, one would have trouble explaining the immediate spread of the practice among the first disciples. Indeed, it is difficult to find precedents among pagan customs. Nor does the baptism of Jewish proselytes offer much support, because of its differences with ecclesial baptism: it was not a ritual washing conferred by a minister, but rather by the neophyte himself; it did not apply to the other members of Israel who were born such; and, finally, it lacked eschatological features.[26] That being the case, only one option remains: to find the roots of the sacrament of baptism in John's baptism, which Jesus himself received.

John's Baptism and Baptism in the Name of Jesus

There are various similarities between John's baptism and Christian baptism: another person administers it (John "the Baptist"); it is directed to all Israel, not only to the proselytes; it is framed in an eschatological perspective, before God's definitive judgment and, therefore, happens only once.

---

24. Before the resurrection, Jesus alludes to baptism in his conversation with Nicodemus (Jn 3:5: "Unless one is born of water and the Spirit, he cannot enter the kingdom of God").

25. Gerhard Lohfink, "Der Ursprung der christlichen Taufe," *Theologische Quartalschrift* 156, no. 1 (1976): 35–54; Wolfhart Pannenberg, *Systematic Theology* III (Grand Rapids, Mich.: Eerdmans, 1998), chap. 13, section III.1.d.

26. Lohfink, "Der Ursprung," 41.

This similarity nevertheless raises a question: why did the disciples take up again the practice of baptism, a practice going back before Jesus, which the master himself did not continue during his public ministry?

In order to answer, it is helpful to explain how Jesus takes up John's ministry and transforms it. According to St. Luke, the Baptist's preaching appears, in many respects, similar to the Savior's. Both speak about the nearness of the Kingdom and about the penitence necessary for the forgiveness of sins. In fact, now in his glorified body, Jesus resumes his missionary mandate with a formula similar to the one that sums up the Baptist's activity. Whereas John had come "preaching a baptism of repentance for the forgiveness of sins" (Lk 3:3), the Paschal Jesus announces to his disciples that "repentance and forgiveness of sins should be preached in His name to all nations" (Lk 24:47).

Note the detail that Jesus adds, which replaces the mention of baptism in Luke 3:3: repentance and forgiveness must happen "in His name" (Lk 24:47). This shows the difference; to the call to conversion announced by John, Jesus adds only one thing: he adds himself. The Baptist, in effect, proclaimed God's future judgment and called for preparation to face it. Christ, for his part, announces that the judgment is already here, as he is this judgment in person. Thus a judgment of mercy is offered which does not require that we convert first: God anticipates us gratuitously, turns toward us, offers us the life of his Son so that, united with him, "in His name," we might be able to abandon sin and be converted. Thus the place occupied by baptism in John's preaching corresponds, in the mandate of the risen Lord, to the name of Jesus, in other words, to the account of his life, which takes up ours. Whereas John baptized with water, the Christian is immersed in the life of Christ, who justifies us in the Father's sight.[27]

We can understand in these terms the preaching of the church that Luke himself relates for us in Acts. The apostles repeat, summarily, the formulas of the Baptist and of Jesus: "*Repent, and be baptized* every one of you *in the name of Jesus* Christ *for the forgiveness* of your sins*" (Acts 2:38). Now baptism reappears, as in John's ministry (Lk 3:3), but associated with the name of Jesus, recalling the master's command (Lk 24:47). Between John's baptism and the church's baptism we encounter therefore, once again, the way of Christ ("in His name"): this is the difference between one kind of water and the other.

---

27. Ibid., 51.

Baptism in the Life of Jesus: The Jordan

We have started to calculate the distance between John's baptism and the Christian sacrament: it is measured exactly as the life of Jesus. Now, in order to explain why the apostles took up the rite of John in order to express bonding to Jesus, it is necessary to find some support in the way of the master. We have to consider, in this regard, one decisive fact. Although Jesus himself would not baptize with John's baptism, he himself was baptized in the Jordan. All the Gospels allude to this incident, pointing out the novelty of the event: the heavens open, the Father's voice is heard, the Spirit descends in the form of a dove (Mk 1:9–11; Mt 3:13–17; Lk 3:21; Jn 1:32–34; Acts 10:38). We understand then: the importance of the scene at the Jordan in Jesus' mission is what decisively roots baptism in his earthly life. Christ's words after Easter, recorded by St. Matthew (Mt 28:19), were not spoken, then, in a vacuum. In order to study them in greater depth it will be important to consider in detail this inaugural episode of his public ministry.

The baptism in the Jordan was certainly not an act of false humility by which Christ lowered himself in order to receive something he did not need. Nor did it involve the mere manifestation to men of a power that he already possessed from all eternity. According to the biblical testimony, Jesus experienced this baptism as a rite that was essential for his mission, in which he received authority and power from the Father. It signified for him, moreover, not only one particular act, but rather the framework that marked out his ministry, which was moved from then on in a singular way by the Holy Spirit.[28]

What happened in the Jordan is understood as the fulfillment of the anointings of the Old Testament, which signified the coming of the Spirit upon men of God, mediators of his love for the people. By being baptized, Christ associated himself in a new way to this history of humanity, which he had already taken up by becoming incarnate, and which advanced in Israel under the guidance of the Spirit.

In the background we find (as we already saw happening in the Eucharist) the idea of the "corporate person," whereby someone can contain the people within himself and mediate divine grace for them, as was foretold about the Servant of Yahweh (Is 42:1).[29] It is no accident that St. Luke places after the scene at the Jordan the genealogy of Jesus, which goes back to

28. Luis F. Ladaria, *Jesús y el Espíritu: la Unción* (Burgos: Monte Carmelo, 2012).

29. H. Wheeler Robinson, *Corporate Personality in Ancient Israel* (Philadelphia: Fortress Press, 1964).

our first father, Adam, "son of God" (Lk 3:23–38). To this stream of generations in which he submerges himself, Jesus brings a new filiation or sonship,
as the Father assures him: "You are My Son" (Lk 3:22).

In this way the Spirit will act patiently on the flesh of the Son, in which
we all find ourselves contained, because we too are sons of Adam; and he
will shape the flesh of Jesus so that it can fully mediate to us his divine sonship. Resting upon Christ, the Spirit will be able to bestow himself in an
unprecedented way upon all flesh (Acts 2:17). Thus we understand why in
Christian baptism the water is connected with the descent of the Spirit,
something that did not occur in the rite of the Precursor: it is because water
and Spirit were united in the scene at the Jordan. Jesus himself later speaks
to the apostles, referring to Pentecost, about a baptism with the Holy Spirit,
which surpasses the one of his cousin John (Acts 1:5).

I will now add another fact to this panorama: the baptism in the Jordan
directs Jesus' life toward the Paschal mystery, toward his death and resurrection. Christ himself interpreted the entire arc of his life in terms of a baptism that he had to undergo, which he identified with the eschatological fulfillment of history. Recall his expressions: "I have a baptism to be baptized
with; and how I am constrained until it is accomplished! (Lk 12:49); "Are
you able to drink the chalice that I drink, or to be baptized with the baptism with which I am baptized? (Mk 10:38). Baptism is thus framed within
the context of the redemptive death of Jesus "as a ransom for many," as the
passage goes on to say (Mk 10:45; Is 53:10), and of his resurrection, when
the Father will start a new age. The formula about the "ransom" alludes to
the Servant of Yahweh, with which the theme reemerges of the "corporate
person" in which the whole people is included.

In summary, in Jesus' life baptism involves, on the one hand, the descent
of the Spirit on his flesh, giving to his entire story a dynamic that leads to
the encounter with the Father; and, on the other hand, the eschatological
action of this Spirit in his death and resurrection. All this is framed within a
view of Jesus as representative of the people, the beginning of a new lineage;
he mediates the Spirit, by his flesh, for all of us.

Baptism, Participation in the Body of Christ

From what has been said we can conclude: the first Christians found, not
only in the Paschal commandment of Jesus, but also in his passage on earth,
the basis for performing baptism and understanding its profundity. As a
context for interpreting Jesus' commandment they preserved in their memory: (1) the baptism of Christ with water in the Jordan, which served as the

start of his mission; (2) the master's words about the baptism that awaited him, which referred to his death and new life; and (3) his announcement of a baptism that they would receive in the Spirit, which was accomplished on Pentecost.

Moreover the disciples set this remembrance or *anamnesis* upon the foundation of the history of Israel and their corporate view of mankind, whereby one person could mediate God's salvation for others. Precisely this unity of the people over the ages was experienced in their memorial acts of worship. It was to be expected, therefore, that the disciples would take for granted also a rite that would accompany their incorporation into Jesus. In fact, the baptismal formula, "in the name of" Jesus, or "in the name of" the God of our Lord Jesus Christ (Father, Son, and Holy Spirit) invokes the ritual biblical *anamnesis* so as to situate us in a lively remembrance of the master. This is because the concepts of "name" and of "memory" are closely related in scripture, which ties personal identity to the story that each one lives through.[30] To invoke the name is, therefore, to evoke the whole way of Jesus (in which his identity is forged), and to associate the life of the believer to that way.[31]

Hence it is easy to understand the process by which Christian baptism originated. The command to baptize that St. Matthew records for us (Mt 28:19), far from appearing out of nowhere, was extensively linked to the history of Israel and to the life of Jesus, to the point where Luke can omit it without damaging the coherence of his account. The immersion of Jesus in the waters of the Jordan began a process that was to culminate in his Passover and would turn him into a wellspring of the Spirit upon mankind; now a similar baptism associated his disciples to this fullness of Christ, configuring them to his death and resurrection, and giving them to drink of one and the same Spirit. Given that the meaning of baptism is understood only in Paschal terms, when we contemplate all together the facts that we have reviewed, it is logical that the glorified Christ should carry out the institution of this sacrament (Mt 28:19).

St. Paul confirms in his letters the interpretation that I have outlined. To the Christians in Rome he speaks about baptism (Rom 6:3–8) precisely in the context of a comparison between Adam and Christ (Rom 5:12–21). We all belong to Adam, our first father, according to the Bible's characteristic

30. Bastiaan van Iersel, "Quelques présupposés bibliques de la notion de sacrement," *Concilium* 31, no. 1 (1968): 11–23, at 19.
31. Thomas F. Torrance, "Ein vernachlässigter Gesichtspunkt der Tauflehre," *Evangelische Theologie* 16, no. 3 (1956): 433–60 and 481–92.

view of corporate personality, which makes the origin of the lineage the representative of the whole people. This connection with Adam helps us to understand our baptismal bond with Christ, into whose new body we have been called to incorporate ourselves. The characteristic feature of baptism is to effect the change of membership: we put off the old body of sin, and we receive a new corporeal existence, that of the risen Christ, placing our members at the service of justice (Rom 6:12, 19). In this way, as St. Paul goes on to explain, the same Spirit can act in us who acted in the flesh of Jesus (Rom 8:11).[32]

Paul's interpretation offers us a final key for understanding how the practice of baptism arises in the church: the influence exercised by the Eucharistic celebration. Indeed, the apostle describes baptism as a birth to the body of Jesus, through which we are clothed with Christ by becoming one with Him (Gal 3:27–28); and precisely this key of the body ("My body which is for you": 1 Cor 11:24) is the one that Jesus offers us in his Last Supper in order to confer on us communion with himself ("The bread which we break, is it not a participation in the body of Christ?": 1 Cor 10:16). Moreover, if the Eucharist contains the memorial of his death and resurrection (1 Cor 11:26), baptism too assimilates us to the death, burial, and glorious rise of Jesus (Rom 6:4). In light of this we may conclude that, if Paul applies to baptism the language about the body of Christ, it is because of the influence of the master's Eucharistic words. In terms of the common basis of the Old Testament ("corporate person," "*anamnesis*"), Paul transposes to baptism the vocabulary that Jesus had used in the Eucharist, and explains the bath in water as a birth to his body.

Conclusion: Toward the Logic of the Sacrament, in Terms of Eucharist and Baptism

We have explored the two principal rites, baptism and Eucharist, to which the New Testament bears witness. From what has been said we can infer common elements that associate the two with each other, in terms of the life of Jesus. In the Eucharist, in continuity with the memory of Israel, Christ interprets his own death as thanksgiving (*todah*) to the Father for the fruitfulness that he communicates to his existence. The flesh and blood of Jesus open up a new space of relation with God and with men, to which Chris-

---

32. The same reasoning, applied in this case to Abraham and Christ, is found in the Letter to the Galatians (see esp. 3:26–29); see Van Iersel, "Quelques présupposés bibliques," 22.

tians are incorporated. It is a dynamic space, where the remembrance of the original action of the Father is preserved and we come to know already the fullness to which his promises lead.

On the other hand, Jesus is baptized in the Jordan: this is a rite that Christ receives from John, in terms of which his work is interpreted as the beginning of a new lineage which mediates the fullness of the Spirit of God. After he has risen, Jesus transmits to his disciples the order to baptize in his name, as a way of incorporating themselves into this life that he is inaugurating. Here too we have the entrance of the believer into the corporeal space of Christ and his adaptation to the rhythm with which he lived, for he is baptized "in His name," in other words, in the remembrance of his way on earth, until his glorious resurrection.

In my explanation the two rites appear to be intermingled with two central traditions of the Old Testament, which will be central also in order to understand the other sacraments. In the first place, we have the concept of *corporate person*: all the members of the people experience the fate of each one, so that Israel is like one person who goes through the ages.[33] This concept is not the primitive abstraction of those who have not yet developed the notion of the individual, but rather the rich vision of the relational, embodied person, the first testimony of which is preserved in familial experiences. Worship, the moment of the people's unity in the presence of God, is precisely what brings about the corporate integration of all Israel in terms of its foundational relation with God.

It is, moreover, the "memory" or *anamnesis*, the actualization of the past, that gives us a presentiment of its fruitfulness so as to illuminate the future; this actualization takes place effectively, once again, in worship. This is about activating the remembrance of God, who saved Israel from Egypt, establishing it as his people, born from the waters of the Red Sea. Having as its contents the actions of the unfathomable God, this memory always gives more than itself, overflowing over the present and the future. It is a living memory that allows each Israelite to consider himself as belonging to the generation that came up from Egypt (Dt 5:3). Israel's remembrance is the remembrance of a promise and thus it is the remembrance of the future that will arrive in this promise: the earth, the construction of the Temple, the happy life of the people with God.

This common background helps us to understand the connection be-

---

33. Robinson, *Corporate Personality in Ancient Israel*; Sang-Won A. Son, *Corporate Elements in Pauline Anthropology: A Study of Selected Terms, Idioms and Concepts in the Light of Paul's Usage and Background* (Rome: Pontifical Biblical Institute, 2001).

tween baptism and the Eucharist: both make present the flesh of Jesus and the recapitulation of history in him. These are the first insights that will illumine, over the course of time, a definition of sacrament. Baptism and Eucharist show that a sacrament revolves around the flesh and its ability to knit relations, with God and with human beings, according to the measure of Christ. The sacraments inaugurate, therefore, a new relational space, that of the body of Jesus, where the believer is enabled to live. This space opened up by the sacrament is, moreover, a dynamic space, which accompanies the way of the person in his story. The sacrament allows us to live according to the temporal rhythm of Jesus, in other words, according to the way in which he acknowledged the origin and destiny of everything in the Father.

Let us add to this picture the primacy that the Eucharist has as the interpretive key of the sacramental logic. Christ's Eucharistic words, which are centered on his body and blood and run along the axis from memory to fulfillment, are the words that offer a framework in which to understand baptism, which is less obvious in the master's explanations. As we saw in St. Paul, baptism is understood as the believer's birth to the flesh offered by Jesus in the Last Supper. Or, in other words, as an extension of the Eucharistic body of Jesus to the body of the Christian.

In light of this, baptism serves as a paradigm by which to understand the relation of the other sacraments to the Eucharist. They, like baptism, are rooted in the earthly ministry of the master, sifted by the Paschal events, and interpreted eucharistically. And they contain the ways in which the body of Christ, constituted in the Eucharist, is associated with the various situations and stages of Christian life. I will return to this subject in chapter 5 when we study the institution of the seven sacraments by Jesus.

In this chapter I started from the life of Jesus and from the rites that he instituted, focusing the analysis on the two major ones: the Eucharist and baptism. They give us the key to understanding how the sacraments mediate the encounter with Christ and our birth and life in him. The basic common coordinates that associate the two rites offer the basis on which is founded the general concept of "sacrament" in the preaching and work of Jesus.

In order to continue a more in-depth study from this perspective it will be important to have recourse to two early readings of this sacramental logic, proposed by St. John and by St. Paul. Although allusions to the sacraments are scattered throughout the New Testament, it is in the Johannine and Pauline writings that we find a first uniform theological explanation of the sacramental outlook.

3 🕊 SIGNS AND WORKS

The Sacramental Outlook of St. John

In order to present to us the earthly Jesus, the fourth Gospel chooses the way of signs. John calls "signs" the prodigious works of the master which, written down one by one, would not fit on all the bookshelves in the world (Jn 21:25). The apostle left us a selection written down, so that we might believe and have life (Jn 20:30–31). John associates these signs with the sacraments: to Nicodemus, attracted by signs (Jn 3:2), Jesus suggests baptism (Jn 3:5); and the sign of the multitude filled with the loaves is clearly Eucharistic (Jn 6:51–58). We will see in this chapter that this is not a matter of isolated details; the signs structure the beloved disciple's testimony about Jesus and lead to the Christian sacraments. Let us begin by discussing a radical objection to this position.

A Sacramental Gospel?

A hasty or fragmented reading of the fourth Gospel could cause one to think that John does not value the sacraments very highly: thus, for example, he does not speak about the institution of the Eucharist, nor does he recount the baptism of Jesus. Bultmann went so far as to say that the fourth Gospel tries to present a Christianity without sacraments: he even speaks about an anti-sacramental text, preoccupied with showing the eschatological presence of the salvation of Jesus, without other mediations. The well-known exegete did recognize undeniable references to baptism and to the Eucharist (Jn 3:5, 6:51–58, 19:34), but he attributed them to a later author who supposedly corrected the tone of the Gospel, harmonizing it with the choir of the universal church.[1]

Today that is an outdated position. The clearly sacramental verses which

---

1. Rudolf Bultmann, *Das Evangelium des Johannes* (Göttingen: Vandenhhoeck and Ruprecht, 1953), 98n2.

Bultmann pointed out form part of the architecture of the passage in which they are found; and they are completely consistent with Johannine language. Moreover, by understanding the symbolic style of the Evangelist, exegesis has discovered other allusions to the sacraments.

Certainly, we must avoid all exaggeration; it seems unlikely, for example, that in the resurrection of Lazarus, John refers to penance (implicit in the words "loose him," as St. Augustine interpreted them),[2] or that the anointing at Bethany is about the anointing of the sick (based on the verse: "that she may keep it against the day of my burial," Jn 12:7). But there are well-founded reasons for discovering many references intended by the Evangelist. Raymond Brown has pointed out these allusions as certain: to baptism (Jn 3:5, the conversation with Nicodemus, and in Jn 9, the man blind from birth); to the Eucharist (Jn 6, discourse on the bread of life, and in Jn 15, the vine and the branches); baptism and Eucharist in the water and the blood which gush from the open side of Jesus (Jn 19:34);[3] penance, when the risen Christ breathes on the disciples (Jn 20:23).[4] Other occasions (such as the wedding at Cana for matrimony in Jn 2:1–11) are, according to him, more dubious, but not to be simply dismissed.[5]

Still, to understand the sacraments in John, it is not enough to give a list of the sacramental passages. For the sacramental element is not just this or that text, but the logic underlying the entire Gospel. This reading, diametrically opposed to Bultmann's, was championed by Oscar Cullmann.[6] According to the latter, John is interested not only in telling the story of Jesus, but in telling it *sacramentally*, approaching it from the viewpoint of the sacraments, the living presence of Christ in the church. That is, in accordance with John, the privileged key—the only key—to remembering Jesus correctly, in such a way that his story is not a thing of the past but a living

---

2. Augustine, *In Iohannis* XLIX, 24 (CCL 36:431); in Nicene and Post-Nicene Fathers [hereafter NPNF-I for first series, NPNF-II for second series], ed. Philip Schaff (London: T and T Clark, 1886–1900), I, 7:277b–278a.

3. Bultmann imagined that Jn 19:34 was an addition by the church and commented on the passage: "It is difficult to find in it any other meaning but this: the sacraments of baptism and the Lord's Supper have their foundation in the death of Jesus on the cross" (Bultmann, *Das Evangelium des Johannes*, 525).

4. This is taught by the Council of Trent (DH 1670).

5. Raymond E. Brown, "The Johannine Sacramentary Reconsidered," *Theological Studies* 23, no. 2 (1962): 185–206; for another interpretation that tends to maximalism, see Bruce Vawter, "The Johannine Sacramentary," *Theological Studies* 17, no. 2 (1956): 151–66. See also Kikuo Matsunaga, "Is John's Gospel Anti-sacramental? A New Solution in Light of the Evangelist's Milieu," *New Testament Studies* 27, no. 4 (1981): 516–24; James W. Bunce, "The Liturgy of the Last Gospel," *Expository Times* 126, no. 6 (2015): 270–80.

6. Oscar Cullmann, *Les Sacrements dans l'Évangile johannique: La vie de Jésus et le culte de l'Église primitive* (Paris: PUF, 1951).

event. We have a Gospel written from the perspective of the sacraments, so as to be understood sacramentally.

Evidence to support this opinion is not lacking, beginning with the general structure of the text. Recall that the fourth Gospel starts with the testimony of the Baptist, who prefigures Christian baptism in water and Spirit, and allows us to recognize Jesus: "for this I came baptizing with water, that he might be revealed to Israel" (Jn 1:31, 32–34; 3:5). This new birth is already present in the prologue, linked with the incarnation of the Word: to believe in Christ makes us sons of God through a generation not by blood or carnal desire (Jn 1:12). On the other hand, the Gospel culminates with the death of Jesus on the cross, from whose side flow blood and water, also an allusion to the sacraments (Jn 19:34, in light of 1 Jn 5:6). Moreover, is this not consistent with the liturgical character of the other Johannine scripture, the Book of Revelation?[7] And with the insistence in the First Letter of John on this birth from God that is baptism (1 Jn 3:9; 5:6)?[8]

To prove the thesis, I will start from the importance that the fourth Gospel gives to the signs and works of Jesus. And we will see how these signs are associated with the Christian sacraments, especially with baptism and the Eucharist. It will help us to keep uppermost in mind a liturgical key to the Gospel of John: the theology of the temple, identified by Christ with his own body, where the divine glory dwells.

The Great Sign: The Temple Destroyed and Rebuilt

It is well known that St. John uses the word "sign" to speak of the miracles of Jesus. In this way he indicates, on the one hand, that he is not just talking about wonders that astonish the onlookers and prove the authority of him who performs them. There is in the miracles, above and beyond all else, a revelation of the mystery of Jesus, who invites us to embrace him.[9]

---

7. King, "*Lex orandi, lex credendi.*"

8. Giuseppe Segalla, "La testimonianza dei sacramenti (1 Giov 5, 6–12)," in *Sul sentiero dei sacramenti: Scritti in onore di Ermanno Roberto Ruta*, ed. C. Corsato (Padua: Messaggero, 2007), 171–88.

9. On the signs of Jesus in John, see Roland E. C. Formesyn, "Le sèmeion johannique et le sèmeion hellénistique," *Ephemerides Theologicae Lovanienses* 38 (1962): 856–94; Sebald Hofbeck, *Semeion: Der Begriff des Zeichens im Johannesevangelium unter Berücksichtigung seiner Vorgeschichte* (Münster: Schwarzach, 1966); Xavier Léon-Dufour, "Towards a Symbolic Reading of the Fourth Gospel," *New Testament Studies* 27, no. 4 (1980–81): 439–56; Donatien Mollat, "Le semeion johannique," *Sacra Pagina* (1959): 209–18; Willem Nicol, *The Semeia in the Fourth Gospel* (Leiden: Brill, 1972); Peter Riga, "Signs of Glory: The Use of 'semeion' in St. John's Gospel," *Interpretation* 17, no. 4 (1963): 402–24; Willis H. Salier, *The Rhetorical Impact of the Semeia in the Gospel of John* (Tübingen: Mohr Siebeck, 2004); and Giuseppe Segalla, "Segno giovanneo e sacramenti," in *Segno e sacramenti nel Vangelo di Giovanni*, ed. P. R. Tragan (Rome: Anselmiana, 1977), 17–44.

Thus we understand that the signs have a structuring role in the fourth Gospel, concerned with arousing faith, that is to say, our Christian discipleship. It is easy to distinguish the book of signs (Jn 1:19–12:50) from the book of glory (Jn 13:1–20:31); the unity of the whole is assured, inasmuch as the distinctive purpose of *signs* is to reveal the *glory* of Jesus (Jn 2:11).

From this point of view the transfiguration of Jesus—the glory in his flesh—could be identified as a key to reading the Gospel.[10] For, although St. John does not recount this mystery, we find two important allusions to it in the text. First, the master, troubled by the nearness of the hour, hears the voice of God which glorifies his name in the Son (Jn 12:27–28). The two central features of the transfiguration transmitted by the Synoptics appear here: the glory of the Father and the passion of Jesus, in which this glory manifests itself (Jn 12:32). All of this recapitulates his entire ministry, precisely in the sight of men who do not believe in his signs (Jn 12:37). We have, then, a *concentration* of the entire episode in just two verses. Second, on the other hand, John *extends* the transfiguration to the whole Gospel. In effect, the prologue already tells of the Word made flesh (Jn 1:14), whose glory is contemplated over the course of his earthly life, and precisely through his signs (Jn 2:11).

This allows us to conclude that the signs flow from Jesus himself, the Word made flesh, as he travels through history; and they are manifested abundantly in the life, death, and exaltation of the Son, which meet with the incredulity of men.[11] For this reason it can be affirmed that "the signs are the flesh of the glory of God."[12]

It is not unusual for the Old Testament to present the life and works of a person, particularly of a prophet, as a sign in which God speaks and acts. Such a thing happens, above all, when worship is in crisis, for this was the sphere in which divine signs normally took place (Ex 3:12). The prophet is the new place where the Spirit moves, when the temple, because of the people's infidelity, is more a prison to God than a home. The novelty that the prophets bring is the fact that the signs are experienced in the flesh of the man of God: "Isaiah has walked … as a sign" (Is 20:3); "I have made you

10. Riga, "Signs of Glory"; on the relation between Jn 1:14 and the transfiguration of Jesus, see Rainer Riesner, "John 1:14 and the Disciple 'whom Jesus loved,'" in *Rediscovering John: Essays on the Fourth Gospel in Honour of Frédéric Manns*, ed. L. D. Chrupcala (Milan: ETS, 2013), 303–36.

11. In the Synoptics we find also the Old Testament concept of sign, which reaches its apogee in Jesus. He is the sign of Jonah (Mt 12:38–45; Lk 11:29–32) which foretells the definitive, eschatological fulfillment of history. Therefore to discern him is to discern the "signs of the (last) times" (Mt 16:1–4; Lk 12:54–59).

12. Léon-Dufour, "Towards a Symbolic Reading," 442.

a sign" (Ezek 12:6).[13] Now the word of God is received and heard when his servant is received and heard; when one enters into the sacred space that the prophet establishes with his own bodily presence.[14]

Indeed, St. John follows this line of thought when he presents the body of Jesus as the new and definitive temple. Whereas from ancient times the glory of God dwelt in the sanctuary, whereas he commandeered the prophets so that they might work in his name and experience his own passion (Jer 20:7), now he has made a place for himself in the flesh of Christ, and he reveals himself in the earthly activity of the Son. The theology of the temple runs through the fourth Gospel and, associated with the liturgy of Israel, intermingles with the signs of Jesus and, as we will see, with the Christian sacraments.

The concept appears on the very first page: "And the Word became flesh and dwelt among us ... we have beheld his glory" (Jn 1:14). "Dwelt" means: he pitched his tent as did Yahweh in ancient times in the midst of his people. The Greek term (*skenóo*) shares consonants with the Hebrew *shekinah*: the presence of the glory of God. Moreover, when John says "the Word became *flesh*" and not simply "became *man*," the theology of the temple also resounds, the presence of God in the midst of the earth. For the human body is a primordial temple, inhabited by the breath of Yahweh (Gn 2:7); and, as we have just seen, the body of the prophet is the place of the revelation of God, when the temple of stone ceases to be hospitable to the Most High.[15]

John adds right away, in the dialogue with Nathaniel, another reference to the temple: "you will see heaven opened, and the angels of God ascending and descending upon the Son of man" (Jn 1:51). This recalls the ladder of Jacob, and the memorial stone which the patriarch anointed, when he understood that he was setting foot in the house of Yahweh (Gn 28:12–22). Thus Jesus surveys, already in the Jordan, the final horizon of his life and work, when he ascends glorified to his Father's dwelling place.

Jesus' first collision with the Pharisees takes up again the image of the temple, this time openly in the context of signs.[16] To the Jews who seek

---

13. Is 8:18: "I and the children whom the LORD has given me are signs"; Is 20:3: "Isaiah has walked naked and barefoot for three years as a sign"; Ezek 12:6, 11: "I have made you a sign. I am a sign for you"; Ezek 24:24, 27: "Thus shall Ezekiel be to you a sign. So you will be a sign to them."

14. Martin Buber, "Sinnbildliche und sakramentale Existenz im Judentum," *Eranos Jahrbuch* 2 (1934): 339–67, at 350: "the prophet not only works in signs but also lives in signs. The sign is not ultimately what he does, but rather, inasmuch as he does it, the prophet himself is the sign."

15. Mario Cucca, *Il corpo e la città: studio del rapporto di significazione paradigmatica tra la vicenda di Geremia e il destino di Gerusalemme* (Assisi: Cittadella, 2010).

16. Scott Hahn, "Temple, Sign, and Sacrament: Toward a New Perspective on the Gospel of

a sign, Jesus offers the sign that forms the foundation and culmination of them all: "Destroy this temple, and in three days I will raise it up" (Jn 2:19); "he spoke of the temple of his body" (Jn 2:21). The signs that will decant the life of Christ point to a supreme sign: the death and resurrection of Jesus as ruin and reconstruction of a temple (Jn 2:18–19).

Although Jesus does not explicitly call the cross and resurrection a "sign," he does so here in a veiled way, at the beginning of his ministry. Recall, moreover, that his first sign at Cana alludes to the decisive hour, when Mary reappears beneath the cross (Jn 2:4; 19:26); and that many signs are performed in the context of the Jewish Passover, which prefigures that of the master. Thus, the Eucharistic sign of the multiplication of the loaves (Jn 6) and that of the resurrection of Lazarus (Jn 11:47) forebode his death and resurrection (Jn 6:51, 62; 11:49–53; 12:7). A distinctive feature of the sign is its paradoxical character, for the zenith of its manifestation coincides with the moment of the greatest scorn for Jesus.[17]

This presentation of signs in the context of the new temple does not appear only at the beginning and end of the Gospel. On the contrary, it is possible to follow the topic throughout the master's journey, for John decants the signs, as we will see, in time with the feasts of Israel, which are located in the sanctuary and confer a chronology on the Gospel. Thus, through the connection with Jewish ritual, the link between the signs and the Christian liturgy is reinforced, especially baptism and the Eucharist.

For now, we can conclude that signs always refer to a space (the temple, which is the body of Jesus) where the full indwelling of God among the people lives. And that they point to a definitive sign through which this space is built: the death and resurrection of the Lord.

Signs and Incorporation into Christ

Signs, we have seen, invite us to enter into the space of the relationship with Jesus; this space is the new temple, where God can be adored in Spirit and truth (Jn 4:23) and unity can be established among men (Jn 11:52). How do signs bring us into this temple of the body? To answer this question, it is necessary to observe the dynamism of the sign, a dynamism which is discov-

---

John," *Letter and Spirit* 4 (2008): 107–43; Mary L. Coloe, *God Dwells with Us: Temple Symbolism in the Fourth Gospel* (Collegeville, Minn.: Liturgical Press, 2001).

17. On the relation of the Johannine signs with the cross, see Jean Zumstein, "Le signe de la croix," *Lumière et Vie* 41, no. 209 (1992): 68–82; this author writes: "the ultimate fulfillment that verifies the seven signs and gives them their full validity takes place in the opposite key, namely, of ridicule and death" (73).

ered both through the connection between sign and faith, and also through the closeness of Christ's *signs* to his *works*.

The Sign and Faith in Jesus

Let us take the multiplication of the loaves as our point of departure (Jn 6). It is a moment which sums up the entire ministry of Jesus, for here this union between sign and the flesh of Christ crops up again, referring us both to his birth (Jn 1:14) and to his passion, death, and resurrection (Jn 6:51). The theme of the dwelling place, which is the temple, also reappears in this passage: to eat the flesh and to drink the blood signifies dwelling in Christ, and Christ in us (Jn 6:56).

The sign, in the first place, invites us to set out on a journey so as to enter into a relationship with Jesus.[18] The multitude, full of bread, wants to crown him king responsible for the security that it needs, but it is mistaken. Anyone who contemplates the sign must be goaded, on the contrary, by uneasiness, by the search for a deeper satisfaction, through God. For this reason, after multiplying the provisions, the master mysteriously crosses over the waters to the other shore, thus inviting us with a new sign to follow him in his journey. Jesus reminds the Jews about something essential to the human experience: the nursing infant, in his mother's milk, does not merely desire a full stomach, either, but rather the relationship with his mother. Similarly, the sign was given so that men, in setting out on the journey, might establish a bond with the living bread, Christ; that is to say, the sign was given in order that faith might spring up.[19]

The Old Testament already testifies that a distinctive property of the sign is that it impels us to walk the path. Think, for example, of the sign that God gave Moses when he revealed his name to him: "I will be with you: and this shall be the sign for you, that I have sent you: when you have brought forth the people out of Egypt, you shall serve [i.e., offer sacrifice to] God upon the mountain" (Ex 3:12; 4:22–23). The sign that God offers to Moses surprises us, because it is a sign that will be given only in the future. Furthermore, it is not enough to open one's eyes to prove it: it is necessary for Moses to set out on the journey and to obey God's command. What is required, then, in order for there to be a sign, is that man accept it and respond to it; the very struggle of Moses, his liberty *en route*, the success of his enterprise,

18. For the following discussion see Paul Beauchamp, "Le signe des pains," *Lumière et Vie* 41, no. 209 (1992): 55–67; Luis Sánchez Navarro, "El misterio del pan," in *La sacramentalidad del ser*, ed. L. Granados (Madrid / Burgos: Didáskalos / Monte Carmelo, 2017).

19. Luis Erdozáin, *La función del signo en la fe según el cuarto evangelio*, Analecta Biblica 33 (Rome: PIB, 1968).

will be part of the sign. And, finally, it will be possible to contemplate this sign only on Sinai, in the space opened up by God for the people's worship.

Manna, administered by Moses himself, constitutes the background of the discourse on the bread of life. Jesus, who on the one hand identifies himself with this bread come down from heaven, does not fail, on the other hand, to highlight the differences. For manna is received passively, without fatigue or effort. It was not yet the food of the Promised Land, which would have to be cultivated. Hence it was forbidden to gather any surplus. On the contrary, the new sign of Jesus indicates entrance into the land, a place where it is possible to dwell and enjoy the fruits of one's own labor: the boy with the few loaves makes his contributions, and the disciples make sure that nothing is wasted. This entrance into the land occurs precisely with Christ; he, in reality, does not just come down from heaven, like the manna, but also rises up from below; he became flesh to fill the flesh with glory through his death and resurrection.[20]

The sign possesses, then, a dynamic character because it sets us on the path to Jesus; and a relational character, because it leads us into the space of bonds opened by him when he came into the world and became flesh. It becomes clear in this light why St. John associated the sign with faith, our personal adherence to Christ in order to become like him. This dynamic and relational character of the sign explains, on the one hand, that he gave the sign to us so that we might believe, for the divine action always precedes us (Jn 20:30–31); and, on the other, that only someone who believes—only someone who sets out on the journey and enters into a relationship with Jesus—can see the sign, for it is hidden from those who trust in the self-sufficiency of their outlook and, having blackened their own eyes, prove that they are blind (Jn 9:41). Entering into the sign, therefore, as we will see below, calls for a work.

Let us note, finally, that the sign has paradoxical features that cause scandal: Jesus' listeners abandon him when he commands them to eat his flesh (Jn 6:66). Jesus applies to stubbornness in the presence of signs the phrase from Isaiah (Is 6:9): so that they may see but not perceive, and may hear but not understand (Jn 12:37–43).[21] This same text appears in the Synoptics in reference to the parables (Mt 13:14; Mk 4:12). Signs and parables go, therefore, hand in hand, as though the sign were a parable incarnated in Jesus. Hence in the signs, as in the parables, the message does not impose itself

---

20. Beauchamp, "Le signe des pains," 62–64.
21. Recall that Ex 10:1 associated signs with the hardness of the pagan heart.

upon us, but appeals to our liberty.[22] That which signs announce, indeed, can be contemplated only if we allow ourselves to be attracted by them, if we enter into their splendor, renouncing judgment of them from without. For the sign opens a perspective opposed to that of the isolated subject, who only seeks security and contentment; the sign is meant to lead us to a different, relational outlook which, although it might seem to make us lose control, broadens our perspective enormously. He who closes himself to signs, on the contrary, entrenches himself ever deeper in his conceit, so that, seeing, he does not see. For this reason the fullness of signs passes precisely through the cross, a sign turned the wrong way around so as to uproot the stubbornness of the isolated subject and to open the space of unity with God and our fellow human beings.

Sign and Work: Common Action with the Father

In this context we can understand that John also refers to the miracles of Jesus as "works." The term recalls the central deeds of Yahweh in the Old Testament: creation and the exodus. As with the signs, we find ourselves within the context of the God who reveals himself in order to establish his presence among men. In fact, works and signs refer to the same reality, but from complementary points of view. The sign is that which everyone sees; it is the action contemplated from outside. The work, for its part, is the sign seen from within, for him who accepts it in his heart. For this reason, when Jesus speaks of himself, he does not refer to his signs, but to his works; works are signs from the perspective of Christ, who dwells at the center of the mystery. Thus, the author who called the sign "the body of the work" said it well.[23]

What is this perspective of Jesus, about which the works inform us? It is about his common action with the Father. He who walks the path opened by the sign discovers the secret of the miracles, not in the autonomous power of the wonder worker, but in the initiative of the Father who sent his Son, thus revealing himself as origin of all. Jesus refers therefore to his works as the works which the Father gave him to accomplish (Jn 5:36).[24] That is to

---

22. On the relation between signs and parables, see Riga, "Signs of Glory"; Enno Edzard Popkes, "'Das Mysterion der Botschaft Jesu': Beobachtungen zur synoptischen Parabeltheorie und ihren Analogien im Johannesevangelium und Thomasevangelium," in *Hermeneutik der Gleichnisse Jesu*, ed. R. Zimmermann (Tübingen: Mohr Siebeck, 2008), 294–320.

23. Xavier Léon-Dufour, "Los milagros de Jesús según Juan," in his *Los milagros de Jesús* (Madrid: Cristiandad, 1979), 268; on the recognition of the works based on the signs, see Riga, "Signs of Glory," 417–23.

24. Albert Vanhoye, "L'oeuvre du Christ, don du Père," *Revue des sciences religieuses* 48 (1960): 377–419.

say, the Father did not just give Jesus static gifts to possess; he went further, giving him works, that is, inciting and accompanying the very action of his Son. Within the heart of the sign, which is the work, the Father's continual self-gift to the Son is discovered; and the Son's giving of himself in response, together with the Father, so as to include mankind in this communion.

We now understand the link between sign and work. Whereas signs, as we have seen, lead us to a relation with Jesus, to a grafting onto him, and culminate therefore in the destruction and raising of the temple of his body; works, for their part, call to mind that this space is the space of the mutual indwelling of the Father and the Son, who come to men to make their dwelling among them. The works corroborate that what has been revealed by Jesus through his signs is the mystery of the God who is a communion of persons.

The link between signs and works is confirmed when we notice that Jesus performs some of his signs on the Sabbath. Surely, his intention is not to trivialize the holy day of the Jews, to show them that all the days of the week are the same. If he favors the Sabbath it is because this is the fitting day for him to manifest himself. Indeed, the Sabbath is called in the Bible, "sign," inasmuch as it recalls that manual labor (the work) bears fruit when it carries the divine blessing (Ezek 20:12). The sign of the Sabbath thus proves to be a memorial sign that testifies to how God precedes, stirs up, invigorates human activity. There is no better framework for the activity of Jesus, whose food is to do the will of the Father.

We will see in the following section that, whereas signs and works tell us about the building of the new temple throughout the life of Christ, the sacraments will be the participation of the faithful in this temple, once it is erected. When speaking of the sign and the work, therefore, St. John prefigures the central elements of sacramental theology: the dimension of *sign* is joined by the dimension of *efficacious work*; and both are directed toward constructing a covenant with God, *communicating the grace of his presence.*[25]

From the Sign to the Sacrament

To prove that the signs worked by Jesus point to the sacraments, it helps to pay attention to the liturgical context within which they are situated. This has to do with the principal Jewish feasts, celebrated in the Temple,

---

25. On the "works" in St. John, see Raymond E. Brown, "Appendix III: Signs and Works," in his *The Gospel according to John* (Garden City, N.Y.: Doubleday, 1966–70), 1:525–33.

which decant the life of Jesus.[26] Given that St. John associates signs with the ancient liturgy, it is not surprising that he also links them to Christian worship. And, in fact, around the account of the signs there are plenty of allusions to baptism and the Eucharist. Let us see the combination of these elements (Old Testament feasts, signs, sacraments) during the three Passovers of the Savior.

The first Jewish Passover that the Gospel tells us about serves as an occasion to present baptism (Jn 2:13–3:21). To Nicodemus, a man who seeks signs (Jn 3:2), Jesus speaks about "being born again" in water and Spirit (Jn 3:5). Two distinct themes run through the text: the Pharisee understands that Christ is inviting him to come nearer to him, to believe in him; the Christians, for their part, discover more: this drawing near happens precisely in baptism.[27] The image used is that of birth (to be born again or to be born from on high), combined with water and the Spirit. The scene of the Samaritan woman shortly afterward again develops the theme of water, associating it with worship "in Spirit and truth" (Jn 4:24), which will no longer occur in the Temple of Jerusalem, but rather in the encounter with Jesus. It is not surprising that, when decorating the catacombs, Christian art should discover in the Samaritan woman a baptismal motif.[28] After this first Passover John mentions another Jewish feast that he does not identify (Jn 5:1), which frames the curing of the paralytic in the pond of Bethsaida, evoking once again salvific water.[29] These episodes bring to mind the Old Testament image of the temple, from which flows water in abundance (Ezek 47:1–12), symbol of the life-giving Spirit.

The second Passover is associated with the multiplication of the loaves, together with the Eucharistic discourse that follows it (Jn 6). We are facing an essential sign, for it is focused on the body of Jesus, at the same time manna and Paschal lamb (Jn 1:29), given by God the Father and sacrificed for the life of the world (Jn 6:51). The liturgical context is obvious if we recall that God had ordered Moses to preserve some of the manna in the temple

26. Gale A. Yee, *Jewish Feasts and the Gospel of John* (Wilmington, Del.: Michael Glazier, 1989); Hahn, "Temple, Sign, and Sacrament"; Coloe, *God Dwells with Us*.

27. According to Léon-Dufour, "Towards a Symbolic Reading," there are two complementary ways of reading the Gospel of John: first, as a fulfillment of the Old Testament in Jesus; second, as access to Jesus through the sacraments. Thus the conversation with Nicodemus was understood by the Pharisee in the first sense, the only one that was comprehensible to him; while Christians grasped it also in the second sense.

28. S. Smalley, "Liturgy and Sacrament in the Fourth Gospel," *Evangelical Quarterly* 29, no. 3 (1957): 159–70, at 168.

29. Tertullian interprets the passage in the baptismal sense: *De Baptismo* V, 5–7 (CCL I, 28:1–282; ANF 3:671b–672a).

(Ex 16:32–34), and that the sanctuary was where the lamb was offered. The master also mentions that to eat of the Eucharist is to enter into a space of mutual indwelling with him (Jn 6:56).

This episode is followed by the preaching of Jesus during the Feast of Tabernacles (Jn 7–8). We find ourselves in the temple, which has been prepared for the occasion with enormous containers of water and candelabra of light. When he identifies himself with the water ("let him come to me and drink, he who believes in me," Jn 7:37) and the light ("I am the light," Jn 8:12), Jesus presents himself once more as a temple. Baptismal echoes resound at the mention of the rivers which flow from the heart of Jesus and of those who believe in him (Jn 7:37), evoking again the temple-spring of Ezekiel.

Finally, John 9 (the curing of the blind man) also alludes to baptism. As with Nicodemus, there is a new illumination: the blind man was blind from birth, and his parents have a prominent place in the story, as if to underscore in this way his new origin, of which they remain ignorant. The aquatic motif reappears in the pool of Siloam, which means "sent" (Jn 9:7), a name which underscores the key to the mystery of Jesus: his procession from the Father, in which we take root through baptism, which begets us as sons (Jn 1:13).

Regarding *the third Passover,* when Jesus dies, the theme of the temple returns. In the farewell discourse, in a liturgical tone, there is an allusion to the many mansions or rooms of the house (Jn 14:2), the "place" or new temple which Christ goes to prepare for his disciples;[30] the context, through the mention of the vine into which the branches are incorporated, is Eucharistic (Jn 15:1–11). This is also the setting of the washing of the feet (Jn 13:1–20). Comparison with the Lucan account of the Last Supper, the outline of which the fourth evangelist adopts, shows that the washing takes place precisely where Luke situates the institution of the Eucharist. According to St. John, Jesus asks his disciples to imitate his humble act, which is possible only for someone who, through having been washed in his water, has a share in Christ. The association with the sacraments, which incorporate us into Jesus, springs up spontaneously.[31] There are even some who point out the link with the purification of the feet which was asked of those who entered into the Jewish sanctuary.[32]

30. James McCaffrey, *The House with Many Rooms: The Temple Theme of Jn. 14, 2–3* (Rome: Pontificio Istituto Biblico, 1998).

31. Francis J. Moloney, "A Sacramental Reading of John 13:1–38," *Catholic Biblical Quarterly* 53, no. 2 (1991): 237–56; Yves-Marie Blanchard, "Lavement des pieds et pénitence: Une lecture de Jean 13, 1–20," *La Maison Dieu* 214 (April 1998): 35–50.

32. Alan Kerr, *The Temple of Jesus' Body: The Temple Theme in the Gospel of John* (Sheffield: Sheffield Academic, 2002), 268–313.

Finally, John 19:34 presents the image of the pierced side from which flows blood and water. The evangelist could have been thinking of the blood of the sacrifices which, having pooled beneath the altar, joined the water of the Cedron and flowed intermingled from one side of the Temple.[33] The definitive sign of Christ (Jn 2:19: "destroy ... I will raise it up ...") establishes a new temple, from whose heart spring streams of living water. Effects of this supreme sign—and, therefore, the place to which all signs point—are baptism and the Eucharist, water and blood which spring from the new sanctuary.

From all this we can conclude that the signs which occur in relation to the liturgical feasts of Israel and to Jesus as temple, point to the Christian sacraments. Two lines of thought come together here. First, *signs*: during his life Jesus opens the space (temple) where the liturgy of Israel arrives at its fullness, and which is the space of his body. This opening culminates in the cross and resurrection, definitive sign of the destruction and raising of the new sanctuary. The rest of the signs point to this final action: little by little, they display the space of relation to Jesus, incorporating into him those who believe. It is a space in which the Father and the Son dwell, *working* together in order to welcome the disciple.

Second, *sacraments*: Jesus glorified is the temple from which the new Christian liturgy is born. These appear similar to signs inasmuch as they too incorporate us into the place where the Father and Son dwell. At the same time, they are different from signs, because the latter led into a temple which was being formed; while the sacraments are expansions of the temple which, once the Passover has run its course, is now present and active in the world.[34]

The sacraments are, therefore, the final perspective for understanding the Johannine signs. The vanishing point of the signs and works of Jesus are baptism and the Eucharist, which spring directly from the great sign and the great work that is the death and resurrection of Jesus, where the new temple is inaugurated (Jn 2:18–21).[35] That is to say, baptism and the Eucharist are about being born into the body of Jesus, being grafted onto him, expanding his growth in history toward the celestial Jerusalem. *While the sign brings us into the space of Jesus, which is becoming established, the sacrament flows from*

---

33. Hahn, "Temple, Sign, and Sacrament," 114n49.

34. A similar relation is spelled out by Hofbeck, *Semeion*, 196: "the signs orient toward the divine life, the sacraments give it."

35. Léon-Dufour, "Towards a Symbolic Reading," 441: "The symbolic operation must be situated in the two dimensions of time defined by the Paschal event, the time of Jesus of Nazareth and the time of the glorified Lord."

this full space, already built, so as to incorporate the believer into it. Everything seems to be summarized in that question of the first disciples: "Where are you staying?" (Jn 1:38). According to the key that we have offered, the master responded a little later, when he spoke to Nathaniel about the "greater things" that the disciple would see, presenting himself as a new Jacob upon whom angels would ascend and descend, and thus alluding to the sanctuary which the patriarch prefigured (Jn 1:50). In the sacraments we can also identify some of those "greater works" that the disciples would perform after the ascension of Jesus, as he himself promised (Jn 14:12).[36]

From what has been said, we can figure out why John does not narrate the institution of baptism and the Eucharist. This absence helps to underscore the theological vision of the fourth Gospel. For thus the sacraments appear, not as isolated events, but as a lens through which to read the entire life of Christ. They are not present principally as an object of the narrative, but as the vanishing point to which everything tends and as the perspective from which everything is understood in unity. It becomes clear, then, that in the sacraments one accesses not only the rites that Jesus lived, but Jesus' life itself.[37] Thus, for example, in the Eucharistic discourse the rite in which the bread is transformed into flesh is not mentioned; taking it for granted, John concentrates on its ultimate fruit: the flesh of Jesus, true food, is the true bread.[38]

Conclusion

The Gospel according to John, beyond testifying to certain concrete rites, contains the principles of a sacramental logic. For the sacraments give the Christian access to Jesus so as to find him, not as a vague historical remembrance, but as the Living One *par excellence* (Rv 1:18). The leading thread is provided by the *signs* worked by Christ, which point to the great sign that is his death and resurrection, when his body is established as the new and definitive temple. Signs prepare this worship space, they disclose it, they explain it: it is the space of the common work of the Father and the Son which is meant to make room for all of humankind. On the other hand, these same signs, framed within the liturgy of Israel, prefigure the *sacraments*. Whereas the signs help us to associate ourselves with the earthly journey of Jesus toward the cross and resurrection, the sacraments (John focuses on bap-

---

36. Hahn, "Temple, Sign, and Sacrament," 130–33.
37. Giuseppe Angelini, *Il tempo e il rito alla luce delle Scritture* (Assisi: Cittadella, 2006), 308.
38. Paul Beauchamp, "Le signe des pains," 66.

tism and the Eucharist, without neglecting others) permit us, starting from this same cross and resurrection, to live on the fullness of the risen Lord. Whatever is said about signs will be completed, sifted through the passion of Christ, and fulfilled in his glorious flesh, in the sacraments. Here are some keys to the sacramental outlook.

The sacramental logic is forged and revealed in the flesh, for that is where we are incorporated into the relational space opened by Jesus, a space that is the temple of his body (Jn 2:21). To be on pilgrimage through the *signs* does not mean, therefore, leaving behind what is exterior so as to settle down in the interior, as if, for example, the curing of the blind man did not really matter, and it was only about gaining acuity in the spiritual senses. On the contrary, the place toward which signs are directed is precisely the death and resurrection of Jesus in the flesh: they are signs that move to the fullness of the bodily encounter with Christ, where the new temple is raised.

The *sacraments,* for their part, receive and consummate these characteristic features of the sign. They flow from a fullness of what is corporeal in Christ, which they never leave behind. Although "the flesh is of no avail" (Jn 6:63), it is not because it has to be overcome in the Spirit; but rather because its vocation is to be filled with the Spirit, the only One who bestows life (ibid.). One distinctive feature of the sacrament consists of becoming rooted in the space of the body which, being the first place in which we are situated in the world and among our brethren, was the place assumed by Jesus in order to build the dwelling place of the Father with us.

The sacramental logic is a logic of active participation: only someone who sets out on the journey sees the sign and, having become a friend of Jesus, allows himself to be transformed by him. To enter into the space-temple of the body of Christ is to dwell in a network of relations animated by continual reciprocal giving, which originates continually from God the Father. This implies that the signs, besides enlightening the understanding, promote the active participation of the whole person. The sign can be understood only if one enters into it, receives it cordially, and follows the road which it opens up. Hence signs are also *works*: the common work of Jesus and his Father, the work of both in the believer. Hence too the deep connection between *sign and faith,* and their virtuous circle: the sign makes faith possible, faith enables us to see the sign.

The *sacrament,* for its part, fulfills what was begun in the signs. The sacramental epiphany, in order to be recognized, brings the whole person into play, introduces him into an action initiated by Christ. We will see that, by defining the sacrament as an efficacious sign of grace (sign that communi-

cates the grace which it represents), the theological tradition has preserved
this double dimension—sign and work—of the Johannine vocabulary.

Finally, the sacramental logic enables us to capture the proper rhythm
of salvation history, from the beginnings of created things up to their consummation in Christ. The signs of Jesus are signs-memorials that review the
history of the Old Testament, which dates back to the dawn of the world.
The space of his body, where the divine glory is manifested, is not foreign to
the other spaces that God opened when he laid the foundations of the cosmos. Thus, the new birth from the waters refers to the old birth (Jn 16:21);
and the Eucharistic bread has as its background work and the fruit of the
earth (Jn 6:27). And this is because these original spaces also take root in the
body of man, ever since the union of Adam and Eve (Jn 2:1–11), the body
that the Word assumed when he was born of Mary.

It is not surprising, in light of what I have said, that tradition has called
John the "Liturgist," nor that iconography has represented him holding a
chalice, just as he appears, for example, on the façade of the Lateran Basilica.[39] There is a profound insight here. If John is honored with the name of
"Theologian," it is precisely inasmuch as he is a "Liturgist." For a theologian
is not only someone who soars, like an eagle, to scrutinize with burning
eyes the splendor of the divinity of the Logos; but someone who adopts
the sacramental outlook, which contemplates God active in the world and
in history, and discovers that the glory of the Most High is reflected in the
flesh of Jesus.

Having explored the Johannine vision, we can focus on other texts of
the New Testament that also offer an overall perspective on the sacraments:
the Pauline corpus. The term *mystery*—in Latin *sacramentum*—will call for
special attention here. Although the theological tradition finds inspiration
in St. John for the definition of sacrament as "sign of grace," St. Paul was the
one who fostered our discourse today about the seven "sacraments."

---

39. On John as a liturgist, see Ethelbert Stauffer, *Die Theologie des Neuen Testaments* (Gütersloh: Bettelsmann, 1941), 45; Angelini, *Il tempo e il rito*, 296. The representation with the chalice is
connected also with a legend about the life of St. John, whom the Romans tried to poison; when the
apostle blessed the chalice, he drove out its poison. The iconography combined legend and Eucharistic
allusion, which are not necessarily antithetical.

4 ❧ FROM ST. PAUL
TO THE *MYSTERION-*
SACRAMENTUM

Someone who investigates in scripture the meaning of the Greek word *mysterion*, translated in Latin as *sacramentum*, may be surprised. For it appears that the term is used in the New Testament in a sense different from the one that it has today, not only in theology but in the practice of the faithful. The Bible, indeed, does not seem to apply the word *mysterion* (*sacramentum*) to the Christian rites, such as baptism and the Eucharist. Is this because our language has moved away from the Gospel usage? And if so, for what reasons, and with what effects?

To answer these questions, I will delve more deeply into the meaning of *mysterion* in the New Testament, above all as St. Paul uses it. In the previous chapter we saw that the fourth Gospel approaches the sacraments starting from the signs and works of Jesus. I will show now that the apostle to the Gentiles bases his sacramental synthesis on the concept of *mysterion*. As I have already noted, later theological tradition would employ the Pauline language of *mysterion* to enumerate the sacraments, and it would prefer the Johannine view of the sign to define them.

From *mysterion* to the Sacraments

What does *mysterion* mean in scripture?[1] St. Paul employs the word to designate God's plan, hidden for ages and manifested with the sending of his Son (Rom 16:25; Eph 3:9; Col 1:26). Christ himself is the mystery of God,

---

1. D. Deden, "Le Mystère Paulinien," *Ephemerides Theologicae Lovanienses* 13 (1936): 405–42; Gunther Bornkamm, "Mysterion," in *Theologisches Wörterbuch zum Neuen Testament,* ed. Gerhard Kittel (Stuttgart: W. Kohlhammer, 1990), 4:809–34; Carolyn Osiek, "Il 'Mysterion' paolino," *Catholic Biblical Quarterly* 44 (1982): 521–22; Benjamin L. Gladd, *Revealing the mysterion: The Use of Mystery in Daniel in Second Temple Judaism with Its Bearing on First Corinthians* (Berlin: W. de Gruyter, 2008); Gregory S. Magee, "Uncovering the 'mystery' in 1 Timothy 3," *Trinity Journal* 29 (2008): 247–65.

manifested in the flesh (Col 2:2; 1 Tm 3:16). In him, particularly in his obedience on the cross (1 Cor 2:1–2) and in his grateful resurrection from the dead, the Father revealed his eschatological design for history (1 Cor 15:51) and carried it to its conclusion.

Note that the *mysterion* does not consist of Jesus alone, isolated from the rest of mankind and from the cosmos, but rather of Christ as the one who recapitulates the ages (Eph 1:9–10): *mysterion* is a relational term that allows the actors in salvation history to be linked with one another. In this way the church too belongs to the *mysterion*, inasmuch as she extends to the world the fullness brought by Jesus (Eph 1:22–23). Therefore the *mysterion* consists in the unity of all, Jews and Gentiles, in one body (Eph 3:4–6, 9–10). The perspective of *mysterion* is thus interwoven with another major theme of the Pauline vision: the church, the body of Christ.[2]

We should add that this union in the body, for Paul, is not only the organic union of the head with the members, but also the personal union of the bridegroom with his bride in "one flesh," according to Genesis 2:24.[3] Paul would call the cohesion of Christ and his church, as the final destination of the way of man with a maiden (Prv 30:19), the "great mystery" (Eph 5:31–32). The expansion of the *mysterion* throughout the world follows the analogy of fertility, just as the union of husband and wife prolongs divine creation in their children.

I already noted that the word *mysterion* is not applied directly to baptism and the Eucharist. This raises the question with which I started this chapter: how can we explain the fact that little by little the Church Fathers and then medieval theologians would use the term *mysterion* and its Latin equivalent *sacramentum* to refer to Christian worship?[4]

Some answer that the church probably spoke about the sacraments as "mysteries" through an adaptation to the mystery religions of Hellenism. In those cults the history of a divinity was represented, for example that of the god Mithra, crowned by the sun and conqueror of the bull whose blood fertilized the earth with life.[5] The follower associated himself with these

2. Charles C. Ryrie, "Mystery in Ephesians 3," *Bibliotheca Sacra* 123 (1966): 24–31; Heinrich Schlier, "Die Kirche als das Geheimnis Christi," in his *Die Zeit der Kirche* (Freiburg: Herder, 1956), 299–307; and Gary W. Derickson, "The New Testament Church as a Mystery," *Bibliotheca Sacra* 166 (2009): 436–45.

3. Andreas J. Köstenberger, "The Mystery of Christ and the Church: Head and Body, 'One Flesh," *Trinity Journal* 12 (1991): 79–94.

4. Herbert Musurillo, "Sacramental Symbolism and the *Mysterion* of the Early Church," *Worship* 39 (1965): 265–74.

5. Franz Cumont, *Les mystères de Mithra* (Brussels: H. Lamertin, 1902); Robert Turcan, *Mithra et le mithracisme* (Paris: Les Belles Lettres, 1993), and *Recherches Mithraiques: Quarante ans de questions et d'investigations* (Paris: Les Belles Lettres, 2016).

events, thus obtaining salvation; in order to participate, it was necessary to go through an initiation rite that required an oath of silence about what was experienced—this feature may be connected with the etymology of *mysterion*, which seems to be derived from the Greek verb "to be silent."[6]

The thesis of this Hellenistic background was defended by some theologians, especially Protestants, of the first half of the twentieth century. The use of the word *mysterion* to speak about the Christian mystery, in this view, was a departure from the original purity recorded by St. Paul. Disappointed in their expectation of the imminent coming of the Messiah, which animated the apostolic community, the faithful transferred their interest to the sacraments, which presented the divine within reach by way of a ritual with a magical twist.[7]

The so-called theology of the mysteries of Odo Casel also supposed Hellenistic influence in the discourse of the Church Fathers. But he gave this finding a positive tone: pagan elements were accepted to convey the Christian newness which, according to the Benedictine scholar, finds no parallels in the Jewish tradition.[8] Still, without denying that there is some adoption of pagan vocabulary and ideas in early Christianity, the Hellenistic background falls short as an explanation of why *mysterion* would later be applied to the liturgy. It is worth the trouble to pursue a more probable line of investigation: the Old Testament.[9] This is recommended, above all, because it is the backdrop of the Pauline terminology of the *mysterion*, and because we find in it an initial *rapprochement* between liturgy and *mysterion* that offers a solid basis for the patristic development. As we will see, in the Bible the *mysterion* is already associated with worship: the first Christians did nothing but elaborate on the original connections.

The trail of the Old Testament leads us to notice the Hebrew term *sod*, a group of counselors with whom God decides the paths of history.[10] The term, which means the meeting of the council, came to signify

6. On the pagan mysteries see Carl Clemen, *Der Einfluss der Mysterienreligionen auf das älteste Christentum* (Giessen, 1913); R. Schulte, "Mysterion en el griego clásico y en el helenismo," in *Mysterium Salutis: Fundamentos de la dogmática como historia de la salvación*, ed. J. Feiner and M. Löhrer (Madrid: Cristiandad, 1969), 4.2:78–81; Tennyson Jacob Wellman, "Ancient Mystēria and Modern Mystery Cults," *Religion & Theology* 12, nos. 3–4 (2005): 308–48.

7. Rudolf Bultmann, *Geschichte und Eschatologie* (Tübingen: Mohr, 1958), 59; Ramón Arnau, *Tratado general de los sacramentos* (Madrid: Biblioteca de autores cristianos, 1994), 58.

8. Odo Casel, "Altchristlicher Kult und Antike," *Jahrbuch für Literaturwissenschaft* 3 (1923): 1–17.

9. Deden, "Le Mystère Paulinien," 442; Karl Prümm, "Mystères," *Dictionnaire de la Bible: Supplément* 6 (1960): 10–225.

10. Raymond E. Brown, "Pre-Christian Semitic Concept of Mystery," *Catholic Biblical Quarterly* 20, no. 4 (1958): 417–33, and "Semitic Background of the New Testament mysterion," *Biblica* 39 (1959): 70–87.

also the decisions made in it, designated with the Hebrew word *raz*, which the Septuagint would translate as *mysterion*. Later on the prophets were admitted to this meeting so that they might reveal those sublime plans to the people. The theme recurs in the wisdom literature, which talks about the divine secrets of creation (Sir 43:32) and associates the *mysterion* with the eschatological fulfillment of everything (Wis 2:22).[11] It is interesting that these pages already contain a certain critique of the mystery cults (Wis 2:22; 14:15) but, at the same time, speak in ritual terminology about Wisdom as an "initiate" (Wis 8:4). The *mysterion* appears forcefully, above all, in the apocalyptic literature: Daniel is the man who knows the divine *mysterion* about history and can therefore interpret the royal dreams (Dn 2:28; Mk 4:11; Rv 10:7).

Based on the Bible, the idea was taken up by the rabbis, who spoke about "the mysteries of the Torah" because in it is found the key that makes it possible to open the book of history and to read between its lines. Someone who knows the Torah can interpret God's eschatological will, the goal toward which he governs the eons.[12] *Mysterion*, in this context, is an exegetical tool for deciphering biblical prophecies.

Well, then, St. Paul assumes this rabbinical use, transforming it in view of his faith in Jesus: for the apostle, the place which the Torah occupied for the Jews is occupied by Christ. He alone, God's definitive Amen (2 Cor 1:20), breaks the seals so that the books might be opened and the fullness of time might be disclosed. Jesus is thus turned into the exegetical key to understanding the history of Israel to which scripture bears witness. Hence, in the Pauline use of the term, as I noted, the *mysterion* is Christ himself.[13] Or, more precisely, the *mysterion* is Christ as the one who recapitulates all things and all events; Christ as the center of the network of relations in which everything finds its order on the journey to the Father. Just as the *mysterion* in the Old Testament contains the way in which the eons point to their consummation, so too St. Paul interpreted the *mysterion* according to the unity of the ages which look to Jesus, who anticipates their definitive fullness.

In order to examine Paul's vision in greater depth it will be important, therefore, to pay attention to the understanding that Israel had of the divine designs for history, and to analyze how Paul took up this perspective from the vantage point of his faith in Jesus. The analysis will show us the pro-

---

11. Brown, "Pre-Christian Semitic," 424–25.
12. Bornkamm, "Mysterion," 823; Ratzinger, "Zum Begriff des Sakramentes."
13. See 1 Cor 2:1, 2:7, 1:23; see also Col 2:2, 1:27, 4:3; 1 Tm 3:16.

found association of the *mysterion* with divine worship, inasmuch as both aim to illuminate the same question: the way in which God works in history, leading the ages to himself.

The Pauline *mysterion* from the Perspective of the Old Testament

How do the people of Israel perceive the unity of salvation history? What key enables them to read the years of it just as the pages of a book are read? One characteristic of Israel is its awareness that it experiences time as a plot, that is to say, with an origin, a conflict, and a resolution, all guided by the divine plan.[14] Other nations may travel through the cyclical time of the seasons or meditate on eternal recurrence: for Israel, on the contrary, history is a journey from the creative origin to a fullness which also will come down from God.

This does not mean that time is a straight line that travels arrogantly toward the future, while rejecting the past. On the contrary, Israel's future is possible only if a deepening of memory corresponds to each new event. Its time resembles a spiral that unrolls and rises only insofar as it turns back on itself; or the wheel of a vehicle that moves ahead because it revolves continually on its axle.

Therefore the key to biblical history lies in typology, whereby each event points to another future event in which fullness will be found. The Bible recounts for us the repetition of types or figures, the resonance of already-familiar musical themes that are performed in a new key. Those who crossed the Red Sea will traverse the Jordan; and those who fled from Egypt through the desert will return from Babylon through other barren regions. Each step forward revives the memory of gifts already received and brings a better appreciation of the fruit that was guarded in the seeds of those gifts.

Well, then, *in Israel the vantage point from which this rhythm of the covenant is discovered is worship*, the place of closeness between God and his people, where Yahweh reveals himself. Why can the unity of biblical history be revealed only from the perspective of the liturgy? As it happens, although Israel experiences time that points in a specific direction, this is not because the Israelites had greater abilities to imagine the progress of history. The explanation must not be sought in man and his plans, but rather in God, who acted on the path of his beloved little one. The explanation

14. José Granados, *Teología del tiempo, ensayo sobre la memoria, la promesa y la fecundidad* (Salamanca: Sígueme, 2012), 57–66.

must be found in Yahweh, who revealed himself as the Lord who saves. Indeed, the reason why Israel is not allowed to forget its *past* is because this past preserves the traces of God's action, and thus it has something unique and unrepeatable, just as God himself is unrepeatable in all that he does. And the reason why the *future* brings to Israel the fulfillment of its hope is because God has established tomorrow as the region of his coming, where his promise will reach maturity. Here, then, is the answer to our question: *because the ages are tied to the action and epiphany of God, only divine worship will succeed in revealing their enigma to us.*

It can be stated, in short, that the history of Israel is deciphered through typology, and that typology is linked with worship as the place where Yahweh's saving action is recalled and faith in his promise is renewed. Thus, only by drawing near to the Temple to offer the first-fruits of the earth that the Lord gave them, can the Israelites tell the mighty deeds of God who guided his people step by step (Dt 26:1–11).

In the third section of chapter 2, above, I introduced two biblical concepts in which this view that Israel has of its history is condensed. Through remembrance or *anamnesis* the blessings received from God are made present and one manages to see the strand that links the ages, which are threaded on Yahweh's irrevocable fidelity. In this way the people can perceive their unity down through the generations, as though they were one corporate person. I already noted that these two concepts (*anamnesis* and *corporate person*) are connected to worship. That is where the Israelites experience the fact that they belong to the whole assembly from the perspective of their common participation in the covenant with God.

From what has been said we can conclude: given that the *mysterion* has to do with the unity of God's plan and with its definitive fulfillment for the whole people, discourse about the *mysterion* presupposes an evocation of the Israelite context of worship where this plan is recognized and put into effect. An example of this linkage between *mysterion* and worship is the fact that the rabbis came to call circumcision a *mysterion*.[15] We can assume that St. Paul, who was well-versed in Jewish scripture, would understand ritual as the sphere in which to recognize God's plan for the world. Would it not be logical then for the apostle, in adopting the term *mysterion*, the revelation of this divine design, to have the Christian liturgy in mind also?[16] Two indications lead us to confirm this conclusion.

---

15. Melchior Verheijen, "Mysterion, sacramentum et la synagogue," *Recherches de science religieuse* 45 (1957): 321–37, at 334, citing *Tanchuma Buber* 6.23 and *Genesis Rabbah* 49.

16. Van Iersel, "Quelques présupposés bibliques."

First, Paul interprets the Christian liturgy precisely in terms of the two concepts—*anamnesis* and corporate personality—that we just saw intermingled with Israelite worship as the key to discovering the unity of history. Indeed, baptism is understood as remembrance in which we relive the death of Jesus and receive the pledge of his resurrection (Rom 6:3–4); the Eucharist too becomes a proclamation of his death, so that Christ hastens his second coming at the parousia ("*so that* he comes," 1 Cor 11:26).[17] On the other hand, the apostle interprets baptism and Eucharist in terms of the corporate unity of the people. Baptism inserts us into the body of Christ because it introduces us into his relational sphere, just as all human beings were already in the body of Adam; or as the Israelites "were baptized into Moses in the cloud and in the sea" (1 Cor 10:2). And according to the same logic, the Eucharist is insertion into the body of Christ (1 Cor 10:16–17). The Christian liturgy appears, in this light, as the fullness of the Jewish liturgy; indeed, from the perspective of the Eucharistic experience Paul can say: "these things happened for your instruction" (1 Cor 10:11).

Second, the apostle explicitly associates the concept of *mysterion* with the types or figures in terms of which the plot of history is interpreted in a unified manner and which, as we know, are linked with Israelite worship. Indeed, *mysterion* is for Paul the creation of Adam from the clay of the earth, which prefigures his resurrection in Christ (1 Cor 15:45–51); and *mysterion* is also the union of Adam and Eve inasmuch as this union proclaims the extreme love of Jesus for his church (Eph 5:31–32).

In short, we can say that for St. Paul the Christian sacraments assume and fulfill both the *typology* that reads history as a unified whole and the *corporate* vision of the person; these two concepts are related both with Israelite worship and with the ability to perceive the *mysterion* or divine plan for the ages. Therefore everything points to the fact that the Christian liturgy was the soil in which the Pauline concept of *mysterion* took root and matured. Is it possible to prove this thesis from the apostle's texts themselves?

The Pauline *mysterion* and the Christian Sacraments

I have highlighted a clear connection, attested in Paul's writings, between the central coordinates of the *mysterion* and the central coordinates of the liturgy, both in the Old and in the New Testament, for both (*mysterion*, worship) illuminate the unity of the history of the people of God in light of

---

17. Hofius, "'Bis dass er kommt.'"

its definitive consummation in Christ. A question then arises: why did St. Paul not articulate more clearly the relation between *mysterion* and liturgy? For, indeed, it seems that when Paul speaks about liturgy (baptism, Eucharist) he does not use the term *mysterion*, and when he does use the term *mysterion*, he is not speaking about the liturgy.[18]

Mysterion, Baptism, Eucharist

Still, a more careful reading discovers the connection of *mysterion* and liturgy in the Pauline corpus. Take, for example, the Letter to the Ephesians, in which the *mysterion* has a predominant role. The purpose of the initial blessing, which presents Christ as the recapitulating *mysterion*, is that Christians might be "holy and blameless before him" (Eph 1:4). The ritual tone is evident: only what is irreproachable is worthy of divine service. Moreover the Letter teaches that the final end of the church is to worship God, as proved by the abundance of liturgical formulas: "To him be glory in the Church and in Christ Jesus to all generations, for ever and ever. Amen" (Eph 3:21).[19]

It should be noted, moreover and above all, that the *mysterion* is joined to the Pauline definition of the church as body. The universal recapitulation in Christ occurs inasmuch as he is head of the church (Eph 1:22–23). And the *mysterion* is completed when Jews and Gentiles are united in one body, now that the wall that once separated them has been broken down (Eph 2:13–16, in light of 3:3). Thus *the Pauline vision of the church as body of Christ arises precisely in the Eucharistic context*. St. Paul speaks about the unity of Christians in one body in terms of his experience of the Lord's Supper and of Jesus' words about offering his body (1 Cor 10:16–17).[20] We can conclude, therefore: if the basis of the *mysterion* is the body of the church, and the basis of the church is the Eucharist, then the Pauline use of *mysterion* rests on Eucharistic foundations.[21]

Thus, even if St. Paul does not describe baptism or the Eucharist as a *mysterion*, liturgical experience inspires his use of the term. Worship is the place where one discovers that the body of Christ, prolonged in the body of the church so as to reunite all creatures in God, is the key to the unity of history and is therefore identified with the *mysterion*. In fact, surrounding the image of the church as body there is no lack of allusions to baptism and

---

18. Eberhard Jüngel, "Das Sakrament—was ist das?," *Evangelische Theologie* 26, no. 6 (1966): 320–36, at 331; Jüngel follows Günther Bornkamm, "Mysterion," 809.

19. Mussner, "Die Kirche als Kultgemeinde," 256–67.

20. Son, *Corporate Elements in Pauline Anthropology*.

21. Schlier, "Die Kirche als das Geheimnis Christi," 306.

the Eucharist. Thus, after associating *mysterion* and body, Paul speaks about "one body and ... one baptism" (Eph 4:4–5).[22] And before speaking about the great mystery of the unity of Christ and his church (Eph 5:31–32), he points out that Christ purified her—his body and bride—in water and the word (Eph 5:26, an allusion to baptism), nourishing her as his own flesh (Eph 5:29, a Eucharistic allusion).

Why does the apostle not refer directly to baptism and the Eucharist with the term *mysterion*? One reason is obvious: in this way he attempts to avoid confusion with the Hellenic mysteries. The warning against these rituals appears already, as I noted, in some books of the Old Testament (Wis 14:15) and continues to be present among the early Fathers. They shied away, at first, from terms related to the theology of the mysteries. Only around the fourth century, when Christianity had established its social presence and dispelled the danger of misunderstandings, did the Fathers apply profusely to the liturgy the vocabulary of the pagan religions, speaking about "mystagogy" and "initiation" and using the "discipline of the arcane."

Distinguishing terminology was useful, moreover, to clarify the novel elements of New Testament worship in comparison to the Hellenic religions. The latter proposed a religious ecstasy that separated the initiate from everyday life so as to enclose him in the secret sphere of the divine. In the Christian liturgy, on the contrary, man does not abandon the creaturely coordinates of his body and his time, but rather encounters them again fully in Jesus. For this reason baptism and Eucharist are not for a few elect; on the contrary, they possess a transparent simplicity because they are anchored in the most elemental features of man's experience, which is taken up and confirmed in Christ; and therefore these rites comes within the reach of everyone. "Rational worship," as St. Paul would say, the acceptance of God's truth that illuminates existence, is not found by distancing ourselves from the concrete reality in which we live, but rather by offering our own body (Rom 12:1–2). This was the conviction that motivated Speratus, a second-century martyr, when he tried to explain to the proconsul Saturninus how close to everyday life the Christian religion was: he called it *mysterium simplicitatis*, in contrast to the complex Hellenic rites.[23]

---

22. Edouard Cothenet, "L'économie du mystère et le baptême selon l'Épître aux Éphésiens," in *Mystagogie: pensée liturgique d'aujourd'hui et liturgie ancienne*, ed. A. M. Triacca (Rome: CLV, 1993), 85–101.

23. *Passio Sanctorum Scillitanorum* 4, in *The Acts of the Christian Martyrs*, ed. Herbert Musurillo (Oxford: Clarendon Press, 1972), 86.

Mysterion and Marriage

Until now I have spoken about baptism and the Eucharist because they are the rites that Paul discusses more carefully. But in his texts on the *mysterion* there are also hints of the presence of another sacrament: matrimony. This proves to be especially interesting because of its connection with the union of Christ and the church in one flesh, the pivotal point of the Pauline *mysterion*.[24] Matrimony is, in fact, the only one of the seven that Paul explicitly relates to the term *mysterion*, in Latin *sacramentum*. It is true that we do not have here the technical usage that theology would employ later in speaking about "the seven sacraments." But this does not diminish the importance of the fact because, as we see, the Pauline *mysterion* is found at the root of Christian worship, which therefore includes marriage.[25]

Furthermore, in the Letter to the Ephesians, marriage is associated with the *mysterion* in the key context of typology. Indeed, in Ephesians 5:31–32 Paul cites a verse from Genesis (2:24: "a man leaves his father and his mother and clings to his wife") to prove that there is a great *mysterion* in the union of Adam and Eve, in relation to Christ and his church. The passage is important because in it the typology dates back from Jesus not only to the history of Israel, but as far as the foundations of creation. The union of man and woman, insofar as it prefigures the union of Christ and his church, contains a leitmotif that explains the unity of the ages from their beginning.

Paul thus follows the logic of the Old Testament: there too the history of the people goes back to creation so as to show that it is universal from its origin. As a result, Israelite worship would reflect man's primordial experiences, and in particular family life. Indeed, God caused Israel to be born of the waters as his Son and led him by way of the desert to educate him through this trial. Then, too, the history of the people is the history of the abandoned woman on whom God looks with life-giving love so as to protect her in a spousal covenant. Or, finally: Israel's future is the hope for a son who will come to fulfill the desires of the people, inaugurating the Holy Land with his flesh and building in it the dwelling place of God with mankind. In short, the time of the covenant is measured with the original time of the family. In fact, when the liturgy of Israel becomes perverted, the

---

24. For the following discussion see José Granados, *Una sole carne en un solo Espíritu: Teología del matrimonio* (Madrid: Palabra, 2014).

25. Of all people, a Protestant theologian advocates stressing the link between matrimony and the concept of sacrament: Wolfhart Pannenberg, *Systematische Theologie* (Göttingen: Vandenhoeck and Ruprecht, 1993), 3:267; translated as *Systematic Theology* (Grand Rapids, Mich.: Eerdmans, 1998), vol. 3.

prophets, in order to replace that corruption, have to decipher the meaning of history in their own body, staking their own life and their family relationships.

Marriage, moreover, belongs to the framework of Israelite worship, inasmuch as the unity of the people through the generations is perceived in the latter. On the one hand, through marriage, creation and the narrative of history are taken up into worship itself, in keeping with biblical *anamnesis*. Is the family not the place where we learn to string our days together, starting from the love that generated us and from the spousal promise that seals this love? Moreover, in the second place, marriage enables us to understand the *mysterion* in its entirety as the unity of all the people, in keeping with the "corporate person" of scripture. Is the family not the place where we perceive for the first time the singular way in which the flesh enables us to become one?

To the extent that Paul, as we have seen, understands Christian worship too in terms of the concepts of *anamnesis* and the corporate person, it was logical that he would assume the backdrop of familial experiences: the relation man-woman goes on to give shape to the *mysterion* in a structural way, as the key with which to decipher it. And in turn, given that Christ inaugurates the full way of being one body and of recapitulating history (*anamnesis*), those who become his members through baptism and the Eucharist (Eph 5:30) will see that their union "in one flesh" is transformed too, and that they are able to love one another at a new level, as Christ loves his church (Eph 5:21–33). The presence of matrimony then adds a profound outlook on how the *mysterion* is rooted in the creaturely condition of the human person; and it attests to Jesus' power to transform our concrete way of life in the body, establishing there his liturgy of oblation (Rom 12:1–2).

Pauline *mysterion* and Johannine Sign

Finally, in order to round off what the Pauline *mysterion* means, it may help us to compare his approach with the one offered by the fourth Gospel (see chapter 3 above). Whereas John made use of the "sign" to describe the sacramental economy, St. Paul adopts the perspective of the *mysterion*. Note the parallelism between the two outlooks. Both are centered on Christ, who with his incarnation brings to fulfillment a process that runs through the Old Testament. For he is, in St. John's writings, the meeting place of all the signs which introduce man into the space of the new temple, or rather, of the glorified body of Jesus. And he is also, in the writings of St. Paul, the *mysterion par excellence*, precisely in his incarnation, death, and resurrection from the dead. This is to say that both the "sign" and the *mysterion* are explained in light of the body of Jesus, who takes upon himself the flesh of Adam. The closeness of these two visions was formulated as follows by St. Irenaeus of Lyons: "For there are many mansions in the Father's house (Jn 14:2), inasmuch as there are also many members in the body (Rom 12:4; 1 Cor 12:12, 20)."[26]

There is, we should add, a common relation of the *sign* and of the *mysterion* with typology. Indeed, recall that the Johannine *signs* (united with the *works* of Jesus) take up the liturgy of Israel, which decants the history of the people; and they point to the Paschal mystery from which the sacraments flow. And the *mysterion*, as I just explained, signals the eschatological fulfillment of the ages in Christ, who recapitulates them.

Certainly the perspective of the sign appears to be centered on the manifestation, while the *mysterion* indicates instead what is hidden. But this is only an apparent contrast, because for Paul *mysterion* is bound up with preaching; it is precisely what the apostle cannot stop saying. There is a paradox here: etymologically "mystery" comes from the verb "to be shut, to keep silent" (*myo*), but Paul relates it to the word. Thus, according to Ephesians 6:19, the *mysterion* is the content of the Gospel; and in 1 Corinthians 2:1 it is associated with announcing the good news.[27] This highlights the fact that the ultimate secret of the biblical God is not that he is beyond words, but rather that he is closer to us than these very words: he is ineffable, not because he eludes all discourse, but rather because he is the very power that allows us to speak.

Based on this harmonious vision of the sign and the *mysterion*, the church went on to develop sacramental theology. As I have already noted, the term *mysterion* (*sacramentum* in Latin) would be used to designate the sacraments, while the Johannine sign would serve to define them. To conclude this chapter, I will show how the Church Fathers take up and develop the content of the Pauline *mysterion*. In chapter 8, below, I will examine the way in which the perspective of the fourth Gospel was received.

Toward the Classical Use of the Term "Sacrament"

I began this chapter by noting the apparent disconnect between the biblical terminology of the *mysterion* and the traditional use of the word "sac-

---

26. Irenaeus of Lyons, *Adversus haereses* III, 19, 3 (SC 211:382; ANF 1:449b).

27. Gene R. Smillie, "Ephesians 6:19–20: A Mystery for the Sake of Which the Apostle is an Ambassador in Chains," *Trinity Journal* 18 (1997): 199–222.

rament" that is connected with worship. I proved that this discrepancy is illusory: St. Paul offers a solid basis for relating the *mysterion* (*sacramentum*) to the Christian liturgy.

Note that the Church Fathers closely follow the Pauline inspiration. Indeed, in their view too, *mysterion* must be combined with typology and explains the definitive meaning of the *historia salutis* (history of salvation) in Christ and his church.[28] Therefore they frequently use the term as an exegetical tool to explore the passages of the Old Testament. The great *mysterion* is Jesus himself in the events of his life; in him is contained the ultimate future of history to which everything tends.[29] And precisely because the Christian, in baptism and the Eucharist, has access to this perfect fullness of the ages from which the coherence thereof can be observed, *mysterion* would be applied to the liturgical rite also.

One of the first witnesses to this connection of ideas is St. Ignatius of Antioch, who speaks in his Letter to the Ephesians about three "mysteries" that the devil did not know because they happened in the hidden depths of God: the conception of Mary, her childbirth, and the cross of Christ. As in Paul's writings, the use of the term is Christological: it deals with events that testify to the truth of the Son's flesh.[30] And, also as in Paul, Ignatius refers the *mysterion* to participation in Jesus, thanks to which "our life has sprung up again by him and by his death."[31] The context allows us to interpret the phrase in a liturgical key: this *mysterion* requires us to live "in observance of the Lord's day," Sunday, which replaces the Jewish Sabbath. Everything leads us to connect the *mysterion* with baptism (the new life "by him") and the weekly celebration of the Eucharist. This reading is confirmed by another passage in which Ignatius refers to "the ministers of the mysteries of Christ Jesus," who "are not ministers of meat and drink, but servants of the Church of God."[32] The martyr is referring again to the Eucharistic service.[33]

We observe the same continuity with Paul in the writings of St. Justin. The martyr is one of the first to develop extensively the typological key: the mysteries inhabit the Old Testament in its reference to Jesus.[34] Therefore

---

28. On the mystery in patristic writings see Bornkamm, "Mysterion," and Eliseo Ruffini and Enzo Lodi, *"Mysterion" e "sacramentum": La sacramentalità negli scritti dei Padri e nei testi liturgici primitivi* (Bologna: EDB, 1987).

29. Pannenberg, *Systematische Theologie*, 3:379–82; Musurillo, "Sacramental Symbolism."

30. Ignatius of Antioch, *Ad Ephesians* XIX, 1 (SC 10:88; ANF 1:57).

31. Ignatius of Antioch, *Ad Magnesians* IX, 1 (SC 10:102; ANF 1:62).

32. Ignatius of Antioch, *Ad Trallians* II, 3 (SC 10:112; ANF 1:67).

33. This is the interpretation of Raphael Schulte, "Los términos *mysterion* y *sacramentum* en orden a una teología de los sacramentos," in *Mysterium Salutis*, 4.2:76–98, 108–9.

34. Justin, *Dialogus cum Thryphone* 74, 3 (PTS 47:197; ANF 1:235b): the saving *mysterion* that

the *mysterion* is an exegetical tool and is applied to phrases of scripture that prophesy future fulfillments. Speaking to Trypho the Jew, Justin argues that Christians know "all the mysteries" (in the plural), because they are able to trace the whole Law back to the mystery (in the singular) of Christ.[35]

It is remarkable that the saintly philosopher, who is well acquainted with the pagan mysteries, does not see them as a source of inspiration to explain the sacraments. Just the opposite happens: for Justin Martyr the mystery religions are the ones that plagiarize Christian worship (baptism and Eucharist) because they have not understood the Old Testament.[36] And this is because the devil, who knows the ancient prophecies only partially, aped them unsuccessfully. The pagan mysteries, then, are derived from an erroneous exegetical reading that is unaware of the fullness of Jesus. Baptism and Eucharist, on the contrary, are part of the *mysterion* inasmuch as they already actualize the fullness of time that Christ brought. Therefore Justin can refer to the mystery of our regeneration, which is baptism,[37] and speak in reference to the Jewish Passover about the "mystery of the Lamb" with whose blood the bodies of Christians are anointed.[38]

The typological reading of the Bible gradually centers the outlook of the Fathers on the ritual prescriptions of the Old Testament, which are interpreted in reference to Jesus. This does justice to the Israelite practice of grasping in ritual the unity of history and anticipating in the liturgy the fulfillment of the promises. Melito of Sardis, in his *Peri Pascha*, gives a good example of this exegesis, speaking about the "Paschal mystery" and describing its prefigurations (types) in the sacrifices of the Old Testament, in which "the mystery of the Lord" was already being fulfilled.[39]

We see, therefore, that the *mysterion* terminology is associated increasingly with the liturgical rites, starting with baptism and the Eucharist. The liturgy is linked with the *mysterion* because it prolongs in history the great *mysterion* of the incarnation, life, death, and resurrection of Jesus, just as

---

is Christ's passion, contained in the church's preaching; ibid., 115, 1 (PTS 47:267; ANF 1:256b): the prophets predicted the mystery of Christ in parables and in a hidden manner; ibid., 138, 2 (PTS 47:308; ANF 1:268b): the story of Noah contains the mystery of the cross, etc.

35. Ibid., 44, 1–2 (PTS 47:142; ANF 1:217a): Christians know "all the mysteries," which is to say, the interpretation of the Law that points to "the mystery of Christ."

36. Justin, *1 Apologiae* 54, 6 (PTS 38:109; ANF 1:181a): "The devils, accordingly, when they heard these prophetic words, said that Bacchus was the son of Jupiter, and gave out that he was the discoverer of wine, and they number wine among his mysteries; and they taught that, having been torn in pieces, he ascended into heaven"; *Dialogus cum Thryphone* 69, 2 (PTS 47:189; ANF 1:233a); *1 Apologiae* 66, 4 (PTS 38:128; ANF 1:185b).

37. Justin Martyr, *Dialogus cum Thryphone* 85, 7 (PTS 47:218; ANF 1:242a).

38. Ibid., 40, 1 (PTS 47:136; ANF 1:214b).

39. Melito of Sardis, *Peri Pascha* 1–3 (SC 123:60–62) and 33 (SC 123:76).

the Old Testament was riddled with mysteries that pointed to Christ. The distinction that Justin makes in the above-cited passage between "the mysteries" and "the mystery" neatly takes up this articulate synthesis.

On the other hand, the first Church Fathers have reservations when it comes time to use terms that belong to the Hellenic religions. Thus, for example, at first they avoid the plural *mysteria*, which was applied more specifically to the cults. Clement of Alexandria is a pioneer in appreciating the similarities between the Hellenic mysteries and the Christian sacraments. He would speak about "the mysteries of the Word (Logos)," "truly sacred mysteries."[40] From him, for example, comes the first mention of the "discipline of the arcane," which commanded Christians to keep silence about the rites of initiation. Clement also called the bread and wine of the Eucharist "mystical."[41] One typical characteristic of the Alexandrian school would be, especially in Origen, the philosophical use of the term "mystery," which was already very common among the Platonists: the true worship is philosophy and the true initiation consists of discovering the foundation of things in the invisible God.[42]

The terminology of the mystery religions was not embraced entirely until the fourth century, when the new religion was established and no longer felt threatened by syncretism. This is demonstrated, for example, by St. John Chrysostom, who states that the "ineffable mystery" is consummated in the stroke of the lance that pierced Jesus' side, and speaks about the "initiated" who are regenerated by the water and are fed by the flesh and blood.[43] The same author situates the *mysterion* along the axis that runs from the visible to the invisible, an axis that one travels along not by merely human wisdom, but rather thanks to the gift of the Spirit, who enables us to receive the unfathomable revelation of God.

The Latin-speaking church, where the term *mysterion* is translated by *sacramentum*, deserves special mention.[44] It is logical to wonder about the

40. Clement of Alexandria, *Exhortation to the Heathen* XII (SC 2:187–93; ANF 2:205a–b); H. G. Marsh, "The Use of MYSTERION in the Writings of Clement of Alexandria," *Journal of Theological Studies* 37 (1936): 64–80.

41. Marsh, "The Use of MYSTERION," 75–80.

42. Henri Crouzel, "Origène et la structure du sacrement," *Bulletin de littérature ecclésiastique* [hereafter *BLE*] 63 (1962): 83–92; Hans Urs von Balthasar, "Le mystère d'Origène," *Recherches de science religieuse* 26 (1936): 513–62; 27 (1937): 38–64.

43. John Chrysostom, *Homily 85 on John 19, 31–37* (PG 59:463b–c); see also *Homily 7 on 1 Cor 2, 6–7* (PG 61:55–56); and, on the mystery in Chrysostom, see Van Roo, *De sacramentis*, 13–17.

44. Joseph de Ghellinck, *Pour l'histoire du mot "Sacramentum." 1. Les Anténicéens* (Louvain-Paris, 1924); Adolph Kolping, *Sacramentum Tertullianeum: Untersuchungen über die Anfänge des christlichen Gebrauchs der Vocabel sacramentum* (Münster, 1948); Christine Mohrmann, "Sacramentum dans les plus anciens textes chrétiens," *Harvard Theological Review* 47 (1954): 141–52, and "Quelques

reason for this step, given that the word *mysterium* existed in Latin and would also be used by the Fathers. Besides the fact that it was common to find a Latin equivalent of every abstract term (as is the case with *mysterion*), there was a weighty reason for the change, which is already familiar to us: avoiding confusion with the pagan rites. And thus, for example, the plural *mysteria* was not used and other terms were avoided, such as *initia, sacra, arcana*, which were proper to those cults; *sacramentum*, for its part, was free of associations with the mystery religions.

Among the ancient Romans, in what senses was the word *sacramentum* used? In general it expressed a certain relation with the sacred; more concretely it referred to an action that consecrates, for *sacramentum* comes from *sacrare*, in the active sense.[45] Moreover *sacramentum* connoted the public character of such an action, which was legally binding; for this very reason it became more difficult for the mystery cults to use this term. Based on these two features (sacred force and juridical weight), the *sacramentum* can be defined as a public *religious obligation*, which gives rise to three meanings of the term.[46] (1) Inasmuch as this obligation incorporates into a new group, *sacramentum* implies an initiation. (2) Based on that, *sacramentum* can refer also to the oath that is taken at the initiation; the word was used in fact for the promise of loyalty to the army (like the pledge of allegiance today) which in those days acquired a sacred force.[47] (3) Finally, *sacramentum* designates the sacred bond itself that is created by this obligation; this usage is reflected, for example, in the expression *sacramentum amicitiae* (sacrament of friendship).[48] The connotation of *sacramentum* as a sacred bond explains why the Fathers call not only the rite of baptism itself a *sacramentum*, but also its permanent effect on the Christian, who is associated in a singular way to God in Christ (what later would be called the baptismal "character").[49]

Why was the term *sacramentum* chosen rather than others? As we have

---

observations sur 'sacramentum' chez Tertullien," in W. den Boer et al., *Romanitas et Christianitas* (Amsterdam: North-Holland, 1973), 233–42; and Joseph T. Lienhard, "*Sacramentum* and the Eucharist in St. Augustine," *The Thomist* 77, no. 2 (2013): 173–92.

45. I follow above all Mohrmann, "Sacramentum dans les plus anciens textes," 146.

46. Ibid., 145.

47. In various passages Tertullian uses *sacramentum* as a synonym for the oath that was taken in the army: *Ad martyras* III, 1 (CCL 1:5; ANF 3:694b); *De corona* XI, 1 (CCL 2:1056; ANF 3:100b); *Scorpiace* IV, 5 (CCL 2:1076; ANF 3:637a); *De idolatria* XIX, 2 (CCL 2:1120; ANF 3:73b). This does not mean, as I have already noted, that he is talking about the original meaning which was, rather, that of a religious bond: Mohrmann, "Sacramentum dans les plus anciens textes," 150.

48. Mohrmann, "Sacramentum dans les plus anciens textes," 146.

49. Nicholas M. Haring, "St. Augustine's Use of the Word 'Character,'" *Medieval Studies* 14 (1952): 79–97; I will study this subject later in chapter 12.

seen, its public and juridical features distanced it from the mystic rites and freed it for Christian use. At the same time, points of contact can be noted between the Pauline *mysterion*, which designated union with Christ (Col 1:27) and the force of the "sacred union" contained in the Latin *sacramentum* (the third meaning listed above).[50] Tertullian was very important in spreading this equivalence between *mysterion* and *sacramentum*, but he only spelled out a fact that was already present in the Christian communities and attested in the ancient versions of the Bible.

The translation of *mysterion* as *sacramentum* left free the term *mysterium*, which is a direct translation of the Greek *mysterion*. Some authors, such as Lactantius, started to use *mysterium* as if it were a synonym of *sacramentum* to indicate the totality of the salvation wrought in Christ and the concrete rites that communicate it.[51] Little by little, in the Latin church, a separation of meanings resulted: *sacramentum* was reserved more for the ritual (according to its Roman use), and *mysterion* was used to designate the ultimate salvific reality that the rites represent.[52] This clear distinction, which would not be available in Greek theology, is useful for the analysis of the structure of the sacrament, provided that one is careful to integrate correctly the distinct aspects of the visible and the invisible.

We can also understand the medieval usage, which grew on the patristic soil, in light of what has been said.[53] I should note in the first place that *mysterion* and *sacramentum* remained broad enough that they could refer to all of salvation history and, concretely, to typological exegesis. Although the word "sacrament" was restricted gradually to liturgical acts, its general scope was never abandoned. Hugh of St. Victor, for example, when he explained the sacraments based on the biblical story of King Hezekiah, who was cured with a poultice, would be able to make this play on words: the account presents to us "a sacrament about the sacraments."[54]

In the second place, given this association with the types of biblical figures, medieval writers see the sacraments accompanying man throughout his history: rooted in creation, they are multiplied by the old covenant; with the arrival of the new covenant they are then concentrated into the

---

50. Mohrmann, "Sacramentum dans les plus anciens textes," 148.

51. Vincenzo Loi, "Il termine *mysterium* nella letteratura latina cristiana prenicena," *Vigiliae Christianae* 19 (1965): 210–32; 20 (1966): 25–44.

52. About St. Augustine, see Lienhard, "*Sacramentum* and the Eucharist."

53. Artur Michael Landgraf, "Die Lehre vom geheimnisvollen Leib Christi in den frühen Paulinenkommentaren und in der Frühscholastik," *Divus Thomas* 24 (1946): 217–48 and 393–428; 25 (1947): 365–94; 26 (1948): 160–80, 291–323, 395–434.

54. Hugh of St. Victor, *De sacramentis christianae fidei* I, 9, 5 (PL 76:325): "magnum de sacramentis sacramentum commendatum est."

seven that we know today. For this reason Hugh of St. Victor can entitle his principal work in which the entire *historia salutis* is set forth: *On the Sacraments of the Christian Faith* (*De sacramentis christianae fidei*). The Middle Ages, moreover, continue to refer all the sacraments to Christ, the incarnate Word, "sacrament of the sacraments," who recapitulates all of history.[55] Following the Church Fathers, the medieval theologians understand the sacraments of Israel as sacraments of the future, of Christ who was to come. The new sacraments, on the contrary, are the remembrance of Jesus who has come and, with his power, colonizes our present while preparing his coming again in glory.

The richness of the term *sacramentum* was important, therefore, in order to keep the Christian rites united with the entire economy of salvation; they prove to be ways of marking time in salvation history. The biblical heritage, recapitulated in St. Paul, continued to be very much alive: the worship of the church, in continuity with Jewish worship, gives us the key with which to understand the unity of history, condensed in the life and work of Jesus. St. Thomas Aquinas shows that he is an heir to this tradition when he says that the sacrament is a sign of three things: remembrance of the past, present manifestation of grace, and a foretelling of future glory.[56]

In the last three chapters I have explored the essential features of the biblical data: the roots in Jesus (chapter 2) and the first sacramental elaboration in the writings of St. John (chapter 3) and of St. Paul (chapter 4). From all this we can draw a conclusion that I will analyze in the following chapter: the sacraments are rooted in Christ's life in the flesh.

---

55. Hugh of St. Victor, *Sententiae de divinitate* II, ed. A. M. Piazzoni, *Studi Medievali* 23 (1982): 912–55, at 921.

56. Thomas Aquinas, *Summa Theologiae* [hereafter *ST*] III, q. 60, a. 3, co.

5 ❧ THE INSTITUTION OF THE SACRAMENTS IN THE FLESH OF CHRIST

Starting with the rite of Jesus, which takes up into itself the whole remembrance of Israel, I described the perspective of the New Testament: the sacraments are the space from which the Christian revelation is contemplated while participating in it. It is not surprising, then, that the early reflection of theology does not address them directly, just as our view does not focus either on the window that opens onto the landscape. What is of primary interest is the encounter with the risen Christ, present in his church, an encounter that the sacraments mediate for us. This gives rise to the foundational question of sacramental theology: what relation do the sacraments maintain with the life and work of Jesus?

The question is decisive in this hour of the faith. Our era, which is fond of the silhouette of the Nazarene, has difficulty encountering him in the church; and if it accepts the church, it does so inasmuch as it expects her to give them understanding, closeness, tolerance ... worrying about the rites, perhaps, only as an expression of this welcome and affection. People today believe, yes, that they can get closer to Christ by communion, but not by the Mass; by authenticity, but not by confession; by love, but not by matrimony. I will attempt to show, nevertheless, that the sacraments are the only way of touching Christ in the flesh, so that his presence becomes real and concrete, without the idealistic, ethereal contours with which we usually imagine him. *Numquam sine aqua Christus*, we can say with Tertullian: one never encounters Christ without the water of baptism and the other salvific rites.[1]

The insight that the sacraments are rooted in Jesus brought to maturity

---

1. Tertullian, *De Baptismo* IX, 4 (CCL 1:284; ANF 3:673b).

a sure article of faith which was defined at the Council of Trent: Jesus instituted the seven of the New Testament.[2] As I study this article of faith in the following pages, I will conclude that the sacraments are not connected with Jesus solely by virtue of a decision of his, as though their effect were comparable to that of a law that is in force. Rather, they are connected with Jesus above all because he himself forged them in his body over the course of his life and continues to make himself present in them, touching the Christian's flesh and conforming it to himself. Hence this chapter is not a prologue to the study of the sacraments, but rather the source from which the following discussion proceeds. Having already distilled in the preceding pages the biblical teaching about the institution of the sacraments, we will start by seeing how the Church Fathers delve into it.

The Sacraments, Starting with the Body of Christ: Fathers of the Church

The Fathers of the Church do not speak yet about the seven sacraments, nor do they outline a common definition for them. Moreover, the term "sacrament" is broader for them; even when it is restricted to worship, it includes the ceremonies of Israel and other liturgical practices of the church. Still, although they recognize this variety of "sacraments," they are well aware of the great differences between rites: what distinguishes the central acts of the Christian liturgy is that they are founded on a command of Jesus.

St. Augustine states, for example, that some sacraments—like baptism or the celebration of his body and blood—were handed on to us by the Lord himself and by the apostolic teaching.[3] Thus there is an essential difference between the rites that are found in the canonical scriptures and others, like the annual celebration of Easter, that do not appear in the biblical text, although they are admitted by the universal church and depend on an ancient tradition, sometimes even one of apostolic origin.[4] In order for a

2. Heinrich Denzinger, *Enchiridion Symbolorum* (43rd ed.), ed. and trans. by Peter Hünermann (San Francisco, Calif.: Ignatius Press, 2012) [hereafter DH], 1601.

3. Augustine, *De doctrina christiana* III, 9, 13 (CCL 32:11; NPNF-I 2:560b): "sed quaedam [signa] pauca pro multis ... ipse Dominus et apostolica tradidit disciplina" (but our Lord Himself, and apostolic practice, have handed down to us a few rites [signs] in place of many).

4. Augustine, *Epistolae* LIV 1, 1 (Corpus Scriptorum Ecclesiasticorum Latinorum [hereafter CSEL] 34.2:159; NPNF-I 1:300a–b): "unde Sacramentis numero paucissimis, observatione facillimis, significatione praestantissimis, societatem noui populi conligauit, sicuti est Baptismus Trinitatis nomine consecratus, communicatio corporis et sanguinis ipsius, et si quid aliud in Scripturis canonicis commendatur, exceptis his quae seruitutem populi ueteris pro congruentia cordis illorum et prophetici temporis onerabant, quae et in quinque libris Moysi leguntur" (He has bound his people under the new dispensation together in fellowship by sacraments, which are in number very few,

sacrament to proceed from Jesus it is necessary, therefore, to have scriptural testimony, which reflects either the authority of the master himself or that of the apostles, his witnesses and envoys. For the distinctive feature of these few rites is having been created by the Wisdom of God made man.[5]

In all this, Augustine's argument runs along the channels of tradition. St. Ambrose had already said: "Who is the author of the sacraments, except the Lord Jesus?"[6] And later on Pope Leo would declare that Christ, after Easter, gave to his disciples "the form and the power to baptize,"[7] that is to say, he not only conferred the authority but also prescribed the rite.

Once that principle is established, the Church Fathers add little concerning the institution of the sacraments; they are not concerned, for example, about enumerating the seven, nor do they specify, based on proof texts, when Christ established each of them. On the other hand, they open up for us another perspective with a greater scope: the sacraments are connected with the whole life of Christ in the flesh. I will examine the case of the Eucharist, and of baptism, because of their foundational character among the salvific signs; then I will draw several inferences that can be applied generally.

The Eucharist Contains the Mystery of Christ

The Eucharist is rooted in Christ; this is proved, in the first place, by the fact that his very words are the ones that are repeated in the rite. As St. Ambrose says: "this sacrament that you receive is brought about by the word of Christ."[8] The bishop of Milan states that at the consecration the priest no longer uses his own words, but rather those of Jesus.[9] That is to say, the ministers do not merely quote the master, but rather he speaks through them so as to lend efficacy to the rite.

---

in observance most easy, and in significance most excellent, as baptism solemnized in the name of the Trinity, the communion of his body and blood, and such other things as are prescribed in the canonical scriptures, with the exception of those enactments which were a yoke of bondage to God's ancient people, suited to their state of heart and to the times of the prophets, and which are found in the five books of Moses).

5. Augustine, *De vera religione* XVII, 33 (CCL 32:14): "ab ipsa dei sapientia homine assumpto, a quo in libertatem uocati sumus, pauca sacramenta saluberrima constituta sunt" (the few most salutary sacraments were instituted by the very wisdom of God, after he had assumed the manhood by which we are called to freedom).

6. Ambrose, *De sacramentis* IV, 4 (SC 25:82).

7. Leo the Great, *Epistolae* XVI, 3 (PL 54:699): "postea quam resurrexit a mortuis, discipulis suis, in quibus omnes Ecclesiarum praesules docebantur, et formam et potestatem tradidit baptizandi" (after he rose from the dead, he handed over to his disciples, in whom all the prelates of the Churches were taught, both the form and the power to baptize).

8. Ambrose, *De mysteriis* IX, 52 (CSEL 73:112).

9. Ambrose, *De sacramentis* IV, 4 (SC 25:82).

Furthermore, what happens when the consecratory formula is pronounced reflects the events themselves of the life of Jesus. Indeed, the *parallel between the Eucharist and the incarnation* is a commonplace in patristic writings.[10] We find this already in St. Justin Martyr: just as the Word took on flesh and blood when he was born among us, so too in the Eucharist the words of the prayer pronounced by the minister transform the bread and wine into the body and blood of Jesus. Therefore, when we eat and drink this food, our body is nourished by immortality, for it participates in the immortal flesh of Jesus.[11] In the Eucharistic rite, then, we see the life of Christ condensed as though in a compendium: his coming from the Father when he became incarnate and his return to the Father when he rose from the dead. Therefore Jesus instituted the sacrament not only inasmuch as he gave an order for the rite to go into effect, but rather because the rite makes present the same mystery of the Word made flesh and of his passage through the earth to lead us on high.[12]

And not only that: the Eucharist, by associating us with the life of Christ, also introduces us into his divine mystery. Given that the Eucharist makes present the Son of God, who feeds continually on the Father, *to eat it is to receive the paternal food, that is, to participate in the eternal generation of the Son.*[13] In this way we delve into the biblical data explored above (chapter 2). For, indeed, the Eucharist of Jesus is his *todah*, his thanksgiving to the Father for having received all gifts from him; still, such an immense gratitude, corresponding to such blessings, reveals that we are in the presence of the only-begotten Son, who came to mold his filiation in our flesh. Hence in the Eucharist we can become sons in the Son, fed by the bread that comes from the mouth of God.

We can then confirm that the Church Fathers understand the Eucharist in close union with Christology. And it could not be otherwise: how could the mystery of Christ's person and the mystery of the sacrament that contains the body and blood of Christ not shed light on each other? From this connection a "Eucharistic Christology" can be developed. It should be

---

10. Johannes Betz, "La Eucharistía, misterio central," in *Mysterium Salutis*, 4.2:186–310, at 210.

11. Justin Martyr, *1 Apologiae* 66 (PTS 38:127; ANF 1:185b).

12. Also Irenaeus of Lyons, *Adversus haereses* IV, 18, 5 (SC 100:117; ANF 1:486a): "Eucharistia, ex duabus rebus constans, terrena et caelesti" (the Eucharist, consisting of two realities, earthly and heavenly), in other words, in the Eucharist there is an earthly reality, the species of bread and wine, and another heavenly reality, the risen body of Jesus. See Dominic J. Unger, "The Holy Eucharist according to St. Irenaeus," *Laurentianum* 20 (1979): 103–64, at 127.

13. Manuel Aroztegi, "Eucaristía y filiación en las teologías de los siglos II y III," in P. de Navascués et al., *Filiación: Cultura pagana, religión de Israel, orígenes del cristianismo* (Madrid: Trotta, 2012), 4:257–89, at 289: "In the second and third centuries there was a conviction that the divine generation that takes place in Christ in the bosom of the Trinity occurs in those who share in the Eucharist."

noted, as we ponder the various opinions that the Fathers support concerning the mystery of Jesus, that when it comes to speaking about the Eucharist they usually agree on one central point: their interest in the flesh of Christ as the key of human salvation. St. Cyril of Alexandria summarizes the common opinion when he calls the Eucharist "Christ in us by means of his sacred flesh."[14]

Furthermore: because it contains the entire life of Christ, *the Eucharist also takes up all of history, which is recapitulated by him, starting with the history of Israel.* For Melito of Sardis, for example, Jesus was present in the Old Testament not only as the preexisting Son, but also because the flesh that he would offer was being prepared then, in the different sacrifices and libations.[15] We speak, therefore, about the "mystery of [Israel's] Passover ... in the Lord's body."[16] St. Ambrose, too, when he says that Christ is the author of the sacraments, is referring not only to the Eucharist, but also to the earlier sacrifices that prefigured it. And he asserts that the Christian sacrament is older than the ones celebrated by Abraham and Moses.[17]

Finally, *the Eucharist expands Christ's life to the era of the church*, between his ascension and his second coming. After the flesh of Jesus goes up to heaven, it is presented before the Father as the first-fruits of humanity, so as to fill the whole cosmos from its place with God: this is why it can take possession of sensible matter in the sacraments. This bodily presence of Jesus on the altar is the seed that generates the church as the communion of those who share not only the same heart and mind but also the same flesh, insofar as they are born as members of a new family. The patristic vision of humanity as a whole into which Christ kneads himself when he becomes incarnate, springs from this Eucharistic terrain.[18]

To summarize: *according to the Church Fathers, the Eucharist is instituted when the flesh of Christ is shaped as glorious flesh that joins with the flesh of believers so as to communicate its life to them.* The preparations for this institution begin with the creation of the world and run through the Old Testa-

---

14. Gaspar Hernández Peludo, "Cristo en nosotros por medio de su santa carne: Trasfondo cristológico y pneumatológico de la doctrina eucarística en Cirilo de Alejandría," in *Sacramentos: historia, teología, pastoral, celebración: homenaje al prof. Dionisio Borobio*, ed. José María de Miguel González (Salamanca: Biblioteca Salmaticensis, 2009), 225–54.

15. Melito, *Peri Pascha* 31–32 (SC 123:76): "Tell me, angel, what frightened you [during the Jewish Passover]? ... The death of the lamb or the prefiguration of the Lord?"

16. Melito, *Peri Pascha* 56 (SC 123:91).

17. Ambrose, *De sacramentis* IV 3, 8–12 (SC 25:81).

18. Emile Mersch, *Le corps mystique du Christ: Études de théologie historique* (Paris: Desclée, 1936), 418–34; José Granados, "Los sacramentos y el don del Espíritu sobre Jesús," in *La unción de la gloria: en el Espíritu, por Cristo, al Padre: Homenaje a Mons. Luis F. Ladaria, SJ*, ed. Manuel Aroztegi et al. (Madrid: Biblioteca de autores cristianos, 2014), 113–42.

ment, from generation to generation, so as to converge with the life of Jesus. Then, during his path on earth, his flesh is slowly shaped by the Spirit until it contains the fullness of communion with God and mankind and ascends into heaven "that he might fill all things" (Eph 4:10). The Eucharistic body is thus forged, which can be called a "narrative body," for it recapitulates the whole story of Christ and expands during the era of the church until it embraces the remotest human spaces.

Baptism, Birth into the Body of Jesus

The preferred image used from antiquity to speak about baptism is birth.[19] Jesus spoke about it with Nicodemus (Jn 3:5); St. Paul assumes it when he presents baptism as the reception of a new body, conformed to Christ's risen body (Rom 6:3–14; see also Ti 3:5: "the washing of regeneration"). Based on this, the Fathers focused not only on the concrete event of the celebration but also on the new being that is received, which embraces the believer's entire life: baptism imprints on a human being a "seal" that makes him like Jesus, and the believer is called to guard it.[20] Taking an image from Origen, we can say that the river in which we baptize, our Jordan, is Jesus himself: baptism plunges us into his life and introduces us into his narrative.[21] Let us study this connection of baptism with the person of Jesus.

Jesus' baptism in the flesh, the foundation of Christian baptism ➣ The first clue linking baptism to Jesus is given to us by the mystery of the Jordan. The Christian's birth is preceded by a new birth of Christ who, in order to institute baptism, performed it first on himself. Clement of Alexandria presents the episode as a model of the baptismal liturgy, with its various stages: we are submerged, we are illumined, we are anointed when we come out of the water, and we then receive the fullness of the Spirit.[22]

---

19. See, among many other authors, Theophilus of Antioch, *Ad Autolycum* II, 16 (SC 20:141): "God blessed the creatures born of the water, because one day men would be regenerated by water"; Pseudo-Barnabas, *Epistolae* VI, 13–15 (SC 172:127): "born again, we received hearts of flesh so as to enter into the promised land inaugurated by the risen Lord"; *Epistolae* XVI, 8 (SC 172:193): "we are new creatures, recreated from the foundations up"; Irenaeus, *Epideixis* 3 (SC 406:89): "This baptism is the seal of eternal life and of the new birth for God"; *Epideixis* 7 (SC 406:92): "the baptism of our new birth"; Augustine, *Sermo* 216, 8 (PL 38:1081).

20. See, for example, Irenaeus, *Epideixis* 3 (SC 406:89): "the seal and the new birth for God"; *Epideixis* 100 (SC 406:220): "the three articles of our seal"; Peter-Ben Smit, "The reception of the Truth at Baptism and the Church as Epistemological Principle in the Work of Irenaeus of Lyons," *Ecclesiology* 7 (2011): 354–73.

21. Origen, *Homilies on Luke* XXI, 4 (SC 87:294).

22. Clement of Alexandria, *Paedagogus* I, 6, 26, 1–2 (SC 70:159; ANF 2:215b): "The same also takes place in our case, whose exemplar Christ became. Being baptized, we are illuminated; illuminated, we become sons; being made sons, we are made perfect; being made perfect, we are made

The fact that Christ was baptized is not due to a sort of humility which necessarily would have been false. At least for the Church Fathers of the Asiatic school, the event is rooted instead in the very truth of Jesus who, as Son, receives everything from the Father. Having taken on flesh, the place *par excellence* of receptivity and openness to God's hands, this flesh requires, for its progressive divinization, that the Spirit be poured out upon it.[23] Moreover, the transformation that the Spirit works in Christ during his mortal life, because it refers to the flesh that he has in common with all mankind, would entail a renewal of those who believe in Jesus. As St. Justin says: Christ is born in the Jordan "for men"; that is to say, he is born so that we can all be reborn as children of God.[24]

The water of baptism is conformed to the flesh of Jesus so as to give us a share of his Spirit 🐟 The link between Jesus' baptism and ours comes about through water. The Fathers commonly teach that Christ transforms the waters when he touches the Jordan with his flesh. Thus, according to Ignatius of Antioch, the Lord is baptized in order to sanctify the water,[25] while Tertullian adds that his flesh communicated his purity to the waters.[26] He did not come to be washed, St. Ambrose states, but rather to wash the waters themselves, so that they might obtain the right to baptism.[27] *Everything happens as though the water were configured with the flesh of Jesus so as then to assimilate Christians to him when it touches them.*

What does the touch of this water communicate to us? Its waves transmit in turn the sanctity that Christ's flesh transmitted to them. Hence Tertullian can describe the baptismal water as filled with the Spirit, who acts in it and communicates himself through it.[28] As we are incorporated by the

---

immortal.... This work is variously called grace, and illumination, and perfection, and washing." Antonio Orbe, "Teología bautismal de Clemente Alejandrino," *Gregorianum* 36, no. 3 (1955): 410–48.

23. Ladaria, *Jesús y el Espíritu.*

24. Justin Martyr, *Dialogus cum Thryphone* 88, 8 (PTS 47:224; ANF 1:244a). I do not follow here the variant put in by the editor.

25. Ignatius of Antioch, *Ad Ephesians* XVIII, 2 (SC 10:86; ANF 1:57).

26. Tertullian, *De pudicitia* VI, 15–16 (CCL 2:60): "[caro] quae munditias suas aquis traderet" ([flesh] that imparted its purity to the waters). See also Tertullian, *Adv. Iud.* VIII, 14 (CCL 2:106): "sanctificante aquas in suo baptismate" (in his baptism that sanctifies the waters).

27. Ambrose, *Expositio evangelii secundum Lucam* II, 83 (CCL 14:1124): "Baptizatus est ergo Dominus, non mundari volens, sed mundare aquas; ut ablutae per carnem Christi, quae peccatum non cognouit, baptismatis jus haberent." See also Chromatius de Aquileia, *In Matthaeum* XII, 4 (CCL 9A:32): "numquam enim aquae baptismi purgare peccata credentium potuissent, nisi tactu dominici corporis sanctificatae fuissent" (for the waters of baptism could never wash away the sins of believers unless they had been sanctified by the touch of the Lord's body).

28. Tertullian, *De Baptismo* IV, 2 (CCL 1:278; ANF 3:671a); also Justin Martyr, *Dialogus cum Thryphone* 86–88 (PTS 47:219–24; ANF 1:242a–244a); Irenaeus of Lyons, *Adversus haereses* III, 17, 1 (SC 211:328–30; ANF 1:444b).

water into the flesh of Jesus, we receive the same Spirit who, after descending upon Christ, now dwells in his flesh.

Complete institution of baptism: from the Jordan to Easter ✒ Although it is certain, as I said, that the foundation of Christian baptism lies in the baptism of Jesus, it should be noted that the latter frames the master's entire life and especially his death and resurrection. Indeed, the baptism in the Jordan, as the descent of the Spirit on the flesh of Christ, contains the code of the entire route traveled by Jesus, which consists of a series of anointings until the definitive Paschal anointing, when his flesh proves to be full of the Spirit of life. Therefore those who see the institution of baptism at the Jordan or on Golgotha are not in opposition. St. Ignatius of Antioch already associates the two moments when he says that Christ purified the waters with his passion.[29] And St. Justin, describing baptism, surveys the cross present above the waters.[30]

This explains why the baptismal liturgy, besides reproducing the Lord's baptism, also represents his burial and return to life. St. Gregory of Nyssa explains the imitation or *mimesis* that occurs in the liturgy through the rite: the passion and resurrection of Jesus is reproduced so that the baptized person can escape with him from the labyrinth of death.[31] St. Basil expresses himself along the same lines, using the image of an athlete who, after completing one course at the stadium, catches his breath before starting the next one; thus Christ paused in death, so as then to rise again.[32] St. Leo the Great, for his part, teaches that Jesus instituted baptism on the cross,[33] and therefore only after Easter he would explain to the disciples how to baptize.[34]

The Christian's flesh is born to the flesh of Jesus ✒ What are the effects of baptism in the believer who receives it? The Christian's flesh, through the water, is touched by the flesh of Jesus and is thus grafted onto his body. This

---

29. Ignatius of Antioch, *Ad Ephesians* XVIII, 2 (SC 10:86; ANF 1:57).

30. Justin Martyr, *Dialogus cum Thryphone* 86 (PTS 47:219–20; ANF 1:242b); also Tertullian, *De baptismo* XI, 4 (CCL 1:286; ANF 3:674a): "Quia tunc utique a discentibus dari non poterat [baptismus] utpote nondum adimpleta gloria Domini nec instructa efficacia lavacri per passionem et resurrectionem, quia nec mors nostra dissolvi posset nisi Domini passione nec vita restitui sine resurrectione ipsius" ([baptism] at that time, of course, could not be given by his disciples, inasmuch as the glory of the Lord had not yet been fully attained, nor the efficacy of the font established through the passion and the resurrection; because neither can our death see dissolution except by the Lord's passion, nor our life be restored without His resurrection).

31. Gregory of Nyssa, *The Great Catechism* XXXV (SC 453:302–6; NPNF-II 5:502b–503a).

32. Basil, *Treatise on the Holy Spirit* XV (SC 17:169–70; NPNF-II 8:21b).

33. Leo the Great, *Epistolae* XVI, 7 (PL 54:701; NPNF-II 12:29b).

34. Ibid., 4 (PL 54:699; NPNF-II 12:28b).

is why we speak about a new birth: one is born to a new flesh, which is the flesh of Christ who died and rose again. It is surprising that authors with very different anthropologies share this perspective, as if they all conformed their thought to the cultic practice. St. Hilary of Poitiers, for example, tells us that baptism regenerates us in a new body that is conformed to the body of the glorified Christ.[35] And according to St. Gregory of Nyssa, in baptism, through the flesh that was assumed and deified by the Word, and through the water, which resembles the earth from which our flesh was molded, this same flesh is saved.[36] St. Leo the Great, for his part, stated the maxim: "the body of the regenerated Christian becomes the flesh of the Crucified" (*corpus regenerati fiat caro Crucifixi*).[37]

New relations in the church open up to the believer when he is associated with the body of Jesus.[38] According to St. Leo the Great, what God conferred on Mary so that Jesus might be born in the Spirit he also conferred on the waters of baptism so as to illuminate believers.[39] The water, therefore, which as we already know is associated with the flesh of Christ, is linked also to a maternal womb, the womb of the church, in which the believer is regenerated.[40]

To summarize, baptism in the Fathers is connected directly with Jesus, for it makes us participate in his life in the flesh. Contact with his body, through the mediation of the water, generates in us a new body, open to the outpouring of the Spirit. The church takes part in this corporeal birth; her maternal body generates and nourishes through the waters of baptism.

The Sacramental Economy, Rooted in the Flesh of Jesus

The Eucharist, therefore, contains the flesh of Christ. Baptism, for its part, engenders us to this flesh. Just as the water serves to knead the flour that will be baked into bread, so too, St. Irenaeus points out, when we are moistened

---

35. Hilary of Poitiers, *De Trinitate* VIII, 7 (CCL 62A:320; NPNF-II 9:139b): "unum sunt in eiusdem regeneratione naturae" (they are one by regeneration into the same nature).

36. Gregory of Nyssa, *The Great Catechism* XXXV (SC 453:303; NPNF-II 5:502a–b).

37. Leo the Great, *Sermo* LXIII (CCL 138A:114; NPNF-II 12:177a): "quaedam species mortis et quaedam similitudo resurrectionis interuenit, ut susceptus a christo christumque suscipiens non idem sit post lauacrum qui ante baptismum fuit, sed *corpus regenerati fiat caro Crucifixi*" (all this is a sort of dying and rising again, whereby he that is received by Christ and receives Christ is not the same after as he was before he came to the font, for the body of the regenerate becomes the flesh of the Crucified).

38. Tertullian, *De Baptismo* XX, 5 (CCL 1:295; ANF 3:679b).

39. Leo the Great, *Sermo* XXV: "dedit aquae quod dedit matri" (he gave to the water what he gave to the mother) (CCL 138:130). See also *Sermo* XXIV: "the same Holy Spirit fills the font, Who filled the Virgin" (NPNF-II 12:135b).

40. Augustine, *Sermo* CXIX (PL 38:674): "vulva matris, aqua baptismatis" (the water of baptism is the mother's womb).

by baptism we form the one lump of dough of the Eucharistic body.[41] Baptism and Eucharist allow an initial general outlook on the sacraments: they cause the human being to take root in the flesh of Jesus. Recall that the word *mysterion* (and *sacramentum*, among the Latin Fathers) is used in patristic writings to describe both the entire salvific work of Jesus upon the flesh, and also the liturgical rite. This is because the two are very closely linked, as St. Leo the Great explains: "that which was visible of our Redeemer has passed into the sacraments."[42]

What has been said is recapitulated in the patristic exegesis of John 19:34: from Jesus' side flowed blood and water.[43] The Fathers, following St. John, interpret this as an allusion to the sacraments. Tertullian applies the passage to the two baptisms, of water and of blood (martyrdom).[44] St. Augustine includes the Eucharist also: "from whence have flowed forth *the sacraments* of the Church."[45] One of his followers, Quodvultdeus, later explained: "immediately blood and water flowed out, the two twin sacraments of the Church. The water, in which the Bride is cleansed; the blood, in which she finds her dowry."[46] The sacraments flow from the Paschal mystery of Jesus at the precise moment when the church is formed.[47]

From this source the other sacraments flow too. In the patristic literature *confirmation* appears as closely united with baptism, for it contains a further gift of the Spirit that perfects the baptismal seal.[48] As for *penance*, it is understood as an arduous return to the vital coordinates of baptism; hence Origen associates it also with the water and blood that flowed from the pierced side: "All purification of sins, even that which is sought through Penance, requires the aid of him from whose side flowed water and blood."[49]

41. Irenaeus of Lyons, *Adversus haereses* III, 17, 2 (SC 211:332; ANF 1:444b–445a).

42. [Translated from Latin.] Leo the Great, *Sermo* LXXIV, 2 (CCL 138A:42; NPNF-II 12:188b): "Quod itaque redemptoris nostri conspicuum fuit, in sacramenta transiuit."

43. Alban A. Maguire, *Blood and Water: The Wounded Side of Christ in Early Christian Literature*, Studies in Sacred Theology 108 (Washington, D.C.: The Catholic University of America Press, 1956), 18–167; Edward Malatesta, "Blood and Water from the Pierced Side of Christ," in *Segni e Sacramenti nel Vangelo di Giovanni*, ed. Pius-Ramon Tragan (Rome: Anselmiana, 1977), 164–81; Sebastian Brock, "The Mysteries Hidden in the Side of Christ," *Sobornost* 7, no. 6 (1978): 462–72.

44. Tertullian, *De baptismo* XVI, 1 (CCL 1:290; ANF 3:677a).

45. Augustine, *In Iohannis* CXX, 2 (CCL 36:661; NPNF-I 7:434b).

46. Quodvultdeus, *De symbolo* I, 6 (CCL 60:16).

47. Leo the Great, *Epistolae* XVI, 4 (PL 54:699; NPNF-II 12:28a–b).

48. Burkhard Neunheuser and Patricio de Navascués, "Confermazione," in *Nuovo Dizionario Patristico e delle Antichità Cristiane*, edited by A. di Berardino (Milan: Marietti, 2006), 1:1150–54.

49. Origen, *Homilies on Leviticus* VIII, 10 (Die griechischen christlichen Schriftsteller der ersten drei Jahrhunderte [hereafter GCS] 29:411; SC 287:50); Isidore, *De ecclesiasticis officiis* II, 25, 3 (PL 83:820); on Origen, see Karl Rahner, "La doctrine d'Origène sur la Pénitence," *Recherches de science religieuse* 37, no. 1 (1950): 47–97, 252–86, 422–56, where he observes the connection between the penitential rite and the baptismal catechumenate.

In the same way, the consideration of *matrimony* revolves around John 19:34, where the Fathers contemplate the mystery of the new Eve, built up from the side of the new Adam. This sacrament contains, therefore, the creaturely language of the body of man and woman, a language that Jesus takes up in order to strengthen it; and it points to the newness of the Eucharistic body, the spousal union between Christ and his church. The ministerial *priesthood*, for its part, is also linked to the spousal body of the Eucharist, for in the ordained minister Christ makes himself present to his church as her head and origin. St. Ignatius of Antioch already saw the image of Jesus in the bishop, as the source of Eucharistic unity for the church.[50] St. Augustine, for his part, later associated matrimony and holy orders with baptism, grouping them together with the term *sacramentum* in its classical sense of a sacred bond. This is because the three rites conform the person to Christ with a unity that remains firm even if we are unfaithful to him.[51]

To summarize, we can conclude: (1) the Fathers are intent on emphasizing the *connection of the sacraments with Christ's life in the flesh*. Rather than focusing on particular gestures or words, they contemplate the whole existence of Jesus in the flesh as the moment of institution. Using a sentence by St. Augustine we can say: "Christ is the life of all the sacraments."[52] (2) Originated by the flesh of Jesus, the sacraments are moreover *the expansion of his bodily presence throughout history*. They are testimony that the life of the Lord confers unity on all time, from creation until the end of the world: he already acted in the ancient sacrifices and, after ascending into heaven, continues to offer himself in his church. (3) *The center is in the Eucharist and in baptism*, which more evidently flow from his side; from them we understand how the rest of the sacraments conform us to the flesh of Christ.

Christ, Author and Cause of the Sacraments: Medieval Theology

The fact that the sacraments are rooted in Christ remained central to theological reflection during the Middle Ages. This is confirmed by the outline that Peter Lombard adopted for his *Sentences*, which would also serve as the

50. Ignatius of Antioch, *Ad Smyrneans* VIII, 2 (SC 10:162; ANF 1:89–90); *Ad Magnesians* VII, 1–2 (SC 10:100; ANF 1:62).

51. Augustine, *De nuptiis* I, 10, 11 (CSEL 42:223), where baptism and matrimony are associated and the bond is compared with the character; *De bono coniugali* XXIV, 32 (CSEL 41:226–27) for the connection between matrimony and holy orders; in *De baptismo* I, 1, 2 (CSEL 51:146) relations between baptism and holy orders appear.

52. Augustine, *Sermo* X, 2 (CCL 41:2): "[Christus] qui omnium sacramentorum vita est"; the context is a discussion of circumcision.

basis for his successors: the explanation of the sacraments follows Christology, because they are medicines of the Good Samaritan.[53] Moreover, in the words of Hugh of St. Victor, Jesus is the sacrament *par excellence*: "sacrament of the sacraments."[54]

The continuity with the patristic era is evident in two other respects. In the first place, the Eucharist, in which Jesus himself is made present in the flesh, continues to exercise a gravitational force that makes the other sacraments revolve around it. Through the Eucharistic prism, as we will see (chapter 9), the main concepts of medieval sacramental theology are forged.

In the second place, the sacraments extend also, and with the very same breadth of outlook, to the entire *historia salutis*, which is recapitulated in the Savior: the old covenant had sacraments and the new covenant has sacraments. Certainly, the latter spring from Christ, like the river that flows from a source, making present his action among the faithful. But the signs of the old covenant too are connected with Jesus, for they arouse faith in the future Messiah and, given that they take up created reality, they rely on the firstborn Son in whom all things were made. This outlook would allow theologians to describe the institution of the sacraments dynamically, taking into account the course of the ages.

What new ideas does the medieval period contribute to this topic? It begins the task of seeking, for each sacrament, the concrete moment in which Jesus established it. This concern, which is less present in the Fathers, arises together with the gradual development of a generic concept of sacrament that is applicable to all seven. From this emerge the first difficulties, as with some sacraments it is not easy to identify the passages that corroborate their institution by Jesus. The Middle Ages saw two different solutions, which we can study in their most highly developed forms in the works of St. Bonaventure and St. Thomas Aquinas.

St. Bonaventure and the Gradual Institution of the Sacraments

St. Bonaventure closely follows the conclusions of Alexander of Hales, one of the first theologians to wonder whether all the sacraments come from Christ.[55] Alexander maintained that the ultimate authority (*auctoritas*) to

---

53. Peter Lombard, *Sent.* III, *Incipit* (SpBon 5:23).

54. Hugh of St. Victor, *Sententiae de divinitate* II, ed. A. M. Piazzoni, *Studi Medievali* 23 (1982): 912–55, at 921.

55. Alexander of Hales, *Summa* IV, q. 1, m. 3, a. 4; q. 5, m. 2–3; q. 9, m. 1, and *Glossa in quatuor libros Sententiarum* IV, d. 7, n. 1, in Bibliotheca Franciscana Scholastica Medii Aevi [hereafter BFSMA] XV (Quaracchi, 1957), 129; on the institution of the sacraments in Alexander of Hales, see E. Guillaume, "De institutione sacramentorum et speciatim confirmationis juxta Alexandrum Halensem," *Antonianum* 2 (1927): 437–68; Joseph Bittremieux, "L'institution des sacrements d'après Alexandre

institute a sacrament belongs to God, for he alone gives grace. At the same time he explained: God can institute a sacrament through human ministry (*ministerium*) and did so throughout salvation history, acting for example through Moses and the apostles. Christ's role is unique because he is at the same time God and man: he has *auctoritas* and also performs a *ministerium*; his, moreover, is a unique ministry from which the other ministers derive their power. The institution of the sacraments will unfold, therefore, in distinct phases, with a distinct intervention of Christ in each one of them. Hence, if Alexander speaks about the institution of any sacrament by the apostles (like confirmation or extreme unction), he always does so based on the central ministry of Jesus.

St. Bonaventure adopts the view of his master and enumerates three sacramental ages: the time of nature, the time of the written Law, and the time of the Gospel.[56] Thus we can distinguish one sacrament from another and their gradated relation with Jesus. First, there are *sacraments of nature, common to the Old and the New Law*. These are matrimony, the union of a man and a woman for the purpose of generating children, and penance, the natural ability of the sinner to repent and turn to God, which had its origin when the Lord said to Adam, "Where are you?" These sacraments, instituted from the beginning by the creator, were then confirmed and approved by Jesus, who furthermore brought them to maturity: with him matrimony proves to be perfectly indissoluble; penance is perfected with auricular confession.

There are also *intermediate sacraments* which run through salvation history. These were anticipated by the figures of the Old Testament and, with the arrival of the Gospel, were instituted by Jesus. These include baptism, the Eucharist, and holy orders. Within the institution by Christ, Bonaventure distinguishes various phases, which extend into the time of the church. Thus, for example, Jesus himself *suggested* baptism (when he was baptized by John and in his conversation with Nicodemus); *instituted* it (for Jesus himself baptized through his disciples); and *confirmed* it (when he had risen and sent his disciples to baptize).[57]

Finally, there are sacraments of the new era, which have no figures in the Old Testament because they are proper to the outpouring of the Spir-

---

de Hales," *Ephemerides Theologicae Lovanienses* 9 (1932): 234–51; Franz Scholz, *Die Lehre von der Einsetzung der Sakramente nach Alexander von Hales* (Breslavia: Franke, 1940).

56. Bonaventure, *In IV Sent.*, d. 2, a. 1, q. 1 (Quaracchi 4:49): "Tempora legis naturae, legis scriptae et Evangelii conveniunt institutioni Sacramentorum, tamen secundum magis et minus"; d. 23, a. 1, q. 2 (Quaracchi 4:591); Bittremieux, "L'institution des Sacraments."

57. Bonaventure, *In IV Sent.*, d. 3, p. 2, a. 1, q. 1 (Quaracchi 4:77–78).

it, which occurred only after Easter. These include confirmation, in which we are anointed as soldiers (for combat); and the anointing of the sick, in which we are anointed as kings (to enter into the Kingdom of God). In these two cases, St. Bonaventure, following Alexander of Hales, says that Christ *suggests* the sacraments, but the Holy Spirit *institutes* them by means of the apostles. And from this perspective he defends the thesis that confirmation and extreme unction were established by the church, as there are no passages that corroborate that they came directly from Jesus.

Later on the Council of Trent would define that the seven sacraments were instituted by Christ.[58] Does this mean that St. Bonaventure's opinion is rejected? Certainly not, because Trent did not wish to settle legitimate debates between the schools, as we will see later.[59] In reality, when we evaluate the position of the Seraphic Doctor we must take into account the fact that in his day the theological vocabulary—the precise scope of terms such as "institute" or "promulgate"—was not yet fixed. In fact, in order to be able to speak about institution Bonaventure demands the presence of all the elements necessary to confect the sacraments—the matter and form of the hylomorphic theory—which from the outset makes it impracticable to trace several of them back to Jesus.

In any case, the learned Franciscan stated that confirmation and extreme unction were at least "suggested" by Christ, thus anchoring all the sacraments in the life of the Lord.[60] Moreover in his opinion the Spirit, when he institutes the sacraments, always works together with Jesus, making explicit what was already contained in the master's words and deeds. The institution of confirmation, for example, thus proves to be the work of the Holy Spirit, who continues in the church the task of Jesus even after the apostles' death.[61] Then, as the Spirit is a doctor too, he can institute sacraments; but it should not be supposed that there are two who institute them, for Christ and the Spirit of Christ do not add up to two distinct legislators, but rather one and the same.[62]

In short the fact that there are sacraments that were not instituted by

---

58. DH 1601.

59. The question, moreover, was introduced at the Council based on the intervention of a Franciscan friar, Richard de Mans; it would have been strange for him to seek the condemnation of two famous Doctors of his order. Ferdinand Cavallera, "Le décret du Concile de Trente sur les sacrements en général," *Bulletin de littérature ecclésiastique* 6 (1914): 401–25, at 416.

60. Bonaventure, *In IV Sent.*, d. 23, a. 1, q. 2, co. (Quaracchi 4:591): "haec duo sacramenta [confirmatio, extrema unctio] a Christo fuerunt insinuata, sed post a Spiritu Sancto fuerunt instituta" (these two sacraments were suggested by Christ but were later instituted by the Holy Spirit).

61. Bonaventure, *In IV Sent.*, d. 7, a. 1, q. 1 (Quaracchi 4:164); q. 2 (Quaracchi 4:166).

62. Ibid., d. 23, q. 1, a. 2, ad 1 (Quaracchi 4:592).

Jesus does not mean that they are unrelated to Jesus. Rather than focus on the term "institution," therefore, it is necessary to look at the connection of the sacraments with Christ as their source, a link affirmed by St. Bonaventure which is, as we will see, what the Council of Trent later sought to save. On the other hand, we can note two advantages of the Bonaventurian approach: his view of the sacraments as a leitmotif of salvation history; and the free space that it opens up for the Holy Spirit, through whom Christ continues to be active in the church. Insisting on these points does not diminish the centrality of Jesus, whose power is displayed in the whole salvific economy and always through the Spirit. To prove this, it is enough to take a look at the summary of sacramental theology that Bonaventure offers in his *Breviloquium*. There every statement, either about the sacraments in general or about one of the seven, is explained in reference to Christ. The thirteen questions posed receive as their first response, thirteen times, this refrain or a similar one: "because the principle that heals us, that is, the Incarnate Word."[63]

St. Thomas Aquinas: Institution from the Space of the Body of Christ

St. Thomas contributes a new approach, the merit of which lies in his having related the incarnation closely to the sacraments. From this perspective he supports his thesis: Christ instituted by himself the seven of the New Law that are recognized by the church.[64] I am interested, above all, in the theological vision on which Aquinas bases his teaching. Christ institutes the sacraments, in the first place, as God, with authority to communicate divine grace—something that is impossible for any human being. Following a common terminology, St. Thomas speaks about a power of authority (*potestas auctoritatis*) that is proper to the author or origin.[65]

To this he adds that Christ institutes the sacraments as man also. That is to say, God communicates grace through the human ministry of his Son, for this is a grace that comes to save what is human. He, by his life on earth, particularly in his passion and resurrection, made himself the channel of sanctity and justice for mankind. Therefore his mysteries in the flesh are not only the meritorious cause but also the instrumental cause of our salvation, as the brush is for the portrait painter.[66] We have, then, a second power of

---

63. Bonaventure, *Breviloquium*, p. 6, c. 1 (Quaracchi 5:265); p. 6, c. 2 (Quaracchi 5:266).

64. Thomas Aquinas, *ST* III, q. 64.

65. On the institution of the sacraments in St. Thomas, see Bertrand-Marie Perrin, *L'institution des sacraments dans Le commentaire des sentences de saint Thomas* (Paris: Parole et Silence, 2008).

66. Humbert Bouëssé, "La causalité efficiente instrumentale de l'Humanité du Christ et des sa-

Jesus, the power of ministry (*potestas ministerii*) which he gains from having established his own body as the principal instrument of salvation.[67] Every sacrament proves to be, therefore, a prolongation of Jesus' humanity, in such a way that he can be conformed with men in the various situations that they go through. Christ associated the material of the sacraments to his own flesh so as to touch us by means of them.[68] Here we find the foundation of the classic principle: *sacramenta sunt propter homines*, the sacraments are for human beings.

Thus it is understood that this ministry of Christ to institute sacraments is quite unique, not comparable to other ministries like that of Moses or that of the apostles. For this reason St. Thomas explains that Jesus' power of ministry is a *potestas excellentiae*: it far exceeds the power that others possess. For, in the first place, he was the only one who did not need rites in order to communicate grace: his humanity, and particularly his passion, is the root of all sacramental efficacy.[69] Moreover, to him alone belonged the power to institute new sacraments by associating a sign with the bestowal of a grace.[70] Finally, it was reserved to Jesus to institute sacraments in his own name, given that they work through faith in Christ's passion.[71]

According to St. Thomas, Jesus in principle could have communicated this "power of excellence" to others. There might have been, then, for example, a baptism "in the name of Paul," or a church capable of increasing the number of the sacraments. But the Lord did not act in that way: the power of excellence is, using an Augustinian expression on which there was much medieval commentary, a power "that Christ could have given but did not give."[72] He decided not do so, according to Aquinas, in order to manifest

crements chrétiens," *Revue Thomiste* 39 (1934): 370–93; Joseph Lécuyer, "La causalité efficiente des mystères du Christ selon saint Thomas," *Doctor Communis* 6 (1953): 91–120.

67. *ST* III, q. 62, a. 5, ad 1.

68. Ibid., q. 66, a. 3, ad 4: "virtus Christi derivata est ad omnem aquam" (Christ's power flowed into all waters). See also Aquinas, *Commentum in quatuor libros sententiarum* (Paris: Parma, 1929–47) [hereafter Parma], d. 26, q. 2, a. 3, ad 1 (7:922): "sicut aqua baptismi habet quod corpus tangat et cor abluat ex tactu carnis Christi" (just as the water of baptism has from the touch of Christ's flesh something with which to touch the body and to wash the soul).

69. *ST* III, q. 62, a. 5: "utrum talis virtus in sacramentis derivetur a passione Christi ... ex latere Christi dormientis fluxerunt sacramenta per quae salvata est Ecclesia" (Whether the sacraments of the New Law derive their power from Christ's passion? ... From the side of Christ asleep on the cross flowed the sacraments which brought salvation to the Church).

70. Ibid., q. 72, a. 1, ad 1: "instituere novum sacramentum pertinet ad potestatem excellentiae, quae competit soli Christo" (The institution of a new sacrament belongs to the power of excellence, which belongs to Christ alone).

71. Ibid., q. 64, a. 3, co.

72. A. Landgraf, "Der frühscholastische Streit um die *potestas quam Christus potuit dare servis et non dedit*," *Gregorianum* 15, no. 4 (1934): 524–72; the reference is to Augustine, *In Iohannis* V, 11 (CCL 36:46; NPNF-I 7:35a).

more clearly the unity of salvation, so that divisions might not crop up in the church, as in the verse: "I belong to Apollo; I belong to Peter" (1 Cor 1:12).[73] For this reason Christ handed over to his followers only the power of ministry (*potestas ministerii*), by which they can administer the sacraments in the name of Jesus, but not institute them. To summarize: Christ possesses a *potestas auctoritatis* as God, and a *potestas ministerii* as man, a power that in him reaches a supreme degree and is therefore called *potestas excellentiae*; this includes the ability to institute sacraments, which is reserved to the Savior.[74]

Having offered this general theological framework, St. Thomas endeavors to ascertain on what occasion of his life Jesus instituted each sacrament. For there to be an institution it is necessary, Aquinas explains, not only for Christ to conform the sacrament to his humanity so as to enable it to be a source of grace, but also for him to transmit to the apostles the concrete rite that they have to celebrate. It is certain that sometimes words of Jesus in this regard are lacking, for example about confirmation or the anointing of the sick. St. Thomas then supposes that the master transmitted them to the apostles in private, and it was up to them to make them public by promulgating the sacrament. His syllogism on this point runs contrary to the one used by St. Bonaventure. The Seraphic Doctor argues: the reason why the words are not in the New Testament is because Jesus did not say them, for how could his followers have forgotten to write them down?[75] Aquinas reasons: even though the words are not found in the New Testament, Jesus must have said them, for how would they have dared to celebrate the sacrament without having sure support in the master's teaching?[76]

We must take into account the fact that Thomas is handling historical data that are not very precise; he thinks, for example, that confirmation was administered with the anointing of chrism from the apostolic age onward. Among other things he relied on the testimony of Dionysius the Areopagite, a fifth- or sixth-century author whom he supposed to be an immediate disciple of the apostles and a good witness, therefore, of their liturgical practices. This limited historical knowledge leads Thomas to think that Christ determined the details of each sacrament, even though there is no record of

---

73. *ST* III, q. 64, a. 4, ad 1.

74. Perrin, *L'institutions des sacrements*, 577–78.

75. Bonaventure, *In IV Sent.*, d. 7, a. 1, q. 1 (Quaracchi 4:164); d. 23, a. 1, q. 2 (Quaracchi 4:591).

76. Thomas Aquinas, *ST* III, q. 72, a. 4, ad 1: "Multa enim servabant Apostoli in sacramentorum collatione quae in Scripturis communiter propositis non sunt tradita" (For the apostles, in conferring the sacraments, observed many things which are not handed down in those scriptures that are in general use).

it in scripture, and to leave unexplained the evolution that history observes in some sacramental rites.

The richness of this perspective, in any case, lies in its having rooted the sacraments in the earthly actions of Jesus, which prefigure or already represent the sacramental event although they do not contain it in all its details.[77] Its weak point is that it required furthermore a complete determination of the rite (matter and form) on the part of Christ. It is true, on the other hand, that St. Thomas distinguishes the two aspects: the institution of the sacrament and the transmission of the complete rite. Thus, for example, baptism is instituted when Jesus is baptized in the Jordan, although he determines then neither the order of baptism nor the formula; or matrimony in the loving self-sacrifice of Jesus on the cross, although without an explicit teaching by the master in that hour about marriage. St. Thomas recognizes, moreover, that to institute a sacrament does not mean to celebrate it: Jesus instituted confirmation by "promising it," for it was administered by the apostles only after Pentecost.[78] Based on these facts it has been possible to establish a distinction, within the thought of Aquinas, between the *institution of the sacrament* (with an action of Jesus that represents the grace) and the *institution of the rite* in matter and form.[79] Later reflection would agree that Jesus performed the first; his role in the second, nevertheless, would need further explanations.

To summarize: the Middle Ages left us a broad framework in which to discover the relation of the sacraments to Christ. St. Bonaventure underscores the unity of all salvation history, in which God sowed the sacraments; and he sees the Spirit as the one who prolongs Jesus' action in the church. St. Thomas, for his part, takes as his basis a firm Christological principle centered in the incarnation and Christ's redemptive death; and he sees the sacraments as extensions of the Lord's humanity, rooted in his concrete life in the flesh—and therefore in concrete acts of the earthly Jesus—which allow him to associate us with himself. The two theologians share a key insight: the connection of all the sacraments with the life of Jesus. They also share a pending question: determining what it means "to institute," in other words, what elements necessarily have to proceed from Christ.

Moreover, although their answers are different, St. Thomas and St. Bonaventure ultimately rely on a common trust in the church, who determines whether a sacrament comes from Jesus, either because she preserves

---

77. Perrin, *L'institution des sacrements*, 584–86.
78. Thomas Aquinas, *ST* III, q. 72, a. 1, ad 1.
79. Perrin, *L'institution des sacrements*, 586–91.

the memory of Christ's words (St. Thomas), or because she prolongs his work (St. Bonaventure). These are precisely the principles that later would be called into question with the arrival of the Protestants, who as a result would deny that various sacraments proceed from Jesus and, therefore, are authentic. This will cause the interest to shift, in Catholic theology too, from the foundations of the sacrament in the life of Christ (the patristic and medieval perspective) to the search for the words and gestures of Jesus that legitimize the existence of the traditional set of seven.[80]

The Protestant Reformation and the Council of Trent

With the Protestant Reformation a new stage in the reflection on the sacraments begins.[81] A debate on the sacraments prompts Luther's denunciation of Rome going astray in sacramental matters and thus sending the church into a new Babylonian captivity. Here too, as in other points, the Reformer asserts his exclusive Christocentrism: by insisting excessively on the institution of the sacraments by Christ he would eliminate the role of the church and, with it, would deprive most of the seven of their basis in Jesus.

Luther: Expurgate the Sacraments Instituted by the Church

The fact on which Luther insists is traditional: that the sacraments are rooted in the Savior. Indeed, for him, if one wanted to follow the biblical language literally, one would have to speak only about one sacrament, Christ.[82] Moreover Luther shares a concern with St. Thomas: finding in scripture—interpreted however without the mediation of the church—explicit proof of the institution of the sacraments, which are, according to his perspective, signs associated with a promise of grace.[83] Based on this premise, Luther drastically reduces the set of seven: in the strict sense he accepts only baptism and the Eucharist; in the broad sense, penance as well.[84] What principles organize his reasoning?

---

80. Colombo, "Dove va la teologia," 697.

81. Josef Finkenzeller, *Die Lehre von den Sakramenten im allgemeinen: Von der Reformation bis zur Gegenwart* (Freiburg: Herder, 1981), 10–13.

82. Martin Luther, *Disputatio de fide infusa et acquisita* 16–17, in *Werke*, Weimarer Ausgabe (hereafter WA), 6:86: "Nullum sacramentorum septem in sacris literis nomine sacramenti censetur. Unum solum habent sacrae literae sacramentum, quod est ipse Christus Dominus" (None of the seven sacraments is mentioned in sacred scripture by the name of sacrament. The sacred scriptures have only one sacrament, which is Christ the Lord himself).

83. Thus Luther denies the sacramental character of extreme unction because it is not given to an apostle "sua auctoritate sacramentum instituere, id est, divinam promissionem cum adiuncto signo dare" (to institute a sacrament by his own authority, that is, to give a divine promise with a conjoined sign).

84. Luther, *On Genesis* (WA 9:349.1–5): "Matrimonium, unctio, Confirmatio non sunt

Luther judges everything in terms of the criterion of justification by faith: God saves us without any work on our part, if only we believe in his forgiveness. The sacraments too obey this logic: they are signs that promise salvation, by way of visible words so as to elicit faith.[85] For this reason, if these promises are not found on the lips of Christ, the only one who can guarantee them, they will be fictions rather than sacraments.

Moreover Luther denounces what he believes are the abuses of the church in regulating the rites. Therefore he insists that the only sacrament that can be accepted is one that with no doubt whatsoever is attested in scripture as coming from the master. As we have seen, medieval theologians resolved the problems about the institution of some sacraments by having recourse to the continuity between the work of Christ and that of the church. Based on the principle "Christ alone" and *sola Scriptura,* Luther, on the contrary, undermines the foundations that anchor the sacraments in Jesus.

To summarize, only two sacraments will be accepted, the ones for which there is irrefutable evidence in the words of the master: baptism and the Eucharist.[86] Based on this conviction, Luther demotes the other sacraments to sacramental rites. And he accuses the church not only of having invented novelties of which Jesus was not aware, but also of having eliminated things

---

sacramentalia signa, quae non habeant annexam promissionem. Ordo figmentum est" (Matrimony, extreme unction, Confirmation are not sacramental signs; they do not have a promise attached to them. Holy orders is a figment). *De captivitate babylonica* (WA 6:501.33): "Principio neganda mihi sunt septem sacramenta et tantum tria pro tempore ponenda, Baptismus, Poenitentia, Panis" (On principle I must deny that there are seven sacraments and reckon only three for the moment: Baptism, Penance, Bread). About priestly orders he goes so far as to say in *De captivitate babylonica* (WA 6:560.20–21): "Hoc sacramentum Ecclesia Christi ignorat, inventumque est ab Ecclesia Papae: non enim solum nullam habet promissionem gratiae ullibi positam, sed ne verbo quidem eius meminit totum novum testamentum" (Christ's Church knows nothing of this sacrament, it was invented by the Pope's Church: not only does it have no promise of grace made anywhere, but the whole New Testament says not even a word about it).

85. Luther, *De captivitate babylonica* (WA 6:550.19–20): "sacramenta servant credentes promissioni divinae" (sacraments preserve those who believe in the divine promise). In a letter to Spalatin (WA Briefwechsel, 1:594) he adds: "quod sacramentum non sit, nisi ubi expressa detur promissio divina, que fidem exerceat, cum sine verbo promittentis et fide suscipientis nihil possit nobis esse cum Deo negotii" (because it is not a sacrament unless an explicit divine promise is given somewhere, which is the object of faith, because without the word of the one who promises and the faith of the one who receives it there can be for us no dealing with God).

86. Luther accepts as actions of God: "Verbum Evangelii, Baptismum, eucharistiam" (The Word of the Gospel, Baptism, Eucharist) (WA 6:560); in the strict sense, in order for a sacrament to exist, a sign is required, which would lead him to exclude penance: "si rigide loqui volumus, tantum duo sunt in Ecclesia dei sacramenta, Baptismus et panis, cum in his solis et institutum divinitus signum et promissionem remissionis peccatorum videamus" (Strictly speaking, there are only two sacraments in God's Church, Baptism and the bread, because in them alone do we see both a divinely instituted sign and a promise of the forgiveness of sins). Penance is, definitively: "via ac reditus ad baptismum" (the way or a return to baptism; WA 6:572).

desired by him, for example, by denying communion under both species for the laity. What Christ established, he argues, must be maintained strictly, for "if we allow even one institution by Christ to be changed, then we annul all his other laws."[87]

To this we must add that Luther evolves in his view of the sacraments. He does so as a result of debates with other reformers who reduce them to a mere sign, denying the presence of Christ in the Eucharist and the necessity of baptism, or insisting that it could be repeated.[88] And in fact, if a sacrament is only a visible word, a divine call to a response of faith, what specific contribution does it make as opposed to preaching? To answer this question, Luther would come to accept the fact that a sacrament saves, not only because we believe in the promise that it contains, but because it was instituted (*quia institutum est*). This means that faith has to accept the concrete signs of water, bread, and wine inasmuch as they are willed by God and keep us from falling into subjectivism. The institution, from this perspective, proves to be decisive, not only in order to establish what rites are sacraments, but also to substantiate their salvific import.

The Response of Trent and of Later Theology

Trent counters, in the first place, the negation of various sacraments, the most serious point of the Lutheran challenge. In its Session VII, when it formulates various canons about the sacraments in general, the Council affirms that seven of them, no more and no less, were instituted by Christ, and it enumerates them.[89] The context is, just as in Luther's writings, the theme of justification, but now in order to affirm that it does not depend on faith alone: it comes about through the sacraments, it grows through the sacraments, and it is regained through the sacraments if it is lost. The doctrine about their institution by Jesus is reaffirmed next when some specific sacraments are discussed.[90]

Still, Luther had also denounced supposed abuses by the church in reg-

---

87. Luther, *De captivitate babylonica* (WA 6:503.13–15).

88. W. Schwab, "Luthers Ringen um das Sakrament," *Catholica* 32 (1978): 93–113; I will return to this point in chapter 10, below.

89. Council of Trent, Session VII, *Decree on the Sacraments*, canon 1 (DH 1601).

90. On the institution of holy orders, see DH 1773; on extreme unction, see DH 1695: "vere et proprie sacramentum Novi Testamenti a Christo Domino nostro, apud Marcum quidem insinuatum, per Iacobum autem Apostolum ac Domini fratrem fidelibus commendatum ac promulgatum" ([it] was instituted by Christ our Lord as a true and proper sacrament of the New Testament. It is alluded to indeed by Mark [Mk 6:13], but it is recommended to the faithful and promulgated by James the apostle and brother of the Lord). See also DH 1716: "a Christo Domino nostro institutum et a beato Iacobo Apostolo promulgatum" (a sacrament instituted by Christ our Lord and promulgated by the blessed apostle James).

ulating the rites. Therefore, after affirming their institution on the part of
Christ, Trent adds that the church's intervention is not illicit interference.[91]
She has the right, for example, to determine that the laity should receive the
Eucharist only under the species of bread. The Council affirms the ecclesial
power to modify aspects of each sacrament according to the diversity of
circumstances, times, and places, taking into account the benefits for those
who receive it and the worthy veneration that is due to them;[92] it does warn
that no one can make such changes on his own initiative.[93]

In order to justify this position it was necessary to respond to the ac-
cusations of Luther, who thought that the church had arrogated to herself
the power to institute sacraments apart from the master's will. Trent wishes
to legitimize the church's intervention without denying that the origin is
always in Christ. And it notes, for this reason, a limit to the ecclesial power:
salva illorum substantia, in other words, while keeping intact what pertains
to the "substance of the sacraments."[94]

What does this expression mean? Some have tried to interpret it in
keeping with the hylomorphic theory that was prevalent then: the substance would be the union of matter and form.[95] Viewed this way, Christ

91. Council of Trent, Session XXI, *Doctrine and Canons on Communion*, chap. 2 (DH 1728); see
also canon 9 of Session XXII, *Sacrifice of the Mass* (DH 1759).

92. Council of Trent, Session XXI, *Doctrine and Canons on Communion*, chap. 2 (DH 1728):
"declarat, hanc potestatem perpetuo in Ecclesia fuisse, ut in sacramentorum dispensatione, salva illorum substantia, ea statueret vel mutaret, quae suscipientium utilitati seu ipsorum sacramentorum
venerationi, pro rerum, temporum et locorum varietate, magis expedire iudicaret" (declares that, in
the administration of the sacraments—provided their substance is preserved—there has always been
in the Church that power to determine or modify what she judged more expedient for the benefit
of those receiving the sacraments or for the reverence due to the sacraments themselves—according
to the diversity of circumstances, times, and places). Next it cites 1 Cor 4:1: "ministros Christi et
dispensatores mysteriorum Dei" (servants of Christ and stewards of the mysteries of God) and 1 Cor
11:34: "cetera, quam venero, disponam" (About the other things I will give directions when I come).

93. Council of Trent, Session VII, *Decree on the Sacraments*, canon 13 (DH 1613); later on I will
say more about the church's authority over sacramental matters (see chapter 14, below).

94. Council of Trent, Session XXI, *Doctrine and Canons on Communion*, chap. 2 (DH 1728);
the very lively debate on the formula subsided around the time of Vatican II. See Heinrich Lennerz,
"Salva illorum substantia," *Gregorianum* 3, no. 3 (1922): 385–419 and 524–57; Adhémar D'Alès, "Salva
illorum substantia," *Ephemerides Theologicae Lovanienses* 1 (1924): 497–504; Johann Baptist Umberg,
"Die Bedeutung des tridentinischen *salva illorum substantia* (s. 21 c. 2)," *Zeitschrift für katholische
Theologie* 48, no. 2 (1924): 161–95; G. Koerperich, "De substantia sacramentorum iuxta Concilium
Tridentinum," *Collectiones Namurcenses* 30 (1936): 325–34; Hyacinthe-François Dondaine, "Substan-
tia sacramenti," *Revue de sciences philosophiques et théologiques* 29, nos. 2/4 (1940): 328–30; André
Poyer, "À propos du *Salva illorum substantia*," *Divus Thomas (Piacenza)* 56 (January–March 1953):
39–66, and "Nouveaux propos sur le *salva illorum substantia*," *Divus Thomas (Piacenza)* 57 (1954):
3–24; Artur Michael Landgraf, "Substantia sacramenti," in his *Dogmengeschichte der Frühscholastik*
(Regensburg: Pustet, 1954), 158–68; Albert Michel, "Modification des éléments sacramentaires par
l'Église *Salva illorum substantia*," *Doctor Communis* 12 (1959): 5–30, and "Salva illorum substantia,"
Doctor Communis 20, no. 3 (1967): 5–32.

95. Peter Lombard already distinguishes: *verbum* and *elementum* are *de substantia*; other things
pertinent ad solemnitatem ejus (have to do with its solemnity). *Sent. IV*, d. 3, c. 1, n. 3 (SpBon 5:244).

would have had to institute, for each sacrament, the material sign and the words that accompany it. Still, let us recall a general principle for interpreting Trent: the Council claims only to rebut the Protestant position, without deciding other debates between the theological schools.[96] Therefore one has to assume that the different opinions continue to be licit, unless it is possible to prove the contrary by the text itself or by the debate conducted during its composition.

We have already seen that some of the theories proposed in the Middle Ages distinguish between one sacrament and another: they are all tied to Christ, but some only indirectly. In order to condemn the Protestant teaching it was enough to affirm that the institution of the set of seven is traced back to Jesus, without any need to specify how this occurs; the Council Fathers were primarily interested in the fact, not in the manner.

Moreover, a study of the acts of the Council reveals that the expression *salva illorum substantia* was not meant to have a technical sense.[97] In other words, Trent does not understand the word "substance" here in the philosophical sense, as the union of matter and form, but rather in a theological sense: substance is what proceeds from Jesus himself and therefore constitutes the nucleus of the sacrament. We must distinguish, then, between the substance of the sacrament (which cannot change) and the substance of the sacramental rite, its matter and form (which can, in some cases, be modified). Pius XII, speaking about the sacrament of holy orders, would describe this *substantia sacramenti* as that which "with the sources of divine revelation [i.e., scripture and tradition] as witnesses, Christ the Lord himself decreed to be preserved in a sacramental sign."[98]

The post-Tridentine theologians would have heated debates about the interpretation of the Council.[99] They ask, for example, whether the institution by Christ has to be immediate or mediated. In the first case, which almost all of them were inclined to favor, Jesus himself would have instituted each sacrament; in the second case he would have delegated (to the apostles or to the whole church) the ability to institute some of them.[100] An immediate institution appears to be more in keeping both with the nature

96. Heinrich Lennerz, "Das Konzil von Trient und theologische Schulmeinungen," *Scholastik* 4, no. 1 (1929): 38–53.

97. Lennerz, "Salva illorum substantia," 524–57; the discussion of the theologians, which revolves around Communion under both species, is found in *Concilium Tridentinum: Diariorum, actorum, epistularum tractatuum* [hereafter *CT*], ed. Klaus Ganzer (Freiburg im Breisgau: Herder, 1901), 8:528.

98. Pius XII, *Sacramentum Ordinis*, Apostolic Constitution, November 30, 1947 (DH 3857).

99. Finkenzeller, *Die Lehre von den Sakramenten im allgemeinen*, 79–93.

100. Pierre Pourrat, *La théologie sacramentaire: Étude positive* (Paris, 1903), 268–72.

of the sacraments, inasmuch as it assures their direct connection with Jesus, and also with the awareness of the church, which never claimed to institute sacraments herself. At least in the case of extreme unction, Trent ruled out the possibility that Christ delegated the power to institute it to James, who limited himself to promulgating it.[101] Later Magisterial declarations against Modernism clarified that the sacraments do not spring from a gradual discernment by the church.[102]

Another question agitates the minds of theologians: is it necessary for Jesus to have determined each sacrament in its particular details, or is it enough that he offered, at least in some cases, a general indication? This is the difference between institution *in genere* (without determining the finishing touches of the sacrament) or *in specie* (establishing concretely the matter and form of each one). As I demonstrated above, the theory that agrees best with the revealed data is immediate institution (Jesus did not delegate to others the institution of the sacraments), but this does not mean that the institution was accomplished *in specie*. If, as Trent asserts, there are differences between one sacrament and another, there will be differences also in the manner of their institution.[103] Historical investigations conducted from the seventeenth century onward to rebut Protestant teachings confirmed that the church in various cases modified the structure of the sacramental rite: the anointing with oil in confirmation appears only in the second century; the handing over of the instruments of priestly orders originated in the Middle Ages; the prayers for the rite of confirmation and of the anointing of the sick varied greatly, even at the dawn of Christianity, from one region to another, and so on.[104] These inquiries promoted the theory of an institution *in genere* of various sacraments, wherein Jesus left some aspects undetermined which the church then specified.

In order to explain why the seven sacraments instituted by Christ were enumerated only with the passage of time, we can turn also to the essay by John Henry Newman about the development of dogma.[105] In light of his arguments, some have proposed an *explicit* institution of baptism and the Eucharist on the part of Jesus, and an *implicit*, as it were "seminal" institution of the rest of the set of seven. This would explain why the ecclesial

---

101. DH 1695 and 1716.

102. Pius X, *Lamentabili Sane*, Decree, pars. 39–51 (DH 3439–51).

103. Council of Trent, Session VII, *Decree on the Sacraments*, canon 3 (DH 1603).

104. Pourrat, *La théologie sacramentaire*, 74–83 and 313–14; Michel, *"Salva illorum substantia,"* 485–87.

105. Pourrat, *La théologie sacramentaire*, 273–74; the English cardinal expounds his teaching in John Henry Newman, *An Essay on the Development of Christian Doctrine* (Notre Dame, Ind.: University of Notre Dame Press, 1989).

awareness about some sacraments had developed only over the course of the years; while continuing to maintain that the essential data are already found present from the beginnings.

Institution of the Sacraments Starting from the Church-Sacrament: Karl Rahner

The concern of post-Tridentine theology with anchoring the individual sacraments in the words and works of Jesus ran into obstacles with the arrival of the modern era. This was due, on the one hand, to a development of our understanding of how revelation is transmitted. Some theories about the institution of the sacraments supposed the existence of traditions that are not reflected in scripture, but were passed on to the church orally from Jesus and the apostles. Today, nevertheless, most scholars reject the thesis that tradition includes a set of sayings not contained in the Bible; tradition is, rather, the way in which the church preserves and interprets scripture and, thanks to apostolic succession, transmits this interpretation.[106] Note that, from this perspective, not only are the sacraments attested in the tradition, but also, in the case of priestly ordination, they are a vehicle by which tradition is conveyed.

Another difficulty arises from the historical-critical investigation into the life of Jesus. According to this approach, it is not enough to cite texts that place the institution on the master's lips, for even these texts could have originated in the early church. Thus it is called into question, for example, that the account of baptism in Matthew 28:19 comes from Jesus. Even the institution of the Eucharist is turned into a debated question: what exact words did Jesus use at the Last Supper? Although for Luther the distance between baptism (which he accepted as a sacrament) and the anointing of the sick (which he rejected because it does not come from Jesus) was clear, it is not as obvious today for historical criticism, which emphasizes the influence of the community on the composition of the Gospel.[107]

To avoid these obstacles, some have proposed starting from a vision of the church as the root-sacrament from which the other sacraments are derived; the chief proponent of this view was Karl Rahner. From this vantage point it is possible to elaborate a theory of institution that avoids a cer-

106. Karl Rahner and Joseph Ratzinger, *Offenbarung und Überlieferung* (Freiburg: Herder, 1965); translated as *Revelation and Tradition* (New York: Herder and Herder, 1966).

107. Pannenberg, *Systematische Theologie*, 3:306–7; Karl Rahner, "What is a Sacrament?," in *Theological Investigations*, vol. 14: *Ecclesiology, Questions in the Church, the Church in the World* (London: Darton, Longman and Todd, 1976), 135–48, at 136.

tain apologetic anxiousness to find in the Bible words of Jesus about the seven sacraments.[108] I will return to this connection between the church-sacrament and the seven sacraments (in chapter 15, below). For now it is enough to say that, for Rahner, Christ is the primordial sacrament who makes himself present in the church, which is the root or stem sacrament, because from her spring the branches of the other seven. From this perspective, Rahner concludes, sacramental theology is a chapter of ecclesiology,[109] and the sacraments are the concrete acts in which the sacramental being of the church is revealed and gains strength.

The way to prove the origin of the sacraments in Jesus is thus expedited: he instituted them in instituting the great sacrament of the church. It is not necessary, therefore, to seek words of Jesus that are the basis of each one of the seven. In fact, again according to Rahner, such words probably do not exist for holy orders, matrimony, confirmation, and extreme unction. And there is no need to choose the easy escape of supposing that Christ made private revelations to the apostles, of which we find no trace in the Gospels. For we do not come across signs of the precise rite of some of these sacraments either in the first three centuries after Christ: if the church had received some word from Jesus on the subject, why would she have delayed so long in identifying the rites?

Does this mean that, in Rahner's view, we must deny the institution of these sacraments on the part of Jesus? Certainly not: it is a fact affirmed by Trent. Rahner's point is that the foundation of some rites in Christ can be ascertained by another path, that of the church as sacrament. Indeed, every act of the church in which she is implied as a historical and eschatological presence of redeeming grace (that is to say, as a radical or root sacrament) has been performed in her by Jesus and is, therefore, a sacrament.

Notice that Rahner is not saying that Christ delegated to the church the ability to institute sacraments. Rather, Jesus included the sacraments, as hidden seeds, in the genome of the church, and she herself is the root sacrament. In this way the church, over the course of history, institutes no sacrament; she limits herself to recognizing within herself the presence of the sacraments implanted by Christ. And thus, for example, because she defined that they are seven in number, there are no new sacraments that she can list.

Rahner's proposal highlights the importance of ecclesial mediation in clarifying the origin of the sacraments in Jesus. Thus he touches on a deci-

---

108. Karl Rahner, *Kirche und Sakramente* (Freiburg: Herder, 1961), 37–67; translated as *The Church and the Sacraments* (New York: Herder and Herder, 1963).
109. Karl Rahner, *Kirche und Sakramente*, 38.

sive point, which is central to the different visions of Trent and Luther. One result of his theory is of interest to us: it is necessary to keep the church in mind, not only because she specifies the rites or promulgates them, but also because she herself belongs to the sacramental act.

On the other hand, some have voiced criticisms of Rahner's position that prompt us to revise some aspects of it or to fill in the gaps.[110] By insisting that the sacraments come from the church, our author overlooks another more primordial side of the story: *the church is born from the sacraments.* As we will see in detail further on (in chapter 15, below), together with the line Christ-church-sacraments and preceding it, we have to draw another line: Christ-sacraments-church. In other words, the sacraments are not only actualizations of the church's ministry, but above all actualization of the mystery of Christ in order to generate the church.[111]

It follows that in order to prove the institution of a sacrament it is not enough, as Rahner intended, to prove that Jesus established the church as a sacrament; it is necessary to prove also that he established the sacraments as the foundation of the community of salvation.[112] Consequently we cannot renounce the exegetical effort to find, in Jesus' earthly life itself, a basis that supports the creation of each sacrament. The church plays a part in discerning and determining the rite, but it is a subordinate part that can never dispense with the figure of Jesus, with his words and works. And this root in the life of Christ must be supported in some way in the Bible, which is the normative testimony of the revelation of Jesus in the flesh. I will attempt to do justice to these facts by offering a synthesis, bearing in mind the central place of the Eucharist, both in order to understand the role of the church and also in order to analyze the connection of the other sacraments with Christ.

Institution of the Sacraments by Jesus: Synthesis from the Perspective of the Eucharist

The seven sacraments are anchored in Jesus, who instituted them; this is an article of faith. In order to explain this truth, theology, because of its internal vicissitudes, has concentrated on the words and gestures with which

---

110. William A. Van Roo, "Reflections on Karl Rahner's 'Kirche und Sakramente,'" *Gregorianum* 44, no. 3 (1963): 465–500, at 493–98. See also Pannenberg, *Systematische Theologie*, 3:375; in Pannenberg's judgment Rahner's theory threatens a central principle of Christian theology, that every sacrament must find its origin in Jesus Christ, the head of the church.

111. Colombo, "Dove va la teologia."

112. Van Roo, "Reflections on Karl Rahner," 497.

Christ determined each rite. The study of patristics and of medieval theology helps us to extend this outlook: the entire life of Jesus in the flesh is what institutes the sacraments. Only in this way can they be an effective radiation of Christ's life and love to mankind. Jesus' decision to institute rites, so that we might participate in his lot, makes sense only in conjunction with the path that he traveled in the flesh.

In order to substantiate this approach and to shed light in turn on the modern question about the institution of the sacraments, it seems appropriate, as I just pointed out, to start from the Eucharist, the true root (or radical) sacrament from which the emergence of the others is understood.[113] For here the institution by Jesus is transparent, attested in all four Gospels, and it allows us to proceed from the clearest so as to illuminate those that are less clear, and thus to outline the connection of the seven sacraments with the words and works of Christ.

Eucharistic Point of Departure

Jesus instituted the Eucharistic rite at a precise moment of his life, to which historical criticism bears witness in its main features (see chapter 2, above). This rite is framed in a Jewish Passover meal: Jesus performs an act of remembrance that gathers up within it the history of the people of Israel from the creation of the world. At the same time there are evocative new features, for the master focuses on the words over the bread and wine, which he identifies with his body and blood and distributes among the Twelve, in gratitude to the Father. Thus he performs a *todah* or sacrifice of praise for the original gift of life and for the definitive redemption thereof that was to arrive on Easter. All this shows us that the institution of this sacrament is not reduced to an isolated moment: it expands its hours to embrace the whole journey of Jesus, from the Father to the Father. The first Christian Eucharist was celebrated perfectly only after the resurrection (the first Sunday), when Christ, reunited with his brothers, lifted up a hymn of glory to the Father.

From these facts we infer that the rite revolves around the axis of the body and blood of Christ: a body received from the Father, filled with the Spirit of life, given up for mankind. That is to say, the rite opens up for us the relational space of the body of Jesus, a most suitable sphere for communion with God and the brethren. And given that this space is forged over the course of his entire earthly journey, the Eucharistic body is a "narrative" body, so to speak: it contains the remembrance of the master's steps and

---

113. Colombo, "Dove va la teologia," 707: "specifically, it is a matter of 'deriving' all the sacraments from the Eucharist, rather than from the Church."

anticipates his glory. The space of this body is generated, in fact, with the incarnation of the Son of God; if every body preserves in some way the marks of the one who shaped it, then Jesus' body points in a unique way to his radical origin in the Father. Moreover, this body receives the Holy Spirit, who comes down upon it and works in Christ over the course of his life, shaping his flesh so as to provide lodging for full communion. At the Paschal mystery of the cross and resurrection, the body of Christ will be associated definitively with the Father's glory and the regeneration of the children of Adam.

I am interested in drawing from all this a twofold conclusion: first, the institution of the rite is based entirely on the space of relations that originates in the body of Christ. Therefore the taking of bread and wine and the distribution of them to the disciples with the words that accompany it is placed at the service of the relational and narrative significance of this body that is offered and of this blood that is shed. Second, precisely because the Eucharistic rite flows from the language of the flesh of Jesus, it not only embraces his personal history but also is open to that of his brothers and sisters. For in the Bible the flesh always bands us together with other: it is flesh of flesh, one flesh, the same flesh, and so on. In fact, Jesus institutes his rite by taking up into it the whole history of salvation experienced in Israel, and by including in himself the body of the church, gathered around her master after Easter to offer the *todah*. The church, therefore, is not foreign to the constitution of the sacrament, but rather takes part in it. Here lies firm support to prove her singular authority over the salvific rites.

To summarize: Jesus institutes the sacrament inasmuch as he associates a material rite to the language of his flesh, which was forged over the course of his earthly journey, from his origin to his destination in the Father. Therefore the institution is not performed only at one moment, but rather embraces the arc of Christ's life, culminating in Easter, when Jesus offers the sacrifice of praise together with his brothers. As a result, the institution is not foreign to the church, for she is attached to the body of Jesus as his bride, one flesh with him.

Baptism, Integration into the Eucharist

It is time now to consider baptism, which illumines us, as we will see, about the connection of the other sacraments with the Eucharistic body. We note right away one difference with the Eucharist: now the rite is on the lips not of the pre-Paschal Jesus—although the master refers to baptism in John 3:5—but rather of the risen Lord (Mt 28:20; Mk 16:16); and the exact formula appears only in Matthew among the four evangelists. This prompts us to think that the baptismal practice of the church was not only based on these words but derived from the entire life of Jesus.

Indeed, as we saw earlier (in chapter 2, above), the apostles preserved in their memory the episode at the Jordan, when the Spirit descended upon the Son of man, who in his flesh represented all of us. And they preserved also the words of Jesus about the other "baptism" that he had to receive by dying and rising from the tomb. These remembrances, heightened by the light and word of the risen Lord, and against the background of the liturgy of the Old Testament, would bring the apostles to practice baptism as a means of being incorporated into Jesus and of receiving his Spirit.

The influence of the Eucharistic celebration was decisive in this step from the remembrance of Jesus to the practice of baptism. In fact, the New Testament interprets baptism in the light of the Eucharist, as putting off the old body of Adam and being engrafted onto the body of Jesus, the true vine. Therefore baptism consists of the transformation of our members so as to work justice (Rom 6:19). Whereas the Eucharist opens the space of the body of Christ (i.e., of the bodily relations that he inaugurates), baptism signifies the incorporation of the believer into this space, in such a way that at the center of the institution stands once again the body of Jesus with the relational meanings that are forged in his flesh.

Thus we understand why the institution of baptism occurs after Easter: it is fitting to establish it when the new body of the risen Lord is already constituted and can receive the believer into itself. We understand also that there is greater participation of the apostolic church in the determination of the baptismal rite. She, born of the Eucharist, is the one who welcomes Christians in her bosom—an image which we know has been connected with the water of baptism from as early as the patristic era.

To understand this intervention of the church it helps to observe the differences between the Synoptics (see chapter 2, above). While in Matthew and Mark the institution of the rite is acknowledged as coming from the risen Jesus, Luke does not mention the institution, but rather narrates for us in Acts how the church baptized in the name of Christ. Thus the rite which in Matthew is on the lips of the risen Jesus is described by Luke in the concrete activity of the apostles.

According to the Lucan account, then, it falls to the apostolic church to perform the baptismal rite, without any need to transcribe explicit words of the master. The firm anchorage in the life of Jesus is given to us by the elements that I have outlined: his baptism in the Jordan, where he received the Spirit in the name of all (Lk 3:21–38); his words about the eschatological baptism that awaited him in his death and resurrection (Lk 12:49–50); the light that the Eucharist shed on the ritual manner in which we participate in the life of Christ (Lk 22:19–20).

In Luke's view, the church preserved these events in her heart and meditated on them against the background of the Old Testament, which already situated in a liturgical context the unity of the people in one mediator. In this way she started to practice the rite, recognizing it as the master's will and capable of incorporating us into him. This step from the life of Jesus to the baptismal rite was possible because of the disciples' encounter with the risen Lord, from which a penetrating outlook on the whole path of Jesus extended. This Paschal light is the one that Matthew mentions explicitly in narrating the institution of baptism: "Go and baptize ..." (Mt 28:19). From the perspective of a holistic reading of the Gospel, it makes little difference whether the church *practices* baptism in terms of its memory of Jesus, as in Luke, or the church *recalls the words* of Jesus who establishes baptism, as in Matthew. This proves to be paradigmatic in understanding the institution of the other sacraments, for which explicit sayings of the master are lacking in the Gospels, as they are lacking for baptism in Luke.

Institution of the Other Sacraments, Starting from the Eucharist and Baptism

We can suppose for the other sacraments a process analogous to what St. Luke allows us to glimpse with respect to baptism. Then, as the first sacramental syntheses in the writings of John and Paul showed us (in chapters 3 and 4, above) and as I will prove in the following pages, the distinct sacraments arise through the branching out of the Eucharistic space of Jesus to all spheres of Christian life, a ramification that is inaugurated in every believer with baptism.

For the church, therefore, it was in the first place a matter of recognizing the different expressions of the body of Christ that follow from the Eucharist and accompany the different places and time of a believer's life. Secondly, it was a matter of associating with each corporeal sign a suitable ritual expression, which is inferred from the words and works of Jesus as a whole, against the background of the Jewish liturgy. The light by which to discern this link between the meaning of the body of Christ and each concrete rite came to the apostles from their encounter with the risen Lord, which according to St. Luke has Eucharistic overtones: "[We] ate and drank with him after he rose from the dead" (Acts 10:41).

Notice that what the apostles achieve is not the union of a ritual sign with the divine grace that accompanies it—only Christ could achieve that, as Scholastic theology correctly reasoned. But rather they limit themselves to testifying as to what ritual sign best captures, from the faithful memory of Christ's life, the different relational meanings that Jesus forged in his body. For it is by adopting these meanings (these ways of being situated in the world, among our fellow human beings, and with respect to God) that we can receive from Christ's very Spirit.

Such an intervention of the church therefore takes nothing away from the immediate institution on Christ's part, which is guaranteed inasmuch as the central sign that constitutes the sacrament is contained in the body of Jesus itself; and inasmuch as the ecclesial verification of the rite proceeds from the deeds and sayings of the master, always against the background of the Old Testament. The apostolic church plays an irreplaceable role in this process: she alone, as witness of the life of Jesus, could identify, in an act of memory illuminated by the resurrection, the authority of Christ as the origin of the sacramental gestures and words. The institution of each sacrament has to find support, therefore, as St. Augustine pointed out, either in the life of Jesus, or in the apostolic preaching, as they are contained in the New Testament.[114] This scriptural basis is necessary in order to determine the *substance* of the sacraments, in other words, those elements of them that are foundational for the church because they came from Jesus himself, the essential memory of whom was preserved and transmitted by the apostles.

It helps to think that a parallel task fell to the apostles themselves: that of composing the New Testament, thus recording the nucleus of Jesus' message and offering their authorized interpretation. This was also an exercise of memory, in that they transmitted faithfully the Lord's preaching and the narrative of his life. It is logical that this role with respect to the word was joined to another similar role with respect to the sacraments, which are the place where the word can resound and be heard.

We understand too now what the patristic contribution was: just as it was up to the Church Fathers to determine the biblical canon, so too they play a decisive role both in verifying which rites proceed from Jesus and are the spinal column of the church, and also in creating "the fundamental forms of the Christian liturgical service."[115] We are talking about a slow

114. Augustine, *De doctrina christiana* III, 9, 13 (CCL 32:11; NPNF-I 2:560a–b); *Epistolae* 54, 1, 1 (CSEL 34.2:159; NPNF-I 1:300a–b).

115. Joseph Ratzinger, *Theologische Prinzipienlehre: Bausteine zur Fundamentaltheologie* (Munich: Erich Wewel, 1982), 139–58, at 155; translated as "Importance of the Fathers for the Structure of the Faith," in *Principles of Catholic Theology: Building Stones for a Fundamental Theology* (San Francisco,

process during which the church became aware of the seeds already sowed by Christ, a process that would lead her to distinguish the seven sacraments as the ones instituted by Jesus. Here too there is a parallel with the canon of scripture: the Council of Trent definitively fixed both the set of seven sacraments and the list of biblical books.[116]

I can now finally indicate the main lines of the institution of each sacrament. *Confirmation* is rooted in the baptismal event, emphasizing its dynamic aspect; the Spirit, after constituting the believer as a child of God in baptism, impels him so that he too generates communion with God and with the brethren, a communion that expands into the missionary witness of faith. Jesus instituted the sacrament inasmuch as the Spirit brought to perfection the love that he lived in his flesh, showing him the way in his ministry and broadening his activity so that it might embrace all the spaces where human beings dwell. The apostles captured this dynamic meaning of the body of Christ in the rite of imposing hands, while praying over the believer (Acts 8:14–17; 19:1–6). The anointing with oil, not attested in apostolic usage, was introduced shortly afterward as necessary for the validity of the rite; given the biblical practice of anointing, this expresses more clearly the language of Jesus' body in the power of the Spirit. The prayer formula was fixed by the church: fidelity to the master required only affirming the harmony between the ritual gesture and the language of Christ's anointed body.

Through *penance*, the believer goes back to the vital coordinates of baptism. Christ instituted this sacrament inasmuch as the relations that he forged during his life in the flesh, and into which we are incorporated when we are baptized, never abandon someone who strays from them, however great his transgression may be. This is because these relations, inaugurated by Jesus in his body when he endured death in his fidelity to the Father, reach to what is most primordial in the human person, that filial foundation that no guilt can blot out and to which it is always possible to convert. Inasmuch as this conversion is capable of regenerating concrete relations in the flesh (and not only in the isolated interior of the individual), reintegrating us visibly into the body of Jesus, the sacrament includes the confession of sin before the church. In order to determine the rite in fidelity to Christ it was

---

Calif.: Ignatius Press, 1987), 133–52, at 150; Eugenio Romero Pose, "Exégesis patrística y liturgia," in *Liturgia y Padres de la Iglesia*, XXIV Jornadas de la Asociación Española de Profesores de Liturgia (Bilbao: Grafite Ediciones, 2000).

116. The presuppositions presented here justify the authority of the church of all ages to modify the rite, provided that she does not alter its substance, an authority that will be the subject of study further on (see chapter 14, below).

enough to indicate, in the absolution, that the sinner is loosed from sin; the fact that the words are pronounced by the priest, the representative of Jesus, clarifies that their purpose is to reincorporate the penitent into the body of Jesus and into the narrative of his life.

Christ carried out the institution of *matrimony* inasmuch as he took up, in his life in the flesh, the creaturely meanings of the body, and brought to fulfillment, in his passion and glory, their ability to express communion. In this way the union in "one flesh" (Gn 2:24) of two persons who, because they are baptized, belong to Christ's flesh, will be a union according to the measure of the flesh of Christ, the bridegroom of the church and one flesh with her. Given that the bodies themselves of the spouses receive a new meaning within the body of Christ when they join in marital union, it is not necessary to add any rite to express the reference to the body of Jesus which characterizes the seven sacraments.

The Savior instituted *holy orders* inasmuch as his body was set up in the Eucharist, culminating in his death and resurrection, as the source of life for the church. Thus his paternity was configured in a new way—that is, his bodily ability to generate life, which now transmits the eternal life of God.[117] The apostolic church, in practicing the imposition of hands to confer holy orders, carried out an act of memory: this is the rite that captures the paternal meaning of the flesh of Jesus and configures the priest to this flesh. Over the course of history the church added elements to the rite, such as the conferral (which was required during the Middle Ages) of the chalice and of other instruments that expressed various functions of the priestly ministry.

The *anointing of the sick* refers to the language of the body in exactly the same existential situation that Christ was going through at the Last Supper when he offered his *todah*, in the midst of sorrow until the resurrection. And it was instituted when Jesus shaped his suffering flesh in openness to the Father and to the brethren, in such a way that his wounds could come to be glorious wounds at his resurrection. The Letter of James, based on his faithful memory of the master, established the rite of anointing with oil and determined that a prayer was necessary (Jas 5:14–15). In this way it captured the meaning of Jesus' body, afflicted and full of hope, in order to bring about the configuration of the sick person to him.

To summarize, the substance of all the sacraments consists of containing and mediating the way of experiencing the body that Jesus forged during his

---

117. To understand these statements, see my discussion in chapter 14, below.

journey so that we might be able to receive a share of his Spirit. The Savior instituted the sacraments in his flesh, shaping it with salvific meaning and incorporating us into it by means of a rite. This centrality of Christ's body, which is entrusted to us in the Eucharist, will be decisive in part 2 of this treatise, in which we will journey toward a definition of sacrament.

PART 2

THE SACRAMENTS, RITUAL OPENING OF THE SYMBOLIC SPACE OF JESUS

After studying how the sacraments are rooted in Christ, I will focus my attention on defining them. Starting, as I have done until now, from the Eucharist, the root-sacrament, a route with three stages rises up ahead of us. First, bread and wine, the body and the blood, invite us to consider how all creation comes to be included in the sacrament and can consequently be understood in a sacramental way (chapter 6). Second, the fact that the rites of Israel (Passover, *todah*) are taken up into the rite of Jesus inspires us to inquire about the manner in which the sacrament takes up into itself the course of the ages, with their destination in Christ (chapter 7). Finally, the Lord's gesture and words complete the overall vision so as to determine what is a sacrament of the new covenant (chapters 8–10). The search for an answer will require us to navigate the meanderings of the theological tradition: from St. Augustine (sacrament as sacred sign: chapter 8), via the Middle Ages (the sacrament as a sign that causes grace: chapter 9) to the modern perspective marked by the Protestant crisis and Trent (chapter 10). Only after this review will it be possible to offer a synthesis that shows the sacraments as an opening, in the life of the church, of this new space of relations inaugurated by Jesus in his flesh (chapter 11).

6 ❧ THE ROOTS OF
THE SACRAMENTS IN
CREATION

The vantage point from which to contemplate the sacraments in their entirety—I have concluded so far—is the Eucharist. The rite performed by Jesus is many-layered; it recapitulates within itself, in chronological order: creation, the history of Israel, and the life of Christ, in which the age of the church is anticipated. I will begin by analyzing the component rooted in creation, which is the task of this chapter; I will go back to the beginning of history so as then to retrace it step by step.

Note that this undertaking is not just a kind of philosophical prospecting so as to become acquainted with the subsoil of human experience and the makeup of the universe. We are dealing, rather, with an intrinsic requirement of Jesus' rite, and therefore this attempt has a theological character. The very rite celebrated by him forces us to return to the beginning in order to understand it fully, because he employs the original language of body and blood, of earth and human work. This subject (the rootedness of the sacraments in creation) is decisive, moreover, in linking the sacraments with our human experience and with our way of understanding the world. What horizons did Jesus open up for us when he introduced creation into his rite? How did he purify and transform created reality by taking it up?

From the Eucharistic Rite to the Creation
of Man and of Things

Jesus himself was the one who, in instituting the sacraments, included in them the language of creation by pronouncing words over the bread and wine and identifying them with his body and blood. He thus performed an act of memory which went back, following the channel of Jewish history, to the dawn of the world: the creation of the cosmos (bread and wine) and the formation of man (body and blood). This recognition of the beginning, which always involves gratitude, was integrated perfectly into the sacrifice of thanksgiving or *todah*, the nucleus of the Last Supper: Jesus thanked the Father who graciously willed to resurrect this flesh that he himself had shaped. It is not surprising that the church would subsequently connect the Eucharist with the creation of the world: Sunday coincides, after all, with the Roman "day of the sun," thus evoking the inaugural day on which God created light.[1] Let us pause to consider the central features of this reference of the Eucharist to creation.

"This is my body"; "this is my blood." In ancient times, God shaped Adam's body from the clay of the earth and breathed into it his breath of life (Gn 2:7). And this exhalation, through the blood, enlivened his flesh. In flesh and blood, therefore, there is a summary of biblical man, flesh in which the breath of Yahweh dwells. This recalls above all his *dependence on the creator*: no one ever gave himself a body or arranged his own members, which reflect a higher wisdom. However much he racked his brains, no one has been able to lengthen one bit the years of his life, the gift of the Spirit or divine breath. From this emerges, moreover, a *relational view of the person*: his body situates him in the world, gives him a surname in a family ("his own flesh") and citizenship in a fatherland. I maintain, then, that the Eucharist quietly pronounces the definition of man: a being who lives in a network of relations, with God and his brethren, a network that he is called to intertwine over time until it is made capable of accommodating full communion.

The memory evoked by body and blood includes furthermore all material creation, starting from the *bread and wine* of the rite. If bread can be body, and wine can be blood, it is because man, in his animated flesh, recapitulates within himself the entire universe. He is a microcosm or, as Leonardo da Vinci said, a micro-atlas, of oceans and continents in miniature. And not only that: Jesus did not pick created elements that sprout spontaneously and hang within hand's reach (he did not choose an ear of grain or a bunch of grapes); bread and wine are possible only through human ingenuity and labor. Thus everything that made Eden pleasant—everything formed by God or produced by man's work—finds room in this rite of Jesus and reaches its maturity therein.

Note, finally, that this creaturely memory of Jesus, which is revived in the liturgy, *receives its definitive light from the glorious resurrection*. For we know that Christ at his Last Supper celebrates the rite as an anticipation of his death and exaltation. Therefore we are confronted with a memory that

---

1. Justin, *1 Apologiae* 67, 3, 8 (PTS 38:129–30; ANF 1:186a).

is reinterpreted, transfigured, from the perspective of its fulfillment; with a route that is considered from the viewpoint of its final summit. That is to say, the rite does not invite us simply to go back to what is created, but rather to reinterpret what is created in light of its destiny, so as to discover its most original secret.

The Eucharist, therefore, offers us an adequate vision of man and of the cosmos. This theme was developed by the Church Fathers: if bread and wine, if body and blood, could find lodgings in the rite of Jesus, it is because the material universe already spoke a language of incipient faith.[2] The sacraments, from the perspective of our daily experience of them in the church, clear a passage for us to discover a cosmic liturgy and to participate in it.[3]

St. Irenaeus gives us an example of this. In order to demolish the Gnostic system that denied the salvation of the flesh, he uses as a supporting argument the Eucharist: the reason why Jesus at the Last Supper takes bread and wine, with which the carnal creature is fed, is because he wants to give eternal life to this same carnal creature.[4] This implies, in turn, that God, in making the sun rise and in sending rain so that the wheat fields and the grapevines sprout, already shares with mankind, through his material creation, a seed of his divine life.[5]

Starting from the Eucharist—the unity of Christ and Christians in one body—the Fathers also illuminate the communional sense of creation, whereby all things are related to each other and with man. In light of St. Paul (1 Cor 10:17), it is a commonplace to see a sign of fraternal communion with Jesus in the many grains that form the loaf or in the abundance of clusters that are turned into one cup.[6] The image is completed, in an allusion to baptism, with the need to moisten the mass of dough; and, finally, with the baking of the bread in the fire of the Spirit.[7] Besides, the same experience of food, which testifies that those who eat a common meal belong to the world together, explains the radical union of Christians in Jesus, as they share in his very nature.[8]

The Eucharist therefore illuminates the primordial vocation of matter

2. Tertullian, *De Baptismo* III, 6 (CCL 1:279; ANF 3:670b): "si materiam quam in omnibus rebus et operibus suis deus disposuit, etiam in sacramentis propriis parere fecit, si quae vitam terrenam gubernat etiam caelesti procurat" (God has made the material substance which He has disposed throughout all his products and works, obey him also in his own peculiar sacraments; that the *material substance* which governs terrestrial life acts as agent likewise in the celestial).

3. Joseph Ratzinger, *The Spirit of the Liturgy*, trans. John Saward (San Francisco, Calif.: Ignatius Press, 2000), 24–34; reprinted in his *Collected Works*, 11:12–19.

4. Irenaeus of Lyons, *Adversus haereses* V, 2, 2 (SC 153:32; ANF 1:528a).

5. Ibid., V, 3, 3 (SC 153:50; ANF 1:530a).

6. For example, *Didache* IX, 4 (SC 248:176); Augustine, *In Iohannis* XXVI, 17 (CCL 36:268).

7. Augustine, *Sermo* 272, 1 (PL 38:1247).

8. Hilary of Poitiers, *De Trinitate* VIII, 13–17 (CCL 62A:325–29; NPNF-II 9:141a–142a).

and of the flesh. The reason why we can receive eternal life in receiving the body of Jesus is because every fruit of the earth can already transmit in some way the life of God. And the reason why the Eucharistic food makes us one with Christ is because all food already in a certain way bands human beings together and situates them in the cosmos, under the provident hand of the creator. From the perspective of the Eucharist, the entire material universe is revealed as a welcoming environment through its common openness to the Father and through fraternal communion. Creation thus acquires sacramental features.

Creation Baptized: The Patristic View

The first Christian writers, although with various emphases, deciphered the being of man and of the world starting from the sacraments. I have noted that the Eucharist is the point of departure for this approach. Let us look now at baptism, which will also give a basis on which to understand better the heart of created reality and its final destiny.

As we already know, the Fathers favor the image of new birth to explain Christian initiation.[9] Their immediate interest, more than the forgiveness of sins, is the appearance of a new creature which, as a result, puts off the body of death (Col 2:11). The outlook is focused, beyond the liturgical event, on the lasting condition in which the believer remains. In fact the name "baptism" refers to the state of consecration at which the believer arrives, rather than to the rite itself. Hence the preferred name for baptism is "seal" and the faithful are insistently exhorted to guard their baptism. This seal represents membership in the body of Jesus, who died and rose again. Because of this new body that the believer receives—because of this new rootedness in Jesus—we are one with each other.[10] This seamlessly harmonizes two traditions: the Johannine, which speaks to us about being born again from above (Jn 3:5), and the Pauline, according to which we are associated through baptism to the death and resurrection of Christ, in other words, to his new risen corporeality (Rom 6:3–23).

In order to understand the new life of baptism we have to ask ourselves, then, about the connection between Christian birth in the water of the font and natural birth on our mothers' knees. Can they clarify each other? The Gnostic heretics saw it as undignified that the ineffable plan of God should

---

9. For the following discussion, see Everett Ferguson, *Baptism in the Early Church* (Grand Rapids, Mich.: Eerdmans, 2009).

10. Hilary of Poitiers, *De Trinitate* VIII, 7–8 (CCL 62:319–20; NPNF-II 9:139a–140b).

be accomplished through the ministry of material creatures.[11] Against them the Fathers defended the harmony between the new body received in baptism and the more original truth of the created body in its state prior to sin. Tertullian argues that, if baptism is the regeneration of man, it must be the work of the same God who engendered man; how can someone who did not generate regenerate?[12] For this reason the oldest baptismal rite contains allusions to Eden: the catechumen, who starts by looking westward, turns eastward, where the first Garden was located.[13]

This congruency (between coming into the world and being baptized) becomes clear, for example, in the commentary by St. Irenaeus of Lyons on the cure of the man blind from birth (Jn 9).[14] Jesus, in making mud with his saliva and smearing it on the darkened eyes, revealed that he was the same hand of the Father (the Logos) which, at the dawn of the world, formed Adam out of clay (Gn 2:7). All the same, this remaking according to the origins was not enough to save the man. It was necessary, Irenaeus adds, for the blind man to be regenerated in the pool of Siloam, which represents baptism. These are two stages of one and the same activity of the creator upon the body: *opera Dei, plasmatio hominis*, the works of God consist of molding man gradually.[15]

The connection between the first and the second birth allows us to state that, if baptism is a new birth, then birth can be seen too as the primordial baptism. In fact, the Fathers project baptismal categories onto the formation of the first man. For Tertullian, for example, the water that would be used afterward in Christian initiation was required in order to moisten the clay with which Adam was molded.[16] Starting from his baptismal destiny, this sheds light on the origin of the person and his place in God's work. In molding man, the creator premeditated the act of conforming him with the glorified body of Jesus, filled with the Spirit.

From the flesh of man, this outlook was projected then onto all of creation. Water is admirable, Tertullian declares (in reference to Gn 1:2, the

---

11. Irenaeus of Lyons, *Adversus haereses* I, 21, 4 (SC 264:71; ANF 1:346a–b): "dicentes non oportere inenarrabilis et inuisibilis Virtutis mysterium per uisibiles et corruptibiles perfici creaturas" (and maintain that the mystery of the unspeakable and invisible power ought not to be performed by visible and corruptible creatures).

12. Tertullian, *Adversus Marcionem* I, 28, 2–3 (CCL 1:472; ANF 3:293b): "Si [baptismus] regeneratio est hominis, quomodo regenerat qui non generavit?" (If the regeneration of man [is the purpose of baptism], how can he regenerate who has never generated?).

13. Cyril of Jerusalem, *Catecheses* I, 8, 18 (SC 126:98).

14. Irenaeus of Lyons, *Adversus haereses* V, 15, 2–3 (SC 153:202–10; ANF 1:543a–b).

15. Ibid., V, 15, 2 (SC 153:204; ANF 1:543a).

16. Tertullian, *De Baptismo* III, 5 (CCL 1:2797): "Non enim ipsius quoque hominis figulandi opus sociantibus aquis absolutum est?" "For was not the work of fashioning man himself also achieved with the aid of waters?" (ANF 3:670a–b).

Spirit who was hovering over the waters), both for its antiquity and for its dignity as the seat of the Spirit.[17] This clarified the lofty vocation of matter, which is called to be part of the sacrament.[18] Then, through water, which represents the origin of all things in God, the whole creation is filled with the Spirit, as if it received a prototype of baptism.[19] Melito of Sardis sings of a baptism of the earth through the rains and rivers, which make it fertile.[20] And he adds that the sun itself is baptized in the waters of the ocean without being extinguished, but rather conquering the darkness and then rising to illuminate everything, like Christ.

This approach results in a baptismal anthropology and cosmology. It is as though the entire cosmos proved to be prebaptized in view of man's creation, and as though man received a prebaptism in view of his definitive baptism in Christ. And just as baptism brings about incorporation in Christ and the infusion of the Spirit, so too the creation of the world is linked to the action of the Word and the Spirit of the Father, which prefigures the future economy of salvation. All creation was constituted in the Logos, and then received order and structure in him; all creation was also anointed by the Spirit, the primordial breath that filled the universe and infused into it a dynamic disposition toward its goal. Let us analyze the presence of these two moments, in the Word and the Spirit.

First, configuration with Christ in baptism reveals the way in which the Logos bestows order on the universe. And given that baptism seals us with the cross of Jesus, the earliest theology discovered in the cross the original architecture of creation: God spread out in the heavens a cosmic cross so as to give firmness to all things; and he shaped Adam as a cruciform being, distinguished in his flesh from the rest of the animals by his ability to assume

---

17. Gn 1:2 appears already in a baptismal context in Justin Martyr, *1 Apologiae* 64, 3 (PTS 38:124); for other patristic texts, see Jean Daniélou, *Sacramento y culto según los santos Padres* (Madrid: Guadarrama, 1962), 108–13.

18. Tertullian, *Adversus Marcionem* I, 14, 3 (CCL 1:455); *De Baptismo* III, 1–2 (CCL 1:278): "ista materia tantae dignationis meruit officium ... habes, homo, inprimis aetatem uenerari aquarum, quod antiqua substantia, dehinc dignationem quo diuini spiritus sedes, gratior scilicet ceteris tunc elementis" (this material substance merited an office of so high dignity.... The first thing, O man, which you have to venerate, is the *age* of the waters, in that their substance is ancient; the second, their *dignity*, in that they were the seat of the Divine Spirit, more pleasing to Him, no doubt, that all the other then existing elements) (ANF 3:670a).

19. Ferguson, *Baptism in the Early Church*, 245–47, a commentary on Tatian, *Oratio* V, 6 (PTS 43:14; ANF 2:67a): "As the Logos, begotten in the beginning, begat in turn our world, having first created for Himself the necessary matter, so also I, in imitation of the Logos, being begotten again, and having become possessed of the truth, am trying to reduce to order the confused matter which is kindred with myself."

20. Melito, *Fragment* VIIIb (SC 123:228–32); Franz Joseph Dölger, *Sol Salutis: Gebet und Gesang in christlicher Altertum* (Münster, 1920), 264–67; Robert M. Grant, "Melito of Sardis on Baptism," *Vigiliae Christianae* 4 (1950): 33–36.

the shape of the cross.[21] In this way the union of human beings among themselves and with God, which is contained in the horizontal and vertical wooden crossbeams, and which Jesus brought to fulfillment in handing himself over to the Father and to the church, is discovered already in the origins of all natural and social spaces; it is as though they had been marked with the sign of the cross through a primordial baptism that would reach its consummation on Golgotha.

Second, the outpouring of the Spirit that is accomplished in baptism also illuminates the constitution of the universe. For in its light some writers would speak about a cosmic anointing: in creating the world and ordering it with his Logos, God sent a share of his Spirit to activate all beings toward their fullness in the Father.[22] Theophilus of Antioch, taking as his inspiration the baptismal anointing with the "oil of God," describes this balm which permeates natural and artificial beings: ships, towers, and houses, newborns, even the entire earth, anointed with air and light.[23]

In short, the point of departure is Christian baptism as the eschatological completion of history, in which the being of matter arrives at its fullness and man's definitive body is born, configured to the glorified Christ. And from the perspective of baptism sacramental features are revealed in the material universe, which announced from the beginning the maturity for which it was destined. The path of the sacrament, from baptism to baptism, runs through human flesh, which is not only testimony of God's first love but also the ultimate recipient of his benevolence.

Toward a Sacramental View of Creation: From the Fathers to the Middle Ages

The outlook of the Fathers, starting from the sacraments, discovers the symbolic architecture of all creation. Two authors, St. Augustine and Dionysius, are important because of their great influence on the Middle Ages.

St. Augustine: Natural Signs and Given Signs

As we will see in more detail in another chapter, St. Augustine pioneered the definition of sacrament as a sign, thus associating it with the signs which,

---

21. On this theory of the cosmic cross, see José Granados, *Los misterios de la vida de Cristo en Justino Mártir* (Rome: PUG, 2005), 393–98.

22. Antonio Orbe, *La unción del Verbo: Estudios Valentinianos* (Rome: Editrice Pontificia Università Gregoriana, 1961), 3:67–82, who refers to St. Justin Martyr and St. Theophilus of Antioch.

23. Theophilus of Antioch, *Ad Autolycum* I, 12 (SC 20:84).

according to him, are sown throughout creation.[24] In order to understand them, it is essential to distinguish between natural signs and given signs. A *natural* sign is traced back to the relation of causes and effects: the paw-prints of the wolf in the snow announce the beast's passage; smoke alerts us to the fire. A *given* sign, for its part, results from a personal will that gives it meaning; note that in this case we are not talking about an arbitrary convention but about a communicative sign, in which someone gives something to another.

We should add that, for St. Augustine, who in this idea innovates with respect to earlier philosophers, the sign *par excellence* is the word, not only as a perceptible expression of the idea or concept, but as call and response, that is, as a vehicle of interpersonal communication. And in fact his model is the biblical word, the sign given by God to human beings to reveal to them his salvation and to invite them to accept it.[25]

It appears, therefore, that the bishop of Hippo is more interested in given signs than in natural ones. Still, both types of signs, distinct in themselves, combine in one case: when the one who gives them is God, who also created nature. Then we have *natural signs* that point to the creator (as though they were his footprints: Rom 1:20),[26] and these signs, in turn, are *given signs*, gifts with which God shows his love for man.

Augustine can contemplate creation, then, as an immense book where each being is a word with which the Lord addresses his creature. And so, in his *Confessions*, he dialogues with created things: "'You have told me concerning my God that you are not He; tell me something about Him.' And with a loud voice they exclaimed, 'He made us.' My questioning was my observing of them; and their beauty was their reply."[27]

In order to understand correctly this Augustinian view of beings as signs-word, it is important to note that each created thing not only reveals the creator's presence but also moves man's desire, impelling him to the love of God. Created beings are a sign because when they are perceived, they raise our consciousness; and also because when they are loved, they propel us toward the final goal, the unequalled rest.

---

24. To supplement what is said in this section about St. Augustine and to substantiate it, see chapter 8, below.

25. Joseph Engels, "La doctrine du signe chez saint Augustin," *Studia Patristica* 6 (1962): 366–73; B. Darrel Jackson, "The Theory of Signs in St. Augustine's *De Doctrina Christiana*," *Revue des études Augustiniennes* 15, nos. 1–2 (1969): 9–49; Tzvetan Todorov, "À propos de la conception augustinienne du signe," *Revue des études Augustiniennes* 31, nos. 3–4 (1985): 209–21.

26. Augustine, *Epistolae* LV, 6, 11 (CSEL 34.2:181): "ducitur … similitudo ad diuina mysteria figuranda … ex omni creatura" (a likeness to symbolize the divine mysteries is derived from all creation).

27. Augustine, *Confessiones* X, 6, 9 (CCL 27:18; NPNF-I 1:144b).

Hence we conclude that in creation there is a dynamism or drive that gives meaning and direction to history. That is to say, cosmic signs, because they are joined with the current of God's love, open a path in time which marches toward its goal in Christ. Augustine preserves, therefore, the biblical typological outlook, which does not move us directly to what is on high, but propels us along the route of history, from its origin to its fullness. I will confirm these findings in chapter 8.

Dionysius: From Sign to Sign, a Ladder of Light

The symbolic theology of Dionysius would also prove to be very influential. Through this unknown author (fifth/sixth century), who is presented under the name of the philosopher converted by Paul in the Areopagus, the symbolic outlook extends from the liturgy to all creation and singularly illuminates the interpretation of the Bible.[28] The model now is not so much the word as the faculty of sight: the light that descends from above and is communicated in distinct degrees to the lower layers of the world so as to enable man to raise his eyes to it.[29] All things are symbols that emanate from God and reflect his glory, leading us to him. Someone who is pure of heart and possesses contemplative strength ascends to supernatural truth, which is more dazzling than the sum of its symbolic reflections.

There is a serious neo-Platonic influence here: from the material world we are raised to the purer strata of being. Still, this does not mean that Dionysius despises material creation. For according to him there is unity between the links that connect the degrees of being: *supremum infimi attingit infimum supremi*—the ceiling of each lower story touches the floor of the next higher one.[30]

On the other hand, it does not appear that this approach grasps the whole richness of biblical thought, in which the flesh and history are the place where the revelation of God and the salvation of mankind occur. In Dionysius the material world—which is subordinated to and hierarchically integrated into the spiritual world—does reflect the perfection of beings

28. Victor V. Bychkov, "The Symbology of Dionysius the Areopagite," *Russian Studies in Philosophy* 51, no. 1 (2012): 28–63; and Nicholas Madden, "Edith Stein on the Symbolic Theology of Dionysius the Areopagite," *Irish Theological Quarterly* 71, nos. 1–2 (2006): 29–45.

29. Marie-Dominique Chenu, "Pour une anthropologie sacramentelle," *La Maison Dieu* 119 (1974): 85–100; contrary to Chenu's opinion, I think that the Augustinian perspective offers more opportunities to translate correctly the biblical heritage than the one opened up by Dionysius.

30. The axiom is inspired by Dionysius the Areopagite, *De divinis nominibus* VII, 3 (PG 3:872b); we find the formula in Thomas Aquinas, *Quaestio disputata de spiritualibus creaturis*, a. 2, co. See Bernard Montagnes, "L'axiome de continuité chez Saint Thomas," *Revue de sciences philosophiques et théologiques* 52, no. 2 (1968): 201–21.

but does not by itself help to forge it.[31] Symbols do not drive us to retrace history, nor do they indicate the maturation of the flesh until it can contain the Spirit perfectly. References to typology, which orients signs toward the life of Jesus, are scarce in the *Corpus Areopagiticum*.

It is interesting to note, on the other hand, and in keeping with this author's negative theology, that the signs suited to revealing the divine which are adopted by scripture are modeled on the most brutish part of nature— for example, the monstrous beasts of the prophet Ezekiel. According to Dionysius, we are confronted with *dissimilar similarities*; their mission is to invite us to overcome all concepts and to ascend to the sublime. In fact, when we call God "sun" (a comparison which in itself is fair), we might confuse him with the noble star, making a serious mistake. But if we compare him with a proud leopard or a rearing horse, which are clearly opposed to his calm essence, it will be clear to us that he surpasses all likeness.[32] Their crass corporeality proves to be, paradoxically, more apt to represent the divine, inasmuch as it preserves its mystery by veiling it.

The Middle Ages: Creation, Included in the Sacraments

Whereas the patristic view of the world and of man starts with the sacraments so as to illuminate creation, the medieval view sets out on a complementary path: it is intent on deciphering the way from creaturely experience to the Christian sacraments, the summit of history. The difficulty is in describing how nature, the bearer of symbolism from the very beginning, is taken up into liturgical language. In order to hit the mark, the masters ask themselves: what is the connection and what is the difference between a "creaturely sign" and a "sacramental sign"?

The question is situated, moreover, in a broader scheme: elucidating a general concept of sacrament. Starting from this, it becomes easier to discover traces of the sacramental logic in the cosmos and in man. In this way the effort to systematize sacramental doctrine opens the door to a major influence of philosophy. As far as the symbolic value of creatures is concerned, the medieval theologians drank from the two springs whose abundance I mentioned: St. Augustine and Dionysius. The framework within which the Middle Ages understand the sacraments is defined by the Augustinian concept of sign, frequently interpreted, however, in terms of the light and vision, according to the approach of Dionysius. This does not always avoid a certain neo-Platonic contagion: diminishing the importance of the material

31. Dionysius the Areopagite, *De coelesti hierarchia* II, 3 (SC 58:80).
32. Ibid., II, 1 (SC 58:74).

sign so as to judge that we can do away with it once we have arrived at what is signified, which is heavenly and spiritual. Let us analyze some features of this synthesis.

Hugh of St. Victor already proposed a definition of sacrament that explicitly integrated the creaturely element. The sacrament—besides the signification (*significatio*) which exists when God institutes it in history, and besides the sanctification (*sanctificatio*) or effective communication of grace through the administration of the sacrament—contains a similitude (*similitudo*) or likeness with the created order, for example, the power of water to cleanse in baptism.[33] What is creaturely, then, becomes included in what is sacramental as an element that is indispensable for an understanding thereof.[34]

Medieval thinkers agree moreover on one point: the economy of signs corresponds to man's condition in the flesh.[35] It is certain that sometimes the necessity of the sacrament is explained only in terms of the fall into sin: the voluntary submission to sensible elements that prostrated Adam requires as a remedy that man humble himself, receiving salvation from what is inferior (the flesh), thus inverting the preeminence of the spirit which our first parents enjoyed.[36] But we find another reason also: the sacrament is adapted to the creaturely condition of man, fashioned by God as body and soul.[37] In light of this the sacraments are given not only to heal sin, but also because they harmonize with human nature and fulfill it.[38]

Could creation itself be described, then, as a sacrament? In the response to this dilemma, the negative opinion of St. Thomas was influential. Aquinas recognizes a sign value in all things, for, according to St. Paul, the invisible nature of God made itself perceptible starting with the creation of the

33. Hugh of St. Victor, *De sacramentis* I, 9, 2 (PL 176:317d; *CV* 1:209–10): "sacramentum est corporale vel materiale elementum foris sensibiliter propositum ex similitudine repraesentans, et ex institutione significans, et ex sanctificatione continens aliquam invisibilem et spiritalem gratiam" (A sacrament is a bodily or material element outwardly and perceptibly proposed, by likeness representing, and by institution signifying, and by sanctification containing some invisible and spiritual grace).

34. Ibid., I, 9, 4 (PL 176:322b: *CV* 1:215): "primum Creator per maiestatem vasa formavit; postea Salvator per institutionem eadem proposuit; postremo dispensator per benedictionem haec ipsa mundavit; et gratiam implevit" (First the Creator formed these vessels by his majesty; next the Savior proposed them by his institution; finally the steward cleansed these same vessels by his blessing, and filled them with grace).

35. Thomas Aquinas, *ST* III, q. 61, a. 1; q. 60, a. 6. For St. Thomas the sacraments were not necessary in the original state in paradise; see *ST* III, q. 61, a. 2.

36. Hugh of St. Victor, *De sacramentis* I, 9, 3 (PL 176:319: *CV* 1:211).

37. Thomas Aquinas, *ST* III, q. 60, a. 6, co.

38. This relation between sacrament and man's incarnate condition is found already in the Fathers. See John Chrysostom, *Homily* 82, 4 (PG 58:743): "If you were incorporeal, [God] would have given you merely incorporeal gifts; but since the soul is united to a body, he entrusted spiritual realities to you through what is sensible."

world (Rom 1:19–20). There is no reality which does not signify something more beyond itself; in other words, every reality is a musical note in the orchestral score of the cosmos. The *doctor communis* prefers, nonetheless, not to apply the term "sacrament" to creatures. For creation, even though it is a sign of its maker, does not represent God to us as sanctifying; it does point to a divine reality, but not to a divine reality that bends down to man to overflow graciously upon him.[39] This is to say, creatures help us to understand the creator, but not to imagine the covenant that he desires to make with human beings.[40]

This conclusion, nevertheless, must be refined in light of the doctrine about the sacrament of matrimony, which acquires a special importance for this topic. Interesting in this regard is the opinion of St. Bonaventure, who says that marriage is the one sacrament that exists before sin, for it is not only a remedy but also an office, that is, collaboration in a mission entrusted by God and a sign of the definitive salvation in Christ and his church.[41] This presence of the sacrament already in Eden is possible because, while the other sacraments are conferred using material elements that are inferior to man, so that he might humble himself and thus receive the suitable remedy for his pride, in matrimony, on the contrary, the material used is the very body of the man and of the woman. This means that, in this sacrament subjecting oneself to what is bodily does not abase a human being but rather integrates his material dimension into the totality of his vocation and path. In fact, according to Bonaventure, in matrimony the body appears as the space of going out of oneself toward the other and of welcoming the beloved into oneself. And it helps us, therefore, to understand our radical dependence on the creator and our destiny of love in him. Matrimony, from this point of view, constitutes the root of the economy of the sacraments in the original constitution of man and of all creation. I will return to this point below.

---

39. Thomas Aquinas, *ST* III, q. 60, a. 2, ad 1: "creaturae sensibiles significant aliquid sacrum, scilicet sapientiam et bonitatem divinam, inquantum sunt in seipsis sacra, non autem in quantum nos per ea sanctificamur" (Sensible creatures signify something holy, *viz.* Divine wisdom and goodness, inasmuch as these are holy in themselves; but not inasmuch as we are made holy by them).

40. On the other hand, according to the same St. Thomas, who follows St. Augustine here, in all creation there are traces of the Trinity; the fullness is attained in man, where not only God's footprints but his very image dwells (Thomas Aquinas, *ST* I, q. 45, a. 7). All things, besides revealing by their form the beauty of the Son-Logos, give us to understand, by their origin from nothing, the generating action of the Father and, by their movement or impulse toward perfection, the dynamism that the Spirit of love imprints on them. This perspective is more open to accept the idea that creation appears to have sacramental features, not only inasmuch as it helps us to know the creator, but also because it leads us into the movement of love toward him.

41. Bonaventure, *In IV Sent.*, d. 26, a. 2, q. 1, resp. (Quaracchi 4:666); for this theme in Bonaventure, see José Granados, *Una sola carne en un solo Espíritu: Teología del matrimonio* (Madrid: Palabra, 2014), 129–34.

In summary, the medieval period confirms the harmony between the created world and the sacraments and delves into this connection. It is true, on the one hand, that medieval theology obscures somewhat the way in which they fulfill man's primordial incarnate condition. For it reinforces an outlook on the sacraments as a humiliation administered to Adam so that he might correct his sin, rather than as the culmination of an original vocation. In the theology of marriage, nevertheless, we can glimpse sacramental features of the body, prior to sin, which are in line with Pauline teaching (Eph 5:32) and the patristic view (in commentary on Jn 19:34 in light of Gn 2:24). In fact, this centrality of the language of the body in interpreting the symbolism of creation has been highlighted by contemporary theology. This language has been necessary in order to respond to some formidable challenges of the modern era; challenges that drastically affect the sacramental concept of the cosmos to which the Bible testifies.

The Modern Crisis of Symbolism and the Response of Catholic Theology

The ancient view of the cosmos was largely modified with the arrival of modernity. Contemporary man, in fact, has given up leafing through the universe as if it were a big book, or listening to it as he enjoys a symphony. What noise hushed this "correct, well-tuned sound / of the lute skillfully plucked" which enchanted Friar Luis de León so much?[42]

It is odd, as the philosopher Hans Jonas has remarked, that the theory which gave rise to the new view of the world, the theory which produced the industrial and technological revolution, was initially devised from the perspective of astronomy, which has so little practical application.[43] Investigating "how the heavens go" modified key presuppositions about the march of history and its direction.

Indeed, from the new outlook on the stars, the following conclusions

42. Creation is described as a big book: Alain de Lille, *Rhythmus alter* (PL 210:579a): "Omnis mundi creatura / quasi liber et pictura / nobis est speculum" (Every creature of the world, / like a book and a picture, / is a mirror for us). Hugh of St. Victor, *De tribus diebus* III (Corpus Christianorum: Continuatio Mediaevalis [hereafter CCCM] 177:9.94): "Universus enim mundus iste sensibilis quasi quidam liber est scriptus digito dei … et singulae creaturae quasi figurae quaedam sunt … ad manifestandam et quasi quodammodo significandam inuisibilem Dei sapientiam" (That entire perceptible world was written like a kind of book by the finger of God … and the individual creatures are like figures … to manifest and in some way to signify the invisible wisdom of God). See also St. Bonaventure, *Breviloquium* II, 12 (Quaracchi, V, line 1).

43. Hans Jonas, "Seventeenth Century and After: The Meaning of the Scientific and Technological Revolution," in his *Philosophical Essays: From Ancient Creed to Technological Man* (Chicago: University of Chicago Press, 1980), 45–80.

were drawn: matter is the same throughout the universe, just as corruptible on earth as between the stars. The moon, as the first telescopes revealed, is not an ideal sphere; and the sun, which was believed to be the image of the divine light, is in reality covered with spots. Therefore there is no cosmos with an orderly architecture, in which the higher spheres move the lower ones in a rhythmic merry-go-round, but rather a topsy-turvy, shapeless space. Moreover, this space has no concrete limits: rather, it is an infinitely expanding reality, almost all of it empty.

This new view of the homogeneous, artless universe fostered the description of every natural movement by means of mechanical laws without a goal or purpose. Once the hierarchy on which the order of the ancient cosmos rested was abandoned, every change was reduced to the agitation of particles, according to forces of action and reaction, which sufficed to explain deterministically the future of the world.

One remarkable consequence is that any personal (free and conscious) cause that might impinge on this closed system ceased to exist. And this referred not only to the intervention of God, but also of man. The iron chains of the laws of physics left no room for the unforeseen caprices of freedom or for the verifying pretentions of logic. This gives rise to an outlook in which nature in itself has no goals, does not triumph or fail, does not arrive at the right or wrong harbor. Everything that has any knowledge with which to understand an end or any will to attain it falls within the realm of the interior, subjective mind. The world proves to be foreign to what is properly human.

Let us consider the new way of understanding the symbolism or language of things that is deduced from this. It becomes impossible to see things as syllables that spell out a horizon of meaning. For the links between objects, their mutual references, are confined to mathematical equations, without origin or goal. If the universe has its own intelligible, profound language this is only a projection by man, by his intentions and plans. If the world can be described as sacramental it is only because the human being imposes meanings on it or because he assigns to objects purposes that are extrinsic to them.

It is true that romanticism later reacted against this loss of enchantment in the cosmos: people once again spoke about the mystery of nature and conceived of it as a space of adventures. And thus there was an attempt to restore to the world and to human life a sacramental sense, some openness to the mystery.[44] However, the Romantics continued to regard man as the

44. Michel Deneken, "Les romantiques allemands, promoteurs de la notion d'Église sacrement

one solely responsible for meaning, this time not insofar as he understands the world, but rather insofar as he feels it and is emotionally moved by it. The cosmos, as such, remained blind to words and meanings; symbols were discerned in the interior looking-glass of emotion without ever passing beyond their subjective limits.

Note: I am not saying that symbolism has disappeared today. There were symbols in antiquity, and there are symbols in modern times. The difference lies not in the number of them, but rather in what a symbol is understood to be. The symbols of yesteryear clarified one another, constituting among themselves a harmony to which the human being belonged; I described them, in chapter 1, as proper symbols of the dwelling place. On the contrary, modern symbols prove to be extraneous to the things themselves: they are projections that man makes between obscure things in terms of his clear mind; the symbols do not form among themselves a space or a fabric, but rather all refer to the isolated, nondimensional point of subjectivity.

The theology of the sacraments can shed light on this crisis of contemporary culture. This is because, starting from the sacraments, the major break between the meaning of life and the architecture of the cosmos is mended. The patristic and medieval view showed us this: Jesus, in bringing history to fulfillment, included all matter in himself, through his body. The human body, then, is precisely the key to reinterpreting in a new form the language of the universe and to recovering it as a possible home for man.[45]

Catholic theology in recent times has again proposed this sacramental outlook on the world.[46] This attempt tries to bring the sacraments closer to man's everyday experience[47] and to present them as the key to any theology of creation. This path promises to be fruitful, provided that deviations and exaggerations are avoided.

Deviations can occur if the symbolism generated by the sacraments ends up being a mere projection of the mind upon reality. For in this way the

---

du salut? Contribution à l'étude de la génèse de l'expression Église sacrement du salut," *Recherches de science religieuse* 67, no. 2 (1993): 55–74.

45. Kenneth L. Schmitz, *The Gift: Creation* (Milwaukee, Wis.: Marquette University Press, 1982).

46. Dionisio Borobio, *Sacramentos y creación: de la sacramentealidad creatural-cósmica a los sacramentos de la Iglesia* (Salamanca: Secretariado Trinitario, 2009); Hans Boersma, *Nouvelle Théologie and Sacramental Ontology: A Return to Mystery* (Oxford: Oxford University Press, 2009); Arno Schilson, "Symbolwirklichkeit und Sakrament: Ein Literaturbericht," *Liturgisches Jahrbuch* 40 (1990): 26–52; Peter Hünermann, "Die sakramentale Struktur der Wirklichkeit: Auf dem Weg zu einem erneuerten Sakramentenverständnis," *Herder-Korrespondenz* 36 (1982): 340–45, and "Sakrament, Figur des Lebens," in *Ankunft Gottes und Handeln des Menschen: Thesen über Kult und Sakrament*, ed. R. Schaeffler and P. Hünermann (Freiburg: Herder, 1977), 51–87.

47. The little work by Leonardo Boff, *Los sacramentos de la vida y la vida de los sacramentos* (Bogotá: Indo-American Press Service, 1975), is effective in this regard, although it tends to understand symbols as a projection of man upon things, and not as their own language.

enterprise is shipwrecked on the same reef that we wanted to avoid. In fact, drawn in by the disincarnate modern trend, some sacramental interpretations of experience have ended up proposing a symbolism on behalf of man, his intentions and ends. And thus, instead of reinterpreting creation in a Christian way, they have reinterpreted the Christian in terms of the modern mindset, reducing the sacrament to a subjective way of looking at things. For example, the doctrines of transsignification or transfinalization, which became fashionable toward the end of the past century to explain the presence of Jesus in the Eucharist, stumbled into this danger.

Exaggerations result when creaturely sacraments are not distinguished from the seven sacraments and theologians act as though the whole world were already a saving sacrament. If that were the case, what would the seven from Jesus do for us? For us to be saved, then, would it not be enough to discover the sacraments of the cosmos in which God revealed himself, through which he was already saving us? In order to differentiate one kind of sacrament from another, it will be essential to recover the vision of biblical typology, according to which signs run through history and have different ways of being actualized in time. I will thus end up distinguishing the sacraments according to the distinct stages of man's salvation, while safeguarding the newness of Jesus.[48]

Creation: Sacramental Space

To propose a synthesis, I will start, true to the method used above, with the Eucharist. Having reached the summit of his journey, Jesus interpreted his work from the perspective of the offering of bread and wine, which he identified with his body and blood given up for mankind. In this way he shed light on the meaning of every human life: it is before all else life in the flesh and, more precisely, life situated in the world, open to brethren, grateful to the creator. Besides, because this life, symbolized by blood, carries within itself the vital breath of the Spirit, it is also life proceeding from God and destined to dwell with him. In addition, by associating his rite with bread and wine, Jesus unveiled the mystery of the cosmos: creation groans with the pangs of childbirth so that it might fulfill its vocation and participate through the human body in the fullness of the Son (Rom 8:19–23). Analyzing these sentences will lead to a description of the whole of creation as a *sacramental space*.

48. Joseph Ratzinger, "Die sakramentale Begründung christlicher Existenz," in his *Gesammelte Schriften*, 11:197–214; "The Sacramental Foundation of Christian Existence," in *Collected Works*, 11:153–68.

The Body, Opening for a Network of Relations

The rite of Jesus invites us to look at life from the viewpoint of its incarnate condition. In the biblical perspective, assumed by Christ, *the body places us in the world*; through it we belong to the environment (of things and persons) that surrounds us. It is possible, in fact, to speak about the body as a first house or home, as it opens up for us the network of familial relations that receives us at birth and always accompanies us as the background of our journey.[49]

This wards off a view of man as an isolated consciousness who looks at the universe from a distance. On the contrary, the human person is always a relational person, who feels from within the surrounding world and who needs a space of interpersonal connections in order to encounter himself and to survey his path. According to this approach, the affective sphere of life plays a leading role: the affections enable us to connect with what surrounds us, to become involved in each tie, to inhabit our surroundings, and allow it to inhabit us.

Still, this habitat of man in the world is always open to something more, to discovery and surprise: before us are unfurled relations into which we can delve and which thus enrich us. It can be said, therefore, that the bodily space in which we live is a *symbolic space*, because it refers us beyond itself.[50] Note that the symbolism proves to be a feature, not of isolated objects, but rather of the space constituted by the encounter between the human being and his world. In this way it becomes clear that symbols do not drive us toward a further, disincarnate reality; rather, they invite us to delve into this network of relations in which our body places us.[51] Abraham went out from his land, but only because God promised him another land that was more filled with his presence. Let us see what depths are hidden in the symbolic space of our belonging to the world.

This bodily space is symbolic, in the first place, *inasmuch as it points beyond itself toward the origin from which we proceed*. Indeed, the body is the emblem of how much in life anticipates us; of how much exists here

---

49. For this reason Gabriel Marcel was able to say in *Homo viator: prolégomènes à une métaphysique de l'espérance* (Paris: Aubier, 1963), 90–91: "Between the mystery of the union of soul and body and the familial mystery there is a profound unity, which sometimes has been little emphasized: in both cases we are in the presence of one and the same fact or, rather, of something more than a fact, because it is the very condition for any possible fact: incarnation."

50. For a more extensive development of this idea, see chapter 11 below.

51. Buber, "Sinnbildliche," distinguishes the sign-epiphany from the biblical sign; the first reveals or shows the covenant and is like the mirror of the invisible; the second establishes the covenant, and is like a hand that meets another hand: "hand in hand the covenant is signed and renewed" (352).

already, welcoming us from the very start, preceding our work and making it possible: the presence of our parents and siblings, our belonging to this place and to this people, and so on. In an immediate way our body refers us to another earlier body: to our mother's womb and to the conjugal love "in one flesh" that generated us and welcomed us into the world. Precisely the sexual difference, set within the bodies of our father and mother, and not designed by them, invites us to open entirely our horizon of memory so that it points to the creator; he united husband and wife and made them fruitful for the sake of children, shaping our embryo in the womb. Thus, through the love of our parents, our body reveals the presence of God as the good origin of life. The symbolic space of the body is constituted as a filial space, entirely oriented around the magnetic pole of an original donation.

If the sexual difference of our parents opens up our origin toward the mystery of love and of God's creative action, this same difference is then experienced in our own body as a vocation to love between husband and wife. The symbolic space that welcomed us when we came into the world asks us to continue building upon this spousal bond. Our sexed condition, by situating us in the presence of the other, male or female, who cannot be reduced to our point of view, prevents us from enclosing in our subjectivity (reducing it to an isolated point) the space of our incarnate presence in the world. For this reason the polarity man-woman is an indispensable hinge for structuring the symbolic space and opening it up to the presence of the mystery. In fact the Song of Songs situates in the bodily union of the lover and the beloved (and not in the solitary body of the human being) the complete microcosm where all creation is gathered to reflect the divine love.[52]

The ability of the symbolic space marked out by the sexual difference to be open to what is beyond it, is revealed radically with *the birth of a child*. Here we plainly discover that the symbolism of the body, pointing to the life that is coming, does not impel us to overcome space in such a way as to leave our incarnate condition behind. For the unheard-of novelty of the child occurs only in the bodily habitat of the union of the parents and needs it in order to subsist: this environment, as a familial network and as a dwelling place, will be the one that welcomes and sustains the new life. Here too, in generation, it becomes evident that the bodily space is open toward the active presence of the creator, the sole source of life. So the first woman sang: "I have gotten a man with the help of the LORD" (Gn 4:1), and the first man discovered this when he generated an heir according to the divine image and likeness (see Gn 1:26 and 5:3).

52. Robert Alter, "The Garden of Metaphor," in his *The Art of Biblical Poetry* (New York: Basic Books, 1985), 231–54.

What I have said confirms that the opening of the space of relations (its symbolism) occurs not through an elevation to other realities foreign to this space, but rather by delving more deeply into the network of bonds that it interweaves within itself. How does this process of deepening come about? The bodily experiences just described, by referring to the memory of filiation, to the fidelity of a spousal relationship, and to the generative openness of the future, reveal that the symbolic space is enriched through maturation in time: *the line that opens the symbolic space to things beyond itself is the line along which history runs.*

We can compare this space in which the body situates us, according to an image taken from Song of Songs 4:16–5:1, with a garden which protects the furrows where its seeds fell (memory of the past) and which shows in hope the sure fruit (fecundity of the future). In fact, in the biblical text cited, the garden refers both to the orchard where the lovers meet and to the union of their bodies. The Eucharist already pointed in this direction, as the sacrament that structures incorporation into Jesus according to a temporal axis, from origin to consummation: "do this in memory of me," "until he comes" (1 Cor 11:26).

Symbolic Language of the Body and Experience of Love

In order to finish describing the symbolic space of the body (which contains the key to the sacramentality of creation), I need to highlight two other dimensions of it. In the first place, this space comes to be symbolic space only because a word crosses through it and thus orders and orients it in time. Without the word, our affective presence among things and persons loses its clear contours and becomes amorphous. In the Eucharist, too, the fullness of all symbolic space, the *words* of Jesus resound, which speak about a "body for you" and, as *todah*, thank the Father for the flesh which he will gave back to him glorified. In the second place, the conjunction of body and word, by itself, would remain a rigid structure; in order to acquire symbolism capable of maturing beyond itself there has to follow within it the experience of personal love, which enlivens and activates the space of our presence in the world. Then, too, the environment of relations opened up by Jesus in his Last Supper invoked the descent of the eternal Spirit, by virtue of whom he was able to offer himself as victim of the sacrifice (Heb 9:14) and rejoin his disciples once he was risen. I will elaborate briefly on these two dimensions of the sacramental space.

First, the symbolic space of the body is a space where the word resounds. The Bible recounts for us how Adam learned to speak: the birth of language did not happen in the depth of the mind, by abstract reflection, but rather required a concrete environment: that of the encounter between the man and his world. First, Adam named the animals, deciphering in this way their essence and thus establishing a place for each one in the totality of the cosmos. Then, upon discovering Eve, the personal word was born, capable of calling the other by his unique name; capable also of being declined for the first time as a verb, and thus of narrating a story of freedom (Gn 2:24: "Therefore a man leaves his father and his mother and clings to his wife, and they become one flesh").

All this confirms that the word is not Adam's projection onto the world, but rather is born in his encounter with creatures; in order to be pronounced, the word needs the cosmic and interpersonal space represented in the Garden. In turn, this space of Eden, without the word, would not be habitable; the word is what configures it, determining the place of each thing (and of each affection) in the whole, and channeling it in time, from its origin in God toward a fruitful destiny according to the divine promise.

In the experience of the children of Adam, too, language is engendered in the space of an encounter. It is, before all else, a word received from our parents, who transmit to us a native tongue, forged from generation to generation. It resounds originally as a proper name that the parents assign to the child, reminding him of his provenance and hinting at his vocation (*nomen, omen*). This elucidates the connection between flesh and word. On the one hand, the name is received only in the generative space of the family, for outside of that space it sounds like an unreasonable, controlling imposition. On the other hand, the name is necessary to order the filial space and to give it a direction in time, as a reminder that one belongs to a tradition and as a preparation for one's destiny.

Another word, that of the spousal promise, also proves to be deeply rooted in the bodily space of our presence in the world, this time in what concerns our sexed condition. Indeed, the conjugal space of the "one flesh" (Gn 2:24), structured according to the difference of male and female, is humanly habitable only when it is crossed by the spousal promise of mutual acceptance and self-giving. Without this word, which assures fidelity all the days of their life, the spouses' exchange of their bodies entails an implicit lie. On the other hand, a word of such great scope, which bonds in such a close union and extends the common history toward the future of children, can be given only in the space of the sexual difference between the spouses.

Word and flesh, then, call for each other. I have already noted that medieval philosophers described the cosmos as a big book, and that this view is rendered unlikely in the sidereal space of modern science. From the perspective of the covenant between flesh and word that I have proposed, nevertheless, it becomes possible to recover such an outlook. For the reason why the incarnate space that situates us in the world is crossed by the word (the reason why in this space one can receive a name and pronounce a spousal promise) is because there is a language of the body. And this language can be expanded to all material things so as to rediscover, with Dante, "how God's love binds the universe together into a book."[53]

Second, for man to be able to inhabit the symbolic space, the network of relations that is interwoven there is not enough, nor is the order that the word confers on it. This space becomes sterile unless it is the scene of a gratuitous experience that cannot be deduced from the bonds alone and the words alone: the experience of love. Thus, the child who is born of his parents is bonded to them indissolubly and his vital space is always configured starting from them; but this relation can turn out to be oppressing, enigmatic for one's own identity (as it was for Oedipus), if it is not inhabited by paternal and maternal love and by the filial response. The same can be said about the encounter of man and woman: only interpersonal love makes the relation between the two habitable, filling it with life; without love, the space opened up by the sexual difference is the space of mutual domination, a space that ends by falling back on two one-dimensional individuals.

The symbolic space of the body invokes, therefore, the experience of love; and for its part, love can be enkindled only within this symbolic space. *On the one hand*, without the space of the body, which affectively links man and his world, love would prove to be superficial, incapable of being a unitive force of two beings or of touching them within and transforming them. Only thanks to the body is it possible for a child to belong to a family, to bear a name and surnames as his own and not as artificial accoutrements; thanks to the body, husband and wife can be radically one and assign a name to the child who is born of their union. *On the other hand*, only thanks to love can the space of relations in which the body situates us enlarge our life. Without filial love, the relationship with one's parents weighs like a chain from which we want to free ourselves without success, for we will always bear their mark. Without conjugal love, the promise of marriage proves to be a yoke that imprisons, obliging us to plow a land that is not ours. Following the saying of Jesus, we could say that the body, by itself, is of no avail; it is love (the Spirit) that gives life (Jn 6:63); without forgetting that this saying

53. See Dante, *Paradiso* XXXIII, 86–87.

comes from the incarnate Word, who dwelt among us (Jn 1:14) to enliven with his love the space of relations opened up in the body.

Marriage, Original Sacrament

What I have said leads to the conclusion: the symbolic space of our installation in the world, a space rooted in the body, ordered by the word and enlivened by love, sets up its pillars on the experiences of marriage and family.[54] This corroborates the insight of Bonaventure mentioned above: marriage is the original sacrament in which the human body, in its ability to express love, reveals the highest vocation of man and woman. It is an insight developed by St. John Paul II, who would call marriage "the primordial sacrament."[55]

This fact is confirmed by the pages of the New Testament. I have already noted that the Greek term *mysterion*, from which the Latin word *sacramentum* is derived, is not applied in the Bible either to baptism or to the Eucharist, but appears in reference to marriage (Eph 5:31).[56] St. Paul discovers in conjugal union a key for interpreting the march of salvation history from its origins down to Jesus. The love of Adam and Eve pointed to the charity that would unite Christ with his church in one flesh. Hence marriage serves as a grammar to express the *mysterion,* that is, the epiphany of the divine plan in the incarnation, death, and resurrection of the Son, who recapitulates all human beings in one body. This insight of the apostle coincides with the teaching of Jesus, for whom marriage is what God has united from the beginning (Mt 19:6–8). In this way the master confirms the opening of conjugal love to the creator's love. Marriage, then, acquires strategic importance in understanding how all creation, through the love of man and woman, becomes open to the presence and action of God and sets out toward Christ.

The Eucharist, too, the central rite of Jesus, takes up the connection between marriage and the *mysterion.* As I mentioned above, when Christ at his Last Supper uses the language of the body given up; when he recapitulates in himself the memory of his people and entrusts it to his disciples; when he anticipates the fruitful future of the resurrection ... he is supposing as a background the familial experiences that enable us to interpret his gift of self. On the one hand, only from the viewpoint of the Eucharist can

---

54. For the following discussion, see Granados, *Una sola carne.*

55. John Paul II, *Man and Woman He Created Them: A Theology of the Body,* catechesis 98, 1–2 (October 20, 1982), 510–11; available at www.vatican.va.

56. It is worth noting that a Protestant theologian has advocated recovering the biblical basis for the sacramentality of marriage, precisely insofar as St. Paul associates it closely with the *mysterion* in Eph 5:31: Pannenberg, *Systematic Theology,* 3:391–98.

we understand the radical goodness of our incarnate condition and of the vocation inscribed in our flesh. On the other hand, only in terms of these experiences, based on marriage, does the meaning of "a body for you" make sense, as well as the participation in his flesh and in his vital narrative, a participation promised by Jesus to his followers.

Precisely because the creaturely symbolism of the body not only prepares for the Eucharist but also is taken up into it and perfected by it, it is possible to speak about marriage as a sacrament of the New Law. This inclusion of matrimony among the seven is based on the continuity (which we saw attested by the Church Fathers) between the original language of the body and the new body inaugurated by Jesus, on which Christians feed. This means that someone who is nourished by the Eucharist and lives according to the measure of the body of Christ, necessarily will experience his bodily relations also in a new way, starting with the most original ones. For this reason baptized spouses, by inaugurating the space of the "one flesh," inaugurate it according to the measures of the space of the body of Jesus. And thus they build a Eucharistic space in which their way of experiencing filiation, fraternity, paternity, and the married state are transformed, for these have always pointed to Christ and have been enriched by him.[57]

I maintain, therefore, that thanks to marriage, the Eucharist, and in it the other sacraments, welcome the original experiences of the creaturely body that I have described as an original symbolic space. In this way matrimony assures that the sacraments are rooted in the flesh and in human history, for it acts as a hinge between the primordial "sacraments" of human experience and the sacraments of the new life of Jesus. Marriage, therefore, besides being one of the seven, proves to belong to the very definition of sacrament, inasmuch as it links the salvific sign to the order of creation.

From the Human Body to the Entire Cosmos

Starting from the Eucharist and still in reference to the body which is handed over in it, a light rises to illuminate the architecture of creation and its path in history. The reason why flesh and blood—taking up the bread and wine—are capable of containing and communicating the communion of God with human beings and of human beings among themselves, is because the human body, taking up into itself the whole cosmos, already and necessarily harbored a seed of that fruit from its very origins.

---

57. Andrea Bozzolo, "Amore coniugale e mistero cristologico: Sulla sacramentalità del matrimonio," in his *Il rito di Gesù: Temi di teologia sacramentaria* (Rome: Libreria Ateneo Salesiano, 2013), 215–304.

Ancient man had intuited this ability of the body to recapitulate the distinct strata of the universe. The Jewish legends explain how God, in forming Adam, took dust from the four corners of the Earth—north, south, east, and west—thus summing up all creation in the first-formed man.[58] This corresponds to the description of the human being as a microcosm, a mortar in which bits of everything that exists are mixed, both bodily and spiritual.

Still, the light that rises from the Eucharist reveals more to us: not only that the body sums up the regions of created being, but also that the body is called to be extended so as to house within it all creation, in such a way that the incipient language of things can come to fulfillment. For one can look at the mountains, the sea, the rivers, and all aspects of creation, sensing that the human body enters into harmony with them, but recognizing at the same time that this body in its littleness is incapable of expressing such immense glory. From Jesus, however, it is confirmed that the glorious language of the mountains, seas, and rivers is a radiance of the glory that is contained in the human body, as Christ experienced it and hands it over to Christians, in anticipation of the final resurrection. For this reason the Gospel of John insists not that bread is made body, but rather that the body is the true bread; for in the body—received from God, open to communion with the brethren—is the fullness of what it means to eat.[59]

From this springs the outlook on the cosmos that draws on the tradition of the bestiaries, begun by the *Physiologus*, in which each animal is interpreted according to its meaning in the order of nature, but with a decisive climax in Jesus and in the narrative of his life. Thus the eagle which, according to ancient science, finds springs of living water so as to rejuvenate itself, prefigures baptism, in which the human being is reborn.[60] And when the serpent, before coming near to drink, leaves its venom in its den, this prefigures that as we approach baptism we must reject the poison of a wicked life.[61]

The sacraments, in short, confirm and enlarge what we intuit in our original experience: the human body, the only one that the creator deemed worthy of shaping with his hands, according to the insight of Theophilus of Antioch,[62] the only one capable of pronouncing in conjugal love the word that lasts until death, the only one that can hope beyond hope and

---

58. Louis Ginzberg, *The Legends of the Jews* (Philadelphia: The Jewish Publication Society of America, 1913), 55.

59. Beauchamp, "Le signe des pains," 66.

60. *Physiologus* 6, ed. O. Schönberger (Frankfurt: Reclam, 2001), 12.

61. *Physiologus* 11 (20).

62. Theophilus of Antioch, *Ad Autolycum* II, 18 (SC 20:145).

bring to the world the personal newness of each birth ... this human body possesses the key to recovering the symbolism of the cosmos and of history. Thus we can understand the comparison used by St. John Chrysostom in his baptismal sermons: just as the grapevine keeps its leaves during the time in which it must protect and nourish the roots, so too the universe keeps its heavenly bodies during the time in which it must protect and nourish the human being.[63]

This final image reminds us once more that the symbolic space in which our body situates us is a space open to maturation. The sacramental features that the cosmos possesses do not imply, therefore, that it already communicates salvation to us, but rather it points toward it in hope, just as the leaves give us a presentiment of the fruit. This opens up for the sacraments a road in history, a road that the people of Israel will travel until its maturity in Jesus. I will dedicate the next chapter to a study of the steps of this route.

63. John Chrysostom, *Eight Baptismal Catecheses* III, 3 (SC 50:152).

7 ✍ SACRAMENTS OF HISTORY

The Old Covenant

The reason that the Christian sacraments can harbor within them the entire creation—water, oil, bread and wine, body and blood—is because they take it up through the history of Israel. Indeed, the rites of Jesus were prefigured in the Old Testament: from the offering of the just Abel and the sacrifice of Abraham, our father in faith; from the anointing of kings and prophets and the consecration of priests. Only this slow novitiate of the old covenant allows us to understand the sacraments of Jesus. For note well: the old sacrifices are not only anticipations of the fulfillment, but integral elements of the new rite, columns used to build it.

This chapter's account of the "sacraments" of Israel is inspired precisely by their inclusion in the Eucharist. I will carry out a *Eucharistic* interpretation of the Old Testament, which will highlight the sacrifice and the covenant, the Passover and the *todah*. In no way does this mean imposing on the Old Testament an outline foreign to it; on the contrary, the Eucharistic outlook will help to make evident from the pages of the Bible themselves the thread that strings them together. The new rites are hidden in the old ones; the old ones manifest their truth by being included in the new ones.

Religious Ritual

The Bible does not present ritual as something belonging exclusively to the holy people of God; on the contrary, it is practiced by the Gentiles and is part of universal culture. Even though foreign worship is frequently denounced as idolatrous, Israel is acquainted with a positive version of it. For from the perspective of the experience of the covenant, in which divine service has an essential place, the religious journey of every human being is illuminated. The history of humanity before Abraham is marked with ritual milestones, like the offering of Abel (Gn 4:3) or the sacrifice of Noah (Gn 8:20).

How did man come to be a "ritual animal"?[1] Modernity accused ritual of being infantile, doomed to give way to the adult forms of progress.[2] Ritual, nevertheless, obstinately reemerged, as noted by contemporary sociology, which assigns it various roles, like helping the individual to perceive the collective consciousness of the group,[3] or lending unity to the heterogeneous functions of the complex society that we live in.[4]

However, can ritual be explained solely in terms of making common life convenient? Modern ritual studies describe it as "formal behavior prescribed for occasions not given over to technological routine that have reference to beliefs in mystical beings or powers."[5] Moreover these features of it are noted: it is *collective*, because it is always celebrated in a group; it is *traditional*, because it is inherited and transmitted with few changes; it has the ability to give *direction* or orientation to life; it is not designed by reflection or thought but instead is inherited as a *space from which one can think.*[6]

All of this shows us that ritual not only discharges a function within society but also is a foundation thereof. This is demonstrated by studies that associate it with the birth of language, with the forging of personality from infancy, with the emergence of the question about meaning, and so on.[7] The Bible, too, for its part, measures the unity and the path of the people in terms of divine worship, and not vice versa: the liberation of Israel, its birth as a people, is entirely oriented toward its adoration of God on the mountain (Ex 3:18).

In fact, in order to do justice to the very experience of ritual we have to

1. On ritual, see Angelini, *Il tempo e il rito*; Louis Bouyer, *Rite and Man: Natural Sacredness and Christian Liturgy* (Notre Dame, Ind.: University of Notre Dame Press, 1967); Mircea Eliade, *The Sacred and the Profane* (New York: Harcourt, Brace and World, 1959); Jean-Yves Hameline, "Éléments d'anthropologie, de sociologie historique et de musicologie du culte chrétien," *Recherches de science religieuse* 78 (1990): 397–424, and "Aspects du rite," *La Maison Dieu* 119 (1974): 101–11; François Isambert, *Rite et efficacité symbolique: Essai d'anthropologie sociologique* (Paris: Cerf, 1979); Victor W. Turner, *The Ritual Process: Structure and Anti-structure* (London: Routledge, 1969), and *From Ritual to Theatre: The Human Seriousness of Play* (New York: Performing Arts Journal Publications, 1982); and Arnold van Gennep, *Les rites de passage* (Paris: Emile Nourry, 1909).

2. Auguste Comte, *Cours de philosophie positive*, vol. 5 (Paris: Baillière, 1864).

3. Émile Durkheim, *The Elementary Forms of the Religious Life* (London: George Allen and Unwin, Ltd., 1915).

4. Niklas Luhmann, *La religión de la sociedad* (Madrid: Trotta, 2007).

5. Victor Turner and Edith Turner, *Image and Pilgrimage in Christian Culture: Anthropological Perspectives* (New York: Columbia University Press, 1978), 243.

6. Ronald L. Grimes, "Defining Nascent Ritual," *Journal of the American Academy of Religion* 50 (1982): 539–55, at 541.

7. Hameline, "Éléments d'anthropologie."

affirm that at its origins we find no human plan that consciously or unconsciously designs it for utilitarian purposes and the common good. Ritual is born from a more original event, which is the manifestation of the sacred or *hierophany*, which appears to the celebrant as the genuine, real thing, as the power that moves and organizes everything. Let us see how authentic life becomes possible only in the space opened up by this presence, as opposed to the emptiness of other mundane spheres not touched by the sacred.

In the first place, the hierophany distinguishes the sacred environment from the profane, thus giving structure to the space of the world. Ritual helps to anchor the earth in the divine, to establish a center that orients the cosmos, orders it and, in this way, allows man to inhabit it.[8] Hence the mission of many rituals is to actualize the cosmogony, the moment in which the first habitable space was generated, assuring the solidity of the pillars that support it against the chaos of matter. The Bible accepts this view: Noah, after the flood, erected an altar; then God promised never again to inundate the ground (Gn 8:20–21).

This sacred place is *par excellence* the *temple*, where the pillars of the universe are raised. But also the rooms of the *dwelling*, inasmuch as one experiences in them the mystery of the beginning and end of life; it is very common, for example, to venerate thresholds, which delimit spaces and allow transitions between them. From this perspective it is understandable that ritual always requires the participation of the *body*, the original "place" where man dwells, where he becomes open to others and is situated in the world. The ritual space is built, in fact, on the connection between body, dwelling, and cosmos. For this reason the form of the altar or sanctuary corresponds to distinct parts of the organism; and the ritual action corresponds to the various organic functions.[9]

In the second place, rites also help us to *orient ourselves in time*. This is the context for the theory about the "rites of passage" described by Arnold van Gennep, the inventor of this terminology, which Victor Turner rediscovered and popularized.[10] Van Gennep spoke of what is "liminal" (from the Latin *limen*, threshold) to refer to the transitions between stages of life. Rituals help man to pass through them, ensuring that as he does so he receives help from on high and does not upset the balance with the community and the cosmos. Van Gennep focuses on the vital steps of the individual

---

8. Eliade, *The Sacred and the Profane*, chap. 1.

9. Ibid., 173.

10. Van Gennep, *Les rites de passage*; Turner, *The Ritual Process*; Mircea Eliade, *Naissances mystiques: Essai sur quelques types d'initiation* (Paris: Gallimard, 1959), translated as *Birth and Rebirth: The Religious Meanings of Initiation* (New York: Harper, 1958).

and distinguishes various rites: of *separation* (as in funerals), of *transition* (a pregnancy, a betrothal), of *incorporation* (such as a marriage, an initiation to adult life).

These transitions refer not only to the individual but also to the community and to the cosmos. So it is, for example, in festivals of the new year. They help to repair the damage or attrition of being that time brings with it, which can be observed in the course of the seasons toward winter. The ritual puts the world in contact with the divine—with a sacred time that does not pass or diminish—so as to reenergize the march of the universe, so that the cycle can begin again and in its dance can follow the wheel of the generations.[11]

In summary, ritual situates us in the space of the world, which is sustained by the power of God, and it allows us to travel through time by means of contact with the divine eternity. The two dimensions are of course connected: when the sanctuary is built one builds the year also, with all its days, as the temple (*templum*) is the place where time (*tempus*) is regenerated—words that are etymologically related.[12]

To conclude, I should add that the dimension of ritual that I have described contains also decadent elements which, far from preserving the genuine experience, smother it. Think of formalism, in which the person hides behind the rite, as though behind a mask, so as not to put himself in jeopardy in his action; or of the kind of ritual falsehood which is idolatry, adoration of oneself in the work of one's own hands; or of magic, in which the ritual intends to dominate reality for the benefit of the isolated individual. Even if they are free of such deformations, primitive rituals suffer from a break with ordinary life: ritual situates man outside of the normal course of his days so as to allow him some contact with the eternal and, only in this way, to reintegrate him into the rhythm of his days, which by themselves are decadent. These limitations, nevertheless, do not contradict our positive appreciation of ritual. On the contrary, only by means of ritual can a space and time be established with horizons sufficiently broad for the person and the community to pass through life.

The Sacraments of Israel over the Course of Its History

The universal experience of ritual just described is included in the Bible, where it is purified and transformed in terms of God's covenant with Israel.

11. Eliade, *The Sacred and the Profane*, chap. 2.

12. As Eliade notes, in some primitive peoples, in order to say that a year has passed, they say that the world has passed (*The Sacred and the Profane*, 73). On the relation *Templum-tempus*, see ibid., 75, and Hermann Usener, *Götternamen* (Bonn, 1920), 191.

Here too there is a relation between rite and man's space and time. Let us begin with the ritual-time connection, given its predominance in scripture.

Ritual: Time of Salvation

A distinctive characteristic of biblical ritual is that it synchronizes man with the rhythm of a history of salvation.[13] This already becomes evident in the Jewish Passover. The sacrifice of the lamb and the blood smeared on the doorposts and lintels ransoms the firstborn sons, the hope of the next generations. This ransom, in turn, implies the new birth in the Red Sea, whose waters are both the tomb of the old life and also like the maternal womb for the new. We see that the ritual is thus bound up with filiation and with the fruitfulness of a new beginning.

Still, the movement that introduces Passover does not end at the Red Sea: it is prolonged until Sinai, which is also a place of worship, according to the sign that Yahweh gave Moses when he spoke to him from the burning bush (Ex 3:12): Israel will go out of Egypt to serve God in the desert. On the one hand, the liturgy of Sinai will be marked by the remembrance of the Red Sea: the rite, from now on, will revive the memory and, in doing so, will actualize this original event that has never stopped happening, for God continually generates his people.

Sinai, moreover, shows that the time of salvation requires patience and maturation. Israel is born of the waters, but that is not enough for it to receive new life from God. It is important for the people to cross the desert, to have a time of trial, when the remembrance of the benefits fades and it has to cultivate faith in the promise. It is a matter of Israel being educated like a son and of generating within itself a freedom that is capable of responding to God. Specifically, the new worship celebrated on the mountain ("they ate and drank": Ex 24:11) and the sacrifices that are commanded there give shape to this path of growth.

Then the Book of Exodus explains that on the holy mountain, in the same environment of worship, the Law of God is entrusted to the people. This is a distinctive feature of biblical ritual that proves to be inseparable from the Torah, which is instruction for the journey of life. On the one hand, worship is already collaboration between God and man and contains the dynamism of moral action. On the other hand, the words of the Law are heard only in the liturgical context in which they were heard and written: the reason why they are not an oppressive command is because they are born of the grateful recognition of divine salvation and of its promises.

13. Hahn, "Canon, Cult and Covenant."

Another contribution of the theophany on Sinai to Israel's route is that it establishes the everyday, institutional moments of worship that accompany the day-to-day activity of the people. Let us consider, on the one hand, the Sabbath; and, on the other hand, the building of the Temple. Thus the stability of ritual begins when Israel arrives in the Promised Land and offers the fruit of the earth that has matured. Whereas the worship started with God's generative action, today the son has grown and can make offerings from his own harvest: gratitude culminates when man gives thanks for the work of his hands blessed by Yahweh (Dt 26:1–3).

Inasmuch as ritual orients man in time, it keeps its relation with the biblical signs. For the sign is, on the one hand, a memorial, a remembrance of the saving action of God, who calls us to respond to his love in the covenant. Thus, in Exodus 13:9, the Passover is "a *sign* on your hand and a memorial between your eyes."[14] And the sign, in turn, reveals a future which requires man's collaboration. For example: God gave to Moses, as a sign, the fact that the whole people would adore him on the mountain (Ex 3:12); in order to be fulfilled, such a sign required that Moses set out on a journey, relying on that voice.[15] Note that the Sabbath too is a sign of the unfailing covenant between God and man (Ezek 20:17), for it reminds us that the creator is the origin of all fruitful activity of the children of Adam.

Worship, finally, in revealing to us the tempo of history, reveals to us also God as the Lord of all ages. In fact, the Israelite's profession of faith, when he presents the first fruits in the temple, consists of narrating the history of Yahweh with his people, beginning with Jacob, a wandering Aramean (Dt 26:1–11). We recognize the God of the Bible, as we recognize any person, when we hear his story. And by understanding in worship the name of the God who saves, Israel also understands itself, in its condition of favorite son.

We can conclude that *worship contains one outlook on the past* (God's blessings) *and another on the future* (the fruitfulness that he lavishes). Ritual is an event of memory, inasmuch as God's deed in rescuing Israel from Egypt is commemorated in it. Inasmuch as this deed is still promising, the remembrance of it, like the remembrance of a promise, will hasten our pace toward the future. For this reason biblical ritual is always open toward a definitive event that will justify the course of history. This event will take the form either of the abundant presence of God when he converts the entire

---

14. Thurian, *L'eucharistie*; P. A. Kruger, "Symbolic Acts Relating to Old Testament Treaties and Relationships," *Journal for Semitics* 2 (1990): 156–70.

15. Buber, "Sinnbildliche," 347.

Holy Land into a temple, or else of the sending of the Messiah, the shoot of the generations and rebuilder of the same sanctuary.

Sacrifice: Interpretation in the Major Key of Fatherhood

Starting from this journey of Israel in time, I can pause to explain the heart of worship: sacrifice. A sacrifice is at the origin of the promise made to Abraham (Gn 15:7–20), a sacrifice initiates the escape from Egypt (Ex 12:2–6), and another sacrifice serves as the goal of Moses's peregrinations (Ex 24:11).

There has been much debate about the significance of sacrifice in the Bible. What meaning does the death of an animal have when it is offered to God in a common meal? Our manner of speaking usually understands "sacrifice" in a negative sense: to make a sacrifice is to lose something; it involves some suffering; we associate it with the bloody death of the victim.

This, nevertheless, is not the original meaning of the term. Today sacrifices, in all cultures and specifically in biblical culture, are interpreted as a gift that unites man with God.[16] Note: God is not the one who needs this gift, but rather, in offering it, man acknowledges it as a previous gift from the Lord, from whom he received life and all things. In other words, the sacrifice expresses gratitude for the prior love of the creator so that his gifts can be received fully.

We should emphasize, therefore, a key element of sacrifice: it does not start with a human action but rather with a gift that is received from God. Therefore a sacrifice is something that Israel can in no way produce. Indeed, the fire that burns the victim has to come down from heaven, as in the story of Elijah (1 Kgs 18:38). In the Temple they preserved a perpetual flame with which to burn the sacrifices; the first spark of it had been taken from on high.[17]

Note how far we are from the extended sense of sacrifice as human loss: it is, on the contrary, a gain in being, and of a being which, because it is sacred, can only come down from God. From this perspective the principal aspect of sacrifice is gratitude which, in giving thanks for the divine gift, places it at God's disposal, so that thus this gift might become greater, inasmuch as it is experienced in communion with Yahweh. It is not surprising, in this light, that the Psalter places the sacrifice of *todah* or praise at the center of biblical spirituality. "I will praise the name of God with a song; I

---

16. For the relation between gift and sacrifice, see Sabourin, "Sacrifice"; Gerardus van der Leeuw, "Die *Do-ut-des* Formel in der Opfertheorie," *Archiv für Religionswissenschaft* 20 (1920–21): 241; and Roland de Vaux, *Instituciones del Antiguo Testamento* (Barcelona: Herder, 1976), 570.

17. Vanhoye, *Tanto amó Dios al mundo*; Robert J. Daly, "The Power of Sacrifice in Ancient Judaism and Christianity," *Journal of Ritual Studies* 4 (1990): 181–98.

will magnify him with thanksgiving. This will please the LORD more than an ox or a bull with horns and hoofs" (Ps 69:30–31).

This gift for which man has given thanks opens the way to unity with God, that is, to the consecration of the one who offers the sacrifice.[18] Therefore the sacrifice can be described also as communion with the divine.[19] Thus we see the importance of the sacred meal: one sits down at table with God so as to share the same life with him. From the perspective of this orbit of unity between God and men, the sacrifice appears also as a meeting of men with each other, resting on one and the same foundation; and therefore it promotes social cohesion.

One fact is especially emphasized in the Bible: *a sacrifice requires that blood be shed.* It is well known that blood is identified with a person's life. The sacrifice indicates, in this way, that the covenant is worth more than life, because without the covenant (without a relationship with God and, through him, with the rest of the people of God), life loses its meaning.[20] Moreover, given that life is not lost in a sacrifice, because the animal dies in man's place, we have to add: *the covenant makes possible a new life,* a life transformed in communion with God. This means that in a sacrifice something is added to life, for it is bound together with its creator. This bond is an increase of being that can be received only from the Lord: hence, as I said, it is up to him alone to initiate the ritual action. This makes it clear that the blood poured out does not signify a settling of accounts with a God who is thirsting for vengeance. Rather, this libation, which represents a person's life, invites the participants to acknowledge an original filial debt: life is possible only if its bond with its giver is accepted; far from shortening life, this bond expands it.

In light of this account of sacrifice we discover a key connection that associates *sacrifice and fatherhood.*[21] With the ransom of the firstborn sons in the exodus from Egypt we are reminded about another sacrifice that is

18. With respect to sacrifice as consecration, see Henri Hubert and Marcel Mauss, "Essai sur la nature et la fonction du sacrifice," *Année sociologique* 2 (1899): 29–138: "The procedure consists of establishing some communication between the sacred world and the profane world, using as the intermediary a victim, that is, a thing destroyed in the course of the ceremony."

19. For sacrifice as communion with the divinity by means of the sacred meal, see William Robertson Smith, *Lectures on the Religion of the Semites* (New York: MacMillan, 1927); Bouyer, *Rite and Man,* 84–85.

20. Paul Beauchamp, *L'uno e l'altro Testamento: saggio di lettura* (Brescia: Paideia, 1985), 279: "The blood speaks, to say that the word of the covenant is worth more than life."

21. Ibid., 279–86. See also Jean-Pierre Sonnet, *Generare è narrare* (Milan: Vita e pensiero, 2014), and Jon D. Levenson, *The Death and Resurrection of the Beloved Son: The Transformation of Child Sacrifice in Judaism and Christianity* (New Haven, Conn.: Yale University Press, 1993). This relation is highlighted as well, although interpreted differently, by *Throughout Your Generations Forever: Sacrifice, Religion, and Paternity* (Chicago: University of Chicago Press, 1992).

at the origin of the people's existence: the sacrifice of Abraham, who was to offer up Isaac, the son of the promise.[22] If blood stands for life, this life is specifically the life of the son, who by prolonging and enlarging the earthly existence of the father is the "life of his life." What this means, then, is not only that the covenant is worth more than one's own life, but also that the covenant is also worth more than the life that one has generated (which is the overflow of one's life), because generating makes sense only in the covenant: generating so as to introduce the son into the covenant. More-over, in the sacrifice God does not allow the death of the firstborn son but rather ransoms him; and he shows us in this way how the covenant makes possible a new generation, with which the life that comes from God can be transmitted.

We understand then that the animal represents the body of the son; and that the son's body testifies to God's generating action, which the father professes in shedding the blood of the victim. This paternal character of the offering appears *sub contrario* in its perverse, degenerate form: the sacrifice of a son to Moloch, which is condemned by the Bible.[23] Then instead of symbolically offering the animal blood (and thereby admitting: "I am not the lord of my son's life"), the father kills his offspring, gobbling it up, de-vouring his own future out of his anxiety to dominate the present.

We can place now in its context the expiatory sacrifice, which brings about the forgiveness of sins. Because the sacrifice restores communion, one of its effects is to eliminate what separates us from God. Hence it appears, on its negative side, as a loss: the shedding of blood and the death of the vic-tim.[24] From this perspective a sacrifice belongs to a world that has strayed from the original divine plan and needs to recover harmony. In any case it should not be forgotten that the final background against which the sacri-fice is situated is that of the generation of a life: professing that goodness is the "root" of all things, deeper than any evil that manages to infect the "plant" of beings, it is possible for everything to sprout again. The suffering that sacrifice involves can be understood only from the perspective of the greater good that it communicates.

---

22. About the ransom of the firstborn sons, see Karin Finsterbusch, "Vom Opfer zur Auslö-sung: Analyse ausgewählter Texte zum Thema Erstgeburt im Alten Testament," *Vetus Testamentum* 56 (2006): 21–45; Hartmut Gese, "Ezechiel 20,25f. und die Erstgeburtsopfer," in *Beiträge zur Alttesta-mentlichen Theologie*, ed. H. Donner (Göttingen: Vandenhoeck and Ruprecht, 1977).

23. Paul Beauchamp, *La ley de Dios: de una montaña a la otra*, Didáskolos 17 (Burgos: Monte Carmelo, 2014), 95–96 (on Moloch and human sacrifices).

24. This aspect has been studied by René Girard, *Violence and the Sacred* (London: Continuum, 2005 [1972]).

Another biblical rite has to be situated in relation to sacrifice: circumcision. On the one hand, it too, like a sacrifice, is related to the covenant, of which it is the sign (Gn 17:12, 14; 21:4; Lv 12:3). The one performing this rite is to say "blood of the covenant" while shedding it,[25] and only circumcised males can participate in the covenantal sacrifice which is Passover (Ex 12:43–49). On the other hand, circumcision too, like sacrifice, is bound up with the descendants promised by God upon sealing his pact with Abraham. In light of this it is not surprising that circumcision affects a man's generative potency. It is a mark received in the flesh precisely inasmuch as that is the place where life is open to the mystery of marriage and fertility; in fact, it seems that this rite was originally performed as a preparation for a wedding.[26]

Worship Generates Space: The Temple and the Body

Central to sacrifice is man's relation with his God and, also, the relation between parents and children, through the generations. In giving to these bonds their full form, sacrifice (and worship in general) *orders the space of relations in which life unfolds*, disposing it in turn to the presence of Yahweh. This gives rise to the theology of the temple, which is built through an original action of God, who orders the measurements of its walls.[27] In worship, the Lord opens spaces of communion with him so as to remind us that his love always precedes us, just as the walls of a home remind the son that certain hands received him when he came into the world.

This primacy of the divine action allows, from the viewpoint of the sanctuary, a retrospect on *creation*, the original space opened up by God. Israel learns, from the encounter with Yahweh, that all of reality is the environment of the divine presence. The Garden of Eden prefigured the temple: one enters into both through the east, and one of the cherubim guards it; God easily passes through both; man tends and cultivates both.[28] Both the instructions given to Moses for building the sanctuary and its execution in

---

25. León Dufour, "Circuncisión," in *Vocabulario de Teología Bíblica* (Barcelona: Herder, 1965), 144; de Vaux, *Instituciones*, 83–86.

26. De Vaux, *Instituciones*, 85; this would explain the mysterious passage Ex 4:24–26.

27. R. E. Clements, *God and Temple: The Idea of the Divine Presence in Ancient Israel* (Oxford: Basil Blackwell, 1965); Yves Congar, *The Mystery of the Temple* (London: Burns and Oates, 1962).

28. Gordon J. Wenham, "Sanctuary Symbolism in the Garden of Eden Story," in *I Studied Inscriptions From Before the Flood: Ancient Near Eastern, Literary, and Linguistic Approaches to Genesis 1–11*, ed. R. S. Hess and D. T. Tsumura (Winona Lake, Ind.: Eisenbrauns, 1994), 399–404, at 399. See Jon D. Levenson, "The Temple and the World," *The Journal of Religion* 64 (1984): 275–98, who points out the relation between the creation of the world in Gn 1 and the instructions for building the temple in Ex 25–40; this author declares: "The temple is to space what the Sabbath is to time" (298).

the edifice constructed by Solomon have parallels with the account of the foundation of the world.[29]

The outlook on creation as a temple includes man as well, into whose flesh God infused his breath from the beginning (Gn 2:7). If, as I have already said, the victim of the sacrifice symbolizes the body, the primordial temple is found in the body too. And this is because the space of relations that is closest to life unfolds there—the first space to be open to the beneficent presence of Yahweh: sons are "flesh of the flesh" of the parents, who prolong the divine creation; siblings share "the same flesh," recognizing a common origin in God; husband and wife are "one flesh," united by the Lord. It is not surprising that, when David proposes building a house for God (a temple), God responds that he is the one who will bestow a "house" on David, that is to say, a family (2 Sm 7:11).

This last-mentioned fact invites us to conclude that the space of the temple is a dynamic space, which grows through the generations. Thus we grasp another feature of ritual that was noted before: its ability to accompany the history of the people. The times of ritual, we can conclude, are times of maturation of the relational space in which man lives, until it is fully inhabited by Yahweh. And thus, the tent of the covenant, where God's glory descends, will give way to the temple, built in the Promised Land and called to fill it with its glory, when everything, down to the bells on the horses and the stew pots, is consecrated to the Lord (Zec 14:20).

The Prophets: Critique and Deepening of Worship

Precisely because God desired to live in our land, he placed himself within man's reach, and he patiently runs the risk that the latter will try to profane his temple. This happened repeatedly in the history of Israel. Failing to fulfill the Law, the people closed off its space of relations in the presence of God by its impurities and abuses against its brother.

This is the context in which to understand the prophetic denunciation of worship. It could appear, on the one hand, that the prophets are the enemies of ritual and that they aspire to suppress it. This approach, nevertheless, springs from a flimsy notion about their ministry. The prophetic message certainly cries out against the rituals. In the first place it denounces assimilation with the idolatrous forms of the neighboring peoples, and also

---

29. Peter J. Kearney, "Creation and Liturgy: the P Redaction of Exod. 25–40," *Zeitschrift für die Alttestamentliche Wissenschaft* 89 (1977): 375–87; Moshe Weinfeld, "Sabbath, Temple and the Enthronement of the Lord: The Problem of the Sitz im Leben of Gen 1:1–2:3," in *Mélanges bibliques et orientaux en l'honneur de M. Henrie Cazelles*, ed. A. Caquot and M. Delcor (Neukirchen: Neukirchner Verlag, 1981), 501–12; and Levenson, "The Temple and the World," 288.

a formalism that has forgotten the ultimate substance of worship, experiencing it in stone but not in the flesh.

Still, this is not about undermining rituals but rather about putting an end to the abuses so that they serve their ultimate truth. What the prophet rejects is the merely external circumcision of someone who does not acknowledge Yahweh as the source of life; or the sacrifices of someone who then, forgetting their logic of communion, robs and abuses his neighbor. Nor does it do any good to venerate the temple when one has expelled God from one's personal relationships, shutting him out of one's own flesh.

We see that in reality the prophet is conducting a critique of worship on the basis of the deepest dynamic of worship itself. For if worship furnishes an environment of openness to the divine, the prophet relocates this environment in the human body—his own—a place where God pronounces his Word and expresses his joy and his sorrow. Moreover, if worship teaches human beings the rhythm of the stages of life, the prophet is the one who reminds the people, so to speak, what time it is on the clock of the covenant.

The *signs* of the prophet, then, acquire great importance; they are the way in which worship continues to be present and alive in his ministry. For these signs have the same task as ritual: to open up a space where the Word of God resounds to teach us to understand his designs on history.[30] Is it the time to sing or to lament? To reinforce the city walls or to escape through its breaches into exile? To eat bread with one's loins girded or to plant vineyards in a foreign land? The prophet announces all this in signs, made up of words, deeds, sufferings [*pasiones*]. The *passage from ritual to sign* centers ritual on the bodily existence of the prophet, where the inspired word pulsates.

We can say, then, that the prophet does not merely spiritualize worship, channeling it toward the internal attitude or toward moral ideals.[31] What happens, rather, is that the prophet embodies the ritual, brings it close to the flesh that is his own, the prophet's.[32] This is a preparation, as we will see, of the salvific signs that Jesus will institute, culminating in the Eucharist, when the master offers his body and blood.[33] Thus we observe the continuity of

---

30. Angelini, *Il tempo e il rito*, 168: "It appears justified to associate the prophetic sign and the ritual; it too, indeed, prepares the space for a word which will have to be added, but which for the time being we can only—and must—hope for."

31. About the "spiritualization" effected by the prophets, Hans-Jürgen Hermisson, *Sprache und Ritus im altisraelitischen Kult: Zur "Spiritualisierung" der Kultbegriffe im Alten Testament* (Neukirchen-Vluyn: Neukirchener Verlag, 1965); and Hans Wenschkewitz, *Die Spiritualisierung der Kultusbegriffe: Tempel, Priester und Opfer im Neuen Testament* (Leipzig, 1932).

32. Cucca, *Il corpo*.

33. For a comparison between the prophetic signs and the Last Supper, Jacques Dupont, "Ceci est mon corps, Ceci est mon sang," *Nouvelle Revue Théologique* 80 (1958): 1025–41, at 1033–36.

Christ with the ancient worship, in which rituals already revolved around the body and its openness toward the sacred.

I should note, in conclusion, that the same critique of worship is present in the Book of Psalms: "Sacrifice and offering you do not desire; but you have given me an open ear" (Ps 40:6); "The sacrifice acceptable to God is a broken spirit" (Ps 51:17). In interpreting these verses let us not forget that they were sung to accompany ritual offerings, for psalms are fashioned in a liturgical context.[34] This confirms that it is not a matter of eliminating worship, but rather of centering it (so that its deepest truth is expressed) on the concrete relations to which the flesh opens us and in which the original love of God is made present.

The Ancient Rites in the Light of Jesus

The rites of the Old Testament, as we have seen, are open toward the future, with a presentiment of a fullness. The Gospel announces that this consummation has been accomplished in Christ and, more precisely, in his Eucharist, which takes up and perfects the liturgy of Israel, refines it, and renews it. From the Eucharistic vantage point, therefore, we get the correct view of the paths taken by worship over the history of the people. Recall that the "sacraments of the Old Law" (so they were called by the theological tradition) are not only precursors of the Eucharist, but also, having been received in it, are an integral part of it in revealing the face of God and communicating his saving action.

The Viewpoint of the New Testament

Jesus lives from the space of the culture and worship of his people Israel. The Gospels present him to us as one who carries out the Law, who did not come to abolish but to fulfill it (Mt 5:17). On the other hand, he distances himself from the interpretation of the Pharisees, Sadducees, and scribes, aligning himself instead with the prophetic critique.[35]

The matter is evident, in the first place, with the polemic surrounding the Sabbath. It is not a question of Jesus wanting to annul the precept by working his miracles in sacred time, as though it were just a day like any other. On the contrary: Jesus chooses the Sabbath as a day suitable for sav-

34. Sigmund Mowinckel, *Psalm Studies* (Nashville, Tenn.: Abingdon, 1962); Katharine J. Dell, "'I Will Solve My Riddle to the Music of the Lyre' (Psalm XLIX 4[5]): A Cultic Setting for Wisdom Psalms," *Vetus Testamentum* 54 (2004): 445–58.

35. Morna D. Hooker, *The Signs of a Prophet: The Prophetic Actions of Jesus* (London: SCM Press, 1997).

ing man and for the coming of the Father's Kingdom, as this day shows the precedence of the divine work. Thus Christ confirms the relevance of this feast in its most profound significance, which will lead to Sunday, the day that the Lord made.

The burning question is the reinterpretation of the sacrifices: they are all consummated in the Eucharist, which frames the death and glory of Jesus. This explains why among the first Christians there was no debate about the value of the Jewish sacrifices, as there was about circumcision and the other precepts of the Law. For it was obvious that the death of Jesus made the old ritual offering superfluous.

What value does Christ confer on the Temple sacrifices? On the one hand, he observes the rites and other holy days that are celebrated there. Indeed, while speaking about the sanctuary (with the Samaritan woman: Jn 4:21–23), he declares that salvation comes from the Jews. According to the chronology of St. John, Jesus himself takes up and lives out his mission against the background of the liturgical calendar of Israel (see chapter 3, above).

On the other hand Christ reaffirms the prophetic denunciation: "I desire mercy and not sacrifice" (Mt 9:10–13, citing Hos 6:6). Very important in this respect is the expulsion of the merchants from the Temple. The gesture was not only a denunciation of abuses, for the vendors were necessary in order to carry on worship properly, in other words, they were an intrinsic part of it even in its original, incorrupt form. Jesus is announcing, therefore, a radical reform, which can be understood only as the eschatological transformation of worship, in keeping with the prophetic hope.

This is made clear by studies of the Last Supper, where Christ refers to himself as the sacrifice mentioned in the Book of Exodus, with its blood of the covenant (Ex 24:8 according to Mt 26:28 and Mk 14:24), and reinterprets it in light of the new covenant announced by the prophets (Jer 31:31 in Lk 22:20 and 1 Cor 11:25) and the sacrifice of praise (*todah*) characteristic of the psalms. The filial logic of the sacrifices, which I described before, is consummated now in the gratitude of the only-begotten Son, who hands over his true body, without lambs that symbolize it, for the eternal life of the world.

In this way Jesus sheds light on the Old Testament: everything points to the gradual centering of the sacrifice on the body of the Son, who hands himself over in a filial offering of obedience to the Father and, in this way, proves to be the source of new communion for his people. While every rite establishes the center of space and time as the place of the epiphany and action of God, the Eucharist, as no previous rite had done, radically identifies this space and time with the body and the life of a human being, Jesus. The body of Christ is the new temple, the new sacred space where the mystery is manifested; and the time of the Eucharist, memorial of the Father and anticipation of his Kingdom, summarizes, over the course of a concrete human life, the ultimate explanation of the ages of the world. In this light we can understand why the New Testament generally does not tie Jewish cultic terms to the Christian liturgy, but rather extends them to the entire existence of Jesus and of those who believe in him.[36]

The disciples promoted this reading of the Old Testament that was inspired by the teaching of Jesus. St. Paul argues polemically with those who base their salvation on the fulfillment of the Law by having themselves circumcised and obeying the dietary laws.[37] For although God conferred salvific importance on those rites, it is not because of what a human being accomplishes in them, but rather because they bear a sign or seal imprinted by God (Rom 4:11). These rites in fact testify to the divine promise which is accomplished gratuitously from generation to generation until it reaches fulfillment in Jesus (Gal 3–4). In celebrating them, the Israelite was called to profess God's gift with the heart of a son, so that he might become rooted in him and bear much fruit. In this way the apostle recovers in the Christian rite the profound filial and generative logic of the Jewish rituals. We are looking, then, not at a condemnation of the old worship, but rather at the discovery of its consummation in Jesus, the Son of God born under the Law.

Hence Paul can interpret the rites of the Old Testament in light of the Christian liturgy: in the desert the people received spiritual food and drink (1 Cor 10:4); through their sacrifices the Jews already entered into communion with the altar of God, prefiguring the Eucharist (1 Cor 10:18). Certainly, the observance of full moons and other holy days is described as a subjection to the elements of the world, which are overcome in Christ (Col 2:8–16). This does not mean that Christian religious practice distances itself from the concrete reality of the flesh, but rather that it is focused on the incarnate Son, the head of the body of the church: if the earlier rite was a shadow, the reality is the body of Jesus (Col 2:17). Consequently St. Paul can identify the temple with the body of the Christian community (1 Cor 3:16) and of each believer (1 Cor 6:19; 2 Cor 6:16), and can talk about the body as a holy offering that is pleasing to God (Rom 12:1).

The most detailed explanation of the value of the ancient liturgy in the

---

36. On this topic see my discussion in chapter 13, below.
37. On worship in St. Paul, see Vahrenhorst, *Kultische Sprache*.

light of Christ is found in the Letter to the Hebrews.[38] There the worship in the Temple is described as an imitation of a heavenly worship: Moses planned the tabernacle according to what had been shown to him on the mountain (Heb 8:5; 9:23). Note that this is not about a Platonic image: the *heavenly temple means that future, definitive temple* in which the plans of the Most High will be completed. God guided the liturgy of the people toward the promise of a consummated union, a promise that is fulfilled, according to Hebrews, in the life and death of Jesus and in his ascension on high, when he enters into the Father's presence through the tabernacle of his own body (Heb 9:11).[39]

Let us point out once again that the old worship does not lead to merely interior and spiritual worship. On the contrary, the blood of the he-goats reaches its fullness in that other blood, which is that of Jesus; and in a temple that is the body of Jesus. This confirms that all the old sacrifices converge in the flesh of Christ. Indeed, if Jesus' sacrifice not only cleanses the outside but also purifies the conscience, it is precisely because it is carried out in a body, a place of communion (Heb 13:3), where the deepest identity of each one as a son and a brother is at stake. In all this it should be noted that Hebrews, although it does not deal explicitly with the Eucharist, presupposes it as a backdrop.[40]

In conclusion, the New Testament, based upon the Eucharist, interprets the old worship in harmony with its most original inspiration. From this we should take away two points: the importance of filiation in offering the sacrifice; and the gradual centering of worship on the flesh of man, victim and temple. This Eucharistic reading of the Old Testament will serve as a basis for the Church Fathers and for the theological tradition.

The Patristic Typological Reading

The first Christians then addressed the question about the value of the Old Testament. There were some who, in their fascination with the newness of Jesus, denigrated the preludes heard before him. The Marcionite and Gnostic heretics, for different reasons, contrasted the just God of the Old Tes-

---

38. Vanhoye, "Par la tente."

39. St. Ambrose lists these three stages (Old Testament, Gospels, eschatological fullness) in *De officiis* I, 48, 239 (CCL 15:88): "Hic umbra, hic imago, illic veritas. Umbra in lege, imago in euangelio, ueritas in caelestibus" (Here a shadow, here an image, but there—truth. A shadow in the Law, an image in the Gospel, truth in heaven).

40. James Swetnam, "Christology and the Eucharist in the Epistle to the Hebrews," *Biblica* 70 (1989): 74–94: "the hypothesis of the importance of the eucharist gives a coherence, relevance, and depth to the letter which is otherwise lacking" (74). See also Arthur A. Just, Jr., "Entering Holiness: Christology and Eucharist in Hebrews," *Concordia Theological Seminary* 69 (2005): 75–95.

tament with the merciful Father of Jesus. The covenants and rites of the two gods, according to them, had to be distinct too. It would be unworthy, for example, for the Father of Christians to contaminate his worship with material elements.

Faced with this challenge, the universal church defended a unified plan of history, wrought by one God who offers the same salvation to all. This meant acknowledging the salvific role of the Old Testament and of its worship. The majority interpreted the rites of Israel as prophecies of Christ. And they maintained that the Jews were asked to perform this worship literally by God's will. What advantage did this practice bring to them?

For some, among whom Origen stands out, the rites symbolize, in their material execution, the justice and goodness to which the soul is called.[41] The Alexandrian theologian cites as an example the offering of two turtledoves, according to Leviticus 5:7. Given that these birds form a stable, faithful couple (the turtledove would be an image of the church, the bride of Christ), someone who performs the rite understands that he must unite his soul in a spousal way with God.[42] The sacrifices of the Old Law were given in order to grasp and fulfill this spiritual meaning. Such ceremonies educated the people, not insofar as they were performed corporeally, but because they invited the faithful to pass from the flesh (the literal fulfillment) to the Spirit (moral behavior).[43] Within the New Testament itself Origen emphasizes the obligatory crossing from the bodily sacrament to its ultimate meaning, in the Spirit.

Other Fathers, besides accepting the prophetic and moral meanings, give weight also to the literal fulfillment of the precept in the flesh. This happens at least insofar as the practice of the ritual helps to set limits on the sinful tendency. Sacrificing to Yahweh, Justin Martyr tells us, avoids the risk of adoring false gods.[44] St. Irenaeus of Lyons goes farther: in their ceremonies the people not only repress the evil that dwells in them but also prepare

---

41. Werner Schütz, *Der christliche Gottesdienst bei Origenes* (Stuttgart: Calwer Verlag, 1984); Francesca Cocchini, "La normativa sul culto e sulla purità rituale nella interpretazione di Origene," *Annali di Storia dell'esegesi* 13 (1996): 143–58; Clementina Mazzucco, "Il culto liturgico nel pensiero di Origene," in *Dizionario di Spiritualità Biblico-Patristica* XII: *Culto divino-Liturgia*, ed. S. Panimolle (Rome: Borla, 1996), 203–20; and Clementina Mazzucco, "Culto," in *Diccionario de Origenes* (Burgos: Monte Carmelo, 2003), 215–21.

42. Origen, *Homilies on Leviticus* II, 2 (SC 286:94).

43. Because this meaning would be accomplished fully in Christ, Origen goes so far as to say that God did not desire the yearly sacrifices of the lamb, but rather that it should be understood that the one Lamb who takes away sin, who is Christ, had to be immolated; see *Homilies on Leviticus* II, 5 (SC 286:116–18).

44. Justin Martyr, *Dialogus cum Thryphone* 19, 6 (PTS 47:101); in this regard, see José Granados, *Los mysterios de la vida de Cristo en Justino Mártir* (Rome: PUG, 2004), 100.

to receive Christ. The carnal rites of the Old Testament had an educational value, not so much to transcend the flesh as to accustom it to the presence and gradual action of the Spirit.[45] In the new covenant, with the arrival of the Son, the Spirit is totally poured out on the flesh, enabling it to perform filial works beyond the habitual servitude of the old covenant.[46] The old and new regulations are not distinguished because one is carnal without the Spirit and the other spiritual without the flesh; rather, they differ by the abundance of the Spirit who, in both, runs through the same channel of the flesh.

Think of Irenaeus's interpretation of sacrifice. The saint considers it through the lens of the gift: recognizing that everything is a gift from the creator, we offer to him what he has communicated to us so as to be united in this way with him. And this is not because the Lord needs what we give him: we sacrifice for our benefit, because only by giving thanks for the gift and placing it at the service of friendship with the donor is it possible for this gift to fulfill us.[47] The bishop of Lyons can thus elucidate the old sacrifices in light of the Eucharistic sacrifice, which is *todah* or thanksgiving. This being so, while the primitive offering was servile, because one gave only a part of what one possessed, the new offering is a filial donation in which the Christian offers everything, because he offers himself.

St. Augustine, whose teaching went on to have great influence, cultivates this positive view of the sacrifices of Israel.[48] The bishop of Hippo, who had once belonged to the Manichean sect which reviled the old covenant, always kept in mind the necessity of interpreting the Bible in an undivided way. In Milan, through St. Ambrose, he learned the allegorical exegesis of Origen and with it managed to escape the difficulties that the disciples of Mani had raised for him. But this was not enough to refute his opponents, for that exegesis did not explain the literal meaning of the Bible, leaving up in the air some vague suspicion about the goodness of matter and of the body. His return to Africa and his contact with the exegetical rules of Ty-

---

45. Manuel Aroztegi, *La amistad del Verbo con Abraham según san Ireneo de Lyon* (Rome: Editrice Pontificia Università Gregoriana, 2004), chap. 5; on circumcision, 208.

46. Philippe Bacq, *De l'ancienne à la nouvelle Alliance selon S. Irénée: Unité du livre IV de l'Adversus haereses* (Paris-Namur: Presses universitaires de Namur, 1978); Antonio Orbe, "El Antiguo Testamento," in his *La teología de los siglos II y III* (Rome / Salamanca: PUG / Sígueme, 1988), 389–415; Ysabel de Andia, "Modèles de l'unité des testaments selon Irénée de Lyon," *Studia Patristica* 19 (1989): 49–59.

47. Irenaeus of Lyons, *Adversus haereses* IV, 18, 1 (SC 199:596): "We are bound, therefore, to offer to God the first-fruits of His creation ... so that man, being accounted as grateful, by those things in which he has shown his gratitude, may receive that honour which flows from Him" (ANF 1:484b).

48. Paula Fredriksen, "Secundum Carnem: History and Israel in the Theology of Saint Augustine," in B. Brown et al., *Augustine and World Religions* (Plymouth: Lexington Books, 2008), 21–36.

conius opened up for him a new perspective with a greater appreciation for the literal meaning of scripture. In his *Contra Faustum* he defends not only the fact that the Law is good, but also the thesis that the carnal observance of the rites was meritorious for the Jews. All Israel is like a great prophet who prepares for the coming of Jesus, not only in words, but in deeds, in the flesh itself. Does this not correspond with its mission of generating the Messiah?

Augustine explains rites starting with their status as signs. Someone who performs the rite without knowing the sign, out of obedience alone, is saved, but under the economy of the slave and not as a free man. In the Old Testament this was generally the case: the signs were profitable because they were made out of obedience to the one God.[49] Only a few just men, with a prophetic gift, knew the ultimate meaning of the rite and, in this way, by their faith in Christ, obeyed as free men.[50] The old and new forms of worship agree therefore in their adherence to Jesus, who reveals the ultimate meaning of them. Both in gathering the manna and in receiving the Eucharist, although the food that is eaten is different, the final grace that is given by the two is the same.[51]

Certainly there is no lack of difference between one rite and the other. In the Old Law the sacraments promised the Savior; in the New Law they communicate salvation.[52] Manna and Eucharist, although bestowing the same grace, do not do so in the same way: the manna is the shadow, the Eucharist is the truth; in the manna the Word was encountered, today the incarnate Word is handed over.[53] Moreover, in the New Law there are fewer sacraments that are easier to celebrate and of transparent significance, closer to the life of man because they spring from the life of Jesus.[54] As a result, the

---

49. Augustine, *Epistolae* LV 7, 13 (CSEL 34.2:183).

50. Augustine, *De doctrina christiana* III, 6, 10 to 9, 13 (CCL 32:83–86; NPNF-I 2:559a–560b).

51. Augustine, *In Iohannem* XXVI, 11 (CCL 36:16; NPNF-I 7:171b): "uisibilem cibum spiritualiter intellexerunt, spiritualiter esurierunt, spiritualiter gustauerunt, ut spiritualiter satiarentur. Nam et nos hodie accipimus uisibilem cibum; sed aliud est sacramentum, aliud uirtus sacramenti" (They understood the visible food spiritually, hungered spiritually, tasted spiritually, that they might be filled spiritually. For even we today receive visible food; but the sacrament is one thing, the virtue of the sacrament another).

52. Augustine, *Enarrationes in psalmos* LXXIII, 2 (CCL 39:1006): "sacramenta novi testamenti dant salutem; sacramenta veteris testamenti promiserunt salvatorem"; also *Contra Faustum Manichaeum* XIX, 16 (CSEL 25:513).

53. Augustine, *In Iohannem* XXVI, 13 (CCL 36:2; NPNF-I 7:172a): "Manna umbra erat, iste ueritas est."

54. Augustine, *Epistolae* LIV 1, 1 (CSEL 34.2:159): "unde sacramentis numero paucissimis, obseruatione facillimis, significatione praestantissimis societatem noui populi conligauit, sicuti est baptismus trinitatis nomine consecratus, communicatio corporis et sanguinis ipsius et si quid aliud in scripturis canonicis commendatur" (Hence by sacraments that were very few in number, very easy to observe, and very distinguished in their significance he gathered together the society of the new

meaning of the sign is revealed to every Christian, and not only to a few elect, so that all can live freely as is fitting for sons.

In any case, the rites of the Old Testament had value also in their carnal observance, inasmuch as they pointed to the coming of Jesus in the flesh. The case of circumcision illustrates this: St. Augustine recognizes its power to obliterate original sin in the Jewish boys. The efficacy of circumcision depends, therefore, not only on the faith of the one who undergoes it, but on the very performance of the rite.[55] The bishop of Hippo arrives at this conclusion by reflecting on original sin and its reverse: universal justification in Jesus. Discovering the salvation offered to all by a common connection with the flesh of Christ helps him to appreciate fleshly membership in the Jewish people as a salvific factor.

The Sacraments of the Old Law in the Theological Tradition until the Middle Ages

The medieval authors make valuable efforts to discussing the connection between the sacraments of the old and the new covenant.[56] In this debate they used a very broad concept of sacrament that extends to the whole history of salvation. At no time was the sinner left without sacraments, for they were the medicine of mercy.

What is the difference between the old and the new rites? To specify it a distinction is made between efficacy *ex opere operantis* (that is, because of the dispositions of faith and charity in the person who performed the act) and *ex opere operato* (that is, by reason of the very work performed with the sacrament). There is no difficulty in agreeing that the old rites act *ex opere operantis*: the love with which the work is performed saves the one who performs it. Can these rites also work *ex opere operato*, as would happen in the sacraments of Jesus?

Hugh of St. Victor thinks so: inasmuch as the rites point to the sacraments instituted later on by Christ, they receive from them in advance the ability to work grace in someone who performs them.[57] Peter Lombard's opinion is different: in the old covenant the rite is one way of expressing faith and charity, like many others. If it produces salvation it is not because

people, for instance baptism consecrated in the name of the Trinity, the communication of his own body and blood, and whatever else is recommended in the canonical scriptures).

55. Augustine, *De nuptiis* II, 11, 24 (CSEL 42:276); *Contra Iulianum* II, 6, 18 (PL 44:686); *Contra litteras Petiliani* II, 72, 162 (CSEL 52:103).

56. Emmanuel Doronzo, *De sacramentis in genere* (Milwaukee, Wis.: Bruce, 1945), 233–62.

57. Hugh of St. Victor, *De sacramentis* I, 8, 12; 11, 5 (PL 176:313 and 345; *CV* 1:204 and 245); St. Thomas expounds this opinion in *Super IV Sent.*, d. 1, q. 1, a. 5, sol. 1 (Parma 6:466).

of what is done but because of the way in which it is done.[58] An altogether different case is circumcision: all agree that this rite works *ex opere operato* to remove original sin, based on the exegesis of scripture (Gn 17:14: a man who is not circumcised will be uprooted from the people) and of the Fathers, especially of St. Augustine.

How do Bonaventure and Aquinas, the two great masters of medieval theology, reply? The Franciscan leans toward following Hugh of St. Victor: the old rites also saved *ex opere operato*. And this is because they were a profession of faith made through a work (*professio fidei facto*). Certainly this capability *ex opere operato* was derivative (*per accidens*), depending on what would have to happen in the rites of Jesus; while in the New Testament the sacraments work by a power inherent in them, inasmuch as God associated them immediately with the work of Christ.[59]

St. Thomas, although he seems to have changed his opinion as his thought matured, tends to see the sacraments of the old covenant only as a condition established by God for giving grace. In the old covenant God saves, we might say, *thanks to* the sacraments, but not *through* the sacraments. The sacraments of Jesus, on the contrary, are themselves the instrumental cause of grace. For Thomas the causality of the sacraments is closely united to the flesh of Christ, and this is why they could not possess the power to justify us until the incarnation burst onto the scene.[60]

Interest in understanding the value of the old rites declined considerably starting with the Lutheran Reformation. The Protestants, as we will see (in chapter 10, below), overlooked the efficacy of the rite, placing the emphasis on the faith of the one who receives it. In this way they found no great difference between the sacraments of bygone days and the new ones. Both are a word of salvation addressed to man, who is called to receive it. Everything depends on the confidence with which this promise is received, and not so much on the sign with which it is expressed.

---

58. Artur Landgraf, "Die Gnadenökonomie des Alten Bundes nach der Lehre der Frühscholastik," *Zeitschrift für katholische Theologie* 57, no. 2 (1933): 215–53.

59. Bonaventure, *In IV Sent.*, d. 1, p. 1, a. 1, q. 5, concl. (Quaracchi 4:25): "Sacramenta novae legis per se iustificant et gratiam conferunt ex opere operato, quod non faciebant Sacramenta legis veteris nisi per accidens" (The Sacraments of the New Law justify and confer grace by themselves *ex opere operato*, which the Sacraments of the Old Law did not do except accidentally).

60. Thomas Aquinas, *ST* III, q. 62, a. 6, co.: "causa efficiens non potest esse posterior in esse, ordine durationis, sicut causa finalis. Sic igitur manifestum est quod a passione Christi, quae est causa humanae iustificationis, convenienter derivatur virtus iustificativa ad sacramenta novae legis, non autem ad sacramenta veteris legis" (The efficient cause cannot in point of time come into existence after causing movement, as does the final cause. It is therefore clear that the sacraments of the New Law do reasonably derive the power of justification from Christ's Passion, which is the cause of man's righteousness; whereas the sacraments of the Old Law do not).

Trent, in its response, intends only to rebut Luther's position, while respecting the legitimate discussion among the schools. Therefore it does not attempt to determine the way in which the Old Testament sacraments act. The Council is content to condemn anyone who equates them with those of the New Testament and thinks that they differ only in the ceremonies and external rites. With Trent we must affirm, therefore, that there is an essential difference between the two rites in their way of communicating grace, while leaving open the question of what this difference is.[61] Later authors would continue thinking that the sacrifices of the Old Law have a certain efficacy to sanctify man by reason of the rite itself that is performed.[62]

After Trent the sacraments of the Old Law occupied a marginal place in the treatises. In them the Council's influence would also have the tendency, which arose from the Protestant opposition between Law and grace, to interpret negatively the salvific economy of Israel. The matter would be aggravated later on, when the anti-ritualist interpretations of Christianity typical of the modern era regarded with suspicion the Old Testament, which emphasizes precisely the literal practice of worship. Not until the twentieth century was the study of the Mosaic sacrifices revived. I already set forth the chief results of this investigation earlier in this chapter. All that remains, therefore, is to draw conclusions that place the topic in the context of a theology of the sacraments.

Conclusion

What is the value of the worship in Israel? The answer is interesting, not only to satisfy the curiosity of historical scholars, but also in order to understand the Christian sacraments. And this is because the old rites, besides preparing for the coming of the new ones, went on to become a constitutive part of them.

Moreover the question sheds light on other subjects. In the first place, in its light we understand better the path of every culture (which grows up around worship) toward Christian culture (structured around the seven sacraments); and the preparatory route by which every believer approaches

61. DH 1602; before Trent, Innocent III declared that circumcision pardoned original sin in *Maiores Ecclesiae Causas* (DH 780); the Council of Florence, for its part, taught that the sacraments of the Old Law did not cause grace (*Exultate Deo*; DH 1310).

62. For St. Robert Bellarmine the old sacraments possessed true efficacy, which he calls legal or typical (they did not confer sanctifying grace, but legal purification), and which surpasses a mere sign; therefore they can already be called sacraments because for the learned Jesuit it is a more proper characteristic of a sacrament to cause grace than to signify it; see *De controversiis*, vol. 3, lib. I, cap. XII (Naples: J. Giuliano, 1858), 34–36.

the grace of the sacraments. Furthermore, in the second place, thanks to the rites of the Old Testament, shaped over centuries, our seven acquire a historic depth with which to accompany the life of mankind and of the church. Each sacrament, like good wine, is not the work of a rapid inspiration but rather accumulates within itself the sediment of the ages. Let us recall now the main conclusions reached in this chapter.

First, the worship of the Old Testament makes transparent the logic of the covenant forged by Yahweh with his people. Just like the covenant, the sacrifice—the ritual *par excellence*—is established by God and is always performed on his initiative. In a sacrifice human beings offer to God gifts that they have received from him and thus, by acknowledging the origin of the goods, manage to reach the donor himself and to establish a filial relationship with him. The offering refers not only to the objects given up, but to man's very life, symbolized by the blood of the libations. In this way he professes that the covenant is worth more than life, because the covenant makes life worthy and fruitful. Moreover, the life that is offered in the sacrifice is the life of the firstborn son, in whom the existence of the parents and of the whole people opens up toward a future full of hope. In shedding the blood of the animal, believers recognize that generating a new life is possible only within the covenant with God. The sacrifice is a guarantee that the relation between father and son, if it acknowledges its origin in Yahweh, will be able to flourish for generations according to the divine promise.

Second, inasmuch as the rite is at the service of the covenant, which is man's relationship with God, it orders in a new way the network of relations in which man lives and, therefore, the space of his settlement in the world. This lends importance to the concrete place (sanctuary or temple) in which the rite is celebrated, because from that place order is conferred on human environments, an order that revolves around the beneficent presence of God. The temple that is at the root of all temples (because it is the original space in which man becomes open to the world and to others) is man's own body, which is configured in the rite as the suitable space for the divine epiphany and blessings.

Third, the relational spaces opened up by the sacrifice, in testifying to God's gift and its fruitfulness, prove to be dynamic spaces that mature in time. Therefore within the rite Yahweh's deeds are recalled and one hopes for the fulfillment of his promises, so that the history of mankind and of the people is a narrative shared with the Lord of history. It is up to the rite, therefore, to narrate the times of personal and community life as times of the covenant. We can say, combining the previous points, that biblical history is the history of a relational space (history of the flesh, of the family, of a people, of the whole earth) which gradually becomes better suited to being a dwelling of God with men, until the definitive Jerusalem.

In light of this, I conclude that ritual effectively mediates for man the experience of the covenant, inasmuch as through it alone the spaces and times are opened up in which God can reveal himself. Therefore Solomon declared that every prayer offered in the sanctuary would certainly be heard: "When your people Israel ... pray and make supplications to you in this house, you will hear in heaven and will forgive" (1 Kgs 8:33). From this perspective the sacrament of the old covenant is efficacious *ex opere operato*, but according to an efficacy that nevertheless is not complete, because the space opened up by the rite awaits its future consummation.

What is then the newness that the Gospel brings, an essential newness that must be maintained according to the teaching of Trent? The new feature of the rite of Jesus is the fact that the celebration is centered on the body of man, opening him up to a relational fullness with God. Indeed, under the Old Law the other material elements, particularly the flesh and blood of the sacrificed animal, spoke for the body, which was incapable of expressing by itself the ultimate mysteries of the origin and end of life. In the new covenant, nevertheless, the body of Jesus, the Son of God, becomes capable of expressing the definitive significance of it all, in being established as the place of maximum openness to the Father and to human beings. The New Testament testifies, then, to the total corporealization, in the flesh of the Lord, to which the Old Testament pointed.

In short, the old worship possessed sanctifying efficacy through the rite itself that was performed, but without managing to regenerate the center of the person. And this is because it did not fully reach his flesh nor, therefore, the relations that spring from it. Based on the work of Christ on the cross, nevertheless, his sacraments acquire an irrevocable efficacy because they seal the covenant with God in the very space of man's body and man's time, as I will confirm in the following chapters. Inasmuch as this fulfillment recovers the original insight that inspired the old worship, we can say, with St. Ambrose, that the Christian sacraments are older than those of Israel.[63]

---

63. Ambrose, *De mysteriis* 44 (SC 25:122): "antiquiora sacramenta ecclesiae quam synagogae" (The sacraments of the Church are older than those of the Synagogue).

8 ❧ SIGNS OF CHARITY

The Sacraments in St. Augustine

Considering the Eucharist has helped us to see how the sacraments include within themselves the language of creation (chapter 6), sifted by the salvation history of Israel (chapter 7). In taking up these two dimensions, Jesus transforms them, giving them a new principle of unity, just as wine, in fermenting, transforms the must and the water that it contains. Only from the perspective of this action of Jesus is it possible to understand what the sacraments of the New Law are, a task that I begin to tackle in this chapter.

Structure of the Sacraments of Jesus in the New Testament and in the Fathers

A definition of sacrament was late in arriving. We already know the reasons for this delay. Just as the spectator focuses on the landscape, not on the window that offers a view of it or on the light and the air that bathe it, so too the Church Fathers did in considering the Christian mystery. They were interested in the sacraments inasmuch as they refer beyond themselves: as a place of encounter with Christ, as an environment that gives access to his life and work. Attention directed to them to delimit them and define them would arrive only in a second phase. One milestone in this process is the Augustinian formula, the influence of which can still be felt in our day: a sacrament is a *sign of a sacred reality*. In order to understand this correctly it is necessary to frame it first within the context of the previous tradition, which had already offered several general traits of the sacraments, although without arriving at a precise formula.

The New Testament

A first insight into the structure of the Christian rites comes from the New Testament, the writings of St. John and St. Paul in particular. The fourth evangelist describes the sacraments in terms of *signs* (see chapter 3, above). The background is the theology of the temple, which is identified with the body of Jesus, where the divine glory is manifested. Indeed, we find the sign *par excellence* in the destruction and raising of this temple of his body, which will come to pass in his death and resurrection. The other signs lead toward this, for they aim to make us enter into the space of relations opened by Christ and his Father through their common action; hence the signs, viewed from within, can also be called works. The Christian sacraments, for their part, preserve the structure of the sign, for through them we are introduced into the space of the body of Jesus that was already built in his passion and glory. Sign and sacrament become tied to the flesh of the Son of God, to the encounter that is produced in it, to the luminous communion that it opens up for us.

In the Pauline writings the term *mysterion* serves as a basis for developing the sacramental view (see chapter 4, above). Here we likewise have an epiphany: God's plan, hidden for centuries, is revealed and completed in the sending of his Son Jesus, in his death, resurrection, and ascension in glory. This *mysterion* is manifested also in the flesh: that of Jesus as the head; that of his church, the union of Jews and Gentiles, as his body or bride. And his revelation unfolds over the course of a history, putting together the distinct events of God's plan, which Christ recapitulates. I should add that St. Paul connects the epiphany of the *mysterion* to the word that is preached, as an event that appeals to the listener, asking him for confident obedience.

We encounter here an initial basis with which to determine the common features of Christian ritual. Although they differ in their approach, both John and Paul encourage viewing the sacrament as the opening of a space of communion (temple or body) rooted in the life of the incarnate Son, a space that matures through God's salvific action in history. Inasmuch as this space is ordered according to the work and the message of Jesus, we can say that it is full of light (sign) and traversed by the word (*mysterion*), a light and a word that are enjoyed by those that dwell in it.

Together with this view of the whole, the New Testament also describes a common ritual structure, composed of a material gesture and a word or prayer. The Eucharist serves as the basic inspiration, when Jesus pronounces his words over the bread and wine. From there the outline is extended to baptism and to other rites. Thus Jesus commands the disciples to baptize in the name of the Father and of the Son and of the Holy Spirit (Mt 28:19); to the Ephesians the apostle speaks about "the washing of water with the word" (Eph 5:26); hands are imposed on Timothy with a prophecy (1 Tm 4:14);

St. James describes the anointing of the sick with oil together with a prayer (Jas 5:14); the apostles impose hands while praying in order to confer the Spirit (Acts 8:14–17) or to ordain (Acts 6:6). In short, the sacraments appear to be described according to an initial axis: bodily action–word.

Other passages show a second axis that runs through the sacrament: from the perceptible rite (bodily action and word) toward an invisible grace or gift of God; from the earthly manifestation to the spiritual and divine. Thus, to Nicodemus Jesus preaches a baptism in which one is born "of water and the Spirit" (Jn 3:5). Paul asks Timothy not to neglect the "charism" that he has within him, received by the imposition of hands (see 1 Tm 4:14). The Letter to the Hebrews, in reference to baptism, speaks about "our bodies washed with pure water" (Heb 10:22). All this reflects the *mysterion* that is Christ himself (Col 2:2), in whom "the whole fullness of deity dwells bodily" (Col 2:9). The point of departure of these formulas is, again, the Eucharistic experience, in which Jesus offers us his risen body, from which the Spirit of God flows.

Structure of the Sacrament in Patristic Writings

We have already seen (in chapter 5, above) how the Fathers were interested above all in the root of the sacraments in Jesus. Only in a second phase were they concerned about investigating the structure of the sacrament in itself. Their point of departure is always Christological: the reason why there is word and matter in the sacrament is because behind it is Christ, the incarnate Word; the reason why grace is communicated in the sacrament through the body is because behind it is Christ, anointed in the flesh with the fullness of the Spirit starting at the Jordan. The mystery of the incarnation and anointing, which culminates in the ascension and on Pentecost, is the basis for understanding the architecture of the sacraments. They are situated in the convergence between the flesh of Jesus and our flesh, upon which the same Spirit rests. Starting from here the first sacramental outlines arise, which emphasize the connection between what is visible and what is invisible, the interior and the exterior, and thus lend initial support to a definition of sacrament as sign, which will reach maturity in St. Augustine.

In the first place, a sacrament is described according to the conjunction of Spirit and flesh, a conjunction that is manifest in the rite.[1] Thus Tertullian says: "The *act* of baptism itself too is carnal, in that we are plunged in

---

1. Edward Yarnold, "The Body-Soul Relationship, mainly in connection with sacramental causality," *Studia Patristica* 35 (2001): 338–42.

water, *but* the *effect* spiritual, in that we are freed from sins."[2] In his treatise *On the Resurrection of the Flesh* he adds:

The flesh, indeed, is washed, in order that the soul may be cleansed; the flesh is anointed, that the soul may be consecrated; the flesh is signed (with the cross), that the soul too may be fortified; the flesh is shadowed with the imposition of hands, that the soul also may be illuminated by the Spirit; the flesh feeds on the body and blood of Christ, that the soul likewise may fatten on its God.[3]

I should note that, in this famous text, among the material elements (water, oil, sign of the cross, shadow of the hands, etc.) we find the body and blood of Christ. Given that this risen body and blood remain forever as the hinge post of our salvation, the passage does not consider matter a mere stairway to the spiritual, which could be dispensed with once the path had been traveled. In fact, according to Tertullian, not only does the flesh become spiritualized, but also the Spirit becomes embodied: "the [S]pirit is corporeally washed in the waters, and the flesh is spiritually cleansed in the same."[4]

St. Irenaeus of Lyons writes, along the same lines: "Our bodies have received unity among themselves by means of that laver which leads to incorruption; but our souls, by means of the Spirit."[5] What the body gains with the washing is not only being free of sweat and dust, thus symbolizing the purity of the soul, but above all the new unity with the body of Christ which already presages the resurrection. Through the sacrament, composed of Spirit and matter, man receives salvation of his entire being. Origen, too, although from a different theological perspective that values the flesh less, associates the structure of the sacrament to our bodily condition: given that a human being is body and soul, the water of baptism is not ordinary water, but water sanctified by an invocation.[6]

How does this passage from corporeal to spiritual occur? The schools give different explanations. The Platonic influence can be felt above all in the Alexandrian tradition of Origen, who holds that the material aspect is only an initial element, necessary for the uneducated. Then it is left behind, for those who are already journeying over the mountains of God do not need it.[7] But another line of thought—present in Justin Martyr, St. Irenae-

---

2. Tertullian, *De baptismo* VII, 2 (CCL 1:282; ANF 3:672b).

3. Tertullian, *De resurrectione carnis* VIII, 3 (CCL 2:931; ANF 3:551b).

4. Tertullian, *De baptismo* IV, 5 (CCL 1:280; ANF 3:671a).

5. Irenaeus of Lyons, *Adversus haereses* III, 17, 2 (SC 211:332; ANF 1:445a).

6. Origen, *Fragmentum in Iohannem* XXXVI (GCS 4:104.15); Crouzel, "Origène et la structure," 90–91.

7. Aroztegi, "Eucaristía y filiación."

us, and others—will prevail: it sees the flesh not as the first step in a path of progressive disembodiment, but rather as the earth to be cultivated so that the fruit of salvation may mature on it. For the Spirit desired to descend precisely on the flesh and to fill it completely, communicating his properties to it. In this way the sacramental signs always move from flesh to flesh, from the flesh that yearns for the Spirit to the flesh that is filled with him. This thought is recapitulated by St. Irenaeus as follows, again traversing the axis from the visible to the invisible: "For what other visible fruit is there of the invisible Spirit, than the rendering of the flesh mature and capable of incorruption?"[8] For the bishop of Lyons, what is visible and manifest in a sacrament (its "flesh") is not the shell of the Spirit that would have to be discarded in order to encounter him, but rather the fruit of the Spirit, which reaches maturity after a patient process.

The Church Fathers present the sacrament not only as a joining of the flesh and the Spirit, but also as divine revelation, which occurs precisely in the dwelling place of the body and along its journey to God. In relation to the Eucharist, for example, to eat bread implies "eating" the Word. For the one who is received in Communion is the *Logos*, the Word of God, who continually "feeds" on the Father, on his knowledge and will. The sacrament, therefore, is also a cognitive event, but not as abstract study, because it is tied, through the act of eating, to the communion between Christ and mankind through the handing over of his body.

This line of thought explains why Christian initiation, specifically baptism, very soon receives the name "illumination" (*photismós*).[9] Note that this light is the one received by someone who is born, someone who "sees the light of day" in a second birth.[10] It does not consist, therefore, of a merely internal enlightenment, but of the light of a bodily childbirth [*alumbramiento*]: just as the baby who is born enters into the light of day and is surrounded, welcomed, and bathed by it, so too the neophyte, when he is born to the communion of the church, the body of Christ, is surrounded, welcomed, bathed, by the splendor of the new relations that are experienced in Jesus. This means that the sacrament brings a clarity that proceeds from the believer's new situation: from the bonds with Christ and with his brethren which give him lodging from now on.[11] Thus the sacrament's light is

8. Irenaeus of Lyons, *Adversus haereses* V, 12, 4 (SC 153:154; ANF 1:538b).

9. Justin Martyr, *1 Apologiae* 61, 11–13 (PTS 38:119; ANF 1:183b).

10. St. Justin speaks about the illumination of baptism in the context of a new birth: Justin Martyr, *1 Apologiae* 61, 9–11 (PTS 38:119; ANF 1:183b).

11. Irenaeus of Lyons, *Adversus haereses* IV, 20, 5 (SC 100:640; ANF 1:489a): "Those who see the light are within the light, and partake of its brilliancy."

the light of love, which is suitable for recognizing Christ and walking in his ways.

Here we find the ability of the sacrament to decipher the course of history. Indeed, it is well known that the Fathers understand the sacraments in terms of typology, that is, a reading of the times that points to the fullness in Jesus. Well, then, in describing this fullness they call it "truth," not as opposed to a lie, but rather in contrast with the shadow and the figure of the preceding times.[12] The sacrament therefore contains a revelation, and what is illuminated in it is precisely the unity and direction of history. From this vantage point a view opens up which allows us to discover the entire route, as it opens up for someone who reaches the crest of a mountain after a long ascent. Here is born a knowledge tied to the tick-tock of time: it is not static contemplation, but rather light that emanates when we set out on a journey.

In short, the most fertile insights of the patristic era present the sacrament as a dynamic conjunction of the flesh and the Spirit, starting from the fullness of Jesus. Moreover, the sacrament is described also as a place of light and truth, inasmuch as it reveals to us how our relations must be ordered for them to dispose the flesh to the action of the Spirit and what path the flesh is called to follow so as to be filled with him. Based on this approach, St. Augustine formulates his proposal.

St. Augustine: Sacrament and Sign

St. Augustine's contribution stands on the pillars of the earlier Fathers. His definition of sacrament as a sign of a sacred reality (*signum rei sacrae*) went on to be very influential. In order to delve into the approach of the bishop of Hippo, I will consider his way of understanding the sign, and will then examine its connection with the sacraments. Note to begin with that St. Augustine uses the word *sacramentum* in several ways: sometimes it is a biblical prophecy, sometimes a divine secret, sometimes the visible manifestation that unites us with what is arcane, and so on.[13] Here we are interested in *sacramentum* inasmuch as it refers to rituals; from this perspective we can grasp the other meanings of the term.

The Sign according to St. Augustine: *De doctrina christiana*

Augustine's analyses of the sign are found, above all, in his work *On Christian Doctrine*.[14] The book expounds a method for reading the Bible and

---

12. Melito of Sardis, *On Easter* 39–45 (SC 123:80–84).
13. Lienhard, "*Sacramentum* and the Eucharist."
14. On the sign in St. Augustine, see Robert A. Markus, "St. Augustine on Signs," *Phronesis* 2

explicating it. This fact is already important: signs are defined in the context of the communication of the Word of God to man. Let us look at their main features.

Signs and the path of love   Augustine begins with a twofold division of the object of all doctrine. Someone who teaches is interested either in the realities about which he speaks (*res*), or in the signs (*signa*) that speak to us about those realities.[15] What matters is the knowledge about these realities; but in order to receive it and, in turn, to transmit it, it is necessary to be clear about signs.

The realities, in turn, are divided into two types: those that exist to lead us to other realities, and those that constitute the final destination of the path. The former are the route to the goal, and therefore we can say that "they are to be employed" (in Latin: *uti*). The latter are the definitive goal of the route, and about them we can say that "they are to be enjoyed" (in Latin: *frui*).[16] This distinction allows Augustine to describe the order of man's movement in the cosmos: only the ultimate reality, God, who is the Trinity, Father, Son, and Holy Spirit, can be loved as the definitive resting place (*frui*),[17] while we seek the other things (which include even the human being who loves) in order to journey (*uti*)—from them, with them—toward the definitive rest.

With this distinction we have not strayed from the biblical context. For everything revolves around the great commandment that sums up the Law: love the Lord above all things (*frui*); and love your neighbor as yourself, in other words, as someone proceeding from God and ordered to him (*uti*). In this way Augustine considers human life to be a pilgrimage which draws near to the creator through what is created.

(1957): 60–83; Ulrich Duchrow, "*Signum* und *superbia* beim jungen Augustin," *Revue des études Augustiniennes* 7 (1961): 369–72; Engels, "La doctrine du signe"; Jackson, "The Theory of Signs"; Douglas W. Johnson, "*Verbum* in the early Augustine (386–397)," *Recherches Augustiniennes* 8 (1972): 25–53; Mauricio Beuchot, "Signo y lenguaje en san Agustín," *Diánoia* 32 (1986): 13–26; Rowan Williams, "Language, Reality and Desire in Augustine's De Doctrina," *Literature and Theology* 3 (1989): 138–50; Daniel Bourgeois, *Le champ du signe: Structure de la sacramentalité comme signification chez Saint Augustin et Saint Thomas d'Aquin* (PhD diss., University of Fribourg, 2007); Phillip Cary, *Outward Signs: The Powerlessness of External Things in Augustine's Thought* (Oxford: Oxford University Press, 2008); and Susannah Ticciati, "The Human Being as Sign in Augustine's De doctrina christiana," *Neue Zeitschrift für Systematische Theologie und Religionsphilosophie* 55, no. 1 (2013): 20–32.

15. *De doctrina christiana* I, 2, 2 (CCL 32:7; NPNF-I 2:523a): "Omnis doctrina uel rerum est uel signorum" (All instruction is either about things or about signs).

16. Ibid., I, 2, 3 (CCL 32:8; NPNF-I 2:523b): "Res ergo aliae sunt, quibus fruendum est, aliae quibus utendum, aliae quae fruuntur et utuntur" (There are some things, then, which are to be enjoyed, others which are to be used, others still which enjoy and use).

17. Ibid., I, 5, 5 (CCL 32:9; NPNF-I 2:524a).

After explaining the realities (*res*), the bishop of Hippo dwells on the signs that serve as vehicles communicating them. A sign is something that the senses perceive and that leads us to another reality that is beyond them. The definition will be repeated from one pen to another in the Middle Ages: "A sign is a thing which, over and above the impression it makes on the senses, causes something else to come into the mind" (*signum est res, praeter speciem quam ingerit sensibus, aliquid aliud faciens in cogitationem uenire*).[18]

It is important to note the parallel between the movement of all that exists toward its goal in God (*uti-frui*) and the movement of signs toward the reality signified (*signum-res*). On the one hand, our love always directs us toward a greater love, until we arrive at the original divine love. On the other hand, our knowledge impels us, from sign to sign, to a deeper reality that will be, at the final end, God also. *The passage from uti to frui, from love for creatures to their source in God, runs parallel with the passage from the sign to the signified.*[19] From this we deduce that signs cannot be understood as merely intellectual. The channel through which the sign flows is the channel of charity, which begins in God and drives everything toward it. The movement of the sign is, so to speak, an affective movement in which the order and the direction of love are revealed to us.

Sign and gift   This connection between the sign and the path of charity is reinforced if we consider the Augustinian distinction between *natural* signs and *"given"* signs.[20] *Natural* signs are, for example, fire, which is announced by smoke, or the wolf's trail, which indicates the passage of the animal. And *given* signs? Some explain them as arbitrary (only the product of an individual's will) or as conventional signs (the result of an agreement). But Augustine's terminology itself evokes another aspect: they are given, that is to say, *donated*, because with them someone communicates something to someone.[21]

In this way the emphasis is placed on the persons who exchange the signs. And this is because in every sign there are two axes: one that goes

18. Ibid., II, 1, 1 (CCL 32:32; NPNF-I 2:535a); this reflection on signs, following the ancient philosophers, had already been stated by Origen, *In Iohannis* XIII, 60 (PG 14:521) (wonders are signs because they point beyond the senses).

19. Todorov, "À propos de la conception"; Williams, "Language, Reality and Desire"; Ticciati, "The Human Being as Sign"; and Eberhard Jüngel, *Gott als Geheimnis der Welt* (Tübingen: Mohr Siebeck, 2010), 2–10. In fact, Augustine relates the distinction between *uti* and *frui* to Rom 1:20, which speaks about perceiving the invisible based on what is visible: *De doctrina christiana* I, 4, 4 (CCL 32:8; NPNF-I 2:523b); I, 34, 38 (CCL 32:28; NPNF-I 2:532b); I, 35, 39 (CCL 32:29; NPNF-I 2:533a).

20. *De doctrina christiana* II, 1, 2 (CCL 32:32; NPNF-I 2:535b).

21. Ibid., II, 2, 3 (CCL 32:33; NPNF-I 2:536a); Engels, "La doctrine du signe," 373.

from the sign to the object signified; the other that goes from the person who communicates to the one who receives the message. St. Augustine underscores this second axis, in keeping with the context of his work: exegesis of the divine Word, given by God to mankind. In view of this interpersonal feature of the sign, we understand why St. Augustine defines a third type together with the realities that are used and enjoyed: we ourselves, who are capable of using (*uti*) and of enjoying (*frui*); beings that desire and love, on a journey toward our final rest in God.[22]

The word, a sign *par excellence* ❧ This interest in the communicative sign leads Augustine to give a privileged place to a certain type of signs: words.[23] It happens that many signs (*signa*) are at the same time realities (*res*)—for example, smoke—which, besides making us think of fire, exist by themselves. Well, then, the specific characteristic of words is that in them almost everything boils down to being signs: take the sign away from the word and what is it except an indistinct noise? Thus words prove to be signs *par excellence*. Is it not certain, Augustine asks himself, that all signs can be enunciated with words, while it is impossible to show all words with visible signs?[24] His proposal to associate language with signs—a proposal unprecedented in ancient philosophy—is a contribution to semiotics which was possible because of Augustine's interest in biblical exegesis.

So central is the word in interpreting signs that, in a certain way, *all signs have something of the word* and can be defined as visible words (*verba visibilia*). As we know (see chapter 6, above), Augustine extends to all creatures this character of given sign, because through them God the creator communicates to us his will and his love. This occurs in a singular way in the types of biblical figures, as realities that point to another in the future: the Paschal lamb can be seen as a lamb and also as a prophecy of Jesus on the cross.[25] From God's perspective, natural signs are also given signs and "visible words," for in them he shows us his will about the ages, until their fullness in Christ.[26]

---

22. *De doctrina christiana* I, 4, 4 (CCL 32:8; NPNF-I 2:523b).

23. The young Augustine considered language the effect of original sin; later on he explained that what was caused by the Fall of man is the confusion of tongues at Babel, not language in itself: Duchrow, "*Signum* und *superbia*."

24. *De doctrina christiana* II, 4, 5 (CCL 32:34; NPNF-I 2:536b).

25. Ibid., I, 2, 2 (CCL 32:7; NPNF-I 2:523a); II, 10, 15 (CCL 32:41; NPNF-I 2:539b).

26. Ibid., II, 5, 6 (CCL 32:35; NPNF-I 2:536b–537a); II, 3, 4 (CCL 32:34; NPNF-I 2:536a–b); also *Sermo* LXXVII, 5, 7 (PL 38:486): "quae a Domino facta sunt, aliquid significantia erant, quasi verba, si dici potest, visibilia et aliquid significantia" (The things made by God were signifying something, like words, so to speak, which are visible and signify something).

Signs in the depth of creation 🐾 Created beings are therefore signs that point toward God, who in turn surpasses all signs. Just as all loves are ordered to rest in him, so too words attempt to pronounce the ineffable God. Still, God is neither just another object of love, superior to the others, nor just another truth that stands out among truths.[27] For if he were simply the final goal to which signs lead (the end of their long series) he would ultimately be comparable with the others. And then love for God would diminish interest in creatures, as though he entered into competition with them. It must be said, on the contrary, that the openness of reality to God is just what allows us to take it seriously and never to lose our passion for it, knowing that it always gives more of itself. The fact that things are signs, far from diluting their consistency, makes them interesting and worthy of esteem. The God of the Christians manifests his greatness, not because his presence makes the world vague, but rather because it confers depth on it.

This is proved by the fact that Augustine points to Christ, the way and at the same time the goal, as the center of all signs.[28] In him it is confirmed once and for all that signs are not only springboards to the eternal, which we can forget after jumping on them, as in the Platonic writings in which Augustine had found momentary comfort. Christ is the supreme sign, the measure of all signs, because his entire being is a radical reference to God; and, at the same time, Christ must never be surpassed, because he himself is God. In Jesus is revealed, therefore, that in every being, as sign, there exists an infinite opening, an unfathomable depth, for through it we can travel toward the Father.

This analysis of signs already brings us close to the sacraments. They, as rites, are also signs given by God, *verba visibilia* that point to the definitive rest in him. Certainly it is important to distinguish one rite from another. The rites of the pagans are for Augustine useless signs, for they lead to nothing good: it is just as harmful to venerate the sign as the reality to which the sign points, that is, the idol. The Israelites, for their part, received useful signs, for such signs were pathways to God. It is true that many Jews did not understand these signs, but at least knew that signs were sent by Yahweh and, by following the signs confidently, they progressed in the service of God, even if as slaves. For the characteristic of a son, who is free in the household, is to understand what the sign is pointing to, so that he can fol-

---

27. *De doctrina christiana* I, 6, 6 to 7, 7 (CCL 32:9–10; NPNF-I 2:524a–b).

28. Ibid., I, 11, 11 (CCL 32:12; NPNF-I 2:525b): "Cum ergo ipsa sit patria, uiam se quoque nobis fecit ad patriam" (Thus, though Wisdom was Himself our home, He made Himself also the way by which we should reach our home).

low it not only because it is commanded, but because he understands what the goal is. So it happened with the patriarchs, prophets, and the just, who by anticipation knew Jesus, the fullness of the signs.[29]

Finally, in the New Testament the light of the risen Lord shines: from the Paschal mystery, in which the glorified flesh of Jesus appears, it becomes evident to everyone where the ritual signs point to.[30] The Christian sacraments, because they are derived from the body of Christ, include every son of Adam, and can be few and simple, accessible to the great multitude. And will not this, the connection between the rite and the risen flesh of Jesus, radiant with light, be the reason why Augustine defines a sacrament as a sign?

The Sacraments, Sacred Signs

Let us explore now the way in which the sacraments, as Augustine describes them in various passages of his work, are "sacred signs."[31] This is a

29. Ibid., III, 8, 12 to 9, 13 (CCL 32:84–86; NPNF-I 2:560a–b).

30. Ibid., III, 9, 13 (CCL 32:85–86; NPNF-I 2:560b): "Hoc uero tempore posteaquam resurrectione domini nostri manifestissimum indicium nostrae libertatis inluxit, nec eorum quidem signorum, quae iam intellegimus, operatione graui onerati sumus" (But at the present time, after that the proof of our liberty has shone forth so clearly in the resurrection of our Lord, we are not oppressed with the heavy burden of attending even to those signs which we now understand).

31. *De civitate Dei* X, 5 (CCL 47:277; NPNF-I 2:183a): "Sacrificium visibile invisibilis sacrificii sacramentum, id est, sacrum signum est" (A sacrifice, therefore, is the visible sacrament or sacred sign of an invisible sacrifice); *Epistolae* LV, 2 (CSEL 34.2:170): "sacramentum est autem in aliqua celebratione, cum rei gestae commemoratio ita fit, ut aliquid etiam significare intelligatur, quod sancte accipiendum est" (For a sacrament exists in some celebration when a deed is commemorated in such a way that it is understood to signify something also which is to be received in a holy manner); *Epistolae* 138, 7 (CSEL 44:131): "[signa] cum ad res divinas pertinent, sacramenta appellantur" (when signs pertain to divine matters, they are called sacraments); *Epistolae* 105, 3, 12 (CSEL 34.2:604): "Operatur per illum [ministrum] Deus visibilem sacramenti formam, ipse autem donat invisibilem gratiam" (God produces through him [the minister] the visible form of the sacrament, but he himself gives the invisible grace); *Epistolae* 98, 2 (CSEL 34.2:521–22): "Aqua igitur exhibens forinsecus sacramentum gratiae, et Spiritus operans intrinsecus beneficium gratiae ... regenerant hominem" (Therefore the water, displaying outwardly the sacrament of grace, and the Spirit, working inwardly the benefit of grace ... regenerate man); *Sermo* 272, 1 (PL 38:1247): "Ista, fratres, ideo dicuntur sacramenta, quia in iis aliud videtur, aliud intelligitur. Quod videtur speciem habet corporalem; quod intelligitur, fructum habet spiritualem" (Therefore, brethren, they are called sacraments because in them one thing is seen, and another is understood. What is seen has a bodily appearance; what is understood has a spiritual fruit); *Quaestiones in Heptateuchum* III, 84 (CCL 33:1882–94): "quomodo ergo et moyses sanctificat et dominus? Non enim moyses pro domino, sed moyses uisibilibus sacramentis per ministerium suum, dominus autem inuisibili gratia per spiritum sanctum, ubi est totus fructus etiam uisibilium sacramentorum. Nam sine ista sanctificatione inuisibilis gratiae, uisibilia sacramenta quid prosunt? ... Nihil quippe profuit symoni mago uisibilis baptismus, cui sanctificatio inuisibilis defuit" (In what way, therefore, do both Moses and the Lord sanctify? For Moses does not sanctify for the Lord, but rather Moses sanctifies by visible sacraments through his ministry, while the Lord sanctifies by invisible grace through the Holy Spirit, in whom is all the fruit of the visible sacraments also. For without that sanctification of invisible grace, what good are the visible sacraments? ... Certainly visible baptism was of no benefit to Simon Magus, who lacked invisible sanctification"; *De catechizandis rudibus* XXVI, 50 (CCL 46:4): "signacula quidem rerum diuinarum esse uisibilia, sed res ipsas inuisibiles in eis honorari" (moreover the signs of divine things are visible, but the invisible things themselves are honored in them).

broad definition that can be applied to anything that guides us from what is earthly and visible to what is invisible and divine; and it embraces both the Mosaic sacrifices and the rites of Jesus or other liturgical gestures. Other examples of sacraments are the full moon or the duration of the Triduum in the celebration of Easter.[32] Let us start by noting what all these signs in this group have in common: the transition or passage from what is created to the Father, through the work of Jesus.[33]

The background of the sacraments—the transition from the world to the Father ✎ I have already noted that the sign serves to introduce us into the movement of charity which, starting in God, runs through salvation history with its center in Christ and its final destiny in the Father. This means that the sacrament is a *sacred* sign, not only inasmuch as it points to knowledge of God, but also inasmuch as it introduces us into a personal dialogue with him, the giver of the signs, until we arrive at full communion. In this way the sacrament helps us to go through the history of the covenant. For Augustine there is a *sacramentum memoriae* (sacrament of memory) and a *sacramentum spei* (sacrament of hope).[34] All biblical signs "help to inflame the love through which we tend to that [final] rest."[35]

This is confirmed in *Letter 55 to Januarius*, a short treatise on the sacraments.[36] Januarius had asked about the rites of the Paschal celebration: spring, the full moon, the explanation of each day of the Triduum, etc. Augustine responds: unlike the nativity, which only commemorates the specific date of a major event, Easter is full of "sacraments," that is, of signs that show us our path through this world to the Father. Everything is centered on the transition of Jesus from death to life, and from the flesh to the Spirit. This passage ("Passover") of the master has repercussions on the disciples, Augustine adds, along two coordinates: it has already occurred in us through faith (because we live in the Spirit), and it will be consummated in

32. *Epistolae* LV, 5, 8–9 (CSEL 34.2:177–80); LV, 14, 24 (CSEL 34.2:195).

33. On the sacrament in St. Augustine: R. Russell, "The Concept of a Sacrament in St. Augustine," *Eastern Churches Quarterly* (1936): 73–79 and 121–31; Henri-Marie Féret, "Sacramentum. Res. Dans la langue théologique de S. Augustin," *Revue de sciences philosophiques et théologiques* 29, nos. 2/4 (1940): 218–43; P. Thomas Camelot, "Sacramentum fidei," *Augustinus Magister* (Paris, 1954), 2:891–96, and "Sacramentum: Notes de théologie sacramentaire augustinienne," *Revue Thomiste* 57 (1957): 429–49; François Berrouard, "Pour une réflexion sur le 'sacramentum' augustinien: la manne et l'eucharistie dans le *Tractatus XXVI, 11–12 in Johannis Evangelium*," in *Forma Futuri: Studi in onore del Cardinale Michele Pellegrino* (Turin: Bottega d'Erasmo, 1975), 830–44; Emmanuel J. Cutrone, "Sacraments," in *Augustine Through the Ages: An Encyclopedia*, ed. Allan J. Fitzgerald (Grand Rapids, Mich.: Eerdmans, 1999), 741–47; Lienhard, "*Sacramentum* and the Eucharist."

34. *Contra Faustum* XX, 21 (CSEL 25:564); XII, 20 (CSEL 25:349).

35. *Epistolae* LV, 12, 22 (CSEL 34.2:193).

36. Camelot, "Sacramentum," 431–40.

hope, when our flesh arises, having become spiritual flesh.[37] Herein lies the
key with which to understand the celebration: the month of the first-fruits
signifies the new Paschal life and the new time that Jesus inaugurates.[38] The
full moon marks the moment in which our satellite starts to draw closer to
the sun, the symbol of God, losing its brilliance on the eyes of this world;
and finally, the Sunday of the resurrection, the eighth day that follows the
seven days of this age, points to that rest where Jesus himself will be our
solace.[39]

This perspective is examined in greater depth in a famous passage from
The City of God, which culminates a long discussion about the right worship of God, a discussion that is conducted during the first ten books of the
work. Augustine tries to describe what the true sacrifice is, and for this purpose reads Psalm 51(50).[40] Sacrifices are not pleasing to God; and nevertheless one does please him: the sacrifice of a contrite heart (Ps 51[50]:16–17).
Does King David contradict himself here? Does God want sacrifices or not?

To answer, Augustine resorts to the concept of "sacrament." Animal sacrifices were sacraments (that is, sacred signs) of the true sacrifice, which consists of ordering everything to the creator. Mercy, the supreme sacrifice (see
Hos 6:6–7) is rooted precisely in this: loving one's neighbors (and oneself)
so as to lead all to God. We have here again, closely united, the cognitive
dynamic of the sign (*sacramentum*) and the dynamic of love (*sacrificium*).
The sign of the sacrificed animal reveals to us the offering of a contrite heart,
which focuses our loves on the divine love. The sacrament, the path of the
signs toward what is true, is associated with the sacrifice, which is a transition of charity toward God. This connection is analogous to the one that
we already observed between the binomial *signum-res* and the binomial
uti-frui.

Christ, dead and risen—sacrifice and sacrament ✎ The passage from
The City of God that I have commented on continues by pointing out the
culmination of this sacrifice *par excellence* which is mercy: Christ's offering
of himself to the Father on the cross. For on Calvary Jesus, who took on
everything that is human, channels this in a well-aimed movement toward
God. This means that the axis of the sacrament does not point simply from
the visible sacrifices of the Old Testament toward a superior, invisible one.
In other words, the axis of the sign does not go from low to high but rather

37. *Epistolae* LV, 2, 3 (CSEL 34.2:171).
38. Ibid., 3, 5 (CSEL 34.2:174).
39. Ibid., 9, 17 (CSEL 34.2:187).
40. *De civitate Dei* X, 5–6 (CCL 47:276–79; NPNF-I 2:183–84).

traverses the ages to culminate in the bodily sacrifice of Jesus. And this sacrifice, because it is offered in the visible flesh, continues to be a sacrament also, or rather, the supreme sacrament. Jesus is, then, the fullness of the *sacrificium* and the fullness of the *sacramentum*.

It is possible then to ask ourselves: if the death and resurrection of Jesus is itself a sacrament, of what is it a sign? To what does it point? St. Augustine distinguishes two directions, according to the pattern that St. Paul offers and to which I have already referred. On the one hand, the death and resurrection of Jesus manifests our death to the old man and our rising to new life (see Rom 6:4). On the other hand, the death and resurrection of Jesus anticipates for us the one that will occur corporeally in those who believe in him, at the end of time (see Rom 6:5).[41] The first axis goes toward the depths, so as to describe from the perspective of faith the change that has already taken place in Christian life. The second goes toward the future, so as to discover in hope what is promised to our body: its glorification.

In other passages St. Augustine refers to these two aspects as *sacramentum* and *exemplum*. *Sacramentum*: what Christ suffers visibly signifies, in Christians, their death to sin and resurrection to the justice that has already occurred in them. *Exemplum*: what happened corporeally to Jesus will happen corporeally to the Christian, who is called to the resurrection.[42] This terminology (*sacramentum-exemplum*) combines the two elements of signification according to Augustine: the sacrament is the passage from the exterior to the interior; but also the passage of all history to its final, eschatological fulfillment in the risen flesh.

In short, in order to point to the body of Christ, the path of signs does not follow the direction indicated by the Platonic books that the bishop of Hippo had read. The sign is not an arrow that moves us away from the world toward the heights, but rather a thread on which history is strung so as to reflect, in this way, the movement of God's love toward his weak creature which needs to mature in time. Within this framework it will be possible for us to define the place of the sacraments instituted by Jesus.

The sacraments of the new covenant, from the body of Christ ☙ We have seen how, in defining a sacrament as a sign in *The City of God*, St. Augustine is thinking about the sacrifices of the Old Testament, for they invite us to look beyond, to the true sacrifice, that of Jesus. Does the name sacra-

---

41. *Epistolae* LV, 2, 3 (CSEL 34.2:172).

42. Basile Studer, "'Sacramentum et exemplum' chez saint Augustin," *Recherches Augustiniennes* 10 (1975): 87–141; the terminology appears above all in *De Trinitate* IV, 3, 6 (CCL 50:49).

ment apply also to the Eucharist, the sacrifice of the Christians? We will see that it does, but with a major difference.[43]

On the one hand St. Augustine links the rites of Israel and those of the church. Both the Jews in the manna and the Christians in the Eucharist receive one and the same spiritual fruit, for they both feed on the Word of God through faith in Jesus.[44] Still, the bishop of Hippo distinguishes between the old worship and the new, resorting for this purpose to a grammatical argument. For in Mosaic times this faith professed that someone "will be born," "will suffer," "will rise." Now, nevertheless, the words have changed, for we say that he "was born," "suffered," "rose again."[45] From this it follows that in these two cases the reality is the same,[46] but whereas then salvation was received only in a promise (the future form of the verb), now we receive the Savior himself who has already come to us (past form of the verb).[47] In short: *the Old Testament drank of Christ in sign; the New Testament receives the true Christ in Word and flesh.*[48] Then in shadow, now in truth.[49]

This mention of the Word and the flesh touches on the crucial point of Augustine's approach, which is based on the incarnation. If the old sacrifices were signs of what was to follow in Christ, the summit of mercy, the Eucharist too proves to be a sign of Christ. It too directs our attention to the sacrifice that is Jesus himself. It too is, for this reason, a sacrament. The difference is that the Eucharist not only points to the incarnation but also flows from it, and therefore allows us to receive the reality that is signified: Christ in Word and flesh, the mystery *par excellence* of God.[50] Hence the Christian sacrament, besides pointing toward Christ, shares in him.[51]

43. Berrouard, "Pour une réflexion sur le *'sacramentum'* augustinien."

44. *De doctrina christiana* III, 8, 12 to 9, 13 (CCL 36:42; NPNF-I 2:560a–b); *In Iohannis* XLV, 9 (CCL 36:392; NPNF-I 7:252): "Fide manente signa variata" (Under different signs there is the same faith).

45. Therefore Augustine joins the sacrament to the celebration of a past event; Augustine, *Epistolae* LV, 1, 2 (CSEL 34.2:170).

46. *Contra Faustum* XIX, 16 (CSEL 25:512–14).

47. *Enarrationes in psalmos* LXXIII, 2 (CCL 39:1006): "sacramenta novi testamenti dant salutem; sacramenta veteris testamenti promiserunt salvatorem" (The sacraments of the New Testament give salvation; the sacraments of the Old Testament promised the Savior).

48. *In Iohannis* XXVI, 12 (CCL 36:366; NPNF-I 7:172a): "Petra Christus in signo, verus Christus in Verbo et in carne" (The rock was Christ in sign; the real Christ is in the Word and in flesh).

49. Ibid., XXVI, 13 (CCL 36:366; NPNF-I 7:172a): "manna umbra erat, iste ueritas est" (The manna was only a shadow, this is the truth).

50. *Sermo* X, 2 (CCL 41:2): "[Christus] qui omnium sacramentorum vita est" ([Christ], who is the life of all sacraments); *Epistolae* 187, 11 (CSEL 57:112): "non est enim aliud dei mysterium nisi Christus" (There is no other mystery of God except Christ).

51. This is demonstrated by François Berrouard, "'Similitudo' et la définition du réalisme sacramentel d'après l'Epître XCVIII, 9–10 de saint Augustin," *Revue des études augustiniennes et patristiques* 7, no. 4 (1961): 321–37.

In order to confirm the relation between Christ and the Eucharist, it is enough to recall how Augustine ascribes a double effect to the Paschal sacrament (passion and exaltation), following the binomial *sacramentum-exemplum*. On the one hand we already enjoy the new life of Jesus (*sacramentum*) and, on the other hand, we will share in his resurrection in the flesh at the end of time (*exemplum*). Well, then, this same double effect is attributed to reception of the Eucharist. In it the new life of Jesus is given to us, even now; and through it the resurrection of the bodies will be given to us at the end of time.[52] In fact, the reason why the New Testament still contains rites is because we have not yet arrived at the resurrection of the body, which is the final cause of these rites.[53] The sacraments of the new covenant are interpreted, therefore, in terms of the great sacrament that is the Passover of Jesus, in which the definitive transition to the Father of all creation is consummated.

From all this we can derive a corollary: the Eucharist, being a *sacrament*, already contains the unity of the body of the church who, in offering it on the altar, offers herself.[54] For this reason Augustine can exhort the Christians who receive Communion: contemplate what you are, become what you receive.[55] In baptism, too, ecclesial communion comes about, for we call "sacrament" not only the rite but also the permanent incorporation of the baptized person into the body of Jesus.[56] Through baptism we are moistened so as to form one mass of dough; and then we receive the fire of

---

52. *In Iohannis* XXVI, 16 (CCL 36:268).

53. *Contra Faustum* XIX, 9 (CSEL 25:507; NPNF-I 4:242b–243a): "nam neque penitus auferri debuit nouae vitae sacramentum, quia restat adhuc in nobis futura resurrectio mortuorum" (For neither should the sacrament of the new life be wholly discontinued, for our resurrection from the dead is still to come).

54. *De civitate Dei* X, 6 (CCL 47:279; NPNF-I 2:184b): "Hoc est sacrificium Christianorum: multi unum corpus in Christo. Quod etiam sacramento altaris fidelibus noto frequentat ecclesia, ubi ei demonstratur, quod in ea re, quam offert, ipsa offeratur" (This is the sacrifice of Christians: we, being many, are one body in Christ. And this also is the sacrifice which the Church continually celebrates in the sacrament of the altar, known to the faithful, in which she teaches that she herself is offered in the offering she makes to God).

55. *Sermo* 227, 1 (SC 116:234): "Si bene accepistis, uos estis quod accepistis" (If you receive worthily, you are what you receive); *Sermo* 272, 1 (PL 38:1247): "Si ergo uos estis corpus Christi et membra, mysterium uestrum in mensa Dominica positum est: mysterium uestrum accipitis. Ad id quod estis, Amen respondetis, et respondendo subscribitis. Audis enim, Corpus Christi; et respondes, Amen. Esto membrum corporis Christi, ut uerum sit Amen.... Estote quod uidetis, et accipite quod estis" (Therefore if you are the Body of Christ and members of it, the mystery that you are is situated in the Lord's Supper: receive the mystery that you are. You respond Amen to what you are, and in responding you agree. For you hear "Body of Christ" and you respond "Amen." Be a member of Christ's Body, so that your Amen may be true.... Be what you see, and receive what you are).

56. Haring, "St. Augustine's Use of the Word 'Character,'" and "The Augustinian Axiom: *Nulli Sacramento Injuria Facienda Est*," *Medieval Studies* 16 (1954): 87–117; and "Berengar's Definitions of Sacramentum and Their Influence on Mediaeval Sacramentology," *Medieval Studies* 10 (1948): 109–46. See chapter 12, below.

the Spirit, which bakes the bread so as to strengthen our ties.[57] In light of this, the scope of the sacraments of the new covenant proves to be coextensive with the scope of the body of Christ and of the church.

This confirms that a general concept of signification (a sort of "sign-arrow" that will elevate us from this world to the heights according to a Platonic axis) is not enough to contain the Augustinian synthesis. For the Eucharist, and baptism too, are not simple signs of something that is encountered beyond them, but rather a real participation in what happened in the flesh of Christ and will be given to us fully when we are raised from the dead. In light of this the equating of sacrament and sign proves to be insufficient, inasmuch as the sacrament, far from sending us to a distant salvific reality, introduces us into the space where this living reality is encountered. Augustine himself emphasized, in the light of St. Paul's teaching, the imperfection of equating sacrament and sign. For the apostle not only declared that in baptism *we signify* Christ's burial, but rather he said that in baptism *we are buried* with him.[58] Therefore we can declare that the sacrament of the body of Jesus is not only a sign of this body but the very body of Jesus.[59]

Structure of the sign—word and element ⬧ This framework allows us to ask, finally, about the structure of ritual. Faithful to the Bible, Augustine discovers in the sacraments a visible element and a word. "What is the baptism of Christ? The washing of water by the Word. Take away the water, it is no baptism; take away the Word, it is no baptism."[60] This unity of matter (water) and word allows Augustine to speak about the sacrament as a "visible word."[61]

How are the word and the material action related in the sacrament? St. Augustine answers in a passage from his *Commentary on St. John* that would become very influential. The water, he says, touches the flesh and cleanses the heart. It cannot do this, of course, by its aquatic properties alone, but

57. *Sermo* 272, 1 (PL 38:1247).

58. *Epistolae* 98, 9 (CSEL 34.2:531) which cited Rom 6:4: "non ait: 'sepulturam significauimus,' sed prorsus ait: 'Consepulti sumus.' Sacramentum ergo tantae rei non nisi eiusdem uocabulo nuncupauit" (He does not say, "we signified Christ's burial," but plainly says, "We are buried with him." Therefore he called the sacrament of such a great matter by the same name and no other).

59. Ibid.: "sicut ergo secundum quendam modum sacramentum corporis christi corpus christi est, sacramentum sanguinis christi sanguis christi est, ita sacramentum fidei fides est" (therefore, just as in a certain way the sacrament of Christ's body is the Body of Christ, and the sacrament of Christ's blood is the Blood of Christ, so too the sacrament [mystery] of faith is faith).

60. *In Iohannis* XV, 4 (CCL 36:152; NPNF-I 7:100a).

61. *Contra Faustum Manichaeum* XIX, 16 (CSEL 25:513; NPNF-I 4:244b): "quod enim sunt aliud quaeque corporalia sacramenta nisi quaedam quasi uerba uisibilia, sacrosancta quidem uerum tamen mutabilia et temporalia?" (For what else are material sacraments but visible words which, though sacred, are nevertheless changeable and transitory?). See *In Iohannis* LXXX, 3 (CCL 36:529).

rather inasmuch as it is accompanied by the word. The word is added to the element, and the sacrament is formed, which is like a visible word (*accedit verbum ad elementum et fit sacramentum, etiam ipsum tamquam uisibile uerbum*).[62] The bishop of Hippo then compares the action of the sacrament with the pronunciation of a word that is heard and passes, whose light and force however remain in the one who listened to it. Note that the word, here, is not composed of matter and idea only, but also of matter and communicative force: it is a saving word, a word of vocation or promise; it is the word of faith, capable of transforming the one who receives it.

Does this mean that Augustine reduces the sacrament to the word alone, diminishing the importance of the material element? That would be a reductive reading. For, on the one hand, the bishop of Hippo makes it clear that without water there is no baptism. Moreover, deep down Augustine has in mind the event of the incarnation, in which the flesh and the Word are united.[63] Christ was able to unite us to himself because he took flesh. We find ourselves, then, in a position diametrically opposed to a kind of spiritualism that dilutes the sign into the word, into a mere message, and forgets the flesh of the sacrament. Recall how Augustine explains, in the same work, the saying of Jesus, "the flesh is of no avail" (Jn 6:63). The flesh is good for nothing if it is separated from the Spirit; it is very beneficial if it is filled with him; and the incarnation took place precisely for this purpose.[64]

Let us add two more details about the structure of the sacrament as the bishop of Hippo understands it. In the first place, because the sacrament is a sign, the symbolism of the material elements used has great value. And thus, for example, the bread and wine remind us of the unity of all Christians in

---

62. *In Iohannis* LXXX, 3 (CCL 36:529; NPNF-I 7:344b); François Berrouard, "Le *Tractatus* 80,3 *in Iohannis Evangelium* de saint Augustin: la parole, le sacrement, la foi," *Revue des études Augustiniennes* 33 (1987): 235–54; see also St. Augustine, *Sermo* 229, 1 (*Miscellanea Agostiniana* 1:29.22): "sed iste panis et hoc vinum accedente verbo fit corpus et sanguis Verbi" (but with the addition of the word, that bread and this wine become the body and blood of the Word); *Sermo* 229, 3 (*Miscellanea Agostiniana* 1:31.15): "nam tolle verbum, panis est et uinum: adde uerbum, et iam aliud est. et ipsum aliud, quid est? corpus christi, et sanguis christi. Tolle ergo uerbum, panis est et uinum: adde verbum, et fiet sacramentum" (For take away the word, and it is bread and wine; add the word, and now it is something else. And what is this other thing? The body of Christ and the blood of Christ. Therefore take away the word, it is bread and wine; add the word, and it will become a sacrament); *Sermo* 234, 2 (PL 38:1116): "[panis] accipiens benedictionem Christi, fit corpus Christi" ([the bread], in receiving Christ's blessing, becomes the body of Christ).

63. Camelot, "Sacramentum," 443.

64. *In Iohannis* XXVII, 5 (CCL 36:272; NPNF-I 7:175b): "Caro non prodest quidquam, sed sola caro; accedat spiritus ad carnem, quomodo accedit caritas ad scientiam, et prodest plurimum. Nam si caro non prodesset, Verbum caro non fieret, ut inhabitaret in nobis.... Caro uas fuit; quo habebat adtende, non quod erat" ("The flesh profiteth nothing," only when alone. Let the Spirit be added to the flesh, as charity is added to knowledge, and it profiteth very much. For if the flesh profited nothing, the Word would not be made flesh to dwell among us.... Flesh was a vessel; consider what it held, not what it was).

one body, like the grains of wheat in one loaf or the clusters of grapes in one and the same cup.[65] In the second place, given that the sacrament situates us in the stream of God's love, the rite communicates its own force, as becomes plain in the expression *virtus sacramenti* (virtue or force of the sacrament). While the sign points to a signified reality (*res sacramenti*) which is ultimately God himself, the *virtus sacramenti* is the divine impulse that carries us in the direction indicated by the sign, until we reach our final goal.[66]

The Sacrament as Sign: Christian Newness and Philosophical Reflection

It remains for us to ask a question about the famous Augustinian definition. In reflecting so much on signs, might Augustine have watered down the Gospel wine with pagan philosophy? In reality, as we have seen, the comparison of a sacrament to a sign draws from two sources: the biblical input, which accepts the Johannine view of the *semeion* and the Pauline view of the *mysterion*, associated with the body of Christ; and philosophical reflection, tinged with a neo-Platonic influence.

The first perspective is the one that gives rise to and invigorates Augustine's thought. As I have shown, he sees the sign as a revelation of God's love so as to lead us to himself; this interpretation overcomes mere intellectualism. The sign is situated in the context of a covenant with God and is always rooted in the flesh and in the relations of communion that arise in it. The distinctive characteristic of the sign is not to elevate us to the heights by transcending what is earthly, but rather to move us along a salvation history which culminates in the resurrection of the flesh. Augustine's approach can be interpreted, in fact, in biblical terms, with a simple equation: the reason why the *mysterium* (or *sacramentum*) is a *signum* is because Paul (*mysterion*) = John (*semeion*).

Furthermore, the bishop of Hippo, by resorting to philosophical reflection, makes sure that the sacraments can be related with the experience of every human being and the culture of every people. For when God reveals himself he does so to human beings and through human beings; hence, in order to grasp his Word, it is necessary to understand the signs proper to

---

65. *In Iohannis* XXVI, 17 (CCL 36:268; NPNF-I 7:173a–b): "Dominus noster Iesus Christus corpus et sanguinem suum in eis rebus commendauit, quae ad unum aliquid rediguntur ex multis. Namque aliud in unum ex multis granis confit, aliud in unum ex multis acinis confluit" (Our Lord Jesus Christ has pointed our minds to His body and blood in those things, which from being many are reduced to some one thing. For a unity is formed by many grains forming together; and another unity is effected by the clustering together of many berries).

66. Berrouard, "Le 'Tractatus 80,3,'" 235–54.

civilization. Thus, a large part of the second book of *De doctrina christiana* is dedicated to showing the importance of history, physics, mathematics, philosophy, etc., in deciphering the divine message.

Moreover, this effort to dialogue with culture allowed philosophical thought to be enriched by the Christian doctrine about the sacraments. Specifically, Augustine contributed to the study of language, being the first to present it as a set of signs. He arrived at this perspective starting from exegesis of the Bible, whose signs could be understood in their entirety as God's language for revealing himself to man.

Finally, the vision of faith also passes a judgment on all human efforts to comprehend. For St. Augustine is well aware of the fact that God appears foolish to the worldly-wise, who miss his humble signs of flesh and cross: "Yet, since we when we come to Him [divine Wisdom] do wisely, He when He came to us was considered by proud men to have done very foolishly."[67] Augustine offers an example of this critical dialogue with philosophy when he describes worship as contemplation of the truth, an idea that he shares with the Platonist sage and which fits nicely with the equating of sacrament and sign.[68] Still, Augustine does not understand this contemplation as the work of the mere intellect which purifies its view, but rather as knowledge that appeals to our heart. Indeed, according to what he had experienced in his conversion, in order to inspect the truth thoroughly, human efforts are not enough. It is necessary to let the truth reveal itself to us and to lead us to itself. This knowledge is the substance of religion (*religio*), which in Augustine's view comes not from the Latin word for "reread" (*re-lego*, Cicero), but rather from "to be reattached," to bind oneself to the source of light.[69] This humble reception is the basis for the full act of worship (sacrifice) by which we are united to God.

Conclusion

In this chapter we saw how Augustine explains the fact that the sacrament is a sign. He understands the sign *from the viewpoint of God's personal communication to man*, in which the important thing, along with what is said and understood, is who says it and to whom. From this perspective the *word* emerges as the suitable referent by which to understand the other signs.

---

67. *De doctrina christiana* I, 11, 11 (CCL 32:12; NPNF-I 2:525b).

68. Theo Kobusch, "Das Christentum als Religion der Wahrheit: Überlegungen zu Augustins Begriff des Kultus," *Revue des études Augustiniennes* 29 (1983): 97–128.

69. *De vera religione* LV, 113 (CCL 32:259); *religio* comes also from "choosing (God) again": *De civitate Dei* X, 3 (CCL 47:275; NPNF-I 2:182a); Kobusch, "Das Christentum," 123.

The biblical context (God who dialogues with man over the course of history) *explains the parallel between the cognitive path of signs and the way of charity*. That is to say, the light that emanates from signs enables us to see history as a route which, with its fullness in Jesus, directs all things from the first love of the Father to their consummation in him. Augustine insists on the harmony between sign and love in associating the *sacramentum* (sign that points to God) with the *sacrificium* (union of all loves in the divine love).

The axis of signs therefore traverses salvation history and culminates in the body of Christ. In Jesus a twofold openness of the sign appears. For he shows us the new life that believers have already received, in communion with God and the brethren, as well as the future resurrection of the body. The sacraments, which are derived from Jesus' side, pierced by the lance, are signs that associate us also with a twofold goal: the body of the risen Christ, inasmuch as it is already the source of new relations between human beings in the church; and the same body of the risen Christ inasmuch as our bodies will be conformed to it at the completion of history. St. Augustine sometimes describes these two dimensions of the sacrament as *sacramentum* and *exemplum*.

Given in the sacrament, then, is a revelation (it is a sign), but not only as cognitive clarity, but rather as a light that is born of love, so as to reveal love's order and path, with its source and destination in God. Hence in the sacrament, as in every sign, a passage occurs from the exterior to the interior; not so that the subject can remain deep in thought, but rather so that he can delve more deeply into these relations and ties with God and with his brethren that constitute the core of personal identity. In this way, sacramental signs, far from being a system of abstract formulas, display a map to guide us in the affective space and to lead us toward perfect rest in God.

To summarize: this connection of the sacrament with the impulse of charity, which traverses the flesh and human history, allows us to do justice to the Augustinian doctrine about the sacrament as sign. It is time to study, in the next chapter, the sometimes reductive way in which the rich and in some respects tortuous heritage of Augustine has been received. This review will confirm the importance of keeping closely linked the view of the sacrament as a sign and the experience of communion in the body of Christ and of the church.

9 ❧ SIGN AND CAUSE OF GRACE

The Sacraments in the Medieval Synthesis

The Augustinian heritage was very much present throughout the medieval period. Recall that Peter Lombard, in his *Sentences*, used as the general outline for his work the division of *De doctrina christiana* by St. Augustine, which distinguishes things (*res*) and signs (*signa*). Lombard deals primarily with things (*res*), to which he dedicates the first three books of his work (God, creatures, Christ); the fourth and last book corresponds to signs (*signa*), which are more precisely the sacraments, both of the Old and of the New Law.[1]

Well, we know that St. Augustine left us a rich, variegated view of the sacraments, and also that he did not order his viewpoint systematically but rather scattered statements throughout his writings. The Middle Ages, which tended to isolate patristic formulas, ran the risk of reducing their scope.[2] Despite everything, theologians were able to gather Augustine's viewpoint; and this was because they were looking at one and the same object, with their faith-lives nurtured by one and the same experience.

Is a Sacrament a Sacred Sign?

It is remarkable that those who read St. Augustine before the twelfth century did not consider his definition of sacrament as a sign to be decisive: this was because the formula was never the focal point of his perspective. The equating of sacrament and sign would be asserted only as a result of the Eucharistic debate, and for reasons that were a little heterodox. Its champion

---

1. See Peter Lombard, *Sent.* I, 1 (SpBon IV:55); *Sent.* IV, *Incipit* (SpBon V:231).

2. See Haring, "Berengar's Definitions of Sacramentum," 112, where the author cites Guitmund of Aversa: "Ex beato Augustino scandali pene totius videtur esse principium" (The beginning of almost the whole scandal seems to be from St. Augustine).

was Berengar of Tours (d. 1088), who was famous for having denied the real presence of Jesus on the altar. For this reason, in order to understand the definition of sacrament as sign it is necessary to consider the Eucharistic debates, both between Paschasius Radbertus and Ratramnus (ninth century), and between Berengar and Lanfranc (eleventh century). We have here another proof of the centrality of the Eucharist with respect to the other sacraments: sacramental language took shape in the controversy surrounding it.

Paschasius Radbertus and Ratramnus: Between Truth and Figure

The first Eucharistic debate took place in the ninth century, and its protagonists were two monks of the Monastery of Corbie, St. Paschasius Radbertus and Ratramnus, who disagreed about the mode of Jesus' presence in the Eucharist.[3] It should be noted, however, that the equating of sacrament and sign was not mentioned, and that the discussion is profoundly influenced by the approach of St. Isidore of Seville, who emphasizes, more than the revealing sign, the salvific activity or force of the sacrament which acts secretly.[4]

This does not keep Paschasius's view from including the chief aspects of Augustine's theology. For Paschasius, the center of the sacramental action is the salvation of the flesh that is consecrated by the Spirit: "they are called sacraments because, beneath their visible appearance, which is seen, the flesh is secretly consecrated by the divine power."[5] Thus the Eucharist gives us the body of Christ and brings about the unity of Christians in one body; baptism, for its part, is birth to this body, incorporation into it; all of which occurs in the power of the Spirit.[6]

---

3. See Celia Chazelle, "Figure, Character and the Glorified Body in the Carolingian Eucharistic Controversy," *Traditio* 47 (1992): 1–36; María Ángeles Navarro Girón, "La eucaristía, memorial del sacrificio de Cristo en la primera controversia eucarística (s.IX)," *Revista española de teología* 55 (1995): 29–63 and 135–79.

4. See Isidore of Seville, *Etymologiae* VI, 19, 40–41 (PL 82:255c): "Sacramenta dicuntur, quia sub tegumento corporalium rerum virtus divina secretius salutem eorundem sacramentorum operatur; unde a secretis virtutibus, vel a sacris sacramenta dicuntur. Quae ideo fructuose penes Ecclesiam fiunt, quia sanctus in ea manens Spiritus eumdem sacramentorum latenter operatur effectum" (They are called sacraments because beneath the covering of corporeal things the divine power secretly effects the salvation of those same sacraments; hence they are named sacraments after those secret virtues or after sacred things. In the Church's possession, therefore, they become fruitful, because the Holy Spirit abiding in her brings about that same effect of the sacraments in a hidden way). See also Paschasius Radbertus, *De corpore et sanguine Domini* III (CCCM 16:23–24).

5. Paschasius Radbertus, *De corpore et sanguine Domini* (CCCM 16:24): "ob hoc sacramenta uocantur, quia sub eorum specie uisibili quae uidetur secretius uirtute diuina caro consecratur, ut hoc sint interius in ueritate quod exterius creduntur uirtute fidei" (They are called sacraments because, beneath their visible species, which is seen, the flesh is secretly consecrated by the divine power, so that they might be interiorly in truth that which they are believed to be externally by the virtue of faith).

6. See ibid., IX (CCCM 16:57).

In this context Paschasius poses the question about the relation between what is visible and what is hidden, which is key to an understanding of sacrament. How can we affirm the presence of Jesus' body on the altar, if it cannot be seen, touched, tasted? Would we not have to say that this body is there *as a figure* or sign, but that it is present *in truth* only in heaven, where it is seated at the right hand of the Father? To answer, Paschasius makes at the same time two statements that could appear contradictory: in the Eucharist the body of Christ is present, both in truth and in figure.

Can something be a figure and, at the same time, be the truth? The answer is based on the difference between the Mosaic Law and the Law of Christ. In the rituals of the Old Testament we had a figure that was a shadow, not the truth; the Eucharist, however, presents a figure that is, at the same time, the true body of Christ. We can distinguish then between the manna received by Israel, which was a figure without truth, and the Eucharist, a figure in which we encounter the truth of the risen body of Jesus.

To show how this is possible, Paschasius's argument starts from an analogy with the incarnation: there the body is the *figure* of the Son of God, inasmuch as it reveals him to us; however, at the same time, the Son of God is *truly* encountered in this body. And what is said about Christ, the incarnate Word, finds a parallel in the corporeal condition of every human person. The person, in fact, is made present in his body (that is to say, is there *in truth*), but as a reality that goes beyond what is corporeal (the body is, therefore a *figure*).

I should add that, according to Paschasius, this going beyond the confines of the body (the body's ability to contain something that surpasses it) refers not only to the presence of Jesus, but also to the presence of other Christians in Jesus, because his body is the place where the relations that bring us together are rooted. That is to say, in the sacrament of the altar the body is opened up beyond itself and accommodates both the mystery of the Person of Christ and the mystery of the communion of human beings in Christ. Here too we encounter harmony with the embodied condition of the human person, for the body reveals the constitutive relations that unite us to the rest of the human family, in which we are children, siblings, spouses, etc., so as to share one flesh. On the altar, therefore, the body of Christ is encountered in *truth*, but at the same time in *figure*, inasmuch as this body is communicated to the church so that she might grow. The body is there *in truth*, because it is really present; *in figure*, because in a dynamism of expansion toward its ecclesial fullness. As the tree of life slowly produced a fruit so that man might receive immortality, so too the true tree of paradise, which is Christ, produces the Eucharist so that the church, his body, might attain the life of God.[7]

And so, in the definition that Paschasius gives of the sacrament, everything moves, not toward an ideal and distant reality, but rather toward consecrated flesh, that of the faithful, which is conformed to the flesh of the risen Lord.[8] Truth and figure do not contradict each other because the body of Jesus is considered in its personal mystery and in its dynamic communication to Christians.

Ratramnus, for his part, proposes a rather meager perspective. This is because for him the truth is the plain appearance of the thing, as opposed to what is hidden and secret. Therefore, without denying the presence of the Eucharistic body on the altar, he argues that it is distinct from the presence of the true body of Jesus, both when it was born of Mary and walked through Galilee, and also when it has ascended into heaven and remains incorruptible. Only in the case of Christ's personal body can it be said that we have the truth, without images or shadows; in the Eucharist, on the contrary, there is figure only, no truth.

Well, such an argument, in which the figure excludes the truth, departs from the patristic concept of sacrament; for a sign is understood now as a reference to something more distant, without realizing that there is a "corporeal sign" which not only points *toward* the person, but contains him in all his richness. Distancing himself from the direct connection with the experience of the body, Ratramnus starts down a slope that leads to difficulties in conceptualizing the Eucharist. The consequences will be clearly evident when the discussion is reframed, two centuries later, with Berengar of Tours.

Berengar and Lanfranc: Sacrament-Sign and Sacrament-Body

Berengar's novel argument is wrapped in traditional clothing; he reasons according to Augustine's definition: *a sacrament is a sacred sign.*[9] Togeth-

---

7. See ibid., VII (CCCM 16:39).

8. See ibid., IX (CCCM 16:57): "Ecce duo ista sacramenta quid efficiunt! Per baptismum ergo renascimur in Christo et per sacramentum corporis ac sanguinis Christus in nobis non solum fide, sed etiam unitate carnis et sanguinis manere probatur. Et ideo iam membra Christi eius carne uescimur, ut nihil aliud quam corpus eius, unde uiuimus, et sanguis inueniamur" (This is what these two sacraments accomplish! Through baptism, therefore, we are reborn in Christ and through the sacrament of the body and blood we experience that Christ remains among us, not only by faith, but also by the unity of flesh and blood. And therefore Christ's members already feed on His flesh, so that we might be found to be nothing other than the body and blood of Him on whom we live).

9. Concerning what I will say about Berengar, see Damien van den Eynde, *Les définitions des sacraments pendant la première période de la théologie scolastique (1050–1240)* (Rome: Antonianum, 1950); William A. Van Roo, *The Christian Sacrament* (Rome: Editrice Pontificia Università Gregoriana,

er with it, he will use this other expression: *visible form of invisible grace*, which is also inspired by the bishop of Hippo. Even though the formulas are Augustinian, Berengar reads them in his own way, then neatly identifies sacrament and sign, forgetting the wide palette of nuances that I noted in Augustine. For there to be a sacrament, Berengar concludes, there has to be a visible reality that points to another distant reality (the one signified by the sacrament), that is, to a final reality that can be grasped only by the reason, not by the senses.[10] An inevitable conclusion then follows: where the sacrament is, the reality to which it points is not.

What happens here is like when we see in the moon at night the reflection of the sun and say that there is a sign of the latter in the former. This way of understanding a sign (sign = reflection or sign = arrow) excludes the real presence: the sun is not in the moon, but much farther away, in a place inaccessible to the sense of sight. The Platonic allegory of the cave, where a bonfire projects shadows on the wall, concurs with this concept of sign: a reflection or an arrow that points beyond the sign.

Applying this definition to the Eucharist, the sacrament is identified with the species of bread and wine, while what is signified by the sacrament is the body of Jesus, which is not on the altar but in heaven. Peter Lombard summarized the erroneous theory as follows: "The body of Christ is there only in sacrament, that is, in sign, and we eat it only in sign."[11] Increasingly forceful responses to Berengar were made by Lanfranc of Bec (d. 1089), Guitmund of Aversa (d. 1095), and Alger of Liège (d. 1131). Indeed, it was clear that Berengar's definition left key points of Eucharistic doctrine unexplained. For in the Eucharist the visible sign and the reality signified cannot be separated (without denying the real presence). On the contrary, the Eucharist is a sacrament because in it the body of Jesus is made present and active.

Lanfranc sees here a clear connection with the logic of the incarnation, a connection that Paschasius Radbertus had already emphasized: Christ the man is the revelation of God and, at the same time, true God. Something similar happens in the Eucharist: on the altar we find a sign, yes, but a sign in

1992), 45; Adriano Caprioli, "Alle origini della 'definizione' di sacramento: da Berengario a Pier Lombardo," *La Scuola Cattolica* 102 (1974): 718–43; Haring, "Berengar's Definitions"; and Irène Rosier-Catach, "Signification et efficacité: sur les prolongements médiévaux de la théorie augustinienne du signe," *Revue de sciences philosophiques et théologiques* 91 (2007): 51–74.

10. See Haring, "Berengar's Definitions," 111.

11. See Peter Lombard, *Sent.* IV, d. 10, c. 1 (SpBon V:290); the retraction that was required of Berengar would read: "non tantum per signum et virtutem sacramenti, sed in proprietate naturae et veritate substantiae" (not only through the sign and power of the sacrament, but in its proper nature and in the truth of its substance) (DH 700).

which Jesus himself is made really present. This confirms that the language of the body underlies the logic of the sacraments, for the body is not only the expression but also the active presence of the person, who is encountered in the body and not beyond it.

In order to respond to Berengar, Lanfranc starts with a traditional formula: St. Augustine had spoken not only about the sacrament *of* the body of Christ, but about the sacrament *which is* the body of Christ.[12] Accepting the definition of sacrament as sign (because of its Augustinian ancestry), Lanfranc argues that the body of Christ that is on the altar is also a sacrament, for it is also a sign that points to another reality. Indeed, the Eucharistic body is *a sign of the historical body of Jesus*, which died on the cross and rose again from the tomb, and *a sign of the resurrected body that is promised to the Christian* when he feeds on the Eucharist.[13] Guitmund of Aversa, for his part, would add that the Eucharistic body is also *a sign of the body of the church*, because the communion of Christians is forged in the space of Jesus' body.[14]

In this way, in contrast to Berengar's reductive approach, a vision of the sacrament is proposed that it not a reflection of some other distant reality ("sign-arrow") but rather the active presence of what is signified. Thereby the incarnation and life of Jesus and our incorporation into him are made central to the sacrament, thus grasping the substance of the patristic approach. The Eucharistic body of Jesus is a sacrament inasmuch as salvation history is recapitulated in it; and inasmuch as it incorporates into itself, through this history, all mankind in the body of the church.

There is an opposition here between two ways of understanding sign or sacrament. On the one hand (Berengar), the sign is understood as a staircase by which to ascend from visible earthly things to heavenly spiritual things. We could speak about a *transcarnal sign*, because it abandons the flesh to arrive at a reality located on other shores. Above, I used the image of the "sign-arrow" which, from the bow of sensible things, propels us to an ideal target; or of the moon that reflects the inaccessible light of the sun. On the other hand, there is a vision of sacrament, not as an external reference to a distant reality, but rather as an open space in which to situate oneself so

12. Augustine, *Epistolae* 98, 9 to Boniface (CSEL 34.2:531): "sicut ergo secundum quendam modum sacramentum corporis christi corpus christi est, sacramentum sanguinis christi sanguis christi est, ita sacramentum fidei fides est" (therefore just as in a certain way the sacrament of Christ's body is the Body of Christ, and the sacrament of Christ's blood is the Blood of Christ, so too the sacrament [mystery] of faith is faith). I spoke about this remark in the preceding chapter.

13. See Lanfranc, *Liber de corpore et sanguine Domini*, ed. M. Aroztegi, in *Lanfranco: El cuerpo y la sangre del Señor* (Madrid: Publicaciones San Dámaso, 2009), 5:70–80.

14. See Guitmund of Aversa, *De corporis et sanguinis Christi veritate* (PL 149:1460–61).

as to encounter the signified reality there, and only there. We could speak, in this regard, about an *incarnate sign*, as opposed to the *transcarnal* sign, because the experience of living in the body is precisely what allows us to understand this type of signs: in the body the person is encountered; in the body are forged the relations of communion that constitute and enlarge personal life.

This latter view conforms with the incarnation event, in which the sign *par excellence* that is present in the Eucharist was given to us. As Lanfranc and his followers pointed out, this sign, rooted in the body of Jesus, runs through history, for it preserves the memory of the life of Christ and keeps alive the anticipation of our glorious fulfillment when we will be conformed to him; and, in turn, the same sign opens relationally toward communion with Jesus in the church. All this, as I will show, invites us to abandon the "sign-arrow" approach so as to speak about a "sign-body," in which life is open to a network of relations (below I will refer to this as "symbolic space") that gradually matures over time.

To conclude, let us recall the paradox to which I alluded earlier: Berengar's definition (sacrament as visible sign of an invisible reality) ended up becoming generally accepted, although his fundamental vision was rejected. Instead of changing the formula, theologians set about correcting, specifying, and completing it. In this way medieval theology succeeded in capturing the patristic experience in a system that was coherent, yes, but also complicated. The situation can be compared to what happened to Ptolemaic astronomy: even though it faithfully reflected the stellar phenomena, it tangled up the mathematical formulas by supposing that everything revolved around the earth. Similarly, medieval thinkers succeeded in grasping the biblical and patristic concept of sacrament, but only by developing a tortuous system which corrected their reductive definition of sacrament. Just as the theory of Copernicus, recognizing the sun as the center, offered a much simpler and straightforward description of the same data, so too it is possible, by situating the body of Jesus at the center of sacramental theology, to offer a view simpler than the medieval one, without having to discard its insights.

In order to complete this limping definition of sacrament as "sign-arrow," the learned doctors explored various paths: they developed a distinction between what is "sacrament only" (*sacramentum tantum*) and what is at the same time sacrament and signified reality (*sacramentum et res*); they discussed the composition of the sacramental sign as matter and form; and they added that the sign not only manifests but also *causes grace*. Let us look at these aspects in more detail.

Res et sacramentum: The Sign, Starting from the Body of Christ

While the Church Fathers understood the sacraments in terms of the body of Christ, the reduction of sacrament to sign brought about by Berengar forced theologians to adopt now as the point of reference, not the body present on the altar, but the species of bread and wine. To the extent that his definition became generally accepted, the tendency spread also to consider the material and visible sign in the rite as sacrament in the proper sense. As we will see, the authors did not stop calling the body of Christ a sacrament too, thus preserving the connection between sacrament and body that is central in the New Testament and in the Fathers. For this purpose they elaborated terminology which, starting with the Eucharist, distinguishes three dimensions of each sacrament.[15] First, *sacramentum tantum*: the mere sacrament or sign of another reality that is signified; in the Eucharist this will be the species of bread and wine. Second, *res et sacramentum*: something that is a signified reality and at the same time sacrament; for the Eucharist this is the body of Jesus which is really present. Third, *res tantum*: the ultimate reality of the signified grace, which in the Eucharist is the communion in charity of Jesus and his church.

What do these dimensions of sacrament mean? The first (*sacramentum tantum*) is the one that best corresponds to Berengar's definition: the species of bread and wine is a sign that points to a further invisible reality. The new feature that corrects the Berengarian lenses is in the second dimension (*res et sacramentum*): the body of Christ, which is at the same time sign and signified reality. For here we do not have a sign that points to a grace situated further on, but rather a sign that is also the event of grace and its continuous presence. For this reason Berengar's sign-arrow is not enough to explain this meaning.

As we saw, according to the medieval authors the body of Christ indicates something beyond itself (it is *sacramentum*), not inasmuch as it lifts us beyond the flesh, but inasmuch as it helps us to grasp the history of the flesh (the *dynamic* dimension of the sign), a history in which Christ makes us one

---

15. On the origin of the expression *res et sacramentum*, see Pedro López-González, "Origen de la expresión 'res et sacramentum,'" *Scripta Theologica* 17, no. 1 (1985): 73–119; Ronald F. King, "The Origin and Evolution of a Sacramental Formula: *sacramentum tantum, res et sacramentum, res tantum*," *The Thomist* 31, no. 1 (1967): 21–82; Ludwig Hödl, "*Sacramentum et res*—Zeichen und Bezeichnetes: Eine begriffsgeschichtliche Arbeit zum frühscholastischen Eucharistietraktat," *Scholastik* 38, no. 2 (1963): 161–82; Emanuele Doronzo, "Originis et evolutionis doctrinae de *re et sacramento* brevis delineatio," *Revue de l'Université d'Ottawa* 4, no. 4 (1934): 213–28.

with him, among ourselves, and with the Father (the *relational* dimension of the sign). What unfolds in this "sign-body" is, therefore, a space of *relations* (the communion of Jesus and his church), a space that *matures* over time, from the incarnation to the final resurrection. Aquinas captured this medieval vision by attributing to each sacrament a threefold sign: commemorating Jesus' passion, representing charity in the church, and anticipating the final resurrection.[16]

To summarize, given the incomplete definition of sacrament as mere sign (to which Berengar was inclined), a distinction came about that helped to recover a richer perspective, by calling the body of Christ *sacramentum et res*.[17] In this way the Eucharistic body of Jesus continues to be the *sacramentum par excellence* and the key to understanding what a sacrament is. And this is because this body, through the relations that open up from it and mature in history, points to the ultimate grace of communion between God and mankind, which will be called *res tantum*. The species of bread and wine (*sacramentum tantum*), for their part, are placed at the service of the central sacramentality of Christ's body, making it visible, but always according to the salvation history and communional traits proper to this body.

Once this distinction was established for the Eucharist, it would then be applied to the other sacraments, with special importance in the case of baptism.[18] In the Eucharist *res et sacramentum* indicates the real presence of the body of Jesus, as distinct from the grace of communion with God and fellow Christians, or *res tantum*; in baptism, in contrast, the terminology helps us to distinguish two effects of the sacrament: the baptismal character, through which we are incorporated into Jesus, and the grace received, which communicates the life of God. While the water that is poured is merely sacrament (*sacramentum tantum*), in the baptismal character we have something that is already a reality of grace and also a sacrament (*res et sacramentum*), for it in turn refers beyond itself, to the believer's living communion with Christ and the church (*res tantum*).

The schema for baptism closely follows Eucharistic theology. In fact, as

16. See Thomas Aquinas, *ST* III, q. 60, a. 3, co.; on the expression *res et sacramentum* in St. Thomas, see I. Bonetti, "*Res et sacramentum* nella concezione tomista dei sacramenti," *Divus Thomas (Piacenza)* 55 (1952): 228–37; Eloy Tejero, "La *res et sacramentum*, estructura y espíritu del Ordenamiento canónico: Síntesis doctrinal de santo Tomás," in P. Rodríguez et al., *Sacramentalidad de la Iglesia y sacramentos* (Pamplona: Universidad de Pamplona, 1983), 427–60.

17. See Haring, "Berengar's Definitions," 146: "Berengar's definitions of *sacramentum* finally had their triumph in the terminology of Duns Scotus, while the formula *sacramentum et res* is a silent tribute to the broader terminology of the Fathers."

18. It was first referred to baptism in the twelfth century, a century after the *Summa Sententiarum* had applied it to the Eucharist: see Haring, "Berengar's Definitions," 145.

I will elaborate further on (in chapter 12, below), the character consists in our permanent incorporation into Christ, which makes us members of his body. For this reason, if in the Eucharist the *res et sacramentum* is the body of Jesus present on the altar, in baptism the *res et sacramentum* continues to be connected to the body, in this case to the body of the baptized person insofar as it is incorporated into Christ's body. In this way the baptized person himself in his body (that is, in the concrete relations rooted in Jesus in which he lives) proves to be the key to understanding the sacrament. Again we can understand the *sacramentum* not as an arrow pointing toward a distant reality separated from the flesh, but rather as entrance into the network or space of relations of Jesus' body, where his grace is received.

Note that with the *res et sacramentum* of baptism, one aspect of the patristic doctrine is captured which was left out by the definition of sacrament as a mere visible sign. Indeed, St. Augustine many times identifies the *sacramentum* with a stable sacred bond that remains in the Christian, associating him to the body of Christ. The bishop of Hippo is faithful to the earlier tradition: the first Church Fathers defined baptism as a seal that is imprinted on the believer, and therefore they urged the faithful to guard it.[19] This is because they saw in the sacrament, beyond the liturgical rite, the new life of the believer, begotten as a member of the body of the church. The doctrine of *res et sacramentum* makes it possible to focus our interest again on the corporeal relations in which the Christian lives and on his journey in time. From there, the foundation is laid to extend the *res et sacramentum* to the whole set of seven sacraments, as I will demonstrate (in chapter 12, below, on the sacramental character).

To summarize, the *res et sacramentum* appears in order to resituate the sacrament in relation to the body, and more precisely with the body of Christ which generates the body of the church. Paschasius Radbertus, as early as the ninth century, had explained sacrament in this way, having recourse to the Gospel image of the treasure buried in the field. The treasure is grace, and the field is the body of Christ, in which all the relations of the church are rooted. Only by entering into the environment of Christ's body (only by digging in its field) can one find that treasure.[20] St. Bonaventure takes a similar position when he writes, in a passage inspired by St. Paul (see Col 2:17): "the sacraments of the first age [creation] were like a shadow of the truth; those of the middle age [the age of the Law]—like a figure or

19. For all of the following discussion, see chapter 5 and chapter 12.
20. See Paschasius Radbertus, *De corpore* XVII (CCCM XVI:98).

image; the last sacraments, that is, the sacraments of grace—like the body."[21]

Little by little, in Scholastic theology, the connection between *sacramentum* and body would weaken, and attention would be focused on the *sacramentum tantum* as the key to interpreting the sacraments. Duns Scotus, for example, restricts the sacrament to *aliquid visibile extra*, something outwardly visible.[22] This tendency leads to a blurring of the patristic insight that identified the *sacramentum* with the body of Christ and our baptismal participation in it. Thus we observe the retreat of sacramental life into the liturgical action, which makes it difficult for the sacraments to branch out into the whole life of the Christian. The effects of this reductive view would be even more noticeable in Protestant teaching, which I will examine in the next chapter.

Matter and Form—Body and Word

In analyzing the sacraments, a twofold structure leaps into view: there are material elements and there are words pronounced, as St. Augustine notes.[23] One statement of his, which we already know, would be very influential: "The word is joined to the element and the sacrament comes about, which is like a visible word."[24] Augustine uses similar expressions for the Eucharist: "This bread and this wine, when the word arrives, become the body and blood of the Word."[25] The place occupied in the first text by the sacrament is taken in the second by the body and blood of Christ. This confirms that the mystery of the incarnation (the Word assumes flesh) is present in Augustine's mind when he speaks about a "visible word." We know that this broader context fell into oblivion in the reductive view formulated by Berengar, who understood sacrament to mean the external rite, forgetting its rootedness in the human body.

Later the Middle Ages took up these two Augustinian aspects (*elementum*, on the one hand; *verbum*, on the other) and described the rite as the union of a material reality and a word.[26] Two ways of analyzing the sacra-

21. Bonaventure, *Breviloquium* VI, 2 (Quaracchi 5:266), following Hugh of St. Victor, *De sacramentis* I, 11, 6 (PL 176:346; *CV* 1:247).

22. On this point see Haring, "Berengar's Definitions," 143.

23. For the following discussion, see Artur Michael Landgraf, "Beiträge der Frühscholastik zur Terminologie der allgemeinen Sakramentenlehre," *Divus Thomas (Freiburg)* 29 (1951): 3–134, at 109–18; Damian van den Eynde, "The Theory of the Composition of the Sacraments in Early Scholasticism (I–III)," *Franciscan Studies* 11, no. 1 (1951): 1–20 and 117–44; 12 (1952): 1–26.

24. Augustine, *In Iohannem* LXXX, 3 (CCL 36:529).

25. Augustine, *Sermo* 229, 1 (*Miscellanea Agostiniana* 1:22.22); *Sermo* 229, 3 (*Miscellanea Agostiniana* 1:31.15).

26. See van den Eynde, "The Theory of the Composition," I, 5.

mental sign arose. The first, used by Hugh of St. Victor, identifies a tripartite composition: things, actions, words (*res, facta, verba*).[27] For Hugh this is a way of speaking about three types of sacraments, in other words, a way of classifying them into objects, deeds, utterances. But one important work compiled in his school, the *Summa Sententiarum*, later adopted this division to enumerate the dimensions of each sacrament, which is composed of material elements, actions, and words.[28] The second, on the other hand, is a bipartite composition, based directly on Augustine. His distinction between the word and the water (element) of baptism is applied to the other sacraments, starting with the Eucharist. We find this method attested in Gerhoh of Reichersberg, and then it was adopted by Peter Lombard (*res et verba*); from his work it spread rapidly.[29]

The first of these two options deals more closely with liturgical celebration; for this reason it includes ritual action and not only the things used in the sacrament. The preoccupation of the second is to determine what parts are essential in order for the administration of the sacrament to be valid. Based on this bipartite schema, the distinction between matter (the sensible element) and form (the words) of the sacrament would arise over the course of the twelfth century.

The first to appear was the term "form," which in patristic writings referred to the visibility of the sacrament, in other words, to the sensible sign, as opposed to the virtue or reality of grace which is communicated in it. Based on this, medieval theologians elaborated two new senses of "form." On the one hand, it is the *formula* pronounced in the sacrament, that is, the words, as distinct from the things used in the rite.[30] On the other hand, "form" denotes the entire ritual structure: thus, for example, they say that the sacraments of the heretics are valid if they are celebrated according to the correct form of the church (*in recta forma* or *in forma ecclesiae*).

The term *matter*, for its part, arises at a later time. It starts by indicating, in general, the entire visible substrate of the celebration: rituals, words, things, etc. Peter Lombard refers it to the water of baptism,[31] and soon we find it applied to the bread and wine of the Eucharist. In this way it comes to be a synonym of the material element used in the sacrament, although this technical sense was slow in arriving. Moreover, in defining the matter of the

---

27. See Hugh of St. Victor, *De sacramentis* II, 9, 1 (PL 176:471d).
28. See *Summa Sententiarum* IV, 1 (PL 176:118c).
29. See Gerhoh of Reichersberg, *De simoniacis*, in *Libelli de Lite* III, 255; cited by van den Eynde, "The Theory of the Composition," I, 8; Peter Lombard, *Sent.* IV, d. 1, c. 5, n. 6 (SpBon V:235).
30. See Landgraf, "Beiträge der Frühscholastik," 118.
31. See *Sent.* IV, d. 3, c. 6 (SpBon V:249).

sacraments, theologians would take into account Hugh of St. Victor's interest in capturing the active component of the rite. For this reason they would
say that the matter consists not only in things, but in the use of things, in
the ritual application of the elements.[32]

Hence I conclude that the terms "matter" and "form" did not enter into
liturgical terminology as a pair, but each one on its own account. Only later
on do we find them associated in referring, on the one hand, to the material
reality of the sacrament, and, on the other hand, to the formula or words
that are pronounced in it. Even so, this original combination of matter and
form that arises during the twelfth century does not depend on Aristotle's
hylomorphism. They are two aspects present in the sacrament, the origin of
which goes back to St. Augustine. And the terms are employed above all for
baptism and the Eucharist, without being applied systematically to all seven
sacraments.

The link between hylomorphism, on the one hand, and the material and
form of the sacraments, on the other hand, was not elaborated until the
thirteenth century. The similarity of vocabulary with the Aristotelian doctrine helped matter and form to be understood in terms of the two principles, determining (form) and determinable (matter), that make up the Philosopher's cosmos: the bipartite view evolved into the hylomorphic view.
In this way a more orderly system was achieved, but at the price of forcing
some sacraments into a mold that does not suit them well. Hugh of St. Cher
(1200–1263) was the first to discover a composition of matter and form for
each sacrament.[33]

Even so, the central inspiration continued to be the Christian mystery,
which took on elements of the most widespread philosophical view. Certainly, the process makes sense inasmuch as the Christian outlook shares
with the Stagirite a uniform view of the cosmos and of the human being.
The sacraments are adapted to man's essence, composed of matter and form
(body and soul), thus reflecting the structure of the whole universe. But
this philosophical heritage is received in the light of the Gospel: Hugh of
St. Cher, for example, when he specifies the matter and form of baptism,
explains the efficacy of the water by its contact with the flesh of Jesus in
the Jordan.[34] The central inspiration is the body of Christ, assumed by the
Son of God and shaped over the course of his life, death, and resurrection, a
body whose structure continues to be present in the sacraments.

---

32. See Arnau, *Tratado general*, 118–21.
33. See van den Eynde, "The Theory of the Composition," III, 12–22.
34. See ibid., III, 15.

It is true that this view is obscured to the extent that it brings about the reduction of the sacrament to what I have called a "sign-arrow" and the sensible ritual is taken as the model of the sacrament. When this happens, the species of bread and wine is the sacrament in the proper sense in the Eucharist, and in baptism it is the water being poured. But then the division into matter and form loses its direct connection with the body of Jesus, present on the altar, to which the baptized person is configured; and, as a result, the hylomorphic schema becomes difficult to apply to other sacraments, such as matrimony or penance, which go beyond the ritual celebration. It is symptomatic that these sacraments, the ones most bound up with man's everyday life and his incarnate condition, have been the most difficult to fit into the hylomorphic schema.[35] Returning the body to its central position will make possible, as we shall see, a more coherent interpretation of the composition of the sacramental sign: I will return to this subject below (in chapter 11), where I will offer a synthetic definition of sacrament.

Efficacious Sign of Grace: The Causality of the Sacraments

The equating of sacrament and sign in Berengar was not suited to capturing the richness of the Christian sacrament because it started from a reductive concept of the sign: an arrow that points to another distant reality. Later theologians, although accepting the aforesaid equation, attempted to correct its deficiencies. We have already explored one way of doing so: insisting that the central thing is not the exterior visible sign (*sacramentum tantum*) but rather the new body that the sacraments make present (the body of Jesus into which ours is incorporated), which is at the same time a sign and the reality signified (*res et sacramentum*). But in order to rectify Berengar's lines of argument it was necessary furthermore to add that the sign not only manifests grace but also communicates it: as theologians would say, it is an *efficacious* sign.[36]

---

35. Alexander of Hales, who was one of the first to offer a systematic explanation of the seven sacraments, accepts the composition of matter and form (without linking it to the hylomorphic theory); for matrimony and penance he does this only on the condition that the acts of those who receive them are understood as the matter. See van den Eynde, "The Theory of the Composition," III, 10–12.

36. See Duns Scotus, *Ordinatio* IV, d. 1, pars 2, q. 1 (*Opera Omnia* XI:66.126): "proprie tamen dicitur signum efficax, si adhibito signo, sequitur significatum" (nevertheless it is properly called an efficacious sign if what is signified follows when the sign is used); pars 3, q. 2 (*Opera Omnia* XI:116.541): "Ista [scil. sacramenta] novae legis causant gratiam tanquam signum efficax" (These [sacraments] of the New Law cause grace as an efficacious sign).

The Sacrament, Cause of Grace

This development incorporated the heritage of the patristic definition of St. Isidore of Seville, to whom I have already referred. In his *Etymologies* he had not defined sacrament as a sign, insisting instead that hidden beneath the corporeal clothing there is a divine force (*virtus*) that saves us.[37] St. Bonaventure follows this line of argument in his *Breviloquium*, when he classifies the sacrament as a sanctifying medicine.[38]

We observe subsequently in theological writings the need to explain what is understood by sign. Hugh of St. Victor, in his influential treatise *On the Sacraments of the Christian Faith*, says that a sacrament, besides being a sign, *contains grace*, and he uses the image of the vial in which a medicine is stored.[39] The *Summa Sententiarum* of Hugh's school develops this idea in a more dynamic key: "A sacrament is the visible form of the invisible grace *which is communicated in it*, that is, *which the sacrament itself confers.*"[40] Peter Lombard, for his part, formulates it as follows: a sacrament is a sign "of a form that bears the image and is a cause"; and he insists: "the sacraments were instituted not only to signify but also to sanctify."[41]

The causality of the sacraments is approached, therefore, without aban-

---

37. See Isidore of Seville, *Etymologiae* VI, 19, 39–42 (PL 82:255c–d): "ob id sacramenta dicuntur quia sub tegumento corporalium rerum virtus divina secretius salutem eorundem sacramentorum operatur unde et a secretis virtutibus vel a sacris dicuntur" (For this reason they are called sacraments because beneath the covering of corporeal things the divine power secretly effects the salvation of those same sacraments; hence they are named sacraments after those secret virtues or after sacred things).

38. See Bonaventure, *Breviloquium* VI, 1 (Quaracchi 5:266): "Patet etiam, quae sit *causa efficiens*, quia divina institutio; quae *materialis*, quia signi sensibilis repraesentatio; quae *formalis*, quia gratuita sanctificatio; quae *finalis*, quia hominum medicinalis curatio. Et quia 'denominatio fit a forma et a fine'; hinc est, quod dicuntur *Sacramenta*, quasi medicamenta sanctificantia" (It is also plain what its *efficient cause* is, for it is a divine institution; what its *material cause* is, for it is the representation of a sensible sign; what its *formal cause* is, because it is gratuitous sanctification; what its *final cause* is, for it is the medicinal cure of mankind. And because a name is assigned according to the form and the end [of a thing], hence they are called *sacraments* as if to say 'sanctifying medications). See *In IV Sent.*, d. 1, p. 1, art. 1, q. 2 (Quaracchi 4:14).

39. See Hugh of St. Victor, *De sacramentis christianae fidei* I, 9, 2 (PL 176:317; *CV* 1:210); I, 9, 3 (PL 176:320; *CV* 1:212).

40. *Summa Sententiarum* IV, 1 (PL 176:177): "Sacramentum est visibilis forma invisibilis gratiae in eo collatae, quam scilicet confert ipsum sacramentum. Non enim est solummodo sacrae rei signum sed etiam efficacia. Et hoc est quod distat inter signum et sacramentum. Quia ad hoc ut sit signum, non aliud exigit nisi ut illud significet cuius perhibetur signum, non ut conferat. Sacramentum vero non solum significat, sed etiam confert illud cuius est signum vel significatio" (For it is not only the sign of a sacred thing but also efficacy. And this is the difference between a sign and a sacrament. For in order to be a sign, all that is required is that it signify a thing of which it presents a sign, not that it confer [that thing]. But a sacrament not only signifies but also confers the thing of which it is the sign or signification).

41. Peter Lombard, *Sent.* IV, d. 1, n. 4 (SpBon V:233): "Ut imaginem gerat et causa exsistat.... Non ergo significandi tantum gratia sacramenta instituta sunt, sed etiam sanctificandi."

doning the definition of sacrament as sign; the authors limit themselves to making this definition more specific.[42] In reality, while the body of Christ itself was considered a sacrament in the proper sense, its efficacy was implicit and it was not necessary to mention it too. Then, indeed, because the body makes the person present, the body of Jesus makes present the person of Jesus, together with the new relations that Jesus generates (the communion of the church). But when the sacrament came to be understood primarily as the species of bread and wine, as it tended to happen after Berengar, then it became necessary to add that this sign really effects the presence of the body of Jesus on the altar. The identification of the sacrament with a generic sign required the introduction of another note: it communicates grace.

It was urgent, then, to explain the manner in which the sign and the infusion of grace are united. The answer was found via an investigation of the difference between the sacraments of the Old and the New Testament.[43] What happens in the transition from one economy of salvation to the other? Is eating the manna in the desert the same things as receiving the Eucharist of Jesus?

In order to answer the question, the theologians had recourse to an important distinction. They agreed that the old sacraments confer grace through the good dispositions of the one who performs the work (they would say: *ex opere operantis*). They debated whether or not grace was conferred also through the work itself that was performed (*ex opere operato*), independently of how it was performed (*ex opere operantis*). The matter could be settled unequivocally (see my discussion in the third section of chapter 7, above) only insofar as the New Testament is concerned.[44] The authors agree in pointing out that the sacraments of the New Law transmit a grace that depends neither on the one who administers them nor on the one who receives the sacrament: they are efficacious through the work itself that is accomplished in them, above and beyond the dispositions and action of the minister or of the recipient.[45]

42. St. Thomas is the one who most forcefully supports a general definition of the sacraments as signs, with which he is able to embrace in one view the sacraments of the old and the new covenant: see Hyacinthe-François Dondaine, "La définition des Sacrements dans la Somme Théologique," *Revue de sciences philosophiques et théologiques* 31 (1947): 213–28.

43. See Landgraf, "Die Gnadenökonomie," 215–53.

44. See Bonaventure, *In IV Sent.*, d. 1, p. 1, a. 1, q. 5 (Quaracchi 4:25): "Sacramenta novae legis per se iustificant et gratiam conferunt ex opere operato, quod non faciebant Sacramenta legis veteris nisi per accidens" (The sacraments of the New Law in themselves justify and confer grace *ex opere operato*, which the sacraments of the Old Law did not do except accidentally).

45. At the origin of the distinction between *opus operantis* (the work of the one who performs it) and *opus operatum* (the work performed) was the exegesis of the betrayal by Judas, which was atrocious according to the *opus operantis* but good according to the *opus operatum*. See Artur Michael Landgraf,

The comparison with the Old Law reveals the reason for this efficacy of the new signs: it is to be found in the master's life itself, in which the novelty of the Gospel in comparison with Israel is enclosed. In other words, the key to the causality of the sacrament is the action accomplished by Jesus himself, especially in his cross and resurrection; the believer receives in the sacrament the benefits of that action. From this perspective we understand better the meaning of the formula *ex opere operato*: *the sacraments save "because of the work performed" by Jesus*; the sacrament introduces the recipients into the action of Christ, who is the one who secures the grace. The collaboration of the recipient is important too, as we will see (in chapter 14, below), but always subordinate to the participation in Jesus.[46]

Two Ways of Understanding the Efficacy of a Sacrament

The authors do not limit themselves to asserting that the sacrament acts *ex opere operato*, but also discuss whether it can also be called the *cause* of grace. This second point requires that the performance of the rite be not only the occasion for grace to be granted to us, but also the channel through which it reaches us. The explanation runs into a considerable difficulty: how can a material action, like bathing in water, communicate invisible, spiritual, divine grace? Moreover, if we know that in the creation of the world God acted without the mediation of any creature whatsoever, can a creature mediate the communication of his sanctity, which is a more excellent work?

To answer this question, it helps to study the opinion of St. Bonaventure, who represents the Franciscan school, which had misgivings about considering the sacrament as a cause.[47] The Seraphic Doctor affirms in his *Breviloquium* that the sacraments contain and cause grace, but explains: in reality grace lodges in the soul alone and God alone infuses it; the sacraments contain and cause grace because "in them and through them, according to a divine decree, it is necessary that the supreme physician, Christ, should draw out the grace of healing."[48]

"Die Einführung des Begriffspaares *opus operans* und *opus operatum* in die Theologie," *Divus Thomas* 29 (1951): 211–23.

46. For St. Thomas, for example, the expression *ex opere operato* refers to the work performed by God or Christ: see *Super IV Sent.*, d. 6, q. 1, a. 3, sol. 2 (Parma 7:559); d. 4, q. 2, a. 2, q.c. 2, ob. 1 (Parma 7:514); ibid., sol. 2, ad 1 (Parma 7:515). On this subject, cf. Pierre-Marie Hombert, "La formule ex opere operato chez St. Thomas," *Mélanges de science religieuse* 49 (1992): 127–41.

47. See Bonaventure, *In III Sent.*, q. 40, d. 3 (Quaracchi 3:893–96); *In IV Sent.*, d. 1, p. 1, a. un., qq. 4–5 (Quaracchi 4:19–26); d. 3, p. 2, a. 1, q. 2 (Quaracchi 4:78–80); and d. 10, p. 2, a. 1, q. 3 (Quaracchi 4:231). See Willibrord Lampen, "De causalitate sacramentorum iuxta S. Bonaventuram," *Antonianum* 7 (1932): 77–86; and François-Marie Henquinet, "De causalitate sacramentorum iuxta codicem autographum S. Bonaventurae," *Antonianum* 8 (1933): 377–424.

48. Bonaventure, *Breviloquium* VI, c. 1 (Quaracchi 5:265): "huiusmodi Sacramenta dicuntur

In his *Commentary on the Sentences*, Bonaventure had gone into more detail on this subject, stating two possible solutions to explain the sacramental communication of grace. The first had been supported by his teacher, Alexander of Hales: the sacrament prepared man to receive the grace by impressing a character on his soul. Once this character is obtained, God infuses grace through it.[49] St. Thomas, also commenting on the *Sentences*, would espouse this opinion (the sacrament as the *causa dispositiva* of grace), although later he retracted it in the *Summa*.[50] The mediation of the character in order to transmit grace is a valid solution, which I will return to further on. It means, as I will explain later, that our adherence to the body of Christ (which is conferred by the character) is required so that the sacrament might introduce us into the living communion of Christ.

According to the second opinion that Bonaventure examines, the sacrament is efficacious only because of a divine pact, in other words, because God has promised to bestow salvation each time the rite is performed. The Seraphic Doctor uses the example of a letter that bears the royal seal, the power of which resides, not in something inherent in the letter, but in the king's mark. In fact, when the monarch dies, the letter will become a useless piece of paper, without anything in it having changed, except in its relation to others (*ad aliquid*). According to this comparison, the sacrament is not efficacious by its internal constitution, but rather by the will of God, who desired to confer grace when the rite is performed. The Seraphic Doctor, without deciding completely in favor of either opinion, leans toward this second one, for it seems to him more in keeping with reason although perhaps less consonant with the statements of the Church Fathers.

What is at stake in this debate? St. Bonaventure describes it this way: "We have to take care to avoid the possibility that, if we give too much praise to the corporeal signs, we will take honor away from the healing grace and from the soul that receives it."[51] The basic question, then, is: can the flesh be the channel of grace? Does this not diminish the dignity of the divine assistance? To answer this question it will help to keep in mind, as we will see,

---

gratiae vasa et causa, non quia gratia in eis substantialiter contineatur nec causaliter efficiatur cum in sola anima habeat collocari et a solo Deo habeat infundi; sed quia in illis et per illa gratiam curationis a summo medico Christo ex divino decreto oporteat hauriri" (Sacraments of this kind are called the vessel and cause of grace, not because grace is substantially contained or effectively caused in them, because grace has to be lodged in the soul alone and be infused by God alone; but rather because it is necessary, according to a divine decree, that the supreme physician, Christ, should draw out the grace of healing in them and through them).

49. See Bonaventure, *In IV Sent.*, d. 1, p. 1, a. un., q. 4, resp. (Quaracchi 4:21).

50. See Thomas Aquinas, *In IV Sent.*, d. 1, a. 4, sol. 1 (Parma 7:462).

51. Bonaventure, *In IV Sent.*, d. 1, p. 1, a. un. (Quaracchi 4:24).

the central position of the Eucharist, the fundamental sacrament. Starting with that, our question then becomes: what place does Christ's flesh hold in explaining God's economy of salvation, to which the sacraments belong?

Aquinas: Instrumental Cause through the Flesh of Christ

That being the case, St. Thomas brings a new light to the development of the concept of *instrumental causality*, which allows him to distinguish between the principal action of God and that of the sacrament.[52] Indeed, an instrument can be called a cause, as a brush causes a painting, without thereby diminishing the original causality of the artist. The same will be true with the sacraments: they are instrumental causes, which act while respecting the unquestionable primacy of the divine author. It becomes unnecessary to say that the sacrament only disposes the recipient for grace (by giving the character) without being able to cause it, as Alexander of Hales had proposed.[53] It *can* cause grace, the answer goes, but always as an instrument. Note that this makes the sacramental character no less important: further on (in chapter 12) we will see that it too acts in the manner of an instrument.

Besides introducing the concept of instrumental cause (which gradually would be accepted by different authors), another Thomistic contribution (more specifically of his school) is the identification of the instrument with the material performance of the rite, which then becomes a channel of grace.[54] It is true that God, in creating the world *ex nihilo*, did not associate corporeal elements with his work. But the redemption of human beings follows a different logic, because it requires their free collaboration, collaboration that God produces by becoming man and assuming flesh, so as to take up our life and transform it. From the perspective of the incarnation, it makes sense that the infusion of grace comes about through matter, for does not the whole economy of salvation hinge on the body of Jesus? St. Thomas discovers in Christ's humanity the first instrument of salvation, which he calls *instrumentum coniunctum*, "conjoined instrument."[55] The seven sacraments, as instrumental causes, prolong this radical instrument that is the Lord's body.

---

52. See Van Roo, *De sacramentis*, 279–83.

53. See Hyacinthe-François Dondaine, "À propos d'Avicenne et de saint Thomas: de la causalité dispositive à la causalité instrumentale," *Revue Thomiste* 51 (1951): 441–53; Nathan Lefler, "Sign, Cause and Person in St. Thomas' Sacramental Theology: Further Considerations," *Nova et Vetera* 4 (2006): 381–404.

54. The opinion of St. Thomas on this topic has been interpreted in various ways: see Domenico Bertetto, "La causalità dei sacramenti secondo S. Tommaso ed i suoi interpreti," *Salesianum* 10, no. 4 (1948): 543–68.

55. See Thomas Aquinas, *ST* III, q. 62, a. 5, co.

In fact, Thomas already advances these concepts in the Christological part of the *Summa*. There Aquinas says, on the one hand, that the passion of Jesus acts with redemptive causality (*per modum redemptionis*), that is, inasmuch as it pays the ransom so that we might be saved. But he adds, on the other hand, that it also possesses an efficient causality, as from one body to another. Indeed, Christ's flesh is the *instrument* of our salvation, for its corporeal actions and passions work with the divine power to banish sin and death.[56] The transformation that Jesus achieved in his flesh, by living and suffering in it, opening it up to the love of God, transforms the flesh of all human beings who are incorporated into him, making them capable of being united in a new way among themselves and with God.

St. Thomas therefore emphasizes corporeality as key to an understanding of a sacrament's efficacy.[57] The causality of a sacrament is the proper causality of the body: in the first place of the body of Christ and then, based on it, of the material elements of the rite (water, bread, wine, oil), which are assimilated in some way to this body of Jesus. Given that the Eucharist contains the presence of the Lord's body itself, it is the principle of the efficacy of the other sacraments. So it happens in baptism, where the water, which had been touched by Jesus in the Jordan, transmits to us the touch of Christ's body, configuring us to him so that grace might be poured out on us.[58] It is understandable then why Aquinas denies that the sacraments of the Old Law had the ability to cause grace, for that power springs from the transformation of the flesh achieved by Jesus, which does not exist until the incarnation.[59] Only in the New Testament is the action of the sacraments

56. Ibid., q. 49, a. 1, co.; see also III, q. 56, a. 1, ad 2 and ad 3; a. 2, resp. and ad 4. Cf. Bouëssé, "La causalité"; Lécuyer, "La causalité"; on the resurrection, see William Van Roo, "The Resurrection of Christ, Instrumental Cause of Grace," *Gregorianum* 39, no. 2 (1958): 271–84; Jean-Pierre Torrell, "La causalité salvifique de la résurrection du Christ selon saint Thomas," *Revue Thomiste* 96, no. 2 (1996): 179–208.

57. St. Thomas relies also on our ordinary experience: does the body not transmit spiritual realities, as when the voice communicates ideas? See Thomas Aquinas, *ST* III, q. 62, a. 4, ad 1.

58. See ibid., q. 62, a. 3, resp.: "gratia est in sacramento novae legis ... secundum quandam instrumentalem virtutem, quae est fluens et incompleta in esse naturae" (grace is in a sacrament of the New Law ... as to a certain instrumental power transient and incomplete in its natural being); and a. 4, co.: "virtus autem instrumentalis habet esse transiens ex uno in aliud, et incompletum; sicut et motus est actus imperfectus ab agente in patiens" (whereas the instrumental power has a being that passes from one thing into another, and is incomplete; just as motion is an imperfect act passing from agent to patient).

59. See ibid., q. 62, a. 6, co.: "causa efficiens non potest esse posterior in esse, ordine durationis, sicut causa finalis. Sic igitur manifestum est quod a passione Christi quae est causa humanae iustificationis, convenienter derivatur virtus iustificativa ad sacramenta novae legis, non autem ad sacramenta veteris legis" (The efficient cause cannot in point of time come into existence after causing movement, as does the final cause. It is therefore clear that the sacraments of the New Law do reasonably derive the power of justification from Christ's Passion, which is the cause of man's righteousness; whereas the sacraments of the Old Law did not).

ex opere operato derived from the "work performed" by Christ in his body.

Together with the Thomistic opinion, the other view of the Franciscan school, which St. Bonaventure had already pointed out, continued to be present. According to the latter, the sacrament does not work by itself, in its concrete materiality, but rather based on a pact by which God has promised to transmit grace when the rite is celebrated. This would be the view defended by Duns Scotus, who sees the sacrament as an occasion for God to bestow his gifts. As I have already noted, the example used was that of a letter from the king which assures us that he will pay us a sum of money. The letter does not obtain the money by its physical properties, but rather inasmuch as it is a testimony of the royal promise.

It is true that this way of explaining the causality takes into account the interpersonal dimension of the sacrament, presenting God as a true guarantor. Some have spoken, therefore, about a "covenantal causality."[60] We must say, however, that this approach does not perceive the centrality of the flesh for salvation, perhaps because it finds it difficult to accept the fact that the body can be a channel of divine grace. Thus it forgets that the place where the covenant with God was definitively established was in the flesh—in the flesh of Christ and in that of Christians. And it tends to separate the two aspects of sacrament, the sign and the cause, which stay united only by God's external will. It would not take long for the slender thread that held these two pieces together to be cut with the arrival of the Protestant Reformation.

Conclusion

Allow me to now summarize some conclusions of this review of the Middle Ages. The common definition of sacrament fundamentally comprises two features: the sacrament of the New Law is a *sign* and *cause* of grace. We noted that this duality becomes necessary in order to neutralize the influence of an incomplete definition of sacrament which became generally accepted with Berengar of Tours. This author understands the sacrament as a sign that reflects a distant reality ("sign-arrow"); and thus this type of sign is separated from the manner of signifying that is proper to the body. Indeed, the body does not refer us to a person who is found beyond it, but rather we en-

60. See William J. Courtenay, "Covenant and Causality in Pierre d'Ailly," *Speculum* 46, no. 1 (1971): 94–119; this author emphasizes that the examples used by the proponents of this theory refer on many occasions to God's covenant with his chosen people, thus overcoming a merely juridical view (99); according to Courtenay, this sacramental debate would have interesting consequences for the medieval development of the economy and of the value of money: see his "The King and the Leaden Coin: The Economic Background of 'Sine qua non' Causality," *Traditio* 28 (1972): 185–209.

counter the person (together with the relations that unite him to the world and to other persons) only in the body and by means of the body. Hence the equating of sacrament and sign proves to be too narrow an explanation of the sacraments, which are rooted in the body of Christ inasmuch as it is open to the bodies of human beings and associates them to itself.

The medieval synthesis overcomes the dilemma by identifying in the sacraments something that is *res et sacramentum*, in other words, an intermediate reality between the mere sign and the mere effect of grace. This *res et sacramentum* refers to the body: first to the body of Christ (in the Eucharist), and then to that of the faithful (in baptism and the other sacraments). Speaking about *res et sacramentum* is tantamount to refining the equating of *sacramentum* and *signum* by saying that the sign is a corporeal sign.

A second aspect helps to correct Berengar's narrow definition: the sacraments are special signs because furthermore they *cause* grace. Various theories are proposed to account for this fact: grace is communicated because God has promised to do so, by a pact; or it is communicated by the performance of the material rite, which is associated with the flesh of Christ, the central instrument of our salvation. I have favored this latter explanation, which is supported by St. Thomas, as the one most closely related to the view of the body as the hinge of our salvation, which is attested in the New Testament and in the Church Fathers. From this perspective the deviations introduced by Berengar are corrected and signification is traced back to corporeality: the sign *par excellence* is the body of Jesus. Thus we can examine in a suitable light the connection between the sign and the efficacy of the sacrament, for the body not only is a sign of a presence, but also materializes it: only in the body do we encounter the person and enter into relation with him; the corporeal sign is *ipso facto* efficacious.

Despite these two corrective measures, the ambiguity connected with a rather unclear definition of sacrament continued to hang in midair. The tendency to identify the sacrament with the external sign or with the rite persisted, relegating the *res et sacramentum* to a secondary plane and conceiving of causality as something external to the sign itself. As we have seen, this tendency affects another question that runs through medieval sacramental theology: the sign as a composition of matter and form. To the extent that interest in the corporeal presence (*res et sacramentum*) was lost, and attention was concentrated on the visible element of the rite, there would be a lack of a single principle to indicate the unity of matter and form in the sacraments, and its application to various individual sacraments (particularly penance and matrimony) would seem forced.

In short, medieval theology remains faithful to the biblical inspiration and to the contribution of the Church Fathers, setting up a coherent system that accounts for all the data of revelation. I have also identified some unresolved tensions that impede a clear vision of what the supporting pillars are amid the jungle of columns. In particular one notices some difficulty in integrating clearly the two central aspects of sacrament: sign and communication of grace. The balance was attained, but not without some wavering. And, as we will see next, it was then broken by the Protestant Reformation, to which it was necessary to respond at the Council of Trent.

10   SACRAMENT, WORD, BODY

Protestant Crisis, Catholic Reform, Modern Perspectives

The central component of the Protestant Reformation has been identified specifically as the rejection of the Catholic view of the sacraments.[1] And even though the Reformers considered the doctrine of justification by faith the chief point of their program, it is certain that that doctrine took on a practical form when they tackled the sacraments, which brought its hidden implications to light. It is not surprising that Trent would dedicate most of its sessions to the sacraments: what was at stake, as we will see, was the sacramental vision of all Christian life and of the church herself. One can infer from this the ecumenical interest of my topic, for in it the interconfessional differences are manifested more clearly, and it requires a greater investment in dialogue. The obstacles in this field, moreover, arise not only in the debates between specialists, but rather affect the believers' everyday visible practice of their faith. Let us begin by studying the Lutheran perspective.

Luther: The Sacrament, God's Promise That Calls for Faith

The first sacrament that attracted Luther's attention was penance, in the context of justification through faith.[2] Does this sacrament justify because

---

1. See Ernst Troeltsch, "Protestantisches Christentum und Kirche in der Neuzeit," in his *Kritische Gesamtausgabe* (Berlin: De Gruyter, 2004), 7:114: "the central religious idea of Protestantism is the dissolution of the concept of sacrament, of the authentic and true Catholic concept of sacrament.... From the viewpoint of the history of dogma, this is the decisive point because of which, for the first time, the Catholic system was definitively broken."

2. On the sacraments in Luther's writings, see Erich Roth, *Sakrament nach Luther* (Berlin: Töpelmann, 1952); Helmut Hennig, "Die Lehre vom *Opus Operatum* in den lutherischen Bekenntnisschriften," *Una Sancta* 13 (1958): 121–35; Erwin Iserloh, *Gnade und Eucharistie in der philosophischen*

we believe that it has the power to pardon or because of the priest's absolution? To answer this question, Luther interprets the minister's words as a divine promise addressed to the penitent. This promise calls for the faith of the sinner: if he gives it his full credence and relies on it, he surely receives forgiveness. The words pronounced by the minister, therefore, are not effective by themselves, but only if they are received with this radical trust in them which is the marrow of the Protestant faith.[3] Later Luther would apply the same schema of penance to baptism and the Eucharist. In them what saves is neither the word pronounced by the minister, nor the actions that he performs, but rather the faith of the one who receives the sacrament, believing that his sins are pardoned by God as the Word promises him.

Starting from this original intuition, the Protestant view of the sacraments is articulated. We will observe in Luther a clear evolution: although at the beginning he insists on the role of faith, later he would emphasize the importance of the sacrament in itself. A decisive factor in understanding this change will be his debates with other Reformers, who diminished the importance of the sacrament so much that they ended up denying the necessity of baptism.

The Sacrament Saves Because of Our Belief in It:
Luther *versus* the Catholic View

In the first phase, Luther was preoccupied above all with promoting the correct use of the sacraments: they do no good unless they are received with faith. This is because Luther interprets the Catholic doctrine, in particular the doctrine expounded by Duns Scotus, as though it did not require being well-disposed in order to receive the sacrament. The sacrament would be reduced, then, to a ritual work that intends to purchase salvation, without the need of being open to the Gospel of divine forgiveness. In light of these assumptions, Luther regards the church's sacraments as a human apparatus that impedes the direct action of Christ. And therefore he wishes to dismantle this structure, which deprives souls of their Christian liberty. To this

---

Theologie des Wilhelm von Ockham: ihre Bedeutung für die Ursachen der Reformation (Wiesbaden: Steiner, 1956), 134–47; Wolfgang Schwab, *Entwicklung und Gestalt der Sakramententheologie bei Martin Luther* (Frankfurt am Main: Peter Lang, 1977), and "Luthers Ringen um das Sakrament"; Karl-Heinz Zur Mühlen, "Zur Rezeption der augustinischen Sakramentsformeln: 'accedit uerbum ad elementum et fit sacramentum' in der Theologie Luthers," *Zeitschrift für Theologie und Kirche* 70, no. 1 (1973): 50–76; Finkenzeller, *Die Lehre von den Sakramenten*, 2–25; Günter Wenz, *Einführung in die evangelische Sakramentenlehre* (Darmstadt: Wissenschaftliche Buchgesellschaft, 1988); and Karl Lehmann and Wolfhart Pannenberg (eds.), *Lehrverurteilungen—kirchentrennend?*, vol. 1 (Göttingen: Vandenhoeck and Ruprecht, 1988).

3. Luther already presents this view in his famous ninety-five theses (theses 6 and 7): cf. Schwab, "Luthers Ringen," 96.

enterprise he dedicates his work *On the Babylonian Captivity of the Church* (1521).

How does Luther substantiate his view of the sacraments? He would employ a saying by St. Augustine with which we are already familiar: "The word is joined to the element and the sacrament comes about, which is like a visible word ... not because it is said, but rather because it is believed" (*accedit verbum ad elementum et fit sacramentum ... non quia dicitur sed quia creditur*).[4] At the initial stage of his thinking Luther focuses on the second half of the statement, where the axis "word-faith" is established. And he accepts the Augustinian definition of sacrament-sign, understanding sign to be not the revelation of something hidden but rather (again following the bishop of Hippo) a *visible word*.[5] The sacrament thus is placed entirely at the service of the Word of God, which promises us mercy. The rite awakens in man the certainty that the Word is at work here and now in his life. This certainty is faith, the only thing which truly saves.

Given this approach, Luther rejects the idea that the celebration of the sacrament by itself causes grace. The sacrament proclaims grace and promises it; but it is nothing more unless it is given to someone who is receptive to it in faith. Faith alone is what saves, and not the work performed in the rite. *Non sacramentum, sed fides sacramenti iustificat*, "it is not the sacrament, but faith in the sacrament that justifies."[6]

This opinion denies, therefore, a doctrine that was common in the Middle Ages: the sacrament communicates grace *ex opere operato*. Luther suspects that this formula reduces the sacrament to a human work regulated by the church, thus robbing God of the primacy; and that it involves a magical concept of the sacraments that spares man the trouble of listening to the Word and converting. This certainly was not the meaning that Catholic theology gave to *ex opere operato*, as Luther's debate with Cardinal Cajetan showed.[7] According to the latter, the formula emphasizes precisely the fact

---

4. See Augustine, *In Iohannem* LXXX, 3 (CCL 36:529).

5. For an up-to-date presentation of Luther's perspective from the Protestant viewpoint, see Gerhard Ebeling, "Erwägungen zum evangelischen Sakramentsverständnis," in his *Wort Gottes und Tradition* (Göttingen: Vandenhoeck and Ruprecht, 1964), 217–26; Ebeling laments the fact that theology (both Protestant and Catholic), in receiving the Augustinian heritage, equated word and sign without further ado, which reduces the richness of the biblical word. The reason why is that the Word of God is not only the sign of a distant reality, but an actual presence that works mightily in the believer; even the Augustinian expression *verbum visibile*, which seems to capture neatly the Protestant view (sacrament in the service of the Word) is misleading for Ebeling, for it gives the impression that the word acts only within the sphere of signification, thus concealing the value of the biblical word as a proper event.

6. Luther, *Sermo de poenitentia* (WA 1:324.16–18).

7. See Finkenzeller, *Die Lehre von den Sakramenten*, 9.

that in the sacrament the divine action precedes the work of man. In other words, far from denying that the believer needs to be open to God, Catholic teaching understands that openness as a response to an original gift that comes from God. As the post-Tridentine theologians would clarify, the work performed in the sacrament is the work of Jesus: "*ex opere operato*, that is, by Christ, meaning *quod operatus est Christus*, 'that which Christ wrought.'"[8]

What is the bottom line with Luther's proposal? His contribution is useful for recalling, on the one hand, that the sign is framed in an interpersonal relationship: it is a sign proceeding from the love of God who communicates himself to us and promises us a future. Already in Augustine, as we saw, the sign is a "given sign," the communication of love, and not only a reference to a hidden reality. Luther, moreover, correctly highlights the importance of faith in relation to the sign: faith is the manner of knowing that is suited to the sign and receives it. In reality, medieval theology had always recognized the necessity of faith in order to receive the fruit of the sacrament; although it understood faith to be not only assurance of salvation but that acceptance of revelation that enables us to participate in the divine knowledge and to orient our life toward God.

On the other hand we have to say that there are several weak points to Luther's emphasis on faith. Indeed, focusing on the axis promise-faith can paradoxically end up emphasizing the human action, and not the divine primacy, which in fact is manifested in the efficacy of the sacrament. Moreover, this perspective does not make clear what the sacrament, as a ritual action, adds to the preaching of the word. Taking this view to its extreme logical conclusion, the sacrament would be an aspect of the word that could be dispensed with. These were not just abstract dangers: within the Reformation itself Karlstadt and Zwingli arrived at this latter conclusion; by considering baptism a mere accessory and by denying that the Eucharist was the body and blood of Jesus, they forced Luther to refine his ideas.

The Sacrament Is Not Only a Word: Controversies within the Reformation

Whereas in his confrontation with Rome Luther had preferred the second part of Augustine's statement, which insisted on faith ("not because it is said, but rather because it is believed"), later he would dwell on the first part ("the word is joined to the element and the sacrament comes about").[9]

8. Johann Adam Möhler, *Symbolism: Exposition of the Doctrinal Differences Between Catholics and Protestants*, trans. James Burton Robertson (New York: Crossroad, 1997), chap. 4, par. 28, n. 4.

9. For all of the following discussion, cf. Schwab, "Luthers Ringen," 106; Mühlen, "Zur Rezeption der augustinischen Sakramentsformeln."

Based on this sentence (Luther goes so far as to say that it is the best one that Augustine ever pronounced), the Reformer insists that the sacrament is not only a word, but also a visible material element and can be defined as "water embraced by the word," "bread and wine embraced by the word."[10]

His perspective continues to be that of the Word of God that summons man, but emphasizing now that this word is heard with sensible sounds, vibrates outside of me, and arrives from outside of me, and thus cannot be reduced to a personal impression. In other words, generic faith in divine forgiveness is not enough, but rather it is necessary to receive the sacrament as it was instituted by God, in order to profess that the forgiveness comes from him. Accepting the concrete existence of the water, bread, and wine emphasizes that the Word comes to man from outside, without being identified with the believer's subjective view: the Word is what saves man; man does not save the Word. In conclusion it could be said that the Reformer, in recovering the importance of the sacrament, recovers with it the corporeality of the divine Word. In light of this, Luther went on to distinguish between the "philosophical sign" that points to an absent reality and the "theological sign" that reveals a reality that is present and active in man's life.[11]

Luther's evolution becomes plain to us when we read, in one of his so-called table talks, that rather than the Augustinian *non quia fit, sed quia creditur* ("not because [the sacrament] is celebrated, but because it is believed"), it is necessary to affirm *non quod fit, sed quod sic est institutum* ("not because [the sacrament] is celebrated, but rather because it was instituted in that way").[12] This is because, Luther comments, Augustine reasoned *a posteriori*, already supposing the divine institution; but in the alternative sentence that Luther proposes the reasoning is *a priori*, determining the true principle of the sacrament: its institution by Jesus.

In order to understand Luther it is necessary to keep in view the two phases that I described: his break with the church, on the one hand; and his dispute with the other confessions of the Reformation, on the other. Trent would respond to the first Luther, whose position is extreme. The second, given his greater insistence on the incarnation, allows some *rapprochement* to the Catholic position: the Word of God, in order to be addressed to man, is a word that resounds in the ears and is connected to the concrete act with

10. The text about baptism is in Luther, *Der kleine Katechismus* (1531), IV, 1 (WA 30:379); the text on the Eucharist is in Luther, *Der grosse Katechismus* (1529), IV, 83 (WA 30:223).

11. Cf. Luther (WA Tischreden, 4:666n5106): "Signum philosophicum est nota absentis rei, signum theologicum est nota praesentis rei" (A philosophical sign is a note of an absent thing; a theological sign is a note of a present thing).

12. Cf. Schwab, "Luthers Ringen," 112, with reference to Luther (WA Tischreden, 1:321n677).

which Jesus instituted the rite. From this point of view Luther could agree that the sacrament communicates grace, though not in itself, but rather based on the divine will. Only thanks to the sacrament can faith be a true exodus from one's own ego and a total reference to another.[13]

The Lutheran Approach and Forgetting the Body

If Luther gradually drew closer to the Catholic position, then what distance was left explaining the major differences in the sacramental practice of the two confessions? This is a key question in order to individuate the topics of greatest interest in the ecumenical dialogue.

In describing the patristic and medieval view (chapters 8 and 9), I noted that it was entirely based on the sacrament *par excellence*, which is the body of Christ, in which we participate through the other sacraments. After that I described a tendency (that had been growing since Berengar) to drift away from this center and to understand a sacrament as an external sign, the ritual celebration. Medieval theology responded both by elaborating the notion of *res et sacramentum* and by insisting on the causality or efficacy of the seven signs. In the Eucharist, the *res et sacramentum* was the body of Jesus; in baptism (and analogously in the other sacraments), *res et sacramentum* was our incorporation into the body of Jesus through the sacramental character.

This rooting of the sacraments in the body of Christ is precisely what proves to be obscured in Protestantism. This is where the major rifts open up, rather than in the relation between faith and sacrament or word and sacrament. In this respect it is essential to understand the disputes surrounding the Eucharist. Confronted by the more spiritualistic Reformers, Luther admits the real presence of Jesus.[14] Thus, whereas in Calvin's view Christ is limited to *acting* in the sacrament, without being present, Luther professes that Jesus is encountered in the bread and wine. Faith therefore is directed toward this presence, which for its part assures the forgiveness of sins, but a Lutheran difference from the Catholic position remains nevertheless. As Trent would define, Christ is not in the Eucharist *together* with the bread and wine, but rather the bread and wine are transformed into the body and blood of Christ.[15] For this reason, while in Luther the presence is oriented to eucharistic communion and has no meaning apart from it, in the Cath-

---

13. Cf. Vinzenz Pfnür, "Die Wirksamkeit der Sakramente *sola fide* und *ex opere operato*," in *Das Herrenmahl*, ed. Gemeinsame Römisch-Katholische/Evangelisch-Lutherische Kommission (Paderborn: Bonifacius, 1978), 93–100.

14. See Ratzinger, "The Problem of Transubstantiation and the Question about the Meaning of the Eucharist," in his *Collected Writings*, 11:218–42.

15. See Council of Trent, Session XIII, *Decree on the Sacrament of the Eucharist*, chaps. 3–4 (DH 1639–42).

olic view the presence is permanent, because it transforms the roots of the reality: this is expressed by the term *transubstantiation*.

Catholic Eucharistic logic leads to the discovery of this sacramental permanence in all of Christian life and in all of the church's work. The negation of the real Eucharistic presence explains also the Lutheran rejection of the sacramental character (*res et sacramentum* in the medieval view), in other words, of the incorporation into Christ of the baptized person's whole life so that in a certain way it might be transubstantiated into him.[16] The controversy would have repercussions on the sacramental architecture of the church, above all as a result of the Protestant rejection of two sacraments: matrimony, through which the sacramental economy is rooted in the cosmos and in social life; and holy orders, which structures the sacramentality of the church herself.

This allows us to observe that Luther's view, although richer and more sacramental than that of the other Protestant denominations, nevertheless in reality becomes rather disincarnate.[17] Yes, the word of God becomes concrete in the sacrament, but only as a personal event that then has no ramifications in the other aspects of the believer's life and of the church's body. While in the grand biblical-patristic view the whole Christian was defined in terms of the sacrament, for Luther the sacrament follows and remains outside of the believer, without including him in itself or renewing him from within. For the Reformer, the event in which forgiveness of sins is offered to me is sacramental, but not the network of relations that sustain man in time so that he might build up the Christian life. This latter view is the one held by the Council of Trent.

Trent: *ex opere operato* and the Sacramentality of Christian Life

The question about the sacraments proved to be decisive at the Council, both insofar as it concerned Catholic doctrine and insofar as it became necessary for the reform of the church. The fundamental concepts were addressed in Session VII,[18] followed by other sacraments at later sessions, until the Council arrived at matrimony in Session XXIV.

---

16. On the Lutheran denial of the sacramental character, see below, chapter 12.

17. Two contemporary interpretations of Reformation theologians propose a synthesis that justifies the sacraments as a reminder that the word of God—which still holds the primacy—is a situated or, we might also say, an incarnate word: see Ebeling, "Erwägungen zum evangelischen Sakramentsverständnis," who is followed by Jüngel, "Das Sakrament," and Jüngel, *El ser sacramental en perspectiva evangélica* (Salamanca: Sigueme, 2007).

18. March 3, 1547 (DH 1600–1613).

The canons on the sacraments in general were preceded only by a short foreword, which highlighted the connection with the doctrine on justification. In the sacraments all true justice "either begins through the sacraments or, once begun, increases through them or, when lost, is regained through them" (DH 1600).[19] This affirms that the sacraments "narrate" grace, that is to say, they articulate it in time so that it might accompany the person's whole journey. While the Reformers focused on the sole point of justification by faith, for Trent faith cannot be limited to receiving the forgiveness of sins, but rather is projected from there into all Christian activity in the world. And the sacraments are precisely the means that allow us to contemplate faith in all its richness, for they unfold from start to finish the story that faith is called to travel through. In part 3, below, I will study the unfolding of the seven sacraments into all areas and all moments of the life of the Christian and of the church.

I am interested now in canons 4 to 8, where the Protestant idea of sacrament is counteracted.[20] Canon 4 clarifies that the sacraments are necessary for salvation (or at least the desire for them is); therefore they cannot be reduced to a mere modality (ultimately a superfluous modality) of the preaching of the gospel, to which one would respond by faith. This doctrine is confirmed in canon 5, where an opinion common among the Protestants is refuted: "If anyone says that these sacraments are instituted only for the sake of nourishing the faith, let him be anathema."

Canons 6 to 8 directly address the efficacy of the sacraments, a sore point of the debate.[21] The sixth reads as follows:

If anyone says that the sacraments of the New Law do not contain the grace they signify [non continere gratiam, quam significant] or that they do not confer that grace upon those who do not place an obstacle in the way [non ponentibus obicem], as if they were only external signs of the grace or justice received through faith and marks of the Christian profession by which among men the faithful are distinguished from the unbelievers, let him be anathema.[22]

---

19. See the Decree on the Sacraments.

20. The Council worked from a list of Protestant errors that were submitted for the examination of the theologians (CT 5:835–36).

21. On the causality of the sacraments at Trent, see Cavallera, "Le décret"; Daniel Iturrioz, "La definición del Concilio de Trento sobre la causalidad de los sacramentos," Estudios Eclesiásticos 24, no. 94 (1950): 291–340; Van Roo, De sacramentis in genere, 267–68; Hubert Jedin, A History of the Council of Trent, trans. Dom Ernest Graf, OSB, 2 vols. (St. Louis, Mo.: B. Herder, 1957–61), 2:370–95; Josep Lligadas Vendrell, La eficacia de los sacramentos "ex opere operato" en la doctrina del Concilio de Trento (Barcelona: Pontificia Universidad Gregoriana, 1983).

22. See Decree on the Sacraments, canon 6 (DH 1606).

We see here the desire to avoid a feeble idea of the sacramental sign, as though it were only an external manifestation that reveals what is internal, in this case the grace or justice received by faith. For, besides being a word, message, or public badge, the sign contains or confers grace. We already know (see chapter 9, above) that the medieval theologians insisted on this point in order to avoid the Platonizing reduction of the sacrament to a sign, which appeared in the proposal of Berengar of Tours.

Canon 7 reinforces this idea: grace is given *through* the sacraments (*per sacramenta*).[23] This formula was preferred to an earlier version which read "*in* the sacraments" (*in sacramentis*) and appeared too weak to express sacramental mediation.[24] Immediately the canon adds that grace, "as far as God's part is concerned," is always communicated to us in the rite. This rejects a Protestant opinion which, based on a presumed arbitrary freedom of God, denied that the sacramental bestowal of grace was assured.[25] Trent confirms, on the contrary, that God has promised to pour out his grace whenever the sacraments are celebrated in a worthy manner. He will not fail to do his part.

The sacramental communication of grace is confirmed in canon 8, where the expression *ex opere operato* is used: "If anyone says that through the sacraments of the New Law grace is not conferred by the performance of the rite itself [*ex opere operato*] but that faith alone in the divine promise is sufficient to obtain grace, let him be anathema."[26] The Latin expression means: not solely through the faith of the recipient (*ex opere operantis*). In the general sense that the formula had at that time it also implied that the efficacy of the sacrament does not depend on the good qualities of the minister (*ex opere operantis ministri*).[27]

Note that no side is taken for any of the theories about the causality of the sacraments that were legitimately discussed in the various schools.[28] The Council limits itself to saying that the sacraments "contain" grace (canon 6) and "confer" it (canons 6 and 8), without even using the verb "to cause." It is

---

23. DH 1607.

24. See *CT* 5:991.

25. The target here was the fifth article of the *Confessio Augustana*, which affirmed that God gave grace wherever and whenever he wished (*quando et ubi visum est Deo*), without mentioning that God has promised to give his grace in the place and at the time of the sacrament; see *CT* 5:836 and Cavallera, "Le décret," III, 21.

26. DH 1608.

27. See Heinrich Lennerz, *De sacramentis novae legis in genere* (Rome: Universitas Gregoriana, 1950), 368.

28. See Lennerz, "Das Konzil von Trient." This explains why no definite formulas of Scholastic theology are embraced: for example, the expression "matter and form" does not appear. The Catechism of Trent would use these terms lavishly.

certain that, in the decree on justification, it is clear that baptism is a cause, and an instrumental cause.[29] But Trent does not explain whether one must teach a causality in the strict sense, as St. Thomas had conceived of it, or in a broad sense, as the Franciscan school maintained. Note that in both cases the theologians of that era classified this causality as "instrumental."

On the other hand, canon 6 indicates a condition for attaining this grace: "not [to] place an obstacle" or an impediment in the way to its reception. The formula "not place an obstacle" was preferred to another one that said "receive correctly and worthily," because the first includes infants who are baptized.[30] Canon 7 teaches the same as the sixth, but in a positive form: in order for the sacrament to produce its fruit it is enough for it to be received properly.

The Protestants rejected the formula "not place an obstacle," for in their view it led to automatism and did not require a change of heart in the believer. As I noted above, the *Decree on the Sacraments* follows the previous one on justification.[31] Given that the latter affirms that the principle of justification is faith, it is clear that Trent does not claim to take any importance away from it, which it in fact considers necessary in order for the sacrament to produce its fruit. What the formula emphasizes, instead, is that the efficacy of the sacrament does not depend on the faith of the one who receives it. In other words, the action that is performed in the sacrament is greater than any disposition or initiative of man, including his very openness to God.[32] This does not mean that faith is being excluded. On the contrary, it is part of "not placing an obstacle" and in an adult it is required at least as unformed faith. Moreover, faith is enlivened and increases with the reception of the sacrament. "Not placing an obstacle" is to be understood also as including the necessary repudiation of sin—a repudiation which is the other side of faith.[33] *Ex opere operato* makes it clear, therefore, that man's part is to be molded by God. The formula indicates, as I have already noted, the

29. See DH 1529: "Huius iustificationis causae sunt ... instrumentalis item sacramentum baptismi, quod est sacramentum fidei, sine qua nulli umquam contigit iustificatio" (The causes of this justification are the following ... the instrumental cause is the sacrament of baptism, which is the "sacrament of faith," without which (faith) no one has ever been justified). The Council of Florence (1439), closely following an opusculum by St. Thomas, had used this language in the *Bulla unionis Armeniorum Exultate Deo* (DH 1310), where the sacraments of the New Law are differentiated from those of the Old Law, because the latter "non causabant gratiam.... haec vero nostra et continent gratiam, et ipsam digne suscipientibus conferunt" (did not cause grace.... These sacraments of ours, however, both contain grace and communicate it to those who worthily receive them).

30. See Cavallera, "Le décret," III, 21.

31. See Finkenzeller, *Die Lehre von den Sakramenten*, 106.

32. See Luis F. Ladaria, *Teología del pecado original y de la gracia: antropología teológica especial* (Madrid: Biblioteca de autores cristianos, 1997), 212.

33. See Bellarmine, *De controversiis*, vol. 3, lib. 1, cap. 12 (22).

primacy of redemption in Christ, which touches, embraces, and transforms the believer, provided only that he puts up no resistance to it.

After setting forth Luther's proposal and how Trent replied, we can ask ourselves whether it is possible to discern a path toward ecumenical reencounter. It must be said, on the one hand, that the identification of some theological misunderstandings, the result of a calm study of the sources, has recently made possible a dialogue that has borne much fruit.[34] On the other hand, in order to promote this dialogue it is necessary to become aware of the differences and to pinpoint them precisely. These are observed, as I said earlier in this chapter, not so much by studying the sacramental event and the role played in it by faith and the rite that is celebrated, but rather by explaining how this event is prolonged and branches out in time, giving shape to the life of the Christian and of the church.

The disagreements arise when we ask, for example, about the *real presence of Christ* in the Eucharist (transubstantiation), from which the sacramental structure of the church springs; about the *character imprinted by some sacraments*, which make all of Christian life sacramental; about the defense of the *sacramentality of matrimony* which confers a sacramental structure on creation and society; and about the *concept of priestly orders* as one basis of the sacramentality of the whole church.[35] In chapters 12 to 15, below, I will dwell on these aspects, where we discover the distance between the Protestant position and the Catholic one. As I have already indicated, these are differences that do not remain on the level of ideas discussed among specialists, but rather intimately affect the life and practice of the faith.[36]

Post-Tridentine Theology: The Physical and Moral Causality of the Sacraments

The lion's share of the Catholic response consisted of reaffirming the sacraments as columns on which the church and Christian life are built. In this

34. See Lehmann and Pannenberg, *Lehrverurteilungen—kirchentrennend?*; Gerhard Ludwig Müller, *Bonhoeffers Theologie der Sakramente* (Frankfurt am Main: Josef Knecht, 1979); Otto Hermann Pesch, "Das katholische Sakramentverständnis im Urteil gegenwärtiger evangelischen Theologie," in Eberhard Jüngel et al., *Verifikationen: Festschrift für Gerhard Ebeling* (Tübingen: Möhr, 1982), 317–40.

35. From one perspective, together with the advances of the ecumenical movement, it is necessary to observe also setbacks in recent years, above all in matters concerning the theology of matrimony and of holy orders: see Karl-Heinz Menke, *Sakramentalität: Wesen und Wunde des Katholizismus* (Regensburg: Pustet, 2013).

36. For a determined attempt at *rapprochement* on the part of a Protestant who addresses the questions that I have pointed out, see Pannenberg, *Systematic Theology*, vol. 3, chap. 12.

way Trent was not limited to offering a clear doctrinal proposal but produced practices for everyday life. In this respect its influence was renovating and broad in scope, although the theological reflection that followed, as we will see, was in many areas shortsighted.

The Catholic theologians insisted, with regard to the Protestant denial, that the sacraments communicate grace: they are signs, yes, but above all *efficacious* signs.[37] In fact, the signification of the sacraments would be forgotten somewhat, as there was a tendency to see it as an aspect juxtaposed to their efficacy. The essential feature of the sacrament, they said, was not primarily to represent grace, but to transmit it.[38] Starting from the controversy with the Reformers, it would become difficult to offer an integral explanation that coordinates these two aspects (sign and cause of grace) of the definition of sacrament.

An example: St. Robert Bellarmine, in considering the role of the *word* in a sacrament, emphasizes its active character in beseeching or obtaining a grace, and not so much its ability to instruct. And thus, when St. Paul describes baptism as "the washing of water with the word" (Eph 5:26), this "word" must be considered *verbum consecrationis* and not *verbum instructionis*.[39] Hence there are no problems with reciting the ritual formula in Latin, although some of the faithful do not understand it, for its role is not to teach, but rather to consecrate with the power of God, who certainly can understand Latin.[40] In this way one important aspect of the word is emphasized—its performative character—albeit by unnecessarily opposing it to its function of transmitting knowledge. Note the mirror-image contrast with the Protestant system, in which the word swallowed up the sacrament. And this is because the controversy made it difficult to reach a fruitful synthesis, which would see the formula of the sacrament both as an efficacious invocation and as a profession of doctrine.

This eagerness to present the sacrament as a cause explains why theologians vigorously resumed a medieval debate: how do the sacraments act in order to confer grace? By raising the issue again the authors clarified the terminology. Then, following Trent, they all affirmed that the sacraments are a cause of grace, whether in the strict sense (Thomists) or understood broadly (the Franciscan school). All of them spoke also about an instrumental cause, that is, one distinct from the principal cause that is God, the sole author of grace.

---

37. On post-Tridentine theology, see Finkenzeller, *Die Lehre*, 68–132.
38. See ibid., 141.
39. See Bellarmine, *De controversiis*, vol. 3, lib. 1, cap. 19 (55–56).
40. See Finkenzeller, *Die Lehre*, 73.

They concurred likewise that, in order to do justice to the causality of the sacraments, it is not enough to consider them conditions *sine quibus non* (i.e., indispensable). This refinement can be illustrated with an example: "that it be nighttime" is a *conditio sine qua non* for us to go out to look at the stars; but "the fact that it is nighttime" is not the cause of our studying the stars. The cause will be, rather, our desire to learn or to enjoy their peaceful beauty, which makes the night a necessary premise for that effect. Starting from the two options already present among medieval thinkers, two theories were outlined: the sacraments act by physical causality or by moral causality.[41]

Let us take, on the one hand, the explanation of *physical causality*, according to Cardinal Cajetan's formula,[42] which was favored in Thomistic circles. It alleges that the sacraments communicate grace through the matter, which is associated in some way with the flesh of Christ. The advantage of this approach is the weight that it confers on the created reality and on the concrete ritual event. On the other hand, if this theory is not explained correctly it gives rise to a certain automatism, forgetting that the sacrament is an encounter between two freedoms. Moreover (but this is not necessarily a defect), this "physical" explanation is the most difficult to understand in the modern world, because of the radical separation that is established today between what is personal and what is material.[43] How can matter—a compound of particles whose movements are governed by mechanical laws—mediate the transmission of grace, which is a personal friendship with God?

Some of these difficulties are avoided when one speaks about a *moral causality*, as was done starting with Melchior Cano.[44] This extends the Franciscan proposal of a causality that some have called "covenantal": the sacrament acts by virtue of the pact with which God bound himself to the salvific rite. Thus, for example, the letter that Uriah carried with him to the battlefield was the cause of his death, not because of the weight of the paper itself but rather because it had been written in the king's hand. Melchior Cano completed this medieval view as follows: in the sacrament

---

41. On this debate, see ibid., 105–16; Doronzo, *De sacramentis in genere*, 159, who reviews the different ancient and modern theories; Bertetto, "La causalità."

42. See Georg Reinhold, *Die Streitfrage über die physische oder moralische Wirksamkeit der Sakramente* (Vienna: Ohlinger, 1899), 19.

43. In this respect, see chapter 6, above.

44. See R. C. González, "La doctrina de Melchor Cano en su *relectio de Sacramentis* y la definición del Tridentino sobre la causalidad de los sacramentos," *Revista Española de Teología* 5, no. 4 (1945): 477–97; Juan Belda Plans, "Melchor Cano: La Relección 'De Sacramentis in Genere,'" in P. Rodríguez et al., *Sacramentalidad de la Iglesia y sacramentos* (Pamplona: Universidad de Navarra, 1983), 651–61.

there is a remembrance of Christ's passion, a moral force that moves God to take action. It is as though, in order to incite us to march into battle, someone sent us the bloodstained shirt of a friend, the sign of his sacrifice for his fatherland. This theory has the advantage of emphasizing the interpersonal aspect of the sacrament. On the other hand, as we will see, it runs the risk of forgetting that the covenant always exists in concrete corporeality because it is rooted in the incarnation of the Word.

In reality it is not a matter of choosing between the two options, because those who defend physical causality accept moral causality too, although they do not consider it sufficient.[45] And in fact the merely moral explanation seems not to do justice to the method of the incarnation, in which matter (of all things!) is capable of mediating the divine presence. For "physical" refers here to the concrete quality of the person's corporeal condition, to his placement in the world and among human beings through the flesh. Hence I propose a "corporeal causality" which will be described in detail in the next chapter. I mention here one advantage of this point of view: it situates the Eucharist, in which the "corporeal" causality is more evident, as the axis around which the constellation of the rest of the salvific signs revolves.[46]

Interesting for my purpose here is the contribution by Matthias Joseph Scheeben. Starting with a reinterpretation of St. Thomas, he already anticipates the place of prominence due to the body.[47] Scheeben understands the sacraments in terms of the incarnation, as its prolongation. And he starts with the Eucharist in order to organize the other six. All of this implies that a corporeal presence and a bodily contact mediate the bestowal of grace. In fact, this author cites radical experiences of our embodied condition, such as fatherhood and motherhood, to explain the causality of the sacraments. According to Scheeben, the corporeal manner of propagating grace was originally a part of creation. If Adam and Eve had not sinned, their conjugal union would have transmitted to us, together with the life of the body, the new life of the Spirit.[48] Scheeben rejects the theory of a solely "moral" causality, that is, exerted by one will on another will, but without passing through the flesh, because it does not correspond to the central tenet of

---

45. See Albert Michel, "Sacrement," *Dictionnaire de Théologie Catholique*, ed. Alfred Vacant et al. (Paris: Letouzey et Ané, 1908) [hereafter *DTC*], 14:485–644, at 614.

46. See Michael Schmaus, *Teología dogmática* (Madrid: Rialp, 1961), 6:91–93, par. 228. Even some defenders of moral causality make an exception for the Eucharist, admitting physical causality there: see José A. Aldama, *Sacrae theologiae summa* (Madrid: Biblioteca de autores cristianos, 1953), 76.

47. See Matthias Joseph Scheeben, *The Mysteries of Christianity* (New York: Crossroad, 2008).

48. See ibid., pars. 78, 81, 85.

faith in the incarnation; and it is not faithful to man's embodied condition. Rather than physical causality, our author prefers to say "hyperphysical," perhaps to avoid reductive ideas that are materialist or magical.[49]

The Sacrament Viewed as Symbol and as Rite: Contemporary Perspectives

The modern era brought with it a devaluation of what is sacramental. Among the causes of this decline we can point to the influence of the Protestant Reformation and of the controversy that followed it. *On the one hand*, the Lutheran view of the sacraments distanced itself from the sacrament-body connection, proposing a kind of disincarnation. This became evident in the denial of the Eucharistic real presence, the baptismal character (which prolongs the rite into the daily reality of the believer), the sacramentality of matrimony, etc. All of this tended to aggravate the split between spirit and matter that proved to be a distinctive feature of modernity. Once the material world was thought to be incapable of harboring the divine, society started down a slippery slope which led, without the Reformers intending it, to contemporary secularization, in which God is present only in the isolated consciousness of the individual.[50]

On the other hand, the difficulty in uniting the signification and the efficacy of a sacrament, which became more pronounced with the post-Tridentine controversy, would enlarge the schism between knowledge and action, between speculation and practice, which is so typical of the modern mindset. This is why contemporary theology finds it difficult to harmonize truth and love, doctrine and pastoral care. In light of this, an urgent attempt was undertaken by theology in the past century to offer a more harmonious vision of the two facets of the sacrament—sign and cause. This effort began with a critique of the Scholastic synthesis, a critique that sometimes was rather hasty and fierce. Hence the contemporary contribution was presented, not only as an adjustment of definite conclusions, but rather as a complete change of paradigm. This created an atmosphere in which the recent and valid contributions frequently led also to a disregard for the fruitful traditional insights. Various factors converged to allow this new approach, which revolves around a greater appreciation for symbolism. Retracing them will allow for the undertaking of a synthesis in the next chapter.

---

49. See ibid., par. 82; the foundation of this causality is found in Christ's flesh (par. 81), and this is proved on the basis of the Eucharist (par. 82).

50. See B. S. Gregory, *The Unintended Reformation: How a Religious Revolution Secularized Society* (Cambridge, Mass.: Harvard University Press, 2012)

Symbolic Causality: Karl Rahner

The modern times of enlightened reason could understand correctly only the "sign" part of the view of sacrament as a sign that causes grace. The rest—that a material action should be a channel of salvation for the spirit—seemed the residue of a magical mentality that the Catholic church was perpetuating in her final throes.

The Romantic movement struck the first blow against this perspective focused on the disincarnate thinking subject. For by reasserting the value of feeling, it reasserted also the perception of mystery, a perception that is awakened, for example, by contemplating nature or by listening to the echoes of history and legend. In fact, theologians turned to speaking about a sacrament as a code or figure for religious ecstasy in confronting life and the cosmos. In reality, nevertheless, the Romantics limited themselves to passing from the realm of knowledge to the realm of feeling, without abandoning the sphere of the subject who measures things in terms of himself.

Even so, this Romanticism fed suspicion of the rationalist system, a suspicion that matured during the twentieth century. In the shadow of Romanticism, the conviction spread that man is not a reflexive consciousness who knows and possesses himself directly. On the contrary, in order to arrive at the knowledge of who he is, he has to go through several mediations: language, community, his memory, his own body, etc., and these mediations affect all perception of himself, of the world, of others.

Then the term "symbol" started to be used to refer, with a thousand nuances depending on the author, to this network of mediations that allow man to know the world and to interact in it. Thus "symbol" is not understood to mean a reference to the reality beyond itself (what I called in earlier chapters a "sign-arrow") but rather the mutual agreement of things with each other and with the subject who contemplates them, an agreement that allows the person to attain a deeper view of his situation and journey in the world. In other words, rather than a "sign-arrow" that propels us toward a distant reality, we are looking at a network or space of symbols, a space of which we ourselves form a part. Recall, in this respect, the Greek origin of the word *symbol*: an object divided into two pieces that, when joined, allow their bearers to recognize each other.[51]

---

51. The use of the term "symbol" differs greatly among authors, according to epistemological distinctions; the reader may consult: Ernst Cassirer, *Philosophy of Symbolic Forms* (New Haven, Conn.: Yale University Press, 1998 [1928]); Jean Daniélou, "The Problem of Symbolism," *Thought* 25, no. 3 (1950): 423–40; Paul Ricoeur, *Philosophy of the Will*, vol. 2.2: *Finitude et Culpability: The Symbolism of Evil*, trans. Emerson Buchanan (New York: Harper and Row, 1967 [1960]); Umberto Eco, "At the

As an example of what I am saying, it is enough to think about the symbolic value of language. This symbolism does not consist in the fact that language refers us to the thought or idea that is expressed in it and would be encountered beyond any word. Rather, the symbolism of language lies in the fact that only by speaking, only by entering into the community of speakers, only by interpreting ourselves with the words that we have inherited and by creating new ones, is it possible for us to think and to elaborate ideas. Thought is not found beyond language, but rather in the active, shared exercise thereof, which is possible only as a result of belonging to the community (that is, to the relational space) where language dwells.

Well, now, in order for this symbolic space to exist truly and not to be reduced to the subjectivity of the one who contemplates it, it is necessary to resolve a dilemma: is such a symbolism of the world a projection of the subject onto things? Or do things themselves have a language that the subject has to learn in order to know himself? Starting from man's incarnate condition (from the fact that we have a body) it becomes possible to establish the second alternative. For the body's own symbolism (its language and what it signifies), though intimate and personal in one of its respects, is found to be, in the other respect, bound up with the materiality of the cosmos, in such a way that it cannot be reduced to subjective impressions and it allows the person to go out of himself toward the encounter with things.

I will leave for later on (chapter 11, below) a more in-depth discussion of these questions and of the way in which they can enrich sacramental theology. For us now it is enough to note that the revived interest in symbols offered an opportunity to reassert the value of the sacraments. Do the sacraments not cultivate the strong concept of symbol that I have just described, as a space or network of relations (the one inaugurated by Jesus) in which the Christian is introduced, a network which in turn takes in the corporeal and cosmic space? The most influential proposal that makes use of this ensemble was elaborated by Karl Rahner.[52]

Roots of the Modern Concept of Symbol," *Social Research* 52, no. 2 (1985): 383–402; Jean Borella, *Le mystère du signe: Histoire et théorie du symbole* (Paris: Maisonneuve and Larose, 1989); Josef Simon, *Philosophie des Zeichens* (Berlin: De Gruyter, 1989); Van Roo, *The Christian Sacrament*; and Fabio Leidi, *Le signe de Jonas: Étude phénoménologique sur le signe sacramental* (Fribourg: Éditions Universitaires, 2000).

52. Karl Rahner, "Zur Theologie des Symbols," in his *Schriften zur Theologie* (Einsiedeln: Benziger, 1964), 4:275–311, trans. Kevin Smyth as "The Theology of the Symbol," *Theological Investigations* (London: Darton, Longman and Todd, 1974), 4:221–52. See also his "Einleitende Bemerkungen zur allgemeinen Sakramentenlehre bei Thomas von Aquin," in *Schriften zur Theologie* (Zurich: Benziger, 1972), 10:392–404, translated as "Introductory Observations on Thomas Aquinas' Theology of the Sacraments in General," in *Theological Investigations*, 14:149–60; and "Fragen der Sakramententheologie," in *Schriften zur Theologie*, 16:398–405 (*Theological Investigations*, 22:189–94).

The German author distinguishes between two meanings of "symbol," thus reflecting the philosophical development just outlined. There is a general, broader sense of symbol as a reality that transports us to another that is not sensible: for example, in mathematics, the addition or multiplication sign. This way of understanding a symbol can be represented as an arrow that is shot from the bow of what is apparent and earthly so as to hit the bullseye of what is substantial and heavenly. According to this meaning, saying that something is a symbol implies saying that it has little ontological density, as when we pay a "symbolic" price.

Nevertheless, Rahner says, there is another type of symbol that is more fundamental and original, which can be called a "real symbol" (*Realsymbol*). A "real symbol" does not point to a reality that is beyond it. It is not necessary to cross through it and leave it behind in order to discover the being of things. And this is because symbol itself belongs to the ontology of the cosmos, for, in Rahner's view, all being is communicative of itself, every being expresses itself in the presence of others, and this is the only way it arrives at really being what it is.

This distinction between a trivial symbol and a strong one (some call the first "sign" and reserve the term "symbol" for the second) was highlighted by some theologians of the nineteenth century, such as Johann Adam Möhler or Matthias Joseph Scheeben, always in relation to the sacraments.[53] Thus Scheeben speaks about "empty sacraments" (which only point to the reality signified) and "full sacraments" (because they communicate this signified reality).[54] These authors offer a clear example of how a truth of faith (the sacraments as efficacious signs) illuminates our understanding of human experience (in this case, its radically symbolic character).

How does Rahner articulate his distinction? Note, in the first place, that Rahner's intention is strictly theological: symbolism starts from God himself as Trinity. Indeed, the Son is symbol of the Father, for the Father gives himself to be known only in the Son, and in such a way that it is not necessary to transcend the Son in order to encounter the Father, because the Son is the Word of the Father that reveals and communicates him to us perfectly.

Starting from the foundational reality of God, the faith perspective discovers this symbolic structure in every corner of the cosmos. All being gives expression to itself; and this expression does not remain outside of it, is not superfluous to it, but rather belongs to its deep identity. In the Christian

---

53. See Johann Adam Möhler, *Die Einheit in der Kirche* (Mainz: Grünewald, 1925); on the theology of symbol in Möhler, see Van Roo, *The Christian Sacrament*, 69–74.

54. See Scheeben, *The Mysteries*, par. 81; cf. Van Roo, *The Christian Sacrament*, 75–77.

universe, a vestige of the Trinity, every creature exists insofar as it communicates itself; and only in this outward expression of itself does it arrive at being what it really is. Consequently a symbol is not only a ladder by which to arrive at what truly counts, but rather the reality itself insofar as it allows itself to be known and attains its fullness only by communicating itself to other beings.

An outstanding example of the "real symbol" is the body, in which the person is manifested. Indeed, in order to know someone I do not have to leave the body behind, because this is the person himself, who is made present and expresses himself in the body. The person always exists united to his body and, therefore, always exists in the symbolic manner of self-communication. In the intersection of these two symbols, the one of the Son that reveals the Father and the one of the body that reveals the person, the symbol *par excellence* takes place: the incarnation.[55] It should be noted that the article in which Rahner advanced his theories about the symbol revolved around the heart of Jesus, the supreme symbol of God's love.

Given that, in the Catholic perspective, the sacrament is a sign that contains the signified reality, Rahner easily deduces the close link between symbol and sacrament. On the one hand, the sacrament is a real symbol of unsurpassable density. On the other hand, and just because everything that exists is a symbol, everything that exists will also be an anticipation or sketch of what is sacramental, so as to communicate to us in the body the divine presence and action. From here Rahner can project his symbolic view onto all of theology, with its center in Christ, the incarnate Word. For the church prolongs in time the fundamental symbol that is Jesus; and thus she herself proves to be an original symbol (sacrament), which is then actualized in the seven sacraments, real symbols of the definitive presence of grace.

Our author then proposes his explanation about the "symbolic causality" of the sacraments, which intends to open up a third way in the debate between physical and moral causality. According to Rahner, the classical theories for exploring how the sacraments cause grace do not take into account their condition as signs. Indeed, if moral causality prevails, then it does not matter, as far as the communication of grace is concerned, that the sign of the sacrament is this one or some other: what counts is that God chose it as an instrument. For its part, the theory of physical causality sees the sacrament as a channel through which grace flows, the efficient cause of its communication; but it does not explain how the type of sign influences

---

55. For discussions of Rahner's proposal that criticize various aspects of it, see Van Roo, "Reflections on Karl Rahner"; and Colombo, "Dove va la teologia."

the grace that is communicated; and this—Rahner argues—is because a sign can never be an efficient cause, but is always a formal cause.

The German theologian insists that the sacraments, according to the Thomistic expression, *significando causant*,[56] and this means according to him: they cause to the extent that they are symbols. Certainly, from an impoverished perspective of sign, causality is not included in the notion of sign, but rather it is necessary to add it from outside (explaining that we are discussing an *efficacious* sign). Nevertheless, if by symbol we understand the "real symbol," this symbol is not only the expression but also the communication of being.[57] To be more concrete, it is helpful if we refer again to the body, which not only reveals the person but also makes him present and active among us. For this reason the real symbol contains, already in its very definition, the two aspects of signification and efficacy that have been split apart since Scholasticism. As a corollary we can deduce that, in Rahner's symbolic panorama of the world, the sacrament is not an exception but rather perfects the rule: it acts as all real symbols act, communicating themselves at the same time that they reveal themselves.

The Rahnerian explanation presents many fertile aspects, although it also invites critics to correct and elaborate several of his points, as we will see in the following chapter. There we will dwell, above all, on the relation between symbolism and body, which is not extensively detailed by the German Jesuit, so as to see that the body is not a symbol of the autonomous subject, but rather of a relational person, a symbol which points, therefore, to the love that fulfills life while containing that love. The different experiences of communion that we have through the body will help us to understand better the valid aspects of the "symbolic causality" proposed by Rahner and will allow us to explore its limits.

Real Presence of the Mystery: Odo Casel

Another tributary that swelled the current of interest in symbolism sprang from the liturgical movement. The central figure was the Benedictine monk Odo Casel. His great insight was to understand the celebration itself as an environment or habitat in which to reflect not only on the sacraments but on theology as a whole. In chapter 1, I adopted this perspective: in the rite a space opens up that mediates knowledge of the mystery. Only by entering

---

56. See Thomas Aquinas, *Quaestiones disputatae de veritate*, q. 27, a. 4, resp. ad arg. 13, line 1 (ed. Marietti, 524); q. 28, a. 2, resp. ad arg. 12, line 1 (536).

57. In continuity with Rahner's thought is the proposal by Alexandre Ganoczy, *Einführung in die katholische Sakramentenlehre* (Darmstadt: Wissenschaftliche Buchgesellschaft, 1979), who sees the sacraments as communicative events.

into this space can one have access to what is revealed. I called this space the symbolic space.[58]

Casel presents the action of the sacraments in a new way: in terms of the liturgical participation that they open up to us. In his view, neo-Scholastic theology adopted a paradigm of efficacious causality that belonged to Aristotelian philosophy. According to such a paradigm Christ's action, which already occurred long ago, set in motion a process whose results are applied to us in the sacraments, as the ripples on a lake transmit the impact of a stone thrown into it.

Well, in Casel's view, arguing in this way involved diminishing the rich heritage of the Church Fathers, for they reason according to Platonic paradigms in which causality occurs through participation in the signified reality. For this reason not only do the grace-filled effects of Christ's passion reach us in the sacraments, but the very passion of the Lord is made present in them. Of course this does not happen because history repeats itself or because we take a trip into the past. Rather, just as the body of Christ is sacramentally in the Eucharist, so too his Paschal mystery occurs sacramentally in each liturgy, because we participate in the eternal action of the risen Jesus, who continues to offer himself to the Father.

Casel does not provide much of an explanation of the meaning of this sacramental way in which the action of Jesus is made present. He contributes more by his insight and his proposed praxis than with a well-furnished theological system. His theoretical contribution, in fact, leaves something to be desired. For, if we follow the Platonizing paradigm that he thinks he discovers in the Fathers, it would appear that in the liturgy we associate with an *atemporal* sacrifice of Christ. The theology of the mysteries, according to this viewpoint and paradoxically, would expel Christianity from history.

The biblical and patristic analysis that I conducted in the preceding chapters prompts me to correct this aspect of Casel's interpretation: the Fathers do not adapt to mere Platonic symbolism, but above all to biblical typology, in which every event is a symbol that captures the past and anticipates the future. For this reason the symbol does not move us toward a disincarnate heavenly region, but rather invites us to traverse the axis of time, from the love of the creator to the definitive Sabbath rest in him. Adopting

---

58. See Casel, *Das christliche Kultmysterium*, trans. Burkhard Neunheuser as *The Mystery of Christian Worship* (Westminster, Md.: Newman Press, 1962). For a complete exposition of Casel's thought, with a complete list of his works, see Schilson, *Theologie als Sakramententheologie*. See also Berenhard Poschmann, "Mysteriengegenwart im Lichte des hl. Thomas," *Theologische Quartalschrift* 116 (1935): 53–116; Sergio Ubbiali, "Il sacramento nella teologia dei misteri," *Teologia (Br.)* (1984): 166–84; Andrea Bozzolo, *Mistero, simbolo e rito in Odo Casel: l'effettività sacramentale della fede* (Vatican City: LEV, 2003).

this viewpoint not only confirms the insight of Casel (who speaks about a presence of the life of Jesus in the celebration of his mysteries), but endows it with historical thickness.

An especially important factor in this respect has been the biblical concept of *memorial*, which is not only a remembrance of the past, but the ability of the past, being pregnant with God's promises, to remain alive in the liturgy. According to this view, which was taken up by Vatican II, the past already anticipates the future and the future confirms and fulfills the past.[59] Moreover this complements Rahner's symbolic vision with a key idea: time is decisive in order to understand what a "real symbol" is. In other words, the sacrament is symbolic inasmuch as it allows us to remember the past by reactualizing it; and inasmuch as it anticipates the future, treating us to its first-fruits.[60] The symbolic space of the liturgy is the space of memory and a space from which the fullness of time is made present, because it is the space dominated by Christ, the Lord of history. I will keep this fact in reserve for the synthesis that I will propose in the next chapter.

Ritual Efficacy: Louis-Marie Chauvet

Along with the line of thought that delves into the sacrament in terms of symbol, and very close to it, the invitation to emphasize the ritual dimension of the sacrament came to fruition during the twentieth century.[61] Here the rediscovery of the primitive rites by cultural anthropology play a major role. In this light, the rite offers an anchor in human experience to explain how the sacraments act. On this point the proposal of Louis-Marie Chauvet is outstanding for its influence.[62]

Chauvet proposes that the efficacy of the sacraments is shaped according to the proper efficacy of the rites. The rites (which I spoke about in chapter 7, above) contain an articulate and dynamic ensemble of symbols which are

59. See Vatican Council II, *Sacrosanctum Concilium*, December 4, 1963 [hereafter *SSC*], no. 47; available at www.vatican.va. See also Thurian, *L'eucharistie*.

60. This historical dimension of the sacrament was highlighted by Joseph Ratzinger, "The Sacramental Foundation of Christian Existence," *Collected Works*, 11:153–68; Walter Kasper, "Wort und Sakrament," in his *Glaube und Geschichte* (Mainz: Grünewald, 1970). Along similar lines is a proposal by Hans Urs von Balthasar that is somewhat scattered throughout his gigantic opus: see Miller, "The Sacramental Theology of Hans Urs von Balthasar"; and Nicola Reali, *La ragione e la forma: Il sacramento nella teologia di H. U. von Balthasar* (Rome: Mursia-Pontificia Università Lateranense, 1999).

61. About the relation of sacrament and rite in recent theology, see Bozzolo, *La teologia sacramentaria dopo Rahner*, 195–219; see also Alberto Dal Maso, *L'efficacia dei sacramenti e la performance rituale: Ripensare l'ex opere operato a partire dall'antropologia culturale* (Padua: Messaggero, 1999).

62. See above all Louis-Marie Chauvet, *Symbol and Sacrament: Sacramental Reinterpretation of Christian Existence* (Collegeville, Minn.: Pueblo Books, 1994), and his "L'avenir du sacramentel," *Recherches de science religieuse* 75 (1987): 241–66. The limitations of Chauvet's proposal are noted by Bozzolo, *Il rito di Gesù*, 82; and Conor Sweeney, *Sacramental Presence after Heidegger* (Eugene, Ore.: Wipf and Stock, 2015).

open to the ultimate mystery of life. Thanks to the rite, indeed, man can situate his space of relationships in the transcendent totality of the cosmos and experience the transitions of his time in relation to an eternal foundation. It can be said that the rite is a symbolic communitarian action that places man in the universe and helps him to traverse history from beginning to end.

On the basis of this, the French theologian presents a harsh critique of the classical view of sacrament as instrumental cause, which he considers characteristic of a utilitarian approach. For an instrument supposes an already constituted subject that operates in the world, whereby said world always remains external to said subject and foreign to its identity.[63] The symbolic order created by the rite, on the contrary, embraces and surrounds the person, so that he needs it in order to be constituted as a person, in order to recognize the world and to recognize himself. Chauvet associates this mediation of the environment, in the first place, with the body (man's original installation in the world) and with language (which situates us in a speaking community and from there mediates all thought).

Our author adds that the symbolic order opened up by the rite cannot be understood solely as a cognitive epiphany that appears before a distant spectator. On the contrary, he is talking about a dynamic order in which the person is called to participate actively. Indeed, the rite is an ensemble of symbols that are set up through work, as indicated by the suffix -urgy present in the word "liturgy" (just as in "metallurgy," "dramaturgy," etc.). For this reason rites, even in primitive cultures, are efficacious in transforming the order of the world; and they do this, not by some magical influence, but rather inasmuch as they revive the original experiences of our dwelling among things and allow us to resituate this dwelling as a whole in relation to a stable center, furnished by the presence of God.

The efficacy of the sacraments is, then, a *ritual efficacy*. Through it, the gift of God in Christ is installed within the symbolic order that surrounds the Christian: a corporeal order, a linguistic order (of scripture, of the profession of faith), an ethical order of relations with the brethren. In this way the sacraments make God present precisely where one would least expect him: in the fragility of corporeal mediations. God preferred to manifest himself in the body, a witness of human weakness, because the body, just when it mediates for us this contact with God, convinces us that God surpasses our experience, and prevents us from possessing him.

63. My historical survey (see above all chapters 8 and 9) has shown how unfounded this judgment is: the background of classical sacramental theology is the incarnation, life, death, and glorification of Jesus; everything revolves, therefore, around this same corporeal mediation that Chauvet thinks that he has discovered.

In his analysis of the symbol Chauvet adds a postmodern note that distances him from Karl Rahner. For Rahner understands the symbol as communication of what is deepest in each being, which reflects the traces of the Trinity and arrives at its fullness in Christ. In Chauvet's view, however, the distinguishing feature of the Christian symbolic order is not presence but rather absence, the negation of the human anxiety about security and appropriating the world. Faced with those who seek solid certainties on which to rely, Chauvet opines that faith aims above all to question certainties and to call everything into doubt.[64] The sacrament, therefore, instead of a real presence, would contain, so to speak, a *real absence*. Are not perhaps the bread broken and shared and the wine poured out the eminent symbol of faith?[65] Paradoxically, according to Chauvet, the sacraments make evident the withdrawal of Christ after Easter. They are the symbol of the empty place, of the "presence of His absence."[66]

What sense can be made of this last-mentioned aspect? It is true that the Christian symbol, having passed by way of the cross, can be received only by way of the refusal to consolidate security in oneself. On the other hand, the ultimate dynamic of the sacrament as symbol cannot be one of an absence, which denies that the deity is among us. True humility is not to remain in continual doubt, but rather to accept the steadfastness that comes from the divine action. The distinctive feature of Christianity is not a negation and an absence, but rather a great "Yes": the original affirmation of the goodness and closeness of God, who allows himself to be touched in the flesh. Only from the vantage point of this radical presence, of this security that the sacraments instill in us, is it possible to confront the difficult times when signs are cloudy. In the next chapter, by exploring the meanings of the body revealed by Christ, we will seek to correct the deviations in Chauvet's perspective, while adopting his valid insights.

Conclusion: The Sacrament and the Return to the Body

The various modern authors surveyed above invite us, from different perspectives, to return to man's incarnate condition as the key to understand-

64. Our author goes so far as to state that the true difference between human beings today is not the one that separates believers from nonbelievers, but rather the one that divides those who are sure of themselves (believers or not) from those (believers or not) who always remain open to questioning their ideas: see Chauvet, "L'avenir du sacramentel," 253, and also, along Chauvet's lines, Lieven Boeve, "The Sacramental Interruption of Rituals of Life," *Heythrop Journal* 44 (2003): 401–17.

65. See Louis-Marie Chauvet, "The Broken Bread as Theological Figure of Eucharistic Presence," in *Sacramental Presence in a Postmodern Context*, ed. L. Boeve and L. Leussen (Louvain: Peeters, 2001), 236–62.

66. See Louis-Marie Chauvet, "L'avenir du sacramental," 265.

ing what a sacrament is. This reorientation coincides with the most certain insights of the patristic and medieval periods, which always worked to keep the sacrament united to the Eucharistic body of Jesus and to our incorporation into it.

I have already indicated that, in Karl Rahner's view, the body is a paradigm of symbolic reality, for in it the person is expressed. The valuable insight of Odo Casel, for his part, argues along the same line, provided that we explain it not in terms of an alleged Platonism of the Fathers but rather in terms of the perspective of Christ's flesh and history, in which the Christian participates thanks to the sacraments. Chauvet, too, in speaking about the symbol and the rite, emphasizes that both revolve around the original language of corporeality: the body is man's first mediation in his self-knowledge and in his knowledge of the world, and therefore establishes the first symbolic order, which is a corporeal order.

This return to the body is necessary because, as the history of the definition of sacrament has shown, starting with St. Augustine, the difficulty in forging a synthesis sprang from disregard for corporeality (and, specifically, the Eucharistic corporeality of Jesus) as the central focus of the sacrament. If the sacrament is a sign, this sign has to be valued in terms of our incarnate condition, in other words, it always has to be thought of on the basis of the body: both the original experience of the body of every man and woman, and the way of experiencing the body inaugurated by Jesus and given to his followers.[67] And remember: by body, I mean our way of making ourselves present to the world and of establishing personal relations that define our identity, all against the constant background of the divine presence and action. For this reason the body is always a cosmic body (it puts us in relation with nature), a familial-social body (experienced in terms of a memory and within the horizon of fruitfulness). Starting from this view of the body, I will draw up, in the next chapter, a definition of sacrament that gathers the facts elaborated by the theological tradition.

67. See Luis F. Ladaria, "Grandeza del cuerpo humano: perspectiva teológica," *Burgense* 56 (2015): 165–81; and Granados, *Teología de la carne*.

11 🐤 ARCHITECTURE OF THE SACRAMENT

The Symbolic Space

My survey to define the sacrament (chapters 8 to 11) concludes in this chapter. I will start from the summary action of Jesus at the Last Supper, an action that reaches its climax in the resurrection. We saw, in fact, that the difficulties in understanding the sacraments over the course of history result from forgetting that they are rooted in the Eucharistic body of Christ. Beginning with the Eucharist will help us to take up again the distinct aspects of the sacrament (signification and efficacy) while integrating them in terms of a cohesive principle: the space of relations inaugurated by the body of Jesus, a body received from the Father and given to the brethren. In order to get their bearings in the following discussion, the readers will have to recall the syntheses that I offered regarding the original creatureliness of the sacraments (chapter 6) and about the path that they open up in history (chapter 7), for those two strata are part of the rite of Jesus.

The Eucharist: The Space of the Body of Jesus

Jesus, at his Last Supper, identified the bread and wine that he distributed to his disciples with his body and blood that were to be handed over. In this way he associated the rite with man's incarnate condition: in other words, according to the biblical view, to man's situation in the world and within the human family, in original dependence on God, the giver of life. The corporeal anchor of the rite assures, therefore, that it will always revolve around a space or network of relations: the rite will aim to order this space, to mature it, to display its fullness. It is, concretely speaking, the relational space *of Jesus* ("this is *my* body"), a space that the rite communicates to human beings ("for you"). I already discussed (chapter 2) the central coordinates of this

Eucharistic space, from which it extends beyond itself, and because of which it deserves to be called a symbolic space (chapter 4).

First, the Eucharist orients the network of Jesus' relations, in the first place, *toward the Father*, to whom the entire ritual action of Christ is referred. Then we recall that here Jesus is offering a sacrifice of praise (*todah*) for the new life that God will give him in raising him from the dead. The body of Christ, prepared already from antiquity by the Father (see Heb 10:5), will be abundant testimony, in the Paschal mystery, to this same paternal goodness. The offering of the chalice, for its part, confirms this openness to God, for blood is the vehicle of life and, consequently, bearer of the Spirit of Yahweh, which filled the flesh of Jesus on that first Sunday; if he calls it "blood of the covenant," it is because with it the pact between God and mankind is sealed seventy times seven times. Hence *in the Eucharist the relational space of Jesus in which Christians participate is constituted as a space of the covenant with God, filially oriented to receive and cultivate the Father's love: it is the new and definitive temple* (see Jn 2:21).

Second, the Eucharist expands the relational space of Jesus *so that it embraces all mankind*. Indeed, over the body and blood of Christ a word of donation is pronounced: "for you," "for many," for the forgiveness of sins (Mt 26:28) and for the life of the world (Jn 6:51). Here the "familial" language of the flesh is employed ("flesh of my flesh," "one flesh," "my own flesh") with which Jesus exposes his fate to ours, in order to entrust to us the life of brothers (see Heb 2:14: "the children share in flesh and blood"). Thus in Christ there is a recapitulation of the "corporate persons" of the Old Testament, like Isaac or the Servant of Yahweh, who had handed themselves over in order to regenerate the people. Moreover the blood, once again in its reference to the Spirit and in the context of the covenant, expresses the unity and reconciliation of all Israel accomplished by the divine favor. *From the flesh of Jesus, therefore, the rite opens up a space of believing fraternity in one body.*

Third, it must be pointed out, finally, that these relations, knit into the flesh and blood of Jesus, give us access to the entire course of his life, in which the history of the world is recapitulated. Indeed, the Lord celebrates his Passover, having loved his own so as to love them to the end (see Jn 13:1); and recognizing his origin in the Father so as to return to him glorified (see Jn 13:3). Moreover the context of the Jewish *pesach* cultivates grateful memory, reviving the awareness of God's original blessings and of the liberation of Israel. The *todah*, too—thanksgiving to the creator (memory) for the forthcoming gift of the risen body (future)—encompasses remembrance and hope in one and the same impulse. In short, the relations into which the rite incorporates us are such that they revive memory and generate the future. *The space opened up by the Eucharist proves, therefore, to be a dynamic space that traverses the ages so as to recapitulate them in the life of Jesus, raising them to their origin in the Father and projecting them toward their definitive destiny in God.*

The coordinates just described set for us the proportions of the basic architecture of the space of relations inaugurated by the rite. In order to complete this view, it is important to recall that this ritual space is not a space foreign to the habitat in which man's life unfolds. By including the body and the blood and the bread and the wine, the rite of Jesus accommodates all the creaturely spaces in which the human person dwells. I studied this aspect in chapter 6; there we saw how the Eucharist defines the human being based on the concrete relations (with the world, with neighbors, with God) in which his flesh places him. I then added that the sacrament of matrimony contains precisely the foundations of this creaturely space: everyone is a son or a daughter, called to be a spouse, and to generate life as a parent, building up a dwelling place and the common city. In chapter 7, I studied moreover how this creaturely space matured over time, centered on the covenant with Yahweh, expanding from rite to rite and from generation to generation.

Well, the high point of this structure arrived with Christ: the ritual space inaugurated by the Eucharist contains the relations that he forged during his life, in which he dwells with his followers (see Jn 1:38). "And the Word became flesh and dwelt among us" (Jn 1:14): the Son of God has settled in the dwelling place of the flesh; he is in radical, full relation to the Father and to his brethren. By assuming a body, he knit together with unsuspected and unsurpassable depth the relations that opened up to him in this very body, filling them with his Spirit of love. In this way he broadened the relational capacity of the flesh and pronounced in it a new language which, thanks to the Eucharistic rite, is definitively forged and can be communicated to his followers. From this perspective I will attempt to develop a general notion of sacrament that is founded on the Eucharist and capable of being applied to the seven sacraments of the New Testament and, analogously, to other salvific rites.

The Sacrament, Opening of a Symbolic Space

Starting from the rite of Jesus, we have seen how a human being's life is situated from its origins in a dynamic space of relations, a space where his body places him. Eucharistic faith proclaims that the Son of God, by becoming incarnate, lived in this space, taking up its coordinates and broadening them according to the dimensions of his love, so as to introduce man into them. I will show presently that this relational space can be described as a *symbolic space*. And I will infer that sacrament is the opening, in the life of human beings, of the symbolic space experienced by Christ in his body.

The Symbolic Space of Jesus

The concept of symbol is very slippery. In general it denotes only the mutual reference between two realities, but without specifying the type of relation that joins them.[1] For this reason we cannot start from symbol to define our view of man or of the world. It makes no sense to say that some eras were more symbolic and others less so, if we do not first distinguish some kinds of symbols from others. It seems more appropriate to define symbol starting from the radical experience of being human. If we take incarnate existence as our point of departure, in other word, the relational life that matures in time, this reveals to us a distinction between two ways of understanding symbol. The first is superficial, the second—fertile.

The symbol can indicate two separate realities: the first is perceived with the senses, the second, the truly real one, is encountered beyond them. The symbol, from this point of view, is a ladder that is stepped on in order to climb, and then it is abandoned after the ascent. A symbol of this type was familiar to the Platonic systems, for they transcend matter toward incorporeal ideas. We can speak in this respect about "sign-arrows," which are lifted up from a carnal, sensible reality to an invisible, spiritual reality that they represent. In this perspective the subject contemplates the symbol from outside, without having to participate in it, without being interpreted by it in turn.

However, this perspective for contemplating signs is not the original perspective of the incarnate person.[2] By living in the body (by *being* the body, too), man finds himself situated in the world, and his identity is con-

---

1. Among the abundant studies on symbol, see Jacques Maritain, "Sign and Symbol," *Journal of the Warburg Institute* 1, no. 1 (1937): 1–11; Daniélou, "The Problem of Symbolism"; Eugen Biser, "Das religiöse Symbol im Aufbau des Geisteslebens," *Münchener Theologische Zeitschrift* 5, no. 2 (1954): 114–40; Borella, *Le mystère du signe*; Simon, *Philosophie des Zeichens*; François Genuyt, "L'économie des signes," *Lumière et vie* 41, no. 209 (1992): 19–35; Mauricio Beuchot, *Las caras del símbolo: el icono y el ídolo* (Madrid: Caparrós, 1999); Giuseppe Mazzocchi, "Segni e simboli nella liturgia: Rassegna bibliografica," *Rivista di pastorale liturgica* 189, no. 2 (1995): 44–46; José María Mardones, *La vida del símbolo: La dimensión simbólica de la religión* (Santander: Sal Terrae, 2003); see also the bibliography offered in note 51 of the preceding chapter.

2. See Marcel, "L'être incarné"; Ricoeur, *Philosophy of the Will*, vol. 2.

stituted on the basis of the network of relations that it establishes with things and persons. And so, by living in the body (by *being* the body, too), man does not contemplate reality from a distance, but rather in reciprocal contact and relation, knowing that he is being looked at and interpreted by it while he looks at and interprets it.

Think about the encounter of a child with his mother, of the painter with his work of art, of spouses in the conjugal embrace. In all these experiences there are symbols, that is, openings of reality toward greater depths. Well, these symbols do not have the form of an arrow that leads further on: it is not necessary to go beyond the mother's face to encounter her smile, beyond the painting to encounter the beauty, or beyond the body of the beloved in order to encounter communion with him or her. On the contrary, the surplus of reality that is given to us here—in the filial or spousal relation, in artistic inspiration—does not come by surpassing these corporeal relations, but only by going deeper into them, for example when we familiarize ourselves with the work of art or our love for the dear person matures. For this reason, instead of a "sign-arrow" that points further on, what we have is a space of relations that invites us to delve more deeply into it: I will speak, therefore, about a "symbolic space."[3]

This symbolic space is offered to man, from his arrival in the world on, as the original environment in which he is born and is welcomed. We already know its basic coordinates, marked by familial relations: the body of the parents who engendered me, the spousal body in which a communion is built up, the generative body that gives life to children, the social body that is consolidated starting from the family. All the relations of this space that receives me and that I inhabit from birth conceal a promise which invites me, not to surpass them in search of another reality, but rather to delve more deeply into them, to tighten the bonds, as one digs in a field to unearth its treasure. The distinctive feature of this space is, moreover, that someone who inhabits it cannot understand himself outside of it. In other words, delving into the symbolism of the things and persons that surround us is the sole way of discovering one's own identity.

In light of this, it is clear that when I speak here about "space" I am referring not to the geometric space of modern physics as an abstract, homogeneous container, but rather to the relational space that is inaugurated by

3. The word "symbol," as we already know, meant for the Greeks an object divided into two that allowed its bearers to recognize each one another. Therefore it seems appropriate to associate the sign to a space of relations, as I am proposing in this chapter. In chapter 1, above, various ways of understanding the symbol were proposed, using for it neatly distinguished descriptions of space: labyrinth, desert, dwelling.

our presence in the body.[4] By space I understand something as concrete as one's own flesh and, proceeding from there, one's dwelling, the city, the temple, the nation, understood first as *affective and interpersonal spaces*, which are made visible then in concrete edifices of brick, logs, stone, etc., which put on different cultural garbs.[5]

The Symbolic Space and Its Maturation over Time

How do we delve into this symbolic space so as to reach the surplus of reality that it contains? According to what I have said, the opening of the symbol does not invite us to transcend it toward a distant, ideal reality. An abstract, archetypal mother is not displayed to a child in his mother's embrace; nor does an artist find a disincarnate beauty behind his work of art. The excess and the surplus of being that is obtained in these experiences occurs within the very bond that we establish with the world and with others, because this bond is called to mature and grow.

This means that the relation in which the flesh connects us to things and persons shows its richness only in the patience and fruitfulness of time. We can say, also, that it is a *promising* or *generative* relation. Consequently, the symbolic space of the body does not unfold from bottom to top, from the material to the ideal; but rather proceeding according to the flow of the hours and of the calendar from a primordial origin to an ultimate destiny. For entering into the space opened by the body means accepting a memory (the body is filial) and having a presentiment of a future (the body—in work, in the generation of a child—is fruitful). For both reasons unreachable horizons loom, toward God: we can always delve more deeply into our origin and aspire more toward our future.

To imagine this symbolic field we can picture a garden or orchard sowed with seeds, which not only preserve the memory of the hand that scattered them, but also await another hand that will harvest its fruits. Someone who lives in the garden experiences a surplus, something that grows slowly and silently, yet never at the edge of the garden, but rather within it, running through its roots and branches. In a similar way, the symbolic space of the body opens up beyond itself because it matures in time from an origin toward a fullness, that is, because it is a space of memory and a fruitful space.

4. To analyze these two ways of understanding space, one author has proposed the distinction between "space" and "place," the latter being what we can call "relational space"; see Edward S. Casey, *Getting Back Into Place: Toward a Renewed Understanding of the Place-World* (Bloomington: Indiana University Press, 2009).

5. Mario Botta and Paolo Crepet, *Dove abitano le emozioni: La felicità e i luoghi in cui viviamo* (Turin: Einaudi, 2007).

This *symbolic space*, intertwined around the body, is where the Son of God revealed himself to the world. For this reason the signs associated with his epiphany and action among men are not "sign-arrows" that draw us out of the body, but rather the plans and pillars of a corporeal *symbolic space*. This space contains the essential ties wrought by Jesus with the world, with his brethren, with God. The openness of this space follows the course of time, from one mystery of Jesus to the next; and it points, on the one hand, to his filial memory, which goes back in a unique way to his Father, and on the other hand to a new fruitfulness which in his risen body transmits the glory of God. St. John spoke about this space as a temple which was to be built and which was identified with the body of Christ (see chapter 3, above); and St. Paul referred, in this same sense, to the *mysterion* of one body, called to expand through the whole world (see chapter 4, above). Let us consider more attentively the way in which Christ inaugurated this new symbolic space of relations in the sacraments.

The Eucharistic Rite, Opening of the Symbolic Space of Jesus

In order to be able to inaugurate the symbolic space and to inhabit it, and to be able to traverse its entire temporal axis, man needs rites. And this is because rites pronounce this ultimate language of the body that the body itself—and here lies its mystery—does not succeed in expressing. The rite gives voice, for example, to the remembrance of the origins from time immemorial; to the unfamiliar novelty of each step toward the future; and to the unforeseeable encounter with the disturbing barrier of death. Earlier (see chapter 7, above) I already concluded that the rite reveals to us—without being able to grasp it—what the vanishing point is of all our relational space, linking it to God; and that it joins our time to the origin and end of history, thus assuring that it can keep marching.

We know that the Old Testament situates cult or worship in relation with familial experiences, particularly paternity and filiation. The rite, on the one hand, saves these experiences from the dangers that threaten them, affirming their goodness. On the other hand, it reveals the ultimate reason for them, preventing us from taking them in an idolatrous fashion as absolute. Thus, for example, sacrificing the lamb (the substitute for the firstborn son) teaches each father to acknowledge the origin of fatherhood in God, so that he can receive and guard the gift of his children, the key to the people's march through the generations.

How is the rite of Jesus situated in this context? The novel feature at the Last Supper was not that it spiritualized and thus distanced itself from the flesh, but, on the contrary, that it corporealized to the extreme: Christ did not offer a lamb, but himself on the cross, expecting that his flesh would be glorified by God. Hence the Eucharist, the central rite of his life, took up the way in which Jesus experienced his body; and it brought to fulfillment the relations that were forged there, inasmuch as it was a body received from the Father (Heb 10:5) and given up for his followers (1 Cor 11:24). In this way the Eucharist offered to Jesus a center in which to unify all the relations of his life as well as a rhythm by which to place landmarks along his way from the Father and to the Father.

At the same time, through the Eucharistic rite, Jesus opened up to his disciples participation in his own environment of life: they will be able to enter now into the space unfolded by Christ's relations, that is, it will be possible for them to be incorporated in him into one body. For the Eucharistic rite magnetizes all our spaces of relations along the forcefield lines of the filiation, fraternity, spousal love, and paternity of Jesus. New filiation, fraternity, spousal love, and fruitfulness now become possible, and they are the pillars of the ecclesial community. The symbolic space of the Eucharist takes up into itself and rescales [*redimensiona*] the original symbolic space of the body, which was built according to the order of familial relations. In celebrating this rite, the original human manner of inhabiting the world is expanded and deepened, according to the measure of Jesus.[6]

The Sacraments, Generation of the Space of Jesus in All Human Spaces

Starting from here, we can consider all the sacraments as a prolongation of the Eucharistic space to the various situations of human life. If the Eucharist is the environment inaugurated by the body of Jesus, the other sacraments incorporate us into this environment. Each sacrament, starting from the space of Christ, colonizes the many dimensions of man's relational space. And all these spaces together constitute the pillars of the church, the house of God (1 Tm 3:15).

Given that the space inaugurated by Jesus takes up into itself the creaturely space, whose most original structure is in the family, it helps to consider matrimony in the first place. And this is because contained here are the primordial relations that welcome a human being when he comes into the world and that form the radical space of his symbolic experience. Indeed, matrimony is a sacrament because Jesus took up and transformed the

6. See Martin Heidegger, "Bauen, Wohnen, Denken," in his *Vorträge und Aufsätze* (Pfullingen: Neske, 1994), 139–56.

ancient space of the children of Adam in order to found his new environment of relations. Therefore when a baptized man and a baptized woman forge the nuptial bond, that is, when they inaugurate the familial space of "one flesh" (Gn 2:24), they always do so as persons rooted in the Eucharistic space of Jesus, which defines them as Christians.

From this perspective, Eucharist and matrimony constitute the two axes or hinges of the symbolic space of the sacramental economy, which takes up into itself the old and the new. The remaining sacraments come about based on the symbolic space that is generated in the Eucharist, the fundamental sacrament; and they refer constantly to matrimony, the sacrament of rootedness [*arraigo*] in creation. In this way, none of the creaturely spaces that accommodate man from the beginning are foreign to the new space of Jesus. From this vantage point, let us look at the other sacraments.

Through baptism the catechumen enters into the symbolic space of Christ's body: it is the portal sacrament. The creaturely reference is birth, by which we are integrated into the cosmos and into society through the body of our family, inheriting its traditions and bearing its name. Once catechumens are baptized, all of their relational space proves to be founded on the space of Jesus and his church. Thus the symbolic ability of their body to knit relations that mature in history is strengthened according to the measure of Christ. The neophytes, engendered in the waters of the womb of mother church, contribute in turn to building up the ecclesial space, so that it expands until it fills all things (see Eph 4:10).

In confirmation the relational space of the baptized Christian gains impetus to mature in the Spirit toward the fullness of Jesus. This sacrament, therefore, makes the space dynamic, transforming it into a space of growth that is capable of generating life in the church and in society. For this reason confirmation is the sacrament of increase or advancement (*sacramentum augmenti*) and also of public Christian testimony, that is, of the courageous opening of the believer's space so as to make fruitful all the relational spaces of humankind.[7]

Through the sacrament of holy orders the space of Christ the head, source of the church, is generated continually in her. As we will see below (in chapter 14), the ordained man is incorporated into the generative space of Christ, who presents himself to his church as father and husband. Here we see again how the relational environment of Jesus takes up the original creaturely bonds into itself and transforms them, this time in matters concerned with the fatherhood of the ordained man.

---

7. See Thomas Aquinas, *ST* III, q. 72, a. 1, co.

Penance is about reopening the baptismal space of the body of Christ that sin has constricted by concentrating everything on the solitary point of the individual. This ability to return to the coordinates of baptism testifies to the supremacy of the communional space of Jesus, which overcomes every effort of sin to close off spaces with its anti-sacramental logic. This reintegration into the body of Christ signifies also a reopening of time, for guilt made the sinner prisoner of his past and thus makes it impossible for his narrative to be open to the future. Confession, by associating the penitent's narrative to Christ's narrative, integrates the guilt into an older and newer story, that of Jesus' forgiveness, and thus reopens the time of memory and of hope. Matrimony, inasmuch as it guards the time of birth and the time of the promise "until death" and "for better or for worse" contains the creaturely basis and support for understanding how penance reopens the original space and time of baptism.

The anointing of the sick, too, is about inaugurating a new space. Precisely when sickness curtails the patient's relational possibilities, confining him to his room and his bed, and confronts him with the final closure of the human space, which is death, the possibility of new relations unfolds for him through participation in the suffering body of Jesus. Pain, which obliges a person to abandon the spaces of autonomy, offers an open flank to the encounter with Christ, who precisely in his passion opened wide his heart to receive the Father's will and to embrace all human beings. Paradoxically, just as the narrowness of the cross points to the four corners of the cosmos, sickness itself can then expand the relational space of the sick person, opening him to the oil of divine compassion and inviting him to share the "world of pain and sorrow" of so many brethren.[8] The promise held by the first dwelling place of the child, signaled by the fruitful difference of man and woman, proves now in Christ to be stronger than suffering and death, and capable of anticipating the sick person's *todah* or praise of the Father, by experiencing already the communional spaces of the future resurrection.[9]

Toward a Definition of Sacrament

From here we can propose a definition of sacrament which, assuming the classic medieval perspective, reinterprets it in terms of its center in the Eucharistic body of Christ. *A sacrament is the opening-up in the life of a human being, by means of a rite, of the symbolic space of relations that Jesus inaugurated in his flesh.* I call this space symbolic because it is capable of maturing

---

8. See John Paul II, *Salvifici Doloris*, Apostolic Letter, February 11, 1984, par. 8; *AAS* 76 (1984): 208.
9. See Leidi, *Le signe de Jonas.*

beyond itself, in the patience of time, toward harboring the presence and love of God, the origin and destiny of history; therefore to say *symbolic* is equivalent to saying *generative*. The ritual opening-up of this space, as we will see, is initiated by Christ through his minister and enlivened by the outpouring of the Holy Spirit.

By *space* I mean a network of relations to which a human being belongs, a network rooted in his body which binds him with the Father, his brethren, and the cosmos. The reference to God is established at the center of this space which is, therefore, a sacred space. The space is *symbolic* because the relations that are forged in it invite us to new depths, as they are capable of containing the divine presence and activity. This space, far from being static, gives more of itself the more it traverses the ages: it is a *generative* space, like a garden, called to mature and to bear fruit. For in the place opened up by the body of Jesus, it is possible both to try to remember the first origin and also to anticipate the eschatological destination.[10] Communion with God proves to be the vanishing point of this dynamism, its principle and its destination. This space of the sacrament includes within it the original *creaturely space* of the body and of its basic relations, which implies that it is not a space separated from the other vital environments, but rather is called to harbor them in itself and, in this way, to fulfill their symbolism or their ability to mature over time.

In order to explore this sacramental space, I will consider next the rite that inaugurates it and, further on, in part 3 of this treatise, its expansion to the rest of life. I will pay attention to two axes that traverse this space and have been elaborated by classic sacramental theology. The first axis relates body and word (*materia–forma*) and thus orders or structures the symbolic space of the sacrament. The second axis takes up again the classic binomial *sacramentum–res sacramenti* (or *gratia sacramenti*), and connects the relations of the sacramental space with the communion that enlivens and animates them.

The Axis Body–Word: Matter and Form of the Sacrament in Light of the Language of Christ's Flesh

We have seen that the sacraments inaugurate a relational space, which, by maturing over time, gives more and more of itself and therefore is symbolic. The opening-up of this space of relations comes about through a rite insti-

---

10. Jean-Jacques von Allmen, *Prophetisme sacramentel* (Neuchâtel: Delachaux et Niestlé, 1964), 10.

tuted by Jesus. I am interested now in describing the composition of this rite, so as to understand better the type of relations that it originates. I will start from the binomial "corporeal action/word" that is derived from the Eucharist; the theological tradition has designated these two terms "matter" and "form" respectively.

Word and Body from the Perspective of the Eucharist

The bread and wine that were distributed to the disciples and identified with Jesus' body and blood connect the rite to his incarnate condition, for food and drink are a figure summing up the corporeal existence of the human person: he who eats assimilates in himself the world and is therefore rooted in his environment, without which he cannot subsist. He who eats, moreover, shares this environment with other humans, who, being *com-mensales* (sharers at one table) and com-panions (eating one bread), are also con-corporeal. He who eats, above all, learns to be grateful in common with others to the fount of life, which is not found in oneself and which ultimately comes from God, whom we taste in tasting his gifts.

Therefore, in giving us his body to eat, Jesus invites us to participate in his way of inhabiting the world, among his brethren and for them, in gratitude to the Father and in readiness to accept his will. The material elements of bread and wine, in representing what is edible, are placed at the service of the language of Christ's body. And this language is precisely the one that the words of institution declare: thanksgiving to God and the offering of his body and blood "for you," "for the life of the world." The rite springs from this indissoluble unity between the corporeal handing-over and the words that express it.

This relation between word and body which is at the center of Jesus' rite belongs to man's original experience, from the moment when he came forth from the hands of the creator. In fact, as I noted in chapter 6, the experiences lived out in the flesh and the encounters that happen in it need the word in order to fit into the totality of our life and history. And the word, for its part, in order to manage to pronounce what is most profound about the personal vocation, needs to resonate in the environment of the relations that the flesh opens up to us.[11] In light of this, we can say that the body possesses a language that the word helps to formulate; and that the word needs a space in which to be pronounced, a space which the body offers to it.

---

11. On the connection between the word and the concrete (incarnate) situation in which it always resounds, see Ebeling, "Erwägungen zum evangelischen Sakramentsverständnis," 217–26; on the efficacy of the word, see Irène Rosier-Catach, *La parole efficace: signe, rituel, sacré* (Paris: Seuil, 2004).

Two examples will serve to illustrate for us this correspondence between body and word. Let us take, on the one hand, the *name* that parents give to their child. If the name comes to define the vocation and identity of the child, it is only because that child was generated from the flesh of his parents, who thus prove to be sharers in the mystery of his origin and can, without abusing their authority, channel his path in life. This means that the giving of a name attains all its efficacy within, and not outside of, a parental-filial space. In turn, the parental-filial space, in order to be fully constituted as a human space, needs the child's name to be pronounced, thus assuring that the parents take charge of their child's destiny.

Let us mention also, secondly, the *promise* that spouses exchange. It is capable, as no other promise is, of giving shape to their whole future (until death parts them) as a future of mutual self-gift, precisely because it is pronounced in the space of "one flesh" (Gn 2:24) where both spouses touch the mystery of their mutual origin in God and collaborate with him in the transmission of life. At the same time, the communion of the spouses in one flesh, in order to be constituted in all its truth, needs this promise of mutual commitment forever to resound within it, a promise which humanizes this union and distinguishes it from other unions in the animal kingdom.

Thus, when Jesus in his rite closely ties word and body, he is bringing to its fullness the architecture of the human space. In assuming flesh he took up the network of relations in which the existence of the children of Adam is interwoven, and expanded it to the measure of his condition as only-begotten Son. At the Last Supper, as he blesses the food, he confesses that his corporeal existence refers him radically to the Father, who shaped his flesh and will not abandon it to corruption. And he also acknowledges, in supping with his disciples, that he shares with human beings one and the same destiny and dares to take it upon himself so as to ransom them from death. In this way he opens up for the disciples, to whom he gives to eat of the same bread and to drink from the same cup (not a custom in the Hebrew Passover), participation in his own way of settling in the world.

The words of consecration clarify precisely how these new ties inaugurated by Christ are ordered, for they express the movement of donation which, from the Father's love ("giving thanks he blessed"), receives his disciples so as to redeem them from being scattered ("the forgiveness of sins") and to make them one ("for you," "for the life of the world"). The Eucharist, through its structure as material action and word, communicates to us, then, the language of Jesus' body, so that we can orient all our relations in a new way.

Word and Body in the Economy of the Sacraments

The structure of word and body is transmitted from the Eucharist to the whole economy of the sacraments. Indeed, as a general rule, they all contain a material action and a word. Baptism is the washing of water and of the word of life (Eph 5:26); the Holy Spirit descends in confirmation when the believer is covered by the hands of the minister, who prays for him (Acts 8:14–17); in ordination hands are imposed and the consecratory prayer is pronounced (1 Tm 4:14; Acts 6:6); another prayer is recited with faith over the sick person when he is anointed (Jas 5:14); and this applies also, as we will see, to matrimony and penance. Light is shed on this structure by the connection between the body and language that Jesus established in the Eucharist:

The material actions with water, bread, wine, oil, etc., acquire meaning based on the radical meanings of the body of Jesus, in other words, based on his way of living out filiation, fraternity, and other relations, bringing to maturity the original meanings of the human body. Through the material of the sacrament Jesus touches our corporeal situation, assimilates it to himself and transforms it, communicating to us his way of dwelling in the world. The water of baptism, for example, is placed at the service of the generative meaning of the body, configuring us to the new filiation (sonship) of Jesus.

The role of the words pronounced in each sacrament, for their part, is to clarify the meaning of the material action (the water poured out, the oil with which we are anointed), associating it with the language of Jesus' body, which the master forged during his life. This is to say that the "form" of the sacrament expresses the order that each rite confers on our space of relations, in order to conform it to the relations experienced by Christ. Thus, for example, in baptism, the birth from the waters corresponds to the invocation of the Trinitarian name, which explains the new filiation that is bestowed here, in light of Jesus' Sonship: the name of God revealed by Christ comes to be the name and the destiny of the neophyte.

Note the luminous circularity of word and body. Thanks to the material action, the words of the formula can resound from the center of human experience, touching the flesh and configuring the relations on which our identity rests. Thanks to the words, on the other hand, the contact with Christ in the sacraments is not a blind encounter in the night, but rather bears a truth about the way to build up relations, in other words, a truth of love. With St. Cyril of Alexandria we can say that the body of Christ, which in touching us generates life, is also a "generator of light."[12]

---

12. See Cyril of Alexandria, *In Iohannem* VI, 9, 6–7 (PG 72:964).

The sacramental signs therefore coincide with the original experience of man (body endowed with word) and of the life of Jesus (incarnate Word). That is to say, the structure of every sacrament is incarnational: a material element so as to touch the human body and a word so as to express the different meanings of the human body (the quality of the relations that are established in it), associating them with the language of Jesus' body. This confirms that the sacraments, according to the classic axiom, are for human beings.

Let us add to this that the rite has a dynamic structure. For, on the one hand, not only is something material used in it, but a material action is carried out. And, on the other hand, the word has a narrative character inasmuch as it is associated with the memory of Jesus' life. Thus the Eucharistic formula summarizes for us Christ's itinerary from the original gift of the Father, to whom he gives thanks, to his total surrender of himself for human beings, for whom he offers his body and blood in hope of the resurrection. In baptism, for its part, the words associate the name of the baptized person to the name of God—Father, Son, and Spirit—revealed during Christ's earthly journey.

This temporal structure of the rite corresponds to our incarnate experience, which also traverses time: the filial meaning of the body reminds us of the origin, the spousal relation speaks about a time shared in the fidelity of the promise, paternity opens up a new future, etc. In all these experiences the time of the flesh (of its desires and affections) is ordered by a word (a name, a promise) that frames it within a personal relation, and thus gives it stability and direction [camino]. The sacrament, therefore, in containing corporeal action and narrative word, is attuned to the structure of our corporeal desires and affections, and becomes capable of conferring on them an origin and a goal. The words of the sacrament reveal the rhythm with which Jesus experienced his time, a rhythm that is made present in the ritual action so as to be communicated to the time of the faithful.

In short, we can distinguish the following strata of the body–word (matter–form) connection. First, the material action already contains a language through its relation to the human body: the bread and wine, to a meal; the water, to cleansing and birth, etc. Second, this action becomes associated, through the word, to the language of Jesus' body, that is, to the way in which he configured his relations: it is his radical openness to the Father, his capacity for communion with human beings, his victory over sin, etc. Third, action and word have a dynamic, narrative sense, for they introduce the Christian into the very story of Jesus: a body that is born, that is received and handed over, that receives the strength of the Spirit, etc. Let us add, finally, an aspect developed in chapter 7: in order to be understood, the words and the meaning of the material action need the background of the whole history of Israel, which Christ included in his rite; thus the water of baptism will recall the Red Sea and the Jordan; the bread and wine recall the Paschal lamb; and so on.

As we have seen, medieval theology framed the structure of the rite in the Aristotelian categories of matter and form. I have already pointed out the advantages and limitations of this proposal (see chapter 9, above). In order to interpret the matter–form division correctly, the crucial thing, as we just saw, is always to keep them joined to man's incarnate, historical condition. Through matter, the flesh of Jesus touches us and conforms us to itself, so that we can live according to the meanings of Jesus' body, as they are contained in the words of the form.

In this way we overcome a difficulty that Scholastic theology ran into in identifying the matter and form of the sacraments of matrimony and penance. They are different from the others, not because they depart from the general rule of body–word but, on the contrary, because they are forged directly in the body and with its language.

And thus matrimony is the environment in which the unity between body and word is perceived, in the original experience of every person, as clarified by the examples of the name and the promise that I used. In fact the spouses come to be "one flesh" (in the consummation of marriage) because they pronounced "one word," their marital consent. Thus it is understood that in a wedding no matter or form is necessary aside from the life and love of the spouses. Given that both of them belong through baptism to the body of Christ, it will be enough for them to express—in word and flesh—their mutual acceptance and surrender in order to signify efficaciously the love of Christ and of the church.

Penance, for its part, has as its material element the path of the penitent's conversion, that is to say, his return to the baptismal coordinates of the body of Jesus. Given that the baptized person is already incorporated into Christ by baptism, and that he simply returns to the space of communion with him, no other additional elements are needed to signify this reincorporation. In order to acknowledge the path of conversion, a spoken confession is to be made, and the grace of the sacrament is received through the priest's words of absolution. These words contain the forgiving story of the life of Jesus, which helps to reinterpret in terms of mercy the story of the believer who had gone astray, freeing him ("I absolve you") from the sin that paralyzes his story.

The Axis Body–Communion: The Efficacy of the Sacramental Sign and the Action of the Holy Spirit

I just described the framework of the sacramental rite, made up of corporeal action (matter) and word (form). This tells us that the sacrament inaugurates a new order of relations in the body (structured according to Jesus' manner of relating to others) and a new way of weaving these relations in time (structured according to Jesus' story). In incorporating us into this relational space of Jesus, the rite also transmits to us the Spirit of Jesus, living communion with him.[13] Then a second axis arises, which goes from the sacramental sign (matter and form) to the grace that is bestowed through it. By exploring this axis we will understand better how the sacrament confers the grace that it signifies.

The explanation has to go back to what was new in the Last Supper, in which we observe a close connection between the structure of Jesus' rite and his communion with the Father in the Spirit. On the one hand, it would have done Jesus no good to perform his rite if it had not been inspired by the Spirit of love that united him to the Father during the passion and brought him back to life on Easter morning. On the other hand, the Spirit could not have descended upon Christ if his life in the flesh had not been ordered according to the words of the rite (in gratitude to the Father, "given up for you"), which opened his life to the will of God and to the love of the brethren. Both aspects, then, are necessary: the corporeal order does no good without the life of the Spirit (see Jn 6:63); and the Spirit can only pour himself out fully upon flesh, the flesh of the Son of God which is disposed to the Spirit's presence and action.

In order to understand this newness it helps us to turn to man's original experience in which, as noted above (chapter 6), the same harmony between body and love is discovered. Man's life in the flesh, ordered according to the familial relations that welcome him into the world, is the support required if love is to flourish in him as the key of his personal identity. Each person understands what it is to receive paternal and maternal love, to be welcomed into a family, only because he has a filial body (because, in the flesh, he was born as a child). Well, now, this relational space of the body can exist without the experience within it of the relations of love that enliv-

13. On the efficacy of the sacraments, besides the modern authors whom I cited in the preceding chapter, the reader may consult Kimberly Hope Belcher, *Efficacious Engagement: Sacramental Participation in the Trinitarian Mystery* (Collegeville, Minn.: Liturgical Press, 2011); Philip McShane, "On the Causality of the Sacraments," *Theological Studies* 24 (1963): 423–36; Otto Semmelroth, "Personalismo y Sacramentalismo," *Orbis Catholicus* 8–9 (1960): 125–44.

en it. Many children, whose bodies recall the relation with their parents and their radical origin in them, are not in fact welcomed or accepted: they will experience their condition as sons and daughters more as a disgrace than as a blessing. Or, having indeed experienced this first love, they reject it in search of independent wanderings, only to end up yearning for husks to eat. In short, belonging to a filial space of relations (through which one bears, for example, one's parental surname) is dead in itself unless there is present in it the love that enlivens these relations.

Another example: two spouses become united in one flesh until death separates them; in other words, they share one and the same corporeal indwelling [*instalación*] in the world, where they no longer dwell as "I" and "you," but rather as "we." In many cultures, from then on, they will join their surnames, now that they share their future project and become capable together of transmitting life to their children. All the same, the community of life that they have forged does not automatically bring love with it; in fact, they can betray this promise of fidelity by taking a stance opposed to the new body that they received in marrying each other. Their familial unity "in one flesh" (see Gn 2:24) is alive only if conjugal love inspires and moves them, and this love in turn can exist only when the spouses have been constituted "in one flesh."

In short, the flesh, by itself, is worth nothing, unless something greater happens in it, which the flesh hopes for without being able to demand it: the love that enlivens the relations in which the flesh situates us. In other words, this love is new with respect to the flesh, cannot be deduced from it, although the flesh calls for it (as filial, fraternal, spousal flesh), and is prepared to receive it, for the flesh is the one place where this love can be kindled.

This relation between flesh and love supplies us with the key to understanding the bond between the sign and the cause of the sacraments. In fact, as the body (whether filial, fraternal, or conjugal) is the channel of love, so in an analogous way the relational space opened up by the sacrament is the channel of grace. Classic theology had difficulty accepting so-called physical causality, because it did not seem logical that spiritual grace should be mediated by a material element (see chapters 9 and 10, above). In this respect it helps to speak about "corporeal causality," thus tracing the matter back to the body, and also to understand that the body is precisely the place where the relations that are constitutive of the person unfold—relations through which God manifests himself and acts. The experience of the creator's fatherhood, for example, is always mediated by the body, the first witness to the fact that life was bestowed on us from a source [*fontalmente*]. The corporeal causality of the sacraments does nothing but corroborate the experience of our incarnate situation, purifying and expanding it.

To this experience Jesus brings a new measure, as Son of God who dwelled in the body and there consummated love for the Father and for mankind. For the creaturely coordinates of the body can never assure the bestowal of a grace. To be born of a mother, to become bound to her forever corporeally as her child, does not unfailingly guarantee her welcome and her embrace. In fact, a mother can forget her suckling child. In a sacrament, nevertheless, once Jesus incorporates us into himself, he offers us without fail the same Spirit that was poured out upon his flesh.[14] It is true, we can place an impediment to his coming and shut ourselves off from his action; but the very fact of being received into the body of Jesus draws down upon us, *per se* and infallibly insofar as God is concerned, the gift of his Spirit.[15]

In short, the sacramental rite configures us to the body of Christ; in other words, it communicates to us the way in which he lived his presence in the world and among men. And when we adopt this way of relating to others, his Spirit can descend on us, as he already descended on the flesh of Jesus so as to dwell permanently in it. Certainly, this descent will always be an overflowing gift that the corporeal rite cannot produce by itself. But, on the other hand, the Spirit of Jesus desired to pour himself out—and promised to do so if he encounters no obstacle—only upon the relational space opened up by the rite, because this is the relational space of Jesus himself. It is possible therefore to call this rite, in its concrete corporeal structure, a channel of grace.

---

14. On the relation between the Spirit and the sacraments, see Boris Bobrinskoy, "L'Esprit du Christ dans les sacrements chez Jean Chrysostome et Augustin," in *Jean Chrysostome et Augustin*, ed. C. Kannengiesser (Paris: Beauchesne, 1975), 247–80; Ignacio Oñatibia, "Por una mayor recuperación de la dimensión pneumatológica de los sacramentos," *Phase* 16 (1976): 425–39; Antolín González Fuente, "El Espíritu Santo y los sacramentos: el dato biblico," *Angelicum* 55, no. 1 (1978): 12–57; Isaac Kizhakkeparampil, *The Invocation of the Holy Spirit as Constitutive of the Sacraments According to Cardinal Yves Congar* (Rome: Pontificia Università Gregoriana, 1995); Ramiro González, "El Espíritu Santo en la economía sacramental de la Iglesia," *Revista Española de Teología* 59, no. 1 (1999): 59–84; Willigis Eckermann, "Neuschöpfung durch den Heiligen Geist in den Initiationssakramenten," in *In der Kraft des Heiligen Geistes: Wovon die Kirche lebt*, ed. W. Eckermann et al. (Kevelaer: Butzon and Bercker, 1998), 91–107; Ephrem Carr (ed.), *Spiritus spiritalia nobis dona potenter infundit: a proposito di tematiche liturgico-pneumatologiche: Studi in onore di Achille M. Triacca* (Rome: Centro studi S. Anselmo, 2005). On some sacraments in particular: Silvano Maggiani, "La mano e lo Spirito: Per una lettura simbolica della imposizione delle mani," *Rivista liturgica* 78 (1991): 391–401; José María de Miguel González, "La acción del Espíritu Santo en la Unción de los enfermos," *Estudio Trinitarios* 30 (1996): 357–84.

15. See Council of Trent (DH 1607).

Summary: Signification and Efficacy, from the Perspective of Christ's Life

In the sacramental perspective just elaborated, sign and efficacious communication of grace call for each other mutually based on what was wrought by Jesus during his life. Indeed, given that the symbolic space opened up by the rite contains Jesus' way of relating (signification), it invokes in and of itself the descent of the Spirit of Jesus (efficacy). And this Spirit, for his part, can be poured out completely, as the Spirit of divine communion that he is, only upon the relational opening of the body of Jesus, the Son of God. The life of Christ, which unfolded in its entirety under the action of the Spirit, constitutes the fundamental reference for understanding the signification and efficacy of the sacraments, and it serves us now as a guide for offering a concluding summary of this chapter.

In fact, the structure of the sacrament can be described in terms of the action of what St. Irenaeus of Lyons called the two hands of God—the Logos and the Spirit—on a third protagonist, the flesh.[16] My proposal is, therefore, to adopt the trinomial *Word–Spirit–flesh* as the key reference of the sacramental dynamism. This trinomial is distributed along the twofold axis that I used to describe the sacraments: *Word–flesh*, as the structure of the rite; and *Spirit–flesh*, in order to understand the bestowal of grace. The theology of the sacraments is thus linked not only with Christology, but also with Trinitarian theology.[17]

We have, before all else, two axes that traverse the experience of the children of Adam (see chapter 6, above). The first indicates *the link between the flesh and the word* and is based on the body's ability to speak a language, the meanings of which are articulated according to the relations that are established in the flesh. We are talking about the filial, fraternal, spousal, generative bonds that open us to the common good and allow us to taste the presence and action of God. Secondly it is *the nexus of the flesh with love* and, therefore, with the presence and work of the Spirit. The language of the body expresses nothing by itself alone until the gratuitous and surprising experience of interpersonal love occurs. And, on the other hand, this experience of love cannot occur except in the body and through the body, because

---

16. See Irenaeus of Lyons, *Adversus haereses* IV, 20, 1 (SC 100:626; ANF 1:487b).

17. See Lothar Lies, "Trinitätsvergessenheit gegenwärtiger Sakramententheologie?," *Zeitschrift für katholische Theologie* 105, no. 3 (1983): 290–314 and 415–29; on the Trinitarian dimension of the sacraments at Vatican Council II, see Henri Bourgeois, "Los sacramentos según el Vaticano II," in *Historia de los dogmas*, III: *Los signos de la salvación*, ed. B. Sesboüé (Salamanca: Secretariado Trinitario, 1996), 185–213, at 205–6.

that is where the person is constitutionally open to relation: filial love exists only toward someone who has generated us; fraternal love exists only toward someone who shares with us the memory of one and the same origin; conjugal love exists only between a man and a woman who form "one flesh."

Well, then, it follows that Christ brought both lines to fulfillment. The first, inasmuch as he *is Word made flesh*, and therefore the one in whom the body attains the expressive summit of its language. No one has woven in the flesh relations of greater density and depth, as son, brother, spouse of the church, father of believers. The second, inasmuch as *the Spirit has rested upon him without measure* (see Jn 3:34), and has slowly acted to shape in his flesh the total communion of God with human beings.

From these two axes we can understand, finally, the structure of the sacraments. The first axis, of body and word, corresponds to the classic structure of the sacramental sign as *matter* and *form*. As I explained above, the matter refers to the body as place of presence to the world and of interpersonal encounter; and the form explains the order and the dynamism of the relations that are rooted in the body. Matter and form are explained, more concretely, in terms of the language of Jesus' body, which was forged during his passage on earth. Thus our body is adapted, in each sacrament, to the different relations that he opened up in his flesh and to the narrative tension of his journey from the Father to the Father. The second axis, *body and communion*, corresponds to the coming of the Spirit upon the flesh. The space opened up by the sacrament now becomes the environment where the Spirit descends, just as the relational body is the space where love occurs. The sacrament is efficacious because, through the rite, it puts us in contact with the flesh of Jesus, on whom the Spirit rests without measure.

The sacraments, we can conclude, generate a relational space in which our life can mature toward its fullness. For through them we are inserted into the fabric of ties that Jesus established and we adopt the concrete rhythm with which he tied together his steps on earth. It is a space that we will never have to abandon, because it is capable of containing within itself the fullness of communion with God. And it is called to expand, as we will see in part 3 of this treatise, to all the environments of human life so as to make them bear fruit abundantly.

PART 3

TOWARD A SACRAMENTAL
WAY OF LIVING

Now that sacrament has been defined as the ritual opening of the space of Jesus' relations in our life, I turn to explore this vital environment that the sacraments inaugurate: what is its architecture, how many pillars does it have, how are its rooms arranged? We will see that this space is founded on the sacramental character (chapter 12); that it is propagated to all the environments where Christians act and suffer (chapter 13); that one essential facet [literally "pole"] of its makeup is the person of the minister (chapter 14); and that it lives and breathes within the great generative symbolic space that is the entire church, the universal sacrament of salvation (chapter 15).

12 ❧ THE SACRAMENTAL CHARACTER

The doctrine about the sacramental character—an indelible sign that some sacraments imprint on the soul—is a hard teaching to contemporary ears. Our age of "fluid relationships" without a fixed form, which can be reinvented at any moment, does not understand that a sacrament produces a radical and irreversible change in a human person. Moreover, in an egalitarian society, the sacramental character seems to insist on a difference: through it baptized persons have an identity distinct from that of the nonbaptized; and priests, in the center of their being, are distinguished from lay people.

In reality, as we will see, the sacramental character is not opposed to the dynamic unfolding of life in time, for it does not consist of a monolithic quality that impedes growth, maturation, risk, and the adventure of a personal story. Nor is the difference that it introduces a barrier that isolates; on the contrary: "As many of you as were baptized into Christ ... are all one in Christ Jesus" (Gal 3:27–28). I will show in the following pages how the sacramental character, far from hobbling the progress and newness of our personal story, is the basis of it; far from separating human beings from each other, it binds them together based on their fruitful differences.

The Doctrine of the Sacramental Character in Scripture and in Patristic Writings

The theology of the sacramental character was developed in the Middle Ages, but its foundations are evident in the Bible and in the Church Fathers.

The Biblical Data

The New Testament conveys the image of the Christian who is "sealed" by God. Thus, for example, St. Paul says: "He has put His seal upon us and given us His Spirit in our hearts as a guarantee" (2 Cor 1:22). Note that the immediate context (2 Cor 1:20) speaks about Jesus as the "Yes" or "Amen" to all the divine promises, thus indicating the definitive character of his work. The topic turns to the seal also in Ephesians 1:13: the Christian has been "sealed with the promised Holy Spirit." Here again the context of the passage alludes to the consummation already inaugurated by Jesus, who gave us the Spirit as a pledge or guarantee (Eph 1:14). The image is confirmed later, in language about "the Holy Spirit of God, in whom you were *sealed for the day of the redemption*" (Eph 4:30).[1]

Certainly we cannot without further ado identify this seal with what would later be called the "sacramental character": the texts may be referring in general to the grace that the believer has received. What does seem probable is the relation of the seal with baptism; and we should take into account the fact that the Jews called circumcision a "seal."[2] This seal, moreover, is described as lasting, as it corresponds to the fullness of time brought by Christ, which anticipates our resurrection in giving us his Spirit as a pledge or security. In short, the language about "seal" suggests the permanence of the baptismal effect in the believer, inasmuch as his time is now under the dominion of the future that has come to pass in Jesus, which surpasses any other future. Thus these texts provide not only a stimulus for developing the doctrine of the sacramental character, but also a picture language in which to propose it.

Well, now, the firmest biblical support of the theology of the sacramental character is found in other passages where, without any mention of a "seal," a permanent effect of the sacrament is acknowledged along the same lines as the verses already cited. Thus baptism is described as a transformation of the believer, who is configured to Christ in his burial and glory (see Rom 6:3–14). Inasmuch as Christ's work has conquered death and has inaugurated the final hour, participating through baptism in his mystery means for the neophyte entering into the definitive reality: it is impossible for him to go back to a past or to escape to a future of which Jesus is not Lord.

Indeed, it is understood that if baptism plunges us into the life of Christ, it also confers the ineffaceable imprint of Christ. And it is not surprising that, according to Paul's teaching, it transforms our very body: we have died

1. Ignace de la Potterie, "L'onction du chrétien par la foi," *Biblica* 40 (1959): 15–22, refers to a number of passages (2 Cor 1:22; Eph 1:14; 4:30) to baptism, with which the seal is identified; and he adds that this is the only possible explanation for the rapid and extensive spread of the equation *baptism = seal* in early Christianity. Another author who associates "seal" and baptism is Thomas Marsh, "The Sacramental Character," in *Sacraments: Papers of the Maynooth Union Summer School 1963*, ed. D. O'Callaghan (Dublin: Gill and Son, 1964), 113.

2. See G. Fitzer, "Sfragis," *Theologisches Wörterbuch zum Neuen Testament* (ed. Kittel), 7:939–54; on circumcision as a seal, see Rom 4:11.

to the body of sin, and our members are now instruments of righteousness (Rom 6:13, 19); we have put on Christ, in other words, we are his descendants (Gal 3:27; Col 3:9–10). For this reason baptism is described as a washing of birth (Jn 3:5) and regeneration (Ti 3:5). The language about being born, or about receiving another body after having overcome death, is evidence of the radical rooting in Jesus, the place where the neophyte now lives. The sacrament is not a transitory action, but rather a living reality that "now saves you" (1 Pt 3:21) and makes the Christian a new creation (2 Cor 5:17).

The image of the seal is clarified from this overall perspective. Through baptism Christians *come to be incorporated into the body of Christ*, that is (according to the biblical view of man), of his very manner of being situated in the world and of living out his relations with God and his brethren.[3] Likewise, baptized persons *adopt the coordinates of Christ's time*, dwelling in this "Yes" of Jesus to all the promises (2 Cor 1:20) which lends a definitive imprint to their adherence to him. Here lies the foundation of the entire theological development concerning the sacramental character.

Patristic Reflection

The first Christians record the image of the seal (Greek: *sfragis*) that the believer receives in baptism.[4] With this expression they refer generally to the sign of the cross, which is traced as the catechumen is anointed. In homilies they would use the comparison of the sheep branded with the mark of Christ so that the Good Shepherd will recognize it and vice versa.[5] These are symbols that help us to imagine the effect of baptism as a permanent reality.

In fact, "seal" would be the most common term with which to refer to baptism without further ado. Thus the expressions "keep the seal" and "keep one's baptism" are used in parallel.[6] As we can see, "seal" is not understood here to mean the sign of the cross alone, but rather the new condition of the

3. See John M. Donahue, "Sacramental Character: The State of the Question," *The Thomist* 31, no. 4 (1967): 445–64; the author emphasizes the importance of the notion of corporative personality in determining the biblical data of the character (450).

4. About the sacramental character in patristic writings, see Biagio Amata, "Il carattere sacramentale: dottrina patristica?," *Rivista liturgica* 85 (1988): 487–522; and David Berger, "Die geschichtliche Entwicklung der Lehre vom *Character indelebilis*," *Una Voce Korrespondenz* 26 (1996): 182–89.

5. See Daniélou, *Sacramento*, 88; cf. Augustine, *Epistolae* 173, 3 (CSEL 44:642): "et uos oues Christi estis, characterem dominicum portatis in sacramento quod accepistis, sed errastis et peristis" (and you are Christ's sheep; you bear the Lord's character in the sacrament that you received, but you went astray and perished).

6. See 2 *Clem* VI, 9; VII, 6. In *Patres apostolici*, ed. F. X. Funk (Tübingen: H. Laupp, 1901), 1:192. Cf. Franz Joseph Dölger, *Sphragis: Eine altchristliche Taufbezeichnung in ihren Beziehungen zur profanen und religiösen Kultur des Altertums* (Paderborn: Schöningh, 1967 [1911]); Everett Ferguson, *Baptism in the Early Church* (Grand Rapids, Mich.: Eerdmans, 2009), 207.

baptized person, whose purity should be preserved. This seal engraves upon us a reflection of the triune God, whose name, revealed in the life of Jesus, the baptismal formula professes.[7]

Together with this terminology there are records of a never-interrupted liturgical practice: baptism is unrepeatable, even if the believer apostatizes from the faith. "Happy the water that washes once," Tertullian exclaims.[8] In order to become reintegrated into the community of baptized persons, the way of repentance, although arduous, is enough. Based on this, it is easy to assume the existence of a constant effect of baptism that cannot be eroded even by the worst sin.[9]

St. Augustine too takes it for granted that baptism is not repeated: if a baptized person strays from the faith through apostasy and then repents, he is not obliged to be washed again. The same applies to schismatics: they will not cease to be baptized Christians and, if they return to the fold, it will be enough to impose a penance on them. Thus patristic writers recognized a mark of baptism that does not disappear even when charity and a living adherence to Jesus die.

In order to explain this permanence of baptism, St. Augustine employs the image of the "character" or mark in the living flesh that soldiers used to receive upon joining the army. A deserter would continue to bear the mark of the Roman Empire; if later on he were to beg for clemency so as to return to the ranks, the emperor would not have a new sign imprinted upon him, but would recognize the old one. Will baptism be worth less in God's sight than the military seal in the sight of Caesar?[10]

The bishop of Hippo uses another simile too: if baptism, as the mark of Jesus, consists of being born again (see Jn 3:5), it will be impossible to cancel its effects, just as it is impossible for a man to return to his mother's womb (Jn 3:4): "I am already born of Adam, Adam cannot beget me a second time. I am already born of Christ, Christ cannot beget me again. As there is no repeating from the womb, so neither from baptism."[11] We should keep in mind this analogy between the body received at birth and the new body assumed by the Christian in being baptized. For it is the most solid patristic witness to the doctrine of the sacramental character: Jesus, the new Adam,

---

7. See Irenaeus, *Epideixis* 3 (SC 406:89): "the seal and the new birth for God"; 100 (SC 406:220): "the three articles of our seal."

8. See Tertullian, *De baptismo* XV, 3 (CCL 1:290): "Felix aqua quae semel abluit."

9. See Haring, "The Augustinian Axiom"; Ernst Dassmann, "Character," *Augustinus Lexikon* 1 (1986): 835–40.

10. See Augustine, *Contra Epistolam Parmeniani* II, 13, 29 (CSEL 51:80); *In Iohannem* VI, 16 (CCL 36:62).

11. Augustine, *In Iohannem* XI, 6 (CCL 36:114; NPNF-I 7:77a).

incorporates us into himself, makes us members of his family by regenerating our flesh.[12]

In reality, St. Augustine refers to the permanent effect of baptism with the term *sacramentum* itself, more than he does with the word "character."[13] For example, someone who feigns receiving baptism, having neither faith nor repentance, will not attain the ultimate reality to which the *sacramentum* points (called the *res sacramenti*) but will receive the *sacramentum* itself—and this, not only as a rite, but as a permanent bond with Christ. For this reason Augustine says that the sacraments adhere to us and dwell in us.[14]

The uniqueness of baptism helps to shed light on another problem, which in turn will serve to frame the doctrine of the sacramental character and to apply it to holy orders. I mean the validity of baptism as conferred by a heretical or schismatic community: do those who were baptized in these communities and then returned to the bosom of the church have to be baptized again? St. Augustine would explore this topic in his debate with the Donatists. They had formed a separate sect and considered Catholic baptism invalid. The Catholics, nevertheless, did not require followers of Donatus to be rebaptized. Even though they do not call us brethren, Augustine says, we call them brethren (alluding to Is 66:5 according to the Septuagint), because we recognize their baptism.[15]

Augustine starts from the fact that baptism cannot be repeated, as the Donatists too agreed. And he applies the same logic, not to someone who receives baptism, but to the one who administers it. Just as the baptized person does not lose his seal if he strays from Jesus and will not need to be rebaptized if he returns, neither will the schismatic priest have to be reordained if he returns to the pale. This implies that the schismatic minister continues to have the right to administer the sacrament (*jus dandi*): he will confer a valid baptism even outside the Catholic church.[16] Because both

12. See Donahue, "Sacramental Character," 454.

13. See Haring, "St. Augustine's Use of the Word Character."

14. See Augustine, *Contra Epistolam Parmeniani* II, 13, 29 (CSEL 51:81): "Haerent sacramenta christiana" (the Christian sacraments adhere); *De baptismo* V, 16, 20 (CSEL 51:279): "baptismus qui in illo est" (the baptism that is in him); *Contra litteras Petiliani* II, 30, 69 (CSEL 52:60): "sacramenta quae in uobis uiolare nolumus" (the sacraments which we do not wish to violate in you); *Epistula ad catholicos* XXII, 61 (CSEL 52:309): "sacramenta insunt" (the sacraments are in [the recipients]).

15. See Augustine, *Enarratio in psalmos* XXXII, 29 (CCL 38:272–73).

16. See *De baptismo* I, 1, 2 (CSEL 51:146; NPNF-I 4:412a): "Sacramentum enim baptismi est quod habet qui baptizatur, et sacramentum dandi baptismi est quod habet qui ordinatur. Sicut autem baptizatus, si ab unitate recesserit, sacramentum baptismi non amittit; sic etiam ordinatus, si ab unitate recesserit, sacramentum dandi baptismi non amittit" (For the sacrament of baptism is what the person possesses who is baptized; and the sacrament of conferring baptism is what he possesses who is ordained. And as the baptized person, if he depart from the unity of the Church, does not thereby lose the sacrament of baptism, so also he who is ordained, if he depart from the unity of the Church, does not lose the sacrament of conferring baptism).

are sacraments (the "sacrament of baptism" and the "sacrament of conferring baptism"), let us treat them in the same way, without doing harm to
either one.[17] In this way, and faithful to the primitive practice of the church,
St. Augustine associates the permanent effects of baptism and holy orders.

Well, now, one clarification is necessary: when someone is baptized in a
schismatic sect he does not receive union with Christ, because he lacks charity, the bond of cohesion that the schismatics have broken. In other words,
baptism can exist outside the church, but it cannot be *of benefit* outside the
church (*potest esse, non prodesse*).[18] Therefore someone who was baptized in
a sect and is now received into the Catholic church, comes to it, not to acquire something that he did not have (for his baptism was valid), but rather
to start to make good use of what he already had.[19]

This means that the schismatic community is not totally corrupt. Augustine compares it to a sick person who has some healthy members and can
perform certain vital functions. In light of this, the question arises: given
that in baptism the church is the one that engenders Christians, must we
say then that the sect of Donatus is the mother of those whom it baptizes?
This question is answered with an image from the Old Testament: Sarah
(the church) is the one that engenders, the children are hers; but she does so
by means of Hagar the concubine (the Donatist party), so that her children
are born in slavery.[20]

Augustine's teaching neatly represents the heritage that the patristic era
would leave on this subject. The Fathers maintain that there is an indelible
effect of some sacraments. And, without much reflection on its essence, they
offer various clear parameters to delimit it. Taking into account a liturgical
fact (baptism is not repeatable), they speak about a new birth that grafts us
onto the body of Jesus through the motherhood of the church. Although
not all of them mention a seal or character, let alone theorize about it, a
unanimous conviction emerges: the radical transformation of the baptized

17. See *Contra Epistolam Parmeniani* II, 13, 30 (CSEL 51:81).

18. See *In Iohannem* VI, 13 (CCL 36:60; NPNF-I 7:44a): "potest fieri ut habeat aliquis baptismum praeter columbam; ut prosit ei baptismus praeter columbam, non potest" (it may be that one
may have baptism apart from the dove; but that baptism apart from the dove should do him good,
is impossible); the dove, in this passage, is the church, which, according to the Song of Songs, is one.

19. See ibid., VI, 14 (CCL 36:61; NPNF-I 7:44a): "Ego, inquit, habeo baptismum. Habes, sed
baptismus ille sine caritate nihil tibi prodest; quia sine caritate tu nihil es.... Veni ergo ad columbam,
dicimus; non ut incipias habere quod non habebas, sed ut prodesse tibi incipiat quod habebas" (I,
saith he, have baptism. Thou hast; but that baptism, without charity, profits thee nothing; because
without charity thou art nothing.... Come, then, to the dove, we say; not that thou mayest begin to
have what thou hadst not before, but that what thou didst have may begin to profit thee).

20. Ibid., XI, 7, 8 (CCL 36:114); *De baptismo* I, 16, 25: "Sara quidem, sed per Agar" (Sarah, indeed, but through Hagar).

person through incorporation into Jesus, so that the sacrament supplies a new flesh and, as it were, a new nature. A permanent effect is caused by holy orders also, through which the ministers acquire the ability to engender others in the faith.

Medieval Theology and the Classical Doctrine about the Sacramental Character

Based on the patristic usage, the permanent effect imprinted by baptism went on to be called "character" in the Middle Ages (adopting St. Augustine's term).[21] This effect is present in the good and the wicked, and therefore is not identified with the state of grace and friendship with God. It will be necessary to distinguish, among the gifts of baptism, those that are, so to speak, "guilt-proof," a distinction that had only started to appear in the Fathers. The doctors are aware of the novelty of their undertaking, which is developed completely only in the thirteenth century; therefore St. Albert the Great says: "little is found in the sayings of the saints about the [sacramental] character, in the sense in which the Teachers debate it."[22]

Theological reflection would find an anchor in the Magisterial statement of Innocent III (in 1201): even when the grace of baptism is not received, for lack of the proper dispositions, the "Christian character" is imprinted.[23] Gregory XI, in his *Decretales* (1230–34), applies it also to the sacrament of holy orders.[24] Then the question arises: what exactly does this character consist of?

The Influence of Dionysius: Sacramental Character as Disposition to Divine Worship

The contribution of Dionysius the Areopagite attracted the attention of theologians from the beginning. Given that medieval theologians iden-

21. See Ferdinand Brommer, *Die Lehre vom sakramentalen Charakter in der Scholastik bis Thomas von Aquin inklusive* (Paderborn: Schöningh, 1908); Grahame J. Connolly, "Sacramental Character in the Teachings of Alexander of Hales," *Collectanea Franciscana* 33, no. 1 (1963): 5–27; Benoît T. D'Argenlieu, "La doctrine d'Albert le Grand sur le caractère sacramental," *Revue Thomiste* 11 (1928): 295–311 and 479–96; Álvaro Huerga, "La teología del carácter en la segunda escolástica," in *Teología del sacerdocio: Escritos sobre el carácter sacerdotal*, ed. J. Ibañes (Burgos: Aldecoa, 1974), 143–82.

22. Albert the Great, *In IV Sent.*, d. 6, c., a. 4, sol., in *Opera Omnia*, ed. Bornget, XXIX:126.

23. See Innocent III, *Maiores Ecclesiae Causas*, 1201 (see DH 781; *Corpus Iuris Canonici*, 2:644–46): "characterem suscipit Christianitatis impressum" (he receives, imprinted on him, the character of Christianity); the sacramental character, which is distinguished from the *res* of the sacrament, is imprinted if there is no "obicem voluntatis contrariae" (obstacle of an opposing will resisting it).

24. See Gregory IX, *Corpus Iuris Canonici*, 2:124: "qui extra tempora statuta sacros ordines receperunt, characterem non est dubium recepisse" (there is no doubt that those who received Holy Orders outside of the appointed times did receive the sacramental character).

tified him as the philosopher converted by St. Paul, they attributed great authority to him. As a contemporary of the apostles, he must have known their rites by heart. Well, then, this author, in describing the new state of life of a baptized person, had mentioned the imprinting of a seal (*sfragis*), in other words, the sign of the cross that the bishop traced on the neophyte's forehead.[25] The doctors refer this expression to the sacramental character and deduce its properties from the text by Dionysius.[26]

The Areopagite argues on the basis of the liturgy: baptism transforms the Christian, so that he offers right worship to God.[27] Only someone who receives it inherits the divine gifts and can participate in the assembly, which is ordered according to various degrees.[28] The medieval theologians deduced that through the sacramental character the person belongs to a new network of relations: with God, from whom all blessings proceed, and to whom the Christian draws near; and with the church, where he will find his place as a member in the body. In this way the sacramental character helps to distinguish between those who have it and those who do not, according to their assigned place in the community.[29]

What was just said corroborates the idea of the sacramental character as a sign imprinted by baptism. How can we describe its traits, given that it is not stamped on the skin but on the soul? Dionysius, who understood baptism as an "illumination," used the metaphor of light to describe its imprint as a radiant reflection.[30] Medieval thinkers deduced: just as the air can be filled with brightness and fire, so too the sacramental character communicates the divine splendor and flame to the soul.[31] Then it follows that the sacramental character belongs to the order of faith, that is, the order of the knowledge of God: it broadens our outlook, allowing us to understand the liturgical language of symbols and their relation to our life. Moreover, this ability to contemplate the divine light makes a human being luminous, capable of radiating to others the gospel of Jesus.

The Areopagite had pictured the baptismal transformation not as a

---

25. See Dionysius the Areopagite, *De ecclesiastica hierarchia* II, 3, 4 (PG 3:400d).

26. See Thomas Aquinas, *Super Sententias* IV, d. 4, q. 1, a. 4, q.c. 3 (Parma 7:510): "Sed contra est auctoritas Dionysii, ex qua characteris traditio derivatur" (Against this view, however, is the authority of Dionysius, from which the tradition about the character is derived).

27. See Dionysius the Areopagite, *De ecclesiastica hierarchia* II, 3, 1–2 (PG 3:397b–c).

28. See ibid., II, 3, 4 (PG 3:400d): "he shares in the inheritance of the divine things and of the sacred order."

29. See Alexander of Hales, *Glossa in quatuor libros Sententiarum* IV, d. 6, n. 2, co. (BFSMA XV [Quaracchi, 1957], 106); St. Bonaventure, *Breviloquium* VI, 6 (Quaracchi 5:270); cf. Thomas Aquinas, *Super Sententias* IV, d. 1, q. 2, a. 4, sol. 1 (Parma 7:472).

30. See Dionysius the Areopagite, *De ecclesiastica hierarchia* II, 3, 3 (PG 3:397d).

31. See ibid., II, 2, 1 (PG 3:393a).

static reflection of the divine life, but as a dynamic ascent of the baptized person toward complete unity with God. The medieval theologians then deduced: the character sets the soul in motion, *tautens* it so that it is lifted up to communion with the Father.[32] This description would encourage an understanding of the sacramental character as disposing the recipient toward grace. In this way it will be possible to distinguish between the two (character and grace), for the character is orientation, path, proximity, but does not imply the full presence of the beloved nor the divine friendship. It is not simply a fire or a heat, but rather a disposition toward heat and fire, just as dry wood is better prepared to catch fire than damp wood.

Here, then, are the main elements with which the Middle Ages interpreted Dionysius: the sacramental character introduces the baptized person into a new visible network of relations, giving him a place in the ecclesial assembly; it imprints upon him the light that reflects the divine vision, turning him into a luminous sign; and it prepares him to know and to receive God, whom he discovers especially in worship. The sacramental character, therefore, *distinguishes* some from others in the body of Christ, *signifies* the grace in which the believer is called to live, and *disposes* him to attain it.

As a summary of these ideas, a definition of sacramental character attributed to Dionysius himself later circulated in the schools, although the text is not found in his works: "the character is a holy sign of the communion of faith and of holy ordination, given by the hierarch."[33] St. Thomas proposes another one, which he says is more in keeping with the Areopagite's teaching: "The character is a sign of the communion of power concerning divine things, and of holy ordination of the faithful, given by the divine beatitude."[34]

Medieval Reinterpretation: The Character in the Christian's Flesh

Medieval thinkers did not limit themselves to accepting the Areopagite's approach, but enriched it. In contrast to his Platonic outlook, which sees man ascending from the tangible toward the divine, they insist on the cor-

---

32. See ibid., II, 3, 8 (PG 3:404c).

33. Thomas Aquinas, *ST* III, q. 63, a. 2, arg. 3; a similar passage is already found in Alexander of Hales, *Glossa in quatuor libros Sententiarum* IV, d. 6, n. 2a (BFSMA XV [Quaracchi, 1957], 105): "Character est signum sanctum communionis fidei et sanctae ordinationis, datum accedenti a hierarcha" (the character is a holy sign of communion of faith and of holy ordination, given to the candidate by the hierarch); see Benoît T. D'Argenlieu, "Note sur deux définitions médiévales du caractère sacramentel," *Revue Thomiste* 11 (1928): 271–75.

34. Thomas Aquinas, *Super IV Sent.*, d. 4, q. 1, a. 2, q.c. 2, sol. 1 (Parma 7:507): "Character est signum communionis potestatis divinorum, et sacrae ordinationis fidelium datum a divina beatitudine."

poreal, earthly aspects of the sacramental economy, bringing their view of the sacramental character closer to our incarnate condition and our journey through time.

This happens, in the first place, when the neo-Platonic doctrine of Dionysius is situated in an Aristotelian mold, which is better suited to deciphering man's natural abilities. This approach has the advantage of better harmonizing the new being of baptism with the person's original creaturely condition. In this context St. Bonaventure sees the sacramental character as a certain habit or disposition toward grace, an openness to receiving it.[35] St. Thomas, for his part, understands it as a power of the soul, an ability to perform certain works, concretely oriented toward worship, but a worship consisting of one's entire life.[36]

This preoccupation with situating the sacramental character in relation to the created structure of the human being is included in one of the definitions that was most widespread among the schools, called the "magisterial definition."[37] According to it, the character is an image imprinted on the soul that configures the "created trinity" to the "creating and recreating Trinity." The "created trinity" is the soul with its three powers (memory, understanding, and will), which are capable of remembering, knowing, and loving the Father, Son, and Spirit, as St. Augustine would teach in his *De Trinitate*.[38] The character is based therefore on the condition of the image that exists in a human being as creature (see Gn 1:26); and it fulfills this image according to the redemptive revelation of the God of Jesus Christ. The sacramental character appears then as the recovery and fullness in Jesus of a certain "creaturely character" that man has by being the image of God. The association of character and image (see Heb 1:3) follows the line of light and vision explored by Dionysius.

Secondly, medieval theologians, assuming the same liturgical background chosen by Dionysius, emphasize the connection between the sacramental character and our incarnate condition. St. Thomas is outstanding

---

35. See Bonaventure, *In IV Sent.*, d. 6, p. 1, a. 1, q. 1 (Quaracchi 4:136).

36. See Thomas Aquinas, *ST* III, q. 63, a. 2.

37. See Thomas Aquinas, *Super IV Sent.*, d. 4, q. 1, a. 2, q.c. 2 (Parma 7:507): "Videtur quod non bene assignetur quaedam alia definitio magistralis quae talis est: Character est distinctio a charactere aeterno impressa animae rationali secundum imaginem, consignans trinitatem creatam Trinitati creanti et recreanti; et distinguens a non configuratis secundum statum fidei" (It seems that no definition can be correctly given other than the magisterial definition, which is as follows: The character is a distinction imprinted on the rational soul by the eternal character according to the image, configuring a created trinity to the creating and recreating Trinity; and distinguishing it from those not configured according to the state of faith).

38. See José Granados, "'Vides Trinitatem si caritatem vides': Via del amor y Espíritu Santo en el *De Trinitate* de san Agustín," *Revista agustiniana* 43, no. 130 (2002): 23–61.

on this point: he understands the character in the mark of our conformity to the body of Jesus, the author of the sacraments inasmuch as he assumed our humanity.[39] Hence Christ's dignity of "eternal character," which he possesses from all eternity as the Word of God and reflection of the Father (see Heb 1:3), does not suffice in order for him to give us the character; but rather the character derives from the incarnation, which establishes Jesus as a corporeal instrument of grace that is able to assimilate corporeal man to itself. And according to St. Thomas, this is because the sacraments are like a prolongation of Christ's body, through which he can enter into contact with every human being, thus transforming his soul.

The sacramental character fits into this perspective—that of Christ, the original instrument, and that of the sacraments, the instruments derived from Christ's humanity. Through the character, the believer is configured to Christ and, so to speak, is turned into a sacramental person. Hence, through the character, the believer himself can be compared with the bread, the wine, or the oil that are sanctified:

> The imprinting of the character occurs through a certain sanctification of the rational soul.... But in this sanctification the soul to be sanctified proves to be no more active than water that is to be sanctified, or oil or chrism in their sanctification, except that man subjects himself to this sanctification by his consent, while the aforesaid objects are subjected because they lack free will; and therefore however the soul may change by its own operations, it never loses the character; just as neither chrism nor oil nor bread that has been consecrated ever lose their sanctification, however they may be changed, as long as they are not corrupted.[40]

Thanks to the character, therefore, it is as if the Christian, now configured to the body of Christ, harbored within himself the sanctified sacramental material; as though he himself became the living, permanent channel of grace. For this reason, if the sacraments work as instruments of Christ, it is also true that "a character is in the soul, as an instrumental power."[41] The character, then, proves to be an intermediate effect ordered to the grace that is communicated, namely communion with God in the church, for only by being conformed to the body of Christ can we receive the Spirit of Christ.

---

39. See Thomas Aquinas, *Super IV Sent.*, d. 4, q. 1, a. 1 (Parma 7:505): "Configuratio [Christo] fit per characterem assimilationis" (Configuration [to Christ] occurs through the character of assimilation [i.e., being made similar]).

40. See ibid., a. 3, sol. 4 (Parma 7:509–10).

41. Thomas Aquinas, *ST* III, q. 63, a. 5, ad 1: "Character est in anima sicut quaedam instrumentalis virtus."

Finally, being bound up with the incarnation and life of Jesus, the sacramental character situates the believer also in the course of salvation history. Indeed, St. Thomas understands the character as a dynamic quality that is oriented to action, for it configures a human being with Christ who acts: *charactere Christi aliquis configuratur ad actiones Christi*, through the character of Christ, someone is configured to Christ's actions.[42] In this way a movement toward his end is imprinted on a human being.[43] God, who with the sacrament entrusts a mission, with the character grants the power necessary to accomplish it.[44]

This end to which the character orients us is the worship of God, which consists, according to Aquinas, of receiving his gifts and sharing them with others.[45] This means that worship leads us to resemble God by entering into his dynamism of communion. Indeed, Trinitarian life is a continual exchange of gifts, which flow from the Father toward the Son and the Spirit so as to return to the Father. Hence the character, as we already saw, stamps the image of the Trinity upon a human being, but not insofar as God is made present through creation, nor inasmuch as he unites us to himself through grace (which can be lacking, even though the character is possessed), but rather inasmuch as we appropriate the power or dynamism that the Trinity possesses, in other words, God's ability to receive and share love.[46]

For this reason, in the case of baptism, St. Thomas speaks about a passive potency, which configures a human being so that he can receive the divine gifts.[47] Confirmation, for its part, confers an active potency, in order to profess the faith publicly. And holy orders, finally, entails an active potency, in this case in order to communicate to others the gifts received from God, generating in them a new being.[48]

In short, in the Thomistic synthesis the sacramental character is a power granted to the believer through configuration with the body of Christ,

---

42. See Thomas Aquinas, *Super IV Sent.*, d. 4, q. 1, a. 1, ad 3 (Parma 7:507).

43. See Thomas Aquinas, *ST* III, q. 63, a. 3, co.: "Character proprie est signaculum quoddam *quo aliquid insignitur ut ordinandum in aliquem finem*: sicut charactere insignitur denarius ad usum commutationum" (A character is properly a kind of seal, whereby something is marked, as being ordained to some particular end: thus a coin is marked for us in exchange of goods).

44. See Thomas Aquinas, *Super IV Sent.*, d. 4, q. 1, a. 1, resp. (Parma 7:506).

45. See Thomas Aquinas, *ST* III, q. 63, a. 2, co.: "Divinus autem cultus consistit vel in recipiendo aliqua divina, vel in tradendo aliis" (Now the worship of God consists either in receiving divine gifts, or in bestowing them on others).

46. See Thomas Aquinas, *Super IV Sent.*, d. 4, q. 1, a. 2, ad 3 (Parma 7:508): "configuratio ista attenditur ad Deum secundum participationem divinae potestatis" (This configuration tends toward God as a participation in the divine power).

47. See Gustave Thils, "Le pouvoir cultuel du baptisé," *Ephemerides Theologicae Lovanienses* 15 (1938): 683–89.

48. See Thomas Aquinas, *ST* III, q. 63, a. 5, co.

which turns him into a sacramental person, a channel of grace for himself and, through himself, for the whole church. This power works by associating a human being, through the mediation of Jesus, to the Trinitarian dynamism. It makes us capable of receiving the divine gifts and sharing them with others, in a continual movement of mutual donation.

To round out the presentation of the medieval doctrine it is helpful to know that the sacramental character is identified with what medieval writers call *res et sacramentum*. Recall that this expression is coined in relation to Eucharistic dogma (chapter 9). It is meant to complete the narrow definition of sacrament as a mere sign (*sacramentum tantum*) of a distant reality (*res tantum*), which would lead to doubt about the real presence of Christ: on the altar would be the sacrament and, therefore, not the reality signified. To say *res et sacramentum* reminds us, then, that the sacrament does not consist primarily of the species of bread and wine, but rather in the body of Jesus. This body is, like every body, at the same time a sign and the signified reality (*sacramentum et res*), in other words, the person's visible form and the active presence of that same person and of the interpersonal relations that constitute him as such.

The terminology *res et sacramentum* would be applied later on to the baptismal character. The reference, again, is to the body, now to the body of the Christian insofar as it is configured to the body of Jesus, a configuration that is the primary effect of baptism. It is interesting to note that baptism, starting with Peter Lombard and following the authority of St. John Damascene, would be identified precisely with the character that it imprints.[49] Here the sacrament in the proper sense is not the *sacramentum tantum*, but rather the *res et sacramentum*, in other words, not the material used in the rite, but rather the Christian who celebrates the rite, insofar as he is incorporated into Jesus. From this follows the patristic usage that I cited earlier in this chapter, which understood *sacramentum* as the permanent effect (or seal) of baptism on the believer. The reflection of St. Thomas moves along these same lines: the baptized person is conformed to the body of Jesus by the character, and comes to be an instrumental cause of grace, turned somehow into a sacrament.

---

49. See Artur Michael Landgraf, "Die frühscholastische Definition der Taufe," *Gregorianum* 27, nos. 2–3 (1946): 200–219 and 353–83, which describes three opinions: baptism is the water (Hugh of St. Victor); it is the ablution to which the believer submits; it is the character (Peter Lombard), which later was called *signum manens* (lasting sign); later Scholasticism would find a synthesis of these three aspects of baptism.

Modern Perspectives Starting from the Protestant Reformation and the Council of Trent

The classic view of the sacramental character would be called into question by theologians subsequent to St. Thomas. Without denying its existence, which as we know was corroborated by Innocent III,[50] some venture to say that it is not a real quality of the soul, but rather a relation that affects a human being from outside, or even a mere relation of reason.[51] In other words, the character is understood as an attitude of God toward us, as one way in which he looks at us that obliges us to perform certain acts, but without this outlook involving a real change in the creature.[52] The problem with this approach is that the content of faith (that the sacrament imprints a character) loses its coupling with human experience. The sacramental character ceases to be a light which, informing man's life, impels him to a work that perfects him. The bond with God that baptism institutes proves to be something extrinsic to the believer, determining him merely from outside. This prepares the ground to the Protestant crisis, which would deny that the character exists.

Luther and the Denial of the Sacramental Character

We are already acquainted with the sacramental view of Luther (see chapter 10, above), who concentrates on justification by faith and tends to reduce the sacrament to a form of preaching the word, to which the believer is confidently receptive. What room is there in his approach for the sacramental character?

Given that the theological development on this subject was relatively

50. DH 781.

51. With different nuances, these are opinions held by Peter John Olivi, Duns Scotus, and William of Ockham: see Jean Galot, *La nature du caractère sacramentel: étude de théologie médiévale* (Paris: Desclée, 1956), 198–220.

52. See Duns Scotus, *Ordinatio* IV, d. 6, p. 4, a. 2, q. 1, n. 235 (*Opera Omnia* 9:368): "non est sacramentum initerabile propter hoc quod imprimat effectum indelebilem, sed ex ordinatione divina" (it is an unrepeatable sacrament not because it imprints an indelible effect, but rather by divine command); ibid., n. 246 (*Opera Omnia* 9:370): "propter igitur solam auctoritatem Ecclesiae—quantum occurrit ad praesens—est ponendum characterem imprimi" (therefore on account of the Church's authority alone—as far as the present is concerned—it is to be assumed that the character is imprinted); according to Scotus, the character is "signum memorativum respectu susceptionis sacramenti quae praeteriit, et signum configurativum, id est significans obligationem animae ad Christum" (a commemorative sign with respect to the reception of the sacrament which took place, and a configuring sign, that is, one that signifies the soul's obligation to Christ); ibid., q. 2, n. 334 (*Opera Omnia* 9:398) and n. 317 (*Opera Omnia* 9:393): "potest dici characterem esse tantummodo quemdam respectum extrinsecus advenientem ipsi animae a Deo immediate in susceptione sacramenti interabilis" (it can be said that the character is only a kind of external regard coming to the soul itself from God immediately upon its reception of an unrepeatable sacrament).

recent, it seems to Luther in the first place that it lacks a basis in scripture, and that philosophy just muddied the waters with its oars. "I admit," he says with some sarcasm, "that the Pope imprints the character behind Christ's back."[53] Calvin, for his part, objects also that the character, being typical of a magical mentality, is a fashionable invention: given that this theory was launched a little while ago, it will cost just as little to demolish it.[54]

But there is, above all, one basic difficulty. To Luther the sacramental character seems to be something possessed by the subject that would incline him to think of himself as the source of his own salvation, separating him from the radical dependence on God that the Reformer wanted to instill. Well, now, it is certain that the character, in the classic Thomistic view, is a power, a dynamism that orients the human being toward his end and helps him to travel toward it. But for St. Thomas this "potency" of man is no reason to boast of his own abilities, but first of all the power to receive (baptism) and, only after having received, to be able in turn to give (confirmation and holy orders).

Underlying the Lutheran view, moreover, is the tendency to concentrate the sacrament on a particular moment in life, suspicious of the permanent donation of God to man. The same logic that leads to denying Eucharistic transubstantiation (accepting the presence of Jesus only in view of Communion) leads to a rejection of the sacramental character, which "transubstantiates" in a way the whole life of the believer.

The Lutheran critique of the baptismal character becomes more evident when it comes to the priesthood: here again, Luther thinks, is this not the long hand of the church's power at work? Holy orders, according to him, must always be linked with the preaching of the gospel. Therefore, if a priest stops preaching he will go back to being merely a layman. This means that the permanent sacramental structure of the church (founded in large part on the priestly representation of Christ) loses its foundation. An act of the church may perhaps be sacramental, but not her being.

Such far-reaching differences with the Catholic perspective do not rule out the possibility of points of contact. As for baptism, Luther defends the idea that it cannot be repeated and agrees that it confers the basic coordinates of all Christian existence. Penance, for example, is explained as a return to life according to baptism. Luther teaches that the latter "lasts forever and, even when we fall and sin, we have access to it."[55]

53. Martin Luther, *De captivitate babylonica* (WA 6:567.23–24).

54. See John Calvin, *Acta Synodi Tridentinae: Cum Antidoto*, ad sess. VII, can. 9, in *Opera* (Brunsvigae, 1868), 7:496.

55. Luther, *Great Catechism* (WA 30:221.19–22).

Response of the Council of Trent

Faced with the Lutheran position, Trent confirmed the existence of the sacramental character. Thus it followed the line of thought initiated by the preceding Magisterium starting with Innocent III and Gregory IX. The Council of Florence, in its *Bull of Union with the Armenians* (November 22, 1439), had taught that three sacraments (baptism, confirmation, holy orders) imprint a character and had defined it as *spirituale quoddam signum a ceteris distinctivum* ("a type of spiritual sign that distinguishes the recipient from others"), imprinted on the soul indelibly.[56] Trent confirms this formula, almost verbatim.[57] Moreover when Trent speaks about baptism it corroborates its nonrepeatable character, even if the recipient had abandoned the faith.[58] In reference to holy orders, over which the noisiest clash with the reformers took place, it insists that the sacramental character cannot be effaced, and therefore an ordained man will not lose his spiritual power even when he ceases to perform his ministry.[59] Trent attributes ecclesial weight to the character of the priest. To deny it is to deny the harmonious, hierarchical unity of the church.[60]

Moreover the Council, faithful to its intention not to settle questions that were disputed among the schools, does not go into defining the sacramental character precisely, a task that it leaves for further theological reflection. The doctors agree, in fact, only on the existence of the character on the soul; and in pointing out the three sacraments that imprint it. The redaction history of the canon shows, for example, that it does not even claim to teach the causal connection between the character that those sacraments imprint and the impossibility of repeating them.[61] What can be inferred from the Tridentine teaching against Luther is that the character prolongs the sacrament in time, accompanying all of Christian life and configuring the being

56. See DH 1313.

57. See Council of Trent, Session VII, *Decree on the Sacraments*, canon 9 (DH 1609): "Si quis dixerit, in tribus sacramentis, baptismo scilicet, confirmatione et ordine, non imprimi characterem in anima, hoc est signum quoddam spirituale et indelebile, unde ea iterari non possunt ... anathema sit" (If anyone says that in three sacraments, namely, baptism, confirmation, and orders, a character is not imprinted on the soul, that is, a kind of indelible spiritual sign by reason of which these sacraments cannot be repeated, let him be anathema). Cf. Cavallera, "Le décret," 74–75.

58. See Council of Trent, Session VII, *Decree on the Sacraments*, canon 11, on baptism (DH 1624) on the condemned assertion of the Anabaptists, see *CT* 5:837.

59. See Council of Trent, Session XXIII, *Decree on the Sacrament of Orders*, chap. 4 (DH 1767), canon 4 (DH 1774): "Si quis dixerit ... [per sacram ordinationem] non imprimi characterem; vel eum, qui sacerdos semel fuit, laicum rursus fieri posse: anathema sit" (If anyone says ... that no character is imprinted by ordination, or that he who has once been a priest can again become a layman, let him be anathema).

60. See ibid. (DH 1767).

61. See *CT* 5:992. For an analysis of the discussion: Cavallera, "Le décret du Concile de Trent," 86.

of the church. Let us consider now some theological developments that are of interest in explaining the character, which will help me to propose a synthesis.

The Character: Configuration to the Body of Christ
(Matthias Joseph Scheeben)

One of the most valuable efforts to delve into the theology of the sacramental character came from the nineteenth-century German theologian Matthias Joseph Scheeben. Scheeben makes the character a key element of his sacramental vision, calling it the soul of the sacraments.[62] For it is, in the case of the three sacraments that produce it, "the center of their entire causality and significance." And it is also "the basis and point of departure of [the] whole activity" of the remaining sacraments.[63]

Scheeben is inspired by the Thomistic view but intends to expand upon its arguments. For to him it does not seem enough to understand the sacramental character as a property of the soul or its power; rather he emphasizes the new being and the new dignity that is conferred on the Christian with the character, transforming his whole person. And this is because the character not only associates us with Jesus' work, but also with the deeper mystery of Jesus. It is assimilation to Christ and to his body and, in light of this, a *consecration*.[64]

The sacramental character of the Christian, in Scheeben's view, proves to be analogous to what the hypostatic union is in Christ, and is based on it.[65] In other words, the character is a sign that configures with Christ "like a similarity, or *rather similarity and union with the sealing that human nature received from the divine Person.*" This Christological basis helps Scheeben to distinguish between the sacramental character and sanctifying grace, in a way that is analogous to the difference between the hypostatic union and Christ's growth in grace over the course of his life.

In order to avoid confusion between character and grace, Scheeben uses an interesting image that emphasizes the believer's participation in the body of Christ:

We are not to think of the character as a vital faculty or a vital form that assimilates us to Christ. Rather we should say that the character is to the mystical body of

---

62. See Francesco Saverio Pancheri, "Il carattere sacramentale in una nuova prospettiva (M.-J. Scheeben)," *Studia Patavina* 4, no. 3 (1957): 459–72; Bernard Fraigneau-Julien, *L'Église et le caractère sacramentel selon M.-J. Scheeben* (Brussels: Desclée, 1958).

63. See Scheeben, *The Mysteries of Christianity*, par. 84 (582).

64. See ibid., par. 84 (584).

65. See ibid., par. 84 (583).

Christ what the general configuration is to the members of the natural human body. This *configuration* is *the form and structure by which the various members* are fittingly accommodated to the structure of the head to which they are to belong, and are therefore adapted, by virtue of their organic union with that head, to receive influence and life from it, [and] also to serve as organs for its activity.[66]

In other words, just as the different organs have their place in the body, connected by veins and tendons, so too the sacramental character grafts us onto the body of Christ. Certainly, the correct placement of an organ is not enough for life to flow into it, but only lays the foundations that allow it to participate in the life and operation of the body, if the blood comes to circulate in it. Analogously, neither does the sacramental character suppose that grace is given to us, even when it situates us in the precise place and among the precise ties through which it can reach us.

When it consecrates us and configures us to the body of Christ, the sacramental character enables us to participate in the church according to our particular vocation, just as each organ of the body, through its situation in the living being, performs different functions. Specifically the character makes us capable of worship—understood in the broad sense as an offering of one's whole life to God—after the image of Christ's priesthood. Together with baptism, confirmation, and holy orders, sacraments that imprint it, Scheeben lists matrimony which, through the indissoluble conjugal bond, consecrates the spouses in Jesus in order to build up the church. In short, Scheeben's perspective situates the sacramental character at the center of Christian life, connecting it directly to the mystery of Jesus and establishing it as the key of the ecclesial structure. For this reason it is up to the sacramental character, in its distinct modalities, to sustain and revitalize the body of Christ.

Scheeben's rich and suggestive proposal has to be clarified with regard to the connection between sacramental character and hypostatic union. Contemporary Christology distinguishes better between that union and the work of the Spirit on Jesus over the course of his life.[67] This action of the Spirit was necessary in order to shape the flesh of the Son, in other words, the exact relational place in which he touches and configures to himself the existence of every human being, a place (the flesh) that Scheeben rightly associates with the sacramental character. Therefore, only at the end of its journey, in the resurrection, is the flesh of Jesus completely disposed to assimilate us to it. The sacramental character is, therefore, the imprint in

---

66. Ibid., par. 84 (589–90).
67. See Ladaria, *Jesús y el Espíritu*.

us, not only of the incarnate Word (as Scheeben points out), but also of the crucified, risen Word that has ascended into heaven and contains in it the full operation of the Spirit. I will take up this element again when I attempt a synthesis in the final section of this chapter.

The Character: Ecclesial Dimension of the Sacrament

As early as the medieval interpretation of Dionysius the sacramental character appears as a distinctive sign that assigns to the recipient a definite place in the church. Rooted in Christ's priesthood, the character signifies membership in a priestly people and is bound up, both with the cultic exercise of the faithful (baptism and confirmation) and with the ordained ministry. We just saw how Scheeben, along the same lines, sees the church as being built on the sacramental character. The theology of the twentieth century took this ecclesial feature as the point of support for a modern explanation of the character.[68]

Karl Rahner, among others, proposed this approach as part of his effort to interpret the entire sacramental economy in terms of ecclesiology.[69] As I will explore further on (in chapter 15), Rahner conceives of the church as an original sacrament from which the other seven are derived as actualizations of it. From this perspective the sacramental character consists precisely of the association with the salvific community that the sacrament gives us. Thus, for example, the character of baptism is the radical membership of the neophyte in the church, through which she claims him as her own forever. From this is deduced the great weight attributed to the character: given that the sacraments derive their force from the original sacrament which is the church; and that the character is precisely the connection of the sacraments with this original ecclesial sacrament; it follows that it is up to the character to mediate all the grace conferred by the sacrament.

Then Rahner states the problem of the visibility of the character. For if the character is a sign, then it will have to be perceived, and not remain hidden in the soul and appear only in the sight of God and the angels. Its visibility, Rahner answers, comes from the place that it confers on the believer in the church. Hence the character is not merely an interior sign, but can be observed in the new relations that the baptized person establishes within the people of God.

---

68. See Huerga, "La teología"; Toshiyuki Miyakawa, "The Ecclesial Meaning of the Res et Sacramentum," *The Thomist* 31, no. 4 (1967): 381–444; Aimon-Marie Roguet, "La théologie du caractère et l'incorporation à l'Église," *La Maison Dieu* 32 (1952): 74–89; and Eliseo Ruffini, "El carácter como visibilidad concreta del sacramento en relación con la Iglesia," *Concilium* 31 (1968): 111–24.

69. See Karl Rahner, *The Church and the Sacraments* (New York: Herder, 1963), 41.

What happens then with those who, possessing the baptismal character, separate themselves from the church? Does the character stop being manifest? Rahner answers: the character is precisely what maintains in them a visible orientation toward full participation in the body of Christ.[70] The sacramental character therefore plays a key ecumenical role, not only because it guarantees the basic unity of Christians in one baptism, but also because it assures that the different churches and ecclesial communities, in their outward appearance and concrete structure (and not only in the hearts of their faithful), contain elements that impel toward unity.

What can we say about this ecclesial dimension [*registro*] of the sacramental character? On the one hand, it highlights an important aspect of its essence, an aspect that we already saw present in the first medieval synthesis. The character introduces us into the network of relations of the body of Christ when it assigns us a specific place in worship—and this worship expands to the whole activity of the church. In this way we understand that the church is not only an interior unity of minds, but rather a communion of visible relations experienced in the flesh. The different ecclesial institutions are built upon this communion, which exercises a beneficial influence on society.

On the other hand this perspective runs the risk of absolutizing a primacy of the church over the character. Indeed, one flaw in Rahner's view (see chapter 15, below) is that he forgets that, besides the line that runs from Christ to the church and then to the sacraments, there is also the line—which proves to be primordial—that proceeds from Christ to the sacraments and then to the church. From this perspective the character is, in some way, the foundation of the very being of the church, where she is generated and is formed in the image of Christ. Said character, therefore, does not fall under her total dominion. In short, the ecclesial interpretation of the character is necessary, but it must take into account not only the fact that the character comes from the church, who claims us for herself, but also, above all, that the character constitutes the church, which is built upon it and, therefore, upon Jesus.

The summary that I will propose next highlights, before anything else, how the character configures us to Christ's life in the flesh. We could say, following Scheeben, that the character is constitutive of the church inasmuch as it makes Jesus' action present in the baptized person. And, only secondarily, inasmuch as membership in Christ is membership in his body, the character is also incorporation into the church, according to Rahner's insight.

70. See ibid.

The Character: Incorporation into the Body of Christ and into the Story of His Life

In the previous chapter, I defined sacrament as the ritual opening of a new space of relations, a space forged by Jesus in the flesh during his earthly journey. We will now see that the sacramental character contains the basic coordinates (the founding pillars) of this space inaugurated by the sacraments.[71] I will focus first on baptism.

Baptismal Character and Physical Birth

Let us start with the biblical data, as received by the Church Fathers: baptism is a new birth that gives us a new body. What is meant by this? To answer this question, we have to take into account, in the first place, what the body signifies in the scriptural perspective. Man is not an isolated, autonomous subject who only secondarily enters into relation with things. On the contrary, as an incarnate being, he is always situated in an environment, and this environment (of objects, persons, memories, encounters) forms part of his deepest identity. Because we have a body we always live in relation and are defined on the basis of this relation with our world.

The first word that our body pronounces is a reminder that we were born. Through the body, whose members we do not shape, we know that we received life from others, that a story preceded us and was entrusted to us as a heritage. Because we are born in a body we always live against an already-existing background: that of our family and native land, of a language and certain traditions, and so on. Corporeality is, then, this original passivity or receptivity that serves as a framework for our whole journey through life.[72]

Of key importance in understanding the background established with our incarnate condition are familial relations: through being born in the body we are children of our parents and share one and the same origin with our siblings. Filiation and fraternity are rooted in the body and fix several permanent coordinates of our settlement in the world, constituting the immovable background of what we endure and achieve. In the body we will later be able to establish other bonds that will also forge our destiny in an irrevocable way, as they are added to the permanent background of our route:

71. See Renzo Gerardi, "Carattere," in *Lexicon: Dizionario teologico enciclopedico*, ed. L. Pacomio and V. Mancuso (Casale Monferrato: PIEMME, 1993), 140–41; Dorothea Sattler, "Charakter, sakramentaler. Begriff," *Lexikon für Theologie und Kirche*, 2:1009–13 (Freiburg: Herder, 1994); and Manlio Sodi, "Cos'è il carattere sacramentale?," *Rivista liturgica* 85 (1998): 451–56.

72. See Paul Ricoeur, *Soi-même comme un autre* (Paris: Éditions du Seuil, 1990), 369–80.

we will be spouses, we will be fathers or mothers, we will build up our native land from generation to generation, etc.

It follows then that, through our incarnate condition, our life unfolds on a framework received from others, a framework whose foundations are the primary relations that the body mediates for us. If a "character" is a mark that is sculpted on stone or wood, we can call "character" also this basic background of ties that confer an original order and direction on our journey. Thus the body of the child has a filial *character*, just like the body of the spouses receives a spousal *character* when they become "one flesh" (see Gn 2:24) and, then, a generative *character*, paternal and maternal.

Note that this background is a symbolic background, inasmuch as it opens a human being to what is beyond himself: as children we inherit from others and belong to others, becoming able to live for others as spouses and to generate life in others as parents. Moreover the symbolism of this relational background is inexhaustible, always overflowing, for it allows us to get a glimpse in our own life of the mystery of God the creator. And thus, for example, the receptivity that we experience in the flesh refers to hands that shaped us in the womb, and to a love that sealed the "yes" of our parents. In short, the original order of relations rooted in our flesh (an order that we called a creaturely "character") opens us to the presence and activity of God, as the first origin and final destination of life.

Sacramental Character and Incorporation in Jesus

The Bible records this fact of experience when it presents every man as being rooted in the history of his ancestors and of his people, and thus it prepares us to understand the work of Jesus. Like every child that comes into this world, he took upon himself the background of a human family, inherited from generation to generation starting from Adam. He appropriated this background in a unique way for, as the only-begotten Son of God and first-born of creation, he lived this original receptivity of the body in radical reference to the Father and communional openness to the brethren, at the same time straightening out whatever was crooked in the legacy from our first father.

Therefore, during his travels through the world, Jesus was able to forge in a new way, under the influence of the Holy Spirit, this original background of relations in which the body situates us. In acting on the flesh of the Son (on his shared way of presence in the world and toward God), the gift of the Spirit modeled for all human beings a new, full way of dwelling in the flesh, in other words, of living out these relations with God and with other human beings. It was a work that culminated in the death, resurrection, and glorious ascension of Christ.

Well, then, in his Eucharist Jesus left us, through the rite, this new space of relations that he inaugurated. "Take my body": Christ offers to us, as a new original background of life, his way of living in the flesh, that is, of being situated in the world and of being bound to the Father and to the brethren. Baptism implies access to this space: through it we receive a new background, a new "origin" on the coordinates of our existence, inherited from Jesus, as though we were born into a new family.

Let us take an example, which also pertains to our coming into the world. With the mother tongue that we learn as children we already inherit an orientation of thought, in which is recorded the history of our people, who for centuries have been speaking the same language. There are languages that are focused more on praxis, others on abstract reason; in every language there are seeds of wisdom; there are also germs of violence. And the language of a people already orients its children toward good or evil, transmitting to them the virtues and defects of their ancestors, simply because with this language we will reason, with it we will understand the world and understand ourselves.

Well, then, in the new birth of baptism, it is as though we received a new mother tongue, with new words and grammar, which will be the point of origin of our speech and knowledge. The language in question was forged by Jesus during his life, death, and resurrection; a language entirely oriented to the service of the truth and of communion. From now on we will be able to speak well or badly, but we will always do it based on a language which, in and of itself, being the language of Jesus, is oriented to a communicative fullness. Similarly, a Spaniard can write rather well or rather badly, but he will always do it with the language of Cervantes.

In short, just as at birth we are received into the network of relations in our family and native land, which forms the constant background of our identity, and from which we inherit our name and destiny, so too baptism offers us a new background, a new familial network of relations on which our life will unfold from that moment on. This new background is the one contained in the body of Jesus, in other words, in the new relations that he inaugurated with the Father and with his church. The Christian will always rely on this background, this family atmosphere: he will either foster it in his life or else stubbornly insist on opposing it. I will call this background a "character."

My approach corresponds with the biblical data, which presents baptism as a new birth (Jn 3:5) in which we receive new members for righteousness (Rom 6:19), as though we had a new corporeality, stripping off the old body of sin (Rom 6:13; Col 3:9–10). We should understand in the same sense the new garment with which the neophyte "is clothed with Christ" (see Gal 3:27). The Fathers deepened this perspective when they insisted on our configuration to the flesh of Jesus. St. Leo the Great speaks for all of them when he teaches that, in baptism, the body of the regenerated person becomes the flesh of the crucified.[73]

The *character* proves then to be a mark inscribed on the body or, better, a new corporeality, a new way of dwelling in the world. Contained in the character are the pillars of the relational space of the Christian, which is the relational space of Jesus. There is no contradiction here with the Tridentine expression to the effect that the character is imprinted on the soul. For the Council wishes only to indicate that this mark is not a tattoo on the skin, but rather is inscribed in the depths of the human person. If by body we understand, as I have stated here, our most original way of being situated in the world and of establishing relations—relations that forge the center of our identity—we do not turn aside from the line of thought marked out by Trent. In configuring our way of living in the body, the character defines us in our deepest core, based on our membership in Christ, and therefore it also seals our soul.

Summarizing: to receive the character is to receive the same corporeal background of Jesus; it is to take up the same basic coordinates of his dwelling in the world and of his ties with human beings and with God, as he acquired them during his life and sealed them with his death and glorification. Thanks to the character one belongs to the relational network of the family of Jesus, and one becomes enabled or disposed to receive the love of this same Jesus, which is his Spirit. If, as Trent teaches, the character is a *spiritual* mark, it is because it configures our flesh so that the *Spirit* of the risen Lord can be poured out completely upon it.[74]

Properties of the Character

The comparison with the corporeal background that we receive at birth explains why *the character cannot be lost, nor should baptism be repeated*. For a son never ceases to be a son, even when he ceases to live like a son, wander-

---

73. See Leo the Great, *Sermo* 63 (CCL 138A:114; NPNF-II 12:177a).

74. DH 1609. Eastern theology insists on this connection of the character with the Spirit: see Martin Jugie, "La doctrine du caractère sacramentale dans l'Église greco-russe," *Ecclesia Orans* 31 (1928): 17–53; Nicola Bux, "Il sigillo dello Spirito nei sacramenti degli orientali," *Rivista liturgica* 85 (1998): 523–28.

ing about the world and squandering his fortune: the filial "character" that his body bears is indelible.[75] In a similar way, the baptismal character that baptism gives us always accompanies us, even when we live in opposition to it. And this brings to fulfillment what happens with natural filiation, for the character is not only the mark of birth to this world, which is threatened by death, but also the seal of the definitive regeneration of Jesus, who trampled death and took the lead into the future of all mankind. In this case we are talking about the filial character of the risen Lord.

Given that the sacraments prolong contact with the flesh of Christ, we can say that *a sacramental body is conferred on us with the character*. According to the insight of St. Thomas that I set forth earlier in this chapter, the role that is played in the rite by water, wine, and oil, which are channels of grace because Jesus touches us by means of them, configuring matter to his body—this role comes now to correspond to the body of the Christian who is incorporated into Jesus, as though the believer himself were turned into a living sacrament, a channel through which runs the communion of grace that associates us to God and to others. Thanks to the character it can be said that in baptism one receives not only a little water but an inexhaustible spring (see Jn 7:37–38).

The character is therefore visible, because it modifies our corporeality and, with it, our concrete way of relating to others. But the visibility of the character, like the visibility of our incarnate condition, is not immediate. For the body, as the primordial dwelling in the world, often remains hidden from our frontal vision.[76] Thus the fact that we are sons and daughters, for example, which is an axis of our space of relations, is not directly visible. It is visible, nevertheless, inasmuch as everything that we do has filial features. Something similar happens with the character, the original corporeality from which the entire life of a Christian unfolds. The character is not seen directly, but is reflected in everything that the believer does, which acquires the familial atmosphere of the Christian. And it is revealed in a particular way by the believer's place in the church, in other words, by the type of relations that have been granted to him to establish in the body of Christ, which are made visible *par excellence* in the worship assembly. And just as our filial condition is perceived even when we live in opposition to our parents, so too the baptismal character can be seen even when we have abandoned Christ, in order to remind us relentlessly that we will find life only in him.

75. See Thomas Aquinas, *Super IV Sent.*, d. 6, q. 2, a. 1 (Parma 7:561): "quia ipsum sacramentum regeneratio quaedam est: cujuslibet autem generatio est tantum semel" (because the sacrament itself is a kind of regeneration: but generation of any sort occurs only once).

76. See Drew Leder, *The Absent Body* (Chicago: University of Chicago Press, 1990).

I should add that this character, as I have described it, is a dynamic reality, that also resituates us in a time of life. This happens, again, in an analogy to our incarnate condition. For the body, inasmuch as it was generated by others, is our oldest memory, inviting us to recognize the good origin that precedes us in everything that we are and do. This memory is taken up and expanded *in baptism, in which we receive the memory of Christ*, which goes back to his transcendent origin as eternal Son of God and as firstborn of creation. Thanks to the character, the Christian's first memory, which serves as a background of all his other memories, is the generative goodness of the Father of Jesus Christ.

At the same time, just as parents, when they give their child his name, situate him within the horizon of a future of hope, so too *baptism, by means of the Christian name received in it, points to a final destiny in God*, to a future that will continually draw the baptized person toward itself. Therefore the character is never a scar of a glorious past, but rather a seal that the age to come places along our journey in time, as an advance or down payment on the eternal life that takes possession of our present. Through the character, the risen body of Christ claims us for itself (see Col 3:1).[77]

In short, *the character adapts the narrative coordinates of our life (its origin, its fidelity, its end) to the story of Jesus*. Therefore, based on the character we can participate in the mysteries of Christ, as they are celebrated in the liturgy: we prove to be configured to the time of Jesus so as to become his contemporaries.[78] In light of this we can understand the connection between *character and participation in the church* that contemporary theology highlights. For the relational coordinates of Jesus into which the character introduces us are the same coordinates that constitute the church. We just need to remember the primacy of entry into Christ, which at the same time makes us members of his body. Therefore, as I have already said, the character is not at the disposal of the church. For her too it constitutes the original receptivity, the memory of her continual birth from Jesus and, therefore, the ultimate, inalienable substrate of her sanctity.[79] From the character, the

77. See von Allmen, *Prophetisme sacramental*, 10: "Sacrament exists wherever the future age chooses, grasps, exorcizes, occupies, and consecrates an element of the present age and thereby becomes present in it."

78. This is a point highlighted by Gottlieb Söhngen (a teacher of Joseph Ratzinger) in his attempt to offer a dogmatic foundation for the "theology of the mysteries" of Odo Casel: see Gottlieb Söhngen, *Symbol und Wirklichkeit im Kultmysterium* (Bonn: Haustein, 1937). For Söhngen, the character is what makes it possible to understand the liturgy not only as a consequence or effect of a past action of Christ, but as the actualization in the life of the Christian of the same events that occurred in his death and resurrection; in this way, thanks to the character, what is celebrated in the liturgy can then expand to the rest of life.

79. See Sergio Ubbiali, "Il carattere sacramentale: La passività costitutiva dell'agire sacramentale," *Rivista liturgica* 85 (1998): 469–86.

church radiates this sanctity to all her visible structures, always with its roots in the sacraments.

What remains now is to describe the different forms that the character assumes. What I said about baptism, connected with the "filial character" of our life, is prolonged in the other sacraments, which accommodate the other dimensions of the language of the body (spousal, paternal and maternal, social, etc.).

The Character in Each Sacrament

Starting with baptism, I described the character as a participation in the corporeal space of Jesus, that is, in his way of dwelling in the world and of initiating relations with the Father and the brethren. This finding invites us to go back from baptism to the Eucharist, for the latter contains the body of Jesus, surrendered to the Father for many in order to reestablish communion. The sacramental character therefore has a Eucharistic form: the character of the remaining sacraments has to be understood from this perspective.

Thomas Aquinas asked himself why the Eucharist imprints no character. Is this perhaps a defect, which does not go well with the excellence of this sacrament? Aquinas answers that every character consecrates the person for worship, and it is like a participation in the priesthood of Christ. Well, now, in the Eucharist we find the perfection of worship, for in it Christ the high priest himself is contained.[80] He concludes, then, that if the Eucharist imprints no character it is by excess, and not by defect. It is the source of every character; it is, one could say, the character of the entire church, in other words, the basic background, the original receptivity that structures the whole being and the work of the body of Christ and makes its common good possible.

If some sacraments (baptism, confirmation, holy orders) imprint a character it is because they communicate the Eucharistic form to the life of the Christian, according to the different states of life. I have already said a great deal about *baptism*, which configures the filial and fraternal structure of the believer to the filiation and fraternity of Jesus, establishing a new background of relations for Christian action.

Confirmation, for its part, is inscribed, not so much in the receptivity of the flesh, but rather in its ability to forge new relations and to grow in them. In our flesh we are endowed not only with a receptive background, but also with an active background which enables us to act. Precisely during a child's

80. See Thomas Aquinas, *ST* III, q. 63, a. 6.

education the orientation of desire and of freedom is generated in him, an orientation that will accompany him during his adult life. Jesus, who took up our journey in time, also received, under the formative action of the Spirit, an orientation of his flesh so that he could preach the Kingdom, make it present in his miracles, and consummate it in his self-surrender on the crossbeams.[81] This active configuration of corporeal relations is what the Lord transmits to us in the chrism. Therefore the character of confirmation is associated with public witness to the faith, which implies the believer's dedication to expanding the Christian spaces, enlivening all dimensions of life from the vantage point of the gospel of Jesus.

Holy orders, for its part, configures the believer to Jesus according to another dimension of the language of the body: paternity. As I will examine this point in depth in chapter 14, it is enough now to outline the analogy that illustrates this for us. When a father engenders a son and receives along with him the task of raising him, his identity is forged in a new way: he not only *has* a son but also *is* a father. This changes the network of corporeal relations that position him in the world, a network that from now on is polarized toward the son as a vector that prolongs the father's future. Well then, in an analogous way, Christ too, over the course of his life, configured his flesh in a generative way as the source and origin of a new lineage. Note that this paternity of Jesus is not merely spiritual but is forged in the body: Christ generates in us a new concrete order of relations, which will attain its fullness in the resurrection of the body, our definitive birth into glory. From this perspective we can understand the distinctive feature of the priestly character, which consists precisely in configuring the body of the ordained man to the paternity of Jesus, enabling him to communicate to human beings sacramentally the abundant life of the master.

The remaining sacraments, although they do not imprint a character, create an analogous configuration to the corporeal background of relations inaugurated by Jesus. I am speaking primarily about *matrimony*. It holds a strategic position because it has custody of those basic meanings of the body that serve as a creaturely analogy by which to understand the sacramental character.[82] The task of matrimony is to introduce these basic meanings into the economy of the sacraments, in such a way that the character imprinted in the sacraments has a direct link with everyday life and the building up of society.

---

81. On the character of confirmation, see Serafino Zardoni, "Il 'carattere' della cresima all'interno di una possibile teologia sul carattere sacramentale," in his *Il sacramento della confermazione* (Bologna: ESD, 1983), 171–98.

82. See Herwi Rikhof, "Marriage: A Question of Character?," *INTAMS Review* 2, no. 2 (1996): 151–61.

Indeed, the formation of the "one flesh" of Adam and Eve (Gn 2:24) already contains a certain character from the perspective of creation. For when a man and a woman marry they specify in a new way their situation in the body: their dwelling in the world will no longer be that of a single person, but of "us," which involves a common way of going through and narrating the stages of life.[83] We can say, taking our inspiration from the biblical expression, that this is a new body which reveals in a new way the action of Yahweh, who formed Eve from Adam's side and joined them through their mutual love, blessing them with the gift of new life. Thus is forged an irrevocable background of the journey of husband and wife, which will serve in turn as the original background for their children, against which they will be able to discover their filial identity. Thanks to matrimony the life of all human persons relies on such a primary background of communion, which is necessary in order to receive one's name wholeheartedly and to find one's path.

The distinctive feature of matrimony as a Christian sacrament is that the two baptized persons who marry already share, through their baptismal character, the corporeality of Christ (his very way of dwelling in the world and of intertwining relations); and therefore they can become "one flesh," according to the new measure of Jesus, and only in this way. Similarly, the common time of the two spouses is conformed to the story of Jesus, to the way in which he paced his time. In other words, the story that they share possesses from now on one and the same origin in the Father of Jesus Christ, where they will find the deep roots of their conjugal love; one and the same fidelity until death and "for better or for worse" which is characteristic of Christ's love; and the capacity to generate children for God, according to the measure of Jesus.

It is not surprising, then, that it is possible to talk about a quasi-character in relation to matrimony, a quasi-character that coincides with the conjugal bond. If there is no "character" here, properly speaking, it is because the union of man and woman belongs to the ancient creaturely order, which was taken up by Christ, but nevertheless not brought to its eschatological consummation: the matrimonial bond is broken by death and the "one flesh" ceases to exist, in the hope of the newness of the resurrected body.

The other two sacraments, penance and the anointing of the sick, being repeatable, do not imprint a character either. All the same, there is in them the reality that the theological tradition called *res et sacramentum* (see chapter 9, above), which shares the stability of the sacramental character.[84] *Pen-*

---

83. See Alain Badiou, *Éloge de l'amour* (Paris: Flammarion, 2009).
84. See Roberto Masi, "La struttura dei sacramenti: *Sacramentum tantum, res et sacramentum,*

ance has to be understood in relation to baptism: it restores the sinner to the relational coordinates that are contained in the baptismal character, as opposed to the coordinates of sin that he had settled on. Forgiveness is received because the penitent turns to embrace the same background of bonds with which Jesus situated himself in the world and opened himself to God and the brethren. Therefore this sacrament would do no good for someone who persists in living in a way contrary to the baptismal configuration of Christian life. The *res et sacramentum* of penance is, in light of this, reintegration into the baptismal body of Christ, which is prolonged in the body of the church.[85]

The *anointing of the sick*, for its part, brings about a particular configuration with Jesus precisely in the hours of his passion and death, in other words, in the same vital context in which the master instituted the Eucharist and gave us his body. Sickness radically affects the corporeality of the sick person inasmuch as it disrupts the equilibrium of the human being with the world, reducing his field of relations. The suffering flesh threatens to restrict altogether the person's range of action, narrowing his world and the bonds that unite him to others. Well, then, the sacrament configures the sick person to the suffering body of Christ who, in similar hours, accepted suffering as the fruitful chalice of the Father in order to ransom mankind, and reopened his life to relations of new communion with God and the brethren. Thus there is a corporeal conformation with Jesus (a conformation which is the *res et sacramentum*) as a lasting effect of the rite, throughout the time in which the sickness runs its course. The sick person now enters into a new space, in which everything invites him to confidence and fruitful self-offering, and if he places no obstacles, Jesus' Spirit of love can be poured out on him, so that he accepts his trial with the same attitude as the master did.

Sacramental Reviviscence in Light of the Character

The doctrine of the character helps to shed light for us on what has been called the "reviviscence" or revival of the sacraments. This can occur if a sacrament was received unworthily but validly. For example: someone is baptized or confirmed without wanting to abandon a life of sin. In this case the recipient is placing an impediment (*obex*, obstacle) to grace, and for this reason grace cannot be communicated to him. The baptism or confirma-

---

res tantum," *Divinitas* 12 (1969): 551–79; Paul F. Palmer, "The Theology of the *res et sacramentum*," in *Readings in Sacramental Theology*, ed. C. Stephen Sullivan (Englewood Cliffs, N.J.: Prentice Hall, 1964), 104–23.

85. See Pedro López González, *Res et sacramentum: origen y aplicación al sacramento de la Penitencia* (Pamplona: Universidad de Navarra, 1991).

tion, nevertheless, is valid and does not have to be repeated. Reviviscence means that, when this person converts and abandons sin, he will receive the special grace of the sacrament that was conferred. Then, St. Augustine notes, what operated before unto death will begin to have its effect unto life.[86]

Theologians have debated how this reviviscence of sacramental grace is produced, using for this purpose the different theories about the causality of the sacraments that I explained in chapters 9 and 10. According to the so-called theory of moral causality, the sacrament accomplishes its effect because God promised to grant his grace whenever the rite is put into effect. From this perspective it is easy to give an account of reviviscence, for it depends only on the will of God, who remembers very well that the sacrament was already conferred in the past and can give his grace when the obstacle disappears.

It is more difficult to explain reviviscence in terms of "physical causality," which views the sacrament, in its material, concrete celebration, as a channel of grace. For if the rite was celebrated some time ago, how will it continue to be the channel of divine favor? The explanation then has recourse to the character (or *res et sacramentum*), which remains in the Christian as a lasting effect, allowing the reviviscence.

The perspective that I proposed in chapter 11 follows physical causality more closely, but takes the person's incarnate condition as central: the sacrament exerts its effect *corporeally*, through our assimilation to the flesh of Jesus, which occurs precisely through the character. Indeed, the character configures the believer to the space which is proper to Christ, in much the same way that we receive at birth the background of basic familial relations that structure our presence in the world and our path through life.

Reviviscence is explained in terms of this permanent background of our relations (a new corporeality) that was received in the sacrament. For when we return to friendship with God, this friendship will adapt to the form contained in the character. Similarly, the son who is reconciled with his father will establish with him, *ipso facto*, a relation of a filial kind, for he keeps forever his name and his surname. This can easily be applied to baptism,

---

86. See Augustine, *De baptismo* I, 12, 18 (CSEL 51:80; NPNF-I 4:419b): "quod ante datum est tunc valere incipiat ad salutem, cum illa fictio veraci confessione recesserit" (what was given before becomes then powerful to work his salvation, when the former deceit is done away by the truthful confession); *De baptismo* III, 13, 18 (CSEL 51:208; NPNF-I 4:441a): "ipse [baptismus] qui propter discordiam foris operabatur mortem, propter pacem intus operetur salutem" (that the very same baptism which was working death by reason of discord outside the Church, may work salvation by reason of the peace within); *De baptismo* VI, 9, 14 (CSEL 51:308; NPNF-I 4:483b–484a); VI, 25, 47 (CSEL 51:324; NPNF-I 4:491). For this doctrine in Thomas Aquinas, see *Super IV Sent.*, d. 4, q. 3, a. 2, q.c. 3, sol. (Parma 7:519–20); *ST* III, q. 69, a. 10.

confirmation, and holy orders. Given that the matrimonial bond is compared with the character, as we saw, here too reviviscence applies. As soon as the validly married spouse is reconciled with God, his love for his wife, or her love for her husband will take the form of the love of Christ and of his church, which is conjugal charity.

Reviviscence exists also in the anointing of the sick, inasmuch as it configures the Christian's flesh to the way in which Jesus experienced his passion and death. As long as the illness for which the anointing was received lasts, this configuration inaugurated by the rite persists. As soon as friendship with God is regained, that friendship will be adapted to the pattern which Jesus forged in order to experience suffering with hope, and to which the sick person was already associated by the sacrament.

With respect to confession, there is no reviviscence. And the reason is that a sacrament revives only when, after being received fruitlessly because the person was attached to his sin, it is conferred validly. However, in penance, repentance for sin is required for the very validity of the rite. Thus, it is not possible for this sacrament to be received fruitlessly and validly.

Finally, the Eucharist is a special case. As I have noted, inasmuch as it contains the "character" of the whole church, the Eucharist is always alive, for the church never ceases to respond faithfully to its grace. As far as the particular individual who receives it unworthily is concerned, his life will recover the Eucharistic form of grace only when he is reintegrated into the body of Christ through the sacrament of reconciliation.

I started this chapter by noting two modern objections to the sacramental character: it seems to separate and isolate Christians from each other, distinguishing those who have it from those who do not; and it seems to make life rigid, binding us forever, so that we cannot undo what we have done. We have seen that the contrary occurs instead: the character broadens our space, for when it configures us to the way in which Jesus lived out his relations, it inaugurates a communion in difference which enriches our horizons; and the character makes existence dynamic by introducing us into the narrative coordinates of Christ, through which we share his memory, his fidelity, and his fruits.

What I have said in this chapter clears the path for the following ones. For from the original space of relations in which the character situates us, the space of Christian action in the world unfolds (chapter 13); we can understand the role of the minister of the sacraments who is configured to Christ the head (chapter 14); and we can discern the sacramental essence of the church (chapter 15).

13 ❧ THE SACRAMENTS AND CHRISTIAN ACTION

A sacrament—as the previous chapter showed us—goes beyond the limits of the celebration. For when the believer receives the character, his very person is assimilated to the sacrament and therefore so will his every act be. We understand, then, that the everyday life of family and friends, work and free time, is entirely sacramental life. In this chapter I will inquire about this connection between the sacraments and Christian action. How is the celebrative action united to the rest of our actions? Without ignoring the classic questions about the requirements for receiving the sacraments validly and fruitfully, my interest will go further: to understand how the sacrament generates the Christian moral subject by promoting a virtuous way of acting, through participation in the action of Jesus.[1] This will show that sacramental action and moral action possess the same logic.

There is a pastoral question at stake which has an effect both on the preparation for receiving the sacraments, and on the cultivation of the gift received in them. For recall that the sacraments inaugurate the Christian space, that is, they forge our situation in the world and our basic network of relations according to the measure of Jesus. They ask us, therefore, to undertake a path which helps us to abandon the coordinates of the old space of sin, closed in on itself. This path opens up when we clear away false foundations and move the pillars onto firm rock. At the same time, once the sacraments have been celebrated, the work begins of building up the relational space of the believer, a space which is called to grow like an animated building or body. The gift received calls for us to accompany its maturation. Our starting point will be a specific aspect of biblical religion: the unity between worship and the moral law which acquires new contours upon the arrival of Jesus.

---

1. See Livio Melina, *Cristo e il dinamismo dell'agire: linee di rinnovamento della teologia morale fondamentale* (Rome: Mursia, 2001).

Worship and Christian Life according
to the New Testament

The worship of Israel, because it remembered the covenant and its promises, was wholly oriented toward moral action. For in the covenant God himself went to work, freeing man from slavery and inviting him to unite his liberty to him. It is not surprising, therefore, that the liturgy of Sinai was centered on the Decalogue, which calls for a thankful response to the saving deeds of Yahweh. The Letter to the Hebrews testifies to this unity: "when there is a change in the priesthood [the key to worship] there is necessarily a change in the Law as well" (Heb 7:12).

The New Testament, which takes a position along these lines, brings new ideas. Note a curious fact: the Jewish cultic vocabulary is not applied in general to the Christian rites, such as baptism or the Eucharist, but directly to the life of the believer. Terms like "priest," "temple," "sacrifice," etc., refer in the first place to ordinary tasks. Thus the Corinthians' offering of charity is liturgical service (2 Cor 9:12); the people of Rome offer their bodies as living sacrifice (Rom 12:1); the Christians of Ephesus are called saints, without ritual defect in God's sight (Eph 1:4); and so on.[2] St. Peter, for his part, describes spiritual sacrifices thus: to avoid evil and live with justice (1 Pt 2:5); and in the Letter to the Hebrews God is pleased with the "sacrifice" of charity (Heb 13:16; see Phil 4:18).

This liturgical language is also applied to the apostolic ministry: St. Paul pours himself out as a libation upon the sacrifice of the faith of the faithful (Phil 2:17); he gives worship to God in his Spirit through the gospel (Rom 1:9); he performs the holy office of the gospel of God, in such a way that the offering of Christians acquires a pleasing odor (Rom 15:16). The fact, then, is clear: cultic language is applied to everyday life and apostolic mission, more than to liturgical celebrations. How are we to interpret this fact?

Some have seen here an indication that Christianity takes importance away from ritual; and in this way they have justified a certain secularized theology. According to them, the gospel does not hold external worship in high esteem, preferring an interest in ordinary action. The more Christians practiced charity, the less necessary it would be to celebrate the faith.[3] The weakest point of this exegesis lies in ignoring the heavy weight given to the

2. See Mussner, "Die Kirche als Kultgemeinde"; Romano Penna, "Cristianesimo e laicità in san Paolo: Appunti," in his *L'apostolo Paolo: Studi di esegesi e teologia* (Cinisello Balsamo: San Paolo, 1991), 562–74.

3. See Bozzolo, *La teologia sacramentaria dopo Rahner*, 196–202.

Eucharistic celebration by the primitive communities: as we already know (see chapter 1, above), the Eucharist is the environment in which many books of the New Testament were written and were read aloud. In fact, would the reason for this novel language not be precisely here, in Jesus' rite?

To prove it let us note that the cultic terminology to which I have alluded, before it is applied to the Christian, refers to Christ himself and to his redemptive action on the cross. St. Paul describes the ritual work of the faithful (Rom 12:1) only after talking about Jesus as the means of "expiation" (Rom 3:25). For the Letter to the Hebrews, the priesthood of Christ, who offered himself (Heb 7:27; 9:14, 25; 10:5–10), makes it possible for his disciples to be "perfected," that is to say, consecrated as priests (Heb 10:14).[4] And if the believers are called priests in the Book of Revelation, it is in relation to the deliverance of Jesus unto death (Rv 1:5; 5:9; 20:4–6). Extending this usage, St. Ignatius of Antioch later described martyrdom, the highest imitation of the Lord, with cultic vocabulary.[5]

Our question, therefore, turns into another one: how did the cultic terms come to be used to explain the death of Jesus? The answer is not difficult: it is enough to look to the interpretation of his death and resurrection that the master himself gave at the Last Supper.[6] Earlier I said that cultic vocabulary is not applied in the New Testament to Christian worship. But it is necessary to make one decisive exception: the institution of the Eucharist. And then we understand: *because Jesus himself closely united his rite to his life and passion, the disciples could interpret in cultic terms the surrender of Jesus on the cross and, based on that, the entire work of the faithful.*

Given that the Eucharist refers to the corporeal life and surrender of Christ, to participate in it is to make of one's own life and surrender in the body a Eucharistic act. The Christian rite, therefore, does not point to a place far from life, from which life is then illuminated and enriched. Rather it looks directly at a human existence in the flesh, that of Jesus—an existence that touches and transforms the life of those who believe in him, drawing them to his fullness in glory.

Here lies the key to understanding the connection between the earth-

---

4. Hence Paul can exhort his readers: "Therefore let us go forth to him outside the camp, bearing abuse for him.... Through him then *let us continually offer up a sacrifice of praise to God,* that is, *the fruit of lips that acknowledge his name*" (Heb 13:13–15). Here the imitation of Jesus' sacrifice on the cross, outside of Jerusalem (against the background of Lv 16:27) is applied to the spiritual praise (*todah*) the psalms call for (Ps 50:14, 23).

5. See Ignatius, *Romans* IV, 2 (SC 10:130; ANF 1:75): "Entreat Christ for me, that by these instruments I may be found a sacrifice to God"; cf. Rudolf Padberg, "Vom gottesdienstlichen Leben in den Briefen des Ignatius von Antiochien," *Theologie und Glaube* 53 (1963): 337–47, at 345.

6. See Joseph Ratzinger, "Eucharist and Mission," in *Collected Works,* 11:330–54.

ly liturgy and the heavenly liturgy, which was already pointed out in the Old Testament and is taken up again in the New. According to the Letter to the Hebrews, the temple that Moses built imitated another higher temple which God showed him on the mountain (see Ex 25:40; Heb 8:5). Is this heavenly sanctuary a Platonic temple, situated in the Empyrean? No, it is the body of Christ, in its resurrected eschatological maturity (see Heb 9:11).[7] That is to say, the plans which God outlined for Moses were taken from the future. And the Christian liturgy is the anticipation of the definitive future, through the Lord's Eucharistic body. The rite is thus closely tied to human action, which is a movement of the rational creature toward his final end in God. Worship gives form to our action inasmuch as it gives us a taste of our destiny and thus propels us toward it.

From all this we can conclude: it is not necessary to make efforts to apply the sacraments to life, for the sacraments already are life, and moreover they communicate to us the full form of life by conforming us to the life of Jesus. We must understand Christ's words to the Samaritan woman in this way: worship will not be given in a temple, but in Spirit and truth (Jn 4:23), that is to say, in the way of loving proper to the Son who reveals (truth) the Father, by giving his love (Spirit).

Sacrament and Christian Moral Action

The theological tradition has delved into this link between ritual action and moral action to which the Bible testifies. Studying it will open for us the door through which to present both the necessary preparation for the sacrament and also the way to cultivate its gift so that it spreads its branches through all the spaces of life.

Lex orandi, lex credendi, lex agendi

The close-knit union of three elements can be observed in the early church: *lex orandi, lex credendi, lex agendi*. For on one hand, the liturgy (*lex orandi*) is the place where the life of Jesus, his whole narrative, is remembered and actualized: he was born of a virgin mother, suffered under Pontius Pilate, rose on the third day, etc., and this is precisely the center of the profession of faith (*lex credendi*).[8] Furthermore, this same liturgy (*lex orandi*) assures us that the body of Jesus is prolonged in the body of Christians who are conformed to him in the sacrament; therefore, the profession of Jesus' narrative

---

7. See Vanhoye, "Par la tente."
8. See de Clerck, "*Lex orandi, lex credendi.*"

or *lex credendi* extends also to the narrative of each believer, that is, to the way in which he is called to build up his life, or *lex agendi*. We observe the pivotal role that the sacrament acquires (*lex orandi*) in associating faith in Jesus (*lex credendi*) and the good works of the Christian (*lex agendi*).

St. Augustine, in his treatise *De fide et operibus*, dwells on the unity of these three dimensions. The holy bishop is fighting against those who, because of a false way of understanding mercy, wanted to administer baptism to those who were living in adultery or other public sins. And his response to them is that in order to be baptized the profession of faith is required, as well as a corresponding moral life. The latter is not something superfluous or subsequent to the faith, but rather belongs to its essence. For it is not enough to profess how Christ lived (who was born of the Virgin, who died and rose and ascended into heaven), if we do not profess how we are called to live as members of the body of Christ.[9] In another text St. Augustine explains from this perspective the "Amen" pronounced when receiving communion: "when they say to you, 'the body of Christ,' you respond, 'Amen': make yourself body of Christ so that your Amen may be true."[10]

The sacrament, we can conclude, is the radical Christian action, as it incorporates us into Jesus' action. St. Hilary of Poitiers frames matters this way when he describes the type of unity created by baptism in the church. According to Hilary this unity is not forged primarily on the basis of the free will of the faithful. That is to say, the reason that we are one (see Jn 17:11) is not that we have decided to love one another much. Such a unity would be very weak compared to the one that baptism bestows on us, which is described thus: "they are one [not because of the conformity of their minds but] in that they have put on one Christ through the nature of one baptism."[11] The same thing happens, Hilary adds, with the Eucharist, which makes us one, not only through a unity of wills but through a radical participation in the flesh of Christ, which generates within us a new way of willing.[12] Something analogous occurs with the children or siblings of a family, whose bonds are anterior to their will because they are rooted in their flesh, which later enables them to have a closer love for each other. In the same way the sacramental event deepens the roots of all union between human beings, establishing them in the love of Jesus and enabling them to carry out the new commandment.

---

9. See Augustine, *De fide et operibus* I, 2 (CSEL 41:36).

10. Augustine, *Sermo* 272, 1 (PL 38:1247): "Audis enim, corpus Christi; et respondes, amen. Esto membrum corporis Christi, ut uerum sit amen."

11. Hilary of Poitiers, *De Trinitate* VIII, 7–8 (CCL 62A:319–20; NPNF-II 9:140a).

12. See ibid., VIII, 13–18 (CCL 62A:325–30; NPNF-II 9:141a–142b).

Participation in the Action of Christ

The Middle Ages collect the patristic heritage into an ordered system and study how our action is grafted onto that of the master. While the Fathers focused on the overall consistency of sacrament, faith, and works, little by little the attention shifts to the celebration itself, analyzing its features in more detail.

Thus, for example, because of the perceived close connection between the celebration and everyday life, medieval theology specified the conditions for an adult's access to the sacraments: (1) in order to receive the sacrament the free intention of the recipient is considered necessary, thus avoiding a magical way of living out the rite; (2) in order for the sacrament to bear fruit, faith and contrition for sins are required; (3) it is admitted, as the church's traditional practice testified, that baptism can be received *in voto* (baptism of desire): this implies accepting a close connection between the baptismal act and conversion, given that they both have the same effects. Later in this chapter, I will return to these questions.

Besides determining these particular cases, the Middle Ages offer an overall framework to explain how liturgy and Christian action are intertwined. Following the Church Fathers, theologians reflect on the sacraments and moral action starting from the difference between old and new covenant. To distinguish the two economies we must focus both on the ceremonial precepts and on morality, thus associating liturgy and life. If the Law of Moses, as St. Paul affirms, was incapable of saving, why did God institute those rituals and write those commandments? Moreover, what is the difference between them and the precepts and rites of Jesus, which do transmit eternal life?

The answer comes in affirming that the Old Law was a servile law of fear; while the New Law is filial, a law of love. The first moderated the *hands* of man, prohibiting or permitting the external work; the second goes straight to the *heart,* regenerating the entire person.[13] How is it, then, that some men of the Old Testament were saved by obedience to the Torah? To answer, a distinction is used that I have already dealt with, one that exercised great influence on the doctrine of the sacraments: the *opus operatum* (the action objectively performed) is one thing, and the *opus operantis* (the action inasmuch as it is caused by the agent) is another. Both aspects, certainly,

---

13. For the following discussion, see Landgraf, "Die Gnadenökonomie." St. Thomas expresses the difference as follows, in *ST* I-II, q. 108, a. 1, arg. 3: "vetus lex cohibet manum, sed lex nova cohibet animum" (The Old Law restrains the hand, whereas the New Law curbs the will).

have to go together, given the unity of the person who acts; yet they can be distinguished.[14]

Now then, what saved when the old precepts and rites were carried out was not, many affirm, the work performed (*opus operatum*) but the good disposition, in faith and charity, of the one who carried it out (*opus operantis*). This helps to understand the novelty of the Gospel: its sacraments do not act solely through the disposition of the one who performs them (*ex opere operantis*), but fundamentally through the work itself that is performed in them (*ex opere operato*).

What is this "work performed" which distinguishes the New Law? This can be nothing but the action of Christ, who concludes the old and begins the new covenant (see chapter 9, above). *Ex opere operato* means, in this light, the work performed by Christ on our behalf (*ex opere operato a Christo*). Hence some medieval writers can affirm: *opus operantis* is that which the believer offers; *opus operatum,* the blood which Jesus shed.[15]

Therefore in the sacrament of the New Law the work of Christ (*opus operatum*) embraces in a synergic way the work of the Christian (*opus operantis*). Thus a close connection is maintained between sacramental practice and the imitation of Christ, which is the source, channel, and end of the moral life. St. Bernard, for example, emphasizes that, thanks to the sacrament, the influence of Jesus on us is not reduced to that of an external model.[16] If our Eucharistic conformity to his life is lacking, the example of his humility and charity would be like a painting without a fabric on which to be set.[17] We can imitate Christ because we have been introduced sacramentally into the current of his action: eating his flesh offers the basis for hearing his words and imitating his works.[18]

14. Medieval authors use this example: the work of Judas, if viewed from the perspective of what happened in itself (Christ's death) is redemptive; but if regarded from the perspective of Judas who performed it (betraying Jesus) it is damning: see Landgraf, "Die Einführung," 245–47.

15. See Landgraf, "Die Gnadenökonomie," 248. Landgraf cites Prepositinus, who records the opinions of others: "Opera operantia appellant actiones offerentium; opera operata sanguis ille oblatus et huiusmodi" (They call the actions of those who offer *opera operantia*; and the blood that was sacrificed and things of that sort *opera operata*).

16. See Jean Leclercq, "Imitation du Christ et sacrements chez St. Bernard," *Collectanea Cisterciensia* 38 (1967): 263–82.

17. See Bernard, *Adversus Errores Abaelardi* (Epistle 190), 25 (ed. Leclercq, *Opera* 8:37): "Quis status gaudio, sive consilio, absque vita? Nempe haud alius quam picturae absque solido. Ergo nec humilitatis exempla, nec caritatis insignia, praeter redemptionis sacramentum, sunt aliquid" (What is the position of joy or counsel, apart from life? Certainly, nothing whatsoever but that of a picture without substance. Therefore neither examples of humility nor signs of charity are worth anything apart from the sacrament of redemption).

18. See Bernard, *Sermones in festivitate omnium sanctorum* I, 3 (ed. Leclercq, *Opera* 5:329): "ipse vos pascit, et operibus, et sermonibus, etiam et carne Filii sui, quae est vere cibus" (He Himself feeds you, both by deeds and by words, and even with the flesh of His Son, which is truly food).

The interest of the medieval writers in exploring the structure of the rite (*opus operatum, opus operantis*) could give the impression that for them the sacrament was an instantaneous event, concentrated in the liturgical celebration. Such a thing was essentially avoided through the very context in which the issue was examined: the entire economy of salvation, new and old, with its center in Christ. To participate in the action of Jesus was, in this light, to participate in a dynamism which recapitulated the ages and included the entire church within itself. Therefore medieval theology could describe the sacraments in a narrative mode, uniting them to the different stages of life, from birth to death; and it took into account not only the life of the person, but that of the entire community.[19]

Another indication of this expansion of the sacraments to all of existence is their pairing with the three theological virtues and the four cardinal virtues. For if at the beginning the grace of the sacraments was viewed as mere medicine that removes threats against health, soon theologians came to understand it as the strengthening of human action. Alexander of Hales formulated one of the first lists that matched the seven sacraments to the seven virtues: baptism to faith; confirmation to fortitude; the Eucharist to charity; penance to justice; extreme unction to perseverance, which is fortitude fulfilled; holy orders to prudence; matrimony to temperance.[20] St. Bonaventure, when proposing this doctrine in his *Breviloquium,* changes the picture slightly: hope is related to confirmation and fortitude to extreme unction.[21] In this way the three theological virtues are associated with the three sacraments of initiation. It makes sense, in fact, to link confirmation and hope inasmuch as this virtue guides the maturation of the Christian in time; a maturation that is possible because, with hope, the final fullness of our life is already anticipated and thus the foundation is given to us on which to launch ourselves toward this fullness.

The connection between celebration and human action is glimpsed also in one of the reasons that theologians usually give for why God instituted the sacraments. According to Hugh of St. Victor they were bestowed so that the believer might be trained (*ad exercitationem*). For man, after the exile from paradise, lives in continual insecurity: when he stops, something pushes him to move; when he moves, he longs for peace and repose.[22] Further-

---

19. See Thomas Aquinas, *ST* III, q. 65, a. 1, co.

20. See Alexander of Hales, *Summa* IV, q. 5, m. 7, aa. 1–2; in his *Glossa in quatuor libros Sententiarum* IV, d. 2, n. 1 (BFSMA XV [Quaracchi, 1957], 40), Alexander speaks about the sacraments as seven different medicines.

21. See Bonaventure, *In IV Sent.*, d. 2, a. 1, q. 3 (Quaracchi 4:53); *Breviloquium* VI, 3 (Quaracchi 5:267). I will discuss St. Albert the Great and St. Thomas in chapter 15, below.

22. See Hugh of St. Victor, *De sacramentis* I, 9, 3 (PL 176:320–22).

more, every time he acts, it is either out of the need for food and clothing, like a slave in perpetual movement; or else it is in the vacillating disintegration of someone who pursues multiple vices. Well, then, frequenting the sacraments frees human action and its path from all slavery and dispersion, by orienting it toward its final destination in the risen Christ. An essential component of this *exercitatio* or training, which extends to all moments of life, is ordering the multiplicity of desires so that they might be directed to their one true end and enable man to ascend continually toward God until he enters into his rest.

The Lutheran Crisis and the Response of Trent

As we already know (see chapter 10, above), one of the elements of the Catholic vision criticized by Luther is the efficacy of the sacraments *ex opere operato*.[23] For him this formula says something very erroneous: the material work performed saves by itself, without any need for conversion. For example, the man who offers a Mass believes that he is justified in God's sight. Thereby salvation remains under his own dominion and, ultimately, under the power of the church, which regulates worship. In this way the Christian exempts himself from faith; as if he could buy salvation without accepting the divine Word into his life. It is a superstitious or magical attitude, which the Protestants think that they are obliged to condemn.[24]

There is clearly a misunderstanding here. As I demonstrated earlier, the formula *ex opere operato* originated to indicate precisely what is proper to the economy of grace, as opposed to a mere fulfillment of the law. *Ex opere operato* refers to the work of God, who gratuitously saves man by going on ahead of the action of the creature. The sacrament sanctifies *ex opere operato a Christo*: thanks to the work performed by Jesus in his passion. Neither is there any foundation for Luther's reproach against an alleged Catholic sacramental automatism which prescinds from conversion. Certainly, abuses may have occurred, but the church has always understood that in order to obtain the grace of the sacrament, openness to faith is necessary, together with the rejection of sin.[25]

Luther, at an initial stage, made the efficacy of the sacraments depend on personal faith, understood as assurance that God forgives. The sacraments are at their root *professio fidei,* visible modes of professing faith, the only

---

23. See Finkenzeller, *Die Lehre von den Sakramenten,* 9.

24. See the *Confessio Augustana* XXIV, 13 (Bekenntnisschriften der evangelisch-lutherischen Kirche 352), where it speaks about a "pharisaica et ethnica persuasio de opere operato" (Pharisaical and heathen conviction about *opere operato*).

25. See Karl Rahner, *Grundkurs des Glaubens* (Freiburg: Herder, 1984), 398–400.

way of salvation, inasmuch as faith receives the saving word of God. There-fore redemption comes to us *solo verbo–sola fide* (by the Word alone–by faith alone), leaving aside the specific features of the ritual. As we know (see chapter 10, above), due to the internal disputes of the Reformation, Luther himself sensed that this position was exaggerated, because when all is said and done one could do without baptism. For this reason he later clarified his teaching, acknowledging the salvific necessity of the sacrament instituted by Christ. Only by immersing themselves in the water and feeding on bread and wine do believers concretely accept the love of God who instituted these signs, and thus accept the proper logic of the incarnation of the Word, which always comes to us from outside ourselves (*extra nos*).[26]

Can we say, then, that Luther maintains the traditional perspective on this point? There is a difference in emphasis, for in the Reformation, the collaboration of man is understood principally as fiducial openness to God; as a firm act of faith in the truth of his promise. This is why everything is concentrated on the instant of the act of faith, where the sinner is justified, without this action tending to branch out to the rest of Christian life, thus accompanying the believer's action in time. In this way, the ritual event nec-essarily turns out to be isolated from the rest of our existence. In fact, the Protestant vision, when it attempts to situate worship within life as a whole, will tend to see it, not in tune with human action, but as an "interruption" that is in discontinuity with it.[27]

Trent responded to Luther's critique by confirming, on the one hand, that faith is part of the sacramental dynamic. As St. Robert Bellarmine would later note, the canons about the sacraments follow the *Decree on Jus-tification*, which affirms that faith is the beginning of salvation, together with repentance.[28] It is false, therefore, to say that the Catholic vision does not take into account the good dispositions of the person who receives the sacrament.[29]

Certainly, on the other hand, these good dispositions are not the rea-son why the sacrament bestows its grace, but only a condition, which the Council formulates negatively: it is incumbent on the faithful not to place

26. See Schwab, "Luthers Ringen."

27. See Angelini, *Il tempo e il rito*, 51–61; Eberhard Jüngel, "Der evangelisch verstandene Gottes-dienst," in his *Wertlose Wahrheit*, 3:16–77; the latter author considers it better not to call worship "priestly" and to reserve that adjective for ordinary life, for the distinctive feature of ritual action is prophetic being—in keeping with the Protestant understanding that regards sacrament in light of the Word.

28. DH 1526.

29. See Bellarmine, *De Controversiis*, vol. 3, lib. 2, cap. 1 (86); on this point see also chapter 10, above.

an impediment or obstacle (*obex*).[30] In other words, the only source and spring of grace is the action of Christ in the sacrament, *ex opere operato*.[31] For man's part, it is enough to let himself be welcomed by Jesus; the primacy of God's action in the salvation of his creature is thus maintained.

The polemic, in reality, dealt not simply with the role of faith in the sacrament, but with the way of understanding this faith. As I have indicated, Luther thought of it as fiducial faith, that is, trusting abandonment to the promise of God who forgives our wickedness. Trent, for its part, understands faith above all as assent to the truth revealed by God, but situates it at the same time in the whole of Christian life: faith is capable of giving us life only if it is united to hope and charity.[32] That is to say, while man is called not to impede the action of grace (not to place an obstacle), the distinctive feature of this grace is that it takes up human action into itself, branching out to the believer's whole life. By means of faith which works through charity (Gal 5:6; see DH 1531), we allow God to work in us, and we prove to be capable of working with God. Accordingly, the Council will see the sacraments, in contrast with Luther, as an organic whole which extends to every area of life. For this reason Trent affirms that they constitute the broad context of human salvation and, so to speak, the narrative that gives meaning to this very salvation: through them all justification is born, grows once it has been received, and is recovered if it is lost.[33]

It could be said that in both—Luther and Trent—the primacy of grace and the necessity of the response of man's faith is preserved; and that both dimensions are found within the rite. The difference appears, nevertheless, when we seek to account for human action. For Luther concentrates the sacrament in the salvific instant of our opening up in the presence of a divine call. Thus the rite inaugurates a life of faith, the only thing that saves, as a receptive attitude of trust in God, which nevertheless does not encompass human action. The Catholic response, on the contrary, sees how the sacrament branches out through the complete history of the person in the flesh.[34] In this way every human action gains a sacramental structure, so that God and his creature work in synergy; and the dynamic of the sacraments can extend to all areas of existence.

30. DH 1606.
31. DH 1608.
32. See Council of Trent, Session VI, *Decree on Justification*, chap. VII (DH 1531); Louis Villette, *Foi et sacrement*, II: *De Saint Thomas à Karl Barth* (Paris: Bloud and Gay, 1964); see Ladaria, *Teologia del pecado original*, 214.
33. See Council of Trent, Session VII, *Decree on the Sacraments*, Foreword (DH 1600).
34. Recall in this respect the importance of the doctrine of the sacramental character, which was denied by the Reformation (see my discussion above in chapter 12).

The influence of Trent on Christian life was very deep because, insofar as it was based on the practice of the sacraments (to which the Council dedicated most of its sessions) its proposal was not limited to the realm of ideas, but rather took flesh in living culture and social customs. Less influential was the result of the theological vision, which during the period after the Council remained stuck in the controversy with the Protestants, so that the overall horizon was lost. Thus, in the explanations of the post-Tridentine theologians, the sacrament became less necessary to explain the form of Christian action, as if it imparted strength to an already-established dynamism, but without informing or reinforcing this dynamism from within. Moral theology, for its part, would cease to be inspired by the logic of the sacraments, focusing on the believer's conscience. Thus the broad horizon of the medieval synthesis is forgotten: the imitation of the life of Jesus, through the virtues, based on being rooted sacramentally in his body. The loss would be more noticeable the more the culture of the sacraments was extinguished, with the secularizing trend of the West. For in everyday life this culture was what maintained the coordinates of belief. Perhaps for that reason the twentieth century, when the erosion was already undeniable, is the one that develops a more integrated theological response, which I will discuss in the following paragraphs.

Once we have verified the close connection between the sacraments and human action, it is important to break down this connection into three moments: the preparation for the rite, the celebration, and the accompaniment of the sacramental gift so that it matures to its fullness. In discussing them, I will invert the order, leaving the preparation for last, because only from the vantage point of the summit can we survey all the bends of the road that leads up to it.

The Celebration of the Sacrament and Human Action

The liturgical movement of the twentieth century and the theological reflection that accompanied it recovered the vision of the sacraments as a participation in the action of Christ. The question arises: how to tie the ritual imitation of Jesus in the liturgy to the imitation of Jesus' virtues in everyday life?

Eucharistic Rite and Redemptive Action of Jesus: Common Coordinates

In order to answer this question, the point of departure has to be the Eucharist, which Jesus associated seamlessly with his redemptive action. And this is because the Last Supper offers us the key to Christ's work, as the course of his life was summarized in the Eucharist: having loved his own (past) who were in the world (present), he loved them unto the end (future) (see Jn 13:1). Well, then, in this rite Jesus acts on the basis of his origin in the Father, giving thanks for his gifts and offering him a sacrifice of praise or *todah*. From this initiative of the Father, which has placed everything in the hands of his Son (see Jn 13:3), Christ gives himself up for his brethren's sake, delivers them from evil, and generates new life within them by reuniting them in one body.[35]

With this last paragraph, did I describe *the Eucharistic celebration of Jesus* or *the redemptive action of Jesus*? The nonexistence of such a dilemma is revealing. It is not just that in the Upper Room Jesus anticipates what would happen later, as if the rite were a prologue to the authentic action. Rather, the rite celebrated is already action, and an especially dense action, which offers him the coordinates by which to map his whole work, making it possible for it to reach its climax. In the following paragraphs I analyze the distinctive features of this ritual action.

Recall that Jesus does not invent his rite out of nothing, but rather adopts the template of the Passover and of the *todah* sacrifice described in the Old Testament, with their origin in God himself. The rite is for Christ, like all prophecies, a gift which his Father prepares for him by means of Israel, a gift which Jesus receives as his own and interprets in a new key. The rite reveals to us, therefore, that the action of Jesus is initiated by the Father, who confers on his Son the ability to participate in a common salvific work (see Jn 17:4; 5:36). By the very fact of celebrating the rite (*opus operatum*), Christ imbues his free surrender with filial logic (*opus operantis*).

Together with this reference to the Father, the rite (again, through its very execution) situates the action of Jesus in a communal key. For at the Last Supper Jesus assumes the tradition of Israel, which he receives through the generations as a child of his people. Moreover, the rite proclaims (pointing toward the future) the unity of the body of the church (1 Cor 10:17), a unity which is the fruit of Jesus' self-surrender (Jn 11:52). The work accomplished by Christ in the rite, by the very form in which it is structured (*opus operatum*), opens his action to all mankind through the generations, and constitutes the communional framework for Jesus to accomplish the gift of himself (*opus operantis*).

35. See Roberto Vignolo, "La rilevanza del rito nella prassi de Gesù," in *La forma rituale del sacramento: Scienza liturgica e teologia sacramentaria in dialogo*, ed. S. Ubbiali (Rome: CLV-Edizioni liturgiche, 2011), 15–44.

In short, through the Eucharistic rite the Savior inserts his work into the divine initiative and opens it to his brethren.[36] This logic of the rite (its structure as initiated and concluded by God, and as shared with other human beings) is precisely the logic of Jesus' offering on his cross, consummated by the Father when he resurrected the Son; and it is the logic of the acts of those who participate in his sacraments.

From the Rite to the Body: The "Literal Action"

Note that this radical unity between rite and action (because of which it can be said that Jesus "offered himself": Heb 9:14) assumes facts of the Old Testament, yet is novel with respect to it. Certainly, in the Israelite covenant too, as in other religious traditions, rite and human action are linked (see chapter 7, above). Given his incarnate condition, man always acts following furrows plowed by others, which he makes his own. In order to act, he must orient himself in the space of relations in which his body situates him, and find the appropriate rhythm to enter into contact with the things of the world. This gives rise to the need for ritual, which fits man's space and time into their final coordinates in God, the center, source, and destiny of all his relationships. In this way ritual, which is rooted in our corporal condition, illuminates this condition and delves into it.

In order to achieve its end, it is necessary for the ceremony to employ material elements external to the human body. For in the rite we relive those moments in life, such as birth and death, which, being in close relation to our final mystery, prove to be inaccessible directly to our corporal acts. Hence, instead of offering the son, the lamb is offered; instead of giving one's own blood, one sheds that of the animal (see chapter 7, above).

Thus shines forth the novelty of Christ who, offering his own body and blood, radically united his ritual to his action in life. He was able to accomplish such a thing because, through a gift of the Father to his Son, which will be consummated in the resurrection, the signifying and relational capacity of his flesh, on which the Spirit of God came to rest, had been reinvigorated to the utmost. What takes place is thus a radical "corporealization" of the Old Testament rites, which now come to be performed directly on the flesh and blood of a human life.

In this way Jesus leaves to his followers a rite which contains the work accomplished by him (*opus operatum a Christo*) in the flesh, which is therefore capable of touching and transforming our flesh. The Christian ritual action thus associates us with Jesus' action and, from there, with the primacy

---

36. See Réal Tremblay, "Sacramenti e vita morale," *Rivista liturgica* 91 (2004): 381–90, at 388.

of the Father's action and with the communal, participatory dimension of ecclesial activity. Moral action, then, acquires the form given by the sacrament: initiated by the Father, accompanied from within the church, capable of fulfilling our relations with God and our brethren. To follow the sacramental channel is to learn to collaborate with the first initiative of another and in communion with others, in order to expand this same communion.

Note that this framework of the sacramental action does not reduce, but fulfills the original experience of human action. For in our action there is always more than what we have put into it; and for that reason we desire, when we act, more than what we think we desire. This explains the fact that our desires manage to hide from us our true desires. Maurice Blondel formulated this mystery well and offered an insight to clarify it, based on what he called the "literal practice,"[37] that is to say, the obedient execution of a fixed rule or of a rite. Although we may perform this rule or rite without understanding it completely, this practice communicates its form to us, shaping our action according to the rite that is performed, which, in the case of the religious rite, is of divine origin. There is the paradox that by following, so to speak, the literal narrowness of the action, we enter into a realm higher than that of our isolated desire (we enter into the sphere of him who shaped the practice), and our will can expand according to the yearning for the infinite that runs through it. Therefore a practical rite, although it may be performed reluctantly, has a beneficial effect, because it contains what others (and the Other) have left inscribed in this practice, which we appropriate as though by osmosis. Thus the insight of St. Augustine: "the affection of the heart, which preceded so that [these rites] will be performed, grows because they have been performed."[38]

All of this is assumed and fulfilled in the sacraments. They act not only, nor principally, through what we put into them, but through what we receive upon entering into their ritual architecture, which was forged by the life of Jesus, who transmits to us in the rite his openness to the Father and the brethren. The practice, by itself, is not enough, but it is the necessary channel in order for us to reach a love that surpasses us. The Spirit of Jesus desired to pour itself out entirely—this is the baffling Christian truth—in the concrete humility of the flesh, because it is in the flesh that are rooted these relationships that the Spirit, as Spirit of love, wants to enliven. The sacramental path leads, then, so to speak, from the outside in, passing through

37. See Maurice Blondel, *Action (1893): Essay on a Critique of Life and a Science of Practice*, trans. Oliva Blanchette (Notre Dame, Ind.: University of Notre Dame Press, 1984), 373–88.
38. See Augustine, *De cura pro mortuis gerenda* V, 7 (CSEL 41:632).

the flesh—which is also the letter, the formula, the rite—so as to give form to our interiority.[39]

The Rite and the Unity of Our Life Narrative

To everything that has been said, it is necessary to add one last feature of the action accomplished in the rite: its ability to situate man's action *in time,* allowing those who participate *to traverse the stages of both personal and community life.* This time dimension is evident in the rite of Jesus, who assumes the memory of Israel and of creation (past) and anticipates the glorious resurrection (future). Within the rite, then, lies the key to understanding his long journey from the Father to the Father, which is capable of recapitulating the whole of the history of the cosmos, from the alpha to the omega. And so the Christian, when he participates in this rite, will be able to extend it to the totality of his own time, conferring on the stages of his life the same unity of Jesus' time.

This means that the *opus operatum* of the rite opens our momentary action to the totality of history, understood as covenant between God and his people. The distinctive purpose of the rite, therefore, is not to explain the simple instantaneous action, but to articulate our actions in time, widening their scope by directing them toward their final end in God.[40] Therefore participation in the liturgy does not rob us of time, but instead grants time to us, for every one of our moments is supported and strengthened by being threaded onto the great journey of life and history into which the rite leads us.

In this light we can explain the relation between sacraments and life with the help of contemporary philosophy, which reflects on how stories and rites configure our actions in time. Taking Paul Ricoeur as an inspiration, we can speak of a movement in three steps, which carries us from life to the rite and, from the rite, leads back to life so as to enrich it.[41] We have as a first step the writing of the story (tale or novel), which is devised by the writer based on his own life experience. He draws from this experience, purifies it, and clarifies it so as to shape on paper its most basic features. The second step is the act of reading the novel. The reader, who receives the story

---

39. See Maso, *L'efficacia;* Rinaldo Falsini, "Il sacramento tra *ex opere operato* e *ex opere operantis,"* *Rivista di pastorale liturgica* 192 (1995): 17–23; Luigi Girardi, *"Conferma le parole della nostra fede":* Il *linguaggio della celebrazione* (Rome: CLV-Edizioni Liturgiche, 1998); Colman O'Neill, "The Role of the Recipient and Sacramental Signification," *The Thomist* 21, no. 3 (1958): 257–301 and 508–40.

40. See my discussion in chapter 7, above.

41. In this respect the reader may consult Paul Ricoeur, *Temps et récit,* 3 vols. (Paris: Seuil, 1983–85); trans. Kathleen McLaughlin and David Pellauer as *Time and Narrative* (Chicago: University of Chicago Press, 1990).

with his imagination, recreates it, adding the harmonies of his memories and hopes. Finally—the third step—the same reader enriches his daily life based on what he read, increasing his capacity to give a narrative unity to his days.

What has been said about the novel can be transposed to the rite, following the same steps. The rite is, in the first place, *instituted* by Jesus, its author, who condenses in it, based on his earthly life, his route from the Father and toward his brethren. Next (second step) whoever *celebrates* the rite, like whoever reads the novel, creatively takes up the narrative of Jesus, rereading it from the perspective of his own experience. A third moment takes place in daily life when the action performed in the rite expands the vital action of the faithful according to the liturgical celebration. In this way he will now be able to live the rite with more intensity, enriching it, not only for himself, but for this great circle of readers that is the church. The movement passes then, as I have said, from life to the rite, and from the rite it returns to life, in a virtuous cycle, richer and richer through the generations.

The role of the Holy Spirit is essential in this transfer between rite and life, so that the two hands of the Father—the Son and the Spirit—participate in the sacrament. As stated above (chapter 11), the Spirit rested upon Jesus during his mortal days, gradually filling all his actions with glory (chapter 2). Well, then, just as the Spirit transmitted the Son's filial disposition to every situation and stage of his path, filially shaping his flesh, so too the Spirit worked in the Eucharistic rite, communicating the filial and communal features of the rite to the concrete existence of Christ, the anointed one. Thanks to the Spirit, Jesus was able to accomplish in his passion and resurrection what he had celebrated at the Last Supper, thus appropriating existentially his ritual self-surrender. For without the Spirit, the rite, in its rigidity, would prove incapable of adapting to all the particular events of Jesus' life.

Similarly, this same Spirit, which is the "communication of Christ" to Christians, works in the sacraments.[42] Firstly, thanks to the Spirit, the sacramental action not only transmits to us the structure of Jesus' life (the letter of his story), but also makes present the very life of Jesus. In the Spirit, therefore, the rite is already life: the life of Christ. Secondly, the Spirit ensures that the rite is made life in the Christian, so that sacramental space expands to all the corners of his world. This expansion is what I will explore in the next section.

---

42. On the Spirit as *communicatio Christi*, see Irenaeus of Lyons, *Adversus haereses* III, 24, 1 (SC 211:472; ANF 1:458b).

Accompanying the Sacramental Gift

In the sacrament God embraces human action, places it in the communion of the church, and accompanies it along a route of hope. This means that the sacramental event does not merely conclude a path, but above all initiates it: the gift received is a promising gift. This corollary sheds light on the pastoral action of the church, which consists not only of preparing the faithful for the sacramental gift, but also of teaching them to cultivate it so that it bears as much fruit as possible. Recall that the early church's catechesis of initiation did not end with the conferral of baptism. Indeed, the so-called mystagogy (introduction to the mysteries) took place during the days following the celebration. The explanation did not precede but followed the gift received, thus dovetailing with the believers' experience.[43]

Eucharist and Baptism: Faith and Charity

The sacramental celebration extends to all of life starting from the Eucharist. This is because the Eucharist contains, so to speak, the genome of the redemptive action of Jesus. For the Eucharistic rite recapitulates not only the life of the master, but the entire history of the world from beginning to end. Baptism, for its part, brings about the incorporation of the Christian into this Eucharistic path.

In light of this, we understand why the Eucharist became associated with two coordinating axes of Christian life: faith and charity.[44] The connection is already present in St. Ignatius of Antioch: "be renewed in faith, that is the flesh of the Lord, and in love, that is the blood of Jesus Christ."[45] Faith associates us with the body of Jesus, for through faith we profess his coming in the flesh and are incorporated into him. Charity springs from

---

43. See, for example, Ambrose of Milan, *De mysteriis* I, 1–2 (SC 25:108). On mystagogy in the patristic era: Hugh M. Riley, *Christian Initiation: A Comparative Study of the Interpretation of the Baptismal Liturgy in the Mystagogical Writings of Cyril of Jerusalem, John Chrysostom, Theodore of Mopsuestia, and Ambrose of Milan* (Washington, D.C.: The Catholic University of America Press, 1974); Enrico Mazza, *La mistagogia: Una teologia della liturgia in epoca patristica* (Rome: CLV-Edizioni Liturgiche, 1988); Christoph Jacob, "Zur Krise der Mystagogie in der Alten Kirche," *Theologie und Philosophie* 66 (1991): 75–89. On the application of the concept today, there is an extensive bibliography: Herbert Haslinger, "Mystagogie–Relecture eines sakramentenpastoralen Leitbegriffs," *Theologie und Glaube* 101 (2011): 92–122. This author erroneously supposes that mystagogy blurs the objective criteria for admission to the sacraments; I will justify the necessity of these criteria later in this chapter.

44. Augustine, *Contra Faustum* XII, 20 (CSEL 25:349), would also call the Eucharist *sacramentum spei*, the sacrament of hope.

45. Ignatius of Antioch, *Ad Trallians* VIII, 1 (SC 10b:116–18; ANF 1:69); see also *Ad Romans* VII, 3 (SC 10b:136; ANF 1:77a): "I desire the bread of God ... which is the flesh of Jesus Christ, the Son of God, who became afterwards of the seed of David and Abraham, and I desire to drink of God, namely His Blood, which is incorruptible love and eternal life."

his outpoured blood, which hands over to us the incorruptible love of the Spirit. In this way, faith roots the believer in salvation, and charity unfolds his path toward consummation, as Ignatius himself declares in another passage.[46]

St. Augustine also develops the connection between Eucharist and charity.[47] Christ, in offering himself on the cross, is the one who channels all creation into a pilgrimage toward the Father, thus bringing to fulfillment the twofold commandment of charity. Christians are associated with this sacrifice precisely in the Eucharist, where the church offers herself in what she offers on the altar.[48] The sacrament, therefore, gathers up the whole movement of love, which comes from God to creatures and guides them all toward himself so as to fulfill them. This connection with charity allows us to call the Eucharist *sacramentum caritatis* and situates it at the center of Christian action.[49]

From the perspective of the Eucharist, *mysterium fidei* (see 1 Tm 3:9), tradition links faith to baptism also as the moment of the Christian's incorporation into the body of Jesus. St. Ignatius associates faith with a "regeneration," a new birth, alluding thus to the baptism that has been received.[50] Soon baptism was called the "sacrament of faith."[51] The expression does not indicate merely that this rite contains the profession of faith and that it communicates faith to the recipient, but rather that baptism itself teaches us what faith consists of: baptism is the visibility of the faith (its visible sign or sacrament). Thus, according to Tertullian, faith, which was naked in the Old Testament, is manifested in the New through its clothing, baptism, which is *vestimentum fidei*.[52] In this way the Fathers seem to suggest: "Do you want to define faith? Look at baptism." We can say, in conclusion, that faith possesses a sacramental structure.[53]

---

46. See Ignatius of Antioch, *Ad Ephesians* XIV, 1 (SC 10b:82; ANF 1:55): "For the beginning is faith, and the end is love."

47. St. Augustine insists, moreover, on the relation Eucharist-faith: *In Iohannem* XXV, 12 (CCL 36:254): "Utquid paras dentes et ventrem? Crede, et manducasti" (Why do you prepare your teeth and stomach? Believe, and you have eaten); see also *In Iohannis* XXVI, 13 (CCL 36:266): "Qui vult vivere, habet ubi vivat, habet unde vivat. Accedat, credat, incorporetur, ut vivificetur" (He who wants to live has somewhere to live and the wherewithal to live. Let him come, let him believe, let him be incorporated, that he might be enlivened).

48. See Augustine, *De civitate Dei* X, 6 (CCL 47:279; NPNF-I 2:184b).

49. See Thomas Aquinas, *Super IV Sent.*, d. 2, q. 1, a. 2, co. (Parma 7:481).

50. Trallians VIII, 1. *Adversus haereses* III, 17, 2 (SC 211:332; ANF 1:444b–445a), Irenaeus defines the bond between Eucharist and baptism by resorting to a similar bakery image: baptism is the water than makes possible the unity of the mass of dough.

51. See Augustine, *Epistolae* 98, 9 (CSEL 34.2:531).

52. See Tertullian, *De baptismo* XIII, 2 (CCL 1:289; ANF 3:676a): the sacrament is "vestimentum fidei ... quae retro erat nuda" (the clothing ... of the faith which before was bare).

53. See Francis, *Lumen Fidei*, par. 40 (582); the relation faith-sacraments appears in Vatican II,

And indeed, by observing a baptism one understands that faith is, before all else, the birth of a new life—this means that the baptism of infants reveals something essential to all baptism. The rite confers on us, in fact, as when we are born, a new name (which implies a new familial bond and a new destiny), which is the divine name of the Father, Son, and Holy Spirit. Inasmuch as faith assigns us this name, it consists in a radical new belonging to the God revealed by Christ. Moreover, the immersion in water, whereby Jesus associates us with his corporeal death and resurrection, shows that the life of faith affects our body, that is, our way of being situated in the world and of establishing relations. Our faith is not only faith in the incarnation, but also an incarnate faith.[54]

In sum, baptism and the Eucharist set up the pillars so as to be able to extend ritual action to the whole time of life.[55] We find this idea in Hugh of St. Victor: "Through faith we receive union; through charity we receive animation. Thus, in the sacrament, through Baptism we are united; through the body of Christ and His blood we are enlivened. Through Baptism we are made members of the body; and through the body of Christ we become sharers in His life."[56] From this perspective it is easy to look also at confirmation. If baptism reminds us of the original receptivity of our work, the sacrament of the chrism emphasizes that man cooperates with God, so that God's gifts in the believer can grow to full maturity. Indeed, in confirmation St. Thomas perceives with greater clarity that sacramental grace not only heals our sin, but also strengthens our action.[57] And St. Bonaventure, as we know, associates confirmation with hope. For this virtue enables us to anticipate the final end of our life in the risen Christ and, in this way, offers solid support for our journey toward him.[58]

Matrimony and Penance: When Human Action Is Sacramental Action

If the sacraments of initiation branch out into all of life through their connection with faith, hope, and charity, two other sacraments harbor within themselves human action in its creaturely and historical depth: matrimony and penance. Matrimony is unique among the seven sacraments because,

---

which says that the sacraments "not only presuppose faith, but by words and objects they also nourish, strengthen, and express it" (*SSC*, no. 59).

54. See Francis, *Lumen Fidei*, par. 42 (583–84).

55. See Livio Melina, Juan José Pérez-Soba, and José Noriega, *Camminare nella luce dell'amore: I fondamenti della morale cristiana* (Siena: Cantagalli, 2008), 256–59.

56. See Hugh of St. Victor, *De sacramentis christianae fidei* II, 2, 1 (PL 176:416; *CV* 1:336).

57. See Thomas Aquinas, *ST* III, q. 72, a. 1; a. 7, ad 1 and ad 3.

58. See Bonaventure, *Breviloquium* VI, 3 (Quaracchi 5:267).

in order for it to be sacramental, the consent through which the baptized spouses surrender themselves and receive each other is enough, without having to add another word or rite *per se*.[59] Here, then, a human action, belonging to the sphere of creation, is taken up without further ado into the economy of the sacraments. And it is not a matter of just any action, but of the one that in a certain way offers the original framework for the other actions that man accomplishes on earth. If we think about the importance that the matrimonial promise has in giving consistency and unity to life; about the value of conjugal love for the education of children, who gain confidence to act because they are witnesses of their parents' fidelity; about the fundamental character of the conjugal life as a means of building up the common good and society, and so on—if we think about all this, we understand that the presence of matrimony among the seven sacraments invites us to include every action of the Christian in the sacramental sphere. It is not surprising that St. Bonaventure set the institution of matrimony in the paradise of Eden itself, when God led Eve into the presence of Adam, who had just awakened.[60]

Something similar happens in penance. It is remarkable that the medieval tradition treats together the virtue of penance and the sacrament of penance.[61] Penance is a sacrament in which God grants us forgiveness; but at the same time it is a virtue, that is, a stable disposition for action, a rational order of our affectivity which moves us to perform good acts—in this case, to abhor our own sin and to cling to the good. For medieval theologians, these two aspects of penance—virtue and sacrament—are inseparable. And this is because the matter of the sacrament of penance consists precisely of the acts of the penitent: the way in which he narrates his life, admitting his guilt, and reopens his future by means of satisfaction for his sins.

This perspective sheds light on what a virtue is, given that it forms part of the sacrament: not man's isolated effort to be just, but the new abilities to act that the gift of a new love arouses within us. On the other hand, we also understand better what the sacrament is, given that it contains within itself a free human act: in the sacrament there is no unilateral concession of a divine favor, but rather a synergetic encounter of God with man in which the working of the creature is seriously assumed.

It should be noted, both in matrimony and in penance, that the sacra-

---

59. See Granados, *Una sola carne.*

60. See Bonaventure, *In IV Sent.*, d. 26, a. 1, q. 2, resp. (Quaracchi 4:664).

61. See Gilles Emery, "Reconciliation with the Church and Interior Penance: The Contribution of Thomas Aquinas on the Question of the *Res et Sacramentum* of Penance," *Nova et Vetera* 1, no. 2 (2003): 283–302.

ment embraces the person's whole narrative, going beyond the moment of the celebration. In matrimony this occurs because of the marriage vows, a promise that embraces the entire life of the spouses. For someone can promise only if he can remember (and thus will not forget the promise) and is able to anticipate his future, come what may (thus saying: "I will be with you always"). Penance, too, expands in time, for time is necessary in order to admit guilt and set out on the road to forgiveness, thus recovering the narrative unity of life that had been broken by sin.

The anointing of the sick is also a witness to this link between sacrament and human action. For in it, the rite embraces the time of sickness, a time that, by placing us before death, is so special and so necessary in order to understand the totality of human life. This particular time has in fact been described as the one most propitious for exercising the will, for it is the time of trial, when the original promise which every human being experiences upon coming into this world seems to be denied categorically.[62] The anointing, then, in light of Jesus' *todah* or praise of the Father before he entered into his passion, strengthens the sick person's ability to remember the primordial and promising goodness of God, to trust in him, and to remain faithful in hope, thus opening up toward light and life.

Sacraments and Practical Reason

Christian initiation, the foundation of the sacramental life, is associated, according to what I have said, with the theological virtues, the foundation of human action. Other sacraments, such as matrimony and penance, take up within themselves the daily action of the faithful. All this frames the question about the way in which the sacraments animate moral life.

A human being is called to order his actions so that they lead him to the final destination of his journey, which is union with God. In order to be guided to this final destination, a fundamental choice is necessary, whereby we adhere radically to God for our fulfillment and happiness.[63] So then, Christ, in baptism, by incorporating us into himself and giving us his friendship, enables us to anchor our route to this final destination of communion with God. In this way, the destination is no longer a distant ideal, because the sacrament has transformed our life, introducing us into the filial dynamism of Jesus. We can now enjoy a foretaste of this destination through connaturality, so that it attracts us forcefully from the depths of our desire.

---

62. See Giuseppe Angelini, *La malattia, un tempo per volere: saggio di filosofia morale* (Milan: Vita e pensiero, 2000).

63. See John Paul II, *Veritatis Splendor*, par. 66.

This orientation toward the final goal, even though it fixes our intention on the proper good, is not enough to govern life. It is also necessary to order every one of our choices so that they lead us toward the destination. For, according to the structure of human action, in order to direct the intention toward the end, we must choose other intermediate actions, which I will call practical operable goods [*bienes operables*]. These are built by practical reason, whose function it is to guide moral action.[64] The task of practical reason consists in offering a kind of knowledge directed toward action, which permits us to choose those practical operable goods which build up our love of God and neighbor. The perfection of practical reason is the virtue of prudence, so that we might work in all things in accordance with the intelligence of love.[65] We should ask ourselves, then: how do the sacraments affect this prudent exercise of practical reason?

In order to answer, it is necessary to remember that practical reason does not act in the abstract, but always from the perspective of our incarnate situation, that is, from our concrete placement in the world and among human beings. Especially important, as the basis on which practical reason may direct us to action, are the affections. And this is because the affections enable us to enjoy the goodness of things through connaturality with them. Thanks to the affections, goods are perceived as goods advantageous to the person (and not just goods in the abstract), so that they concretely move the person to act.

Well, then, as we know, the sacraments bestow on us a new membership in Christ and in the church. Through them we are rooted in the corporeal situation that Jesus experienced and left to his followers. We have thus received a new relational background (based on the character: see chapter 12), on which the love of Christ, his Holy Spirit, can be poured out, so as to form our affectivity according to the affectivity of Jesus. This new body and these new affections are like a new substrate of our free actions; from this vantage point, practical reason can perceive as advantageous the goods that lead us with Christ to the Father, and can choose them. Through the sacrament, therefore, his Spirit works within us so that we follow God by fulfilling his will, "whether we eat or drink, or whatever we do" (see 1 Cor 10:31). Thus, the ultimate end of union with the Father turns into the end of every one of our works, as was the case in the life of Jesus. Thanks to the

---

64. See Thomas Aquinas, *ST* I-II, qq. 12–13; cf. José Noriega, "Movidos por el Espíritu," in *La plenitud del obrar cristiano*, ed. Livio Melina, J. José Pérez-Soba, and José Noriega (Madrid: Palabra, 2006), 183–200.

65. See Livio Melina, *La conoscenza morale: Linee di riflessione sul Commento di san Tommaso all'Etica Nicomachea* (Rome: Città Nuova, 1987).

sacraments, moreover, our action, by being affectively rooted in Jesus and in the church, will always be a common act, performed out of harmony with our brethren, directed toward goods that hold us together.

Why, from this perspective, is the range of seven sacraments necessary? Thanks to this variety, the fundamental choice of our final end is specified for each different area of human life. The choice that every sacramental rite involves, together with the particular gift of the Spirit that it bestows on us, configure our affectivity according to the basic human goods, which are always ordered to the final end. Therefore the sacraments accompany all the stages of the journey. The specification given by matrimony, for example, is that from the wedding on, the final end of communion with God will be achieved for the spouses through their mutual relation and through the procreation and education of children. And holy orders, to give another example, specifies for the priest the final end of his life in terms of his conformity with the paternity of Jesus, which I will discuss in the next chapter.

Sacraments, Virtues, and Christian Culture

The link between the sacraments and human action is strengthened when these are associated not only with faith, hope, and charity, but also with the cardinal virtues.[66] As I have already noted, Alexander of Hales, later followed by Bonaventure and Thomas Aquinas, paired the two lists.[67] What are the consequences of linking virtues and sacraments? Although certainly the equivalence elaborated by medieval theologians can prove to be a bit artificial, it still can help us consider the basic intention that guided them.

The Middle Ages assumed the Greek doctrine of the virtues with the end of developing a Christian culture that integrated within itself the various dimensions of human existence. This is because the virtues embrace the totality of life, orienting it toward its fullness; and they include life in a communal tradition, placing it at the service of the common good.[68] Therefore only through the virtues does faith fully take root in human life (which runs through history and is communal) and does evangelization reach its fullness.

To link the virtues to the sacraments means, therefore, in the first place, to extend them to the whole course of life. For the virtues make sense only if there is a shared vision of what a flourishing human existence is; and in

66. I will discuss the harmony among the seven sacraments in chapter 15.

67. See Alexander of Hales, *Glossa in quatuor libros Sententiarum* IV, d. 3, nn. 2–3 (BFSMA XV [Quaracchi, 1957], 47–48).

68. Here I follow the diagnosis by Alasdair MacIntyre, *After Virtue: A Study in Moral Theory* (Notre Dame, Ind.: University of Notre Dame Press, 1984), 165–80.

order for this vision to exist, it is necessary to offer a unifying narrative of our days, with a beginning and an end. In this light it is interesting, as I have noted, that St. Thomas links the sacraments to every stage of life, inasmuch as the sacraments contain the fulfilled narrative of any human existence.

Moreover, and in the second place, the virtues, which need a community in order to be practiced and a tradition in order to be inherited and transmitted, are resources for building the common good of the church. And in this they accord with the sacramental action, which is always a communal action, performed within the body of Christ. Recall in this regard the saying of Augustine: "men cannot be joined under the name of any religion ... unless they are bound by some partnership of visible signs or sacraments."[69] The sacraments offer, then, the basis whereby men may act in harmony of heart.

In our contemporary situation, the loss of the virtues as a reference for moral action has led to an emotivism which concentrates such action in the ephemeral moment, and judges everything from the perspective of isolated subjectivity. Recovering the sacraments and uniting them to virtuous action becomes urgent, therefore, so as to confer narrative unity on the life of the person and of society. Only in this way will it be possible to build a Christian culture which serves as a foundation and horizon for the new evangelization. Having explored how the sacrament founds and strengthens moral action and guides it to its end, I can now enumerate the milestones of an adequate preparation to receive them.

Preparation to Receive the Sacrament

Given that human action participates in sacramental action, it will always be necessary to prepare oneself to receive the sacrament fruitfully. This is the only way to make sure, on the one hand, that the person does not place an impediment (*obex*) to the action of grace within him. Another benefit is that he will receive the divine gift more fully, according to the measure of his faith.[70]

Note that this road toward the sacrament is already in some way under the influence of the sacrament that will be received. In other words, one does not only travel a path prior to the action of Jesus, as if the path were to be traveled without depending on him, apart from the sacramental logic. In order to understand this, it helps to consider the path of the Old Testament,

---

69. See Augustine, *Contra Faustum* XIX, 11 (CSEL 25:510).
70. See Origen, *In Matthaeum* XI, 14 (SC 162:347).

which not only was always oriented toward Christ already, but also was preceded by Jesus, inasmuch as he is the firstborn of all creatures and the summit to which the Father's plan pointed from the beginning. Similarly, each time we encounter Christ in the sacrament, we discover that he was already there from the beginning, guiding the path, and that everything good that we sensed from the beginning is received and confirmed in him.

To give an overview of the path of preparation it is important to keep in mind the order in which the sacraments are received. Baptism, the doorway, is necessary in order to be admitted to the rest, because with it we are born into the body of Christ and are enabled to receive other gifts from God.[71] Penance reincorporates us into this visible body of Christ, and therefore it is a preliminary step, if one has committed grave sin, in order to approach the remaining sacraments.[72] Baptism and penance are known as "sacraments of the dead," because they give divine life to those who receive them. The rest are "sacraments of the living," because they presuppose the state of grace if they are to be received fruitfully. I will now examine two specific questions regarding this preparation: the dispositions necessary to receive the sacrament, and the possibility of receiving the sacrament *in voto* or "by desire."

Conditions for Receiving the Sacrament

Coherence between sacramental action and Christian life implies that the subject is well disposed to celebrate the sacrament. The baptismal scrutinies from olden days show great concern with making the sacrament the initiation to a good life.[73] The *Apostolic Tradition* of Hippolytus, for example, calls for the abandonment of sinful professions: idol-makers, pimps, gladiators, magicians, etc.[74] St. Cyril of Jerusalem recalls that before baptism the candidate must expressly reject the pomps of the devil, and he describes how the catechumen turned from west to east, that is, from the demon and the darkness toward Christ and the light.[75] With respect to the Eucharist, St. Justin teaches that only those can participate in it who, having already re-

---

71. See Jerome, *In Sophoniam* I (CCL 76A:441): "per has enim duas portas baptismi et paenitentiae in hierusalem, id est in ecclesiam dei uel introitus uel reditus est" (for through these two doors, baptism and penance, one enters or returns to Jerusalem, that is, the Church of God).

72. See Council of Trent, Session XIII, *Decree on the Eucharist*, chap. 7 (DH 1647).

73. See Augustine, *Sermo* 216, 6 (PL 38:1080).

74. See Hippolytus of Rome, *Traditio Apostolica* XV–XVI (SC 11:69–74).

75. See Cyril of Jerusalem, *Catecheses* I, 9 (SC 126:98–100); the same Cyril (II–IV; PG 33:335–41) reprimands the curious, who come only to pry into what baptism consists of; and later, against sinners, he uses the parable of the man invited to the wedding feast who did not come properly clothed: upon entering the church and observing what garments are customary there, he ought to have learned during the time of the catechumenate to prepare himself properly. Tertullian, for his part, recommends the confession of sins before baptism; see *De Baptismo* XX, 1 (CCL 1:294).

ceived baptism, profess the doctrine proclaimed by Jesus and live according to what the master taught us.[76]

The necessary preparation explains the long catechumenate that developed after Christianity became an official religion, when many who sought to be admitted continued to live in a way contrary to the gospel.[77] This forbearing catechumenate supposed a period of time without a fixed term, for it was adapted to the person's progressive conversion. It was thus distinguished from another, immediate catechumenate, limited to the Lenten season, for those whose situation in life did not contradict the teaching of Jesus.

Even though this preparation was required, it was well known that the saving power was in the sacrament, and not in human action. St. Cyril of Jerusalem, for example, who asks of the catechumen a good intention in order to approach baptism, ceaselessly reminds him that, if he is found among this number, it is because of the power of the cross.[78] Why, then, is this period of exercise required, given that man's works cannot save him? In the first place, because he could close himself off from the divine action, which would render the sacrament ineffective or even nonexistent. In the second place, because the grace of God will bear more fruit the better disposed the person is.

Earlier in this chapter, I discussed the historical background in which the question arose concerning the minimum required for the sacrament to have its effect: was the baptism received by heretics and schismatics valid? A similar question was applied to the Catholic believer: what would happen if someone approached baptism without the right dispositions, lacking faith or living a wicked life? St. Augustine answers, as we know, that the baptism is valid and that there is no need to repeat it; although it will not profit the one who receives it.[79] The Middle Ages inherit and clarify the Augustinian vision, delving into the doctrine of the sacramental character. It remains clear that some sacraments confer the character even on those who reject the faith or live dissolutely, although in these cases they will not give grace or be profitable for salvation.

Going deeper still, the medieval theologians wonder: is some minimal

76. See Justin Martyr, *1 Apologiae* 66, 1 (PTS 38:129; ANF 1:185b).

77. On the baptismal catechumenate, see Gerard A. M. Rouwhorst, "Christian Initiation in Early Christianity," *Questions liturgiques et paroissiales* 87 (2006): 100–119; Paul F. Bradshaw, "The Gospel and the Catechumenate in the Third Century," *Journal of Theological Studies* 50, no. 1 (1999): 143–52; Giuseppe Groppo, "L'evoluzione del catecumenato nella Chiesa antica dal punto di vista pastorale," *Salesianum* 41, no. 2 (1979): 235–55; Aimé-Georges Martimort, "Les rites du Baptême à la lumière de l'histoire," in his *Les signes de la nouvelle alliance* (Paris: Ligel, 1966), 143–52; Michel Dujarier, *Le parrainage des adultes aux trois premiers siècles de l'Église; recherche historique sur l'évolution des garanties et des étapes catéchuménales avant 313* (Paris: Cerf, 1962).

78. See Cyril of Jerusalem, *Catecheses* XIII, 40 (PG 33:820).

79. See Augustine, *In Iohannem* VI, 13 (CCL 36:60).

condition necessary in the subject, even to receive the character? And they answer, yes, because he ought at least to accomplish a human act. Innocent III considers the case of someone who is baptized while feigning (*ficte*), that is, who performs the exterior rite but does not have faith or is living in sin.[80] The pope considers the baptism valid, but requires that he at least have the intention of receiving it. What intention does he mean? On this subject theologians debate at length.[81] Although the terminology changes, in general it is accepted that a *positive intention* is required (it is not enough to be indifferent), and at least an *implicit intention* (desire to do what the church does or what Jesus instituted).[82] In most of the sacraments a *habitual intention* is sufficient (an intention that was formed and not retracted); in penance and matrimony the subject ought to have a *virtual intention* (that is to say, directed to this specific occasion) although it may be lacking at some moment of the celebration because the subject is distracted (thus it is distinguished from an *actual intention*).

Having set this minimum, one might wonder: how can the sacraments be conferred validly (and imprint the character) if the one who receives them lacks faith? Is that not to accept a certain automatism which does not take human participation into account? To respond one must remember, first, that faith has a communal structure, in other words, it is not measured solely by considering the individual. It comes to us, like other essential things in life, based on the relations in which we participate and live. This explains, for example, why an infant can be baptized in the faith of the church. He lives in relation to those who generated him and have welcomed him into life, and he thus participates in a communion from which he obtains his name and his destiny. Inasmuch as faith is set upon this same filial background, the infant can be received in the faith of others (in the faith of the Church) and can participate in it.

Certainly, someone will say: this works for the child, but not for an adult who freely rejects faith. To which we must answer with the poet: "no man is an island." Life continually flows to all human beings from the relations in which they live. And through these relations which constitute him, the adult, too, can be received in some way into the world of faith, further than he knows or desires. As a matter of fact, it is up to the rite and its ob-

---

80. See Innocent III, *Maiores Ecclesiae Causas* (1201) (DH 781).

81. See Van Roo, *De sacramentis*, 192; Albert Michel, "Si l'intention de recevoir un sacrement comme *rite sacré institué par le Christ* est nécessaire à la validité, comment admettre que la foi ne soit pas nécessaire?," *Amicler* 74 (1964): 523.

82. I will go into this question in more detail in the next chapter, when I discuss the intention that is required of the minister.

jective performance to bring about this relational, communal structure of faith. Therefore, to accept the rite, to accomplish it literally, desiring to do what the church does, is to accept implicitly her mediation and thus to be open to the influence of her faith. Certainly this faith is foreign to this baptized person (who does not embrace it personally). However, paraphrasing St. Augustine, we can add: *aliena est, sed materna est*. It is foreign, but it is not totally foreign, because it is maternal, it is the faith of mother church.[83] And every human being can receive it inasmuch as he has been and is, in his most original experience, the child of a mother, and he carries this receptivity engraved at the center of his person.

The situation is different when we consider the conditions for the sacrament to bear fruit, that is, for it effectively to enliven the one who receives it. Here more is demanded on the part of the subject, for the fruit consists precisely in a personal friendship with God, which cannot be experienced if someone is closed to it. We will always be the children of our parents, even though we may reject our father's house; but we will be good children only if we gratefully and cordially accept the name and surname that have been given to us as a founding pillar of our identity and life.

We already know the formula of Trent whereby the sacraments confer grace on someone who "does not place an obstacle" or impediment in the way.[84] While this doctrine insists that a human being is not the cause of his own salvation, it points out at the same time his necessary openness and willingness to embrace grace. In fact, the same Council had described, in its sixth session, the preparatory steps of justification.[85] The theologians after Trent specified further what it means "not to place an obstacle." For the sacraments of the dead (baptism and penance, which confer friendship with God), someone who does not reject mortal sin places an obstacle. For the sacraments of the living (which are received in friendship with God) the obstacle is produced by someone who is conscious of living in mortal sin.[86]

"Not to place an obstacle" means, therefore: the recipient is called to open up in vigilant hope of the divine action, and to admit that he finds himself empty and in need of it.[87] It is his duty to plow the earth, laying

83. See Augustine, *Contra Iulianum opus imperfectum* I, 28 (CSEL 85.1:40). The statement appears in the context of original sin, which affects us even though it is not our own: "aliena sunt, sed paterna sunt, ac per hoc iure seminationis atque germinationis et nostra sunt" ([these sins] are not our own, but they are paternal, and therefore by the law of begetting and sprouting they are ours too).

84. See Council of Trent, Session VII, *Decree on the Sacraments in General*, canon 6 (DH 1606).

85. See Council of Trent, Session VI, *Decree on Justification*, chap. 6 (DH 1526–27).

86. See Aldama, *Sacrae theologiae summa*, 67; Van Roo, *De sacramentis*, 193. For Van Roo, a lack of faith (that is, a lack of *fides informis* or unformed faith), hope, and attrition is an *obex* in the sacraments of the dead.

87. See Johann Adam Möhler, *Neue Untersuchungen der Lehrgegensätze zwischen den Katholiken*

out its furrows, knowing that God is the one who sows the seed and makes it grow. Note that this does not mean a passive attitude, but rather one that is receptive, welcoming, permeated with the desire for the divine gifts. And do not forget either that the grace given to someone who does not place an obstacle regenerates this person's love, so that he may be able to work from now on in synergy with it.

Someone who receives the sacrament while entrenched behind an impediment (*obex*) is said to receive it in a feigned way (*fictus*) inasmuch as it seems that he approaches to receive the gift, but has his fists clenched so that it does not fit into his hands.[88] Let us add that the formula "not to place an obstacle" can apply in a broader sense to the reception of the sacramental character. In this case someone who does not harbor even an intention to carry out the rite as the church performs it, places an impediment.

This conclusion helps the believer to discern whether or not he is properly disposed to approach the sacrament, as St. Paul had already warned concerning the Eucharist (1 Cor 11:28). Another question arises in this respect: should the church herself in some cases postpone admission to the sacrament until the person is properly disposed? The question now is framed not from the perspective of the person who approaches the rite after examining his life but rather from the viewpoint of the church and her discipline, which is based on the gospel. Indeed, Jesus grants authority to the community to verify whether someone has strayed from it and to act accordingly (see Mt 18:15–18).

In the answer it is necessary to distinguish between hidden sins and manifest sins. When a sin is hidden, that is to say, when it does not affect the visible body of the church, it is the responsibility of the one who receives the sacrament to know whether he can approach it worthily. But if it is a matter of a manifest, obstinate sin, which he does not want to renounce, the church herself, in her minister, is the one who cannot admit the person, because of her adherence to the gospel of Jesus.[89]

Indeed, as we have seen from the beginning of this treatise, the sacrament is not a mere intimate encounter of a human being with God (in his conscience or in his private feelings) but the adoption of the relational space which Christ inaugurated in his flesh so as to be able to receive his Spirit.

---

und Protestanten (Regensburg: Verlags-Anstalt Manz, 1893), 276; Finkenzeller, *Die Lehre von den Sakramenten*, 138.

88. See Thomas Aquinas, *ST* III, q. 69, a. 9, ad 3: "Fictus dicitur aliquis ex eo quod demonstrat se aliquid velle quod non vult" (A man is said to be insincere who makes a show of willing what he wills not).

89. See *Codex Iuris Canonici* [hereafter *CIC*] 915.

Someone who is living in manifest sin has settled into a way of initiating relations and structuring the narrative of his life which is contrary to the one that Jesus practiced during his life, which he communicates to us in the sacrament. It would be contradictory if, on the one hand, the person did not want to abandon a relational space contrary to Jesus, and, on the other hand, he wanted to adopt the relational space of Jesus, into which we are incorporated by the sacred rite.

Therefore, if the church were to admit that person, this would only lead to evils, for him and for the church. It would do violence to the person, by trying to impose on him the way of living relations, contained in the sacrament, to which he does not wish to conform;[90] and it would not respect God's sacramental method, which regenerates first the visible relations in the flesh, conforming them to Jesus' way of living his relationships, so that the Spirit of Jesus may be able to descend on them. In addition, the church would betray her profession of faith, because she would commit a "falsehood in the sacramental signs,"[91] which are a visible expression of this faith; and finally, by granting a citizenship card to sin, the ecclesial environment and the common good of the church would be damaged, harming those who inhabit it.

The Sacrament *in voto*

Within the context of preparation for the sacrament, another question arises: is it possible to receive sacramental grace even if the rite is not celebrated? Under certain conditions the answer is yes, which leads us to talk about a sacrament *in voto*, or of desire. This topic highlights the link between moral action and sacramental action, because they can come to have the same effects; and it prompts us to formulate a question: what novelty, then, does the celebration of the rite bring about?

The Gospels testify to the necessity of the sacraments for salvation: "he who believes and is baptized will be saved" (Mk 16:16). At the same time, the converse refers only to faith, not to baptism: "he who does not believe will be condemned" (Mk 16:16). The church understands that baptism is necessary for salvation; but she also knows that, when baptism cannot be performed due to reasons apart from the subject, God counts it as fact. St. Augustine gives the example of the good thief, who arrived in paradise without baptism. Although the bishop of Hippo would later doubt whether or not he was baptized (could the water flowing from the side of Christ have

---

90. See Thomas Aquinas, *ST* III, q. 68, a. 5, ad 3.
91. See ibid., a. 4, resp.

splashed him?), he thinks that, even if he were not baptized, he did attain salvation.[92] The thief would have been saved, not by the baptism of water, but by his faith and his conversion. The same applied to the catechumens who die before baptism and to the martyrs who were not baptized.

The Middle Ages followed the line of thought initiated by the Fathers. Innocent II examines the case of a pious priest who dies without baptism: he can be saved.[93] Innocent III comments on the story of a Jew who baptized himself: although it was not a valid baptism, he would go to heaven if he died, because, without "the sacrament of faith" he had "faith in the sacrament."[94] Peter Lombard distinguishes three situations: there are those who receive the sacrament but not the grace, because they are not properly disposed; there are those who receive grace by means of the sacrament, and this is the ordinary way; and there are also (our case) those who without celebrating the sacrament attain the grace.[95] This last situation is possible, according to Lombard, because "God did not bind his power to his sacraments" (*Deus potentiam suam sacramentis non alligavit*).[96] In light of this, medieval theologians speak about a threefold baptism: baptism of water (*fluminis*) which is sacramental; baptism of blood (*sanguinis*), that is, martyrdom; and baptism of fire (*flaminis*), the one that interests us here, in other words, in the Spirit—this is the baptism that is received through having charity or through contrition of the heart.[97]

A doubt arises, then: does this not make the sacraments superfluous, as their effect can be received without passing through them? Medieval theologians clarify that the sacrament is received *in voto* only if someone wants to celebrate it but it is impossible for him to do so. They had very much in mind an Augustinian maxim: "what you want to do and cannot, God counts as done."[98] Thus, in every case, the effect of grace passes through the sacrament inasmuch as eagerness to receive it is required. If such a requirement is rejected, grace could not come to us. Therefore Trent defines that the sacraments are necessary for salvation, at least *in voto*.[99]

---

92. See Augustine, *De Baptismo* XXII, 29 (CSEL 51:257); cf. *Retractiones* II, 44 (CSEL 36:152).

93. See Innocent II, *Apostolicam Sedem* (DH 741); for the following discussion of the Middle Ages, see Artur Michael Landgraf, "Das sacramentum *in voto*," in his *Dogmengeschichte der Frühscholastik* (Regensburg: Pustet, 1954), 3.1:210–53.

94. See Innocent III, *Debium pastoralis officii*, 1206 (DH 788).

95. See Peter Lombard, *Sent.* IV, d. 4, c. 1, n. 1 (SpBon V:251).

96. See ibid., d. 1, c. 5, n. 5 (SpBon V:235).

97. See Bonaventure, *In IV Sent.*, d. 4, p. 2, a. 1, q. 1 (Quaracchi 4:106–7).

98. See Augustine, *Enarrationes in psalmos* LVII, 3 (CCL 39:6; NPNF-I 8:231a): "Quidquid vis et non potest, factum Deus computat" (Whatever thou willest and canst not, for done God doth count it). St. Augustine refers in this context to works of iniquity.

99. See Council of Trent, Session VII, *Decree on the Sacraments*, canon 4 (DH 1604): "sine eis

This doctrine can be applied also to those who, by no fault of their own, have not encountered Christ and have not approached baptism and the other sacraments, but would have done so had they known about them. God can save them apart from the sacraments, inasmuch as it is supposed that this desire would have existed if they had acquired knowledge about baptism.[100]

Note that the possibility of being saved without carrying out the rite does not imply that redemption is extra-sacramental. Recall, indeed, that the meaning of the rite springs from the language of the body of Christ, into which the Christian is incorporated. Hence a person's salvation does not occur in the hidden depths of the soul, but always in a corporeal way, that is, through our relations with the world and other human beings. The rite can be lacking; what cannot be lacking is the corporeal assimilation to Jesus and to his brethren. If every man of good will manages to be saved, it is because the Spirit grants to him that he may be connected in some way to the Paschal mystery so as to add him to the people of God.[101] Therefore, in the end, those who enter into the Kingdom will do so by participating in a sacramental body, configured to that of Christ.[102] And already in this life, therefore, they participate somehow in Jesus' way of relating, which is present as a seed in the original experiences of every human being and in the different cultures.

From this perspective it must be said that the logic of the sacraments, or rather, the communication of grace through the relations rooted in the flesh of Jesus, is the only one chosen by God to bring us to himself. And that it becomes true (in this broad sense) that *God has bound his grace to his sacraments*. The reason for this is that it befits the sanctity and justice of the human being, a corporeal creature called to glorification in his flesh. This is an absolute necessity on man's part (*ex parte subjecti*) in what concerns not the performance of the rite, but the entrance in the relational space of Jesus,

---

aut eorum voto" (without the sacraments or the desire for them). When we speak about the necessity of the sacraments this is understood, not as an obligation that constrains God, but rather on the part of man, who must be saved: *ex parte subiecti*. This is a necessity of means and of precept (*necessitas medii et praecepti*), in other words, the sacraments are necessary not only because God commands them, but also because they are the suitable means through which he transmits his grace in order to save the man formed of clay.

100. Some have spoken, in this case, about an *intentio interpretativa*; it is assumed that, because certain conditions were present, the intention existed: see Doronzo, *De sacramentis in genere*, 345.

101. See Vatican Council II, *Gaudium et Spes* [hereafter *GS*], December 7, 1965, no. 22; available at www.vatican.va.

102. For this reason Fulgentius of Ruspe, *De fide* 43 (CCL 91A:875) already said that the sacraments were instituted by Christ for the purpose of faith in his incarnation (*quae ad fidem incarnationis suae Christus instituit*).

the only Savior. In short, God's ransom of those who are his own always follows a sacramental logic, even if the sacrament does not take place.

"'Are you able to drink the chalice that I drink, or to be baptized with the baptism with which I am baptized?' And they said to Him: 'We can!'" (Mk 10:38). The enthusiastic answer of the sons of Zebedee expresses great confidence in human action. They do not know it yet, but this "being able" is possible thanks to the sacraments suggested in Jesus' question: the baptism and the chalice. By entering into them, as we have seen in this chapter, the disciples will be able to participate in Christ's action. Only then will there be foundations for the hope which they expressed when they answered "we can!"

14   MINISTRY

Sacramental Fatherhood

The sacraments are received from others: we are baptized, confirmed, and anointed by priests. This reminds us that we do not obtain grace through a direct divine infusion: it comes to us through an encounter with Jesus who calls us, touches us, and transforms us.[1] An integral part of the sacraments is, therefore, the minister. Reflecting on his role, we will illuminate his identity also: someone who, by representing Jesus, becomes a living channel of God's grace. In this chapter, after distilling the biblical message, I will review the theological tradition so as then to propose a synthesis based on the experience of fatherhood.

The Minister, from the Perspective of the Eucharist: Biblical Testimony

The New Testament writings present a ministry, for instance St. Paul's, which in preaching the gospel actualizes the saving work of Jesus on the cross and in his resurrection.[2] As I already showed (see chapter 13, above), the priestly vocabulary that Paul applies to Christ's offering is used also to describe the apostle's mission. Hence he presents himself as a liturgist of Jesus Christ for the sacred service of the gospel (see Rom 15:15–16).

This public ministry, entrusted to him by God, consists not only of transmitting a message, but also of reliving the Paschal power of Christ in Paul's activity and sufferings. Therefore the apostolic word is not just the teaching of ideas, but rather an event that occurs in history in order to make the "mystery" present: the fulfillment of God's hidden plan that culminates

---

1. See Johann-Baptist Umberg, "Sacramenta alii conficiunt, alii suscipiunt," *Periodica* 21 (1932): 74–88.

2. See Heinrich Schlier, "Grundelemente des priesterlichen Amtes im Neuen Testament," *Theologie und Philosophie* 44 (1969): 161–80.

in the cross and glorification of Jesus. Hence Paul describes his commission as follows: "stewardship of the mysteries of God" (see 1 Cor 4:1–2), mysteries that he proclaims not with human wisdom, but rather in the glory and power of the Spirit (see 1 Cor 2:1–5). The apostle places this priestly task, which is performed in preaching, at the service of another sacrifice, that of the faithful, about which he speaks in Romans 12:1–2: "present your bodies as a living sacrifice, holy and acceptable to God." Therefore he teaches the Christians of Philippi that he pours out his blood upon "the sacrificial offering of your faith" (Phil 2:17).

What is the origin of this way of speaking about ministry? In the previous chapter, we saw that it is a distinctive feature of the New Testament to connect worship with other vital activities: "Whether you eat or drink, or whatever you do, do all to the glory of God" (1 Cor 10:31). We saw that precisely the Eucharist, which Jesus closely associated to his death and resurrection, makes possible such a transfer of cultic terms to everyday life. In other words, a new language is justified based on a new liturgical experience inaugurated by Christ at the Last Supper. In light of this, it is revealing that cultic terminology is also applied to the whole activity of ministers, to their preaching and to their hardships for the sake of the Gospel. So we recognize the Eucharistic background of the apostolic commission, although it does not appear as plainly connected with presiding at the Eucharist.[3] In order to see this Eucharistic background it is enough to list several features that distinguish the minister.

In the first place, it is up to him to proclaim the gospel in such a way that the death and resurrection of Jesus is made present in his preaching. His word, as we pointed out, is an efficacious word, which recalls and actualizes the Paschal event.[4] In this way preaching follows the same logic as the Eucharistic rite, as the apostle to the Gentiles teaches: "As often as you eat this bread ... *you proclaim* the Lord's death" (1 Cor 11:26). The proclamation of the word and the celebration of the sacrament share one and the same structure.

Moreover, in Paul's description of the body of Christ, the apostolic ministry corresponds to a task that is of capital importance, because it is the first of the charisms that edify, followed by the charisms of prophecy and teaching (see 1 Cor 12:28). This fact is crucial if we recall that this description of

---

3. See however Acts 20:7–11, where Paul is the one who preaches and breaks the bread; cf. Schlier, "Grundelemente des priesterlichen Amtes," 175; and André Feuillet, *Le sacerdoce du Christ et de ses ministres d'après la prière sacerdotale du quatrième évangile et plusieurs données parallèles du Nouveau Testament* (Paris: Téqui, 1972).

4. See Schlier, "Grundelemente des priesterlichen Amtes," 166.

the church-body has its origin in the Lord's Supper, where believers become one as the bread is one (see 1 Cor 10:17).

Note, finally, that the election of the Twelve Apostles as a symbol of the new people is sealed precisely at the Last Supper, the place where the church is born, as the people of God was born when it sacrificed the Passover lamb and on Mt. Sinai. The Twelve are established as pillars of the new Israel based on the offering of the new covenant.

This confirms that the Eucharist is found at the root of apostolic ministry. Later texts, such as the pastoral letters, already present this structured ministry: it is received through the laying on of hands (1 Tm 4:14; 2 Tm 1:6) and it entails a specific authority over the community. For us it is interesting to note that administering the sacraments is among its functions. Thus baptism is conferred by the apostles (Mt 28:18–20; Acts 2:41; 16:15, 33; 1 Cor 1:14–17) and by the deacons (Acts 6:8; 8:12–13, 38); it is up to the apostles to impose hands so that the Spirit might descend (Acts 8:14–17; 19:1–6); penance is reserved to the priests (see Jn 20:23; 1 Tm 5:20–22), as is the anointing of the sick (Jas 5:14); for ordination to the ministry, the apostles impose hands (Acts 6:6; 1 Tm 4:14; 2 Tm 1:6); and so on. This connection between ministry and sacraments has its logic, inasmuch as the sacraments, as we know, transpose participation in the Eucharistic body (the key of ministry) into the different times and situations of life and of the community.

The Minister's Goodness and Faith

Based on this biblical reflection the early church testifies to a constant practice: no one administers the sacraments to himself.[5] This is an undisputed fact, which only needed the confirmation of the Magisterium in the Middle Ages. Innocent III, for example, considers the baptism of a Jew who, in danger of death, threw himself into a pool saying, "I baptize myself in the name of the Father, and of the Son, and of the Holy Spirit." The Pope explains that the act was not valid, because one person baptizes and another is baptized. Innocent cites a saying of Jesus: "make disciples . . . baptizing them" (Mt 28:19).[6]

At the same time we find from the very beginnings of Christianity that the sacraments are normally administered by ordained persons.[7] Listen to

---

5. One exception, in a way, is the Eucharist, which the priest administers to himself; but this is an exception that proves the rule, for in this sacrament the priest is personally configured to Christ the head, the key of his own ministry, as we will see further on in the chapter.

6. See Innocent III, *Debitum Officii Pontificalis*, August 28, 1206 (DH 788).

7. See Charles de Clerq, "Ministre et sujet des sacrements dans les anciens canons et aujourd'hui," *Kanon* 1 (1973): 54–58.

St. Ignatius of Antioch: "it is not lawful either to baptize or to celebrate a love-feast [*agape*, the Eucharist] without the bishop," whom he compares to Jesus.[8] He adds: "do nothing without the bishop and priests ... all of you therefore run together as into one temple of God, as to one altar."[9] Pope Clement expresses a similar opinion: "Our sin will not be small, if we eject from the episcopate those who have blamelessly and holily fulfilled its duties."[10] And St. Justin, when he describes the Eucharist, assigns the prayer to the one who presides over the brethren.[11] Tertullian, for his part, affirms that the ordained minister has the duty to confer baptism, while also admitting that lay persons can do it.[12] He adds that it is up to the bishop to administer penance and to celebrate the Eucharist.[13] Gradually the texts that presuppose the priest as the minister of the sacraments become more plentiful.[14]

While the need for the minister is clear, it is debated what sort of a man he should be and how he should act. The reflection starts with the pitfalls the ancient church must avoid when she observes that the life of the minister is not always in keeping with his lofty vocation. The topic becomes more serious when it is a question of heretical or schismatic priests: are the baptisms that they confer valid?

One Church Father who answered in the negative was St. Cyprian.[15] He does admit that baptism is not lost, as long as it was received in the Catholic church; but he denies that someone who administers it outside of the church confers it validly. Someone like Novatian, who has strayed from unity, keeps his baptism; but the baptisms that he celebrates are useless unless he returns to the fold. For how could someone without life give life? And how could life exist outside of the one church, which professes one faith and one baptism?[16]

The insight that motivates Cyprian is correct: the minister does not act on his own account but rather based on his membership in the body of

---

8. See Ignatius of Antioch, *Ad Smyrneans* VIII, 2 (SC 10:162; ANF 1:90).

9. See Ignatius of Antioch, *Ad Magnesians* VII, 1–2 (SC 10:100; ANF 1:62).

10. See Clement of Rome, *Ad Corinthians* XLIV, 4 (SC 167:172; ANF 1:17a).

11. See Justin Martyr, *1 Apologiae* 65, 3.5 (PTS 38:126; ANF 1:185a).

12. See Tertullian, *De Baptismo*, XVII, 1–2 (CCL 1:291; ANF 3:677a–b), and *De corona* III, 2 (CCL 2:1043; ANF 3:94b).

13. On penance: Tertullian, *De pudicitia* XVIII, 18 (CCL 1:1319; ANF 4:95a); on the Eucharist: Tertullian, *Apologia* XXXIX, 5 (CCL 1:150–51; ANF 3:46b), and *De corona* III, 3 (CCL 2:1043; ANF 3:94b).

14. See Congregation for the Doctrine of the Faith, *Sacerdotium Ministeriale*, August 6, 1983 (Rome: LEV, 2016).

15. See Cyprian, *Epistolae* LXX–LXXV (CSEL 3.2; ANF 5:377–402).

16. See ibid., LXX, 2 (CSEL 3.2:768–69; ANF 5:377b).

Christ. The conclusion that he draws, nevertheless, is wrong and was rejected by the church, which condemned the practice of rebaptizing.[17] Augustine states that the bishop of Carthage atoned through his martyrdom, which he suffered in union with the church, for whatever may have been deficient in his teaching.[18]

The debate was reignited with Donatism, which arose in the fourth century, again in Africa. The schism came about when the election of Cecilian was rejected. It was alleged that the bishop who ordained him, Felix, was unworthy, because he had surrendered the sacred books during the Diocletian persecution. The Donatists demanded not only that the minister (of baptism or holy orders) not be a heretic; if he behaved publicly in an unworthy manner, the sacraments that he conferred would not be valid either. The sect gained great strength in northern Africa, where it continued to be present until the seventh century.

It would be St. Augustine's job to offer an initial theological explanation for the practice of the church, which accepts the sacraments celebrated by abominable ministers.[19] His reasoning is based on the baptism in the Jordan: John already knew that Jesus is the Christ, but there is something that he nevertheless did not know, which surprised him: the Lord's humility in asking for baptism.[20] The Baptist then exclaimed, "This is the one who baptizes" (Hic est qui baptizat), which means, according to St. Augustine: whoever the one who administers baptism may be, Jesus has reserved for himself the action of baptizing. In Christ's humiliation John discovers an invitation to humility when faced with an unworthy priest, for Christians know that it is the Lord himself who baptizes.

The reason why Jesus reserved for himself this power, which he could have communicated to his disciples, was to preserve the unity of the church, about which the Song of Solomon says: "One is my dove: my perfect one is but one. She is the only one of her mother" (Song 6:8, Douay-Rheims).[21]

---

17. During his lifetime St. Cyprian clashed with Pope St. Stephen (see DH 110–11); and the practice of rebaptizing was condemned at the Councils of Arles (314 A.D.) (DH 123), Nicaea (325) (DH 127–28), and Carthage (348) and by Pope Siricius (DH 183).

18. See Augustine, Epistolae XCIII 10, 40 (CSEL 34.2:484).

19. See Rémi Crespin, Ministère et sainteté: Pastorale du clergé et solution de la crise donatiste dans la vie et la doctrine de saint Augustin (Paris: Études Augustiniennes, 1965); G. Rosemary Evans, "Augustine, the Donatists and Communion," Augustinus 38 (1993): 221–30; Adam D. Ployd, "The Power of Baptism: Augustine's Pro-Nicene Response to the Donatists," Journal of Early Christian Studies 22 (2014): 519–40.

20. See Augustine, In Iohannem VI, 5–26 (CCL 36:56–67; NPNF-I 741–48).

21. See ibid., VI, 6 (CCL 36:56; NPNF-I 7:41a): "Per hanc enim potestatem, quam Christus solus sibi tenuit, et in nullum ministrorum transfudit, quamuis per ministros suos baptizare dignatus sit, per hanc stat unitas ecclesiae, quae significatur in columba, de qua dictum est: Vna est columba mea, una est matri suae. Si enim, ut iam dixi, fratres mei, transferretur potestas a Domino ad ministrum,

For, Augustine continues, if this power were transmitted to many ministers, there would be as many baptisms as ministers, which would call into question the unity of the body (see Eph 4:4–5). Christ is the one who baptizes, in other words: "Peter may baptize, but this is He that baptizeth; Paul may baptize, yet this is He that baptizeth; Judas may baptize, still this is He that baptizeth."[22] There is a second side, then, to the acceptance of an unworthy minister: the defense of the church's unity and of the ecclesial dimension of the sacrament, so that we can salvage the insight that inspired Cyprian.

All this is for Augustine proof of the greatness of the sacrament, which is so holy that it cannot be defiled, however dirty the minister's hands may be.[23] For even if a drunkard, a murderer, or an adulterer baptizes, as long as they baptize into Christ's baptism, Christ is the one who baptizes.[24] There are plenty of testimonies in other patristic works that confirm this opinion. For St. Gregory of Nazianzen, for example, the good priest and the bad priest are like two seals, one made of gold, the other of iron; although they are different, the image that they imprint on the wax is identical.[25] Several later Magisterial interventions followed this line of argument: Anastasius II, in the year 496, compares the evil minister to the fetid air that does not sully the light that passes through it.[26] Nicholas I, in his reply to the Bulgarians, uses the simile of a wax candle that harms itself but sheds light all around.[27]

The argument can be applied also to the problem of the minister who has fallen into schism or heresy. This case is more difficult, because here the priest's wickedness pertains to communion with Christ and the church, which is vital for the validity of the sacrament. In resolving this problem Augustine insists that the grace poured out does not have its source in the

---

tot baptismata essent, quot ministri essent, et iam non staret unitas baptismi" (For by this authority, which Christ has retained to Himself alone, and conferred upon none of His ministers, though He has deigned to baptize by His ministers; by this authority, I say, stands the unity of the Church, which is figured in the dove, concerning which it is said, "My dove is one, the only one of her mother." For if, as I have already said, my brethren, the authority were transferred by the Lord to His minister, there would be as many baptisms as ministers, and the unity of baptism would no longer exist).

22. See Augustine, *In Iohannem* VI, 7 (CCL 36:57; NPNF-I 7:41b).

23. See ibid., V, 19 (CCL 36:52; NPNF-I 7:38b): "Quod sacramentum tam sanctum est, un nec homicida ministrante polluatur" (That sacrament is so sacred that not even the ministration of a murderer pollutes it).

24. See ibid., V, 18 (CCL 36:51; NPNF-I 7:38b): "Sic ergo quos baptizauit ebriosus, quos baptizauit homicida, quos baptizauit adulter, si baptismus Christi erat, Christus baptizauit. Non timeo adulterum, non ebriosum, non homicidam; quia columbam adtendo, per quam mihi dicitur: *Hic est qui baptizat*" (In like manner, then, they whom a drunkard baptized, those whom a murderer baptized, those whom an adulterer baptized, if it was the baptism of Christ, were baptized by Christ. I do not fear the adulterer, the drunkard, or the murderer, because I give heed unto the dove, through whom it is said to me, "This is He which baptizeth").

25. See Gregory Nazianzen, *Oratio* 40, 26 (PG 36:395).

26. See Anastasius II, *Exordium Pontificatus Mei*, 496 (DH 356).

27. See Nicholas I, Responses *Ad consulta vestra*, 866 (DH 645).

minister, but rather in the sacrament of holy orders, through which Christ lives and works in the priest. Ordination, like baptism, is a sacrament, in other words, a sacred bond that conforms the recipient to Jesus. And the two sacraments therefore have equal dignity: if baptism persists even when someone leaves the church, so do holy orders persist. The schismatic, therefore, not only keeps his baptism, but also keeps the *jus dandi*: the right to give baptism to others. Contrary to Cyprian's opinion, then, it is possible for valid sacraments to be administered outside of the church. We are familiar with the image used by Augustine: the church is like Sarah, who begets children through Hagar also, who represents the schismatic sect.[28]

Note that Christ's action in the minister, which guarantees the unity of the church, paradoxically implies a limit to her authority: the church cannot prevent sacraments such as baptism or holy orders from being conferred validly outside of her. And this is because otherwise she would have to identify the source of the sacrament with the righteousness of the minister, and not with the action of Jesus, thus denying a central element that constitutes her as church: she is born of baptism, born of the sacraments, born of the primacy of God's action in Christ, as the bride formed from his side. This implies that there are elements of salvation that belong to the church but are situated, so to speak, beyond her reach, because they refer to the very act by which Christ engenders her. The church's inability to prevent the effect of some celebrations is, therefore, a sign of her greatness, for it shows that she comes from God. As we see, the debate about the minister of the sacrament is also a debate about who the church is.

The problem solved by Augustine cropped up again between the eighth and twelfth centuries in matters pertaining to the sacrament of holy orders, partly because the Augustinian doctrine had fallen into oblivion. Then there were those who denied the validity of ordinations conferred by men who were living in concubinage, simoniacs, or excommunicated.[29] One example: Stephen VI convoked a council in the year 897, which is known as the "cadaver council," at which he hauled into court the cadaver of the accused, his predecessor, Pope Formosus, in order to declare invalid the ordinations that had been performed by the deceased.

The question was discussed by the canonists and theologians of the twelfth century. Peter Lombard continued to doubt the validity of sacra-

---

28. See Augustine, *In Iohannem* XI, 7, 8 (CCL 36:114; NPNF-I 7:77); *De baptismo* I, 16, 25 (CSEL 51:169).

29. See Heinrich Heitmeyer, *Sakramentenspendung bei Häretikern und Simoniten nach Huguccio* (Rome: Gregorian Biblical Book Shop, 1964); and Doronzo, *De sacramentis in genere*, 477–78.

ments administered by a bishop who is separated from the body of Christ.[30] It was not an easy topic because what was at stake was the church's legitimate authority to decide questions that concern her own life and government, and the limits of that authority were not clear. At that time there was no neat distinction between the validity of the ordination that had been received and the exercise of the authority connected to the sacred order, which the church can indeed limit.

The distinction gradually became clearer,[31] and the principle became generally accepted: the faith or goodness of the minister is not necessary for the validity of the sacrament. This was the teaching of Innocent III in the profession of faith that he prescribed for the Waldensians in 1208.[32] And thirteenth-century theology would accept it unanimously. In the context of this question, in fact, the distinction between *ex opere operato* and *ex opere operantis* appears for the first time.[33] The sacrament acts through the work itself that is performed, which represents the action of Jesus, and not through the work of the minister, which is not productive in itself if faith or the proper dispositions are lacking. We find in St. Thomas a balanced synthesis. According to him, it belongs to the minister, as instrument, to transmit the grace that proceeds from someone else. If it depended on the integrity of the minister, we would be placing our trust in a man, and therefore we could never be sure of the validity of the rite.[34]

Trent addressed the subject based on the concurring development of Scholastic theology, thus confirming a traditional teaching by its authority. The problem did not arise with respect to Luther (for whom the minister was only the spokesman of the Word, and it was enough for him to transmit this Word), but rather with respect to the Anabaptists, who claimed that a wicked minister did not confer the sacrament. The Council condemned this doctrine, assuming that "wicked" in this context meant someone in a state of mortal sin. For he could have other defects of his own, such as negligence in celebrating the rite, which would make his act invalid. In other words, if the minister observes what is essential to confect or confer the sacrament, then he confects and confers it.[35] This means that the church can still state

---

30. See Peter Lombard, *Sent.* IV, d. 25, c. 1 (SpBon V:408–13).

31. See, for example, Thomas Aquinas, *Super IV Sent.*, d. 25, q. 1, a. 2, ad 3 (Parma 7:907).

32. See Innocent III, *Professio fidei Waldensibus praescripta* (DH 793–94).

33. The distinction is used in this sense by Petrus Pictaviensis, *Sententiae* V, 6 (PL 211:1235); Innocent III, *De sacro altaris mysterio* III, 5 (PL 217:844).

34. See Thomas Aquinas, *ST* III, q. 64, aa. 5 and 9; *Summa Contra Gentiles* [hereafter *SCG*] IV, 77 (Rome: Leonine Commission, 1930), 15:244.

35. See Council of Trent, Session VII, *Decree on the Sacraments*, canon 12 (DH 1612): "si quis dixerit, ministrum in peccato mortali exsistentem, modo omnia essentialia, quae ad sacramentum

conditions, in some cases, for the validity of the sacrament. This happens in the sacrament of penance when it is administered without having ordinary or delegated jurisdiction—and this is because in this sacrament it is a matter of being integrated into the full visible communion of the church, which depends directly on her authority.[36] And it happens also in matrimony, the validity of which normally depends for Catholics, since Trent, on the canonical form.[37]

The Minister's Intention

Granted that the holiness of the minister is not necessary for sacramental efficacy, it might seem that he is merely passive, an automaton carrying out the rites that bestow grace. This view is not accurate: the free action of the minister is required for the validity of the sacrament. If he is not involved in a minimal way, the celebration will be void.

St. Augustine had already explored the case of baptisms that were administered in jest (playacting) but were received piously by the neophytes.[38] He does not decide the question with a clear answer about its validity, but he does seem to require at least that the act have an ecclesial dimension, in other words, that it be performed in a community of Christians, even though they are wrong about what the true church is because they are heretics or schismatics.

The question is debated among medieval theologians, who conclude that the intention to administer the sacrament is necessary in order for it to be valid. Two reasons are especially weighty. In the first place, given the requirement that the minister be a human being, he has to perform a human act and, consequently, freely will to celebrate the sacrament.[39] Secondly,

conficiendum aut conferendum pertinent, servaverit, non conficere aut conferre sacramentum: anathema sit" (If anyone says that a minister in the state of mortal sin, though he observes all the essentials that belong to the effecting and conferring of the sacrament, does not effect or confer the sacrament, let him be anathema). For the history of the canon: Cavallera, "Le décret," 170–75. Concerning baptism, Trent adds that, when heretics administer it in the name of the Father and of the Son and of the Holy Spirit with the intention to do what the church does, then it is valid (Session VII, *Decree on the Sacraments*, canon 4 on baptism: DH 1617); with respect to penance, the Council teaches that even priests in a state of mortal sin have the power to remit sins "as ministers of Christ through the power of the Holy Spirit conferred in ordination" (Session XIV, *Doctrine on the Sacrament of Penance*, chap. 6; DH 1684); and in speaking about the Eucharist it affirms that the offering cannot be defiled by the unworthiness or malice of the one who presents it (Session XXII, *Doctrine on the Holy Sacrifice of the Mass*, chap. 1; DH 1742).

36. See Council of Trent, Session XIV, *Doctrine on the Sacrament of Penance*, chap. 7 (DH 1686).

37. See Council of Trent, Session XIV, *Decree Tametsi* (DH 1813–16).

38. See Augustine, *De Baptismo* VII, 53, 101–2 (CSEL 51:372).

39. See Hugh of St. Victor, *De sacramentis* II, 6, 13 (PL 176:460; *CV* 1:395): "rationale esse oportet opus ministeriorum Dei, nec propter solam formam praejudicare ubi intentio agendi nulla est"

the words pronounced are essential to the rite; well, then, these words, by themselves, without taking into account who pronounces them, prove to be ambiguous signs, which can indicate various things: only the minister's intention resolves this uncertainty.[40] In order to weigh the significance of this doctrine it is important to emphasize, above all, its positive aspect. The minister is not merely an inanimate channel through which grace passes, but rather by his free act he participates in the confection of the sacrament. Therefore, the more he is configured to Christ, the more readily the sacramental grace will flow through him, redounding moreover to his own sanctification.

Presupposing the minister's necessary intention, a question arises: what is the minimum required in order for the sacrament to be valid? Because validity exists in the case of heretical ministers, understanding or sharing the full meaning of what takes place cannot be demanded, as that eludes someone who has strayed from the faith. On the other hand, because it is characteristic of the minister to act on the part of Jesus (*in persona Christi*), it is necessary to require at least the intention to identify with him, dispensing "what Christ instituted."[41]

Together with this way of formulating the minimum that is necessary, another expression appeared that became well known, which emphasizes the ecclesial import of ministry: the minister is required to have "the intention to do what the church does" (*intentio faciendi quod facit Ecclesia*). Indeed, since the days of St. Cyprian there is a concern that the sacraments should take place within the walls of God's house. Even though the minister continues to be a minister after separating from communion, he must maintain some connection to the church in order to work as one. Well, then, precisely by wanting to do what the church does, the minister binds himself to her in a certain way. Together with the formula *in persona Christi* another one would become widespread: *in persona Ecclesiae*.[42] In fact, through this

---

(The exercise of God's ministries must be rational, and it must not be decided beforehand according to the form alone when there is no intention to act).

40. See Thomas Aquinas, *ST* III, q. 64, a. 8, co.

41. See Bonaventure, *In IV Sent.*, d. 4, p. 2, a. 2, q. 1 (Quaracchi 4:153): "et ideo ad hoc, quod ordinentur, necessarium est, intervenire intentionem ministri, qua intendit illo actu et verbo talem effectum dare, vel saltem quod facit Ecclesia facere, vel saltem quod Christus instituit dispensare" (And therefore in order for them to be ordained it is necessary for the minister's intention to intervene, whereby he intends by that act and word to produce that effect, or at least to do what the Church does, or at least to dispense what Christ instituted).

42. "In the person of the Church." See in this regard: Thomas Aquinas, *ST* III, q. 64, a. 8, ad 2: "minister sacramenti agit in persona totius Ecclesiae, cuius est minister" (the minister of a sacrament acts in the person of the whole Church, whose minister he is); a. 9, ad 1: "minister sacramenti agit in persona totius Ecclesiae, ex cuius fide suppletur id quod deest fidei ministro" (the minister of a sacrament acts in the person of the whole Church, by whose faith any defect in the minister's faith is made

intentional union of the minister with the church, she can supply the defect in his faith.

As with many other aspects of sacramental theology, Luther brought with him an all-encompassing change of perspective. His presuppositions led him to diminish the role of the minister, for in his view everything plays out between the believer and God, through the faith-filled acceptance of the divine promise that the sacrament contains. The only thing that matters, then, is that the minister transmit the divine word and gesture: it makes no difference whether or not he has the intention, whether he acts seriously or in jest.[43]

Trent discussed the minister when it defended priestly orders, which it associates with the Eucharist.[44] This ministry cannot be reduced to a mere function, but rather implies an ontological change through the character that it imprints.[45] This gives rise to the priest's power to confer the sacraments, which in general is not true of lay people.[46] At the same time the Council reaffirms, contrary to Luther, the requirement of the active participation of the minister, who is not a mere sounding board for the forgiving word. The minimum required is defined by the formula that we saw the medieval theologians use: at least (because more could be demanded in some cases) the intention to do what the church does (*saltem intentio faciendi quod facit Ecclesia*).[47]

After Trent theologians attempted to explain what kind of intention is necessary for sacramental validity. Certainly a "habitual intention" is not enough, for we have that even when we are asleep. On the other hand it is too much to demand an "actual intention" (which is the equivalent of "attention"): if that were so, then the sacrament would not be valid if the minister became distracted, for example. They conclude that what is called

---

good). Aquinas follows Albert the Great, *In IV Sent.*, d. 6, a. 12 (*Opera Omnia*, XXIX:140); see also Bernard-Dominique Marliangéas, *Clés pour une théologie du ministère: In persona Christi, in persona Ecclesiae* (Paris: Beauchesne, 1978), 69–170.

43. In *De captivitate babylonica* the Reformer had said that in the sacrament we truly receive what we believe we are going to receive "quicquid agat, non agat, simuletur aut iocetur minister" (WA 6:571); "whatever the minister does, does not do, pretends to do, or does in jest." See Pablo Blanco, "El ministerio en Lutero, Trento y el Vaticano II: Un recorrido historico-dogmatico," *Scripta Theologica* 40, no. 3 (2008): 733–76.

44. See Council of Trent, Session XXIII, *Doctrine on the Sacrament of Orders*, chap. 1 (DH 1764).

45. See ibid., canon 4 (DH 1774).

46. See Council of Trent, Session VII, *Decree on the Sacraments*, canon 10 (DH 1610).

47. See ibid., canon 1 (DH 1611); cf. *CT* 5:991: "In 11. ibi *intentionem faciendi* ut addatur *saltem*; item dixerunt quidam advertendum, quod in Eucharistia requiritur propria intentio conficiendi" (In canon 11, let the phrase *at least* be added where it reads *the intention to do*; likewise some said that it should be noted that in the case of the Eucharist the proper intention to confect the sacrament is required).

a virtual intention (*intentio virtualis*) is sufficient: deciding to perform this specific act, although sometimes one is not thinking about it at the precise moment of performing it.

On the other hand, a distinction is made and the difference between *intentio interna* and *externa* is discussed. Starting with Ambrosio Catarino [Politi], at the time of Trent, some teach that the *external intention* is enough, which they define as the intention to perform the external rite, that is, to carry out the ceremonial gestures and to pronounce the words. Others, in contrast, advocate an *internal intention* and require moreover that the minister, in performing the external rite, intend to perform a sacred act, as the church desires.

We will search the documents of Trent in vain for a solution to this debate, for their purpose was only to condemn the Lutheran position. It is true that, as far as penance is concerned, the Council affirms that the priest has to desire to act seriously and truly to absolve.[48] On the other hand, this sacrament demands more of the minister, for it requires for its validity that he form a judgment on the penitent's situation. In 1690 Alexander VIII condemned a proposition of the Belgian theologian François Farvacques, for he considered valid a baptism by someone who, while performing all the external rites, resolves in his heart not to desire to do what the church does.[49] At least the conscious denial of the internal intention, therefore, invalidates the sacramental act.[50]

What can be said about this discussion, which is important in order to decide about the validity of some sacraments? The necessity of the *intentio interna* is more in keeping with the human participation of the minister, whom St. Thomas calls *instrumentum animatum*.[51] On the other hand, from the perspective of contemporary reflection on the incarnate condition of the human person and of his actions, it is not possible to dissociate the *intentio interna* and the *intentio externa*. And this is because the body has inherent meanings which the acting subject cannot simply set aside. The action performed, in its corporeal visibility, channels the internal intention,

---

48. Council of Trent, Session XIV, *Doctrine on the Sacrament of Penance*, chap. 6 (DH 1685): "sacerdoti animus serio agendi et vere absolvendi" (the priest has [a] mind to act seriously and to absolve truly).

49. The condemned proposition is: "Valet baptismus collatus a ministro, qui omnem ritum externum formamque baptizandi observat, intus vero in corde suo apud se resolvit: Non intendo, quod facit Ecclesia" (Baptism is valid when conferred by a minister who observes all the external rite and form of baptizing but within his heart resolves, I do not intend what the Church does) (DH 2328). See Giacomo Rambaldi, "La *intentio externa* de Fr. Farvacques," *Gregorianum* 27, no. 3 (1946): 444–57.

50. See in this regard Thomas Aquinas, *ST* III, q. 64, a. 8, ad 2.

51. "Living instrument." See Thomas Aquinas, *Super IV Sent.*, d. 18, q. 1, a. 3, q.c. 1, co. (Parma 7:813); *SCG* IV, 77 (15:244); *ST* III, q. 64, a. 10, co.

which does not depend on the arbitrary judgment of an allegedly isolated inner will.[52] Unless the intention is positively excluded, and this decision is manifested somehow, we must assume that the internal intention exists when the rite in its essential components is performed.

I should add one additional detail to this picture, however: the minister could limit his intention in such a way that he wishes to celebrate the sacrament only if certain specific conditions are fulfilled (the sacrament is then administered *sub conditione*, conditionally). This happens in cases where, on the one hand, doubts arise about elements that are necessary for validity (whether the material is suitable, for example, or whether the subject is alive); and, on the other hand, serious harm would result if the sacrament were not administered (e.g., in danger of death, or when there is a doubt as to whether the recipient has already been baptized or confirmed). In limiting his intention, the minister assures the dignity due to the sacrament, on the one hand, and its fullest beneficial effect, on the other hand.[53]

To conclude, we can observe that the debate about the role of the minister usually revolves around minimalism (of goodness, of faith, of communion with the church, of intention). In the following section I will highlight the importance of his full participation based on an analogy with the human experience of fatherhood, as it is taken up and fulfilled by Jesus.

Priestly Ministry and Fatherhood in Christ

The role of the minister, as I have described it, is intertwined with the theology of holy orders, inasmuch as the priest is the minister of almost all the sacraments. Understanding why a sacrament needs a minister then sheds light on the nature of the priesthood, and vice versa. Thus it follows that priestly ordination is not simply one of the seven sacraments which is studied after clarifying the general concept of sacrament. Rather, the figure of the priest belongs to the essence of the sacrament, as he is the minister *par excellence*. Recall that one of the most influential definitions of sacrament during the Middle Ages, the one proposed by Hugh of St. Victor, includes among its terms the minister, given that he participates in the bestowal of grace.[54]

52. See Jean Marie R. Tillard, "A propósito de la intención del ministro y del sujeto de los sacramentos," *Concilium* 31, no. 1 (1968): 125–39; the author leans toward defending the sufficiency of the *intentio externa*.

53. See Miralles, *Los sacramentos cristianos*, 345–46.

54. See Hugh of St. Victor, *De sacramentis* I, 9, 2 (PL 176:317; *CV* 1:209–10); it is remarkable that Hugh himself, in his classic treatise, speaks about priestly ordination before addressing the other sacraments: ibid., II, 3 (PL 176:421; *CV* 1:343).

Just as understanding matrimony helps us to understand the rootedness of each sacrament in the created order, as I noted above (see chapter 6), so too studying the priesthood clarifies the structure of the sacrament as a salvific encounter with the person of Jesus. Christ, thanks to the minister, continues to be corporeally present as the source and summit of all grace. Through the minister, we could say, not only Jesus' word comes to us, but also his voice. This chapter then is essential in exploring the relational space that the rite opens up in the life of the faithful (see chapter 11, above): this is a space polarized around Christ, whom the minister represents and in whose presence the church is situated.

The Sacramental Fatherhood of the Priest

Although the question about the minister's goodness and faith, which dominated the debates in the early centuries, was centered on baptism and holy orders, the facts explored in the New Testament prompt us to take as our reference point the Eucharist, to which ministry is closely associated, as we have seen. In the Eucharist we discover an action of Jesus which is, in the first place, a total reference to his Father, to whom he offers his *todah* sacrifice. Thus he expresses to him his gratitude for the life which he has already given him and which he will restore to him fulfilled in the resurrection. Moreover, by his Eucharistic action, Christ communicates this life to us: the mention of the body broken and shared among the disciples recalls for us the context of the corporate personality. Jesus, like Isaac and the Suffering Servant, becomes one with humankind, shares humankind's destiny in sharing the flesh, and will be capable of regenerating this same flesh by breathing into it new life that is accessible to all his brethren.

We know that this idea of corporate personality arose in Israel based on familial experiences, in which we share one and the same life and belong to each other, with bonds that are rooted in the body. So it happens in the union of the man and the woman in one flesh, resulting in the unity of parents and children, which assures moreover the cohesiveness of the people of God through the generations.

In this context Jesus' action, because it transmits a new life to those whom God has given to him (see Heb 2:13), can be understood as a paternal action. Note that this fatherhood springs from the surrender of his body so as to introduce us into the relations of his new family, and it transforms our flesh so that it matures toward the resurrection. This fatherhood, therefore, is not merely of the Spirit but also corporeal.

In fact, according to biblical anthropology, fatherhood joins father and son in one flesh: the father gives as an inheritance to the son his way of being situated on earth and of narrating his story, which the son will prolong in his days. This placement of fatherhood in the flesh helps the father to be aware that the life which he transmits comes from someone else and not from himself: it comes, ultimately, from God the creator, who formed and joined husband and wife, and engraved on every child his image and likeness (Gn 5:3), shaping his members in his mother's womb (Gn 4:1; Ps 139:13). But the flesh also helps the father to remember that this life passes through him, that it is entrusted to his responsibility as pro-creator and that it will bear his surname so as to prolong his days on earth. Part of the mystery of fatherhood, in light of this, is assigning a name, that is, offering a word that illuminates the path of the son, reminding him that the most ancient origin of his steps is a gratuitous love, and situating him in the covenant with his God.

Well, then, Jesus assumes, refines, and fulfills all this, forging a new fatherhood. This is deduced, most importantly, from the biblical figure of Christ the new Adam, head of a new lineage (see Rom 5:12–21; 1 Cor 15:45–49), a figure that acquires ritual features in the Eucharist. Indeed, in this sacrament, like any father, Jesus constantly refers to his heavenly Father, to whom he addresses the *todah* or thanksgiving for the risen life that he will be able to transmit to his followers. And here too, like any father, Jesus participates actively in the transmission of life, surrendering his body so as to introduce us into the network of corporeal relations that he inaugurated. Here, finally, like any father, Jesus gives us the word (the Eucharistic formula) which, as with the assigning of a name, reminds us of the origin of our life ("giving thanks [to the Father]," "my body for you") and directs us toward a risen destiny ("for the life of the world": Jn 6:51).

Based on this fatherhood it is possible to clarify the role of the minister, which springs precisely from representing Jesus in the Eucharist, as the testimony of the Bible records. The theme appears with ever-increasing frequency in the Church Fathers. We already saw that Ignatius of Antioch relates the liturgical presidency of the bishop with the presence of Jesus, associating both in turn with the divine Fatherhood as their source.[55] St. Cyprian, for his part, writes that in the Eucharist the priest "stands in for" Christ.[56] Later St. John Chrysostom speaks about the minister as a figure, for Jesus himself is the one who transforms the bread and wine into his

---

55. See Ignatius of Antioch, *Ad Smyrneans* VIII, 2 (SC 10:162; ANF 1:89), and *Ad Magnesians* VII, 1–2 (SC 10:100; ANF 1:62).

56. See Cyprian, *Epistolae* LXI, 14 (CSEL 3.2:713; ANF 5:362b): "uice Christi fungitur" (discharges the office of Christ).

body and blood.[57] St. Ambrose too teaches that Christ continues to offer himself today, given that the sanctifying words of the priest work by Christ's power and are his.[58] The priest's task, therefore, is to represent in the sight of the church the fontal position of Jesus, as the father from whom God's life flows.

The formulas with which the sacraments are administered help us to verify this point. It is necessary to distinguish between two types of ministerial words: "I baptize you," "I absolve you," on the one hand, and "this is my body," on the other. What is the relation between them? According to St. Thomas Aquinas, at work in the Eucharist is a configuration of the person of the minister with the person of Jesus. Hence the priest imitates perfectly what Christ carried out in the Last Supper, reciting the words in the master's name, while in the other sacraments he pronounces them in his own name.[59] Indeed, the formula of consecration does not read: "he said that everyone should take and eat of it because it was his body," but rather: "he said: 'Take and eat of it, all of you, for this is my body.'"[60] Thus the priest calls the very body of Jesus his own body, showing that he has become one with him. Here the formula *in persona Christi* is applied in its full meaning.

At this point we find a difference in relation to the other rites. For what is configured to Christ in them is not the person of the minister, but rather his action.[61] In these cases, there is an identification with Christ in the act of administering the sacrament, not in the manner of naming oneself by

57. See John Chrysostom, *In proditionem Iudae homiliae*, hom. 1, n. 6 (PG 49:380); *In epistulam II ad Timotheum homiliae*, hom. 2, n. 4 (PG 62:612): the one who acts in the Eucharist, as in baptism, is Christ.

58. See Ambrose, *Explanatio Psalmorum XII*, 38, 25, 3 (CSEL 64:203): "etsi nunc Christus non videtur offerre, tamen ipse offertur in terris, quia Christi corpus offertur; immo ipse offerre manifestatur in nobis, cuius sermo sanctificat sacrificium quod offertur" (Although now Christ does not seem to offer, nevertheless he is offered on earth, because Christ's body is offered; indeed, he himself is shown to offer among us, for his word sanctifies the sacrifice that is offered).

59. See Thomas Aquinas, *Super IV Sent.*, d. 8, q. 2, a. 1, sol. 2 (Parma 7:591): "Verba enim formae hujus sacramenti proferuntur a ministro in persona Christi quasi recitative.... Aliorum autem sacramentorum formae ex persona ministri proferuntur" (For the words of the formula of this sacrament are pronounced by the minister in the person of Christ, as though in the recital of a legal document.... Whereas the formulas of the other sacraments are pronounced in the person of the minister).

60. See Robert Sokolowski, *Eucharistic Presence: A Study in the Theology of Disclosure* (Washington, D.C.: The Catholic University of America Press, 1994), 13–21.

61. See Artur Michael Landgraf, "Die Ansicht der Frühscholastik von der Zugehörigkeit des *Baptizo te* zur Taufform," *Scholastik* 17 (1942): 412–27 and 531–55; on penance, see Thomas Aquinas, *De forma absolutionis paenitentiae sacramentalis ad Magistrum Ordinis* (Rome: Leonine Commission, 1968), 45:33: "Unde sicut conveniens est forma Baptismi ut minister dicat: ego te baptizo, quia dominus ministris *actum baptizandi* attribuit; ita conveniens forma est ut dicatur: ego te absolvo, quia dominus ministro *actum absolutionis* attribuit" (Hence, just as it is appropriate that in the formula of Baptism the minister says: I baptize you, because the Lord attributes *the act of baptizing* to his ministers, so too it is appropriate that in the formula [of Penance] he should say: I absolve you, because the Lord attributes *the act of absolving* to his minister).

affirming: "this is my body." When Peter or Paul baptize, Christ is the one who baptizes, because Jesus associates himself with the minister in the act of baptizing. But the "I" in "I baptize you" refers to the specific minister who baptizes; whereas the "my" in "this is my body" refers to Jesus. Only the priest says, therefore, "this is my body," "this is my blood"; and based on this he becomes specially enabled to be a channel of grace in the other sacraments, although in the case of baptism someone who is not ordained can be the minister.[62]

We can conclude from this that the priest is a minister inasmuch as he is a father. In fact, the body of Christ in the Eucharist is a generative body, which communicates new life to Christians. Therefore, the reason why the priest can say "this is my body" is because he is configured to the paternal body of Jesus, who now raised from the dead presents himself to the Father together with the children whom God has given to him (see Heb 2:13). In other words, the priest acts *in persona Christi capitis*, in the person of Christ the head,[63] or (and this is the same thing) in the person of Christ as paternal source of life for the church. The fatherhood of the minister consists of introducing human beings into a new body (into the new relations of Jesus), and of pronouncing a name (the words of each sacrament) that associates us with the narrative of Jesus and thus reveals to us the origin and the destination of our journey. Hence the words of the apostle: "I became your father in Christ" (1 Cor 4:15) can be applied to the priest in the sacraments, as this sermon by St. Pacian attests: "Thus Christ begetteth in the Church by His priests, as says the same Apostle, *For in Christ Jesus have I begotten you*. And so the seed of Christ, that is, the Spirit of God produces, by the hands of the priests, the new man conceived in the womb of our Mother [the church], and received at the birth of the font, faith presiding over the marriage rite."[64]

In this light, the debates about the goodness of the minister and his intention, which I summarized earlier, can be framed in these terms. On the one hand, the key of fatherhood helps the priest to understand that he is not the origin of the life of grace that is communicated, which comes from God the Father.[65] In the minister, as in a natural father, a mystery comes

---

62. I will speak about matrimony later on in this chapter.

63. See Vatican Council II, *Presbyterorum Ordinis*, December 7, 1965, no. 2; available at www.vatican.va.

64. Pacian, *De baptismo*, 5–6 (PL 13:1092–93): "Christi semen, id est Dei Spiritus novum hominem … manibus sacerdotis effundit." *Discourse on Baptism*, trans. C. H. Collyns in *The Extant Works of S. Pacian*, Library of Fathers of the Holy Catholic Church 17 (Oxford: John Henry Parker, 1842), 378–84.

65. On the action of the minister, which is united to God's action and therefore more fully human, see Hugh of St. Victor, *De Sacramentis* I, 9, 4 (PG 176:322; *CV* 1:215–16).

about which goes beyond him: he is the channel of fruits that surpass his abilities. Hence "Christ is the one who baptizes" and a wicked minister can celebrate sacraments validly. On the other hand, again as it happens in our experience of fatherhood, the fruits of the sacrament do not arrive apart from the minister, but rather through him, permeating his action. Hence the free intention of the minister is necessary. The priest does not simply speak through another person, nor is he limited to repeating like an automaton what someone else said; but rather he makes it his own, thus turning into a living sacrament of the Lord Jesus.

The Priestly Character and Fatherhood

What has been said helps us to understand better the priestly character. As we know, the character effects a specific conformation to the body of Jesus in the three sacraments that confer it, and in an analogous way in matrimony. Indeed, I defined said character as the acquisition of a new corporeality, that is, of a new way of being rooted relationally in the world, among human beings, in the presence of God, according to the measure of Christ.

Thus baptism can be compared with a birth. And just as when we are begotten we receive, through our body, an original background of relations to which we will always belong—with our parents and siblings, with our fellow citizens and contemporaries, etc.—so too baptism grafts us onto the relational trunk of Jesus, onto the family of the church, which will always remain as the ultimate background of our works and sufferings.

Well, then, the priestly character is rooted in the body, too, but not inasmuch as it is a body taken from others that proclaims our filial roots; rather, inasmuch as the body is the transmitter of life. Therefore the basic experience by which to understand it is not birth, but rather fatherhood. The father, in fact, when his son is born, radically reconfigures his relational space: he has taken upon himself the destiny of another human being; he has given a name to his own future, extending it immeasurably; he has given to his wife the gift of fruitfulness, while also receiving it from her; the space of the "one flesh" that they constructed by marrying expands. Fatherhood means, therefore, receiving a new incarnate form of being situated in the world and of journeying through history, which forges one's personal identity. Not only does something happen to the father (*he has* a son), but now and forever he *is* a father.

In a similar way, the priest configures his fatherhood to the new fatherhood of Jesus: this is what the sacramental character consists of. Through it he receives a new dwelling place in life, in other words, a new body: a new way of relating with human beings and with God, a new way of understanding his memory and his future, all of this based on a new power of engendering the life of Jesus. Therefore St. Augustine could speak about the priest's office as a *ius dandi*, the right to give.[66] This idea was later developed in the Middle Ages: the priestly character consists of an ability to "bestow" eternal goods, an ability that springs from configuration with the priesthood of Christ.[67] For the distinctive feature of this fatherhood of Jesus, to which priesthood is conformed, is that it does not transmit the corporeal life of this world, but rather mediates the risen life (both spiritual and corporeal) of the world to come.

We understand that, just as a father is one forever, even if he carries out his mission reluctantly or abandons it, so too for the priest. Configured forever to the fatherhood of Christ, he has the ability to receive a specific grace: that of being a source of grace, inspired by pastoral charity.[68] This implies that the administration of the sacraments, as an exercise of fatherhood, contains the key to the sanctification of the priest himself: by giving life to his children he fulfills himself in his deepest identity, which is a paternal identity.[69] Moreover the sacraments uncover for him the key for the rest of his ministry: introducing human beings into the relations of Christ and of the church, giving a name to their desires and affections, so that they are channeled to their ultimate destination in God. St. John Chrysostom confirms this connection between priesthood and sacramental fatherhood:

These [priests] verily are they who are entrusted with the pangs of spiritual travail and the birth which comes through baptism: by their means we put on Christ, and are buried with the Son of God, and become members of that blessed Head. Wherefore they might not only be more justly feared by us than rulers and kings, but also be more honored than parents; since these begat us of blood and the will of the flesh, but the others are the authors of our birth from God.... Our natural parents generate us unto this life only, but the others unto that which is to come.[70]

---

66. See Augustine, *Contra Epistolam Parmeniani* II, 13, 28 (CSEL 51:79).

67. See Thomas Aquinas, *ST* III, q. 63, a. 3, co.; a. 6, co.: "per hoc sacramentum [ordinis] deputantur homines ad sacramenta aliis tradenda" (by this sacrament [of Holy Orders] men are deputed to confer sacraments on others).

68. See John Paul II, *Pastores Dabo Vobis*, Apostolic Exhortation, March 25, 1992, pars. 21–23, in *AAS* 84 (1992): 691–94.

69. See Aimond-Marie Roguet, "La sanctification du prêtre par l'administration des sacrements," *Vie spirituelle* 89 (1953): 8–14.

70. See John Chrysostom, *De sacerdotio* III, 6 (SC 272:150–56; NPNF-I 9:47b–48a).

Ministry of the Church in the Sacraments

The outline that I have presented relates the minister with Christ. There is still another question to elucidate: what connection associates him with the church? The question already preoccupied the Church Fathers, who wanted to know not just whether the minister is good or bad, a believer or not, but rather what degree of membership in the church he has, so as to understand the way in which he communicates sacramental grace.

In persona ecclesiae

Recall the teaching of St. Cyprian, who says that sacraments exist only within the church. St. Augustine corrects this position, admitting that the sacraments may be valid outside. All the same, for the bishop of Hippo this does not diminish the value of the church. On the contrary, it shows that she can generate even beyond herself, as Sarah was the one who engendered in Hagar.[71] Thus he testifies that the original principle of the church is not in herself but rather in God.

The matter involves, on the one hand, the fact that the church does not have absolute authority over the sacraments so as to deprive them of efficacy when they are celebrated far from her bosom. It is possible that they may exist among schismatics and heretics who reject her. This is due to the fact that the church receives her being from Jesus precisely through the sacraments. It is not within her reach to prevent them from springing up beyond her borders, for they come from the wellspring from which she herself issues.

This does not mean, on the other hand, that those sacraments are disconnected from the church. Even there, where they are celebrated behind her back, they put someone who receives them in relation with the Catholic church, incorporate him into her. She is the one who engenders and enlivens those Christians. St. Augustine regarded as indispensable for the validity of the sacrament a communal sense that is found also among schismatics, although they are wrong about the true church.[72] This means that in order

71. See Augustine, *De baptismo* I, 14, 22 and 15, 23 (CSEL 51:167; NPNF-I 4:421a–b): "Non Baptismum vestrum acceptamus, quia non est Baptismus ille schismaticorum vel haereticorum, sed Dei et Ecclesiae, ubicumque fuerit inventus et quocumque translatus.... Ecclesia quippe omnes per Baptismum parit, sive apud se, id est ex utero suo; sive extra se de semine viri sui: sive de se, sive de ancilla.... Ecclesiae jure quod est in Baptismo, nascuntur quicumque nascuntur" (We do not acknowledge any baptism of yours; for it is not the baptism of schismatics or heretics, but of God and of the Church, wheresoever it may be found, and whithersoever it may be transferred.... For it is the Church that gives birth to all, either within her pale, or her own womb; or beyond it, of the seed of her bridegroom, either of herself, or of her handmaid.... it is by the right of the Church, which exists in baptism, that whosoever is born receives his birth).

72. See Augustine, *De baptismo* VII, 53, 101–2 (CSEL 5:371; NPNF-I 4:512b–513b).

to celebrate the sacrament it is not enough to refer to the fact that Christ instituted it; necessary also is the intention to belong to his body, embracing Christ's plan for communion. Therefore the minimal intention required of the minister would be formulated also in the Middle Ages as the intention to do what the church does (*intentio faciendi quod facit ecclesia*).

Granted, St. Augustine, faithful now to Cyprian's insight, had explained that outside of the church baptism certainly may exist (*esse*) but cannot be profitable (*prodesse*).[73] Medieval theologians would teach that if the sacrament is to bear fruit, it is necessary for it to work, not only *in persona Christi*, but also *in persona ecclesiae*.[74] Indeed, although the minister may lack faith, if he acts as a minister of the church, she makes up for his incredulity, inasmuch as the minister is connected with her in administering the sacrament.[75]

The perspective of the minister's fatherhood also helps to explain what it means to work *in persona ecclesiae*. Even in natural experience, no one can be a father without the assistance of the mother: the husband joins with the wife, and in this union they receive life from God. For the child, being born of this loving bond of his father and mother proves to be decisive: thus he will understand that, as he was generated in a relation, he is always called to live in relation, to belong to his family and to his people; and that a relation is what mediates his access to God.

Well, then, through the new generation that Jesus brings, the believer is introduced also into the network of relations of the church, of which Christ is head and bridegroom. Therefore she herself participates in this generation, as the Church Fathers testify when they associate the church's womb and the baptismal font.[76] Hence the fatherhood of the priest should be experienced within the people of God, with a particular concern for its

---

73. See Augustine, *In Iohannem* VI, 14 (CCL 36:60; NPNF-I 7:44a).

74. See Thomas Aquinas, *ST* III, q. 82, a. 7, ad 3.

75. See ibid., q. 64, a. 9, ad 1: "minister sacramenti agit in persona totius Ecclesiae, ex cuius fide suppletur id quod deest fidei ministro" (the minister of a sacrament acts in the person of the whole Church by whose faith any defect in the minister's faith is made good).

76. See Augustine, *In Iohannem* XII, 5 (CCL 36:123; NPNF-I 7:82b): "Si propter haereditatem patris hominis temporalem nascitur, nascatur ex visceribus matris carnalis: si propter haereditatem patris Dei sempiternam, nascatur ex visceribus Ecclesiae. Generat per uxorem filium pater moriturus successurum: generat Deus de Ecclesia filios non successuros, sed secum mansuros. Et sequitur: *Quod natum est de carne, caro est: et quod natum est de Spiritu, spiritus est.* Spiritaliter ergo nascimur, et in spiritu nascimur verbo et sacramento" (If one is born to the temporal inheritance of a human father, [let him be] born of the bowels of a carnal mother; if one is born to the everlasting inheritance of God as his Father, [let him be] born of the bowels of the Church. A father, as one that will die, begets a son by his wife to succeed him; but God begets of the Church sons, not to succeed Him, but to abide with Himself. And He goes on: "That which is born of the flesh is flesh; and that which is born of the Spirit is spirit." We are born spiritually then, and in spirit we are born by the word and sacrament).

common good.[77] The distinctive feature of his task is not to promote isolated individuals, but rather to introduce the human person into living ties and to cultivate these ties, so that all their seeds sprout.

In light of this, it is up to the priests, on the one hand, to be living reminders of the fact that the church's motherhood springs from Christ, the origin of all the relations that structure his body. As St. Thomas teaches, "in Baptism, he that baptizes takes the place of the father, while the very water of Baptism takes the place of the mother," symbolizing the maternal womb of the church.[78]

On the other hand, the minister also works *in persona ecclesiae*, representing the church herself. We are speaking, above all, about the church inasmuch as she, by her motherhood, prolongs the action of Christ the head: *in persona ecclesiae matris*, in the person of mother church. In other words, the minister participates in the hierarchical work of the church, who is in a certain way the minister of the sacraments. Thus, according to the teaching of St. Thomas, a schismatic priest who celebrates the Eucharist acts *in persona Christi* and truly consecrates, but being separated from the church he does not act *in persona ecclesiae* and his prayer does not bear fruit.[79]

Finally, the minister acts *in persona ecclesiae* too inasmuch as he represents the whole people of God. For Christ, too, in his intercession with the Father, contains within himself his whole body, forming the whole Christ.[80] Therefore, as Vatican Council II teaches, the ordained minister "in the person of Christ ... effects the Eucharistic sacrifice and offers it to God in the name of all the people."[81] To summarize: in the sacraments the priest represents Christ to the church; he represents all of mother church inasmuch as she prolongs Christ's action; and he represents the entire church which, together with Christ, offers herself to the Father.[82]

The Church's Authority over the Sacraments

These distinctions help us to understand the church's authority and function in administering the sacraments, for they highlight the fact that the

---

77. Therefore, according to Aquinas, *ST* III, q. 65, a. 4, co.: "the sacrament of order is necessary to the Church." Aquinas cites Prv 11:14: "where there is no guidance [governance], a people falls."

78. See Thomas Aquinas, *ST* III, q. 67, a. 7, obj. 2.

79. See ibid., q. 82, a. 7, obj. 3 and ad 3.

80. See Augustine, *In epistola Iohannis* I, 2 (PL 35:1979; NPNF-I 7:461b): "quia Verbum caro factum est et habitauit in nobis. Illi carni adiungitur Ecclesia et fit Christus totus, caput et corpus" ("The Word was made flesh, and dwelt in us." To that flesh the Church is joined, and so there is made the whole Christ, Head and body).

81. Vatican Council II, *Lumen Gentium* [hereafter *LG*], November 21, 1964, no. 10; available at www.vatican.va.

82. See Gisbert Greshake, *Ser sacerdote hoy* (Salamanca: Sigueme, 2006), 153–79.

minister shares in a larger ministry, the ministry of the church herself, which can be called, as I pointed out, *sacramentorum ministra*.[83] From this follows her authority over the sacraments, while never forgetting that they originate from Jesus.

First, *the church has a certain authority to establish the sacramental rites.* She possesses authority over the liturgy to arrange the sacramental event in an orderly, beautiful way. I should explain that this responsibility depends solely on the ecclesiastical authority, "that is, on the Apostolic See, and, as laws may determine, on the bishop," for the liturgy is a common good and a sign of unity of the whole people of God.[84] Therefore I am talking here about the church inasmuch as she is incorporated into Christ the head and gives testimony to his dominion over the sacraments and his ability to generate life.

All the same, in establishing and modifying the rites, the church has to respect what was established by Jesus. The Council of Trent expressed this limit with the formula *salva illorum substantia*, with which we are already acquainted (see chapter 5, above).[85] The "substance," as I put it, has to be interpreted in the theological sense, in other words, as referring to the nucleus of the sacraments that proceeds from Christ. Inasmuch as the church safeguards the memory of Jesus, it is her duty to interpret, in obedience to the Word of God, what this substance consists of.

Note, on the other hand, that the context of the formula was the Tridentine debate about the possibility of giving Communion under one species, which Luther denied. The expression *salva substantia sacramenti* sets a limit, then, on the church's authority, but within the framework of affirming it. The church, accordingly, without affecting what was instituted by Christ, can influence in some cases the concrete structure of the sacramental sign in its matter and form. This has happened, for example, in the rites of confirmation (the anointing with the sacred chrism blessed by the bishop was added) and of priestly ordination (during the Middle Ages the conferral of the instruments was added).[86] The church also established, in matters pertaining to matrimony, new conditions (canonical form) for its validi-

---

83. "Ministry of the sacraments." See Emmanuel Doronzo, *De sacramentis*, 425–27.

84. See *SSC*, no. 22. Trent, for its part, condemns anyone who maintains that the rites can be revised on the initiative of any pastor; see Council of Trent, Session VII, *Decree on the Sacraments*, canon 13 (DH 1613).

85. See Council of Trent, Session XXI, *Doctrine and Canons on Communion*, chap. 2 (DH 1728); Pius XII, Constitution *Sacramentum Ordinis*, par. 1 (DH 3857).

86. See Michel, "*Salva illorum substantia*"; Ramón Arnau, *Orden y ministerios* (Madrid: Biblioteca de autores cristianos, 1995), 223–24.

ty between Catholics.[87] Moreover it is her responsibility to institute and celebrate the sacramentals, which I will speak about below (in chapter 15).

Second, *the church judges concerning the validity and liceity of the sacraments*. If the church has an influence on the constitution of the sacramental rite, discerning which elements are rooted in Christ, with all the more reason she will be competent to decide about the validity of a specific celebration and to set conditions for its liceity, while always respecting the "substance" of the rites. Once again, the task belongs to the Roman pontiff and to the diocesan bishop, inasmuch as the sacraments represent the seamless unity of the church. The case of matrimony is especially delicate, because in it ground is shared with the civil authority, which is interested in marriage as a pillar of the common good of society as a whole.[88]

Third, *the church in some cases can prevent the sacraments from being administered outside of her*. We already know that the sacraments can exist outside of the church too. As I noted, this is not a limitation of her salvific mediation. On the contrary, it testifies to the fact that the grace administered by the church comes to her from a higher source, as she is a mystery originating in God.

All the same, the church makes her authority felt also in cases of the administration of the sacraments beyond her boundaries. For, in the first place, outside of the church, when the exclusion was culpable, the sacraments are administered fruitlessly and the minister commits a grave sin. Secondly, the church is able to set a limit on the *exercise* of the ordained man's authority. And thus, for example, as we already know, she can impede the validity of the absolution given by a priest by denying him faculties. In matters pertaining to matrimony, because of its social importance in building up the people of God, she can also set conditions for validity, as in the case of canonical form after Trent. It is true that she is not permitted—not in this case either—to prevent any and all sacramental marriages celebrated outside of her fold; for we are considering a natural right of the faithful, which can be limited only for serious reasons that affect the common good.

This is the place to mention the principle that the church often "supplies" what is lacking in the celebration of the sacraments.[89] In some cases in which the minister does not have the faculty to exercise his power—for

---

87. See Council of Trent, Session XIV, *Decree Tametsi* (DH 1813–16).

88. See Granados, *Una sola carne*, 319–29.

89. *CIC* 144. See Yves Congar, "Propos en vue d'une théologie de l'économie dans la tradition latine," *Irénikon* 45 (1972): 155–206, at 194–97; Horst Hermann, *Ecclesia supplet: Das Rechtsinstitut der kirchlichen Suppletion nach c. 209 CIC* (Amsterdam: B. R. Grüner, 1968); the case of the "sanatio in radice" of a marriage is also considered part of the maxim *Ecclesia supplet* ("the church supplies").

example, to confirm (*CIC* 882–83), hear confessions (*CIC* 966), or assist at a marriage (*CIC* 1111)—the church herself can supply, that is, act as minister. For this to happen there has to be *common error* or *positive and probable doubt* about whether or not the minister has faculties. Note that the question affects the exercise of the power of jurisdiction, because the church cannot supply concerning the power of holy orders: there will never be a Eucharist, for example, if the person who celebrates the rite is not a priest; nor will there be a baptism if the baptismal formula is not used. We can summarize the ministry of the church with respect to the sacraments as follows: it is her responsibility to preserve them, to govern their administration, and to give the final form to their rites.[90]

The Seven Sacraments, Different Forms of the Minister's Fatherhood

Each sacrament calls priestly fatherhood into play in a different way. The common measure is found in the Eucharist, inasmuch as Christ himself is present there, as the source of life for the church. Indeed, this is the sacrament in which Jesus brings forth the common good of the whole family of God, with paternal magnanimity.[91] The promotion of this common good is entrusted, then, to priests according to the different degrees of holy orders. Acting in the person of Christ, they help to generate the dwelling place of the one body according to the architecture of the Eucharist, in thanksgiving to the Father and in self-sacrifice for the brethren. They are relational men who foster environments where the human person can flourish.

Oriented toward the Eucharist is baptism, the portal sacrament as birth and incorporation into the body of Jesus. Here the priest's fatherhood shines forth inasmuch as his responsibility is to introduce the catechumen into the network of relations inaugurated by Christ. This is what is signified by the symbolism of immersion into water, which is at the same time a tomb in which the body of sin dies and a virginal womb in which the church

90. See Emmanuel Doronzo, *De sacramentis*, 425–27: "Ecclesia est infallibilis sacramentorum conservatrix, sacramentorum administrationis sapiens gubernatrix; quodammodo et indirecte sacramentorum perfectrix. Ecclesia dici quodammodo potest sacramentorum ministra" (The Church is the unfailing preserver of the sacraments, the wise regulator of the administration of the sacraments; in a way and indirectly she is the perfecter of the sacraments. The Church can be said to be, in a way, the minister of the sacraments).

91. See Thomas Aquinas, *ST* III, q. 65, a. 3, ad 1: "bonum commune spirituale totius Ecclesiae continetur substantialiter in ipso Eucharistiae sacramento" (The common spiritual good of the whole Church is contained substantially in the sacrament itself of the Eucharist).

begets us.[92] The priest appears as a father also when he communicates to the catechumen a new name, at the moment when he recites the Trinitarian formula. In this way he connects the identity of the neophyte (his vocation, his destiny) with the definitive name of God that was revealed in Christ (Father, Son, and Holy Spirit): no fatherhood is capable of opening broader horizons for the child's journey.

In baptism, by way of exception, the minister can also be a layperson, even a nonbeliever, as long as he has the intention to do what the church does. And this is because this "portal sacrament" confers on us the most basic of all gifts: the ability to receive the other gifts of God as his children. Given that this filial receptivity from the creator is both the most original sphere of the fraternal vocation of all humankind, and the meeting point of Jesus with all persons from their birth, it is logical that anyone can represent this basic dimension of incorporation into Christ, which is necessary for our salvation.

Confirmation, for its part, completes what is initiated in baptism, inasmuch as it makes more dynamic the relations in which the believer lives, enabling him to mature in love. The role of the minister can be compared to human fatherhood, for a father typically not only generates the flesh, but also generates desire and freedom, giving them an environment and a direction in which they can be strengthened. In this way the son is taught to look beyond the protective walls of his home, and he is impelled toward social life. Similarly the priest performs this paternal ministry for the maturation of the believer, helping him to allow himself to be led by the Spirit and to be introduced further into the ecclesial ties, while expanding them to all of society. It is not surprising, in light of this, that the minister of confirmation is *per se* the bishop, as sign and foundation of the unity of the local church.

In penance too the priest exercises his fatherhood, now by accompanying the regeneration of the believer. Here the minister works as father in pronouncing the word which, recalling the radical forgiveness of Jesus, helps the penitent to recover the original meaning of his filial identity. It is a matter of telling him: "You are worth more than your wicked deeds, because a radical love that is deeper than any sin that you have committed, holds the secret of your name and destiny; from the perspective of this love it is possible for you to go back to narrating your story, including your history of sin, as the story of a son who goes back home." Once again, the responsibility of the minister, as father of the family, is to reintegrate the believer into the home, in other words, into the network of the church's relations, which regenerates those who dwell in it.

---

92. See Cyril of Jerusalem, *Catechesis* III, 4 (SC 126:112; NPNF-II 7:15a).

The anointing of the sick is also a generative sacrament, in the midst of suffering and prostration. For it can teach the recipient that pain is productive, capable of opening up a path and bearing fruit (see Col 1:24). And it does this precisely by confronting what seems to be the definitive victory of sterility: sickness and death. Moreover the sacrament promises to the sick person, through his configuration to Jesus, the fruit of eternal life, at the gates of the final birth to which a human being is called, when he hears the final call of the Father, the last "Come!" to which faith responds.[93] Death can be seen then, as the poet Rilke affirmed, not as a fatal necessity that is imposed, but rather as the mature fruit that hangs from the tree of a flourishing life. Well, then, for this generation too (for this arduous birth into eternity), a father is necessary, represented by the priest, the minister of the sacrament as a Jesus-figure.

Matrimony has a singular place as far as the minister is concerned. This is due to its unique position among the other sacraments. Indeed, they are all the efficacious presence of the body of Jesus that he assumed in the incarnation—a body which shared the human narrative/story, was given over to death, and was filled with the Spirit when it rose again. The distinctive feature of matrimony is precisely that it preserves the connection between this new body of Christ and the original "one flesh" body (Gn 2:24) for the generation of children. For Christ did not abandon the old body, but rather assumed it and integrated it into the sacramental organism, imparting a new measure to it. The sacrament of matrimony guarantees the presence of the created body, recapitulated in the love of the spouses, within the new body of Christ, who has become one with his church.

It is understandable, then, that the spouses themselves can be the ministers of matrimony, inasmuch as they act while personally representing Christ and the church. This ministry complements what I have said about the priest as minister. For here the lay faithful enter with full initiative into the mediation of sacramental grace, specifically commissioned to build a family by raising their children for God, and to contribute to the common good of human society. They too have a ministry, through which the church is made present in all the everyday concerns of life and of society.

Matrimony proves to be indispensable, moreover, in understanding the priest's own ministry, which I have described as a paternal ministry. For marriage is where the human experience of fatherhood is kept, and Christian marriage attests that this fatherhood has been assumed by Christ, who offers to man a new way of living it out. In order for the priest to learn to be

93. See Francis, *Lumen Fidei*, par. 56 (594).

a father in a sacramental way, he will always have to keep in mind this original reference to fatherhood that is experienced in every Christian family.

Recall, moreover, that the presence and work of the priest is not something external to the ministry of the spouses. For the distinctive feature of matrimony is to live out conjugal love according to the new love of Christ and the church, of which the priest proves to be a privileged witness, being the minister of the Eucharist. Therefore he is singularly well-positioned to assist at the ceremony where the spouses exchange vows, reminding them that the bond with Christ is central to their mutual love.

Finally, the priest lives this responsibility of his as father in Christ based on the memory of his own ordination, in which the bishop was the minister. Here the sign—the hands that cover the head of the ordinand, and the prayer that is pronounced over him, configuring him to Christ the head in the power of the Spirit—makes it clear that his fatherhood springs from the memory of an original gift, a memory that effectively and perpetually keeps the strength of the sacrament enkindled (1 Tm 4:14).

15 ❧ SEVEN SACRAMENTS IN THE CHURCH-SACRAMENT

I concluded the previous chapter by stating that the church can be called in a certain way the minister of the sacraments. I was referring to her above all inasmuch as she is configured to Christ the head through holy orders. This statement about the church considers her as being represented in her pastors, who are responsible for conferring the sacraments and regulating their use. All the same, this view has to be broadened in order to discover the sacramental feature of the entire church, and not only of the ordained ministry. The church proves to be more than a minister of the sacraments: she herself is a sacrament.

This topic belongs to the treatise on ecclesiology, where this title (the church as sacrament) is studied in more detail.[1] Nevertheless, sacramental theology too has something to say about the subject. Indeed, this demonstrates the close proximity of these two areas of dogma. It is interesting to note, on the one hand, that the reason why medieval theologians did not need a treatise on ecclesiology is because they explained it in discussing the sacraments: the power of the keys, for example, was addressed together with penance.[2] On the other hand someone recently wrote what appears to be the exact opposite: that sacramental theology in general is nothing but a part of ecclesiology.[3] What should we say: is sacramental theology a chapter in the doctrine about the church, or is ecclesiology a chapter in the treatise on the sacraments? As we will see, the two areas are mutually enriching, according to a luminous circularity that will enable us to consider the seven sacraments as seven columns that give support and shape to the house of the church.

---

1. See Eloy Bueno de la Fuente, *Eclesiología* (Madrid: Biblioteca de autores cristianos, 1998), 73 87.
2. See Peter Lombard, *Sent.* IV, d. 18–19 (SpBon V:355–71); Doronzo, *De sacramentis in genere*, xvii.
3. See Rahner, *The Church and the Sacraments*, 41.

The Church as Sacrament: Vatican II and
Twentieth-Century Theology

Let us start with the description of the church as "sacrament" as proposed by Vatican II and with the way in which it has been received after the Council.[4]

Church-Sacrament in Vatican II

The vision of the church presented by Vatican II starts by affirming that she, "in Christ, is in the nature of a sacrament—a sign and instrument, that is, of communion with God and of unity among all men."[5] In order to understand this statement we must note, first, that the church is a sacrament in relation to Christ, whom scripture and the Church Fathers call the sacrament *par excellence* (see Col 2:2). The word "sacrament" is used here, therefore, in its biblical and patristic meaning, and not in the classic sense of the seven salvific sacraments. This is why *Lumen Gentium* says that the church is "in the nature of" (*veluti*) a sacrament.

It must be admitted, nevertheless, that the patristic support for describing the church as a sacrament is meager.[6] It is true that St. Cyprian, who is cited by the Council, mentions an *inseparabile unitatis sacramentum* (inseparable sacrament of unity) in order to emphasize the importance of belonging to the church.[7] All the same, the bishop of Carthage speaks about *sacramentum* in a broad sense, referring in general to the divine plan for mankind, which is a design of unbreakable union (see Eph 3:3, read in light

---

4. See Henri Bourgeois, "Les sacrements selon Vatican II," in *Histoire des dogmes*, vol. 3: *Les signes du salut*, ed. Bernard Sesboüé (Paris: Desclée, 1995), 243–82.

5. *LG*, no. 1. See Cándido Pozo, "La Iglesia como sacramento primordial: Contenido teológico real de este concepto," *Estudios Eclesiásticos* 41, no. 157 (1966): 139–59.

6. This is recognized by Pieter Smulders, "L'Église sacrement du salut," in *L'Église de Vatican II*, vol. 2: *Commentaires*, ed. G. Baraúna (Paris: Cerf, 1966), 311–38. Among the patristic passages that he cites are *Didaché* XI, 11 (SC 248:186), an enigmatic reference to the "cosmic mystery of the Church" used to describe the surprising behavior of some Christian prophets, and which could allude to the spousal union of Christ and the church. He also cites Gregory of Nyssa, *In Canticum Canticorum* IX (PG 44:949), and St. Cyprian, *Epistolae* 55, 21 (CSEL 3.2:639): "the indivisible sacrament of the Catholic Church." St. Cyprian speaks about the "sacramentum unitatis" (sacrament of unity) in reference to the unity of the church in *De unitate ecclesiae catholicae* IV (CSEL 3.1:213). Smulders also cites Ambrose, *Expositio evangelii secundum Lucam* VII 96 (CSEL 32.4:323), which discusses the "mysterium ecclesiae" (mystery of the Church) by referring to its prefigurations in the Old Testament, such as the Ninevites or the Queen of Sheba.

7. In *LG*, no. 9, the definition of the church as sacrament reappears, and a note cites St. Cyprian, *Epistolae* 69, 6 (CSEL 3.2:754) on the *inseparabile unitatis sacramentum*; the martyr does not apply the term to the church directly, but rather to the divine design of unity that takes concrete form in her. We have also, by the same Cyprian, *Epistolae ad Pompeium* 74, 11 (CSEL 3.2:808–9): there he speaks about a mystery of unity proclaimed in the Song of Solomon, where the beloved is called, through the mouth of Christ, enclosed garden, my sister, bride, Noah's ark. See Ulrich Wickert, *Sacramentum unitatis: Ein Beitrag zum Verständnis der Kirche bei Cyprian* (Berlin: De Gruyter, 1971).

of Eph 2:16) and, as such, includes the unity of the church. We will see, however, that even though the term itself does not often appear in the Fathers, the idea expressed by the Council is found frequently, combined with the presentation of the church as body.

Together with this patristic aspect of the notion "church-sacrament," another note is added immediately afterward, which is now in keeping with the outline of classic sacramental theology: a sacrament is a "sign and instrument."[8] In other words, to describe the church-sacrament the document has recourse to the medieval tradition, in which, as we know, the formula "instrumental sign of grace" was elaborated. Therefore the Council is not simply going back to the patristic perspective, but rather is also applying to the church the Scholastic reflection on the seven sacraments. Sacramental theology, with the twists and turns of its history, becomes necessary in order to enter into ecclesiology.

Of what is the church a sacrament—a sign and instrument? The Council answers: of the unity between God and humankind and of human beings among themselves. In an earlier draft of the text the terms were reversed: first love among men, then love for God. The definitive version correctly restored the order of charity, which always begins in God as in its paternal source and therefore discovers in the neighbor a brother.[9] From this we can conclude: the church is the sign and instrument of a communion, a communion so ordered as to reflect the love of the Trinity, which begins in the Father as in its source.

Further on, *Lumen Gentium* returns to our topic: Christ "sent his life-giving Spirit upon his disciples and through him set up his Body which is the Church as the universal sacrament of salvation."[10] In this way the Council insists that all human fulfillment passes in some way through the church. And, moreover, the notion of "sacrament" is associated with the notion of "body," with weighty consequences: the church is sacrament inasmuch as she is a body that springs from the body of Jesus, the place where the mystery of God is manifested fully. Although I will explore this link "sacrament-body" later on, we should note now the continuity with the historical process by which the sacrament was defined, a process started by St. Augustine that has always revolved around the Eucharistic body of Christ.

8. *LG*, no. 1.

9. See Pozo, "La Iglesia como sacramento," 139–59.

10. *LG*, no. 48. For other references to the church-sacrament in the conciliar documents, see *LG*, no. 9: "established ... the Church, that it may be for each and everyone the visible sacrament of this saving unity"; *SSC*, no. 5: "from the side of Christ as he slept the sleep of death upon the cross ... came forth 'the wondrous sacrament of the whole Church'"; *SSC*, no. 26: "the Church which is the sacrament of unity"; *Ad Gentes*, no. 5: "founded his Church as the sacrament of salvation." See also *GS*, no. 42, citing *LG*, no. 1.

Let us inquire, finally, about the background for the use of this term in the conciliar documents. As there was no clear patristic basis, as I have said, its origin must be identified in contemporary theological reflection, which occurred especially in German-speaking countries.[11] Romanticism (from 1830 on) had already developed an appreciation for the "mystery-sacrament": Goethe, for example, had praised the sacrament as the noblest aspect of religion.[12] Based on this, the nineteenth century elaborated a vision of the church as an immense living organism, which advanced through the ages while allowing the mystery of God to show through: she is a "Great Sacrament" (Heinrich Klee) or a "sacramental mystery" (Matthias Joseph Scheeben).[13]

Later on, twentieth-century theology, the heir of this development, placed the term "sacrament" at the center of its vision of the church.[14] Highly influential was the proposal of Karl Rahner, who was joined by Otto Semmelroth: these authors went on to speak not only about the church as a "great sacrament," but about the church as the "original sacrament" or "root sacrament" (*Ursakrament / Wurzelsakrament*).[15] By this they meant that the church prolongs the true "original sacrament" which is Christ; and that from her the seven sacraments are derived as from one source. Their approach involved a determined precedence of ecclesiology over sacramental theology, a precedence that is the most debatable novelty of this proposal, as we will see.

The influence of this current was such that in the early drafts of *Lumen Gentium* the church is called *sacramentum fundamentale*, alluding to the Rahnerian term *Ursakrament*.[16] The expression then disappeared in the final text, and furthermore the application of the term *sacramentum* to the church was relativized (by adding *veluti*). We can conclude from this that the Council did not adopt the particulars of Rahner's proposal (which postulated the precedence of the church-sacrament over the seven sacraments)

11. See Colombo, "Dove va la teologia," 679: "German theology of this period advanced more by speculative vigor than by historical investigation."

12. See Matthäus Bernards, "Zur Lehre der Kirche als Sakrament: Beobachtungen aus der Theologie des 19. und 20. Jahrhunderts," *Münchener Theologische Zeitschrift* 20 (1969): 29–54; and Deneken, "Les romantiques allemands."

13. See Jean-Marie Pasquier, *L'Église comme sacrement: Le développement de l'idée sacramentelle de l'Église de Möhler à Vatican II* (Fribourg: Academic Press, 2008), 24.

14. See Rahner, *The Church and the Sacraments*, 9–10; Otto Semmelroth, *Kirche als Ursakrament* (Frankfurt am Main: Knecht, 1953); Dennis M. Doyle, "Otto Semmelroth and the Advance of the Church as Sacrament at Vatican II," *Theological Studies* 76 (2015): 65–86.

15. See Otto Semmelroth, "La Iglesia como sacramento de la salvación," in *Mysterium Salutis* 4.1:321–70, at 330.

16. See Pasquier, *L'Église comme sacrement*, 207–16.

but only referred to the general idea of the church as sacrament, pointing out the patristic soil in which it sprang up and associating it with the development of classic sacramental theology (*signum et instrumentum*). At Vatican II, moreover, this idea was linked both to the visibility of relations in the church-*body* and to the *communion* that is forged and manifested in this body.

Church-Sacrament: Theological Potential and Postconciliar Evolution

After it was mentioned at Vatican II, theology delved into the concept of church-sacrament, highlighting several of its features. First, calling the church a sacrament allows for a *comprehensive view that keeps the communion of the church united with the person of Christ and with the seven sacraments of salvation*. In this regard, as we will see, it will be important to clarify correctly the connection between the church and the sacraments, which is not just unidirectional (the church gives us the sacraments), but a two-way relationship: when she celebrates the sacraments the church is engendered by them. Strictly speaking, this latter dimension has the primacy. Vatican Council II accepts both aspects; for, on the one hand, it publishes in the first place the Constitution on the Liturgy, which says that the liturgy is the source and summit of the church's action;[17] and, on the other hand, it enumerates the sacraments within the discussion about the church, affirming that she is actualized in the seven sacraments.[18]

Second, to speak about the *church-sacrament* is to point out the *unity of the visible and the invisible in her*. Therefore, based on the concept of sacrament, two complementary ways of considering the church are unified: as a visible society and as a communion of persons. Thus we understand that the ecclesial institution is not a bureaucratic framework, but rather the manifestation of divine grace and the channel through which it comes to us. This confirms then that the "church-sacrament" cannot be separated from the "church-body," for the body is the place where the mystery is manifested. This view is completed, indeed, by the analogy that Vatican II proposes between the nature of the church and the incarnation.[19] The Word is to the human nature that he assumed what the Holy Spirit is to the visible face of the church.

Third, the concept of church-sacrament has been used to explain *the way*

---

17. See *SSC*, no. 10.
18. *LG*, no. 11.
19. *LG*, no. 8.

in which all human beings are saved by her. As Yves Congar noted, "universal sacrament of salvation" would amount to a contemporary formulation of the ancient axiom *extra ecclesiam nulla salus* (outside the church there is no salvation).[20] This would be saying the same thing, but in a positive way: through the church God's entire blessing comes to every human being.

Certainly some have misused this concept to relativize the church's place in the work of salvation. And they have used the term sacrament, understood as sign of a higher reality, to emphasize the distance between the church and Christ, or between the church and the Kingdom. If this idea is taken to extremes, the church could appear to be one avatar of the Kingdom of God among others, and the missionary urgency on which the gospel insists would be reduced to a clanging cymbal.[21]

All the same, without denying the necessary distinction between sign and signified, it must be said that these authors assume an impoverished view of "sign" that is more Platonic than Christian. Indeed, the sacrament, as the previous chapters showed, is not a "sign-arrow" that points to something beyond it, an arrow that could be dispensed with when it reaches the target, but rather the opening of the symbolic space where the encounter and communion with God and other human beings occurs. Therefore a correct understanding that the church is a sacrament impels a believer even more to mission: the church, as a place or space where salvation happens, is called to expand so as to welcome beneath its branches a multitude of birds. This is the right way in which the sacrament indicates precisely this openness of the church to what is beyond her, toward a greater gift of which she is the servant, for all sacramental space springs from God and is adjusted to the humble pattern of the cross. But this openness will exist, not by a flight toward another separate space, but rather by deepening the relations that are founded on Jesus and weave through the very space of the church.

Finally, the concept of church-sacrament has been criticized for its apparent inability to *include the social concern and action of Christians.*[22] And is this not, in fact, an intra-ecclesial term, embracing only those who are already inside? We will see, nevertheless, that speaking about the "sacrament" proves to be of key importance for the cultural and social mission of the church in the postmodern world, which more than ever is ignorant of spaces

---

20. *LG*, no. 48. See Yves Congar, *This Church that I Love*, trans. Lucien Delafuente (Denville, N.J.: Dimension Books, 1969), chap. 2.

21. Michael Amaladoss, *Beyond Dialogue: Pilgrims to the Absolute* (Bangalore: Asian Trading Corporation, 2008).

22. See Avery Dulles, "The Church as Sacrament," in his *Models of the Church* (New York: Doubleday, 1987), 63–88; I will respond to these critiques in the course of this chapter.

and times where God's presence and action can be experienced; in other words, it is ignorant of sacramental spaces and times.[23] To offer my synthesis at once and to elucidate the questions that have been posed, I will start with the relation between the church and the seven sacraments and, more concretely, between the church and the Eucharist.

The Church Is Sacrament as Body of Christ: Synthesis Based on the Eucharist

The formula in *Lumen Gentium* (no. 1) invites us to study the "church-sacrament" based on the definition for the seven sacraments that was worked out in the Middle Ages: *sign and instrumental cause of grace*. Still, such a general formula must not make us forget the distinctive features of each one of them. Concretely speaking, this means, as we know, that the nature of the sacrament is perceived only in terms of the Eucharist, which can very well be called the "fundamental sacrament." In light of this, to say "church-sacrament" is to say "church-Eucharist." And indeed the title *sacramentum salutis*, "sacrament of salvation," has been applied both to the church and to the Eucharist.[24] As Joseph Ratzinger wrote: "The Eucharist is the *sacramentum Christi* [sacrament of Christ] and, because the Church is *Eucharistia*, she is therefore also *sacramentum*—the sacrament to which all the other sacraments are ordered."[25]

Church-Sacrament as Church-Eucharist

Based on the Eucharist, I will elucidate the general relation between church and sacraments. In order to do this it is necessary to consider first the influence of Karl Rahner, who called the church "the original sacrament" (*Ursakrament*) from which the seven sacraments emanate. In his view these are different actualizations of the church, her actions in which she says and carries out fully who she is. Otto Semmelroth insistently proposed the same view, speaking about the sacraments as differentiations of the root sacra-

23. On the pastoral consequences of the concept of church-sacrament, see Otto Semmelroth, "Pastorale Konsequenzen aus der Sakramentalität der Kirche," in Leo Scheffczyk et al., *Wahrheit und Verkündigung: Festschrift Schmaus* (Paderborn: Schöningh, 1967), 1499–1505.

24. See *LG*, no. 48. See Paul McPartlan, *Sacrament of Salvation: An Introduction to Eucharistic Ecclesiology* (London: T and T Clark, 1995), xv; the author cites Jn 6:54 ("he who eats my flesh and drinks my blood has eternal life") to justify the application of the expression "sacrament of salvation" to the Eucharist.

25. See Ratzinger, "The Church as the Sacrament of Salvation," in his *Principles of Catholic Theology*, 53.

ment of the church.[26] Certainly, for both authors the church derives from Jesus, who is the true original sacrament.

This theory of Rahner possesses the valuable aspects that I have already noted, recorded in *Lumen Gentium*; but it also suffers from a serious deficiency. For while it emphasizes that the sacraments are derived from the church, it does not fully embrace the complementary and even primordial line of argument: the church is born of the sacraments, principally from the Eucharist. Henri de Lubac was the one who insisted most on this point, coining the formula: "The Eucharist makes the Church."[27] Thus the route that goes from the church to the sacraments is preceded by another one: from the sacraments to the church.

A similar primacy of the Eucharist over the church is found already in the writings of St. Paul. In fact, the apostle associates the church with the *mysterion* (in Latin, *sacramentum*) precisely inasmuch as she is the body of Christ, who brings the fullness of the head to the cosmos (see Eph 1:9, 22). Therefore the *mysterion* is the unification of Jews and Gentiles in one body, tearing down the walls that separated them (see Eph 2:13–14; 3:3–6).[28] If the "church-sacrament" is connected to the "church-body," then the church's sacramentality proceeds from the Eucharist, for that is where the one body of Christians is formed (see 1 Cor 10:16–17). Patristic reflection started from this Pauline basis: the concept of church-sacrament can be found in the Fathers only if we keep it connected with the concept of the church-body, which in turn is derived from the Eucharistic practice.[29]

In conclusion, we have two lines of argument: first, the church springs from the Eucharist, as the fruit that matures on the tree; second, the church celebrates the Eucharist, offering the body of Christ on the altar, and in this way she fully actualizes her being. The first line starts from Christ and, through the sacraments, reaches the church—it can be represented with the statement by Henri de Lubac that I cited above: "The Eucharist makes the Church." The second line—pointed out by Karl Rahner and Otto Semmelroth—runs from Christ, through the church, to the sacraments.

26. See Rahner, *The Church and the Sacraments*; Semmelroth, *Kirche als Ursakrament*; Nicolás López Martínez, *Sacramentología General* (Burgos: Aldecoa, 1989), 183; Doyle, "Otto Semmelroth and the Advance of the Church," 84n62.

27. For a comprehensive view of the origin of this phrase, see McPartlan, *Sacrament of Salvation*, 30; Henri de Lubac uses the expression in his *Corpus Mysticum: the Eucharist and the Church in the Middle Ages*, trans. Gemma Simmonds et al. (Notre Dame, Ind.: University of Notre Dame Press, 2007), 88, and *The Splendor of the Church*, trans. Michael Mason (San Francisco, Calif.: Ignatius Press, 1999), 133.

28. See Rowan Williams, "The Church as Sacrament," *International Journal for the Study of the Christian Church* 11 (2011): 116–22.

29. See Mersch, *Le Corps Mystique du Christ*.

How can we articulate these two lines of argument? It is important to understand that the body of Christ is not just a unidirectional prolongation of what happened in Jesus with respect to his church. This image is derived from a view of the body as an organism made up of head and members. This explains Rahner's proposal: from the head (Christ) it passes to the torso (church), which is then prolonged in the seven sacraments (members).

There is, nevertheless, a broader way of thinking about the unity in the body, which is more inclusive of the Pauline proposal. It is contained in the nuptial experience of man and woman who have become "one flesh" (see Gn 2:24; Eph 5:31). Here head and body are husband and wife; and their unity is not only organic but also interpersonal, according to the fidelity of love. In this case the influence is twofold: first, Jesus engenders the church, giving life to her; immediately afterward, Jesus associates the church to himself, so that life can flow from both to all human beings.

In the first place, therefore, the church is born from the Eucharistic body of Jesus, which engenders her. In the Eucharist Christ communicates to his disciples the way of loving God and human beings that he forged during his life in the flesh, and thus establishes them as his body. The church is built on these foundations laid by Jesus. He washes her in the bath of water in the word, so as to present her to himself without spot or wrinkle (Eph 5:26–27); he gives her food and care with his body and blood (see Eph 5:29). From this perspective the sacraments have precedence over the church; ecclesiology is derived from sacramental theology.

In the second place, the church not only is born from Christ but also, as his bride, is associated with his mystery, so that with him she can call human beings to salvation. If the sacraments are the pillars that establish the dwelling place of the church, it is her task to inhabit the house and to enlarge it, celebrating in turn the sacraments according to the mandate received from Jesus. The sacraments now spring from the church so as to incorporate into her the life of human beings and to expand through the cosmos. In other words, having been born of the Eucharist, the church contributes to the formation of the Eucharistic body. Therefore St. Augustine said that, when she offers the offering on the altar, she offers herself.[30] This is the complementary and subordinate line which leads from Jesus and his church to the Eucharist. Ignatius of Antioch spoke in this light about the church as "altar of the sacrifice" and concluded: "if any one be not within the altar, he is deprived of the bread of God."[31] Although the walls of the church are raised

---

30. See Augustine, *De civitate Dei* X, 6 (CCL 47:279; NPNF-I 2:184b).
31. See Ignatius of Antioch, *Ad Ephesians* V, 2 (SC 10b:72; ANF 1:51). Ignatius is probably referring

on the sacraments, they, in turn, have to be celebrated on ecclesial ground.

Thus the church is *ecclesia congregata* (called together by God) and *ecclesia congregans* (which, with Christ, her head, calls Christians together for God).[32] In other words, the church is generated and generating: generated from the Eucharist, inasmuch as she becomes bride through Christ's love; generating through the Eucharist, inasmuch as she, united with her bridegroom, becomes a mother.

The Church as Sacramental Space

The origin of the church in the Eucharist confirms that it is necessary to combine church-sacrament and church-body. Recall that the centrality of the Eucharistic body was our thread through the labyrinth enabling us to follow the tangled historical process in which the definition of sacrament was forged (see chapters 10 and 11, above). Based on this, I defined the sacrament as the opening up of a symbolic space of relations, rooted in Christ's flesh, a space to which Christians come to belong. In light of this, calling the church a sacrament entails thinking about her as a network or space of personal ties (the body of which Christ is head), a space in which full communion with God can be experienced.

The church-sacrament is the corporeal space of relations that Jesus forged during his life and communicated to human beings. Every human place is prepared so as to welcome us and to foster particular relations with the world and with others. Thus, when we are received into a house, we find a structure designed by an architect, who raised its walls so that it would contain a particular style of life. There is a big difference, for example, between an arrangement of isolated apartments with few common areas, resembling a hotel, and another with ample places to converse and live together. The first will foster individualism; the second will serve as a channel for communion.

All this is an image of the more original dwelling place that is the family itself, rooted in the flesh of man and woman and built with the living stones of personal relations. The family possesses a framework of relations (the relation of husband and wife, that of the parents with their children, and so on), in which is contained the original intention of the creator-architect; and it makes it possible to build an environment of ties where communion flourishes. The familial space is then extended in other relations of the house, the city, the temple. All these spaces are symbolic, not inasmuch as they point

---

to the church as a worshipping community: see Juan José Ayán (ed.), *Padres Apostólicos* (Madrid: Ciudad Nueva, 2000), 238n23.

32. See de Lubac, *The Splendor of the Church*, 102–11.

to a further reality, but because one can always delve deeper into them and thus discover the mystery of man and of God.

This approach coincides with the Pauline concept of the church, which belongs to the *mysterion* because she is the body of Christ, in other words, a family rooted in his incarnate love.[33] The apostle, indeed, delights in images of the household (1 Tm 3:15), the wife (Eph 5:24–25), and the temple (Eph 2:21) in order to refer to the church, which is also called a city (Rv 21:2). And recall the similes that St. Cyprian uses in speaking about the sacrament of unity: enclosed garden, Noah's Ark, house, well of living water, garden of luscious fruit, etc.[34]

In light of this, the church can be called a sacrament inasmuch as she is a space rooted in the flesh, with a fundamental framework that she has received from Christ, the plans of which were designed to promote Jesus' way of loving. The foundations of this space are contained in the seven sacraments, preeminently in the Eucharist. Earlier (in chapter 12) I proposed that, whereas through the baptismal character each believer's space of relations is conformed to the body of Jesus, the Eucharist contains a sort of global "character" of the whole church. And this is because in the sacrament of the altar the church receives the plans and pillars established by Jesus. Here lies the order of her relations, where her original holiness is made visible in the world's sight. Starting from the Eucharist, this space takes on concrete form, as I will show later in this chapter, in the other sacraments, especially in those which, by imprinting a character (or, in matrimony, by forging the conjugal bond), involve a new configuration of the Christian's relational spheres.

Therefore, in the space that the sacraments generate we find the first visibility of the church, who is rooted directly in the flesh of Christians. For the household of God (see 1 Tm 3:15) is not built primarily on bricks of clay (although it then needs also an architecture and a form of city planning), but rather on the new relations between believers established by Jesus in his flesh, into which relations we are incorporated by the sacraments. Projected from there are the other visible places that she occupies, which branch out into institutions, customs, laws, rites, and so on.

The church, therefore, is not a gathering of individuals, each of whom has been touched interiorly by God, who now wish to praise him togeth-

---

33. See Friedrich Bechina, *Die Kirche als Familie Gottes: Die Stellung dieses theologischen Konzeptes im Zweiten Vatikanischen Konzil und in den Bischofssynoden von 1974 bis 1994 im Hinblick auf eine Familia-Dei Ekklesiologie* (Rome: Gregorian University Press, 1998).

34. See Cyprian, *Epistolae ad Pompeium* 73, 11 (CSEL 3.2:808–9; ANF 5:389b); *De ecclesiae catholicae unitate* 8 (CSEL 3.1:217; ANF 5:424a).

er. On the contrary, she exists because God acted not in isolated subjects but rather in their mutual relations and, therefore, in the corporeal space that unites them, the space that originated in Jesus' life in the flesh. We can conclude from this that the church is born together with the space of the sacraments as a great family or dwelling place which, on the one hand, is built on them (along the line Christ-sacraments-church) and, on the other hand, offers the environment where they can be celebrated (along the line Christ-church-sacraments).

The church is sacrament because into her corporeal space of relations the Holy Spirit descends and dwells definitively as the communication of Jesus' love. Precisely because the habitat of the church is ordered according to the sacraments, which contain the way of life proper to Jesus, the church is the suitable space in which this Spirit who animated Jesus' life can descend and rest. Outside of this space the Spirit is poured out into incomplete molds that are unable to accommodate his fullness. Only within this space which is the church does the Spirit breathe with the creative power of all his charisms. We can draw an analogy here with what we said about the baptismal character, which orders the believer's relations so that the Holy Spirit can be poured out onto them (see chapter 11, above). All the same, there is also a difference: the life of the believer could become configured according to the relations of Jesus (by the baptismal character) without the believer having the love of Jesus, for lack of faith and charity. This, nevertheless, does not happen in the church-sacrament: the distinctive feature of this ecclesial space is that Christ has assured the sanctifying presence of his Spirit and the faith with which the church receives him, so that the fruit of his love is never lacking. The church is sacrament because the Spirit of communion that Jesus gave us dwells permanently in her, who is the relational dwelling place that reflects the life of Jesus. Therefore we can say, with St. Irenaeus of Lyons: "Where the Church is, there is the Spirit of God; and where the Spirit of God is, there is the Church, and every kind of grace."[35]

Everything that I have said can be summed up with the help of a passage from the Book of Proverbs: "Wisdom has built her house, she has set up her seven pillars. She has slaughtered her beasts, she has mixed her wine, she has also set her table" (Prv 9:1–2). Medieval commentators saw in this house the church, built by Wisdom, Jesus. Given that the passage speaks about sacrifices, and then mentions wine, inviting people to "eat of my bread and drink of the wine I have mixed" (Prv 9:5), it was easy to read it from a Eu-

---

35. See Irenaeus of Lyons, *Adversus haereses* III, 24, 1 (SC 211:474; ANF 1:458b).

charistic perspective,[36] and therefore to find in the seven columns the seven sacraments, on which the church is founded and which, in turn, allow the church to expand and to be built up until she fills the whole world.

Universal Maturation of the Church-Sacrament

Calling the church "sacrament" emphasizes that the space of relations in which she consists (built on the seven sacraments) is an open space that spreads out beyond itself (with the "beyond" which is proper to symbols). This expansion takes place not simply because the church refers us to other external spaces that do not belong to her, but rather because the relations that form the church's space conceal ever-greater depths and, by delving into these relationships, and by helping them mature in time, the church is capable of taking up into herself all of the spaces of human life: the space of the family, the space of work and leisure, the space of commerce and politics, and so on. Besides the image of the house, another simile may inspire us: that of a vegetable garden full of seeds which, in time, bear fruit. The space of the church is sacramental because it is a fertile, generative space.[37]

This entails the fact that *the perspective of the church-sacrament is a dynamic perspective*: that of a dwelling place being built up at the initiative of God who gives the increase. Inasmuch as this space of the church refers to the original gift of Jesus and points to the resurrection as its horizon of fulfillment, the church-sacrament is also church-pilgrim. Recall that, already in the writings of St. Paul, the sacrament is presented as a recapitulation of all the eons in Christ and his church, thus constituting the fullness of time. And that the Church Fathers saw the sacraments, in this light, as the key to conducting typological exegesis, connected with the *historia salutis* (salvation history).

Within this temporal framework, the church's sacramentality illuminates, first of all, *the future*. Given that the church is generated from the resurrection of Jesus, *a space* opens up in her *where the next world is anticipated in glorified flesh*. Entering the church is like entering a force field magnetized by Christ's parousia, which takes possession of our present and attracts it toward itself.[38] In other words, the church is the environment where ev-

---

36. See Bonaventure, *Sermones de diversis* XI, 6, ed. Jacques Guy Bougerol (Paris: Les Éditions Franciscaines, 1993), 1:209; Carl-Gustaf Andrén, *De Septem Sacramentis: En Sakramentsutläggning från vadstena Kloster* (Lund: Gleerups, 1963). The Church Fathers, for their part, referred the passage to the incarnation, identifying the house with the body that the Wisdom of God had knit for himself in Mary's womb.

37. See Irenaeus of Lyons, *Adversus haereses* V, 20, 2 (SC 153:258; ANF 1:548a): "Plantata est enim Ecclesia paradisus in hoc mundo" (The Church has been planted as a garden [*paradisus*] in this world).

38. See Liam Bergin, *O Propheticum Lavacrum: Baptism as Symbolic Act of Eschatological Salvation* (Rome: Editrice Pontificia Università Gregoriana, 1999).

erything can be seen and evaluated according to what it is called to be in its fullness, in accordance with God's hope. She is the garden in which the seeds that are sown there bear plenty of fruit and where the time of maturity is already experienced in a certain way. This is how the church-sacrament is a missionary church. What does mission consist of if not in calling all things together to the fertile ground where they can reach their maximum fruitfulness?

We can conclude then that the church is sacrament of the future, "the seed and the beginning of [the] kingdom" and *sacramentum spei* (sacrament of hope), according to the Augustinian formula.[39] In the words of an Orthodox theologian: "The Church is what she is by becoming again and again what she will be."[40] The Letter to the Hebrews presents the liturgical assembly precisely as a place where the future world is attained—as though we were passing through a time tunnel (see Heb 12:18–24). There Christians are joined, not so much to a heavenly community as to the church that has arrived at her destination, that is, "to the spirits of just men made perfect" (Heb 12:23).

In the second place, the church's sacramentality refers *to the past*: *she is sacrament because she opens up a space of memory*, from which it is possible to remember every origin. We know, in fact, that memory is connected with certain places: just by entering the house where we spent our childhood, we evoke many memories of what happened. Well, then, the church is the dwelling place where it is possible to remember the essential events of history. We remember, in the first place, Jesus and his life; and in Christ we recall the first origin of all things in God, the origin full of purity and promises. Therefore, at the entrance to the church the baptismal font flows, the footprint of God's original love, of his first creation and of his recreation of the cosmos through the death and glorification of Jesus.

This means that the church is entitled to reclaim the original goodness of the world, as it was in the beginning and as Jesus made possible once again.[41] Given that the church keeps this memory, the Fathers were able to

---

39. *LG*, no. 5. See Augustine, *Contra Faustum* 12, 20 (CSEL 25:349; NPNF-I 4:190a): "quando erit sanctorum requies non adhuc *in sacramento spei*, quo in hoc tempore consociatur Ecclesia, quamdiu bibitur quod de Christi latere manavit; sed iam in ipsa perfectione salutis aeternae, cum tradetur regnum Deo et Patri" (when … the rest [i.e., repose] of the saints shall no longer be *in the sacrament of hope*, as now, while in the communion of the Church, they drink what flowed from the side of Christ, but in the perfection of eternal safety [i.e., salvation], when the kingdom shall be delivered up to God and the Father).

40. See Ioannis D. Zizioulas, *The One and the Many: Studies on God, Man, the Church, and the World Today* (Alhambra, Calif.: Sebastian Press, 2010), 138.

41. See von Allmen, *Prophetisme sacramentel*, 35.

see her present already in Abel the just man,[42] and to hear Adam's words to his wife as a prophecy about Christ and the church.[43] Therefore her mission includes not only announcing that everyone is called to fullness in Jesus, but also reminding every human being and society about the order of created reality, according to God's will. Relying on St. Augustine we can speak about the *sacramentum memoriae* (sacrament of memory),[44] just as St. Cyprian had referred to the *sacramentum traditionis*.[45]

In short, the sacramentality of the church indicates, from the past and toward the future, her maturation in time, as the Orthodox theologian Alexander Schmemann nicely puts it: "The nature of the institution can be termed *sacramental,* and this means not only a given or static interdependence between the visible and the invisible, nature and grace, the material and the spiritual, but also, and primarily, the dynamic essence of the Church as passage from the old into the new, from this world into the world to come, from the kingdom of nature into the Kingdom of Grace."[46]

In this way the church, in the concrete space in which she dwells, reveals God as *beginning and end* of all history. The dynamic perspective thus helps us to see that this space is not a closed space for a few people. Given that the common origin of each human being in Christ is remembered in this space, and given that the destiny of the cosmos at the end of time is anticipated in this space, it follows that to inhabit this space and to build it up is to foster the reconciliation and unity of all mankind. This is the ecumenical and missionary power that is lodged in the vision of the church as sacrament of salvation. The Catholic church can be called *sacramentum salutis mundi,* sacrament of the full salvation of the world, inasmuch as all the other spaces that are habitable for human beings find in her their foundation and their crown.[47]

Precisely because the sacramental space of the church comes to her from Christ and thus surpasses her, there are sacramental elements outside of her

---

42. See Gregory the Great, *Homilae in Evangelia* I, 19, 1 (CCL 141:143).

43. See Sebastian Tromp, "Ecclesia Sponsa Virgo Mater," *Gregorianum* 18 (1937): 3–29.

44. See Augustine, *Contra Faustum* XX, 21 (CSEL 25:564; NPNF-I 4:262b): "Huius sacrificii caro et sanguis ante adventum Christi per victimas similitudinem promittebatur, in passione Christi per ipsam veritatem reddebatur, post ascensum Christi per sacramentum memoriae celebratur" (Before the coming of Christ, the flesh and blood of this sacrifice were foreshadowed in the animals slain; in the passion of Christ the types were fulfilled by the true sacrifice; after the ascension of Christ, this sacrifice is commemorated in the sacrament).

45. "Sacrament of the divine tradition"; see Cyprian, *Epistolae* LXXIV 11, 1 (CCL 3/1:808; ANF 5:389b).

46. See Alexander Schmemann, "Ecclesiological Notes," *Saint Vladimir's Seminary Quarterly* 11 (1967): 35–39, at 36.

47. Jan L. Witte, "L'Église, 'sacramentum unitatis' du cosmos et du genre humain," in *L'Église de Vatican II* (ed. Baraúna), 457–91.

full visible communion too. Consequently, the Kingdom of God spreads outside the church not as an invisible, purely spiritual reign, but also sacramentally, in the different relational spaces that shelter the divine presence, spaces that orient those who inhabit them toward the full unity of the Catholic church. Recall that the other churches and ecclesial communities are such insofar as they have sacraments (at least baptism and matrimony) which cause them to tend visibly toward complete union. To summarize, to think about the church as a sacrament, based on the seven sacraments, is to think about her as a space (family, dwelling place, city, temple, garden) of fertile relations which are received from Jesus, which she is called to extend over the course of history through the other spaces that human beings inhabit.

The Sevenfold Harmony of the Sacramental Space

Now that the church has been defined as a sacramental space (body, family and household, city and temple, etc.), a space built on seven columns and called to expand to the whole world and to all time, let us investigate the sevenfold architecture of this space. In this way we address an important task of general sacramental theology: showing the interconnections among the sacraments, explaining their place in the totality of the body of Christ and of the church. This is the proper moment to do so, for only in the context of the church-sacrament can we express clearly the order and connection of the seven. I will begin by examining the different ways in which tradition has ordered them.

The Economy of the Seven Sacraments

The Church Fathers speak about the sacraments one by one, without developing a general concept that associates them. For them the preeminence of the Eucharist and of baptism is clear.[48] They associate baptism with confirmation (these were initially combined in the same rite) and with penance, which is a laborious baptism, the possibility of returning after sin, as it were a second plank of salvation after the shipwreck.[49] The set of seven was progressively outlined during the Middle Ages, in parallel with the search for a precise definition of "sacrament" as sign that communicates grace. The

48. See Yves Congar, "L'idée des sacrements majeurs ou principaux," *Concilium* 31 (1968): 25–34, translated as "The Idea of 'Major' or 'Principal' Sacraments," *Concilium* (English edition) 4 (1968): 12–17.

49. See Jerome, *In Ezechielem* V, 16 (CCL 75:713); cf. Council of Trent, Session XIV, *Decree on the Sacrament of Penance*, chap. 2 (DH 1672).

process culminated in the mid-twelfth century in the *Sentences* of Peter Lombard, who enumerates the seven.[50]

From then on, prefigurations were found in scripture for this number "seven." Did Naaman the Syrian not bathe seven times in the river to be cured of leprosy?[51] And does the Book of Proverbs, as we saw, not speak about the seven columns on which is built the house that is the church?[52] In the number seven medieval commentators find, moreover, a symbol of the totality of salvation accomplished by the Holy Spirit.[53] In this way the sacraments are not only momentary events, but rather branch out into all of Christian life and culture. Let us look at the different ways in which the salvific signs are ordered among themselves, according to medieval commentators.

Above all, theologians consider the different remedies that the sacraments offer, as medicine used by the Good Samaritan. St. Albert the Great, for example, lists the seven sacraments in a way corresponding to the capital sins.[54] Baptism conquers *pride*, for water is the humblest element. The Eucharist overcomes *envy*, which is the opposite of charity. Confirmation casts down *sloth* (*acedia*), infusing joy for good deeds. Holy orders drives out *avarice*, for the Levites choose God alone as their lot and inheritance. Extreme unction eradicates *anger* by the sweet oil that it pours out. Penance uproots *greed*, the symbol of a disordered appetite. And matrimony, obviously, remedies *lust*. St. Bonaventure draws up a list of the sacraments as medicine for the different kinds of evils that afflict man: baptism alleviates original sin, penance removes mortal sin, extreme unction removes venial sin; the distinctive purpose of confirmation is to remedy weakness, while the Eucharist counteracts malice; matrimony is supposed to provide against concupiscence, and holy orders to provide against ignorance, given the competence to instruct that is bestowed on the priest.[55]

---

50. See Bernhard Geyer, "Die Siebenzahl der Sakramente in ihrer historischen Entwicklung," *Theologie und Glaube* 19 (1918): 325–48.

51. See Alexander of Hales, *Glossa in quatuor libros Sententiarum* IV, *Introitus* (BFSMA XV [Quaracchi, 1957], 1–8), where he offers an allegorical exegesis of 2 Kgs 5.

52. As I already noted: see Bonaventure, *Sermones de diversis* XI, 6 (ed. Bougerol), 1:209.

53. These attempts could find support in St. Augustine, *De Genesi ad litteram* V, 5 (CSEL 28:147): "unde ipsum septenarium numerum sancto spiritui quodammodo dedicatum, commendat scriptura et nouit ecclesia" (hence Scripture recommends and the Church recognized the number seven itself as being dedicated somehow to the Holy Spirit); *Epistolae* LV 5, 9 (CSEL 34.2:179–80): "propter ipsum numerum septenarium, quo universitatis significatio saepe figuratur, qui etiam ipsi ecclesiae tribuitur propter instar uniuersitatis" (on account of the number seven itself, by which the universality is often symbolized, which is also attributed to the Church herself as an image of universality).

54. See Albertus Magnus, *In IV Sent.*, d. 2a, a. 1 (*Opera Omnia*, XXIX:42–43).

55. See Bonaventure, *In IV Sent.*, d. 2, a. 3, q. 3 (Quaracchi 4:53); this list is mentioned by Thomas Aquinas, *ST* III, q. 65, a. 1, co.

Another scheme connects each sacrament to a virtue, thus showing that sacramental grace manages not only to defend us against evil, but also to promote and develop good. We are already familiar with the proposal of Alexander of Hales and of St. Bonaventure (see chapter 13, above). St. Albert the Great follows this current also: first he enumerates the theological virtues: baptism is the *sacramentum fidei* (sacrament of faith), extreme unction is the *sacramentum spei* (of hope), the Eucharist is the *sacramentum caritatis* (of charity); and then he links the cardinal virtues to the other sacraments: confirmation to fortitude, penance to justice; holy orders to prudence; matrimony to temperance (moderation).[56] I have already pointed out the greater advantage of Bonaventure's proposal, which associates the three sacraments of initiation to the three theological virtues by pairing chrismation and hope.

St. Thomas situates these two traditions (fighting against faults and promoting the virtues) along the narrative axis that runs through *the different stages of life*. Baptism is birth, confirmation helps us to mature, the Eucharist give the daily food that restores the strength of the traveler, penance lifts up the fallen, the anointing of the sick gives strength in sickness and prepares for the final journey. Two sacraments have a communal character, for they build up not personal life, but the church: these are matrimony and holy orders, as what is at stake in both is the ability to generate, prolonging one's own life in others.[57]

This last observation alerts us to the fact that the sacraments refer not only to the individual but to the entire community of the church. St. Albert the Great speaks about the sacraments of active life, which are necessary for those who join the church (baptism), fight in her (confirmation), or have to heal the wounds of combat (penance); and also to generate new soldiers (matrimony) or to equip those who depart after fighting the good fight (extreme unction), while the purpose of holy orders is to produce good leaders to guide the battle. Albert assigns the Eucharist to the contemplative life, which is dedicated to pleasing God.[58] St. Bonaventure, adopting a similar approach, sees the sacraments as the weapons necessary to supply the army of the church.[59]

These lists confirm that the key to the medieval proposal is the branch-

---

56. See Albertus Magnus, *In IV Sent.*, d. 2a, a. 1 (*Opera Omnia*, XXIX:43).

57. See Thomas Aquinas, *ST* III, q. 65, a. 1, co.; *SCG* IV, 58 (Leonine ed., 15:193–94); *Super IV Sent.*, d. 2, q. 1, a. 2, sol. (Parma 7:481).

58. See Albertus Magnus, *In IV Sent.*, d. 2a, a. 1 (*Opera Omnia*, XXIX:43).

59. See Bonaventure, *In IV Sent.*, d. 2, a. 3, q. 3 (Quaracchi 4:53); *Breviloquium* VI, 3 (Quaracchi 5:267).

ing out of the sacraments to all aspects of life: the battle against evil and the ongoing effort to attain the different goods, on the road through time and in service to the community.[60] Indeed, according to St. Bonaventure there are seven sacraments because they embrace the entire course of this world, in the hope of the eighth day.[61] This is diametrically opposed to a merely intimate and private experience of the sacred rites. Certainly, in explaining this sacramental architecture, it must be understood that the keystone cannot spring from a philosophical analysis of human experience but rather, above all, from the very life of Jesus: he is the measure by which to determine how the salvific signs are associated with one another.

Medieval theology inquired also about the order among the sacraments. It discovered in the Eucharist the most excellent sacrament, because it contains the very person of Jesus, and not only the communication of one of his acts. This is, indeed, according to St. Thomas, the *sacramentum sacramentorum*.[62] If we consider the necessity of a sacrament for salvation, baptism has precedence and, for someone who finds himself in serious sin, penance. Holy orders stands out inasmuch as it assures the constitution of the church, with her origin in Jesus the head, and explains the manner in which the other sacraments are transmitted; therefore Hugh of St. Victor begins his treatise with this sacrament.[63] Matrimony, for its part, even though considered inferior in other aspects, prevails with regard to what it signifies: Christ and the church, in other words, the totality of the Christian mystery. Augustine of Dacia expressed these hierarchies in verse for four sacraments: "Baptism is greater by its effect, the Body [the Eucharist]—in its being, / Matrimony—by its sign, Chrismation [confirmation]—because it has a greater minister."[64]

The Protestant Reformation modified the perspective. Luther's concept of the sacraments as a response of faith to the Word distanced them from the complexity of human action and made it difficult to distinguish one

---

60. See Elio Mitre Fernández, "Los 'sacramentos sociales': La óptica del medievalismo" *Ilu, Revista de Ciencias de las Religiones* 19 (2014): 147–71.

61. See Bonaventure, *Breviloquium* VI, 3 (Quaracchi 5:267).

62. "Sacrament of sacraments." See Thomas Aquinas, *Super IV Sent.*, d. 25, q. 3, a. 2, q.c. 1, arg. 4 (Parma 7:912).

63. See Hugh of St. Victor, *De sacramentis* II, 3 (PL 176:421; *CV* 1:343). Another author who follows this order is Aime-Georges Martimort, *Les Signes de la nouvelle Alliance* (Paris: Ligel, 1966), 77, who cites, as his reason for doing so, the fact that most of the sacraments have an ordained person as minister, and that the liturgical environment in which all the sacraments are celebrated is structured hierarchically.

64. See Augustine of Dacia (d. 1285), *Rotulus pugillaris*: "Maior in effectu baptismus, corpus in esse, / Coniugium signo, maiori chrisma ministro." The text is published in Angelus M. Walz, *Angelicum* 6 (1929): 254–78 and 548–71, at 561.

sacrament from another. Moreover, the strict search for sayings of Jesus that testified to the promise of grace associated to each sign led him to reduce the sacraments to the Eucharist and baptism. Furthermore, in denying that a character is imprinted in the latter, he curtailed the extension of the sacraments to the entire life of the Christian. Finally, with the loss of the sacrament of matrimony, he lost at the same time the sacramental vision of creation, with its basis in the body. In this way the sacraments tended to be concentrated on the individual, without bringing community into play. This drastically pruned the sacramental ramifications—the power of the sacraments to reach every area of common life among human beings and to serve as a foundation for the architecture of the church.[65]

The Council of Trent responded, on the one hand, that there are seven sacraments, no more, no less.[66] Moreover it defended an order and a hierarchy among them.[67] The Magisterium had already taught that baptism is the doorway and the most important one inasmuch as it is necessary for salvation.[68] Now it confirmed that the Eucharist surpasses the others in dignity.[69] One essential contribution of the Council, as I noted above (see chapter 10), was to reaffirm that the sacraments branch out through the life of a person, to the whole plot of his narrative, and to the entire architecture of the ecclesial communion. In this regard it is interesting that Trent, although referring to a definite number, does not deny the symbolic value of the number seven.[70] Precisely this symbolism helps us to see the sacraments as the expression of a totality that confers structure on the church's being and, at the same time, expands her presence in the cosmos and in social life. It is not true, therefore, that the specific number (exactly seven)

---

65. For a valuable attempt, in the area of ecumenical dialogue, to arrive at the seven sacraments starting from the preeminence of baptism and the Eucharist, see Pannenberg, *Systematic Theology*, vol. 3. Pannenberg starts from Luther's perspective, which views baptism as embracing all of life; and he associates to this sacrament confirmation, penance, and the anointing of the sick as different realizations of it. Moreover he accepts the fact that matrimony is a sacrament, relying on the Pauline use of the term. The greatest difference can be observed in his exposition of the theology of holy orders. For his part, Gerhard Ebeling, *Dogmatik des christlichen Glaubens* (Tübingen: Möhr, 1979), 3:319, distinguishes as follows the two sacraments that he accepts as a Protestant: through baptism we come to be Christ's property; through the Eucharist Christ comes to be our property.

66. See Council of Trent, Session VII, *Decree on the Sacraments in General*, canon 1 (DH 1601). There were already earlier Magisterial statements: Innocent III, *Profession of Faith prescribed for the Waldensians* (DH 793–96); Gregory X, *Profession of Faith of Emperor Michael Paleologus* (DH 860); Council of Florence, Bull of Union with the Armenians, *Exultate Deo* (DH 1310).

67. See Council of Trent, Session VII, *Decree on the Sacraments in General*, canon 3 (DH 1603).

68. See Council of Florence, Bull of Union with the Armenians, *Exultate Deo* (DH 1314).

69. See Council of Trent, Session XIII, *Decree on the Eucharist*, chap. III (DH 1639).

70. See Michael Seybold, "Die Siebenzahl der Sakramente (Conc. Trid. Sessio VII, can. 1)," *Münchener Theologische Zeitschrift* 27 (1976): 113–38; Jacques Dournes, "Pour déchiffrer le septénaire sacramentel," *Concilium* 31, no. 1 (1968): 63–76.

is a limitation, given the openness that the New Testament announced.[71] On the contrary: its symbolism assures this universality and in turn its concreteness, avoiding the arbitrary expansion thereof by anchoring it to what was instituted by Jesus.

Noteworthy among the post-Tridentine proposals concerning the order of the sacraments is the one formulated by Scheeben.[72] In his view the Eucharist is a root sacrament, whose logic embraces all the sacraments and whose presence precedes the complete structure of the church. Next our author distinguishes, in the first place, the consecratory sacraments: the ones that imprint a character and structure ecclesial life. Included among them is matrimony, because the conjugal bond is considered to be analogous to the sacramental character, inasmuch as it is a stable vocation within the church for the purpose of building it up. The consecratory sacraments are followed by the medicinal sacraments, penance and extreme unction.

A common division today that is used by the *Catechism of the Catholic Church* (taking St. Thomas as its inspiration) distinguishes between sacraments of initiation, sacraments of healing, and sacraments at the service of communion and the mission of the faithful.[73] This account, which nicely shows the organic quality of the seven sacraments, does not exclude other possible groupings. Above all it is necessary to keep in mind the vision of the sacraments as the architecture of the entire Christian life and of the space of the church. From this perspective all the sacraments are medicinal and all of them build up the good life and communion.[74]

Sacramental Harmony: Architecture of the Christian Space

The ways in which theological tradition has ordered the sacraments testify that they contain the structure that sustains the life of the church and the plot of her journey in time. Based on this I can offer a synthesis, combined with the vision of the church-sacrament. If the church is a space of relations where life opens up to communion, then the seven sacraments will be the basic architecture of this space, the columns on which it arises and which make possible its missionary expansion to other cosmic and social spaces. I will develop what I have already said in defining the sacraments (see chapter 11, above) from the viewpoint of their ecclesial dimension.

Let us start with the Eucharist: this sacrament contains the logic of the

---

71. Despite the contrary opinion of von Allmen, *Prophetisme*, 30.

72. See Scheeben, *The Mysteries of Christianity*, par. 78 (542) and par. 83 (572–82).

73. See *Catechism of the Catholic Church* (Vatican City: Libreria Editrice Vaticana, 1992), 1211.

74. See Revel, *Traité des sacrements*, 1:34–39, who notes, for example, that the Eucharist is the social sacrament *par excellence*.

ecclesial house, the plans and pillars that constitute it as a dwelling place. In the Eucharist the church is born as a space of relations rooted in the body and blood of Jesus, ordered according to his way of being situated in the world, of loving the Father and human beings. Thus the Eucharist is the fundamental sacrament insofar as the other sacraments are expansions of the Eucharistic space to all the moments in the life of the Christian and of the church. They are born of the Eucharist and lead to it. Therefore Vatican II states that the Eucharist is the source and summit of the entire Christian life.[75]

Through baptism the space of Christ's body is inaugurated for each believer. This is the doorway that gives access to the sphere of relations into which Jesus welcomes us. The baptismal character (as we saw in chapter 12) is, as a matter of fact, the inclusion of the space of the catechumen (of his body as a way of being placed in the world and of relating with human beings) into the relational space of Jesus. Baptism thus testifies that the dwelling place of the church is not primarily her own work, but rather a space continually being built up by the Father through the life of his Son, although she also participates in this work of construction. In the center of the church's house a spring flows unceasingly, according to the image of the well of living water used by the Fathers to describe her. The church is a continuous baptismal birth, an uninterrupted memory: of God who generated her in Christ and of the original vocation of the cosmos that attains fulfillment in her. In this way her space is capable of continual newness, for it causes all the seeds of hope that are sown in it to sprout.

In the sacrament of confirmation the relational spheres of the baptized person are made more dynamic so as to mature toward their fullness. This sacrament, so to speak, converts the dwelling place that is the church into a space of growth and expansion. This means that the Christian space is capable of taking up into itself the profane spaces of the world. Therefore this is the sacrament of testimony and of mission, in other words, of the courageous openness of the believer's space in order to make all relational human spheres fruitful.

Holy orders generates in the ecclesial space the presence of Christ, as origin of grace, in other words, as head, bridegroom, and father. As I noted above (chapter 14), the ordained man configures his fatherhood to that of Jesus, thus settling in a new way in the world and among human beings. Thanks to this sacrament, the ecclesial space always has as the focal point of all its perspectives the person and action of Christ, the source of life for the church.

Penance is necessary because the relational space of the church has not

75. See *LG*, no. 11.

yet reached its fullness, and she doubles back and falls short, during her journey in time, because of the sins of her members. For the logic of sin, being an individualistic logic of self-affirmation, is an anti-sacramental logic, in which the symbolic spaces disappear, and everything bends back on itself until it is reduced to a point. The sacrament of reconciliation then reopens the relational spaces proper to baptism and makes it possible again in them to remember God's first love (a love which annuls the obsessive return of sin) and to generate a future in hope.

The anointing of the sick too is about opening a new space of relations. Sickness typically curtails the sick person's capacity to establish ties with the world and with other persons, prostrating him in a way that cripples his prospects, cornering him in front of the final impasse: death. The anointing opens up for the sick person, and for the whole church, a new sphere of life, conformed to the suffering body of Jesus who, precisely while facing death, brought about the maximum openness of the world to God's love, and attracted thus the descent of the Spirit. Through the anointing, the church appears as a great suffering body, hard pressed on all sides but not demolished, which expands in the love of Jesus to the hope for the fully communional space of the glorified flesh.

What I have said about penance and the anointing of the sick shows that the sacramental space of the church is a space marked by the cross, the sign of contradiction. And this is because this space is not measured by our capacity for independent movement, but rather it is a communional dwelling place, which unfolds only when we inhabit it with our brethren under the common fatherhood of God.

Matrimony acquires a central role from the perspective of the church as a sacramental space. The Eucharist, in inaugurating the new space and time of Jesus, refers to the space and time of creation, as he assumed flesh like ours and dwelled on the same earth as we do. As we have seen, matrimony preserves precisely the experience of the body as the original space of relations, based on the "one flesh" of man and woman and of its expansion in their children, flesh of their flesh. Indeed, the archetypal images of the sacramental space spring from the family and the household, out of which the city is formed and the temple arises.

We can understand then why matrimony is a sacrament. When a man and a woman belong through baptism to the space of relations inaugurated by Jesus and share in the Eucharist, they cannot leave outside of Christ their other relational spaces. Above all, they cannot leave out the radical space of "one flesh," which can now be experienced according to Jesus' own measure, and only in this way. Thus matrimony helps us to understand that the church-sacrament,[76] being a dwelling place and family,[77] consists of the opening up of a fruitful sphere of relations. And, at the same time, thanks to matrimony, this sacramental sphere that is the church does not grow apart from the other human spaces (cultural, commercial, political spaces, etc.), but rather in the midst of them and from within them.

All this helps us to see the church-sacrament in the light of the seven sacraments. In order to know who the church is, we have to enter into the Eucharistic space and discover that it is a "baptized" space (which is always being born of God in Christ), upon which the Spirit rests, making it fruitful (confirmation), a cruciform space capable of regenerating the closed spaces of sin (penance) and of discovering new spheres in the anguish of pain and death (anointing of the sick); a space that is ordered in terms of the fontal presence of Christ as father and bridegroom (holy orders) and takes up into itself all the creaturely spaces, starting with the primary space of personal-identity-in-communion that is the family (matrimony).

Sacramentals

Besides the sacraments, the sacramentals are liturgical acts of the church. I discuss them here because they are a further expansion of the ecclesial space into the space of the world, unfolding it even more, so that it contains the presence and power of God. The Old Testament is riddled with rites that are adapted to the various circumstances of human life and to the different transitions of nature. While Yahweh redeems his people with surprising acts, he knows another gentler way of acting, in the midst of everyday occupations and the rhythms of the seasons: his *berakah* or blessing. This guarantees the divine presence in the created order and results, above all, in making the earth and human love fruitful.[78]

Jesus adopted these ordinary rites of life in his preaching and miracles: he gave thanks for food, blessed children, and took up the symbolism and fruitfulness of the earth, as when he smeared the eyes of the blind man and told him to wash in the pool. Indeed, the final image of Christ engraved on the retinas of the apostles was of him blessing them as he ascended on high (see Lk 24:50).

The Church Fathers made good use of this abundance of signs, which

---

76. *LG*, no. 1.

77. See *GS*, no. 48.

78. See Claus Westermann, *Der Segen in der Bible und im Handeln der Kirche* (Munich: C. Kaiser, 1968); and Dorothea Greiner, *Segen und Segnen: eine systematisch-theologische Grundlegung* (Stuttgart: Kohlhammer, 1999).

incorporates all creation into the Christian liturgy. Think of the salt that was given to the catechumens, or the mixture of milk and honey that was tasted after baptism.[79] In the early Middle Ages, many of these rites which accompanied the celebration, or which prolonged it in ordinary life, were indiscriminately called sacraments.[80] Peter Lombard would be the one to call for some of them, such as catechesis or exorcism, to be designated as "sacramentals" instead, reserving the term "sacrament" for the set of seven.[81] The suggestion was accepted by the theological tradition, which from then on thought of sacramentals in relation to the sacraments, while taking care to distinguish them. The Second Vatican Council offers us a very complete descriptive definition: "Holy Mother Church has, moreover, instituted sacramentals. These are sacred signs which bear a resemblance to the sacraments. They signify effects, particularly of a spiritual nature, which are obtained through the church's intercession. By them men are disposed to receive the chief effect of the sacraments, and various occasions in life are rendered holy."[82]

The whole paragraph situates the sacramentals within the orbit of the sacraments, preparation for them, and their expansion to the rest of life. A sacramental, like a sacrament, is a sacred sign, accompanied by a prayer in which some blessing is requested, especially a spiritual one (e.g., to forgive venial sins or to exorcise demons). The main difference is that the sacramental was not established by Christ, but rather derives from the church's authority. The institution of a sacramental is reserved to the Apostolic See, as is its authentic interpretation and possible suppression (*CIC* 1167). The sacramentals can be found within the celebration of a sacrament (e.g., sprin-

79. See Johannes Betz, "Die Eucharistie als Gottes Milch in frühchristliche Zeit," *Zeitschrift für katholische Theologie* 106, no. 2 (1984): 167–85.

80. See Hugh of St. Victor, *De sacramentis* II, 9 (PL 176:471d; *CV* 1:413), who speaks about the "lesser sacraments," which are given so that we might practice piety: sprinkling with water, signing with ashes, the blessing of branches and candles, the sign of the cross, genuflection, etc.

81. See Peter Lombard, *Sent.* IV, d. 6, c. 7, n. 3 (SpBon V:276): "Catechismus et exorcismus neophytorum sunt, magisque sacramentalia quam Sacramenta dici debent" (Catechism and exorcism are for neophytes; they should be called sacramentals rather than Sacraments).

82. See *SSC*, no. 60; see also *CIC* 1166–72 and 1667–79. On the sacramentals see Wilhelm Arendt, *De sacramentalibus disquisitio scholastico-dogmatica* (Rome: Apud Analectorum, 1909); Arnau, *Tratado general*, 359–68; Karin Bommes, "Die Sakramentalien der Kirche," in *Christusbegegnung in den Sakramenten*, ed. H. Luthe (Kevelaer: Butzon and Bercker, 1981), 597–671; Adriano Caprioli, "Presupposti antropologici per un recupero della categoria di sacramentale," *Rivista liturgica* 73 (1986): 153–65; Antonio Donghi, "Sacramentali," in *Nuovo Dizionario di Liturgia*, ed. D. Sartore and A. M. Triacca (San Paolo: Milano, 1995), 1253–70; Pedro Farnés, "Los sacramentales," *Phase* 82 (1974): 330–31; Magnus Löhrer, "Sacramentales," in *Enciclopedia Teológica Sacramentum Mundi*, ed. Karl Rahner (Herder: Barcelona, 1969), 4:341–47; Albaric Michel, "Sacramentaux," in *DTC* XIV, cols. 465–82; and A. M. Triacca and A. Pistoia (eds.), *Les bénédictions et les sacramentaux dans la liturgie* (Rome: Centro Liturgico Vincenziano, 1988).

kling with holy water, or the imposition of ashes), helping at that time to define the form of the liturgy.

Properly speaking, the ritual action that consecrates persons, objects, or places is a sacramental; but the term can be applied also to the lasting effect of the consecration. Thus we can distinguish between transitory sacramentals (mainly blessings) and permanent sacramentals, like the consecration of persons (a monk or a nun), things (for example, sacred vessels), or places (a temple, an altar). There is an analogy with the use of the word "sacrament," which can also refer either to the rite celebrated or to its definitive effect, the character.

It is said that the sacramentals do not act *ex opere operato*. This means that they do not confer grace through the performance of a rite in which the work of Jesus is made present. On the other hand, a grace is given in a sacramental that goes beyond the dispositions of the believer, in other words, they do not act *ex opere operantis* alone. What is its specific type of efficacy? Theology has described it as *ex opere operantis Ecclesiae*, a formula that Pius XII adopted in his 1947 Encyclical Letter, *Mediator Dei*.[83] In other words, the efficacy comes from the action of the church that instituted these rites and connected them to the power of her prayer. From this perspective one could say that the sacramental is efficacious *ex opere operato* (by the performance of the rite itself) inasmuch as it is not reduced to the good dispositions of the person who performs it. Yet this efficacy proceeds, not from the work accomplished by Jesus, but rather from the praying communion of the church, which "is holy and acts always in closest union with her Head."[84] In any case, in order to avoid creating confusion and because of constant usage, it is better to reserve the expression *ex opere operato* for the sacraments.

The *Catechism of the Catholic Church* adds that the sacramentals proceed from the baptismal priesthood, inasmuch as "every baptized person is called to be a 'blessing' and to bless."[85] Therefore several of them can be performed by lay persons. Think, for example, of the role assigned to the father of a family in the blessings of everyday life, as scripture testifies (see Gn 49:28). To summarize, the sacramentals are expansions of the space of the sacraments to the other areas of life in order to open them up to the relation with God. It remains for us to consider this expansion, not inasmuch as it concerns religious matters specifically, but rather as it is capable also of informing profane life in order to serve the common good of human beings.

---

83. "By the action of the acting Church." See DH 3844.
84. See ibid. and Thomas Aquinas, *ST* III, q. 64, a. 1, ad 2.
85. See *Catechism of the Catholic Church*, 1669.

Sacraments and Christian Space in Society and in the World

One might think that the title "sacrament" applied to the church is useful only to describe her openness to the mystery of God, but that it does not take into account the social function of faith in service to the common good. This critique, nevertheless, would be shortsighted, both in its way of understanding what the church-sacrament is, and also when it comes to diagnosing the crisis of contemporary culture. Indeed, calling the church a sacrament is of key importance in understanding her social function today.

In fact, the great evil that afflicts the postmodern subject is his isolation in the cell of subjectivity. What remains is a weak individual who moves to the tune of his most intense feeling, with no relations to sustain him and with no path to bring him to his destination. We will not cure this sickness by proposing that he encounter God in the depths of his soul. For his real problem is the lack of relational environments that would enable him to understand his true identity, which is always discovered and forged in an encounter and a communion. The Christian God is accustomed to revealing himself and acting precisely in these relational environments that affect the flesh and accompany man's narrative, so as to point out in this way the human person's vocation to love. I have called these spaces sacramental spaces.

Society today, on the contrary, abounds in what have been called "non-places."[86] These are the surfaces of the great metropolis (supermarkets, the subway [*metro*], airports, etc.) or of the digital continent with its social networks. They are "non-places" because in them our identity does not come into play, nor do we forge in them stable bonds that thread the narrative of our life. This lack of spaces isolates the human being in his individualism, robbing him of a fabric of relations in which his identity is rooted, and it makes it impossible for the God of Christians, who is God-communion, to reveal himself and act. In order to evangelize this society, therefore, it is of little use to strengthen the private consciences of individuals. On the contrary, it is essential to expand the sacramental spheres.

Consequently, understanding the church as sacrament (in other words, as a space of relations where greatness of life can mature) helps us to identify the best service that Christianity can render to contemporary man. In confronting contemporary man who has no dwelling, no places or times, the "church-sacrament" does not propose initially an interior inspiration and a

86. See Marc Augé, *Non-Lieux: Introduction à une anthropologie de la surmodernité* (Paris: Seuil, 1992).

subjective mysticism, but rather a practice and a lived tradition, which conform us to Jesus' life in the flesh. She is dedicated to building up a human environment, a way of common life that follows the logic of the Eucharist and is rooted socially in the family, then branching out into all sectors of existence, in common ways of working, celebrating, building, welcoming, etc.

It can be helpful, in contrast, to describe the anti-sacramental attitudes, in which Christian life and its presence in the world withdraw from the relational logic that I have described.[87] There is, on the one hand, a *mysticist* vision of the church as a merely interior communion of those who follow Jesus. In reality, this is attuned to the mood of modern secularization, which has identified subjective consciousness as the place where transcendence is encountered. Faith, according to this approach, discovers God in isolated personal experience, and discerns this presence and this voice interiorly. The transmission of Christian faith is conceived of in a way that is in harmony with fashionable subjectivism and emotionalism. Mission reaches the great mass of people, and sometimes very rapidly, but diluting the relevance of the faith along the way. As a result, instead of alleviating the contemporary evil of self-referential subjectivism, this makes it more acute, and the church makes herself superfluous, like salt that has lost its savor.

Another nonsacramental way of situating Christianity is by reducing faith to a convenient or even necessary ingredient for healthy coexistence. The temptation for the church is to resign herself to this "functional" role, thinking that her mission consists of nothing more than resolving tensions and offering resources for common life. Christianity, nevertheless, has always understood the sacramental spaces that it generates, not as additional floors to embellish or balance the building, but rather as foundations to support and orient the rest of society. And this is because in these sacramental spaces the radical ties of man with God and of human beings among themselves are forged, and these are precisely the ties that give rise to human society. Indeed, neither are sacraments measured by the service that they render to the church. Instead they are the origin and goal of all her action.

Finally we have the attitude of the ghetto-minority, which closes itself off from the world in a defensive attitude, attempting to preserve a way of life that it regards as threatened. Here too the sacramental logic is diluted, because the sacrament can be understood only as a symbol of the whole, as capable of embracing in itself the entire richness of existence, which cannot be confined within narrow protective walls. The sacramental space of the church is either Catholic, in other words, with a vocation to embrace the

---

87. See Menke, *Sakramentalität*, 277–319.

material and social universe, or else it ends up bending back over itself until it disappears in a point. As John Henry Newman pointed out, the vigor of Christianity is shown in its ability to assimilate into itself what is foreign, and not to be assimilated by it.[88]

After describing these deviations we can turn to the sacramental view. The church-sacrament distinguishes herself not primarily by the vigor of the interior experience of her members, but rather by creating relational spaces and proposing "rites of passage" that accompany the stages of life, so that the human person can grow and mature. The Eucharistic space is situated at the center, as the place where the church is born and where she learns a new order of relations according to Jesus' love. The sacraments inspire the route of the church not only as celebratory moments, but also inasmuch as they expand to her entire communal life and give shape to her, thus opening her up to the cosmos and to society.

Given that nowadays the broad context of the culture is nonsacramental, this presence of the church will necessarily be experienced as a minority. But it will be a creative minority, according to the expression used by Benedict XVI, because it will generate a dwelling place among the deserted spaces of postmodernity, and it will recount narratives with an origin and a destination when faced with its scattered way of narrating human time.[89] The effort will be aimed precisely at generating cultural environments where it will be possible to experience the human and Christian fulfillment that Jesus has brought us. Did St. Paul not understand the church's mission precisely as edification, the building of a house (oiko-domeo)?[90] And did Jesus not promise us that he himself would prepare his many rooms for us (see Jn 14:2)? He was speaking, no doubt, as St. Irenaeus of Lyons understood it, about the house of the church, who is the body of Christ, that is, the sacramental space where we are called to be grafted until the final resurrection of the flesh, "for there are many mansions in the Father's house, inasmuch as there are also many members in the body."[91]

88. See John Henry Newman, *An Essay on the Development of Christian Doctrine* (Notre Dame, Ind.: University of Notre Dame Press, 1989).

89. See Luis Granados and Ignacio de Ribera, *Minorías creativas: El fermento del cristianismo* (Burgos: Monte Carmelo, 2012).

90. See Rom 14:9 and 15:2; 1 Cor 14:5, 26; 2 Cor 12:19; Eph 4:12.

91. Irenaeus of Lyons, *Adversus haereses* III, 19, 3 (SC 211:382; ANF 1:449b).

Selected Bibliography

Primary Sources

Compendiums

Denzinger, Heinrich. *Enchiridion Symbolorum.* 43rd edition. Edited and translated by Peter Hünermann. San Francisco, Calif.: Ignatius Press, 2012.

Ancient, Medieval, and Early Modern

Alain de Lille. *Rhythmus alter.* PL 210.

Albert the Great. *Commentarii in quartum librum Sententiarum.* In *Opera omnia,* vols. 29–30, edited by Auguste Borgnet. Paris, 1890–99.

Alexander of Hales. *Glossa in quatuor libros Sententiarum Petri Lombardi.* 4 vols. BFSMA, vols. 12–15. Quaracchi: Collegii S. Bonaventurae, 1951–57.

———. *Summa theologica.* Edited by Bernardini Klumper and the Quaracchi Fathers. 4 vols. Rome: Collegii S. Bonaventurae, 1924–48.

Ambrose. *De sacramentis.* SC 25. *De mysteriis.* CSEL 73. Both are translated by Roy J. Deferrari in Fathers of the Church (hereafter FOTC) 44. Washington, D.C.: The Catholic University of America Press, 1963.

———. *Explanatio Psalmorum XII.* CSEL 64.

———. *Expositio evangelii secundum Lucam.* CCL 14.

Anastasius II. *Exordium pontificatus mei.* DH 356.

Augustine of Dacia. "Rotulus pugillaris." Edited by Angelus M. Walz. *Angelicum* 6 (1929): 253–78 and 548–74.

Augustine. *Confessiones.* CCL 26. Translated by Vernon J. Bourke in FOTC 21. Washington, D.C.: The Catholic University of America Press, 1953.

———. *Contra Epistulam Parmeniani.* CSEL 51.

———. *Contra Faustum Manichaeum.* CSEL 25.

———. *Contra litteras Petiliani.* CSEL 52.

———. *De baptismo contra Donatistas.* CSEL 51.

———. *De bono coniugali.* CSEL 41. FOTC 27. Washington, D.C.: The Catholic University of America Press, 1955.

———. *De catechizandis rudibus.* CCL 46.

———. *De cura pro mortuis gerenda.* CSEL 41. FOTC 27. Washington, D.C.: The Catholic University of America Press, 1955.

———. *De doctrina christiana.* CCL 32. Translated by John J. Gavigan in FOTC 2. Washington, D.C.: The Catholic University of America Press, 1950.

————. *De fide et operibus*. CSEL 41. FOTC 27. Washington, D.C.: The Catholic University of America Press, 1955.

————. *De Genesi ad litteram*. CSEL 28. Translated by Roland J. Teske in FOTC 84. Washington, D.C.: The Catholic University of America Press, 1991.

————. *De nuptiis et concupiscentia*. CSEL 42.

————. *De Trinitate*. CSEL 62A. Translated by Stephen McKenna in FOTC 45. Washington, D.C.: The Catholic University of America Press, 1963.

————. *De vera religione*. CCL 32.

————. *Enarrationes in psalmos*. CCL 39.

————. *Epistula ad catholicos de secta donatistarum*. CSEL 52.

————. *Epistolae*. CSEL 44. Translated by Wilfrid Parsons and (vol. 81 only) Robert B. Eno. FOTC 12, 18, 20, 30, 32, 81. Washington, D.C.: The Catholic University of America Press, 1951, 1953, 1955, 1956, 1989.

————. *In Iohannis evangelium tractatus*. CCL 36. Translated by John W. Rettig. FOTC 78, 79, 88, 90, 92. Washington, D.C.: The Catholic University of America Press, 1988, 1993, 1994, 1995.

————. *Quaestiones in Heptateuchum*. CCL 33.

————. *Sermones*. PL 38.

Basil the Great. *De Spiritu Sancto*. SC 17. Translated by Stephen M. Hildebrand in Popular Patristics 42. Crestwood, N.Y.: St. Vladimir's Seminary Press, 2011.

Bellarmine, Robert. *De controversiis*. Naples: J. Giuliano, 1858.

Bernard. *Epistula de erroribus Petri Abaelardi*, in *Sancti Bernardi Opera*, vol. 8. Edited by Jean Leclercq and H. M. Rochais. Romae: Editiones Cistercienses, 1977.

————. *Sermones in festivitate omnium sanctorum*, in *Sancti Bernardi Opera*, vol. 5. Edited by Jean Leclercq and H. M. Rochais. Rome: Editiones Cistercienses, 1968.

Bonaventure. *Breviloquium*, in *Opera omnia*, vol. 5. Translated by Dominic V. Monti, OFM. St. Bonaventure, N.Y.: Franciscan Institute Publications, 2005.

————. *Commentaria in quatuor libros sententiarum*, in *Opera omnia*, vol. 1–4. Quaracchi: Collegii a S. Bonaventura, 1882, 1885, 1887, 1889. Portions translated by R. E. Houser and Timothy B. Noone; Wayne Hellmann, Timothy LeCroy, and Luke Davis Townsend. Works of St. Bonaventure 16 and 17. St. Bonaventure, N.Y.: Franciscan Institute Publications, 2014 and 2016.

————. *Sermones de diversis, Opera omnia*, vol. 9. Quaracchi: Collegii a S. Bonaventura, 1901.

Calvin, John. *Acta Synodi Tridentinae: Cum Antidoto*, in *Opera* VII. Brunsvigae, 1868.

Clement of Alexandria. *Paedagogus*. SC 70. Translated by Simon P. Wood. Washington, D.C.: The Catholic University of America Press, 2008.

Clement of Rome. *2 Clement*. In *Patres Apostolici*, vol. 1, edited by F. X. Funk. Tubingen: H. Laupp, 1901. Translated by James A. Kleist in ACW 1. Westminster, Md.: Newman Press, 1946.

————. *Epistle to the Corinthians*. SC 167. Translated by James A. Kleist in Ancient Christian Writers (hereafter ACW) 1. Westminster, Md.: Newman Press, 1946.

Cyprian. *De ecclesiae catholicae unitate*. CSEL 3.1. Translated by Roy J. Deferrari in FOTC 36. Washington, D.C.: The Catholic University of America Press, 1956.

————. *Epistolae*. CSEL 3.2. Translated by Sr. Rose Bernard Donna in FOTC 51. Washington, D.C.: The Catholic University of America Press, 1964.

Cyril of Alexandria. *In Iohannem*. In Patrologia Graeca (hereafter PG), edited by J.-P. Migne (Paris, 1854–66), vol. 72. Translated by David R. Maxwell in Ancient Christian Texts 12–13. Downers Grove, Ill.: InterVarsity Press, 2013.

Cyril of Jerusalem. *Catecheses*. SC 126. Translated by Leo P. McCauley and Anthony A. Stephenson in FOTC 61 and 64. Washington, D.C.: The Catholic University of America Press, 1970.

Dante. *Paradiso*. Translated by Anthony Esolen. New York: Modern Library, 2004.

Didache. SC 248. Translated by Francis X. Grimm in FOTC 1. Washington. D.C.: The Catholic University of America Press, 1947.

Dionysius the Aeropagite. *De coelesti hierarchia*. SC 68.

———. *De divinis nominibus*. PG 3. Translated by John D. Jones. Medieval Philosophical Texts in Translation 21. Milwaukee, Wis.: Marquette University Press, 2011.

———. *De ecclesiastica hierarchia*. PG 3.

Duns Scotus. *Ordinatio*, in *Opera Omnia*, vol. 9. Rome: Commissio Scotistica, Typis Poliglottis Vaticanis, 1950.

Fulgentius of Ruspe. *De fide*. CCL 91A.

Gerhoh of Reichersberg. *Libelli de Lite*, vol. 3 (Hanover: Hahn, 1897).

Gregory Nazianzen. *Orationes*. PG 36. Selection translated by Martha Vinson in FOTC 107. Washington, D.C.: The Catholic University of America Press, 2004.

Gregory of Nyssa. *In Canticum Canticorum*. PG 44. Translated by Richard A. Norris, Jr. Atlanta, Ga.: Society of Biblical Literature, 2012.

———. *The Great Catechism*. SC 453.

Gregory the Great. *Homiliae xl in Evangelia*. CCL 141. Translated by David Hurst. Piscataway, N.J.: Gorgias Press, 2009.

Gregory IX. *Decretals*. In *Corpus Iuris Canonici* II, edited by A. Friedberg. Leipzig, 1879.

———. *Profession of Faith of Emperor Michael Paleologus*. DH 860.

Guitmund of Aversa. *De corporis et sanguinis Christi veritate*. PL 149. Translated by Mark G. Vaillancourt in FOTC Medieval Continuation 10. Washington, D.C.: The Catholic University of America Press, 2009.

Hilary of Poitiers. *De Trinitate*. CCL 62A. Translated by Stephen McKenna in FOTC 25. Washington, D.C.: The Catholic University of America Press, 1954.

Hippolytus of Rome. *Traditio Apostolica*. SC 11 bis.

Hugh of St. Victor. *De sacramentis christianae fidei*. In *Corpus Victorinum*, vol. 1, edited by R. Berndt. Frankfurt: Aschendorff, 2008.

———. *De tribus diebus*. CCCM 177.

———. *Sententiae de divinitate* II. Edited by A. M. Piazzoni. *Studi Medievali* 23 (1982): 912–55.

———. *Summa Sententiarum*. PL 176.

Ignatius of Antioch. *Epistles*. SC 10. Translated by Francis X. Grimm in FOTC 1. Washington, D.C.: The Catholic University of America Press, 1947.

Innocent III. *De sacro altaris mysterio*. PL 217.

Irenaeus of Lyons. *Adversus haereses*. SC 263–64; 293–94; 210–11; 100; 152–53. Translated by Dominic J. Unger and Matthew C. Steenberg in ACW 55, 64, 65. New York: Newman Press, 1992 and 2012.

———. *Epideixis*. SC 406. Translated by Joseph P. Smith in ACW 16. London: Longmans, Green, 1952.

Isidore of Seville. *De ecclesiasticis officiis*. PL 83. Translated by Thomas Knoebel in ACW 61. New York: Newman Press, 2008.

———. *Etymologiae*. PL 82. Translated by Stephen A. Barney. Cambridge: Cambridge University Press, 2011.

Jerome. *Commentariorum in Ezechielem Prophetam Libri Quatuordecim*. CCL 75. Translated by Thomas P. Scheck in ACW 71. New York: Newman Press, 2017.

———. *Commentariorum in Sophoniam Prophetam*. CCL 76A. Translated by Thomas P. Scheck. Ancient Christian Texts 1. Downers Grove, Ill.: InterVarsity Press, 2016.

John Chrysostom. *De sacerdotio*.

———. *Eight Baptismal Catecheses*. SC 50 bis. Translated by Paul W. Harkins in ACW 31. Westminster, Md.: Newman Press, 1963.

———. *In epistulam II ad Timotheum homiliae*. PG 62.

———. *In proditionem Iudae homiliae*. PG 49. Translated by Paul W. Harkins in FOTC 68. Washington, D.C.: The Catholic University of America Press, 1979.

Justin Martyr. *Apologia*. Patristische Texte und Studien 38. Translated by Leslie William Barnard in ACW 56. Westminster, Md.: Newman Press, 1963.

———. *Dialogus cum Thryphone*. Patristische Texte und Studien 47. Translated by Thomas B. Falls in FOTC 6. Washington, D.C.: The Catholic University of America Press, 1948.

Leo the Great. *Epistolae*. PL 54. Translated by Edmund Hunt. Washington, D.C.: The Catholic University of America Press, 1957.

———. *Sermones*. CCL 138A. Translated by Jane Patricia Freeland and Agnes Josephine Conway. FOTC 93. Washington, D.C.: The Catholic University of America Press, 1995.

Lombard, Peter. *Sententiae* I. Spicilegium Bonaventurianum 4. Rome: Collegii S. Bonaventurae Ad Claras Aquas, 1971. Translated by Becket Soule, OP. Ave Maria, Fla.: Sapientia Press of Ave Maria University, 2016.

Luther, Martin. *De captivitate babylonica*. WA 6. Translated by Erik H. Herrmann. Minneapolis, Minn.: Fortress Press, 2016.

———. *Der kleine Katechismus* (1531). WA 30. Edited by Mary Jane Haemig. Minneapolis, Minn.: Fortress Press, 2016.

———. *Disputatio de fide infusa et acquisita*. WA 6.

———. *Great Catechism*. WA 30. Edited by Kirsi I. Stjerna. Minneapolis, Minn.: Fortress Press, 2016.

———. *On Genesis*. WA 9. Translated by J. Theodore Mueller. Grand Rapids, Mich.: Zondervan, 1958.

———. *Sermo de poenitentia*. WA 1. Translated by Dirk G. Lange. Minneapolis, Minn.: Fortress Press, 2015.

Melito of Sardis. *Peri Pascha*. SC 123.

Nicholas I. *Ad consulta vestra*. DH 645.

Origen. *Homilies on Leviticus*. SC 287. Translated by Gary Wayne Barkley in FOTC 83. Washington, D.C.: The Catholic University of America Press, 1990.

———. *Homilies on Luke*. SC 87. Translated by Joseph T. Lienhard in FOTC 94. Washington, D.C.: The Catholic University of America Press, 1996.

———. *In Matthaeum*. SC 162. Translated by Ronald E. Heine. Oxford Early Christian Texts. Oxford: Oxford University Press, 2018.

Pacian. *Discourse on Baptism*. PL 13. Translated by C. H. Collyns in *The Extant Works of S. Pacian*. Library of Fathers of the Holy Catholic Church 17. Oxford: John Henry Parker, 1842.

Pascal, Blaise. *Pensées*. Paris: Edition Sellier, Le Livre de Poche, 1992.

———. *Sententiae* III/IV. Edited by I. Brady. Spicilegium Bonaventurianum 5. Rome: Collegii S. Bonaventurae Ad Claras Aquas, 1981. Translated by Giulio Silano in Medieval Sources in Translation 45 and 48. Toronto: Pontifical Institute of Mediaeval Studies, 2010.

Physiologus. Edited by O. Schönberger. Frankfurt: Reclam, 2001.

Pictaviensis, Petrus [Peter of Poitiers]. *Sententiae* V. PL 211.

Pseudo-Barnabas. *Epistulae*. SC 172.

Quodvultdeus. *De symbolo*. CCL 60. Translated by Thomas M. Finn in ACW 60. New York: Newman Press, 2004.

Radbertus, Paschasius. *De corpore et sanguine Domini*. CCCM 16.

Tatian. *Oratio ad Graecos*. Patristische Texte und Studien 43.

Tertullian. *Adversus Marcionem*. CCL 1.

———. *Apologeticus pro Christianis*. CCL 1. FOTC 10. Washington, D.C.: The Catholic University of America Press, 1950.

———. *De baptismo*. CCL 1.

———. *De corona militis / De pudicitia / De resurrectione carnis*. CCL 2.

Theophilus of Antioch. *Ad Autolycum*. SC 20.

Thomas Aquinas. *De forma absolutionis paenitentiae sacramentalis ad Magistrum Ordinis*. Edited by H.-F. Dondaine. Leonine edition, vol. 40. Rome: Ad Sanctae Sabinae, 1969.

———. *Quaestio disputata de spiritualibus creaturis*. Edited by J. Cos. Leonine edition 24.2. Paris: Cerf, 2000.

———. *Quaestiones disputatae de veritate*. 2 vols. Edited by P. M. Pession. Rome: Marietti, 1965.

———. *Scriptum Super Sententias*. Edited by P. Mandonnet (Books I–II). 2 vols. Paris: Lethielleux, 1929. Edited by M. F. Moos (from Book III to distinction 22 of Book IV). 2 vols. Paris: Lethielleux, 1922–37.

———. *Summa contra Gentiles*. Leonine edition, vols. 13–15. Rome: Typis Riccardi Garroni, 1918–30.

———. *Summa theologiae*. Leonine edition, vols. 4–12. Rome: Ex Typographia Polyglotta S. C. de Propaganda Fide, 1888–1906.

Modern Magisterium

Unless otherwise noted, these documents are available on the Vatican website (www.vatican.va).

Catechism of the Catholic Church. Vatican City: Libreria Editrice Vaticana, 1992.

Congregation for the Doctrine of the Faith. *Sacerdotium Ministeriale*: *Letter to the Bishops of the Catholic Church on Certain Questions Concerning the Minister of the Eucharist*. August 6, 1983.

Council of Trent. Session VI, *Decree on Justification*, Chapter VII. DH 1531.

———. Session VII, *Decree on the Sacraments*, canon 1. DH 1601.

———. Session XIII, *Decree on the Sacrament of the Eucharist*, Chapters III–IV. DH 1639–42.

————. Session XIV, *Doctrine on the Sacrament of Penance*, Chapter VII. DH 1686.

————. Session XIV, *Decree Tametsi*. DH 1813–16.

————. Session XXI, *Doctrine and Canons on Communion*, Chapter II. DH 1728.

————. Session XXIII, *Doctrine on the Sacrament of Orders*, Chapter I, Chapter IV, canon 4. DH 1764, 1767, 1774.

Francis. *Lumen Fidei*. Encyclical Letter. June 29, 2013.

John Paul II. *Salvifici Doloris*. Apostolic Letter. February 11, 1984.

————. *Pastores Dabo Vobis*. Apostolic Exhortation. March 15, 1992.

————. *Veritatis Splendor*. Encyclical Letter. August 6, 1993.

————. *Man and Woman He Created Them: A Theology of the Body*. Translated by Michael Waldstein. Boston: Pauline Media, 2006.

Pius X. *Lamentabili Sane*. Decree. July 3, 1907. DH 3401–66.

Pius XII. *Sacramentum Ordinis*. Apostolic Constitution. November 30, 1947.

————. *Mediator Dei*. Encyclical Letter. November 20, 1947.

Vatican Council II. *Gaudium et Spes*. Pastoral Constitution on the Church in the Modern World. December 7, 1965.

————. *Lumen Gentium*. Dogmatic Constitution on the Church. November 21, 1964.

————. *Presbyterorum Ordinis*. Decree. December 7, 1965.

————. *Sacrosanctum Concilium*. Dogmatic Constitution on the Sacred Liturgy. December 4, 1963.

Secondary Sources

Aldama, José A. *Sacrae theologiae summa*. Madrid: BAC, 1953. Vol. 4 was translated by Kenneth Baker as *On the Sacraments in General: On Baptism, Confirmation, Eucharist, Penance, and Anointing*. Ramsey, N.J.: Keep the Faith, 2015.

Aletti, J.-N. "Signes, accomplissement et temps." *Recherches de Science Religieuse* 75, no. 2 (1987): 305–20.

Alter, Robert. *The Art of Biblical Poetry*. New York: Basic Books, 1985.

Amaladoss, Michael. *Beyond Dialogue: Pilgrims to the Absolute*. Bangalore: Asian Trading Corporation, 2008.

Amata, Biagio. "Il carattere sacramentale: dottrina patristica?" *Rivista Liturgica* 85 (1988): 487–522.

Andrén, Carl-Gustaf. *De Septem Sacramentis: En Sakramentsutläggning från vadstena Kloster*. Lund: Gleerups, 1963.

Angelini, Giuseppe. *La malattia, un tempo per volere: saggio di filosofia morale*. Milan: Vita e pensiero, 2000.

————. *Il tempo e il rito alla luce delle Scritture*. Assisi: Cittadella, 2006.

Arendt, Wilhelm. *De sacramentalibus disquisitio scholastico-dogmatica*. Rome: Apud Analectorum, 1909.

Arnau, Ramón. *Tratado general de los sacramentos*. Madrid: BAC, 1994.

————. *Orden y ministerios*. Madrid: BAC, 1995.

Aroztegi, Manuel. "Eucaristía y filiación en las teologías de los siglos II y III." In *Filiación: Cultura pagana, religión de Israel, orígenes del cristianismo*, vol. 4, edited by Patricio de Navascués Benlloch, Manuel Crespo Losada, and Andrés Sáez Gutiérrez. Madrid: Trotta, 2012.

Augé, Marc. *Non-Lieux: Introduction à une anthropologie de la surmodernité*. Paris: Seuil,

1992. Translated by John Howe as *Non-places: Introduction to an Anthropology of Super-modernity*. London: Verso, 2008.

Ayán, Juan José. *Padres apostólicos*. Madrid: Ciudad Nueva, 2000.

Badiou, Alain. *Éloge de l'amour*. Paris: Flammarion, 2009.

Bartholomew, C. G. *Canon and Biblical Interpretation*. Grand Rapids, Mich.: Zondervan, 2006.

Beauchamp, Paul. "Le signe des pains." *Lumière et Vie* 41, no. 209 (1992): 55–67.

Bechina, Friedrich. *Die Kirche als Familie Gottes: Die Stellung dieses theologischen Konzeptes im Zweiten Vatikanischen Konzil und in den Bischofssynoden von 1974 bis 1994 im Hinblick auf eine Familia–Dei Ekklesiologie*. Rome: Gregorian University Press, 1998.

Belcher, Kimberly Hope. *Efficacious Engagement: Sacramental Participation in the Trinitarian Mystery*. Collegeville, Minn.: Liturgical Press, 2011.

Belda Plans, Juan. "Melchor Cano: La Relección 'De Sacramentis in Genere.'" In *Sacramentalidad de la Iglesia y sacramentos*, edited by P. Rodríguez. Pamplona: Universidad de Navarra, 1983.

Berger, David. "Die geschichtliche Entwicklung der Lehre vom *Character indelebilis*." *Una Voce Korrespondenz* 26 (1996): 182–89.

Berger, Peter L. "The Desecularization of the World: A Global Overview." *The Desecularization of the World: Resurgent Religion and World Politics*. Grand Rapids, Mich.: Eerdmans, 1999.

Bergin, Liam. *O Propheticum Lavacrum: Baptism as Symbolic Act of Eschatological Salvation*. Rome: Gregorian University Press, 1999.

Bernards, Matthäus. "Zur Lehre der Kirche als Sakrament: Beobachtungen aus der Theologie des 19. und 20. Jahrhunderts." *Münchener Theologische Zeitschrift* 20, no. 1 (1969): 29–54.

Berrouard, François. "'Similitudo' et la définition du réalisme sacramentel d'après l'Epître XCVIII, 9–10 de saint Augustin." *Revue des études augustiniennes et patristiques* 7, no. 4 (1961): 321–37.

———. "Pour une réflexion sur le '*sacramentum*' augustinien: La manne et l'eucharistie dans le *Tractatus XXVI, 11–12 in Johannis Evangelium*." *Forma Futuri: Studi in onore del Cardinale Michele Pellegrino*. Turin: Bottega d'Erasmo, 1975.

———. "Le *Tractatus* 80,3 *in Iohannis Evangelium* de saint Augustin: la parole, le sacrement, la foi." *Revue des études augustiniennes et patristiques* 33, no. 2 (1987): 235–54.

Bertetto, Domenico. "La causalità dei sacramenti secondo S. Tommaso ed i suoi interpreti." *Salesianum* 10, no. 4 (1948): 543–68.

Betz, Johannes. "La Eucaristía, misterio central." In *Mysterium Salutis: Fundamentos de la dogmática como historia de la salvación* 4.2, edited by J. Feiner and M. Löhrer. Madrid: Cristiandad, 1969.

———. "Die Eucharistie als Gottes Milch in frühchristliche Zeit." *Zeitschrift für katholische Theologie* 106, no. 2 (1984): 167–85.

Beuchot, Mauricio. "Signo y lenguaje en san Agustín." *Diánoia* 32 (1986): 13–26.

———. *Las caras del símbolo: El icono y el ídolo*. Madrid: Caparrós, 1999.

Biser, Eugen. "Das religiöse Symbol im Aufbau des Geisteslebens." *Münchener Theologische Zeitschrift* 5, no. 2 (1954): 114–40.

Bittremieux, Joseph. "L'institution des sacrements d'après Alexandre de Hales." *Ephemerides Theologicae Lovanienses* 9 (1932): 234–51.

Blanchard, Yves-Marie. "Lavement des pieds et pénitence: Une lecture de Jean 13, 1–20." *La Maison Dieu* 214 (April 1998): 35–50.

Blanco, Pablo. "El ministerio en Lutero, Trento y el Vaticano II: Un recorrido historico-dogmatico." *Scripta Theologica* 40, no. 3 (2008): 733–76.

Blondel, Maurice. *Action (1893): Essay on a Critique of Life and a Science of Practice*. Translated by Oliva Blanchette. Notre Dame, Ind.: University of Notre Dame Press, 1984.

Bobrinskoy, Boris. "L'Esprit du Christ dans les sacrements chez Jean Chrysostome et Augustin." *Jean Chrysostome et Augustin*. Edited by C. Kannengiesser. Paris: Beauchesne, 1975.

Boersma, Hans. *Nouvelle Théologie and Sacramental Ontology: A Return to Mystery*. Oxford: Oxford University Press, 2009.

Boeve, Lieven. "The Sacramental Interruption of Rituals of Life." *Heythrop Journal* 44, no. 4 (2003): 401–17.

Boff, Leonardo. *Los sacramentos de la vida y la vida de los sacramentos*. Bogotá: Indo-American Press, 1975. Translated by John Drury as *Sacraments of Life: Life of the Sacraments*. Washington, D.C.: Pastoral Press, 1987.

Bommes, Karin. "Die Sakramentalien der Kirche." In *Christusbegegnung in den Sakramenten*, edited by H. Luthe. Kevelaer: Butzon and Bercker, 1981.

Bonora, Antonio. "Dalla storia e dalla natura alla professione di fede e alla celebrazione (Dt 26, 1–5)." *Parola di Spirito e Vita* 25 (1992): 27–39.

Borella, Jean. *Le mystère du signe: Histoire et théorie du symbole*. Paris: Maisonneuve and Larose, 1989.

Borges, Jorge Luis. "Los dos reyes y los dos laberintos." In *El Aleph: Obras completas*. 2 vols. Buenos Aires: Emecé, 1974.

Bornkamm, Gunther. "Zum Verständnis des Gottesdienstes bei Paulus." In *Das Ende des Gesetzes: Paulusstudien*, 113–32. Munich: Kaiser Verlag, 1958.

———. "Mysterion." In *Theologisches Wörterbuch zum Neuen Testament*, edited by Gerhard Kittel, 4:809–34. Stuttgart: W. Kohlhammer, 1990.

Borobio, Dionisio, ed. *La celebración en la Iglesia*. 3 vols. Salamanca: Sigueme, 1987–90.

———. *Sacramentos y creación: de la sacramentealidad creatural-cósmica a los sacramentos de la Iglesia*. Salamanca: Secretariado Trinitario, 2009.

Botta, Mario, and Paolo Crepet. *Dove abitano le emozioni: La felicità e i luoghi in cui viviamo*. Turin: Einaudi, 2007.

Bouëssé, Humbert. "La causalité efficiente instrumentale de l'Humanité du Christ et des sacrements chrétiens." *Revue Thomiste* 39 (May–June 1934): 370–93.

Bourgeois, Daniel. *Le champ du signe: Structure de la sacramentalité comme signification chez Saint Augustin et Saint Thomas d'Aquin*. PhD diss., University of Fribourg (Switzerland), 2007.

Bourgeois, Henri. "Les sacrements selon Vatican II." In *Histoire des dogmes*, vol. 3: *Les signes du salut*, edited by Bernard Sesboüé. Paris: Desclée, 1995. Translated into Spanish as "Los sacramentos según el Vaticano II," in *Historia de los dogmas*, vol. 3: *Los signos de la salvación*, edited by Bernard Sesboüé. Salamanca: Secretariado Trinitario, 1996.

Bozzolo, Andrea. *La teologia sacramentaria dopo Rahner: il dibattito e i problem*. Rome: Libreria Ateneo Salesiano, 1999.

———. *Mistero, simbolo e rito in Odo Casel: l'effettività sacramentale della fede*. Vatican City: LEV, 2003.

———. *Il rito di Gesù: Temi di teologia sacramentaria*. Rome: Libreria Ateneo Salesiano, 2013.

Bradshaw, Paul F. "The Gospel and the Catechumenate in the Third Century." *Journal of Theological Studies* 50, no. 1 (1999): 143–52.

Brock, Sebastian. "The Mysteries Hidden in the Side of Christ." *Sobornost* 7, no. 6 (1978): 462–72.

Brommer, Ferdinand. *Die Lehre vom sakramentalen Charakter in der Scholastik bis Thomas von Aquin inclusive*. Paderborn: Schöningh, 1908.

Brown, Raymond E. "Pre-Christian Semitic Concept of Mystery." *Catholic Biblical Quarterly* 20, no. 4 (1958): 417–43.

———. "Semitic Background of the New Testament mysterion." *Biblica* 39 (1959): 426–48.

———. "The Johannine Sacramentary Reconsidered." *Theological Studies* 23, no. 2 (1962): 183–206.

———. "Appendix III: Signs and Works." In *The Gospel according to John*. Garden City, N.Y.: Doubleday, 1966–70.

Buber, Martin. "Sinnbildliche und sakramentale Existenz im Judentum." *Eranos Jahrbuch* 2 (1934): 339–67.

Bueno de la Fuente, Eloy. *Eclesiología*. Madrid: BAC, 1998.

Bultmann, Rudolf. *Geschichte und Eschatologie*. Tübingen: J. C. B. Mohr, 1958. Translated as *History and Eschatology: The Gifford Lectures, 1955*. Edinburgh: Edinburgh University Press, 1957.

———. *Das Evangelium des Johannes*. Göttingen: Vandenhhoeck and Ruprecht, 1953. Translated by G. R. Beasley-Murray as *The Gospel of John: A Commentary*. Oxford: Blackwell, 1971; reprinted in Eugene, Ore.: Wipf and Stock, 2014.

Bunce, James W. "The Liturgy of the Last Gospel." *Expository Times* 126, no. 6 (2015): 261–69.

Bux, Nicola. "Il sigillo dello Spirito nei sacramenti degli orientali." *Rivista Liturgica* 85 (1998): 523–28.

Bychkov, Victor V. "The Symbology of Dionysius the Areopagite." *Russian Studies in Philosophy* 51, no. 1 (2012): 28–63.

Camelot, P. Thomas. "Sacramentum fidei." In his *Augustinus Magister*, 2:891–96. Paris: Études Augustiniennes, 1954.

———. "Sacramentum: Notes de théologie sacramentaire augustinienne." *Revue Thomiste* 57 (1957): 429–49.

Caprioli, Adriano. "Alle origini della 'definizione' di sacramento: da Berengario a Pier Lombardo." *La Scuola Cattolica* 102 (1974): 718–43.

———. "Presupposti antropologici per un recupero della categoria di sacramentale." *Rivista Liturgica* 73 (1986): 153–65.

Carr, Ephrem. *Spiritus spiritalia nobis dona potenter infundit: a proposito di tematiche liturgico-pneumatologiche: Studi in onore di Achille M. Triacca*. Rome: Centro studi S. Anselmo, 2005.

Cary, Phillip. *Outward Signs: The Powerlessness of External Things in Augustine's Thought*. Oxford: Oxford University Press, 2008.

Casel, Odo. "Altchristlicher Kult und Antike." *Jahrbuch für Literaturwissenschaft* 3 (1923): 1–17.

———. *Das christliche Kultmysterium.* Regensburg: Pustet, 1935. Translated by Burkhard Neunheuser as *The Mystery of Christian Worship.* Westminster, Md.: Newman Press, 1962.

Casey, Edward S. *Getting Back Into Place: Toward a Renewed Understanding of the Place-World.* Bloomington: Indiana University Press, 2009.

Cassirer, Ernst. *Philosophy of Symbolic Forms.* New Haven, Conn.: Yale University Press, 1998.

Cavallera, Ferdinand. "Le décret du Concile de Trente sur les sacraments en général." *Bulletin de littérature ecclésiastique* 6, no. 9 (1914): 401–25.

Chauvet, Louis-Marie. *Symbol and Sacrament: Sacramental Reinterpretation of Christian Existence.* Collegeville, Minn.: Liturgical Press, 1994.

———. "The Broken Bread as Theological Figure of Eucharistic Presence." In *Sacramental Presence in a Postmodern Context,* edited by L. Boeve and L. Leussen, 236–62. Louvain: Peeters. 2001.

Chazelle, Celia. "Figure, Character and the Glorified Body in the Carolingian Eucharistic Controversy." *Traditio* 47 (1992): 1–36.

Chenu, Marie-Dominique. "Pour une anthropologie sacramentelle." *La Maison Dieu* 119 (July 1974): 85–100.

Clemen, Carl. *Der Einfluss der Mysterienreligionen auf das älteste Christentum.* Giessen: Alfred Töpelmann, 1913.

Coloe, Mary L. *God Dwells with Us: Temple Symbolism in the Fourth Gospel.* Collegeville, Minn.: Liturgical Press, 2001.

Colombo, Giuseppe. "Dove va la teologia sacramentaria?" *La Scuola Cattolica* 102 (1974): 673–717.

———. "Teologia sacramentaria e teologia fondamentale." *Teologia* 19, no. 3 (1994): 238–62.

———. "Introduzione." In *La teologia sacramentaria dopo Rahner: il dibattito e i problemi,* edited by Andrea Bozzolo. Rome: Libreria Ateneo Salesiano, 1999.

Congar, Yves. *The Mystery of the Temple.* London: Burns and Oates, 1962.

———. "L'idée des sacraments majeurs ou principaux." *Concilium* 31, no. 1 (1968): 25–34. Translated as "The Idea of 'Major' or 'Principal' Sacraments." *Concilium* (English edition) 4 (1968): 12–17.

———. *This Church That I Love.* Translated by Lucien Delafuente. Denville, N.J.: Dimension Books, 1969.

———. "Propos en vue d'une théologie de l'économie dans la tradition latine." *Irénikon* 45 (1972): 155–206.

Connolly, Grahame J. "Sacramental Character in the Teachings of Alexander of Hales." *Collectanea Franciscana* 33, no. 1 (1963): 5–27.

Cothenet, Edouard. "L'économie du mystère et le baptême selon l'Épître aux Éphésiens." In *Mystagogie: pensée liturgique d'aujourd'hui et liturgie ancienne,* edited by A. M. Triacca. Rome: CLV, 1993.

Council of Florence. Bull of Union with the Armenians, *Exultate Deo.* DH 1310.

Courtenay, William J. "Covenant and Causality in Pierre d'Ailly." *Speculum* 46, no. 1 (1971): 94–119.

———. "The King and the Leaden Coin: The Economic Background of 'Sine qua non' Causality." *Traditio* 28 (1972): 185–209.

Crespin, Rémi. *Ministère et sainteté: Pastorale du clergé et solution de la crise donatiste dans la vie et la doctrine de saint Augustin.* Paris: Études Augustiniennes, 1965.

Cross, F. L., ed. *Studia Patristica* 6. Berlin: Akademie-Verlag, 1962.

Crouzel, Henri. "Origène et la structure du sacrement." *Bulletin de littérature ecclésiastique* 63, no. 2 (1962): 83–92.

Cucca, Mario. *Il corpo e la città: studio del rapporto di significazione paradigmatica tra la vicenda di Geremia e il destino di Gerusalemme.* Assisi: Cittadella, 2010.

Cullmann, Oscar. *Les Sacrements dans l'Évangile joahnnique: La vie de Jésus et le culte de l'Église primitive.* Paris: PUF, 1951.

Cumont, Franz. *Les mystères de Mithra.* Brussels: H. Lamertin, 1902. Translated as *The Mysteries of Mythra.* Chicago: Open Court, 1903.

Cutrone, Emmanuel J. "Sacraments." In *Augustine Through the Ages: An Encyclopedia,* edited by Allan J. Fitzgerald. Grand Rapids, Mich.: Eerdmans, 1999.

Dal Maso, Alberto. *L'efficacia dei sacramenti e la performance rituale: Ripensare l'ex opere operato a partire dall'antropologia culturale.* Padua: Messaggero, 1999.

D'Alès, Adhémar. "Salva illorum substantia." *Ephemerides Theologicae Lovanienses* 1 (1924): 497–504.

Daniélou, Jean. "The Problem of Symbolism." *Thought* 25, no. 3 (1950): 423–40.

———. *Sacramento y culto según los santos Padres,* Madrid: Guadarrama, 1962.

D'Argenlieu, Benoît T. "Note sur deux définitions médiévales du caractère sacramentel." *Revue Thomiste* 11 (May–June 1928): 271–75.

———. "La doctrine d'Albert le Grand sur le caractère sacramental." *Revue Thomiste* 11 (July–September 1928): 295–311.

Dassmann, Ernst. "Character." In *Augustinus Lexikon,* edited by C. Maye, 1:271–75. Schwabe: Basel, 1986.

De Certeau, Michel. "La faiblesse de croire." *La faiblesse de croire.* Paris: Seuil, 1987.

De Clerck, Paul. "*Lex orandi, lex credendi*: sens originel et avatars historiques d'un adage équivoque." *Questions liturgiques et paroissiales* 59, no. 4 (1978): 193–212.

De Clercq, Charles. "Ministre et sujet des sacrements dans les anciens canons et aujourd'hui." *Kanon: Jahrbuch der Gesellschaft für das Recht der Ostkirchen* 1 (1973): 54–58.

Deden, D. "Le Mystère Paulinien." *Ephemerides Theologicae Lovanienses* 13 (1936): 405–42.

De la Potterie, Ignace. "L'onction du chrétien par la foi." *Biblica* 40 (1959): 12–69.

De Miguel González, José María. "La acción del Espíritu Santo en la Unción de los enfermos." *Estudios Trinitarios* 30 (1996): 357–84.

———. *Sacramentos: historia, teología, pastoral, celebración: homenaje al prof. Dionisio Borobio.* Salamanca: Biblioteca Salmaticensis, 2009.

Deneken, Michel. "Les romantiques allemands, promoteurs de la notion d'Église sacrement du salut? Contribution à l'étude de la génèse de l'expression Église sacrement du salut." *Recherches de Science Religieuse* 67, no. 2 (1993): 41–57.

Derickson, Gary W. "The New Testament Church as a Mystery." *Bibliotheca Sacra* 166 (October 2009): 436–45.

Dölger, Franz Joseph. *Sol Salutis: Gebet und Gesang in christlicher Altertum.* Münster: Aschendorff, 1920.

———. *Sphragis: Eine altchristliche Taufbezeichnung in ihren Beziehungen zur profanen und religiösen Kultur des Altertums.* Paderborn: Schöningh, 1967 (1911).

Donahue, John M. "À propos d'Avicenne et de saint Thomas: de la causalité dispositive à la causalité instrumentale." *Revue Thomiste* 51 (1951): 441–53.

———. "Sacramental Character: The State of the Question." *The Thomist* 31, no. 4 (1967): 445–64.

Dondaine, Hyacinthe-François. "Substantia sacramenti." *Revue de sciences philosophiques et théologiques* 29, nos. 2/4 (1940): 328–30.

———. "La définition des Sacrements dans la Somme Théologique." *Revue de sciences philosophiques et théologiques* 31 (1947): 213–28.

Donghi, Antonio. "Sacramentali." *Nuovo Dizionario di Liturgia*, edited by D. Sartore and A. M. Triacca, 1253–70. San Paolo: Milano, 1995.

Doronzo, Emmanuel. "Originis et evolutionis doctrinae de re et sacramento brevis delineatio." *Revue de l'Université d'Ottawa* 4, no. 4 (1934): 213–28.

———. *De sacramentis in genere*. Milwaukee, Wis.: Bruce Publishing, 1945.

Dournes, Jacques. "Pour déchiffrer le septénaire sacramentel." *Concilium* 31, no. 1 (1968): 63–76.

Doyle, Dennis M. "Otto Semmelroth and the Advance of the Church as Sacrament at Vatican II." *Theological Studies* 76, no. 1 (2015): 65–86.

Duchrow, Ulrich. "*Signum* und *superbia* beim jungen Augustin." *Revue des études augustiniennes et patristiques* 7, no. 4 (1961): 369–72.

Dujarier, Michel. *Le parrainage des adultes aux trois premiers siècles de l'Église; recherche historique sur l'évolution des garanties et des étapes catéchuménales avant 313*. Paris: Cerf, 1962.

Dulles, Avery. *Models of the Church*. New York: Doubleday, 1987.

Ebeling, Gerhard. "Erwägungen zum evangelischen Sakramentsverständnis." In his *Wort Gottes und Tradition: Studien zu einer Hermeneutik der Konfessionen*, 217–26. Göttingen: Vandenhoeck and Ruprecht, 1966.

———. *Dogmatik des christlichen Glaubens*, vol. 3. Tübingen: Möhr, 1979.

———. *El ser sacramental en perspectiva evangélica*. Salamanca: Sigueme, 2007.

Eckermann, Willigis. "Neuschöpfung durch den Heiligen Geist in den Initiationssakramenten." In his *In der Kraft des Heiligen Geistes: Wovon die Kirche lebt*. Kevelaer: Butzon and Bercker, 1998.

Eco, Umberto. "At the Roots of the Modern Concept of Symbol." *Social Research* 52, no. 2 (1985): 383–402.

Emery, Gilles. "Reconciliation with the Church and Interior Penance: The Contribution of Thomas Aquinas on the Question of the *Res et Sacramentum* of Penance." *Nova et Vetera* (English edition) 1, no. 2 (2003): 283–301.

Engels, Joseph. "La doctrine du signe chez saint Augustin." Edited by F. L. Cross. Studia Patristica 6.

Enno, Edzard Popkes. "'Das Mysterion der Botschaft Jesu': Beobachtungen zur synoptischen Parabeltheorie und ihren Analogien im Johannesevangelium und Thomasevangelium." In *Hermeneutik der Gleichnisse Jesu*, edited by R. Zimmermann. Tübingen: Mohr Siebeck, 2008.

Erdozáin, Luis. *La función del signo en la fe según el cuarto evangelio*. Analecta Biblica 33. Rome: PIB, 1968.

Evans, G. Rosemary. "Augustine, the Donatists and Communion." *Augustinus* 38 (1993): 221–30.

Falsini, Rinaldo. "Il sacramento tra *ex opere operato* e *ex opere operantis*." *Rivista di Pastorale Liturgica* 192, no. 5 (1995): 17–23.

Farkasfalvy, Denis. *Inspiration and Interpretation: A Theological Introduction to Sacred Scripture*. Washington, D.C.: The Catholic University of America Press, 2010.

Farnedi, Giustino, ed. *Paschale mysterium: Studi in memoria dell'Abate Prof. Salvatore Marsili (1910–1983)*. Rome: Studia Anselmiana, 1986.

Farnés, Pedro. "Los sacramentales." *Phase* 82 (1974): 324–36.

Féret, Henri-Marie. "Sacramentum. Res. Dans la langue théologique de S. Augustin." *Revue de sciences philosophiques et théologiques* 29, nos. 2/4 (1940): 218–43.

Ferguson, Everett. *Baptism in the Early Church*. Grand Rapids, Mich.: Eerdmans, 2009.

Fernández, Emilio Mitre. "Los 'sacramentos sociales': La óptica del medievalismo." *Ilu, Revista de Ciencias de las Religiones* 19 (2014): 147–71.

Fernández, Pedro. "Liturgia y teología: La historia de un problema metodológico." *Ciencia Tomista* 99 (1972): 134–79.

Feuillet, André. "La recherche du Christ dans la Nouvelle Alliance d'après la Christophanie de Jo. 20,11–18." In *L'Homme devant Dieu: Mélanges offerts au Père Henri de Lubac*, vol. 1. Paris: Aubier, 1963.

———. *Le sacerdoce du Christ et de ses ministres d'après la prière sacerdotale du quatrième évangile et plusieurs données parallèles du Nouveau Testament*. Paris: Téqui, 1972.

Finkenzeller, Josef. *Die Lehre von den Sakramenten im allgemeinen: Von der Reformation bis zur Gegenwart*. Freiburg: Herder, 1981.

Fitzer, G. "Sfragis." In *Theologisches Wörterbuch zum Neuen Testament*, ed. G. Kittel, 7:939–54. Stuttgart: Kohlhammer, 1933–79.

Formesyn, Roland E. C. "Le sèmeion johannique et le sèmeion hellénistique." *Ephemerides Theologicae Lovanienses* 38 (1962): 856–94.

Fraigneau-Julien, Bernard. *L'Église et le caractère sacramentel selon M.-J. Scheeben*. Brussels: Desclée, 1958.

Galbiati, Enrico. "I segni sacri dell'Antico Testamento." *Sacra Doctrina* 45 (1967): 13–36.

Galot, Jean. *La nature du caractère sacramentel: étude de théologie médiévale*. Paris: Desclée, 1956.

Ganoczy, Alexandre. *Einführung in die katholische Sakramentenlehre*. Darmstadt: Wissenschaftliche Buchgesellschaft, 1979. Translated by William Thomas and Anthony Sherman as *An Introduction to Catholic Sacramental Theology*. Preston: Mosaic Press, 2011.

Geldhof, Joris. "Liturgy as Theological Norm: Getting Acquainted with 'Liturgical Theology.'" *Neue Zeitschrift für Systematische Theologie und Religionsphilosophie* 52, no. 2 (2010): 155–76.

Genuyt, François. "L'économie des signes." *Lumière et Vie* 41, no. 209 (1992): 19–35.

Gerardi, Renzo. "Carattere." In *Lexicon: Dizionario teologico enciclopedico*, edited by V. Mancuso and L. Pacomio, 140–41. Casale Monferrato: Piemme, 1993.

Gese, Hartmut. "Psalm 22 und das Neue Testament: der älteste Bericht vom Tode Jesu und die Entstehung des Herrenmahles." *Zeitschrift für Theologie und Kirche* 65, no. 1 (1968): 1–22.

———. "Die Herkunft des Herrenmahls." *Zur biblischen Theologie: Alttestamentliche Vorträge*. Tübingen: J. C. B. Mohr, 1983.

Geyer, Bernhard. "Die Siebenzahl der Sakramente in ihrer historischen Entwicklung." *Theologie und Glaube* 19 (1918): 325–48.

Ginzberg, Louis. *The Legends of the Jews*. Translated by Henrietta Szold. Philadelphia: The Jewish Publication Society of America, 1913.

Girardi, Luigi. *"Conferma le parole della nostra fede": Il linguaggio della celebrazione*. Rome: CLV Edizioni Liturgiche, 1998.

Giraudo, Cesare. *La structura letteraria della Preghiera eucaristica*: *Saggio sulla genesi letteraria di una forma*: *Toda veterotestamentaria, Beraka giudaica, Anafora Cristiana*. Analecta Biblica 92. Rome: Biblical Institute Press, 1981.

———. *In unum corpus*: *Trattato mistagogico sull'eucaristia*. Rome: San Paolo, 2000.

Gladd, Benjamin L. *Revealing the mysterion*: *The Use of Mystery in Daniel in Second Temple Judaism with Its Bearing on First Corinthians*. Berlin: W. de Gruyter, 2008.

González, Antolín. "El Espíritu Santo y los sacramentos: el dato biblico." *Angelicum* 55, no. 1 (1978): 12–57.

González, Ramiro. "El Espíritu Santo en la economía sacramental de la Iglesia." *Revista Española de Teología* 59, no. 1 (1999): 59–84.

González, R. C. "La doctrina de Melchor Cano en su *relectio de Sacramentis* y la definición del Tridentino sobre la causalidad de los sacramentos." *Revista Española de Teología* 5, no. 4 (1945): 477–96.

Granados, Carlos. "El Espíritu de Yahvé y el dinamismo de la creación en el Antiguo Testamento." *Anthropotes* 26, no. 1 (2010): 45–64.

Granados, José. "'Vides Trinitatem si caritatem vides': Via del amor y Espíritu Santo en el De Trinitate de san Agustin." *Revista Augustiniana* 43, no. 130 (2002): 23–62.

———. *Los misterios de la vida de Cristo en Justino Mártir*. Rome: Editrice Pontificia Università Gregoriana, 2005.

———. "Taste and See: The Body and the Experience of God." *Communio* 37, no. 2 (Summer 2010): 292–308.

———. *Teología de la carne*: *el cuerpo en la historia de su salvación*. Burgos: Monte Carmelo, 2012.

———. *Teología del tiempo, ensayo sobre la memoria, la promesa y la fecundidad*. Salamanca: Sígueme, 2012.

———. "Los sacramentos y el don del Espíritu sobre Jesús." In *La unción de la gloria: en el Espíritu, por Cristo, al Padre*: *Homenaje a Mons. Luis F. Ladaria, SJ*, edited by Manuel Aróztegi. Madrid: BAC, 2014.

———. "Los sentidos de la fe." In *El que cree ve*: *Reflexiones en torno a la enciclica Lumen fidei*, edited by José Granados and Juan de Dios Larrú. Burgos: Monte Carmelo, 2014.

———. *Una sola carne en un solo Espíritu*: *Teología del matrimonio*. Madrid: Palabra, 2014.

Granados, Luis, and Ignacio de Ribera. *Minorías creativas*: *El fermento del cristianismo*. Burgos: Monte Carmelo, 2012.

Grant, Robert M. "Melito of Sardis on Baptism." *Vigiliae Christianae* 4, no. 1 (1950): 33–36.

Gregory, Bradley S. *The Unintended Reformation*: *How a Religious Revolution Secularized Society*. Cambridge, Mass.: Harvard University Press, 2012.

Greiner, Dorothea. *Segen und Segnen*: *eine systematisch-theologische Grundlegung*. Stuttgart: Kohlhammer, 1999.

Greshake, Gisbert. *Ser sacerdote hoy*. Salamanca: Sigueme, 2006. Translated by P. M. Seumais as *The Meaning of the Christian Priesthood*. Westminster, Md.: Christian Classics, 1989.

Grillo, Andrea. "La nozione di sacramento: da Trento al Vaticano II fino al Terzo Millennio: Dal 'sacramentum in genere signi' al 'sacramentum in genere ritus'?" *Annali di studi religiosi* 1 (2000): 239–63.

Groppo, Giuseppe. "L'evoluzione del catecumenato nella Chiesa antica dal punto di vista pastorale." *Salesianum* 41, no. 2 (1979): 235–55.

Grossi, Vittorino. "*Regula veritatis* e *narratio* battesimale in sant'Ireneo." *Augustinianum* 12, no. 3 (1972): 437–63.

Guillaume, E. "De institutione sacramentorum et speciatim confirmationis juxta Alexandrum Halensem." *Antonianum* 2 (1927): 437–68.

Hahn, Ferdinand. "Zum Stand der Erforschung des urchristlichen Herrenmahls." *Evangelische Theologie* 35 (1975): 553–63.

Hahn, Scott. "Canon, Cult and Covenant: The Promise of Liturgical Hermeneutics." In *Canon and Biblical Interpretation*, edited by C. G. Bartholomew, 207–35. Grand Rapids, Mich.: Zondervan, 2006.

———. "Temple, Sign, and Sacrament: Toward a New Perspective on the Gospel of John." *Letter and Spirit* 4 (2008): 107–43.

Haring, Nicholas M. "Berengar's Definitions of Sacramentum and Their Influence on Mediaeval Sacramentology." *Mediaeval Studies* 10 (1948): 109–46.

———. "St. Augustine's Use of the Word 'Character.'" *Mediaeval Studies* 14 (1952): 79–97.

———. "The Augustinian Axiom: *Nulli Sacramento Injuria Facienda Est.*" *Mediaeval Studies* 16 (1954): 87–117.

Haslinger, Herbert. "Mystagogie: Relecture eines sakramentenpastoralen Leitbegriffs." *Theologie und Glaube* 101, no. 1 (2011): 92–122.

Heid, Stefan. *Kreuz. Jerusalem. Kosmos. Aspekte frühchristlicher Staurologie.* Münster: Aschendorff, 2001.

Heidegger, Martin. "Bauen, Wohnen, Denken." In his *Vorträge und Aufsätze*, 139–56. Pfullingen: Neske, 1994.

Heil, John Paul. *The Letters of Paul as Rituals of Worship.* Eugene, Ore.: Cascade, 2011.

———. *Worship in the Letter to the Hebrews.* Eugene, Ore.: Wipf and Stock, 2011.

Heitmeyer, Heinrich. *Sakramentenspendung bei Häretikern und Simoniten nach Huguccio.* Rome: Gregorian Biblical Book Shop, 1964.

Hennig, Helmut. "Die Lehre vom *Opus Operatum* in den lutherischen Bekenntnisschriften." *Una Sancta* 13 (1958): 121–35.

Henquinet, François-Marie. "De causalitate sacramentorum iuxta codicem autographum S. Bonaventurae." *Antonianum* 8 (1933): 377–424.

Hermann, Horst. *Ecclesia supplet: Das Rechtsinstitut der kirchlichen Suppletion nach c. 209 CIC.* Amsterdam: B. R. Grüner, 1968.

Hernández Peludo Gaspar, and José María de Miguel González. *Sacramentos: historia, teología, pastoral, celebración: homenaje al prof. Dionisio Borobio.* Salamanca: Biblioteca Salmaticensis, 2009.

Hödl, Ludwig. "*Sacramentum et res*—Zeichen und Bezeichnetes: Eine begriffsgeschichtliche Arbeit zum frühscholastischen Eucharistietraktat." *Scholastik* 38, no. 2 (1963): 161–82.

Hofbeck, Sebald. *Semeion: Der Begriff des Zeichens im Johannesevangelium unter Berücksichtigung seiner Vorgeschichte.* Münster: Schwarzach, 1966.

Hofius, Otfried. "'Bis dass er kommt' I. Kor XI.26." *New Testament Studies* 14, no. 3 (1967–68): 439–41.

Hombert, Pierre-Marie. "La formule ex opere operato chez St. Thomas." *Mélanges de Science Religieuse* 49 (1992): 127–41.

Houssiau, Albert. "La liturgie, lieu privilegié de la théologie sacramentaire." *Questions liturgiques et paroissiales* 54 (1973): 7–12.

Huerga, Álvaro. "La teología aquiniana de los carácteres sacramentales en la perspectiva eclesiológica contemporánea." *Revista Española de Teología* 33, no. 2 (1973): 213–44.

———. "La teología del carácter en la segunda escolástica." In *Teología del sacerdocio: Escritos sobre el carácter sacerdotal,* edited by J. Ibañes. Burgos: Aldecoa, 1974.

Hünermann, Peter. "Sakrament, Figur des Lebens." In *Ankunft Gottes und Handeln des Menschen: Thesen über Kult und Sakrament,* edited by R. Schaeffler and P. Hünermann, 51–87. Freiburg: Herder, 1977.

———. "Die sakramentale Struktur der Wirklichkeit: Auf dem Weg zu einem erneuerten Sakramentenverständnis." *Herder-Korrespondenz* 36 (1982): 340–45.

Iserloh, Erwin. *Gnade und Eucharistie in der philosophischen Theologie des Wilhelm von Ockham: ihre Bedeutung für die Ursachen der Reformation.* Wiesbaden: Steiner, 1956.

Iturrioz, Daniel. "La definición del Concilio de Trento sobre la causalidad de los sacramentos." *Estudios Eclesiásticos* 24, no. 94 (1950): 291–340.

Jackson, B. Darrel. "The Theory of Signs in St. Augustine's *De Doctrina Christiana.*" *Revue des études augustiniennes et patristiques* 15, nos. 1–2 (1969): 9–50.

Jacob, Christoph. "Zur Krise der Mystagogie in der Alten Kirche." *Theologie und philosophie* 66, no. 1 (1991): 75–89.

Jedin, Hubert. *A History of the Council of Trent.* Translated by Dom Ernest Graf, OSB. 2 vols. St. Louis, Mo.: B. Herder, 1957–61.

Johnson, Douglas W. "*Verbum* in the Early Augustine (386–397)." *Recherches Augustiniennes* 8 (1972): 25–53.

Jonas, Hans. "Seventeenth Century and After: The Meaning of the Scientific and Technological Revolution." *Philosophical Essays: From Ancient Creed to Technological Man,* 45–80. Chicago: University of Chicago Press, 1980.

Jugie, Martin. "La doctrine du caractère sacramentale dans l'Église greco-russe." *Ecclesia Orans* 31 (1928): 17–23.

Jüngel, Eberhard. "Das Sakrament–was ist das?" *Evangelische Theologie* 26, no. 6 (1966): 320–36.

———. "Der evangelisch verstandene Gottesdienst." In his *Wertlose Wahrheit: Zur Identität und Relevanz des christlichen Glaubens: Theologische Erörterungen,* vol. 3. Munich: Kaiser, 1990.

———. "Sakrament und Repräsentation: Wesen und Funktion der sakramentalen Handlung." In his *Ganz Werden: Theologische Erörterungen,* vol. 5. Tübingen: Mohr Siebeck, 2003.

———. *Gott als Geheimnis der Welt: Zur Begründung der Theologie des Gekreuzigten im Streit zwischen Theismus und Atheismus.* 8th ed. Tübingen: Mohr Siebeck, 2010. Translated by Darrell L. Guder as *God as the Mystery of the World: On the Foundation of the Theology of the Crucified One in the Dispute between Theism and Atheism.* Grand Rapids, Mich.: Eerdmans, 2014.

Kahanâ, Rav. *Pesikta de-Rav Kahana.* Mandelbaum edition. New York: Jewish Theological Seminary of America, 1962.

Kasper, Walter. "Wort und Sakrament." *Glaube und Geschichte.* Mainz: Grünewald, 1970.

Kavanagh, Aidan. *On Liturgical Theology.* Collegeville, Minn.: Liturgical Press, 1992.

Kerr, Alan. *The Temple of Jesus' Body: The Temple Theme in the Gospel of John.* Sheffield: Sheffield Academic, 2002.

King, Fergus. "*Lex orandi, lex credendi*: worship and doctrine in Revelation 4–5." *Scottish Journal of Theology* 67, no. 1 (2014): 33–49.

King, Ronald F. "The Origin and Evolution of a Sacramental Formula: *sacramentum tantum, res et sacramentum, res tantum.*" *The Thomist* 31, no. 1 (1967): 21–82.

Kizhakkeparampil, Isaac. *The Invocation of the Holy Spirit as Constitutive of the Sacraments According to Cardinal Yves Congar.* Rome: Pontificia Università Gregoriana, 1995.

Klinger, Jerzy. "La *koinonia* comme sacramentelle: Perspectives actuelles." *Istina* 20 (1975): 100–111.

Kobusch, Theo. "Das Christentum als Religion der Wahrheit: Überlegungen zu Augustins Begriff des Kultus." *Revue des études augustiniennes et patristiques* 29, nos. 1–2 (1983): 97–128.

Koerperich, G. "De substantia sacramentorum iuxta Concilium Tridentinum." *Collationes Namurcenses* 30 (1936): 325–34.

Köstenberger, Andreas J. "The Mystery of Christ and the Church: Head and Body, 'One Flesh.'" *Trinity Journal* 12 (Spring 1991): 79–94.

Ladaria, Luis F. "Grandeza del cuerpo humano: perspectiva teológica." *Burgense* 56, no. 1 (2015): 165–81.

———. *Jesús y el Espíritu: la Unción.* Burgos, Spain: Monte Carmelo, 2012.

———. *Teología del pecado original y de la gracia: antropología teológica especial.* Madrid: BAC, 1997.

Lampen, Willibrord. "De causalitate sacramentorum iuxta S. Bonaventuram." *Antonianum* 7 (1932): 77–86.

Landgraf, Artur Michael. "Die Gnadenökonomie des Alten Bundes nach der Lehre der Frühscholastik." *Zeitschrift für katholische Theologie* 57, no. 2 (1933): 215–53.

———. "Der frühscholastische Streit um die *potestas quam Christus potuit dare servis et non dedit.*" *Gregorianum* 15, no. 4 (1934): 524–72.

———. "Die Ansicht der Frühscholastik von der Zugehörigkeit des *Baptizo te* zur Taufform." *Scholastik* 17 (1942): 412–27.

———. "Die frühscholastische Definition der Taufe." *Gregorianum* 27, nos. 2–3 (1946): 200–219 and 353–83.

———. "Beiträge der Frühscholastik zur Terminologie der allgemeinen Sakramentenlehre." *Divus Thomas (Freiburg)* 29 (1951): 3–34.

———. "Die Einführung des Begriffspaares *opus operans* und *opus operatum* in die Theologie." *Divus Thomas (Freiburg)* 29 (1951): 211–23.

———. *Dogmengeschichte der Frühscholastik* III/1. Regensburg: Pustet, 1954.

Lanfranc. "Liber de corpore et sanguine Domini." In *Lanfranco: El cuerpo y la sangre del Señor*, edited by M. Aroztegi, 5:70–80. Madrid: Publicaciones San Dámaso, 2009.

Leclercq, Jean. "Imitation du Christ et sacrements chez St. Bernard." *Collectanea Cisterciensia* 38 (1967): 263–82. Translated as "Imitation of Christ and the Sacraments in the Teaching of St. Bernard." *Cistercian Studies* 9, no. 1 (1974): 36–54.

Lécuyer, Joseph. "La causalité efficiente des mystères du Christ selon saint Thomas." *Doctor Communis* 6 (1953): 91–120.

Leder, Drew. *The Absent Body.* Chicago: University of Chicago Press, 1990.

Lefler, Nathan. "Sign, Cause, and Person in St. Thomas's Sacramental Theology: Further Considerations." *Nova et Vetera* (English edition) 4 (Spring 2006): 381–404.

Lehmann, Karl and Wolfhart Pannenberg, eds. *Lehrverurteilungen—kirchentrennend?*, vol. 1. Göttingen: Vandenhoeck and Ruprecht, 1988.

Leidi, Fabio. *Le signe de Jonas: Étude phénoménologique sur le signe sacramental.* Fribourg: Éditions Universitaires, 2000.

Lennerz, Heinrich. "Salva illorum substantia." *Gregorianum* 3, no. 3 (1922): 385–419.

———. "Das Konzil von Trient und theologische Schulmeinungen." *Scholastik* 4, no. 1 (1929): 38–53.

———. *De sacramentis novae legis in genere.* Rome: Universitas Gregoriana, 1950.

Léon-Dufour, Xavier. "Los milagros de Jesús según Juan." In his *Los milagros de Jesús.* Madrid: Cristiandad, 1979.

———. "Towards a Symbolic Reading of the Fourth Gospel." *New Testament Studies* 27, no. 4 (1980–81): 439–56.

———. *Le partage du pain eucharistique selon le Nouveau Testament.* Paris: Seuil, 1982. Translated by Matthew J. O'Connell as *Sharing the Eucharistic Bread: The Witness of the New Testament.* New York: Paulist Press, 1987.

Lienhard, Joseph T. "*Sacramentum* and the Eucharist in St. Augustine." *The Thomist* 77, no. 2 (2013): 173–92.

Lies, Lothar. "Trinitätsvergessenheit gegenwärtiger Sakramententheologie?" *Zeitschrift für katholische Theologie* 105, no. 3 (1983): 290–314.

Lligadas Vendrell, Josep. *La eficacia de los sacramentos "ex opere operato" en la doctrina del Concilio de Trento.* Barcelona: Pontificia Universidad Gregoriana, 1983.

Lohfink, Gerhard. "Der Ursprung der christlichen Taufe." *Theologische Quartalschrift* 156, no. 1 (1976): 35–54.

Löhrer, Magnus. "Sacramentales." In *Enciclopedia Teológica Sacramentum Mundi*, edited by Karl Rahner, 4:341–47. Herder: Barcelona, 1969.

López-González, Pedro. "Origen de la expresión 'res et sacramentum.'" *Scripta Theologica* 17, no. 1 (1985): 73–120.

———. *Res et sacramentum: origen y aplicación al sacramento de la Penitencia.* Pamplona: Universidad de Navarra, 1991.

López Martín, Julian. *La liturgia de la Iglesia: Teología, historia, espiritualidad pastoral.* Madrid: BAC, 1996.

MacIntyre, Alasdair. *After Virtue: A Study in Moral Theory.* Notre Dame, Ind.: University of Notre Dame Press, 1984.

Madden, Nicholas. "Edith Stein on the Symbolic Theology of Dionysius the Areopagite." *Irish Theological Quarterly* 71, nos. 1–2 (2006): 29–45.

Magee, Gregory S. "Uncovering the 'mystery' in 1 Timothy 3." *Trinity Journal* 29 (Fall 2008): 247–65.

Maggiani, Silvano. "La mano e lo Spirito: Per una lettura simbolica della imposizione delle mani." *Rivista Liturgica* 78 (1991): 391–401.

Maguire, Alban A. *Blood and Water: The Wounded Side of Christ in Early Christian Literature.* Studies in Sacred Theology 108. Washington, D.C.: The Catholic University of America Press, 1956.

Marcel, Gabriel. "L'être incarné, repère central de la réflexion métaphysique." *Du refus à l'invocation.* Paris: Gallimard, 1940.

———. *Homo viator: prolégomènes à une métaphysique de l'espérance.* Paris: Aubier, 1963. Translated by Emma Craufurd as *Homo Viator: Introduction to the Metaphysic of Hope.* South Bend, Ind.: St. Augustine's Press, 2010.

Mardones, José María. *La vida del símbolo: La dimensión simbólica de la religión.* Santander: Sal Terrae, 2003.

Marías, Julián. *La perspectiva Cristiana.* Madrid: Alianza Editorial, 1999. Translated as *The Christian Perspective.* Houston, Tex.: Halycon Press, 2000.

Maritain, Jacques. "Sign and Symbol." *Journal of the Warburg Institute* 1, no. 1 (1937): 1–11.

Markus, Robert A. "St. Augustine on Signs." *Phronesis* 2, no. 1 (1957): 60–83.

Marliangéas, Bernard-Dominique. *Clés pour une théologie du ministère: In persona Christi, in persona Ecclesiae.* Paris: Beauchesne, 1978.

Marsh, Thomas. "The Sacramental Character." In *Sacraments: Papers of the Maynooth Union Summer School 1963,* edited by D. O'Callaghan. Dublin: Gill and Son, 1964.

Martimort, Aimé-Georges. "Les rites du Baptême à la lumière de l'histoire." In his *Les signes de la nouvelle alliance.* Paris: Ligel, 1966. Translated as *The Signs of the New Covenant.* Collegeville, Minn.: Liturgical Press, 1963.

Masi, Roberto. "La struttura dei sacramenti: *Sacramentum tantum, res et sacramentum, res tantum.*" *Divinitas* 12 (1969): 199–210.

Matsunaga, Kikuo. "Is John's Gospel Anti-sacramental? A New Solution in Light of the Evangelist's Milieu." *New Testament Studies* 27, no. 4 (1981): 516–24.

Mazza, Enrico. *La mistagogia: Una teologia della liturgia in epoca patristica.* Rome: CLV Edizioni Liturgiche, 1988. Translated as *Mystagogy: A Theology of Liturgy in the Patristic Age.* New York: Pueblo, 1989.

Mazzocchi, Giuseppe. "Segni e simboli nella liturgia: Rassegna bibliografica." *Rivista di Pastorale Liturgica* 189, no. 2 (1995): 44–46.

McCaffrey, James. *The House with Many Rooms: The Temple Theme of Jn. 14, 2–3.* Rome: Pontificio Istituto Biblico, 1998.

McPartlan, Paul. *Sacrament of Salvation: An Introduction to Eucharistic Ecclesiology.* London: T and T Clark, 1995.

———. *The Splendor of the Church.* Translated by Michael Mason. San Francisco, Calif.: Ignatius Press, 1999 (1953).

———. *The Eucharist and the Church in the Middle Ages.* Translated by Gemma Simmonds et al. Notre Dame, Ind.: University of Notre Dame Press, 2007.

McShane, Philip. "On the Causality of the Sacraments." *Theological Studies* 24, no. 3 (1963): 423–36.

Melina, Livio. *La conoscenza morale: Linee di riflessione sul Commento di san Tommaso all'Etica Nicomachea.* Rome: Città Nuova, 1987.

———. *Cristo e il dinamismo dell'agire: linee di rinnovamento della teologia morale fondamentale.* Rome: Mursia, 2001. Translated by William E. May as *Sharing in Christ's Virtues: For a Renewal of Moral Theology in Light of Veritatis Splendor.* Washington, D.C.: The Catholic University of America Press, 2001.

———. "The Eclipse of the Sense of God and of Man." *Communio* 34, no. 1 (2007): 100–116.

Melina, Livio, J. José Pérez-Soba, and José Noriega. *Camminare nella luce dell'amore: I fondamenti della morale cristiana.* Siena: Cantagalli, 2008.

Menke, Karl-Heinz. *Sakramentalität: Wesen und Wunde des Katholizismus.* Regensburg: Pustet, 2013.

Mersch, Emile. *Le corps mystique du Christ: Études de théologie historique.* Paris: Desclée, 1936. Translated as *The Theology of the Mystical Body.* St. Louis, Mo.: Herder, 1951.

Michel, Albaric. "Sacramentaux." In *Dictionnaire de Théologie Catholique,* edited by A. Vacant, E. Mangenot, and E. Amann, 14:465–82. París: Letouzey et Ané, 1913.

Michel, Albert. "Modification des éléments sacramentaires par l'Église *Salva illorum substantia.*" *Doctor Communis* 12, no. 1 (1959): 5–30.

———. "Salva illorum substantia: Contribution à la solution de quelques difficultés de théologie sacramentaire." *L'Ami du clergé* 74 (1964): 481–87.

———. "Si l'intention de recevoir un sacrement comme *rite sacré institué par le Christ*. est nécessaire à la validité, comment admettre que la foi ne soit pas nécessaire?" *L'Ami du clergé* 74 (1964): 523–24.

———. "Salva illorum substantia." *Doctor Communis* 20, no. 3 (1967): 5–32.

Miller, Mark. "The Sacramental Theology of Hans Urs von Balthasar." *Worship* 64, no. 1 (1990): 48–66.

Miralles, Antonio. *Los sacramentos cristianos: Curso de sacramentaria fundamental*. Madrid: Palabra, 2014.

Miyakawa, Toshiyuki. "The Ecclesial Meaning of the Res et Sacramentum." *The Thomist* 31, no. 4 (1967): 381–444.

Möhler, Johann Adam. *Die Einheit in der Kirche*. Mainz: Grünewald, 1925. Translated by Peter C. Erb as *Unity in the Church, or, The Principle of Catholicism*. Washington, D.C.: The Catholic University of America Press, 2016.

———. *Symbolik, oder Neue Untersuchungen der Lehrgegensätze zwischen den Katholiken und Protestanten*. Regensburg: Verlags-Anstalt Manz, 1893. Translated by James Burton Robertson as *Symbolism: Exposition of the Doctrinal Differences Between Catholics and Protestants*. New York: Crossroad, 1997.

Mollat, Donatien. "Le semeion johannique." In *Sacra Pagina: Miscellanea Biblica Congressus Internationalis Catholici de re Biblica*, edited by J. Coppens, A. Descamps, and E. Massaux, 2:209–18. Paris: J. Duculot, 1959.

Moloney, Francis J. "A Sacramental Reading of John 13:1–38." *Catholic Biblical Quarterly* 53, no. 2 (1991): 237–56.

Montagnes, Bernard. "L'axiome de continuité chez Saint Thomas." *Revue de sciences philosophiques et théologiques* 52, no. 2 (1968): 201–21.

Müller, Gerhard Ludwig. *Bonhoeffers Theologie der Sakramente*. Frankfurt am Main: Josef Knecht, 1979.

Mussner, Franz. "Die Kirche als Kultgemeinde nach dem Neuen Testament." In his *Praesentia Salutis: Gesammelte Studien zu Fragen und Themen des Neuen Testaments*. Düsseldorf: Patmos-Verlag, 1967.

Musurillo, Herbert. "Sacramental Symbolism and the *Mysterion* of the Early Church." *Worship* 39 (April 1965): 265–74.

———. "*Passio Sanctorum Scillitanorum*" *The Acts of the Christian Martyrs*. Edited by Herbert Musurillo. Oxford: Clarendon Press, 1972.

Navarro Girón, María Ángeles. "La eucaristía, memorial del sacrificio de Cristo en la primera controversia eucarística (s.IX)." *Revista española de teología* 55, no. 1 (1995): 29–63.

Neunheuser, Burkhard, and Patricio de Navascués. "Confermazione." In *Nuovo Dizionario Patristico e delle Antichità Cristiane*, edited by A. di Berardino, 1:1150–54. Milan: Marietti, 2006.

Nicol, Willem. *The Semeia in the Fourth Gospel*. Leiden: Brill, 1972.

Noriega, José. "Movidos por el Espíritu." In *La plenitud del obrar cristiano*, edited by Livio Melina, J. José Pérez-Soba, and José Noriega, 157–68. Madrid: Palabra, 2006.

Orbe, Antonio. "Teología bautismal de Clemente Alejandrino." *Gregorianum* 36, no. 3 (1955): 410–48.

———. *La unción del Verbo: Estudios Valentinianos*. Rome: Editrice Pontificia Università Gregoriana, 1961.

Oñatibia, Ignacio. "Por una mayor recuperación de la dimensión pneumatológica de los sacramentos." *Phase* 16 (1976): 425–39.

O'Neill, Colman. "The Role of the Recipient and Sacramental Signification." *The Thomist* 21, no. 3 (1958): 257–301.

Osiek, Carolyn. "Review of *Il 'Mysterion' paolino: Traiettoria e costituzione (Associazione biblica italiana, Supplementi alla Rivista Biblica* 10) by Romano Penna." *Catholic Biblical Quarterly* 44, no. 3 (1982): 521–22.

Newman, John Henry. *An Essay on the Development of Christian Doctrine.* Notre Dame, Ind.: University of Notre Dame Press, 1989.

Padberg, Rudolf. "Vom gottesdienstlichen Leben in den Briefen des Ignatius von Antiochien." *Theologie und Glaube* 53 (1963): 337–47.

Palmer, Paul F. "The Theology of the *res et sacramentum*." In *Readings in Sacramental Theology,* edited by C. Stephen Sullivan. Englewood Cliffs, N.J.: Prentice Hall, 1964.

Pannenberg, Wolfhart. *Systematic Theology,* vol. 3. Translated by Geoffrey W. Bromiley. Grand Rapids, Mich.: Eerdmans, 1998.

———. *Systematische Theologie,* vol. 3. Göttingen: Vandenhoeck and Ruprecht, 1993.

Pasquier, Jean-Marie. *L'Église comme sacrement: Le développement de l'idée sacramentelle de l'Église de Möhler à Vatican II.* Fribourg: Academic Press, 2008.

Penna, Romano. "Cristianesimo e laicità in san Paolo: Appunti." *L'apostolo Paolo: Studi di esegesi e teologia.* Cinisello Balsamo: San Paolo, 1991.

Perrin, Bertrand-Marie. *L'institution des sacraments dans Le commentaire des sentences de saint Thomas.* Paris: Parole et Silence, 2008.

Pesch, Otto Hermann. "Das katholische Sakramentverständnis im Urteil gegenwärtiger evangelischen Theologie." In *Verifikationen: Festschrift für Gerhard Ebeling,* edited by Eberhard Jüngel, 317–40. Tübingen: Möhr, 1982.

Peterson, Erik. *Das Buch von den Engeln: Stellung und Bedeutung der heiligen Engel im Kultus.* Leipzig: Jakob Hegner, 1935. Translated as *The Angels and the Liturgy: The Status and Significance of the Holy Angels in Worship.* London: Darton, Longman and Todd, 1964.

Pfnür, Vinzenz. "Die Wirksamkeit der Sakramente *sola fide* und *ex opere operato*." In *Das Herrenmahl,* edited by the Gemeinsame Römisch-Katholische/Evangelisch-Lutherische Kommission. Paderborn: Bonifacius, 1978.

Ployd, Adam D. "The Power of Baptism: Augustine's Pro-Nicene Response to the Donatists." *Journal of Early Christian Studies* 22, no. 4 (2014): 519–40.

Poschmann, Berenhard. "'Mysteriengegenwart' im Lichte des hl. Thomas." *Theologische Quartalschrift* 116, nos. 1–2 (1935): 53–116.

Pose, Eugenio Romero. "Exégesis patrística y liturgia." *Liturgia y Padres de la Iglesia* 26 (2000): 13–62.

Pourrat, Pierre. *La théologie sacramentaire. Étude positive.* París: Lecoffre, 1903. Translated as *Theology of the Sacraments: A Study in Positive Theology.* St. Louis, Mo.: B. Herder, 1910.

Power, David N. "Unripe Grapes: The Critical Function of Liturgical Theology." *Worship* 52, no. 5 (1978): 386–99.

Poyer, André. "À propos du *Salva illorum substantia*." *Divus Thomas (Piacenza)* 56 (January–March 1953): 39–66.

———. "Nouveaux propos sur le *salva illorum substantia*." *Divus Thomas (Piacenza)* 57 (January–March 1954): 3–24.

Pozo, Cándido. "La Iglesia como sacramento primordial: Contenido teológico real de este concepto." *Estudios Eclesiásticos* 41, no. 157 (1966): 139–59.

Prümm, Karl. "Mystères." In *Dictionnaire de la Bible. Supplément*, edited by H. Cazelles, 6:10–225. Paris: Brepolis, 1960.

Rahner, Karl. "La doctrine d'Origène sur la Pénitence." *Recherches de Science Religieuse* 37, no. 1 (1950): 47–97, 252–86, 422–56.

———. *Kirche und Sakramente*. Freiburg: Herder, 1961. Translated as *The Church and the Sacraments*. New York: Herder and Herder, 1963.

———. "Zur Theologie des Symbols." In his *Schriften zur Theologie*, 4:275–311. Einsiedeln: Benziger, 1964. Translated by Kevin Smyth as "The Theology of the Symbol," in *Theological Investigations,* 4:221–52. London: Darton, Longman and Todd, 1974.

———. "Frömmigkeit heute und morgen." *Geist und Leben* 39, no. 5 (1966): 326–42.

———. "Einleitende Bemerkungen zur allgemeinen Sakramentenlehre bei Thomas von Aquin." In *Schriften zur Theologie*, 10:392–404. Zurich: Benziger, 1972.

———. "What is a Sacrament?" In *Theological Investigations*, vol. 14: *Ecclesiology, Questions in the Church, the Church in the World*, 135–48. London: Darton, Longman and Todd, 1976.

———. *Grundkurs des Glaubens*. Freiburg: Herder, 1984.

Rahner, Karl, and Joseph Ratzinger. *Offenbarung und Überlieferung*. Freiburg: Herder, 1965. Translated as *Revelation and Tradition*. New York: Herder and Herder, 1966.

Rambaldi, Giacomo. "La *intentio externa* de Fr. Farvacques." *Gregorianum* 27, no. 3 (1946): 444–57.

Ratzinger, Joseph. "Die Bedeutung der Väter für die gegenwärtige Theologie." In his *Theologische Prinzipienlehre*: *Bausteine zur Fundamentaltheologie*, 139–58. Munich: Erich Wewel, 1982. Translated by Sr. Mary Frances McCarthy, SND, as "Importance of the Fathers for the Structure of the Faith," in Ratzinger, *Principles of Catholic Theology*: *Building Stones for a Fundamental Theology*. San Francisco, Calif.: Ignatius Press, 1987.

———. "The Church as the Sacrament of Salvation." In *Principles of Catholic Theology*.

———. "Die sakramentale Begründung christlicher Existenz." In *Gesammelte Schriften*, vol. 11: *Theologie der Liturgie*. Freiburg im Breisgau: Herder, 2008. Translated as "The Sacramental Foundation of Christian Existence," in *Collected Works*, vol. 11: *Theology of the Liturgy*. San Francisco, Calif.: Ignatius Press, 2014.

———. "Eucharist and Mission." In *Collected Works*, vol. 11.

———. "Gestalt und Gehalt der eucharistischen Feier." In *Gesammelte Schriften*, vol. 11; *Collected Works*, vol. 11.

———. "The Problem of Transubstantiation and the Question about the Meaning of the Eucharist." In *Collected Works*, vol. 11.

———. "Zum Begriff des Sakramentes." In *Gesammelte Schriften*, vol. 11. Translated as "On the Concept of Sacrament," in *Collected Works*, vol. 11.

———. *Jesus of Nazareth*, vol. 2: *Holy Week*: *From the Entrance into Jerusalem to the Resurrection*. San Francisco, Calif.: Ignatius Press, 2011.

Reali, Nicola. *La ragione e la forma*: *Il sacramento nella teologia di H. U. von Balthasar*. Rome: Mursia-Pontificia Università Lateranense, 1999.

Reinhold, Georg. *Die Streitfrage über die physische oder moralische Wirksamkeit der Sakramente*. Vienna: Ohlinger, 1899.

Revel, Jean-Philippe. *Traité des sacrements*, vol. 1: *Baptême et sacramentalité*: *Origine et signification du Baptême*. Paris: Cerf, 2004.

Ricoeur, Paul. *Philosophy of the Will*, vol. 2.2: *Finitude and Culpability*: *The Symbolism of Evil*. Translated by Emerson Buchanan. New York: Harper and Row, 1967.

———. *Temps et récit*. 3 vols. Paris: Seuil, 1983–85. Translated by Kathleen McLaughlin and David Pellauer as *Time and Narrative*. Chicago: University of Chicago Press, 1990.

———. *Soi-même comme un autre*. Paris: Éditions du Seuil, 1990. Translated by Kathleen Blamey as *Oneself as Another*. Chicago: University of Chicago Press, 2008.

Riesner, Rainer. "John 1:14 and the Disciple 'whom Jesus loved.'" In *Rediscovering John: Essays on the Fourth Gospel in Honour of Frédéric Manns*, edited by L. D. Chrupcala, 303–36. Milan: ETS, 2013.

Riga, Peter. "Signs of Glory: The Use of 'semeion' in St. John's Gospel." *Interpretation* 17, no. 4 (1963): 402–24.

Rikhof, Herwi. "Marriage: A Question of Character?" *INTAMS Review* 2, no. 2 (1996): 151–64.

Riley, Hugh M. *Christian Initiation: A Comparative Study of the Interpretation of the Baptismal Liturgy in the Mystagogical Writings of Cyril of Jerusalem, John Chrysostom, Theodore of Mopsuestia, and Ambrose of Milan*. Washington, D.C.: The Catholic University of America Press, 1974.

Robinson, H. Wheeler. *Corporate Personality in Ancient Israel*. Philadelphia: Fortress Press, 1964.

Roguet, Aimon-Marie. "La théologie du caractère et l'incorporation à l'Église." *La Maison Dieu* 32 (October 1952): 74–89.

———. "La sanctification du prêtre par l'administration des sacrements." *Vie spirituelle* 89 (July 1953): 8–14.

Rosier-Catach, Irène. *La parole efficace: signe, rituel, sacré*. Paris: Seuil, 2004.

———. "Signification et efficacité: sur les prolongements médiévaux de la théorie augustinienne du signe." *Revue de sciences philosophiques et théologiques* 91, no. 1 (2007): 51–74.

Roth, Erich. *Sakrament nach Luther*. Berlin: Töpelmann, 1952.

Rouwhorst, Gerard A. M. "Christian Initiation in Early Christianity." *Questions liturgiques et paroissiales* 87, nos. 1–2 (2006): 100–119.

Ruffini, Eliseo. "El carácter como visibilidad concreta del sacramento en relación con la Iglesia." *Concilium* 31, no. 1 (1968): 111–24.

Russell, Ralph. "The Concept of a Sacrament in St. Augustine." *Eastern Churches Quarterly* (1936): 73–79.

Ryrie, Charles C. "Mystery in Ephesians 3." *Bibliotheca Sacra* 123 (January 1966): 24–31.

Sabourin, Leopold. "Sacrifice." *Dictionnaire de la Bible: Supplément*, vol. 10, edited by H. Cazelles and A. Feuillet. Paris: Letouzey and Ané, 1985.

Salier, Willis H. *The Rhetorical Impact of the Semeia in the Gospel of John*. Tübingen: Mohr Siebeck, 2004.

Sánchez Navarro, Luis. "El misterio del pan." In *La sacramentalidad del ser*, edited by L. Granados. Madrid / Burgos: Didáskalos / Monte Carmelo, 2017.

Sattler, Dorothea. "Charakter, sakramentaler. Begriff." In *Lexikon für Theologie und Kirche*, 2:1009–13. Freiburg: Herder, 1994.

Saverio Pancheri, Francesco. "Il carattere sacramentale in una nuova prospettiva (M. J. Scheeben)." *Studia Patavina* 4, no. 3 (1957): 459–72.

Savoia, L. "La funzione ecclesiale del carattere sacramentale." *Sacra Doctrina* 12 (1967): 106–12.

Scheeben, Matthias Joseph. *The Mysteries of Christianity*. New York: Crossroad, 2008.

Schillebeeckx, Edward. "La liturgia, lugar teológico." *Revelación y teología*. Salamanca: Sigueme, 1968. Translated as *Revelation and Theology*. London: Bloomsbury, 2014.

Schilson, Arno. *Theologie als Sakramententheologie: die Mysterientheologie Odo Casels*. Mainz: Matthias Grünewald, 1987.

———. "Symbolwirklichkeit und Sakrament: Ein Literaturbericht." *Liturgisches Jahrbuch* 40 (1990): 26–52.

Schlier, Heinrich. "Die Kirche als das Geheimnis Christi." In his *Die Zeit der Kirche*, 299–307. Freiburg: Herder, 1956.

———. "Grundelemente des priesterlichen Amtes im Neuen Testament." *Theologie und philosophie* 44, no. 2 (1969): 161–95.

Schmaus, Michael. *Teología dogmática*, vol. 6. Madrid: Rialp, 1961.

Schmemann, Alexander. "Ecclesiological Notes." *St. Vladimir's Seminary Quarterly* 11, no. 1 (1967): 35–39.

———. *Liturgy and Tradition: Theological Reflections of Alexander Schmemann*. Crestwood, N.Y.: St. Vladimir's Seminary Press, 1990.

———. *Introduction to Liturgical Theology*. Third edition. Crestwood, N.Y.: St. Vladimir's Seminary Press, 2003.

Schmitz, Kenneth L. *The Gift: Creation*. Milwaukee, Wis.: Marquette University Press, 1982.

Scholz, Franz. *Die Lehre von der Einsetzung der Sakramente nach Alexander von Hales*. Breslavia: Franke, 1940.

Schulte, R. "Mysterion en el griego clásico y en el helenismo." *Mysterium Salutis. Fundamentos de la dogmática como historia de la salvación*, edited by J. Feiner and M. Löhrer, 4.2:78–81. Madrid: Cristiandad, 1969.

Schürmann, Heinz. "Die Gestalt der urchristlichen Eucharistiefeier." *Münchener Theologische Zeitschrift* 6, no. 2 (1955): 107–31.

Schwab, Wolfgang. *Entwicklung und Gestalt der Sakramententheologie bei Martin Luther*. Frankfurt am Main: Peter Lang, 1977.

———. "Luthers Ringen um das Sakrament." *Catholica* 32 (1978): 93–113.

Segalla, Giuseppe. "Segno giovanneo e sacramenti." In *Segno e sacramenti nel Vangelo di Giovanni*, edited by C. Corsato, 17–44. Rome: Anselmiana, 1977.

———. "La testimonianza dei sacramenti (1 Giov 5, 6–12)." In *Sul sentiero dei sacramenti: Scritti in onore di Ermanno Roberto Ruta*, edited by C. Corsato. Padua: Messaggero, 2007.

Semmelroth, Otto. *Kirche als Ursakrament*. Frankfurt am Main: Knecht, 1953. Translated as *Church and Sacrament*. Notre Dame, Ind.: Fides, 1965.

———. "Personalismo y Sacramentalismo." *Orbis Catholicus (Barcelona)* 8–9 (1960): 125–44.

———. "Pastorale Konsequenzen aus der Sakramentalität der Kirche." In *Wahrheit und Verkündigung: Festschrift Schmaus*, edited by Leo Scheffczyk et al. Paderborn: Schöningh, 1967.

———. "La Iglesia como sacramento de la salvación." In *Mysterium Salutis: Fundamentos de la dogmática como historia de la salvación*, edited by J. Feiner and M. Löhrer, 4.1:321–70. Madrid: Cristiandad, 1969.

Sequeri, Pierangelo. *Il Dio affidabile: Saggio di teologia fondamentale*. Brescia: Queriniana, 1996.

Seybold, Michael. "Die Siebenzahl der Sakramente (Conc. Trid. Sessio VII, can. 1)." *Münchener Theologische Zeitschrift* 27, no. 2 (1976): 113–41.

Simon, Josef. *Philosophie des Zeichens.* Berlin: W. de Gruyter, 1989. Translated as *Philosophy of the Sign.* Albany: State University of New York Press, 1995.

Smalley, Stephen. "Liturgy and Sacrament in the Fourth Gospel." *Evangelical Quarterly* 29, no. 3 (1957): 159–70.

Smit, Peter-Ben. "The Reception of the Truth at Baptism and the Church as Epistemological Principle in the Work of Irenaeus of Lyons." *Ecclesiology* 7, no. 3 (2011): 354–73.

Smulders, Pieter. "L'Église sacrement du salut." In *L'Église de Vatican II,* vol. 2: *Commentaires,* edited by G. Baraúna, 311–38. Paris: Cerf, 1966.

Sodi, Manlio. "Cos'è il carattere sacramentale?" *Rivista Liturgica* 85 (1998): 451–56.

Söhngen, Gottlieb. *Symbol und Wirklichkeit im Kultmysterium.* Bonn: Haustein, 1937.

Sokolowski, Robert. *Eucharistic Presence: A Study in the Theology of Disclosure.* Washington, D.C.: The Catholic University of America Press, 1994.

Son, Sang-Won A. *Corporate Elements in Pauline Anthropology: A Study of Selected Terms, Idioms and Concepts in the Light of Paul's Usage and Background.* Rome: Pontifical Biblical Institute, 2001.

Stauffer, Ethelbert. *Die Theologie des Neuen Testaments.* Gütersloh: Bettelsmann, 1941. Translated by John Marsh as *New Testament Theology.* London: SCM Press, 1955.

Studer, Basile. "'Sacramentum et exemplum' chez saint Augustin." *Recherches Augustiniennes* 10 (1975): 87–141.

Stuhlmacher, Peter. "Das neutestamentliche Zeugnis zum Herrenmahl." *Zeitschrift für Theologie und Kirche* 84, no. 1 (1987): 1–35.

Sweeney, Conor. *Sacramental Presence after Heidegger.* Eugene, Ore.: Wipf and Stock, 2015.

Taylor, Charles. *The Ethics of Authenticity.* Cambridge, Mass.: Harvard University Press, 1991.

———. *A Secular Age.* Cambridge, Mass.: Harvard University Press, 2007.

Tejero, Eloy. "La *res et sacramentum* estructura y espíritu del Ordenamiento canónico: Síntesis doctrinal de santo Tomás." In *Sacramentalidad de la Iglesia y sacramentos,* edited by P. Rodríguez. Pamplona: Universidad de Pamplona, 1983.

Terrin, Aldo N. *Liturgia e incarnazione.* Padua: EMP, 1997.

Theobald, Michael. "Das Herrenmahl im Neuen Testament." *Theologische Quartalschrift* 183, no. 4 (2003): 257–80.

Thils, Gustave. "Le pouvoir cultuel du baptisé." *Ephemerides Theologicae Lovanienses* 15 (1938): 683–89.

Thurian, Max. *L'eucharistie: Mémorial du Seigneur: Sacrifice d'action de grâce et d'intercession.* Neuchatel: Delachaux et Niestlé, 1963. Translated as *The Eucharistic Memorial.* Richmond, Va.: John Knox Press, 1960.

Ticciati, Susannah. "The Human Being as Sign in Augustine's *De doctrina christiana.*" *Neue Zeitschrift für Systematische Theologie und Religionsphilosophie* 55, no. 1 (2013): 20–32.

Tillard, Jean Marie R. "A propósito de la intención del ministro y del sujeto de los sacramentos." *Concilium* 31, no. 1 (1968): 125–39.

Todorov, Tzvetan. "À propos de la conception augustinienne du signe." *Revue des études augustiniennes et patristiques* 31, nos. 3–4 (1985): 209–14.

Torrance, Thomas F. "Ein vernachlässigter Gesichtspunkt der Tauflehre." *Evangelische Theologie* 16, no. 3 (1956): 433–57.

Torrell, Jean-Pierre. "La causalité salvifique de la résurrection du Christ selon saint Thomas." *Revue Thomiste* 96, no. 2 (1996): 179–208.

Tragan, Pius-Ramon. *Segni e sacramenti nel Vangelo di Giovanni.* Rome: Anselmiana, 1977.

Tremblay, Réal. "Sacramenti e vita morale." *Rivista Liturgica* 91, no. 3 (2004): 381–90.

Triacca, Achille M., and A. Pistoia, eds. "'Liturgia' 'locus theologicus' o 'Theologia' 'locus liturgicus'? Da un dilemma verso una sintesi." In *Paschale mysterium: Studi in memoria dell'Abate Prof. Salvatore Marsili (1910–1983)*, edited by G. Farnedi, 193–233. Rome: Pontificio Ateneo S. Anselmo, 1986.

———. *Les bénédictions et les sacramentaux dans la liturgie.* Rome: Centro Liturgico Vincenziano, 1988.

Troeltsch, Ernst. "Protestantisches Christentum und Kirche in der Neuzeit." In his *Kritische Gesamtausgabe*, vol. 7. Berlin: W. de Gruyter, 2004.

Tromp, Sebastian. "Ecclesia Sponsa Virgo Mater." *Gregorianum* 18, no. 1 (1937): 3–29.

Turcan, Robert. *Mithra et le mithracisme.* Paris: Les Belles Lettres, 1993.

———. *Recherches Mithraiques: Quarante ans de questions et d'investigations.* Paris: Les Belles Lettres, 2016.

Ubbiali, Sergio. "Eucaristia e sacramentalità: Per una teologia del sacramento." *La Scuola Cattolica* 110 (1982): 540–76.

———. "Il sacramento nella teologia dei misteri." *Teologia* 9, no. 2 (1984): 166–84.

———. "Il carattere sacramentale: La passività costitutiva dell'agire sacramentale." *Rivista liturgica* 85 (1998): 469–86.

Umberg, Johann Baptist. "Die Bedeutung des tridentinischen *salva illorum substantia.* (s.21 c. 2)." *Zeitschrift für katholische Theologie* 48, no. 2 (1924): 161–95.

———. "Sacramenta alii conficiunt, alii suscipiunt." *Periodica* 21 (1932): 74–88.

Unger, Dominic J. "The Holy Eucharist according to St. Irenaeus." *Laurentianum* 20, no. 1 (1979): 103–64.

Vahrenhorst, Martin. *Kultische Sprache in den Paulusbriefen.* Tübingen: Mohr Siebeck, 2008.

Van den Eynde, Damian. *Les définitions des sacraments pendant la première période de la théologie scolastique (1050–1240).* Rome / Louvain: Antonianum / E. Nauwelaerts, 1950.

———. "The Theory of the Composition of the Sacraments in Early Scholasticism (I–III)." *Franciscan Studies* 11, no. 1 (1951): 1–20 and 117–44; 12, no. 1 (1952): 1–26.

Van Der Meer, Frits. "Sacramentum chez St. Augustin." *La Maison Dieu* 13 (1948): 50–64.

Van Iersel, Bastiaan. "Quelques présupposés bibliques de la notion de sacrement." *Concilium* 31, no. 1 (1968): 11–23.

Van Roo, William A. *De sacramentis in genere.* Rome: Typis Pontificis Universitatis Gregorianae, 1957.

———. "The Resurrection of Christ, Instrumental Cause of Grace." *Gregorianum* 39, no. 2 (1958): 271–84.

———. "Reflections on Karl Rahner's 'Kirche und Sakramente.'" *Gregorianum* 44, no. 3 (1963): 465–500.

———. *The Christian Sacrament.* Rome: Editrice Pontificia Università Gregoriana, 1992.

Vanhoye, Albert. "L'oeuvre du Christ, don du Père." *Revue des sciences religieuses* 48 (1960): 377–419.

———. "Par la tente plus grande et plus parfaite." *Biblica* 46 (1965): 1–28.

———. *Tanto amó Dios al mundo: Lectio sobre el sacrificio di Cristo.* Madrid: San Pablo, 2005.

———. *Accogliamo Cristo nostro sommo sacerdote: Esercizi spirituali con Benedetto XVI.* Vatican City: LEV, 2008. Translated as *Christ Our High Priest: Spiritual Exercises with Pope Benedict XVI.* Leonminister: Gracewing, 2010.

Vawter, Bruce. "The Johannine Sacramentary." *Theological Studies* 17, no. 2 (1956): 151–66.

Verheijen, Melchior. "Mysterion, sacramentum et la synagogue." *Recherches de Science Religieuse* 45 (1957): 321–27.

Vignolo, Roberto. "La rilevanza del rito nella prassi de Gesù." In *La forma rituale del sacramento: Scienza liturgica e teologia sacramentaria in dialogo*, edited by S. Ubbiali, 15–44. Rome: CLV Edizioni Liturgiche, 2011.

Villette, Louis. *Foi et sacrement*, vol. 2: *De Saint Thomas à Karl Barth.* Paris: Bloud and Gay, 1964.

Vitta, Maurizio. "La stufa di Cartesio." *Dell'abitare: Corpi spazi oggetti immagini.* Turin: Einaudi, 2008.

Von Allmen, Jean-Jacques. *Prophetisme sacramental.* Neuchâtel: Delachaux et Niestlé, 1964.

Wellman, Tennyson Jacob. "Ancient Mystēria and Modern Mystery Cults." *Religion & Theology* 12, nos. 3–4 (2005): 308–48.

Wenz, Günter. *Einführung in die evangelische Sakramentenlehre.* Darmstadt: Wissenschaftliche Buchgesellschaft, 1988.

Westermann, Claus. *Der Segen in der Bibel und im Handeln der Kirche.* Munich: C. Kaiser, 1968.

Wickert, Ulrich. *Sacramentum unitatis: Ein Beitrag zum Verständnis der Kirche bei Cyprian.* Berlin: W. de Gruyter, 1971.

Williams, Rowan. "Language, Reality and Desire in Augustine's *De Doctrina*." *Literature and Theology* 3, no. 2 (1989): 138–50.

———. "The Church as Sacrament." *International Journal for the Study of the Christian Church* 10, no. 1 (2010): 6–12.

Witte, Jan L. "L'Église, 'sacramentum unitatis' du cosmos et du genre humain." In *L'Église de Vatican II*, edited by G. Baraúna, 457–91. Cerf: Paris, 1966.

Wittgenstein, Ludwig. *Tractatus Logico-Philosophicus.* New York: Routledge, 2005.

Yarnold, Edward. "The Body-Soul Relationship, mainly in connection with sacramental causality." In *Ascetica, Gnostica, Liturgica, Orientalia*, edited by Maurice F. Wiles and Edward Yarnold, 338–42. Studia Patristica 35. Leuven: Peters, 2001.

Yee, Gale A. *Jewish Feasts and the Gospel of John.* Wilmington, Del.: Michael Glazier, 1989.

Zardoni, Serafino. "Il 'carattere' della cresima all'interno di una possibile teologia sul carattere sacramentale." *Il sacramento della confermazione.* Bologna: ESD, 1983.

Zizioulas, Ioannis D. *The One and the Many: Studies on God, Man, the Church, and the World Today.* Alhambra, Calif.: Sebastian Press, 2010.

Zumstein, Jean. "Le signe de la croix." *Lumière et Vie* 41, no. 209 (1992): 68–82.

Zur Mühlen, Karl-Heinz. "Zur Rezeption der augustinischen Sakramentsformeln: 'accedit uerbum ad elementum et fit sacramentum' in der Theologie Luthers." *Zeitschrift für Theologie und Kirche* 70, no. 1 (1973): 50–76.

Theology Coursebooks from The Catholic University of America Press

Sacra Doctrina series:

Ecclesiology by Guy Mansini, OSB

Fundamental Theology by Guy Mansini, OSB

The Godly Image: *Christian Satisfaction in Aquinas* by Romanus Cessario, OP

An Introduction to Vatican II as an Ongoing Theological Event by Matthew Levering

John Henry Newman on Truth and Its Counterfeits: *A Guide for Our Times* by Reinhard Hütter

The One Creator God in Thomas Aquinas and Contemporary Theology by Michael J. Dodds, OP

Catholic Moral Thought series:

Introduction to Moral Theology, Revised Edition by Romanus Cessario, OP

Biomedicine and Beatitude: *An Introduction to Catholic Bioethics* by Nicanor Pier Giorgio Austriaco, OP

Church, State, and Society: *An Introduction to Catholic Social Doctrine* by J. Brian Benestad

Sex and Virtue: *An Introduction to Sexual Ethics* by John S. Grabowski

Other coursebooks in theology:

The Light of Christ: *An Introduction to Catholicism* by Thomas Joseph White, OP

Children of God in the World: *An Introduction to Theological Anthropology* by Paul O'Callaghan

Christ Our Hope: *An Introduction to Eschatology* by Paul O'Callaghan

Introduction to Mariology by Manfred Hauke

Inspiration and Interpretation: *A Theological Introduction to Sacred Scripture* by Denis Farkasfalvy, O. Cist.

Scriptural Index

General Index

Abraham, 10, 46n32, 137, 312n45; sacrifice of, 87, 146, 154
Admission to the sacraments, 300, 324–25; *sub conditione*, 341. *See also* Catechumenate; Validity
Alain de Lille, 133n42
Albert the Great, St., 269, 302n21, 339n42, 373–74
Aldama, José A., 227n46, 323n86
Aletti, J.-N., 2n3, 34n9
Alexander of Hales, 94, 204, 208–9, 270n29, 271n33, 302, 318, 373n51, 374
Alexander VIII, Pope, 340
Alger of Liège, 195
Alter, Robert, 138n52
Amaladoss, Michael, 362n21
Amata, Biagio, 265n4
Ambrose, St., 87, 89, 161n39, 163, 169, 312n43, 344, 358n6; on the institution of the sacraments, 85
Ambrosio Catarino, 340
Anabaptists, 336
Anamnesis, 45–47, 70–71; and marriage, 75
Anastasius II, Pope, 334
Andia, Ysabel de, 163n46
Angelini, 64n39, 147n1, 157n30, 304n27, 316n62
Anointing of the sick, 248, 252; as a column of the church, 379; institution, 116; minister, 355; and moral action, 316
Arendt, Wilhelm, 381n82
Aristotle, 203, 234, 254, 272
Arles, council of, 333n17
Arnau, Ramón, 67n7, 203n32, 351n86, 173n7, 196n13,
Augé, Marc, 383n86
Augustine of Dacia, 375
Augustine, St., xivn2, 4, 5n16, 50n2, 81n52, 88n19, 92–93, 98, 123n6–7, 130, 163,

164–66, 170–190, 191–96, 201, 203, 216n4, 217, 238, 265n5, 266–68, 299, 312n44, 313n47, 313n48, 313n51, 319n69, 320n73, 321n79, 323n83, 326n92, 326n98, 309, 325–26, 333–35, 337, 347–49, 350n80, 359, 370–71, 373n53; on charity and the Eucharist, 313; on the communal dimension of the rites, 319; on the institution of the sacraments, 84–85, 114; on reviviscence, 293; on sacraments and creation, 127–129; on the validity of a sinner's baptism, 321
Ayán, Juan José, 366n31

Bacq, Philippe, 163n46
Badiou, Alain, 291n83
Balthasar, Hans Urs von, 235n60
Baptism, 247, 252; as birth from the womb of the Church, 91, 349–50, 353–54; as a column of the church, 378; and creation, 124–27; of desire and of blood, 326; doorway to the other sacraments, 320; and faith, 312–314; as illumination, 174; incorporation into the Body of Christ, 41–46; institution of, 41–46, 88–91, 111–13; minister of, 353–54; as a new birth, 174; rebaptizing, 332
Baraúna, G., 358n6
Bartholomew, C. G., 3n5
Basil of Cesarea, St., 4n15, 90
Beauchamp, Paul, 55n18, 56n20, 144n59, 153n20–21, 154n23
Bechina, Friedrich, 367n33
Belcher, Kimberly Hope, 255n13
Belda Plans, Juan, 226n44
Bellarmine, Robert, 223n33, 225, 304
Benedict XVI, 385
Berengar of Tours, 192, 194–97, 204, 211–12, 219, 222
Berger, David, 265n4